Dr Raj Persaud is a consultant at London's Maudsley Hospital, the author of the critically acclaimed books *Staying Sane* and *From the Edge of the Couch*, and the presenter of Radio 4's *All in the Mind*. Unusually for a psychiatrist he also holds a degree in psychology which he obtained with First Class Honours. He has received numerous academic awards and prizes for the innovative nature of his research, including the prestigious Royal College of Psychiatrists Research Medal and Prize and The Maudsley Hospital's own Denis Hill Prize, as well as the exclusive medical award the Osler Medal. In 2004 he was appointed Gresham Professor for Public Understanding of Psychiatry. In 2002 the *Independent on Sunday* conducted a poll amongst members of the Royal College of Psychiatrists and the Institute of Psychiatry to discover who were the top ten psychiatrists in the UK as rated by fellow clinicians. Dr Raj Persaud was the youngest doctor to make it into this esteemed list. He lives in London.

Also by Raj Persaud

STAYING SANE
FROM THE EDGE OF THE COUCH

and published by Bantam Books

THE MOTIVATED MIND

Dr Raj Persaud

BANTAM BOOKS

LONDON • TORONTO • SYDNEY • AUCKLAND • JOHANNESBURG

THE MOTIVATED MIND
A BANTAM BOOK: 0 553 81345 5
9780 553 81345 6

Originally published in Great Britain by Bantam Press,
a division of Transworld Publishers

PRINTING HISTORY
Bantam Press edition published 2005
Bantam edition published 2006

5 7 9 10 8 6 4

Set in 10/11½pt Sabon by
Falcon Oast Graphic Art.

Bantam Books are published by Transworld Publishers,
61–63 Uxbridge Road, London W5 5SA,
a division of The Random House Group Ltd,
in Australia by Random House Australia (Pty) Ltd,
20 Alfred Street, Milsons Point, Sydney, NSW 2061, Australia,
in New Zealand by Random House New Zealand Ltd,
18 Poland Road, Glenfield, Auckland 10, New Zealand
and in South Africa by Random House (Pty) Ltd, Isle of Houghton,
Corner of Boundary and Carse O'Gowrie Roads, Houghton 2198,
South Africa.

Printed and bound in Great Britain by
Cox & Wyman Ltd, Reading Berkshire.

Papers used by Transworld Publishers are natural, recyclable
products made from wood grown in sustainable forests. The
manufacturing processes conform to the environmental
regulations of the country of origin.

This edition published 2007 for Index Books Ltd

This is for my parents, Professor Bishnudat and Dr Lakshmi Persaud, who always set themselves and others exceptionally demanding goals. I suspect they consider only serious aims will challenge us to reflect on how we will achieve them, and therefore force us to confront what our lives are really all about.

If you are fully in control, then you aren't going fast enough

Mario Andretti, racing car driver

CONTENTS

ACKNOWLEDGEMENTS

This is my third book, and the fact I am still writing outside the walls of an asylum – although I work in one – can only be down to the unstinting support of a very special group of people.

Heading the list is my wife, Francesca, who inspires 'shock and awe' (a concept of successful married life I introduced in my first book, *Staying Sane*) in all who meet her given her ability to combine being an eye surgeon with bringing up our two children, Sachin and Asha. All this while keeping a psychiatrist together.

My parents Bishnudat and Lakshmi are the two most motivated people I have ever met, and inspired this book; my siblings Avinash and Sharda are both eminent economists, and most of the sensible advice I give comes from them.

The assiduous support of Olivia Jack, Precy Menique and my in-laws, Lira, Rufino, Mary-Anne and Lucinda Cordeiro all ensure that my wife and I can combine busy professional lives with bringing up our children, who have yet to display any of the typical characteristics of psychiatrists' offspring.

My indefatigable personal assistant, Sheila Banks, is the key reason I have continued to progress in the NHS despite the stressful conditions. She is a member of the most resilient and cohesive psychiatric team I have ever met (and my BBC World Service Series *Travels of the Mind* has led me to examine mental-health services all over the world), and which I am incredibly lucky to be part of. The team consists of Iqbal Surfaz, Asha Tait, Pauline LaForge, Sandra Binney, Janette Nixon, Michael Larkin, Chris Powell, Lucricia Taylor and Bibi Doolare.

At Transworld Publishers, Patrick Janson-Smith, Brenda Kimber, Emma Dowson and Alison Tulett have remained bafflingly loyal, despite having to wade through volumes of my favourite obscure psychiatric theories.

My brilliant literary agents Maggie Pearlstine and Jamie Crawford have politely endured mystifying games of poker at my home while patiently waiting for the latest excuse for non-delivery of the manuscript.

Thanks also to Roger Highfield, the eminent Science Editor of the *Daily Telegraph*, Simon Singh, the famous maths and science author, and Mark Wnek, the legendary advertising guru. They are the core of my notorious weekend Dads' Breakfast Clubs. On Sundays in particular we strike terror in the heart of Greenwich Maritime Museum officials as our children go missing there regularly. *The Motivated Mind* was honed during various Breakfast Clubs, and coffee was spilt over it.

At the BBC a host of outstanding broadcasters have supported the public-health-education enterprise in which I attempt to disseminate information about mental health, including Rami Tzabar, Deborah Cohen, Andrew Caspari, Rebecca Asher, Robert Thirkell, Pam Rutherford, Fiona Couper, Tony Phillips, Mark Damazer, Maire Devine, Angharad Law, Katy Hickman, Jo Coombs and Sally Flatman.

Since my last book appeared, the ancient and illustrious Gresham College has generously bestowed on me the title of Gresham Professor for Public Understanding of Psychiatry. Given the recent role they have played in dramatically raising the academic profile of the public understanding of psychiatry, I am naturally indebted to Lord Sutherland of Houndwood, Barbara Anderson and Helene Murphy, all of Gresham College.

Writing rigorously for the lay public about the complex science of the brain and mind is always going to be a challenge, and I have received much insightful editorial input from national newspapers, magazines and academic journals, including the *Independent* and *Daily Telegraph*, the *Financial Times* magazine, *Health Service Journal*, *The Times Educational Supplement* and the *British Medical Journal*. In particular, enormous gratitude is due to Ian Birrell, Matthew Hoffman, Rachel Forder, Simon Hogg, Sam Baker, Rachel Baird, Linda Gray, Rosemary Conley, Jill Craven, Nick Edwards, John Mayberry, Rhona MacDonald, Trevor Jackson and Graham Watts.

Finally, the group who, as ever, have taught me most about the resilience and wonder of the human spirit are my patients. I would dearly like to list them all, but rules of confidentiality mean that the names of those to whom I owe the most must remain forever outside the public domain. But they know who they are.

AUTHOR'S FOREWORD

You may still recall the childhood instruction to 'be content with what you've got', but consider that every great thing begins as discontent, with a desire for something different. The challenge is to refine our longings and discontents into a single powerful purpose

Robert Collier

Great souls have wills; feeble ones have only wishes

Chinese proverb

This book is about how to get what you want in life. Strong motivation has to be part of any formula for achieving your desires, if what you yearn for is more than the mundane. You will require drive and enormous enthusiasm in order to overcome the obstacles and do the hard work necessary to attain the enviable and the sought after.

But to be compelled by a forceful drive is actually much more vital for the life worth living. Yes, it's the key tool you will need in order to lose weight, become rich and attract who you desire. But beyond that, above all its material benefits, motivation is advantageous because at a spiritual or transcendent level it brings real meaning to our lives.

I will, of course, defend and assert these claims later in this book, and not just leave these astounding assertions hanging there.

However, motivation also has a dark side, for it is what drives us to the deepest despair in the face of disappointment. The clinically depressed and suicidal are often the casualties of failed aspiration. I will examine this issue later in the book and suggest ways of avoiding the pitfalls associated with a strong sense of being impelled forward.

The key is for you to be in charge of your motivation, rather than for it to be in control of you.

So motivation is clearly a psychological conundrum because on the one hand it is what takes us to the pinnacle of success, but on the other it plunges us into the abyss of hopelessness when we encounter setbacks. I contend in this book that the answer to the conundrum won't come from motivational gurus or life coaches, but instead lies firmly in the scientific study of the psyche.

Academic psychology and psychiatry have in recent years become divorced from the public understanding of the brain and mind, despite having been more firmly wedded in the first half of the twentieth century, when it seemed part of any intelligent person's obligation to have some awareness of thinkers like Freud and Jung.

Nowadays, most are at least dimly aware that Freud has fallen out of favour – but the latest fashions in psychology and psychiatry seem strangely absent from the catwalk of everyday life, and instead all that makes an appearance in the media are what you would dig out of musty high street charity shops!

Throughout this text the emphasis on pragmatism is juxtaposed with, I hope, scientific rigour. When this book refers to strategies to assist in obtaining what you 'want' or 'desire', I mean goals as diverse as losing weight or improving your career or your relationships. While I draw on academic research, the emphasis is how this translates into what you can effectively do on a daily basis to improve your situation.

I passionately believe that it's important to draw on science to support the arguments about the often surprising tactics you should adopt in a motivational strategy, while at the same time explaining these in ways more familiar to the general public than the accounts found in obscure academic journals.

There are many volumes available to the lay reader and much advice on how to get what you want, but I am not aware of any that depict what is known for certain about the science of motivation from academic research and this is what I hope sets this work apart. I hope my academic colleagues at The Bethlem

Royal and Maudsley Hospitals as well as the Institute of Psychiatry will also find this work of interest, placing as it does motivation centre stage in any attempt to understand and help the public.

I also believe that mainstream modern psychiatry and psychology have remarkably neglected the issue of motivation or have tackled it in profoundly unhelpful ways, as for example in Freud's approach. Freud was absolutely right to question people's motivations. Clients often came to him complaining that they did things they really didn't want to do – and yet they persisted with remarkable tenacity with these repetitive unhelpful behaviours. Freud suggested that their true motivation was unconscious – inaccessible even to them.

I contend that while we need to use certain techniques like the 'perfect day' exercise you will be shown later in this book to properly get at what we really want, as opposed to what we say we want, we don't need to employ a psychoanalyst five days a week for twenty years to better understand and improve our motivation.

The example I will give later of *practical* intelligence also emphasizes the point that a key issue isn't just discovering what would make you truly fulfilled if you attained it – the problem is what *strategy* to adopt in life to get there. This book is all about strategy. When you find you are not attaining an important goal, it's time to go back and re-evaluate your tactics and approach. It is no accident that the only previously available works on stratagem when it came to human affairs were books like *The Art of War* by Sun Tzu and *The Prince* by Machiavelli – which use metaphors of war to help us defeat our opponents.

You will find throughout this guide frequent analogies to war and the military and this is because getting what you really want is indeed a battle – only the enemy is actually within, and the war is with yourself. The book in your hands should provide the necessary intelligence to find out more about the enemy within, and how to expose the double agents of misunderstood emotions that lurk beneath us all.

Although I discuss how to defeat your external enemies, slaying your personal demons is a vital first task.

This volume is a route map to success but also, unlike other so-called inspirational tools, isn't afraid to embrace and confront frailty, weakness and failure, because this is the territory where the battle between success and failure is fought.

I am only too aware of the fine line between triumph and disaster. I won't burden you with excessively fraught examples from my own life (after all, the classic psychiatrist's mantra is 'We are not here to talk about me') but will use a relatively trite example.

On one occasion I was presenting a TV programme on phobias, and as they had an interview with a patient suffering from a serious bird phobia, I was asked to talk while walking towards the camera in the middle of Trafalgar Square. The idea from the 'creative' team was that the pigeons would fly up from around my feet as I strode through them, talking to camera, so making the usual talking-head piece more visually striking.

Unfortunately the rather jaded pigeons of Trafalgar Square are now so used to millions of tourists and camera crews that no amount of striding purposefully through them could get them to fly up. The director was getting anxious as our permit to film expired soon, so he asked me to walk faster and faster in order to try to agitate the pigeons, but all to no avail.

Soon, if he had had his way, I would have been running full pelt to camera while delivering my lines, in order to get the pigeons moving. He even demonstrated that if he ran towards the camera flapping his arms wildly as he did so, the normally indifferent pigeons eventually took fright and indeed flew up. I had to patiently explain that running towards the camera while flapping my arms would seriously damage the credibility of anything I was trying to say. Despite the pressure of the director, and the whole of Trafalgar Square, whose traffic had ground to a halt to witness the spectacle, I held firm and eventually we filmed the sequence in another way.

I think it ended up looking fine but behind the scenes, which the audience never sees – in any TV or actually any kind of endeavour – are all the ridiculous and calamitous incidents that comprise the true story of how any of us stumbles towards achievement.

Perhaps a feat of which I am most proud occurred when I studied psychology at University College London back in the early 1980s, eventually gaining a First Class Honours Degree. This was in no small part due to a certain obsessiveness that seemed to take over during the time I spent in the department. For example, I would be the first to arrive in the library each day and the last to leave, so I developed my own favourite seat, and would be seized by an obsessional crisis if I arrived to find someone else occupying *my* chair.

Soon I was such a regular fixture the other students would ask me where materials they were looking for were, and then eventually the *librarian* would consult me when she couldn't find something. My residence in the department seemed to develop an almost official status – the porters at the front desk once rang the halls of residence to check I was OK when one day I wasn't there as usual when they opened the doors.

It will come as no surprise to those who know something of the autistic behaviour spectrum to learn that every Saturday I *still* spend the whole day at this same library, as I now live just half a mile from the university (that's not why I moved there; honest).

This behaviour may seem strange but I find the subjects of psychology and psychiatry fascinating and have done so ever since I got bitten by the bug, which started with reading Professor Hans Eysenck's popular paperback accounts of scientific psychology in the early 1970s. I was just a teenager then, but he inspired me to take up the subject, and I suspect it was no accident that I ended up at his own Alma Mater, The Maudsley Hospital, where I am now a Consultant Psychiatrist.

The decision to become a doctor and psychiatrist rather than to pursue psychology further was a difficult one. After I had gained the First in my degree, the Psychology Department at UCL brought strong pressure to bear encouraging me to consider doing a Ph.D. there, and I was sorely tempted. I decided to proceed with my medical training, though, because I still wasn't entirely sure that psychology was really the only coherent way of understanding people.

My clinical practice as a psychiatrist today is, however, much more psychological than it is strictly medical. As a result of my student psychology days, I retain a healthy scepticism of the medical model as a frame for mental illness, which often produces conflict between myself and medical colleagues at The Maudsley Hospital and The Institute of Psychiatry.

I fervently believe that psychology is an extremely consequential discipline but that its body of knowledge needs to be celebrated more effectively in our wider culture. This is part of my mission with the BBC Radio 4 series *All in the Mind*, which I now present.

However, the narrowing of vision produced by the scientific quest means other bodies of knowledge like anthropology, economics and sociology – all of which have profound and empirically grounded things to say about human behaviour – are neglected by psychology and psychiatry. Back when I was studying for my psychology degree I seemed to be the only student willing to attend lectures given by other degree courses. Indeed, I probably failed anatomy first time round in my initial year at medical school because I was too busy attending a sociology course rather than my anatomy lectures! (My current patients will be relieved to hear I did pass anatomy second time round during the retake exams at the end of the summer.)

It is interesting to note in terms of the psychology of motivation that the fear of failing again – following my anatomy failure in the first year at medical school – led to such an over-reaction that I gained First Class Honours in my psychology degree, two years later.

Failure and success so often seem to go hand in hand – a key to understanding how to attain your goals is the knowledge that the successful themselves frequently experience failure. The key difference between them and the rest of us is not that disappointment has never been a feature of their lives, but that they try to learn from their mistakes in order to improve performance for next time. The 'mistake' is teaching them how to be better – not that they are never going to make it.

Motivation is not a state of mind that is either there or not. It's a journey. A journey where learning from things going wrong provides the essential route map to the summit of ambition.

This approach means that the key question isn't what did you *earn* today – instead it's what did you *learn* today.

INTRODUCTION

It's fun to do things that people don't think are possible or likely

Michael Dell

People can work very hard climbing the ladder of success only to discover it's leaning against the wrong wall

Stephen R. Covey

George Eastman was on the verge of living a life of ease after building the billion-dollar company Eastman Kodak, but the suicide note he left on his desk when he put a bullet through his head read, 'My work is done, why wait?'

To explain this puzzling phenomenon the new notion of 'success depression' has been invoked in the latest branch of psychology, a field now buzzing with terms like the 'entrepreneurial arsonist', who unconsciously ignites unhelpful interpersonal conflict in the thriving business he founded, just to keep life interesting.

But these ideas do have a respectable heritage in academic psychology. Freud based his psychoanalytic theory on the assumption that people fall ill with psychological problems as a result of not being able to satisfy their needs, be they sexual, aggressive or whatever.

So he was understandably shocked to find several patients attending his practice who had attained everything they ever wanted in life, and then promptly become emotionally disturbed. He concluded in some bewilderment, 'People occasionally fall ill precisely because a deeply rooted and long-cherished wish has come to fulfillment. It seems as though they could not endure their bliss.'[1]

But, since Freud, the problem of helping the ultra-successful cope with the burdens of achievement has been somewhat neglected by clinicians, bogged down with the more obvious problems of the rest of us failures. Psychologists recently began to see cases where problems like 'post-Olympic depression' are described. This is where you win your gold medal in the Olympics, and then promptly get so depressed you can't even get out of bed, far less go training again.[2]

Successful people, according to some psychologists, don't just suffer from burnout; instead they get a version on steroids, termed 'supernova burn-out'. This is the result of achieving all that you want in life, and then asking, 'Is that all there is?' Exposing the myths that surround success is devastating, for we live in a culture obsessed with achievement.

One theory is that we pursue attainment because we believe it will change our lives, when in fact it rarely does.

A rather more prosaic reason for why those who finally attain all that they ever wanted might then find their lives rather barren is precisely because single-minded ambition in the pursuit of a solitary goal does tend to empty your life along the way of competing concerns, like family, friends or hobbies. Of course you will only ever discover this when you finally have time on your hands to explore what else you want to do with your life, once you have attained the summit of your ambitions.

But does this kind of straightforward analysis explain why there are so many well-publicized cases of Wall Street tycoons getting caught in white-collar crimes such as insider trading, illicit sexual affairs or violence? Some psychologists conclude that the underlying cause of these 'inexplicable' acts is often an inability to admit that living the good life is anything other than psychological purgatory.[3]

One famous Los Angeles rock band consulted a psychologist named Dr Berglas complaining that it didn't matter how they played any more at concerts: they had achieved such success that their fans and groupies would now still follow and sleep with them no matter how badly they played.[4] I am still trying to work out what they were complaining about . . .

Certainly the stereotypical successful person doesn't bend to the needs of others – their mantra is 'I'm not the type to get ulcers; I give them', so differing viewpoints from their own are usually seen as obstacles to be hurdled or bulldozed aside, rather than to be nurtured. If you care too much about stepping on toes you won't win any races. Yet the very qualities that produce success in a competitive world also result in loneliness, because to grab first prize you need to push others out of the way rather than embrace them. As John Steinbeck wrote, 'Money's easy to make if it's money you want. But with few exceptions people don't want money. They want luxury and they want love and they want admiration.'[5]

The other central problem that belies all success in life is that the qualities required to achieve prosperity are not those required to maintain it. The restlessness, dissatisfaction and ambition that drove you to take risks are no longer appropriate when you are simply required to calm down and keep an even keel. But the incessant appetite for risk that often characterizes high achievers can compel them to push boundaries unnecessarily, in a way that may end up getting them into trouble, hence the classic mid-life crisis.

The really mysterious conundrum at the heart of success depression is surprisingly ignored by psychologists specializing in the study of motivation, and that is: why do those with the drive, incisiveness and ability to overcome practically any external obstacle get so weak-kneed when confronting their own internal demons? Psychologists are particularly struck by the shallow analysis otherwise intelligent and resourceful people bring to bear on themselves when they are put on the couch.[6] Perhaps a core issue is that many people confuse success with validation, and assume that if the world has rewarded them hugely for being as they are, there is no need to change.

Personal change, however, is at the heart of motivation because it is highly likely that you are going to have to become a different person in order to achieve your goals. This means you need to think about the kind of person you will have to become in order to reach your targets – yet most focus on the dream, and neglect what it's going to take to get there.

For example, a recent survey conducted by a bank launching an exclusive credit card, solely for those earning over £70,000 a year, examined what the average person in Britain today aspired to.[7]

BMW motor cars, trendy warehouse-style apartments, a house in the country, throwing lavish parties, having personal staff to cater to your every need and possessing your own private island were revealed to be the main choices of the public, when asked what they dreamed of.

Obviously the main purpose of such surveys is to raise publicity for the launch of a new product, and the materialism-obsessed press duly obliged, with many focusing on the finding that owning your own island was now the ultimate status symbol. But these findings were clearly regarded as little more than idle pipe dreams, as the survey rapidly went the way of yesterday's papers, and was soon forgotten.

However, psychologists are interested in whether our aspirations and dreams are important in determining where we ultimately end up in life, and recent scientific research confirms that aspirations are a key issue in determining our futures. For example, a study only just published by educational psychologists Ingrid Schoon and Samantha Parsons of City University and the Institute of Education has found that your aspirations as a teenager unerringly predict your eventual occupational status many years later.[8]

Most intriguingly they found that aspirations were more important than actual educational attainment in determining a young person's future career. It would seem that your ambitions are partly so vital because they help you compensate for momentary poor performances that would hold back most people with lower aspirations.

But psychologists have also tended to view aspirations as a double-edged sword – great in helping you succeed, but a large factor in your getting depressed if you don't. High aspirations combined with low actual achievement, plus no hope of altering attainment levels, appear the ideal recipe for personal misery.[9]

If that is the case then the fact that we as a society are generally getting wealthier, and therefore our attainment is rising, should mean that we are becoming happier. However, social psychological surveys tend to find the happiness of wealthy societies in the West remains stubbornly static. Although the majority of the population tends to rate themselves as fairly happy, we are not closing the gap on ultimate contentment, despite getting enormously richer with each generation.[10]

Part of the answer to this mystery comes from looking at not just how much we have, but also whether what we want is changing over time. For example, in 1972 the number of consumer goods (e.g., cars, televisions, microwaves) that individuals cited as part of the good life averaged four, but had risen to over five by 1994.[11] So the more we have, the more we want.

Ralph Waldo Emerson in 1860 put it well when he said, 'Want is a growing giant whom the coat of Have was never large enough to cover.'[12]

This takes us back to that recent credit card survey because what is striking about those results is that although it was the general population being surveyed, and not the super-wealthy, in fact what the ordinary person wants converges increasingly today with what those with means also covet. This more than anything else is symbolic of a modern breakdown in class divisions, as what separated 'us' from 'them' in the past was not just what we earned, but what we aspired to.

This meant the educated middle classes would snigger behind their hands at the ostentatious taste of the Pools winner, even if they did drive the biggest car in the street. But the credit card survey indicates no one is sniggering at anyone's aspirations today, because desires are converging rapidly.

The longing for the private island indeed coincides with recent reports from estate agents that inaccessible properties in remote areas of Britain, which were previously difficult to sell, have now become hugely desirable, in the new yearning to escape the madding crowd.

Remember as well that having a huge entourage was regarded as a coveted status symbol in the credit card survey, so the psychological theme here appears to be we now hanker for the ability of the wealthy to minimize hassle from others. After all, the survey also found that people in Wales and East Anglia were especially impressed by people who own a bullet-proof vehicle(!).

The problem is that if our aspirations keep rising ahead of our attainment and the ultimate status symbols are those that make us stand out from the crowd, most of us, doomed to experience an average improvement in our status, will find our outlook bleak; the majority are condemned to never obtaining what our society currently deems the secret to happiness. Psychologists term this problem being caught on the 'hedonic treadmill'.[13] No matter how fast most of us run we will never catch up with our expectations.

It seems there is a role for charities and voluntary organizations to step in at this point, as one of the few non-materialistic forces in our society, and point out that there is another solution to contentment beyond the ultimate exhaustion of the hedonic treadmill. This is to derive satisfaction from alternative values in life other than materialistic ones. Charities should take more interest in the happiness surveys that psychologists conduct, which, for example, found that only 42% of the population identified a job that contributes to the welfare of society was part of the 'good life', compared with 63% preferring a job that pays more than average. 90% rate a home you own as part of the good life, compared to only 77% indicating a happy marriage.[14]

The con trick at the heart of materialism is the idea that if we work hard we will gain attention – but the fact is most of us are doomed to be average. So the only real way of acquiring significance in the eyes of those around us, which is what we are really pursuing through coveting the BMW car or Rolex watch, is to be noticed and valued by our fellow human beings. And actually this is what charitable work or selfless activity is really all about.[15]

This is not so much modern psychological thinking about fulfilment, more ancient wisdom; the Buddha (563BC–483BC) said: 'If you knew what I know about the power of giving, you would not let a single meal pass without sharing it in some way.'[16]

To me, the key reason for being ambitious and motivated is that this produces personal transformation, which usually means your enhanced abilities and capabilities (e.g., being an eye surgeon) render you someone more useful and helpful to others. An eye surgeon, in alleviating blindness, is a more useful and appreciated member of society than someone whose lack of personal development renders them unable to provide services for which there is much demand in human society.

In this way, ambition and motivation are powerful tools, which, in the right hands, can help fit you into a community, rather than isolate you from it, as tends currently to happen to the enormously successful.

Although this book might at first glance appear to be about ruthless ambition and how to get what you want, it's actually concerned with ultimate fulfilment and so avoiding the kind of success depression we discussed at the very beginning. This in no sense means I am going to discourage you from realizing your dreams even if they are materialistic or narcissitic ones. I will still show you the behavioural technology you need to get there, but I also want you to consider some of the wider issues around the goals that you might set for yourself in terms of what leads to ultimate contentment.

But the inescapable fact remains that achieving your goals in life, not necessarily synonymous with being recognized as successful though often this is the case, does have a major impact on our lives. We like to gossip and be negative about the successful but it's important not to forget that publicly acknowledged achievement is also good for the psyche. The nourishment of success operates at a surprisingly fundamental level, which makes it even more astonishing that success has been so neglected by academic psychologists and psychiatrists.

Actors and actresses at the annual Academy Awards should in their acceptance speeches also thank the Academy for helping them live longer – according to research recently published by doctors at the University of Toronto. The startling finding is that winning an Oscar dramatically increases performers' life spans to such an extent that it is equivalent to rendering them immune from cancer.[17]

The study into the longevity of actors and actresses compared all those who had been nominated for an Academy Award with those who actually won in the seventy-two-year history of the ceremony. By the time the study began, 772 nominated performers had died and were available to be included in the research.

The amazing result is that winning an award leads to an increase in average life expectancy of almost four years compared to those who are merely nominated, and almost six years to those who appear in the same films but don't even get nominated.

Winning an Academy Award more than once was even better for your health than winning just once – multiple winners lived almost three years longer on average than those who had just the one lonely Oscar on the mantelpiece.

The finding has generated a flurry of comment amongst doctors arguing about why winning an Academy Award should be so good for your health, particularly as nominated and winning performers were not likely to be significantly different in wealth, in ways that should have any impact on health.[18]

Others have focused on the possible health significance of differences in social status and prestige, after a recent famous British study on civil servants found that those in lower status positions died at three times the rate as those in higher status jobs.[19] This was despite the fact that lower status jobs were hardly financially deprived, so possible income effects like malnutrition could be ruled out.

Instead the crucial factor seems to be that those in higher status positions have more control over their work compared to lower status colleagues, and it now appears that a sense of control over your life has huge stress and health implications. Academy Award winners undoubtedly gain significantly in prestige over those merely nominated, and are likely to be more in control of their careers. They are usually more able to choose which films they want to work on compared to those left in the audience merely applauding the victors.[20]

Another theory is that self-esteem is the crucial factor, as gaining an award is undoubtedly a massive boost to the ego – as witnessed by the best acting in the whole evening being displayed by nominees covering up their disappointment. That the secret ingredient to a longer life might be self-esteem is supported by research that confirms that heart disease and cancer are more likely in those suffering from depression.[21]

Further support for this theory comes from a follow-up study done by the same Toronto doctors who had done the initial work on Oscar-winning actors and actresses – they have now published data in the *British Medical Journal* on screenwriters who gain an Academy Award. Screenwriters are an interesting contrast to performers, as most labour in anonymity, unlike actors and actresses.[22]

The amazing finding was that winning an Academy Award if you are a screenwriter is actually very bad for your health – winners live on average almost four years *less* than nominees. This is equivalent to an almost 40% increase in death rates by dint of being handed the poisoned chalice of an Oscar.

The correspondence in the *British Medical Journal* from doctors responding to this bizarre result suggested that perhaps a writer's initial exultation at winning an Oscar soon evaporates as it becomes obvious that the fascination and acclaim are concentrated on the leading actors and directors. Oscar ceremonies are primarily about acting honours rather than writing credits. Therefore the Academy Awards ceremony could actually intensify scriptwriters' convictions that they are not properly recognized for their contribution to a film, and even an actor's success. This situation could further corrode a writer's self-esteem, thereby attacking their psychological and physical health.[23]

But if self-esteem and the boost or adulation from your peers are the vital ingredients in helping us to live significantly longer, is it then not a good thing that in our media-soaked age we might all eventually get our fifteen minutes of fame?

Not really, because fame seems to be one of those commodities, like holidays in exotic locations and housing in good settings, that loses value by wider availability. After all, those nominated for an award are already much more famous than most can ever dream of, yet they didn't live as long as the rarer folk who make it on to the stage on Oscar night.

So as award ceremonies proliferate, it is likely the health benefits of receiving an honour will diminish, which should cheer up those remaining in their seats throughout these events.

If being recognized as successful can have such a major impact on your longevity then success is worth understanding, even if you are not a particularly competitive person. The fact that which award you win dramatically alters your longevity demonstrates that the psychology of winning is complex and needs careful explication but has profound effects on our psychology and biology.

One issue, however, that is at last beginning to be understood more widely outside the narrow confines of academic psychology and psychiatry is that achievement is a peculiarly profoundly psychological enterprise. For example, even if you are a world-class footballer it's more about what's going on in your mind rather than in your boot.

Winning in any tough competitive situation, be it work, play or sport, is in large part determined by mental attitude, which boils down to motivation. This has remained obscure to many because the widest celebration of competitive success in our culture tends to be for athletes and sports stars whose achievements appear primarily physical.

For example, when it comes to exercise or sport, how

motivated you are will predict how fit you become, because it determines your persistence in the face of obstacles when in training. All fitness and exercise regimes test resolve because it is how committed you are to your goals that will determine your willingness to roll out of bed early in the morning to go jogging, or to persist in finding that fourth for tennis every week.

The mystery over motivation has always been why some are so much more tenacious when pursuing their goals than others, but now part of that enigma appears to have been resolved by some intriguing new research by psychologist Tory Higgins at Columbia University in New York. Higgins has established that all motivation is basically of two types, which he calls 'promotion' or 'prevention' pride, and depends on whether you have experienced success in the past or not.[24]

Challenging situations remind those with promotion pride of their past achievements and galvanizes them to try to do even better than before. But often a competitive situation merely reminds those dogged by memories of past failures to try to avoid a repetition of the humiliation of previous defeats – so these people, who have prevention pride, work mostly to prevent failure rather than achieve success. Failure avoidance often leads you to be primarily cautious when confronted with a goal, so you tend to skirt risks and perhaps even evade challenging situations altogether.

Promotion pride leads to a more adventurous and experimental approach, as you don't mind risking failure in your attempts to attain success. The key lesson from this new understanding that all motivation is one of two types is that if you suffer from prevention pride you should make a conscious effort to remind yourself of past successes, particularly during training when you hit a tough spot. It may be that some of your caution over really going for it, linked to your obsession with not landing flat on your face, means you have failed to understand that no achievement can ever occur unless you expose yourself to the risk of failure. So if you avoid practising or exercising as much as you can because you are afraid of looking bad in front of others, remember all those who eventually succeed and look fantastic as they stoop for the gold medal to be placed over their heads – they are only there because they weren't afraid of failing.

Again as we shall discover it is the fear of not achieving certain goals that actually stops us getting what we want. We fear failure so much that it stops us succeeding. Fear of public failure is actually visible all around us and perhaps is the great unspoken motivation.

Oddly enough over and over again psychologists find that those who are most successful in business – in particlar self-made millionaires – tend to be those who fear public failure least.[25] Because they don't mind falling flat on their faces in public, they are willing to take the kind of risks that are associated with the big prizes in life.

If you care too much about how you look to others then you will indeed be terrified of being seen to fail. Better then not to openly aspire to be anything other than what you are already.

In fact, fear of failure is often a revealing sign of low self-esteem – it is those with the greatest self-confidence who don't mind looking bad to others by being seen to have cocked up. Before we can risk the damaging blows to our self-esteem of failure we need to shore up our self-confidence.[26]

It is this fear of public failure that actually stops most of us putting our heads above the parapet, and trying for a goal that might improve our lives endlessly. We are so afraid of public failure, particularly here in the UK, that some of our most popular TV progammes are actually exercises in the unconscious exploration of the dread of failing in front of others.[27]

For example, everyone is puzzled by the success of *The Weakest Link* – after all, the sums of money at stake are pitiable compared to rival programmes like *Who Wants to be a Millionaire*. Plus Anne Robinson seems to relish finding new ways of being peremptorily unpleasant to everyone taking part, so unlike most TV shows with a strong presenter presence, she hardly seems the kind of person you want to curl up with on your sofa.

In fact, part of the secret to its success involves the psychology of the situation, and is embedded in code in its very title. The name refers interestingly to the losers – 'the weakest links' – while other quiz shows' associations are with winning – like *Who Wants to be a Millionaire*. So intriguingly a large part of our interest for the first time in this quiz show is in the losers, and not the winner.

The camera that tracks the losers as they shuffle away lingers on their faces for longer than we see the victor at the end enjoying triumph. Such cutting-edge TV quizzes are now not so much about rewarding skill and knowledge as about punishing ignorance.

But the penalty is meted out by the other contestants, who decide which of the stragglers is for the axe after each round, so borrowing a significant element from Channel 4's *Big Brother*. Only this time the voting isn't secret; you unflinchingly parade the name of the person you want ejected. So lucky escapees can target you in the next round. This introduces back-stabbing and personal politics into the quiz show, with the rejected able to vent their spleen to camera afterwards.

Unlike presenters of other shows who might support and encourage the contestants, Anne Robinson castigates them for being stupid, and reminds them how badly they are doing. But the contestants can't band together against her, as they have to vote each other out, so you really are out there on your own – very alone with no friend to phone or audience to ask.

Even the bright light shining in the contestants' faces and the darkened studio backdrop cleverly but subtly recreate the interrogation room. This again is in marked contrast to the cheerful illumination of most game show studios, which don't depict the contestants as rabbits caught in the glare of headlights, as *The Weakest Link* does.

The arrangement of the studio – with the contestants all facing Robinson side by side and being summarily dismissed by her to endure the 'walk of shame' – has uncanny echoes with the childhood situation we have all endured of being grilled by an intimidating school mistress. Indeed, the contestants meekly obey her every command – for example, to defend their choice of the next person to be dumped. No one dares argue with her – they have all regressed into obedient childhood in the face of the stern teacher.

But Robinson has attracted huge fascination precisely because of her awfulness, which echoes a principle well known in forensic psychology, where we pay much more attention to, obey and try to please a person who has the power to hurt us. It is named 'The Stockholm Syndrome' after a famous siege in Sweden in which victims appeared to develop a strong attachment to their hostage takers.[28] Robinson demonstrates this principle in the way she commands the hushed respect of her charges.

Perhaps part of the success of *The Weakest Link* is because we have grown tired of the good-natured bonhomie of the traditional quiz show, where the consolation prizes and host's commiseration seek to bolster the loser with tea, sympathy and an 'It's only a game show' philosophy. Indeed since the contestants chanted this on *Big Brother* as a way of allaying their anxiety before finding out who was for the axe, the mantra has gained an ominous edge.

Maybe we watch because we want to see how others deal with stress and failure. We know the contestants are upset as they trudge the walk of shame, but we want to see how good they are at hiding it. We are gripped by the bitterness and resentment of the losers. Perhaps we are gripped because we too have experienced public humiliation when we failed at school or at work, or were told off by someone in authority. There is a kind of comfort and curiosity in seeing how others cope with similar stress.

But fundamentally what is most intriguing about *The Weakest Link* is how uncompromisingly hard line it is, from how horrible the contestants are to each other in naming the candidates for rejection, to complaining on camera off set afterwards. Trashing them all is Anne Robinson's virtuoso performance as the interviewer from hell.

Is this because the cosy 'tea and sympathy' of the traditional quiz show just got too far away from how we all experience the reality of life?

Now our solidarity is with the loser, because we have all been there. The problem is that our fear of losing, of doing the walk of shame, stops us trying to be winners. In fact, the weakest link is not someone who volunteers to appear on the show, it's the millions watching who are too scared even to try.

Our fear of failure has dramatic implications; it often stops us dreaming and wishing and this stops us thinking deeply about what might make us really happy.

This fear of failure is something we shall explore later in this book, but another issue that immediately raises its head is how much we can alter our mental attitude and motivation – are these not all determined by our childhoods, as many pop media therapists today are likely to maintain?

Some answers are provided by analysis of why some people are more successful in sport than others. Obviously natural sporting prowess and physical ability plus fitness must be a factor, but new research for the Department of Preventive and

Social Medicine at the University of Otago in New Zealand has come up with a surprising answer.[29] The researchers followed up children from the age of five until the age of twenty-six and examined what predicted who ended up representing their local area or region in sports competitions.

They found that certain aspects of personality at the age of five anticipated who would end up playing sports at the highest levels. The key seemed to be how fearful a person you are, in particular if you worry a lot, and especially if you are fearful of new situations. It seems fear is a major handicap if you want to perform well on the pitch or the court. The reason low levels of fearfulness in personality seem to predict future sporting success is that to go all out to win you have to be unafraid of how you appear to others, and of failure or looking foolish. It would seem high levels of fearfulness distract you from focusing entirely on the game itself, and cause you to be concerned about getting an injury or perhaps falling ill as a result of over-exertion.

As a child you might have avoided playing sports because you were afraid of being made to look weedy, or because of your general fear of new situations. The key implication of this research for adults is to examine how much your fears might be holding you back in your fitness regime or your sporting ability.

It could be you don't go to the gym as often as you should because you are afraid of how you appear to others, or you hate being beaten badly on the court so you avoid playing as much as you should. It is important to put your fears to one side if you are going to achieve all you want to performance-wise. So in order to perfect your body, you have to stop your mind getting in the way.

If how you feel about failure at the age of five determines your sporting prowess as an adult, as this research shows, does this mean you can't do anything about your motivation once you achieve adulthood? Again, as I will show later in this book, there is much you can do to alter your motivation no matter what age you have attained. However in order to do this the latest research into the psychology of success, goals and motivation will need to be understood properly and not misunderstood, as is commonly the case.

Many trying to improve their fitness and health have goals like losing a certain amount of weight or running a mile in a certain time – but the brutal truth, according to the latest psychological research, is that most of us will fail to achieve our goals. Yet despite persistently failing, we seem to try and try again. Psychologists call this 'False Hope Syndrome' and we shall discuss it at some length later.

Although certain basic drives are determined by our genes, this doesn't mean they can't be altered using many psychological and some pharmacological techniques. For example, we will be exploring the use of testosterone in altering female and male drive later in the book.

But it is intriguing to note how culturally shy we are of openly talking about and considering how to improve our performance in any sphere of life.

Yet for the rest of us remaining in our seats while others go up to get their awards, we do need cheering up as, to be brutally frank, we often hate seeing others doing better than us. It seems mysterious to us how others do indeed achieve what we covet but seem unable to attain ourselves. The basic mechanism of achievement seems opaque to the rest of us. It also seems to many of us that the price you have to pay to get what you aspire to might be too great – it seems a Faustian pact, whereby you have to do things you don't really morally agree with or find unpleasant to get a foot on the ladder of success.[30]

But is it also possible that this view is merely a rationalization that helps us explain to ourselves why we don't push ourselves harder to get what we secretly really want: more money, more success, a better body, a superior relationship?

Another piece of popular culture that nicely illustrates our ambivalent attitude to motivation and ambition is the popular TV sitcom *Frasier*.

Frasier made history by becoming the first TV series ever to achieve a record five consecutive Emmy wins, nosing ahead even of the enormously successful sitcom *Cheers*, the series from which *Frasier* was originally 'spun-off'.

Yet, ironically, the character of Dr Frasier Crane was not initially planned to become such a TV phenomenon. He was brought on to *Cheers* to serve as a temporary obstacle in the romantic relationship between Sam, the owner of the bar, and Diane, his long-term love interest. But he has now been around for fifteen years, and Kelsey Grammer, who plays the insecure, pompous but curiously likeable radio psychiatrist, has become the world's highest-paid TV star, clinching a £1.17m-per-episode fee.

Frasier left the Boston bar of *Cheers*, where he was a regular customer, for Seattle, where the twice-divorced doctor's peaceful home life of fine cigars and *haute cuisine* is shattered when his gruff, ex-cop father, Martin, is injured in the line of duty and forced to move in with him. But Dad brings with him a down-to-earth manner and a duct-taped recliner that clashes with Frasier's more aesthetic ambitions and fancy furniture.

You might have thought that the programme would rely on Frasier's agony advice for a major source of comedy. It is true that the tired TV device of the psychiatrist beset with more neuroses than his patients, and who doesn't take his own advice, is indeed wearily ground out once more – remember ITV's *Cracker* and Channel 4's *Psychos*?

But the real dynamic on the show is the hyper-competitive relationship between Frasier (a Freudian) and his brother Niles, also an insecure psychiatrist (but an arch Jungian). This is sibling rivalry on steroids as both constantly compete to finally arrive in high society, and it is really through this device that Frasier comes to say something actually pretty subversive and scathing about middle-class aspirations.

For example, in one famous episode Frasier mistakenly receives a mysterious invitation to an exclusive locale. Frasier and Niles are upset to have been left out of the loop about this new hot spot, and become obsessed with getting in to find out what it's all about. They can only access what turns out to be an upmarket spa after complex machinations whereby Niles has to pose as someone else. He and Frasier enjoy all of the amenities, but then are disturbed to learn that the spa has a 'gold level' area to which they are denied access. They constantly complain about being left out but through yet more convoluted conniving they finally get into this area, and are appeased, until they spot a platinum door . . .

Actually, *Frasier* isn't much about psychiatry at all, and after more than 200 episodes I have yet to spot a genuine diagnosis (except in Frasier himself who seems to be a walking textbook).

Instead, *Frasier* merely exploits the device of two psychiatrists competing with each other to poke fun at expertise in all its guises, particularly those who smugly claim to know more than us and patronizingly bestow *advice*. But above all else, and this is *Frasier* at its most sinister, it is really satirizing the middle-class 'over-intellectualization' of life. The device of the psychiatrist is just a metaphor for the middle-class exhibitionist tendency to use a complex Freudian or literary allusion when a short one would do.

Remember Frasier does find the Junior Existentialist Club. Plus he does try to give a bar mitzvah speech in Hebrew, only the friend who he picks to learn Hebrew from plays a practical joke and teaches him a *Star Trek* language instead, so Frasier ends up delivering the solemn bar mitzvah address in Klingon. Maybe we really love laughing at *Frasier* because deep down we want to snigger at all those who try to be better than us.

TEN STEPS TO MORE CONFIDENCE

(1) *Being shy is not a handicap – it's a bonus*
   In fact, shyness is usually an extremely attractive personality trait; often the shy are found more appealing than the socially assertive. So don't see your shyness as a handicap to social intercourse – instead see it as a part of you that many other people will identify with (almost 50% of people rate themselves as shy). Your shyness can be a part of you that connects you with others, not distances you from them, if you have the right attitude to it.

(2) *Before you leap in to talk to someone, do a bit of reconnaissance*
   Starting off a conversation with someone you don't know well, or have only just met, is particularly difficult for the shy, so take a tip from the more socially assertive who, before they leap in, check the situation out as much as possible. You need to focus on what is going on around you (rather than on how inadequate you are feeling) and in particular observe others closely to pick up as much as you can about how they are feeling and what their interests are. Great conversationalists kick off by making comments that are connected to what is going on for the person they are talking to. To overcome shyness you need to take

an active and acute interest in what is going on around you, so you can adapt yourself to it and fit in smoothly.

(3) *Timing is everything in joining a conversation*
A terrible moment if you are shy is at a party when you are at the periphery of a group who are animatedly discussing something and you are trying to join in. The big mistake the shy make is to leap in and interrupt a free-flowing conversation in order to gain entry into the group – everyone feels irritated at you for having disrupted the flow. Instead have the patience to keep waiting until a natural lull occurs before then inserting an open-ended question that lets others participate; but once you have got the conversation moving again, back off talking and give others a chance. The most boring people are those who feel a need to dominate or be the constant centre of attention.

(4) *Don't keep comparing yourself with the wittiest person you know*
Psychological research has found that one reason the less socially confident feel inadequate is that whenever they are at a social gathering, they tend to pay attention to the most socially outstanding person there – the life and soul of the party – against whom they compare themselves unfavourably. Such a comparison will only heighten self-consciousness and inhibit social performance. Instead, start making a conscious effort to see how many people at a social gathering are not holding the whole gathering in idolizing rapture, and notice that you don't have to be an outstanding wit to find gatherings worthwhile and enjoyable.

(5) *Don't try to meet people by only going to places where the very assertive are to be found*
New technology means it is easier than ever before for shy people to meet each other via the internet or on the phone via chat-lines. These ways of encountering people, before an actual 'in the flesh' meeting, might be good for practising social skills, in situations where

there is less pressure and need for assertiveness than in a crowded bar or nightclub.

(6) *Don't see awkwardness as defining all your interactions with others*
Another way of looking at shyness is that you are simply slow to warm up socially – you merely need more time to adjust to new or stressful situations – so give yourself longer, rather than simply abandoning a party or social encounter early.

(7) *If you don't think people are worth getting to know, you won't overcome your shyness*
Psychologists have recently identified a new group of shy people called the cynically shy, who, because they feel rejected by others, tend to feel that making the effort to socialize is pointless, because people are not worth it. As a result they adopt a superior stance, looking down on others. This is unhelpful and merely compounds your isolation. If you are finding it difficult to connect with those you meet, then spread your net wider and make more of an active effort to meet those who share your interests. Everyone has within their lives some achievement that makes them worth looking up to, not down on, and if you can make an effort to find this, you will be everyone's friend.

(8) *Not everything you say to others has to be immediately absorbing*
Shy people tend to have mistaken expectations about socializing and believe everything they say has to come out perfect and witty, so their life has to be like some kind of seamlessly scripted sitcom. In fact, times when a conversation is a bit boring, or you make social faux pas, are entirely part of real life, and unless you don't feel mortified when these things inevitably happen and take them in your stride, you won't overcome your shyness.

(9) *Don't arrive late at parties – get there early*
Because the shy try to put off social encounters, they

often arrive later than usual at gatherings; they reason that it should be easier to mingle when the party is in full swing, plus they hate the idea of standing out by arriving too early. Yet if you are shy, trying to break in to groups of people already vigorously chatting is difficult. So get there early – precisely because there are so few other people around, everyone is grateful to talk to anyone else; they are much less likely to have time for you when all their usual friends arrive.

(10) *Fight the modern plague of 'cocooning' by being constantly open to more small talk with relative strangers*

Increasingly we sit on trains buried in our books, tapping on laptops or talking into our mobile phones, and this all means we are cocooning ourselves from interacting with others on a casual basis via small talk. Also our tendency to rush from one appointment to the next contributes to this gradual social de-skilling. Aim to enter into small talk in at least one casual social encounter each day as part of your programme to overcome your shyness, and soon you will find you have more new friends than you know what to do with.

1

WHY DO YOU DO THAT THING YOU DO?

You can judge the height of someone's talent by what he aspires to. Only a great thing can satisfy a great talent
Baltasar Gracian

Focus less on whether an event is good or bad, but whether or not it involves an important change of life for you
William Bridges

Most psychological work suggests that mentioning how exercise will improve your sex life is much more likely to motivate you than just suggesting it will help you live longer.[1] Unfortunately in many instances people are so keen to get the proposed benefit, e.g., more sex, they don't bother to evaluate the evidence critically, and so are motivated when in fact the goal isn't achievable.[2] Many products like luxury cars are sold on exactly this premise.

It is interesting that at the heart of many motivating strategies is this notion of the covert goal. It is the prospect of more sex that drives us to the gym, or just drives us in the case of expensive automobiles, and this has to be hinted at rather than explicitly directed.[3]

Often it seems the things that really do determine our behaviour – sex, money, power – are not the kind of motivations it's possible to discuss openly in polite company. Why should this be – that so many of our drives are surrounded by taboo? One possibility is that civilization hinges on the issue of controlling our impulses – keeping our animal instincts in check.[4]

So civilization determines that when we sit down to a meal in company we wait for others to be served before starting to eat. This is about expressing our control over our desire to eat, and at the heart of civilization is the principle of control over basic instincts. The problem is that our motivations then become repressed and even obscure to us.[5] At the heart of this book is the idea that we need to become more aware of what really drives us in order properly to harness our drives and direct them in a way that helps us achieve what will really bring fulfilment.

The classic Freudian view was that our core motivations remained buried deep in our unconscious where they were likely to lie undisturbed unless we had the benefit of a trained analyst for therapist.[6]

While Freudian thinking now no longer dominates psychology or psychiatry, a new field has emerged called evolutionary psychology with surprisingly similar conclusions – that what drives us is often below conscious awareness because it is about achieving a long-term evolutionary benefit.[7]

Evolutionary psychology hinges on the idea that much of our motivational and emotional machinery evolved to help us survive in an ancestral environment. The argument is that much of our behaviour and sentiment makes more sense if we begin to consider the possible advantages to our ancestors from hundreds of thousands of years ago.[8]

Making our fundamental aspirations clearer to us is not an overtly easy task. This is illustrated by these recent developments in psychology – particularly in the arena of evolutionary psychology.

For example, in a recent research paper entitled 'Teaching could be hazardous to your marriage', sociologists have found that male university professors and secondary school teachers have a significantly higher than expected divorce rate.

Satoshi Kanazawa of Indiana University of Pennsylvania and Mary Still of Cornell University in New York say their data points to the theory that constant exposure to young female students leads male teachers to eventually find women of their own age less attractive, due to contrast and comparison effects.[9]

In previous laboratory experiments psychologists have found that men who were exposed to photographs of physically attractive women subsequently became less satisfied with their current heterosexual relationships, expressed less commitment to their relationships, and rated their partners less attractive.[10]

These previous brief experiments raised the question to Drs Kanazawa and Still of what would be the cumulative effect on older men's relationships of being constantly exposed to young attractive women. Evolutionary psychologists argue that men, even those much older, are genetically programmed to find women in their late teens and early twenties the most attractive, because this is when women are at their most fertile.

Few occupations and professions afford greater opportunities to come into contact with women in their late teenage years and early twenties than secondary school and college teaching. Teachers and lecturers therefore experience the cumulative effect of exposure to young attractive women, who are at their peak reproductive phase, more acutely than people in most other occupations.

Female teachers and university lecturers are also exposed to young attractive men, but evolutionary psychologists argue this would not have a comparable effect on women's relationships, as women do not value youth and physical attractiveness in mates as much as men do. If the findings of previous experiments imply that the contrast effect could be cumulative, then male teachers of young people should be more dissatisfied with their mates than other people.

To test this theory Kanazawa and Still analysed one of the largest social science data sets available on marital status of the US population, the General Social Survey collected annually for the last twenty-five years involving a sample of almost 33,000 adults. They published their findings in the prestigious journal *Evolution and Human Behavior*.

In the sample, there were 235 college professors and 414 high school teachers. While being a female teacher or lecturer did not predict a higher chance of being divorced compared to women generally, being a male secondary school teacher or university lecturer did predict a much higher chance of being divorced and also not remarrying after divorce than men in the general population. Also male teachers of kindergarten and very young children were not more likely than the general population to have a higher divorce rate, suggesting it is something about exposure to a particular age group of students that is having the effect on male teachers' and university lecturers' marriages.

Kanazawa and Still suggest also that the 'slow to remarry' rate they found among male teachers and university lecturers is due to the cumulative contrast effect. After all, any adult woman these men might meet and date after their divorce would still pale in comparison to the young attractive women with whom they come in daily contact.

The data did not find that male teachers or university lecturers had more casual sex or extramarital affairs than men in the general population. So Kanazawa and Still do not believe the higher divorce rate among male lecturers is due to their having affairs with students. Rather they are suffering a contrast effect, the consequence of constant exposure to younger women with whom they inevitably compare adult women of their own age unfavourably.

Kanazawa said that no other occupation besides university and school teaching seems to have a similarly high proportion of young women among the people that the occupants deal with, rendering confirmatory research on other professions difficult. 'The only other possibility that I could think of is movie producers and directors (who also, I might add, have a high divorce rate). But I'm not sure if there are enough of these people in any representative sample of the United States population for the statistical analysis to yield a significant result,' Kanazawa stated.

Although Kanazawa said he wanted to avoid giving advice to male university lecturers on the basis of his results, he did say, 'What we discover in our study is an innate tendency of men to prefer younger women, just like the innate tendency of men to be aggressive and competitive. If one wants to avoid the consequences of one's innate tendencies, then one needs to be carefully mindful of the fact that one does have such tendencies. If male teachers and their wives want to "save" their marriages, then they need to accept the fact that men are innately predisposed to prefer young women as mates, and be particularly mindful of the potential consequences.'

So according to evolutionary psychology it seems that our drive to pass on our genes is so hardwired into our brains that it leads to behaviour that produces quite a lot of conflict and unhappiness (e.g., divorce).[11]

Evolutionary psychology has permeated every aspect of human experience and even claims to explain why we bother to compose music or do science. For example, new research from this American sociologist also reveals that peak scientific creativity and productivity is closely linked to the time in their lives when scientists are trying hardest to get a mate. This suggests scientific creativity is basically an attempt to show off intellectual prowess to potential marriage partners, in order to attract them.[12]

The research arises from a question posed by evolutionary psychologists: why do we bother to make scientific discoveries at all? If evolutionary theory is correct then these examples of 'cultural display' should produce some benefit in passing on our genes to future generations.

Evolutionary psychologists have recently come up with the radical suggestion that intellectual creativity and productivity are really attempts to display our intelligence. IQ is a characteristic that potential mates find attractive, as traditionally, in the adverse environments we used to live in, intelligence boosts the survival chances of offspring with your genes.[13]

If this is true then as evolutionary psychologist Geoffrey Miller from University College London predicts, 'Cultural production should increase rapidly after puberty, peak at young adulthood when sexual competition is greatest, and gradually decline over adult life as parenting eclipses courtship.'[14]

Indeed, Miller found support for his theory in data on the producers of jazz albums, modern paintings and books; in each case he found that cultural production rapidly increased after puberty, peaked in early to middle adulthood, then declined throughout adulthood.[15]

But Satoshi Kanazawa, the sociologist from the Indiana University of Pennsylvania mentioned earlier, has now uncovered further startling evidence supporting the idea that scientists do science partly in order to attract a mate.

The proof of the theory comes from an investigation into the timing of career peaks of 280 of the most eminent scientists living from the eighteenth century to the present day, and the data is published in a recent issue of the journal *Evolution and Human Behavior*.

Kanazawa analysed the date of the discovery or experiment listed in *The Biographical Dictionary of Scientists* as the most significant contribution of each scientist, to ascertain their ages at the peak of the careers. The mean age of pinnacle scientific achievement among male scientists (only 2.5% of the sample were female) was 35.4, with 50% of scientists peaking within six years before or after the age of thirty-five.

But if this courtship model of scientific productivity is correct and 'cultural display' declines through adulthood, because 'parenting eclipses courtship', then a different pattern should hold for men who had not mated and reproduced. There would be no reason for these men, who had not successfully reproduced, to cease their 'cultural display'. Instead they should be driven to continue being scientifically productive until they attracted a mate.

Indeed Kanazawa found that male scientists who never marry do not decline in productivity as sharply with age as those who do: 50% of unmarried scientists make as great a contribution in their late fifties as they do in their late twenties; the corresponding percentage among married scientists is 4.3%.[16] The average age for peaking in career for unmarried scientists is 39.9, while for married scientists it is 33.9. This difference in the average age for career peaking between married and unmarried scientists is statistically highly significant.

Nearly a quarter of all male married scientists have made their greatest contribution within five years after marriage and the average delay between getting married and experiencing a career peak is a mere 2.5 years. It would therefore appear that once scientists get married, they quickly cease their cultural displays, while unmarried scientists continue to make great scientific contributions later in their lives.

But evolutionary psychology arguments such as these attract criticism because they appear rather sexist – for example, 'cultural display' or intellectual and creative activity is seen as a male strategy to attract female mates because biologists argue that men compete for mates more fiercely than women.[17]

Dr Geoffrey Miller points out in support of his argument that men produce twenty times as many jazz albums, eight times as many modern paintings and three times as many books as women. As a result, Kanazawa only tested his theory using data on marriage and peak productivity on male scientists, explaining that only 2.5% of the 280 scientists listed in *The Biographical Dictionary of Scientists* are female.[18]

Kanazawa comments: 'Contemporary men think that getting married means having to take over half the childcare responsibilities and household work because their wives work as corporate executives. However, the majority of the scientists in my data come from the eighteenth and nineteenth centuries, when married men made very little contribution (in terms of time and energy) to household chores and childcare responsibilities. If anything, married men in the eighteenth and nineteenth centuries had *more* (rather than less) time than single men because now they had someone in the house to cook for them and take care of their needs at all times.'

Evolutionary psychology can even explain who it is you find attractive in terms of the fine details of their personal appearance.

We tend to think of beauty as being in the eye of the beholder, and that physical attractiveness is at least partly down to individual aesthetic judgement. But the very latest scientific research into facial attractiveness claims finally to have unlocked the mystery of what makes a face beautiful, and can even predict what faces will be found most attractive, using precise mathematical formulae for various face measurements.[19]

Evolutionary theory predicts that individuals gain some aspect of quality for their offspring by mating with attractive individuals, perhaps by obtaining good genes.[20]

That we may be biologically or genetically predetermined to find certain faces attractive is demonstrated by experimental work over the past fifteen years that confirms babies as young as a few days old stare longer at the same attractive faces that mirror the preferences of adults. These findings have proved remarkably robust, and have been replicated with babies preferring to play with facially attractive dolls and strangers.[21]

One explanation for this effect is that we are drawn to attractive faces because you might indeed be able to judge a book by its cover, and the face could reveal something important about the brain encased within.

Dr Robin Hennessy and Dr John Waddington at the Royal College of Surgeons Research Unit in Dublin have recently pioneered a Laser Surface Scanning technique that allows for the first time a 3D analysis of how facial shape might vary with brain structure. This team argues that in early foetal life brain and face development are intimately connected, and abnormalities in brain elaboration probably affect face development as well. Their research suggests strong links between the differences in size between male and female brains and the contrast in size in male and female faces.

Hennessy and Waddington point out that numerous developmental disturbances like Down's Syndrome demonstrate a link between brain alteration and striking facial features. Using similar techniques this team recently demonstrated that other disorders linked to brain aberrations are also associated with facial alterations. For example, they have shown that those suffering from schizophrenia are more likely to have, amongst other facial differences, an overall narrowing and elongation of the mid and lower front of the face, with reduced mouth width.[22]

Further support for these theories comes from a study just published by Professor Leslie Zebrowitz and psychologist colleagues at Brandeis University in the USA who have demonstrated that there is an association between facial attractiveness and the IQ of the possessor of the face.[23] Furthermore, strangers were found to be able to correctly judge intelligence at levels significantly better than chance from brief exposures to a target's face. The research found that the widespread assumption in the population that more facially attractive people are more intelligent was borne out to be true to a surprising extent.

Does this mean that your face really could be your fortune?

Sociologists Dr Ulrich Mueller and Dr Allan Mazur of the University of Marburg in Germany recently analysed the final-year photographs of a cohort of graduates of the class of 1950 of the elite United States Military Academy at West Point. Dominant facial appearance in the final-year graduate photograph was a consistent and important predictor of rank attainment in the Army over twenty years later.[24]

Having a more dominant-looking face (strong jaws, broad cheekbones, thin lips or a prominent forehead) predicted getting further up the ranks in the Army, but exactly why remains a mystery. One theory is that dominance in facial features is a marker of higher testosterone levels in the body and as testosterone is known to be associated with competitiveness and aggression, the dominant face is actually signalling us about an important aspect of the physiology of that person.

Or it could be a self-fulfilling prophecy. Because some men appear dominant they get more respect and obedience from others, which assists their rise through the ranks.

There was some support for a self-fulfilling prophecy effect in Professor Zebrowitz's just-published work, as that team found past facial attractiveness predicted future intelligence scores better than past intelligence results. In other words how you looked predicted how intelligent you apparently became more accurately than your past intelligence. Perhaps because the more attractive were treated as more intelligent, they ended up having more stimulating and therefore intelligence-enhancing lives.[25]

But if dominant features in a male face significantly help you get promotion in the Army, is it possible using similar research techniques to ascertain the facial features that render us the most attractive?

Prior to puberty, the lower jaw of the male and female face are similar in length; at puberty, however, men undergo a rapid growth spurt in the lower jaw, driven by testosterone and related hormones. The female jaw undergoes a similar but much reduced growth surge due to their much lower levels of testosterone-like hormones. In order to signal lower testosterone and higher female hormones conducive to female fertility, the shorter the lower jaw the better in women. Indeed a shorter than average lower jaw in women appears to account for most of the attractive female facial proportions (eye-chin, eye-nose, eye-mouth and mouth-chin).[26]

Recent research confirms that the most beautiful female faces have lower jaws that are shorter than two-thirds of the jaw of the average female. Like the jaw, female lips vary with age, and fullness appears to depend on female hormones like oestrogen. As optimal female fertility appears to hinge on a combination of low testosterone-like hormones and high oestrogen, this supports the idea that the attractive female face will be found to have full lips and a short lower jaw.[27]

But why didn't evolution then ensure that women over hundreds of generations had jaws that just got smaller and smaller, and lips that got larger and larger? Of course, functional requirements for chewing, vision and brain development probably account for major constraints on human facial structure.[28]

Also, different environments will have selected different facial features as advantageous. For example, a long nose with narrow nostrils is best suited for a cold arid climate in order to add moisture to and warm cold air. Conversely a short nose with wide nostrils is a better adaption to a hot tropical climate.[29]

But the very latest research on facial attractiveness, just about to be published by psychologists Dr Caroline Keating and Dr James Doyle based in New York, has found that the most attractive faces contain a mixture of features signalling warmth, power and dominance, with no one characteristic eclipsing the others.[30]

A new intriguing theory to explain this finding is based on the idea that the facial features a woman passes on to her offspring include an anti-cuckoldry mechanism, to ensure that she continues to get parental investment from her mate. The danger of an overly striking female face that varies too extremely from the average is that this might make it more difficult for a man to discern his own features in their offspring. A face tending towards a balance of features allows more room for the man's characteristics to show through in the facial appearance of their children, so reassuring him these really are his, and that he should hang around to assist in their raising, so preserving his genes for the future.[31]

Also, in separate recent work, psychologists Dr Penton-Voak and Dr Perrett from St Andrews University found that what kind of male face women were attracted to depended on where they were in their menstrual cycle.[32] Around the time of ovulation they were more attracted to hyper-masculine male faces, but during menstruation they preferred more feminine male faces. The evolutionary theory is that when they are most likely to conceive, women aim to mate with a man signalling the most dominant and aggressive characteristics, because as a survival strategy it is best for her offspring to have these tough genes. However, it might be best to have these children raised by a partner who is more nurturing, though unknowingly cuckolded.

New York psychologists Keating and Doyle's work on the idea of an ideal balance of facial features now makes sense, if we are being pulled in different directions in terms of facial attractiveness depending on our goals and circumstances.

The experimental data supporting this overall 'average is beautiful' position is based on an image-processing technique whereby individual faces are photographed and the images are digitally combined and then printed as a simulated photograph. This method has revealed that average faces are judged to be more physically attractive than the individual faces that make up the average. Furthermore, the attractiveness of a multi-face composite increases with the number of faces in the average.[33]

So although the enhancement of facial beauty supports a multi-billion-dollar industry, and many spend a great deal of time, effort, cost and pain in an endless attempt to improve their faces, the very latest scientific research ironically suggests that they shouldn't try to look too obviously different from the average.[34]

Even if you don't want to buy into evolutionary psychology, and this is an extremely controversial area of psychology, it is still the case that more conventional psychological thinking leads us to the conclusion that our drives are often obscure from our conscious awareness.

For example, if you want to get a date, or choose someone who is likely to stay committed to you for a long time, a new tactic has been suggested by recent psychological research that could increase your chances of success – go for someone whose face resembles your own![35]

The evidence now is that someone who looks a bit like you facially is more likely to find you attractive. This is the conclusion of a series of recent startling psychology experiments conducted both in Britain and the USA.

Attraction to faces is a vital aspect of relationships, with scientific research confirming that the single best predictor of satisfaction with a 'blind date' is facial attractiveness for both men and women.[36]

The problem before now has been trying to predict who would fancy what, given the individual variation in preferences in facial appearance. But now the answer appears to be much simpler than previously realized – people who look facially like you are much more likely to go out with you, marry you and even stay married to you.

Dr Penton-Voak, a psychologist at the University of Stirling, has recently published a study where, using computer graphic technology, he transformed photographic images of women into equivalent male faces. In other words, he showed how these women would look if they had been born men, but with very similar facial features to their own.

He then asked each of the women whose faces had been photographed to rate her attraction to a variety of pictures of male faces, including the one of her own face looking like a man. None of the fifty-two women involved in the experiment realized that one of the male faces they were being presented with was in fact their own face digitally manipulated.

The startling finding was a strong tendency for women to be more attracted to men who looked facially like themselves.

But it was Verlin Hinsz, a psychologist from North Dakota State University in the USA, who first discovered that couples tend to look more like each other facially than could be accounted for just by chance.[37]

This was uncovered by experiments where photographs of individual members of engaged and married couples were compared with other random photographs of faces in terms of who resembled who. Information about who were in relationships with each other was hidden from raters, who had to pair faces up in terms of resemblance. Faces of those who turned out to be in relationships with each other were rated by independent observers as looking more like each other than could be accounted for by just chance pairing. No two photographs of faces were taken with the same background to reduce possible clues that two individuals were partners.

The results provide strong support for the theory that people who are attracted to each other tend to facially resemble each other.

Yet another study found that the longer couples seemed to have successfully stayed together the more they appeared to resemble each other facially – suggesting that a key to viable long-term relationships is choosing someone who looks a lot like you.[38]

One theory to explain these startling findings is referred to as the 'repeated exposure' hypothesis.[39]

It seems we spend an awful lot of time looking at our own faces – in mirrors every day as we check we look OK before going out – and also in our own photographs on passports as well as ID and travel cards. This means the face we probably see more of than any other is actually our own. Also we were surrounded as we grew up by those who were facially similar to us because of genes, in our family environment. This means that we are very familiar with facial characteristics close to our own, and perhaps through this repeated exposure to our own face and to the faces of others genetically similar to ourselves, we develop an attraction to faces similar to our own.[40]

Similarly you could be genetically endowed with a facial

characteristic that is not commonly seen as desirable (e.g., large nose, receding chin, overbite, etc.) but after repeated exposure to this facial characteristic from the mirror and family, you might become much more comfortable with such an attribute than others. So when you are selecting a partner, you would be more appreciative of that facial characteristic than would most others, and so have a greater attraction to a face having that feature than might others. This explains why people with similar looks tend to gravitate to each other.[41]

But one other possible explanation for this odd finding comes from perhaps the most established previous psychological 'law' of physical attraction: the 'matching hypothesis'. This is that people tend to end up choosing those who match themselves in terms of desirable qualities. So all other things being equal, we tend to go for those in our own league in terms of physical attractiveness.[42]

If you are average looking you will tend not to try and chat up someone as stunning looking as Brad Pitt or Michelle Pfeiffer. The key phrase here is 'all things being equal', as elderly tottering billionaires seem to be able to pull young attractive partners, because they have compensating qualities outside the arena of looks.

A good reason for going for someone in your attractiveness league rather than too far above you is that this makes it more likely you won't be rebuffed, or that you won't be dumped when a more desirable prospect comes along.[43]

However, Dr Hinsz took this 'matching' theory into account when he analysed his data on independent observers pairing up photographs of couples in terms of facial similarity. He still found it was actual physical facial resemblance that more powerfully predicted who was seeing each other rather than levels of attractiveness.[44]

It was possible to distinguish between the two theories because, for example, often a female visage resembling a male face would render the woman's face significantly less attractive than the man's. Yet it was facial resemblance that still seemed to account most for why two people were together.

All of this research raises the spooky possibility that when you fall in love with someone else, although you don't consciously realize it, you are really unconsciously falling in love with the bit of them that reminds you of yourself.[45]

Twenty Tips on Improving your Motivation

What do self-made millionaires, Olympic medal winners, or those who have lost weight, reached the top of their profession, picked up Oscars, passed difficult exams, raised happy self-fulfilled children or engaged in fruitful long-term relationships all have in common? They are all extremely motivated because it takes strong personal drive in order to do what is hard in life.

Yet the issue of motivation is fundamentally neglected in our culture – for example, the flaw at the heart of all diets is that they require motivation in order to be completed and yet they don't give any advice on this area.

We get concerned about our children's academic performance and obsess about the quality of their schools and teachers, yet all the evidence is that children can get top grades despite appalling disadvantages if they are motivated enough and yet we do little, if anything at all, to motivate our children, or for that matter ourselves or our colleagues or spouses or relatives or friends. So a key issue is not just how to motivate ourselves but how to motivate others.

Our culture has become obsessed with advantage and disadvantage, fairness and the level playing field, support and assistance, without realizing that in so doing it has completely misunderstood that in life the ability to overcome obstacles is a key part of any success strategy. As a result we have become a society unable to attain our personal goals, because we don't appreciate the key role of inner drive and motivation.

In fact strong motivation is available to us all if we follow the tips below, distilled from years of research.

(1) Set a goal
Don't be vague about your goal – i.e., 'I want to lose weight.' Be as specific as possible – state how much weight you want to lose. Know clearly what the goal is, i.e., what precisely your target weight might be and how many pounds that means you have to lose to get there. Know precisely where you are now and where you have to get to. So don't say you want more pay or a better job – fix exactly how much you want to be earning and what job precisely you want, i.e., Prime Minister and 100K a year.

(2) Set a time

Having fixed your goal clearly, set a date by which you will achieve it. So, for example, now you know you are going to have to lose a stone, set a date by which this will be done. The date puts you under pressure and constrains your options in terms of helping it become clear when you are backing out of doing what you need to to attain your goal.

(3) Set a timetable

Now you know exactly what you want and when, you can work backwards and establish some sub-goals that are closer in time to where you are now. So if you have to lose a stone in six months you can work out how much you need to lose per week in order to attain your goal.

(4) Start tracking your progress

Using the weight-loss example, now you know how much you need to lose per week in order to attain your goal in six months' time, start tracking your progress by measuring your weight regularly. Tracking progress is an essential step to goal attainment because it helps you know how to adjust performance in order to attain your target. Tracking is unpopular as a motivational strategy because it often involves receiving unpleasant feedback about how badly you are doing. If however you don't track and don't get this feedback you can't adjust your strategy and performance in order to raise your game to get what you want.

(5) Get the resources you need to implement your plan

Now you know exactly what you want, when you want it, and what sub-goals you need to achieve to stay on track, you need to think about what resources you need in order to attain your goal. In the weight-loss example you will need perhaps weighing scales and access to healthy low-fat food plus emotional resources like stress-relieving techniques other than comfort eating. It may be you need to join a gym or set aside time to go jogging. Resources are not just physical, but they are emotional, temporal and psychological as well.

(6) Make it difficult for yourself to back out

Failing is much easier if only you know you have failed, so it's best to ensure that failure is going to be public. This is so much more embarrassing that it tends to ensure failure is not an option, which is a great motivational strategy. So tell others about your goals and publicly display your tracking system – for instance by showing everyone else how your weight is doing on a plotted graph in comparison with your weekly target weights.

(7) Make your goal attainment strategy part of your routine
The more you have to make a conscious decision to do the right thing the more likely you are to fall at the early hurdles, so take decision-making out of the scenario by ensuring that you develop the necessary routine habits. If you are on a weight-loss regime, ensure your meals are pre-planned and easy to get at. Organize for a jogging partner to call on you every day at a set time so you get into the habit of jogging as part of your routine.

(8) Get information
Going back to setting your target weight – how did you decide this? Get as much information as you can about your target – what is a realistic weight to aim for? How do doctors calculate what is the right weight for someone of your height? How do others successfully lose weight? Any difficult goal is only ever attained after a formidable amount of research. You need to become an expert in the area so that you are not pushed off course by competing theories about what to do, e.g., going for hypnotherapy as part of the latest craze technique to lose weight and so abandoning your earlier preferred strategy of jogging regularly.

(9) Ask yourself why you have chosen that goal
It's vital to know fully and absolutely why you have opted to devote yourself to a particular goal. If you are suffering from false beliefs about yourself, your goal is unlikely to make full sense and therefore is less likely to be attainable. So why do you want to lose weight? What benefits do you think will accrue from this? Or is it really the case that you yourself don't mind what weight you are and you are only dieting because of what your partner has said? The more you are doing something for yourself and the more it fits into the structure of your core beliefs and values the more likely your goal is going to be achieved.

(10) Make sure you are not suffering from goal conflict

Oftentimes the reason people don't attain a goal is not that they don't desire the goal, it's more that other competing goals produce goal conflict. So if you have a goal of losing weight but also the goal of not being stressed by a feeling of hunger then it's likely that weight loss won't be achieved because there is fundamental goal conflict here. Check that the goals you have set yourself are really top of your list of priorities and make sure the subsidiary goals in your life are not in conflict with the primary goals. List your hierarchy of goals and check for conflicts between key goals. Be prepared to reconcile or reduce goal conflict by reducing the number of goals in your life.

(11) Learn from failure

If your goal is difficult to achieve rather than trivial then almost certainly there will be setbacks on the long journey to eventual success. The key is not to let failure put you off persisting. The successful differ from the rest of us not in that they never experience disappointment – rather in their reaction to frustration, which is to investigate what went wrong, see it as a learning opportunity, and to get right back on track with the plan and executing it.

(12) Don't get complacent

Achieving your goals boils down to evolving a plan and executing it. Even if things are going well never stop getting out the plan and looking at it critically and considering how the execution is going. Circumstances are almost inevitably going to change over time from the period you conceived the plan and started implementing it. It's vital to be flexible and to adapt your plan and its implementation with evolving circumstances. It might even be that as your goals start to be realized you should re-evaluate, setting the bar higher and changing your goals to tougher ones! Gold medal winners at the Olympics when asked what they are going to do next after their victory lap usually ponder for a moment and then reveal they are now going to try and get a second gold.

(13) Find a role model

Whatever your vision, it's extremely useful to investigate

whether others have travelled the path you are on before you. In all likelihood you are trying to repeat a task that has been achieved before and therefore if the goal is difficult it's vital to find out how previous successful journeyers have managed to overcome the difficulties you are now experiencing. Most, however, for reasons of lack of assertiveness and embarrassment, avoid asking advice from those who have attained the goal they now seek. One key theme that emerges from research into self-made millionaires and Olympic medal winners is their unembarrassability. They are willing to do whatever it takes, regardless of the social consequences, in order to attain their goal.

(14) Don't be a loner
Pursuing a goal can often be a lonely business but if you can find others who share your vision then you should try and link up with them. A group of people trying to lose weight are much more likely to succeed than just one, as the shared experience and social element, including the implicit competition, add to the motivating forces at work. With the internet, it's now possible to find others living in other countries who share your desires and are willing to communicate with you and so become a kind of virtual group that can assist you on your journey to success.

(15) Take a long look inside
The issue raised before about goal conflict is related to the dark problem that there may be hidden drives within you conspiring to prevent you from attaining your goal. All successful people have good self-knowledge – they know themselves and they are aware of their weaknesses and the conflicts that are likely to get in the way of attaining goals. Knowing yourself means you can develop strategies to overcome the weak or resistant parts of yourself.

(16) Look into the future
The successful tend to have a personality disposition that is future oriented – this means they are constantly looking forward to the longer-term consequences of present-day actions. Those who keep reaching for that cream bun instead of jogging round the park but say they want to lose weight are basically not see-

ing the long-term consequences of present-moment actions clearly enough. If you are to overcome the resistances present today you need to live in the future and see clearly how what you do today has future implications. Present-oriented people or those who live for the moment never attain difficult goals that require long-term planning and execution.

(17) Be afraid – very afraid

One of the most powerful motivators in life is fear and so the strongly motivated are usually gripped by a deep terror of the consequences of not achieving their goals. The self-made millionaire often fears being poor much more than the poor do, which is why they have worked tirelessly to avoid that outcome. If not achieving your goals has few negative consequences as far as you are concerned it may be you don't have enough fear in your life to drive you forward to overcome difficulty.

(18) Give yourself a break

Achieving goals can be a tough, relentless treadmill so it's also important to be able to take a break occasionally. If you are excessively demanding of yourself you could turn the whole process into such a miserable enterprise that you are in serious danger of getting upset or depressed. You aren't always going to be happy trying to achieve your goals but you need to be able to be kind to yourself as well.

(19) Have a supporters club

While not everyone is going to share your goals you will need people around you and close to you who encourage you on your journey. This is a vital issue because often people embark on the attainment of a difficult goal while their spouse is not at all on board the project and so subtly or not so subtly tries to sabotage the process. Get those close to you to support your project and ensure they are going to be cheerleaders because in the dark moments to come you are going to need shoulders to cry on and strong arms to support you when you feel weak.

(20) Remember goals are worthwhile

The life worth living – if it is about changing and developing yourself to becoming a better human being – must involve goals.

If you meet someone without goals then be kind, but you have met someone who is heading for deep unhappiness in the long run, as we feel best about ourselves when we are proud of our achievement in doing something others regard as difficult. All personal pride, self-esteem and self-confidence stem from the realization of difficult worthwhile goals.

2

HOW TO HAVE A PERFECT DAY

People do not wander around and then find themselves at the top of Mount Everest

Zig Ziglar

We become what we envisage
Claude M. Bristol

There is a problem for motivational theory at the heart of evolutionary psychology, which is that this fundamentally biological view hinges on the idea that our basic drives boil down to an incessant need to pass on as much as possible of our genetic material to future generations – hence the centrality of sexual and affiliative behaviour to much of this theorizing.[1]

This naturally leads to the notion that a lack of motivation may be blamed on your genes.

So how much of success in life is down to raw talent – and how much is due to your drive or motivation?

Many think it's practically all down to motivation, as shown in Thomas Edison's famous quote, 'Genius is 1% inspiration and 99% perspiration,' or the popular saying, 'If one has the will, one can succeed.'

Others think the issue is more finely balanced. In his famous book *Hereditary Genius*, Francis Galton (1869–1962) circumscribes the roots of eminence in the following way: 'By natural ability, I mean those qualities of intellect and disposition, which urge and qualify a man to perform acts that lead to reputation. I do not mean capacity without zeal, nor zeal without capacity, nor even a combination of both of them, without an adequate power of doing a great deal of very laborious work.'[2]

In Galton's terms, reputation (talent, eminence) will emerge from proper qualifications (high capacities, gifts), urges and zeal (needs, passions), as well as the power for laborious work (will-power, persistence).

These 'ingredients' of exceptional performance identified by Sir Francis Galton more than a century ago have reappeared again and again in the psychology of talent emergence as well as biographical analyses of eminent historical figures, according to a recent review by psychologists Françoys Gagné and François St Père.

Intelligence (or talent) and motivational factors are probably the two most commonly mentioned determinants of academic achievement. The most common belief within the general population is that both factors exert approximately equal causal influences on talent development. When people try to explain why they succeed or fail in their aspirations, not only in the academic world, but also in music and sports, effort and ability are by far the two major causal explanations.[3]

Currently when psychologists attempt to study scientifically the issue of which is more important – motivation or intelligence – in success they come up with a very surprising result. Intelligence or talent seems to account for a large proportion of achievement success while motivation counts for relatively little.[4] At best, the ratio of intelligence to motivation reaches 2:1; at worst, it can be as low as 13:1.[5]

How to explain this result? One possibility is that while the measurement of IQ is fairly well established, maybe when psychologists try to measure motivation scientifically they do a bad job of it.[6] It is probably hard to properly measure motivation using psychological testing, as who is going to own up on a questionnaire to not being very motivated?[7] Particularly if the test is administered in a work or school environment and you are aware your boss or teacher has their eye on you and your answer.

But in contrast to the odd result we get when we ask people to rate their own motivation, there is a much closer relationship between motivation and future outcome when you ask other people to assess your motivation.[8]

Françoys Gagné and François St Père of the Department of Psychology, University of Quebec in Montreal, Canada, examined the issue in a recent study and found that parents' ratings of their children's persistence predicts school achievement better than the students' theoretically more valid self-ratings.[9]

The most plausible hypothesis to explain this relates to the parents' perception of their child's motivation and their knowledge of his or her achievement. The parent notes the child does well at school and assumes this has something to do with their motivation and so gives them a high score on effort without actually knowing how much real drive is present. Consequently, if the parents observe that their child is achieving, they will tend to readjust their persistence judgements to a slightly higher level, doing the opposite when the child fails. These influences are sufficient to inflate the association between their persistence ratings and achievement, and create a low-level artificial causal relationship.

So we come back to the problem that it's very difficult to demonstrate scientifically that variation in effort plays a significant role in eventual achievement.[10]

One possible explanation is that having a high IQ is probably very motivating in itself, just as having little talent might be demotivating.[11] If you find you have to try very hard to get anywhere while others do just as well with little effort this will eventually sap your persistence. This could explain why raw talent often seems to predict more than motivation.[12]

On second thought, that lack of relationship can also be easily explained if we understand that in many test situations the task being given a talented subject is usually so well below what is required to challenge their skills that they need no motivation to perform well.[13]

For example, it is a well-known fact that the secondary school curriculum offers little challenge to bright students.[14] The lack of challenge impacts on both motivation and persistence. It decreases the desire to learn in those students who were hoping for new and fascinating knowledge presented at a fast rate. They are seldom working at the upper limit of their zone of proximal development. On the other hand, bright students can achieve very well without even trying.[15]

So one problem, argue psychologists Françoys Gagné and François St Père, is that we live in an environment that often doesn't really challenge the talented and so it can appear that all that really matters is talent and not motivation. Gagné and St Père conclude that the real test is to compare the equally talented with each other and see how differences in motivation then explain future achievement.[16]

Lewis Terman, a famous American psychologist, compared the 150 most successful and 150 least successful participants of his immense longitudinal study of talent development, when they attained mid-life; he found that they did not differ to any extent in intelligence as measured by tests. But there were significant differences: 'the four traits on which they differed most widely were "persistence in the accomplishment of ends", "integration towards goals", "self-confidence" and "freedom from inferiority feelings". In the total picture the greatest contrast between the two groups was in all-round emotional and social adjustment, and in drive to achieve.'[17]

So although motivation matters, it's difficult to measure it scientifically. This explains why it has been neglected by behavioural scientists, when it might actually be the most important variable of all in human behaviour.[18] It is vital, however, at a personal and scientific level to get a sense of where one's motivational levels are in order to better appraise what needs to be done to alter one's motivational strategy.[19]

I therefore want to try out a measure of motivation that I have developed, which I believe gives a better assessment of motivation than most of the tests currently being used in the field.

For this exercise I want you to use your imagination in as unfettered a way as possible. This is not something most people are used to doing, so it might take a few dry runs before you feel comfortable with this rather strange procedure.

It's called the 'perfect day' exercise. I am going to give you a metaphorical blank cheque – you could be anywhere in the world, be with anyone, do anything at all, and basically I want you to outline for me something of what your most perfect day would look like.

If on your perfect day you wake up in Buckingham Palace then tell me about that; if in your perfect day you are an astronaut taking the first step on Mars – or a film star opening the shooting for a new blockbuster – then tell me about that. The key point is that I don't want to hear about a good day or a very excellent day – I want to hear about your absolutely most perfect day. A day such that at the end of it you turn to whoever you were with and say to them, 'This has been the absolutely most perfect day of my life – it cannot get any better than this.'

A few rules.

I want you to tell me about the day in as much detail as possible. Where in the world do you wake up? Do you wake up late or early? Who are you with when you wake up – are you alone or are you with Michelle Pfeiffer or George Clooney? Or perhaps Michelle Pfeiffer *and* Julia Roberts . . .

Remember, it's your perfect day – no one else's. Also I am not here to judge your perfect day – you can be as outrageous as you like. Tell me what you would have for breakfast – would a large staff bring you breakfast in bed? Would you wake in your own Romanesque villa in Tuscany or a modest hotel in New York? What do you do after breakfast? How do you spend the day – is it busy or very relaxed? Do you meet someone famous for lunch?

What kind of person are you in your perfect day? Are you taller than you are now – thinner – richer – wittier?

When I have asked people to describe their perfect day, a surprisingly common recurring event is that many people are picking up an award at a huge ceremony and being acknowledged by their peers as outstanding for particular achievements.

It is also surprising how few men tell me they are waking up with their wives on their perfect day – indeed the male perfect day is often pretty pornographic, but let's draw a hasty veil over that . . .

One client of mine (I will disguise his details to protect his anonymity) came to me because he could never finish any of the books he was trying to complete yet he fervently wanted to be a novelist.

He related a perfect day that starts with him waking on his own private Caribbean island in his own private beachfront villa. Bobbing gently on a pier that he steps on to from his bedroom is his own seaplane – in his perfect day he has a private pilot's licence – and he flies to a nearby island where he breakfasts with the Spice Girls – who are of course good friends of his. Later in the day he scores the winning goal in a World Cup final for England against Brazil. And he ends the day dancing the night away in a very exclusive club in downtown Manhattan. It was important to him that there was a long impatient queue outside the club but that he was immediately waved through by the intimidating doormen, who recognized him from TV.

Would you mind having a go at the perfect day exercise right now? It is vitally important that you do it before you read any further, as if you try to do the exercise after reading what comes below then the point of the exercise will be ruined and you will be left lacking a vital bit of self-knowledge that will prove extremely helpful in gaining a deeper insight into your motivation.

So before turning the page please have a go at the exercise. It doesn't matter if it feels awkward or unfamiliar, just try it and we can always come back and work on it some more later.

Now the interesting thing about the perfect day exercise is that if you do it properly it can be very revealing about your psychology and in particular your motivation.

If you look back at my failed novelist client and his perfect day, does it reveal why he can't actually finish any books? Indeed it does, and also, unless his perfect day changes, why he is highly unlikely ever to complete a novel.

The perfect day exercise is intended to be enjoyable, by the way – that is part of its lure – so if you did it and didn't find it a pleasurable exercise then we will have to talk; but actually it's also deadly serious.

This is because the perfect day technique reveals something of your real motivation – what it is that you would really like to do with your life and what would give you real pleasure. Part of the secret of happiness is not necessarily to eventually achieve your perfect day but to be able to arrive somewhere near it at some point in the future.

If I were to directly ask you what your long-term goals are then you would probably respond with something rather worthy or what you think I wanted to hear. By asking about your goals in a more roundabout, perhaps even sneaky way, disguised as the perfect day exercise, then I get at what would really make your day, so to speak – what it would take to make you really happy and so what you are driven to achieve.

The perfect day exercise is what we term in my trade a 'goal clarification' exercise because it helps illuminate what people's real goals are, not what they think they are. Surprisingly most people don't actually know, or are not being honest with themselves about what would really make them content.[20]

Let me illustrate the power of the approach.

Remember our failed novelist? Well, let's analyse his perfect day – what does it tell us about him? I don't know if you noticed but, surprisingly for someone who supposedly wants to make it in the world of books, there was nothing literary about his perfect day at all. While it is true that his perfect day could not be achieved without a fair amount of wealth and sporting prowess, he didn't have to have anything to do with books to achieve it. Also he did nothing literary in it at all – there was no reading of books, no writing, no meeting literary figures or taking part in any activity remotely connected with literature.

It now becomes clear that this man wanted to write because it might bring him fame or wealth but not because he enjoyed writing. This helps illuminate why he is always going to have difficulty finishing books – he sees writing as a means to an end, an end that might be achieved in many different ways – but he really has no interest in writing for its own sake. It is also likely that writing will probably not bring him the kind of fame that he is really seeking.

Of course it is entirely possible that he might be able to finish books and achieve success without any real interest in literature, but if you are going to achieve your goal the key is to understand why you are doing something. What the perfect day exercise illustrates in this case is that what he really wants is fame and money and the writing is merely a means to an end – it's not the end in itself. What he should really come to his psychiatrist for help with is difficulty achieving the end of fame and wealth, not problems completing books.

Defining a problem in the first place precisely and accurately is a giant step towards solving that problem.[21]

Now many of you may be scoffing at the idea that the perfect day exercise is that powerful a psychological tool – an idle day-dream of this man who suffers from writer's block is that he will score the winning goal in the World Cup final, so what? Well, remember that you have complete freedom to choose whatever you want to do on your perfect day – this allows you to project on to the blank canvas your ultimate fantasies – so it's actually a kind of ink blot test or Rorschach Test.[22] In this test the ink blot shapes a psychiatrist shows are amorphous and ambiguous, so if on prompting you say the shapes remind you of a murdered body then this must tell us something about how you differ from someone who sees a flower instead. Any differences are coming from you and not the shape or test itself.[23]

Let me give another illustration that might help demonstrate the power of the exercise.

I had another client who was a highly successful female senior manager working for a large investment bank. She had achieved in her career everything she could hope for and ten years earlier than many of her contemporaries. However, she came to see me suffering from a mysterious depression – perplexing because she thought she had everything she had ever wanted in life.

We did the perfect day exercise together and to our mutual surprise it turned out that a key element of her perfect day was her singing the lead soprano at the New York Metropolitan Opera. Now this was a lady who had never sung a note of opera in her life. But it now seemed clear that her love of opera had to be dealt with more in her life and that perhaps she needed to sacrifice some of her career ambitions in order to attain real happiness. She started doing some amateur opera and became much more content as a result.

I am not saying you have to ultimately achieve your perfect day in order to become happy but you do have to be heading in a direction that roughly approximates the destination that your perfect day signposts. So if you come to me and you are an employee in a large organization but in your perfect day you are self-employed then it may be that some reconsideration of your employment plans is going to be required if you are to achieve ultimate happiness.

At the heart of the perfect day exercise is a fundamental problem for evolutionary psychology, which is that when people are given free reign to design their days as a vehicle to ascertain their ultimate wishes, sex doesn't usually play as big a role as evolutionary psychology should predict.[24] Wherever you lie on the debate, though, I maintain that the perfect day exercise remains the most powerful way of examining clearly what really drives us and what would really make us happy.

A fascinating but also rather robust variation on the technique is to ask your partner or someone close to you for their perfect day (sneakily without telling them the point of the exercise). How accurate were you in predicting what their perfect day was like? If there were a lot of surprises, might this tell you something about the state of the relationship? Did you feature in their perfect day? Did they feature in yours? Were both perfect days compatible with each other? In other words, could you both have the same perfect day together?

I had better leave the questions at that point, but suffice it to say that my marital therapy sessions at The Maudsley Hospital can get rather lively at this juncture . . .

But why is a book on how to get what you want – or how to motivate yourself to achieve your desires – spending so long at the beginning on goal clarification?

Because there are, in fact, only three reasons why people don't achieve their goals. Goal clarification relates to the first: 'goal conflict'.

We have usually more than one goal in life, but the goal that we have placed great store on yet seem doomed to fail to achieve is perhaps in conflict with another priority. For example, many people want to lose weight but find they are hampered by other goals – the goal to have nice taste sensations in their mouths or to enjoy the feeling of fullness after a meal.

Often it's easiest to lose weight when you are pursuing another goal that synchronizes with the weight-loss goal.[25] Sometimes people start to lose weight for the first time when they suddenly become very busy at work or pursue an absorbing leisure interest, i.e., they don't have time to eat and are distracted from their hunger pangs by whatever is making them so busy.

So in order to achieve your goal it is vital to get a good sense of where this goal lies in your hierarchy of other goals and make sure it really is a top priority or aligns with other goals.

One very common source of goal conflict is having short-term goals that are very different or incompatible with long-term goals. If your short-term goal is to see a lot of TV tonight this is probably incompatible with the long-term goal of passing your exams in a month's time.

Repeatedly, psychological experiments have found that we have a preference for valuable outcomes sooner rather than later. This is known as 'positive time preferences' or an 'inability to delay gratification'.[26]

The delay of gratification experiment is commonly used to investigate the psychology of saving. Subjects are given a choice between an immediate reward and one obtained after a certain time delay. Usually the choice is between a small immediate prize and a larger delayed reward. Almost universally subjects tend to show a preference for the smaller immediate reward – a failure to delay gratification.[27]

Most normal adults show a puzzling failure to delay gratification – for example, in one experiment when offered a choice between five pounds now and ten pounds in two months' time, they chose the five pounds now. Unless there is a very high death rate in you or your experimenter, or interest rates are currently at 5,000% – this is essentially an irrational choice.[28]

One theory about why we tend to spend now rather than save for later, even though this is often the better long-term decision, comes from evolutionary psychology, which points out that wired into our genes is behaviour designed for the environment we evolved into several hundred thousand years ago.[29] This is essentially very unlike the circumstances that we live in today. Hundreds of thousands of years ago the future was extremely uncertain and the concept of next week was not one we were equipped to grasp, given everyday survival was a minute-by-minute affair.[30] In that situation it makes sense to go for definite gains or pleasures now rather than some hypothetical benefit in the very uncertain future.

This theory is very powerful in what it explains of current behaviour.

For example, it accounts for why we find it so difficult to diet or exercise to keep looking trim and attractive. Our stone-age genes still figure it is better to eat that chocolate biscuit now and gain the definite certain pleasure today than to sacrifice it, putting up with the pain of hunger.[31]

Incidentally, this theory has an interesting tip to help you exercise and diet and keep fit. In front of your rowing machine at home you should put up a poster of Claudia Schiffer to motivate you to keep exercising, by making your possible future reward more salient and concrete to you. You should also put this picture up on your fridge door. Obviously you need to adopt these techniques with extreme caution if you are married – in my experience wives, husbands and partners in general seem not to understand the finer details of evolutionary psychology when they come home to find posters of Claudia Schiffer or George Clooney everywhere. Though you could protest that this is what your psychiatrist advised.

Making distant rewards seem closer or more real and concrete – making people more aware at crucial decision moments of the distant implications of their choices now – is the essence of how you motivate people to delay gratification.[32]

Most research indicates we are impatient and have an irrational preference for immediacy, and so make poor choices when it comes to any product that offers rewards in the distant future.[33] This partly explains why pensions are a peculiarly difficult product to interest consumers in. Indeed, the research indicates that most people are liable to be extremely grumpy about purchasing products like pensions because they entail making sacrifices today for a distant hypothetical future.

However, it is not always the case that we cannot delay gratification.[34]

Often we do things like save the best chocolate in the box for last, or do the chores before going out to enjoy ourselves. Indeed, saving the best chocolate for last or putting off the favourite film until after doing the chores seems to add to the piquancy and pleasure of that last chocolate or delayed movie. Psychologists refer to this process as savouring, looking forward to, or anticipating a future pleasure.[35]

But we can only do this if we are very confident we know what is in that last chocolate – we usually have to have had it before and know we really will like it. In a sense then you can only savour certainty – you can only look forward to that film and make sacrifices for it if you are fairly confident you are going to enjoy it because it is by your favourite director, or Claudia Schiffer is in it.

I really must see someone about this Claudia Schiffer fixation . . .

So here we have a fundamental problem. We find it difficult to save or delay gratification or make choices that involve future planning because we discount the future, as we find it difficult to take account of something ephemeral, cloudy and uncertain, in contrast to the present, which is immediately obvious.[36]

How then to assist people to make choices about their futures, which they will feel positive about now?

Another key problem is that people tend to think retirement planning is impossible because they don't know what kind of preferences they will have. They tend to assume that in the future they could be in a very different situation and have very altered predilections to those they have now. If they assume that then obviously retirement planning and pension choices become fraught and unpleasant.[37]

But the science of psychology today has the technology to get a surprisingly accurate idea about the kind of person you will be in the future. This is a result of the branch of psychology known as psychometrics – some of which is more popularly known to the public as personality testing. Done properly personality testing is a highly effective tool in predicting future behaviour.[38]

This is because personality is remarkably consistent across time. For example, recent research has demonstrated that how you spent your first pocket money as a young child is remarkably strongly associated with your spending preferences as an adult.[39] If you tended to spend all your pocket money within a few days or hours of getting it, you will tend not to be a good saver as an adult. If you still had last week's pocket money when next week came round, you are more likely to have bulging high-interest accounts now.

This is not to say that all behaviour is completely determined by the past. A spendthrift who for example marries a sensible saver can be transformed into a more prudent financial planner. But, generally speaking, across populations, personality is a massive force across time.

We are often reluctant to embrace this idea because our personal feeling is that we have changed a great deal with the passing years. But a good demonstration of the power of personality as a relatively enduring force is what is known as 'the school reunion effect'.[40] How many of you have been to a school or university reunion recently? You probably went along convinced you had certainly changed, but when you got there you were amazed at how everyone else, though a bit wider and more wrinkly than you remember them, had extremely similar characters to how you recollected them. In fact, they felt the same about you.

Psychologists have repeatedly confirmed that we are impressed with our own personal change much more than it is apparent to others, or can be demonstrated by our behaviour.

So goal conflict is often something rooted fairly deep in your personality and needs to be explicated and dealt with before you can achieve the goal that has so far eluded you.[41]

Goal conflict only becomes an issue in explaining our failure to achieve our goals when we are considering difficult ambitions. In order to gain the gold medal at the 100 metres race in the Olympics it is likely, given how difficult an aspiration this usually proves, that we have to make this our chief un-adulterated goal for many years, possibly even decades. It is highly probable that goal conflict will endanger the achievement of this aim, for example, conflict with goals of preserving one's marriage or a good relationship with neighbours or children. These other goals will almost certainly have to be sacrificed on the altar of top objective, gold medal at Olympics.[42]

The clarity and simplicity in top achievers' lives – the fact they tend not to have goal conflict – explains why top sportsmen, for example, make such boring interviewees at the press conferences after their stunning successes. If you only have one goal in life you won't have much else to talk about.

The second reason why most people fail to achieve their heart's desire is 'resource depletion'.[43] This means that although you are keen to lose weight you lack the resources to achieve this. For example, you may be tired or upset or unable to afford healthy food and as one tends to overeat when tired or upset or when presented with unhealthy food in the absence of alternatives, your diet is frequently broken.

In order to achieve a goal it is likely that certain resources are required, like time, emotional energy, perhaps physical resources as well. So a key step to achieving an objective is to first go about garnering the necessary resources or plan what to do in the eventuality of a key resource lack. For example, if you are a dieter you should plan what you will do instead of snacking in the case of finding yourself upset or hungry and near a chocolate bar. A key concept here is that resources can be physical but also emotional and therefore it might be that you need emotional support, encouragement or help with negative emotions in order to attain your aims.

The final reason for defeat over objectives is a failure to adequately monitor progress towards attaining your aim. No one attains a goal (at least a worthwhile one) immediately. Instead you move gradually towards it, gaining closer and closer approximations to your final result. At school you would have done essays and practice exams before the final big test at the end of your school career. These mock tests were there to help you monitor your progress towards attaining your final exam result.

You could not hope to get a good final score if you had no idea how you were doing in the years running up to the final exam. Measuring progress gives you valuable feedback that lets you know how much harder you have to work in order finally to close on your target. It's amazing, given the essential nature of feedback and monitoring, how often people attempt to realize a difficult goal, like losing weight, without any monitoring of their progress. In order to hit a weight target in six months' time you need to be measuring your weight every week and plotting this on a graph so you know whether you are hitting your weekly or monthly weight targets that will take you on to your final weight goal.

The reason why people hate monitoring their progress is that it reminds them of how far away they really are from their final goal, but this knowledge is extremely valuable and can be turned around to help you get where you want to go.[44]

So now we can see that the science of motivation helps us understand there are only three key reasons why people don't achieve what they want, despite assuring us these are their most ardent desires. The three reasons are goal conflict, resource depletion and inadequate tracking.

What the science of motivation tells us is that if you don't have significant goal conflict, you are absolutely clear about your goal, you track diligently, and respond proficiently to what the tracking is telling you, plus you ensure your resources are adequate to the task, then the world and all that is in it is yours for the taking.

Now you never imagined it was *that* simple, did you?

How Motivated Are You?

MOTIVATION SCALE

Each statement is followed by two possible responses: agree or disagree. Read each statement carefully and decide which response best describes how you feel. Then tick the corresponding response. Please respond to every statement. If you are not completely sure which reply is more accurate, put the one that you feel is most appropriate. Do not read the scoring explanation before filling out the questionnaire. Do not spend too long on each statement. It is important that you answer each question as honestly as possible.

		AGREE	DISAGREE
1	Hard work explains success more than natural talent	A	B
2	How I spend my leisure time should have no bearing on my long-term goals	B	A
3	So far my rewards are not as much as the work I have put in	A	B

4	When people get in my way it's not because they are trying to be obstructive	B	A
5	I have specifc plans for achieving my goals	A	B
6	I always seek advice from others before making a decision	B	A
7	I don't believe other people when they tell me that I have done a good job	A	B
8	If the obstacles become bigger I will change my goals and abandon current aims	B	A
9	I know my strengths (what I can do well)	A	B
10	What other people think matters a lot to me	B	A

Score

Add up your score by totalling the number of As and Bs you have ticked.

8 or more As: You are scoring very high indeed as a highly motivated person – you are the kind who has even assertively asked the boss for benefits like promotions. Beware of coming over as too pushy.

Between 5 and 7 As: While you are not racked with the constant feeling of drive that besets higher scorers, you are scoring higher than average on motivation – you will tend to work out solutions to the obstacles you face without relying on others for help. However, beware of expecting everyone else to be as motivated as you – this will help you not be so irritated with the less driven.

Between 2 and 4 As: Although you are scoring around average to just below average for motivation you are perhaps more motivated from time to time depending on whether you are doing something of genuine interest to you. Remember that the truly motivated are able to make themselves *become* interested in whatever it takes to succeed. Don't rely so much on a problem or subject interesting you before you get going on it.

Between 0 and 1 A: You are scoring very low on motivation and this may be because you have experienced setbacks in the recent past that have now sapped your confidence. Remember that it's not defeat that determines who eventually succeeds, but instead *response* to setbacks. Perhaps you need to take longer after a disappointment to understand what it truly means to you and why it happened.

3

WHY WILL-POWER DOESN'T EXIST

Blessed is the man that endureth temptation: for when he is tried, he shall receive the crown of life
Bible, New Testament, James 1:12

What would you do if you weren't afraid?
Spencer Johnson

The absolutely last thing we do each year, in its very dying moments, is make a New Year's resolution – and usually the very first thing we do each year, just as it is starting, is break it.

One simple test of how ineffective most of our New Year resolutions are is whether you can even remember whatever it was you so solemnly resolved to do last year. In fact, how many past New Year's resolutions can you remember at all?

But a New Year presents an opportunity to turn over a new leaf in our lives, and this may explain the regularity of this apparently fruitless annual cycle. Yet New Year's resolutions remain resolutely popular. Surveys have found the majority of adults make New Year's resolutions, typically three per 31 December.[1]

Even if none gets carried through, the number of resolutions you make can be revealing. The more resolutions, the wider the gap between the person you would like to be and the way you find yourself now.[2] In other words, the greater your dissatisfaction with yourself. If the number of resolutions you make has been going down over the years, perhaps you are growing more content with yourself. But the dark side to resolutions is the research finding that failing to keep resolutions does lower self-esteem in the long run.[3]

Just in case this tempts you to give up on resolutions, in fact psychologists have found when they follow up people who make resolutions that 40% have actually kept to their resolutions by six months into the New Year.[4] But around 50% of us have already failed in our resolution by the end of January – so the lesson seems to be that getting past the first month with your resolution intact predicts long-term success.[5]

When psychologists have investigated precisely what we resolve, it appears we are terribly self-centred – primarily pre-occupied with our health and looks. Smoking cessation and weight loss together account for over two-thirds of all resolutions, while only 5% are about improving our relation-ships and just 2% concern saving more money.[6]

All resolutions fall into two basic types: start resolutions – where you aim to take up or increase an activity, like exercising more – and stop resolutions, like giving up smoking.[7]

Interestingly, some odd gender differences emerge from psychological research into New Year's resolutions. Women tend to make more start resolutions than men, and women are better than men at keeping to start resolutions, while men are better than women at sticking to stop resolutions.[8] This would suggest men are better at self-denial than women, but women are better at fitting a new activity into their lives. Perhaps men are more rigid and are better at sticking to a routine that helps eliminate a bad habit, while women are more flexible, which helps them take on new things, but also makes them vulnerable to a bad habit worming its way back into their lives through a new loophole.[9]

'Lack of will-power' appears to be the most common reason given to psychologists for breaking a resolution, with most people giving up with exhaustion at having to force themselves to persist with the discomfort of change. But therein lies a clue as to how best to stick to your New Year's resolutions this year.[10]

Resolutions will indeed become a chore if you have to exercise will-power to resist temptation every day – be it the temptation to not get out of bed early for that newly resolved morning jog, or the allure of just one more biscuit. So instead psychologists advise changing your environment so enticement is not so easily put your way.[11]

For example, if you are a biscuit binger and you get ship-wrecked on a desert island for a year without biscuits, no matter how weak your will-power, I can guarantee you will not eat biscuits for that year, because temptation will not arise. In fact, you will not find it at all exhausting forcing yourself to resist temptation, because none will have been put your way.[12]

So you need to create your own personal desert island in the middle of where you live, by throwing away all those fattening foods you binge on, so making it more difficult to binge. For example, I advise my alcoholic patients to take the long way home from work daily if that helps circumvent their favourite pub – the same principle applies to that newsagent from which you normally get the chocolate bar that undermines your diet. The secret is to make your resolution assuming you have no will-power, and that you will succumb to temptation at any opportunity, and plan to avoid situations where will-power will be needed.[13]

After all, you can only continue to be a shopaholic, for example, if you keep finding yourself in shops with money to hand.

Another way people self-sabotage their resolutions is by keeping them secret. While there is an element of superstition to this habit, more pragmatically, it also makes it less personally humiliating when you break your resolution. But you can use this embarrassment factor to help motivate you. Go public with your resolutions – by telling everyone you are giving up smoking, and that you will need their assistance in resisting temptation, you enlist others' support (and make your resolution sound more convincing to yourself).[14]

Ways you can change your environment for start resolutions include getting someone to go jogging with you first thing in the morning; that way when they turn up at your front door it makes it more difficult to succumb to the temptation of staying in the warm bed.

But perhaps the commonest reason why psychologists believe New Year's resolutions fail lies in the way they are worded – the vaguer the resolution the less likely it is to be carried out.[15] For example, 'becoming a better husband' is too ambiguous. But 'becoming a better husband by helping my wife more around the house, for instance by taking out the rubbish and hoovering every week, plus looking after the kids for one evening a week so she has more time to herself' is more specific and therefore more likely to be implemented.

Setting clearly specified goals and target dates by which they will be achieved, and then checking regularly how we are doing, is useful, because it helps us get some idea about how to alter our efforts to ensure we achieve our ambition. So if you aim to lose eight pounds by 1 June, knowing you have lost only two pounds by March gives you more precise and valuable feedback about how you need to alter your current efforts.[16]

So the first step to making sure your New Year's resolution this year really is the start of turning over a new leaf to a new you is to remind yourself what your specific resolution is regularly over the next year, say at the end of each month, so you check your progress towards your goal.

Perhaps that is in fact why so many of our resolutions fail. After all, we only appear to think seriously about them once a year.

The reason it's so tempting to turn over a new leaf at that precise moment is that our environment, full of people drunkenly also making resolutions, makes us sentimentally and over-confidently feel that we can change.

The key here is the power of our environment.

Everyone wanting advice on how to become more motivated feels that if somehow the doctor or psychologist could just throw some inner switch in the brain then they would get it and start working relentlessly towards their goals. In fact, the secret at the heart of motivation is that it's not an internal change that is required but an external one.[17] If we clear out all the fattening foods from our homes then it's impossible to snack and so we will lose weight. We change our environment, which in turn forces us to change. We change the environment because we are sceptical we will resist the presence of fattening foods at home.

Simply trying to anticipate the problems of resisting temptation and taking a few practical steps to limit your ability to respond when in the grip of strong emotions, while you have a chance to plan coolly, is probably the biggest contribution to self-control. This is called pre-commitment.[18] Perhaps the earliest recorded example of this principle appears in the *Odyssey*, in which Odysseus had to sail past the sirens. Because the sound of their voices was so alluring, other sailors had always rowed towards them and foundered on rocks. Odysseus had to pre-commit to stop this from happening to him. Before he was close to the sirens, and therefore under their influence, Odysseus planned how to resist temptation when he heard them. He asked his crew to tie him to the mast and ordered them not to untie him until they had reached their goal. Meanwhile his crew had to be free to row, so he stopped their ears with wax to prevent them from hearing the sirens' calls.

You may have a sneaking suspicion that, in some instances (the alcoholic who forever seems to be 'just passing' his favourite pub) people not only verge on having poor self-management but seem almost to go out of their way to create situations (or antecedents) that will endanger their resolve.

The kind of behaviours addicts indulge in, such as while off drugs offering to post a letter that will take them near their favourite dealer and so increase the likelihood of relapse, are so frequent that a term has been created to describe them: Seemingly Irrelevant Behaviours, or SIBs.[19] The beauty of SIBs is that they seem, at first glance, irrelevant to the temptation, which is why long-suffering spouses or friends innocently allow them to happen. But, sure enough, this behaviour does make relapse more likely.

We have all indulged in SIBs. You just happen to glance through the paper, just happen to see what is on TV, which seems to be an important programme, which means that the planned evening's revision for your exam goes pear-shaped. Looking through the papers and not doing revision do not, at first glance, appear connected, but by a chain of events a relapse is engineered. Effective self-management means learning from past SIBs and avoiding the first event in the chain. Once the sequence begins it is more difficult to stop than it is to prevent it starting in the first place.[20]

A good way to avoid SIBs is to examine them carefully. Start with the final behaviour, which you now regret doing, and work backwards through the sequence of events that led you there. Examine at which stages you could have decided to do something else that would have prevented the undesirable behaviour occurring. In particular, look for the moment at which choosing another more helpful path would have been easiest, and aim to ensure that you do not find yourself at the early part of the progression again. The mentally unhealthy tend to focus only on the final episode in the chain of behaviour and wonder how to stop it happening when they get to this end stage. The mentally healthy go back further and anticipate which behaviours will lead to unhelpful actions in the future.[21]

For example, I often see women alcoholics who can clearly identify that being alone at home precipitates their drinking. They try to fight the urge to drink alcohol under these conditions when they should instead prevent themselves from being alone at home in the first place. Being alone at home is the antecedent that needs to change.[22]

The alcoholic resolves not to drink again because alcohol is destroying his life. However, one day he passes a pub and needs to make a decision about whether to go in for a quick drink or not. He (almost) inevitably goes in and, after his first drink, finds himself back on the treadmill of alcoholism.

He may later bitterly regret his decision but, in order not to repeat it, once he has become sober again, he must examine what was going through his mind at the time of his decision to drink, and see what was uppermost and what was suppressed. He needs to ensure that when he finds himself in the same position again, he does not make the same decision. He will have a different set of priorities, and be more aware of the negative consequences of his decision to have a 'harmless' drink.

It is not reasonable to blame yourself the first time you make an error, but if you repeat your mistakes, it is appropriate to question your decision-making skills and obvious that you need to improve them. If you would like to minimize your mistake-making capacity, then try to consider as much as possible the consequences of your decisions before you make your choice.

One of the reasons people repeat errors is they fail fully to understand themselves. The alcoholic fails to appreciate his inability to control himself and how great his need for alcohol is, and perhaps what role it plays in his life, which is why he has difficulty comprehending that everyone else seems to know he will go in for a drink if he walks past his favourite pub, while he believes he has the will-power not to go in.[23]

Those with addictions, habit problems or who basically suffer difficulty resisting temptation tend to have a misplaced faith in the concept of will-power.[24] They believe they can just will themselves, for example, not to drink if they put their mind to it. Whereas psychologists believe it is probably wisest to assume will-power does not exist as it is such an unreliable entity. Better instead not to go anywhere near a pub, or the scene of any temptation, so your will-power does not get tested. Indeed the further you are from the source of temptation, the longer you give yourself to change your mind as you start the journey towards the object of your desire and weakness.[25] It is also easier to turn down an invitation to go to a pub in the first place than to sit in a bar refusing drinks all evening.

Psychologists point out there are two kinds of self-control being exercised here – in decisional self-control you make a single choice, such as turning down an invitation to go to the pub, whereas in protracted self-control you have to resist temptation continually over a long period of time, for example, if you are sitting in the pub trying to refuse the offer of drinks or trying to avoid looking at the bottles behind the bar. Decisional self-control is clearly the better one to go for.[26]

A good example of this principle is the group of people who have difficulty controlling their excessive spending. Instead of carrying around credit cards, relying on will-power to curb their spendthrift tendency, they would be wise to tear up their credit cards and only take as much cash as they need for basic necessities. Assume that will-power does not exist and that if you face temptation you will succumb, and plan to avoid enticement – this is the only sure way to start to break a dependency.[27]

But to change as people we actually need to change our external environment to encourage us to become the kind of person we aspire to. This is a fundamental issue in the science of motivation, which many people misunderstand. They believe that motivation is about tinkering with the inner self primarily and they want to know how to achieve more will-power.[28]

In fact, the secret is to use your internal desire to act upon the world so it changes to help us become the people we want to be. Take an example – giving up smoking. You need to change your external environment so it's one where you don't encounter the temptation to smoke by removing all easy access to cigarettes. Once your external environment becomes one that shapes or encourages the behaviour you desire then personal change becomes easier.[29]

Ten Steps to Making Better Decisions

(1) *Make sure you haven't decided already*

Often people make bad decisions because they haven't considered the alternatives properly and that is because they have already really made the decision. They may have already decided to buy that expensive item or date the alluring prospect – but they pretend to themselves they are going through some kind of decision-making process. This is only to render legitimate a choice they have already impulsively made. So before you start thinking about your choices be honest with yourself – have you decided already, in which case should you not go back and reconsider all your options more carefully?

(2) *Gather as much information as possible before deciding*

People often rush into a decision because they think they know what to do. In fact, gathering as much information as possible is often very helpful because in the absence of information gathering, you may jump to unwarranted conclusions about your situation. For example, are you sure you know precisely how much disposable money you have? Have you taken into account unexpected bills like household repairs? When a new predicament looms, don't panic and take decisions before you are certain of all the facts. In particular, double-check what you have been told, as others may simply be reporting hearsay. Don't jump to the worst possible conclusion about why the police have brought your children back in a van – ask a lot of questions first before deciding on what to do about your kids! Information is the most valuable commodity when it comes to assisting decision-making, so invest a lot in gathering as much of it as possible. Often people employ more resources in taking the decision than in assembling information first, but investment in information always pays dividends.

(3) *Imagine the consequences of your decision*

Don't neglect the possible long-term as well as short-term consequences of your decision – you might feel happier with certain options in the short term, but how will you feel about your decision in a year's time – or ten years' time? Try to imagine yourself looking back from the future giving your present self advice about the decision – what would that advice be? Consider as well all the possible ramifications in terms of consequences for others. If you indulge yourself and buy the sports car, how will you feel when you can't afford to help your children with the expenses of those upcoming university fees?

(4) *Think about bad similar decisions you have made in the past*

Shopaholics frequently impulsively buy yet another pair of shoes without stopping to consider that although they succumbed to similar temptation in the past, those designer shoes are now languishing in the wardrobe unused for many months. Before coming to a decision, recall similar situations in the past about which you now have regrets and focus on where your bad past decisions have tended to go wrong. Were you too impulsive? Did you not properly take certain issues into account – in which case are you merely repeating your error now? In the stress or excitement of a predicament it is easy to neglect considering what uncomfortable lessons the past might teach you about yourself.

(5) *Consider all the possible alternatives*

There are usually other options that you haven't considered, for example buying a similar item, only a cheaper one, or putting off the decision for a little while longer, or simply hiring the item rather than buying it. In the haste to make a decision it is easy to skate over the universe of other possibilities. Bad decisions are often made because a better alternative was not even considered when it was possible to opt for it instead of what was chosen. Get used to generating a list as long as possible of other options, before you sit down to decide what to do.

(6) *Get some help*
Sometimes a major decision cannot be discussed with other people because some things have to remain private – but it might be worth talking about a part of the issue with someone so that your privacy is maintained but you still get to air the problems. Discussion with others helps explore the issue from perspectives you may not have considered. In particular, dialogue helps reveal your own personal prejudices that could lead to bad decision-making.

(7) *Pay particular attention to worst-case scenarios*
Consider what are the worst possible things that could happen as a result of each option you might choose and be particularly cautious over any choice that has a risk of a particularly bad outcome, even if this appears a remote possibility. For example, even if an option could only remotely lead to a criminal record, or serious injury, then be particulary wary of adopting that course of action.

(8) *Observe good decision-makers in action*
Good decision-makers are not always apparent, but clearly if you have problems over spending decisions, for example, then people who appear to be sensible financially and have a better standard of living than you, but earn the same, might be making better decisions than you. Perhaps you could learn something from them. Successful people in any sphere are partly achieving at a good level because of their good decision-making – what do they take into account before making decisions that you are neglecting?

(9) *Sometimes simply waiting is a good decison*
Often we are forced into making a decision when waiting a bit longer helps clarify things and makes a decision easier. Taking decisions when it is not strictly necessary is a symptom of our ever increasing

'busyness' – we sometimes feel we should take the plunge and get the decision out of the way, so clearing the decks for the next thing we have to do. Sometimes it could be better to just wait and see, but this option requires greater organization so that the decision does not get forgotten about. To help your decision-making get the relevant part of your life organized so that decisions can be put off actively, but then not forgotten.

(10) *Don't get so obsessed with always making the right decision that you put off making decisions for ever*
There are a group of people who are so worried about making errors when they take decisions that they postpone for ever, or an extremely long time, actually making choices in life. They often prefer to delegate decision-making to others rather than shoulder the burden of taking the risk of making mistakes. Errors are inevitable in life as you don't have perfect foresight. Instead, realize that once you have taken the precautions in the previous steps, you have done all you can to safeguard your decisions, so go ahead and make them. You can only learn how to make better decisions in the future by taking the bull by the horns and actually make choices in life. If you don't make a few wild decisions as well then life would hardly be worth living!

HOW STRONG IS YOUR WILL-POWER QUIZ

WILL-POWER SCALE

Each statement is followed by two possible responses: agree or disagree. Read each statement carefully and decide which response best describes how you feel. Then tick the corresponding response. Please respond to every statement. If you are not completely sure which reply is more accurate, put the one that you feel is most appropriate. Do not read the scoring explanation before filling out the questionnaire. Do not spend too long on each statement. It is important that you answer each question as honestly as possible.

		AGREE	DISAGREE
1	I like more extremes than my friends	A	B
2	My parents approved of practically all my friends	B	A
3	I often feel lonely	A	B
4	I usually have no difficulty getting to sleep	B	A
5	A bad habit controls you more than you control it	A	B
6	I try to buy insurance whenever it is available	B	A
7	Everyone has vices so others should not be upset by my habits	A	B
8	It is impossible to break an ingrained bad habit easily	B	A
9	I am only aware of how bad my habits are after doing them	A	B
10	I would never sacrifice a relationship to my bad habits	B	A

Score

Add up your score by totalling the number of As and Bs you have ticked.

8 or more Bs: You are scoring very high on will-power and the ability to break bad habits once you set your mind to it. This is partly because you are more concerned by the effects of your behaviour on others than lower scorers and so would hate the idea of an addiction of yours causing others to suffer. Of course this means you might be vulnerable to a secret addiction, which you are able to control, and which only you know about . . .

Between 6 and 7 Bs: You are scoring above average for the will-power needed to break bad habits, which means your life is fairly free of addictions. But at times of stress you are prone to take up old habits long relinquished or even experiment with new ones. However, on balance you have more will-power than lower scorers and are able to tolerate personal sacrifice and suffering better than them. You also have higher self-esteem and a greater belief in your own personal power compared to the power of any addiction. The bottom line is if you want to stop a habit, you, more than lower scorers, can.

Between 3 and 5 Bs: You are scoring around average to below average for will-power, which means the great danger for you is of cross-addiction; no sooner do you crack one habit than another aspect of your addictive personality appears in another part of your life. Thus you may cut down your drinking or binge-ing, only to take up smoking or gambling instead. While you may believe you have no serious addictions just yet, if you find you need increasing amounts of your favourite support to obtain the same mood-elevating effect, you are well on the way to an addiction.

Between 0 and 2 Bs: You are scoring very low on will-power and this is partly because you mistake the immediate pleasure a bad habit gives you as a sign it cannot be too harmful, so you pay less attention to the long-term consequences of your addictions. If you have no clear-cut habit yet, you are in danger of developing one in the future, especially when under stress and when you need some-thing to take your mind off things, or to cheer yourself up.

Using this approach – that in order to transform ourselves we first have to change our environment and this forces us to change – leads to a radical revision of the explanation for many common problems usually attributed to a lack of will-power. For example, why so many of us are overweight today.

Modern medical research is now suggesting a novel approach to understanding why obesity is such a common problem in the relatively wealthy parts of the world, like North America and Europe (in the US 61% of the adult population is overweight or obese and the UK is not that far behind).[30]

The new theory, proposed by Dr James Hill and colleagues at the University of Colorado in the USA, is that the massive rise in the number of overweight people is not down to any in-dividual propensity to be greedy when eating. Instead this increase in fatness represents a basic mismatch between our environment and our metabolism.[31]

We evolved hundreds of thousands of years ago into an environment very different to the one we live in now and our biology is designed to cope with the rigours of ancient lifestyles we no longer have to endure.[32] In the distant past high levels of physical activity were needed in daily life, and food was inconsistently available. We had to work in fields to harvest what we planted, flee from predators, or run at prey to hunt it for food. As a result, for most of our history physical activity 'pulled' appetite, so the primary challenge to our bodies' weight-control system was to obtain sufficient energy to prevent a negative energy balance producing weight loss.[33]

How different things are today! In our current environment minimal physical activity is required for daily life and food is abundant, relatively inexpensive, high in energy and easily available.[34] In this modern environment food intake 'pushes' the system, so the challenge to our bodies' weight-control system is to increase physical activity sufficiently to prevent positive energy balance leading to weight gain.[35]

What makes keeping slim today even more difficult is that there is, in fact, no apparent drive in most of us to exercise or even to increase our exercise as we eat more. So the prevailing environment actually represents a constant background pressure that promotes weight gain.[36] This is because our bodies evolved a system where the body's natural instinct whenever it finds enough to eat but has no obvious need to exercise (like running away from a predator) is to conserve energy by resting and laying down fat stores.[37]

Our bodies are used to a past environment where food supply is inconsistent, so whenever we find enough food we eat as much as we can, in anticipation of a famine, or at least scarcity, just around the corner.[38]

The modern world has transformed body-weight control away from a largely instinctual or unconscious process. In the ancient world you didn't have to worry about your weight because you did so much running around and little eating that you naturally stayed slim, without having to give it a second thought.[39]

In the current environment, according to the new theory from Dr Hill and colleagues, those who do not devote substantial conscious effort to managing body weight are probably gaining weight.[40]

Our biology is at fault because our bodies have developed processes whereby people eat when food is available and rest when physical activity is not required.[41] The big problem is that food is nearly always available and physical activity is seldom required.

Consequently, just living naturally in the current environment of modern Western countries exerts a consistent one-directional influence on energy intake and energy expenditure, which results inevitably in a positive energy balance and therefore weight gain.[42]

Our environment promotes low-energy expenditure because little or no physical activity is required for daily living, and simultaneously it also encourages overeating through an abundant food supply that is high in fat and energy, easily available, good tasting, inexpensive and served in large portions.[43]

So basically our bodily systems that worked so well in the past are now contributing to the problem of obesity.

In today's environment physical activity is no longer the stimulus that pulls appetite, but rather food intake is now pushing the system, and energy expenditure is struggling to keep up. This situation creates constant background pressure on the system towards positive energy balance that in most people will lead to weight gain and obesity, unless a conscious effort is made to limit energy intake and/or increase physical activity.[44]

As a result in the USA it is estimated that 61% of the adult population is overweight or clinically obese. But the question then arises: if our tendency to become overweight recently is down to our environment, how come not all of us are too fat? Statistically 39% of the US population appear to have a healthy body weight.[45]

There are probably three different groups. One is called by doctors 'genetic superstars' – those lucky enough to have a genetic predisposition to low weight. Then there is the group of people whose daily employment requires strenuous physical activity. But the final group probably interests us the most – these are the people who maintain a healthy weight through sheer determination to stay physically active and to restrain their intake.[46]

In the USA, a long-running study of those who maintain a healthy lower weight over a long time, called the National Weight Control Registry (NWCR), looks at people who have managed to maintain an average weight for at least five and a half years.[47] What is intriguing about this group is they themselves declare that they have to make strong conscious efforts to eat healthily and engage in high levels of physical activity.

Indeed they report a very high level of physical activity, on average the equivalent of walking briskly for about six and half kilometres a day. In other words, the people on this fitness register report taking the equivalent of 11,000 steps a day, and this compares with step-counter measurements of people engaged in typical office work who take the equivalent of 3–5,000 steps a day.

It is sobering to note that the US Surgeon General recommends daily exercise equivalent to 5,000 steps of brisk walking a day. The NWCR group are taking exercise at a level which is roughly double the Surgeon General's recommendation. Little surprise that they confirm that the effort required to maintain this level of activity is substantial.[48]

These individuals appear to be relying on intellect and not instinct for success.

This new thinking suggests that to lose weight and maintain a healthy figure you need to construct a different environment around you that does not expose you to temptation or bad habits.[49]

It is clear that our physical environment, whether for example there is food present or not, influences our behaviour. But we often forget that our environment doesn't just have a physical dimension but also a social and psychological one. For example, if we are surrounded by an environment that doesn't encourage us to become self-reliant then this may produce psychological damage in the long run. It is possible that an environment that is too helpful could actually produce a population of the more emotionally immature. Maybe if you give too much to those who don't have to work for it, they don't end up learning how to stand on their own two feet.[50]

It is widely accepted as a truism in liberal educated middle-class circles that *money can't buy you happiness*, but does this also apply to the poor? It is indeed one of the foundation principles of the modern progressive economy that government-provided social security is effective in easing the sufferings of unemployment, but now new research calls this previously unassailable assumption into question.

Examining data from forty-two nations around the world, a study recently published in an academic journal specializing in well-being research has found that countries that spend more on social security do not end up with happier populations.

Even more startling was the finding that the unemployed are specifically no happier on average in nations with higher welfare expenditures, yet this is a key group who theoretically should benefit most from living in a more generous welfare state.

Overturning the assumption that we already know what will make people happy, the researchers relied on actually measuring personal happiness by asking people directly how content they were with their lot. Their world-wide surveys involved over 58,000 respondents and used the last available figures for social security spending.

The data was collated and analysed at the foremost university department specializing in measuring happiness, Erasmus University in Rotterdam, Holland, and published in the key academic journal for the study of well-being, *The Journal of Happiness Studies*.[51]

What is astonishing about the findings is that they seem to apply to Second and Third World nations as well as First World. For example, in the former Eastern European Bloc, Poland has the highest average score on happiness amongst its unemployed, while it spends the least on social security (8% of GDP). The Czechoslovakian unemployed, on the other hand, are only half as happy as on average the Polish, while they spend the most of the Eastern Europeans on social security (22% of GDP).

Nigeria has one of the highest scores on unemployed happiness across developing countries, yet its government spends almost the least on social security.

But the analysis is probably at its most precise in terms of examining the specific effects of welfare on happiness when the sixteen First World nations are analysed. This is because these all share certain basic social structures like democracy, ensuring that unhappiness due to other social or cultural factors doesn't intrude so much on the comparison.

Those countries that traditionally spend less than the First World average on social security (like USA, Britain and Canada) have much happier unemployed than countries that spend significantly more on welfare, like Finland, France and Italy.

But the researchers weren't content to draw their conclusions from this already convincing set of data. They dug deeper and reasoned that an even more rigorous test of whether welfare makes you happy or not if you are unemployed is whether your happiness rises in countries that increase welfare expenditure over time.

When all sixteen rich nations are considered there is no statistical association between rises in social security spending in the 1980s and 1990s and increased happiness.

For example, in the USA, Norway, Ireland and Argentina there was a relative decrease in welfare spending in the 1980s but a rise in life satisfaction in the unemployed living there. Meanwhile there was an increase in social security spending in Canada, Holland, Japan and Finland but an overall decline in well-being in their unemployed.

Why is it that spending more on welfare produces no measurable beneficial effect on the unemployed's sense of well-being?

One possible explanation, suggests the study's author Dr Piet Ouweneel, arises from the fact that high welfare-expenditure countries tend to be richer ones and it is these economies that generally appear also to have larger income differentials between the rich and the poor. Psychologists have long maintained it's not what you have that makes you ultimately happy but who you compare yourself to.

Across the world it is the countries that are often most generous to the unemployed in terms of welfare payments who also tend to produce more very wealthy people with which to compare yourself unfavourably, perhaps lowering contentment if you don't have much.

Another theory, according to Dr Ouweneel, is that in non-welfare states other institutions like church and community organizations might form surprisingly viable alternatives for state welfare services. Family ties might even be stronger in these countries and relatives may perform a network of care services that function even better than state care. Indeed, sometimes welfare inadvertently encourages the break-up of families by providing extra housing and funding for the disgruntled, young or pregnant who want to move away from their families where otherwise dependency would produce a tighter family unit.

This leads to the provocative idea that maybe the reason why the unemployed are not made happier by more welfare is that the financial advantages of social security benefits are annulled by their unintentional but deeply negative side effects.[52]

Dr Ouweneel contends that the millstone of government bureaucracy in welfare states probably frustrates people and saps their self-esteem, while negative reactions towards the unemployed 'who are living off the back of others who pay taxes' probably make them feel they are spongers.

Generous income supplementation may also have a negative influence on motivation for the unemployed to find a new job, which will have the effect of keeping them unemployed for longer. We know that happiness in the unemployed is surprisingly high for the first few months of unemployment, but usually begins to plummet as the period of joblessness lengthens. In reducing the urgency to return to work, welfare could inadvertently lead to more unhappiness.[53]

Whatever the ultimate reason for these important findings, they suggest that liberal economists who believed you could tweak personal well-being as a macro-economic variable are now dramatically out of step with the latest thinking in psychology.[54]

Perhaps ultimately what the advocates of welfare forget is that too much government interference takes away self-initiative and frustrates an individual's feeling of self-determination, and actually it is these that are the essential prerequisites of happiness.[55]

We also create our environments with our basic attitudes. For example, new research from sociologist Dr William Cockerham and colleagues from the University of Alabama in the USA has found that dramatic differences in attitudes to looking after your body and your health are predicted by your political allegiances.[56]

It seems that those who believe the state should take responsibility for most aspects of life also tend to eschew personal responsibility for taking care of themselves. As a result, they are more likely to engage in lifestyles hazardous to health, including drinking to excess and not exercising.

The research was conducted amongst Russians and compared those who currently longed for a return to the old-style Soviet system with those who preferred the free-market economy. The study, consisting of personal interviews with almost 9,000 Russians, found significant differences in how much you looked after your own health depending on where you placed yourself on the political spectrum.

The old divisions between socialists and capitalists may have largely disappeared in modern Britain, but elsewhere in Europe, particularly in the old eastern-bloc countries, the political conflict remains. These countries have experienced unprecedented upheaval since the collapse of the old Soviet system, and it is still not clear to large sections of the electorate whether abandoning the old centrally planned economies has brought any real benefits.

A key reason why Russia and Eastern European countries are currently attracting the particular interest of health researchers like Dr William Cockerham and colleagues is that one of the most striking developments in world health today is the dramatic decline in life expectancy in these parts of the world. The situation is without precedent in modern history – nowhere else has health generally worsened among industrialized nations.

Russian male life expectancy stood at sixty-four years in 1965 but steadily decreased to around sixty-two years by 1980. Male longevity improved during Gorbachev's brief (1984–7) anti-alcohol campaign, reaching almost sixty-five years in 1987, and then entered a period of accelerated decline – centred around the fall of the communist regime – in which life expectancy fell to a modern low of roughly fifty-eight years in 1994. The most recent figures for 2000 show Russian males living fifty-nine years, on average some five years less than in 1965. Now only 76.2% of Russian men and 91.3% of women currently reach the age of fifty years.

This puzzling situation occurred even though Russia, the dominant state of the former Soviet Union, was not involved in a major war and was a military superpower with a stable government, industrial economy and free medical care.

Dr William Cockerham's research, just published in the prestigious *Journal of Health and Social Behaviour*, concludes that negative health lifestyles appear to be the primary determinant of the decline in life expectancy in the former socialist nations. This conclusion is partly based on the observation of a particularly strong relationship between recent increased alcohol consumption in former communist countries and declining male longevity.

Health lifestyle research on Russia specifically describes an endemic entrenched pattern of excessive alcohol consumption, heavy smoking, high-fat diet and lack of exercise. These lifestyle practices are especially characteristic of middle-age, working-class males whose high mortality rates from heart disease, alcohol poisoning and alcohol-related accidents seem largely responsible for the overall decline in male longevity.

Although the purchasing power of the average wage fell by nearly one half in 1992–3, relative to the price of vodka it *increased* three times, as the Russian government ended its monopoly on vodka production, allowed unrestricted sales from sources at home and abroad, and consumer costs dropped significantly.

As a result, by 1994, Russia had the highest per capita consumption of pure alcohol in the world: 14.5 litres per annum. Given that adult males consume 90% of the alcohol in Russia, yet comprise only 25% of the population, it is obvious that the drinking practices of this group far exceed per capita consumption and reflect a tremendous concentration of drinking.

Cynics have even suggested that in view of the country's economic woes low alcohol costs were a conscious attempt by the Yeltsin government to anaesthetize social discontent.

But such centrally planned economic strategy could perhaps have wider implications beyond mere short-term political ends – perhaps decades of such manipulation of the people have left a long-standing psychological imprint that influences the individual's health choices.

Cockerham, the lead author of this study, suggests that psychologists identify a common person-type found in Russia known as *Homo Soveticus*, defined as a person with a collectivist orientation who does not like to assume any individual responsibilities.

The theory is that Soviet-style socialism eventually induces passivity towards health promotion in the population. After all, previously the state provided for personal needs and the individual in turn gave up personal reliance and freedom. The state was a shelter as it provided free health care and education, old-age pensions, low-cost housing plus food and guaranteed employment.

However, the totalitarian nature and paternalism of such a system has been viewed as responsible for the development and spread of a psychology of passivity and irresponsibility. If they got sick, people knew that the government would take care of them, and so they were not likely to have a strong sense of personal responsibility for health.

For example, one study found that almost all Russian cancer patients (94%) after surgery had no plans to do anything themselves to promote their health; instead they were going to rely solely on medical professionals.[57]

If a socialist heritage, negating individual health promotion, is operative in Russian society as some suggest, it could be predicted that those in favour of returning to socialism would be especially passive with respect to healthy lifestyles.

The theory that your political orientation could influence how much responsibility you took for your health was recently tested by Dr William Cockerham and colleagues by investigating the health practices of a national sample of Russians who wished for a return of socialism as it was before Gorbachev. They were compared with a group who did not wish to return to socialism, and instead favoured staying with a free-market economy.

The data was collected through personal interviews by the Russian Longitudinal Monitoring Survey, a series of nationally representative surveys of the Russian Federation, and consisted of almost 9,000 adults.

The results were that pro-socialists are nearly one and a half times more likely to be frequent drinkers than anti-socialists. Anti-socialists are also significantly more likely to take exercise; in fact, being pro-socialist decreased your chances of exercising regularly by almost 50%. Furthermore, anti-socialists were almost 25% more likely to go for preventive health check-ups compared to pro-socialists.[58]

It is clear the Soviet government promoted neither individuality nor individual initiative in health matters as they imposed a collective-oriented ideology on the population.

If, as it is argued, this heritage has fostered a lack of responsibility for individual health promotion in Russia, then those persons wishing to return to this system would seem most likely to practise a negative health lifestyle. The data from this recent research suggests that this is indeed the case, as pro-socialist respondents generally demonstrated fewer positive health-promoting activities than anti-socialists.

This new research is important because it suggests that a vital aspect of a nation's health status has been neglected, and previously even not measured at all, which is how prevalent the culture of personal responsibility for health is. Self-reliance would seem to be something to be encouraged rather than a passive over-reliance on the state, as those who take more responsibility for their health seem to be healthier as a direct result.

Anti-socialists in Dr Cockerham's research not only had healthier lifestyles but they also rated themselves as generally more healthy than pro-socialists.

The dilemma in politics is that some kind of safety net for those unable to look after themselves seems desirable, yet if the net becomes too extensive it may act as a disincentive for fostering personal responsibility for one's own health. Solving this dilemma is an urgent requirement of modern politics because it could even determine how long we live.

To conclude, we have seen that the best motivational strategy is actually to assume will-power doesn't exist at all. This is a key lesson at the heart of motivation that often comes as a surprise to people outside of the world of academic psychology.

Those who achieve their goals are precisely the same as those who believe the least in will-power and assume they don't have any.

4

HOW TO BIN FRIENDS
AND DISREGARD PEOPLE

*The successful person has unusual skill at dealing with
conflict and ensuring the best outcome for all*
From *The Art of War* by Sun Tzu

*Heroes are not judged for their prowess in hunting and
shooting tigers, but rather for their strength and ability to
endure the humiliation of being pigs*

Chin-Ning Chu

There is accumulating psychological evidence that much of the
stress of work arises from interaction with people rather than
things.[1]

It has long been said that Britain, like other modern post-
industrial societies, has a workforce that is moving relentlessly
through a key transition – from manufacturing to service-
oriented work. This means that we are increasingly in jobs
where we don't deal so much with 'things', like components on
an assembly line, but more with other people. But what hasn't
been realized fully is that having constantly to deal with people
rather than 'things' often brings a unique constellation of
stresses, which the modern workplace or workforce doesn't
seem at all prepared for.

Much medical training, for example, at one level appears to
be focused on how to deal with 'things', like a liver or a liver
function test result, rather than how to cope with people, like
patients and colleagues. This lack of training could mean
doctors are ill equipped when it comes to a vital part of their

jobs, and this explains much of their subsequent stress. Remember also that doctors are often dealing with people at one of the most difficult times in their lives and so at their most complex in terms of the psychological handling they require.

Some recent psychological research has established that a large part of the stress of working in the rapidly expanding sector of call centres is the strain of having to be remorselessly cheerful to callers.[2] The so-called 'Have a nice day' syndrome is about the 'emotional labour' we have to do on a daily basis to keep ourselves appearing fairly reasonable to all around us, no matter how ragged we are really feeling, and to smilingly absorb the difficulties of dealing with problematic customers, when you really want to wring their necks. Psychologists are now increasingly recognizing that this 'emotional labour' may in fact be more mentally taxing than the more physical toil required of us in the past.

Psychologists use the term 'surface level emotional labour' to capture the basic fact that a large part of dealing with people at work is basically 'faking it' – pretending to feel emotions, like feigning interest, sympathy or understanding.

But now new research by occupational psychologists Celeste Brotheridge and Alicia Grandey at the University of Pennsylvania in the USA has found that the more your job requires you to fake emotions, the more likely you are to become emotionally detached from those around you at work, and detached from your own emotional state (you may not realize how depressed and upset you truly are) and the greater therefore will be your future job dissatisfaction.[3]

It seems that there are two key emotional labour tasks required of doctors: to hide negative emotions and to display positive feelings even when these are not residing within one. Psychologists believe that constantly hiding the deep hatred you feel for colleagues and difficult patients might be fairly stressful in itself, but having to go beyond this and portray positive emotions when you really feel the opposite must be even worse and surely pushes you nearer to 'burn-out'.[4]

Burn-out is the state of mind you reach as a result of stressful work when you feel spent. In addition to suffering from emotional exhaustion, you display a detached attitude towards others, perhaps behaving like a psychopath towards them rather than genuinely caring. As a result of this you experience a low sense of effectiveness at work and therefore diminished personal accomplishment.[5]

Burn-out is strongly linked to a tendency to leave the job, hating your work and lowered performance at work. It's also possible that personal detachment in jobs that require high levels of caring, like nursing and medicine, could even be positively dangerous – resulting in such negative behaviour towards patients or clients that they end up suffering grievously as a result.

Jobs that are thought to be particularly prone to burn-out are those where you have to be relentlessly positive – for example, the caring professions like medicine, nursing, social work and teaching, where there is a large amount of personal interaction requiring deep personal attention and concern and therefore perhaps a huge amount of emotional labour.[6]

However, the very latest research on the link between burn-out and emotional labour by Brotheridge and Grandey suggests that the key issue isn't the acting you have to do at work. It is the *way* you try to act that predicts whether you are going to suffer from burn-out or not. Indeed they found that in some jobs the high emotional labour actually predicted a greater sense of personal accomplishment.[7]

The key seems to be whether at work you are performing emotional labour requiring 'superficial' acting or 'deep' acting.

Superficial acting is where you just pretend to be pleased to see someone while deep down you are plotting how to cut the brake cables of their car. Deep acting, on the other hand, is where you try to change your basic attitudes towards the people you interact with by altering your thoughts and deeper feelings, so as to try and make them more positive to those around you.

So, for example, if you are in child-care work it could be that many of the young children you are looking after eventually get your goat, but you make a conscious effort to remain positive and not snap at them because deep down you believe that this is a better emotional state to be in than one of irritability towards young children.

The key finding of Brotheridge and Grandey was that those who seemed to engage in deep acting actually found jobs that demanded high levels of emotional labour more personally rewarding.[8]

You set about deep acting by using the self-same techniques

Hollywood actors who take their job seriously go about researching a part. If, for example, an actor is to play the role of a cop, he will go and hang out with real policemen – immerse himself in that world, as it were – and adopt a role model whom he observes closely, trying to understand his motivation. So you need to find a role model or hang out with those who display the kind of behaviour you are trying to adopt. It could be there are people at the reception desk who are relentlessly good natured no matter how awkward the client or patient – what drives them? How do they see the world?

Another key technique that actors use is to develop a sympathy for the part they have to play no matter how distasteful it might be. To do this they create a back story, which helps generate compassion when this might be a difficult emotion to access. This back story helps the actor develop the right attitude to the part they have to play. In the same way, a doctor might think of an exasperating patient who they have to be nice to as someone who may be having a very bad day or may be dealing with terrible problems in their own personal life.

The answer seems to be that if it's the people at work who you feel are driving you round the bend, you need to find a way of emotionally reacting to them by changing your deeper attitudes, and you will actually begin to enjoy your work.

Then, when you pick up your award or 'Oscar' for outstanding performance at work you can genuinely start your thank-you speech by saying, 'I should like to thank the Academy . . .' because you will have got to the podium as a result of deep acting.

We raised the issue earlier of the fact it's curious that so many of our motivations tend to revolve around taboo subjects. You may be rather keen on sleeping with the new arrival at work, or want more money or power, but you usually can't articulate these desires without at least losing your friends or becoming a social pariah.

It seems that our desires need to be managed to ensure we don't alienate those around us. Why can't we be more open about what really drives us rather than only sharing that with our psychiatrists in the privacy of the consulting room?

One reason for this might be the notion that being driven by a sexual desire or by the need for more money or power is scary to whoever we propose this to. This is because it raises the spectre that we are not concerned about others in our lives, and indeed might manipulate or use them merely as stepping stones to our next goal. For society to function it is vital that we appear to hold the primary goal of getting on with and facilitating the lives of others. If instead it is blatantly obvious our goals are only about ourselves then society rapidly breaks down.

It is also frequently forgotten that many of our goals today are social ones – in order to get on at the office, win the attractive date or attain a higher salary we have to persuade others to give us these things. This means that certain social skills lie at the heart of most achievement. Even in the arena of sport, your personality still has to be one where the manager won't keep benching you even if you have the strongest right foot in the football team.[9]

Many think of these social skills as basically revolving around the capacity to manipulate others.[10]

The appeal of popular reality TV programmes like *Big Brother* and *Survivor* is the unique opportunity they give us to see more clearly, with the benefit of twenty-four-hour fly-on-the-wall cameras, the manipulative personality type in action.

Indeed recent research from psychologists at the State University of New York found that getting people to imagine how to survive with others on a desert island – the scenario of the *Survivor* series – brought to the fore whether their personality was prone to manipulativeness or not.[11]

In other words, the slightly odd predicaments reality TV sets up are designed to elicit and test the manipulative side of our characters – and this is why we watch. We are curious about how others manipulate as we realize we could be unwitting victims of manipulators in real life.[12]

Because manipulative personality types tend to rise up through the ranks of power – many believe our current governments are the most manipulative on record – psychologists now believe manipulators have a huge but often hidden impact on our lives and so have turned increasingly to studying them.[13]

Research has uncovered that not only do super-manipulative personality types exist – and these have a superficial charm, a grandiose sense of self-worth, an ability to lie and manipulate, plus a lack of remorse with shallow emotions – but they will also tend to be hard to uncover.[14]

Without the benefit of the all-seeing eyes of TV cameras, these slippery characters usually get away with their conniving behaviour, undetected by the rest of us. For this reason many are unaware of the true depths to which the manipulative personality can sink.[15]

But while psychologists have been studying this personality type intensively recently, and have now come up with new ways of uncovering the manipulator in action, in fact schemers are not a new phenomenon: they have been with us for a very long time, long before reality TV finally exposed them.

In 1532 an Italian intellectual, Machiavelli, published a book entitled *The Prince*, widely regarded by historians as the first modern treatise on the art of politics. Since then Machiavelli has become synonymous with the use of guile, deceit and opportunism in human relations. Psychologists have thus categorized people into high or low in machiavellianism, or High Mach and Low Mach.[16] The term used within psychology to describe when you have been successfully and secretly manipulated by a machiavellian is to say you have been 'Mached'.

High Machs, or arch manipulators, advocate lying as a preferred policy because they deem it 'necessary in an imperfect world'. Beyond this, machiavellians understand the importance of maintaining a public appearance of virtue while practising whatever is required to achieve their ends.[17]

Manipulators relentlessly approach each new social scenario with the question, 'What kind of person does this situation call for, and how can I best be that person?' The rest of us take a more relaxed view of life and are not incessantly plotting to advance ourselves by trying to suss out how to turn any situation to our advantage.[18]

For example, we may accidentally observe a weakness in another, but we do not always make a note to remember it and later try to work out how to use that vulnerability to our advantage – but that is precisely what the manipulator is up burning the midnight oil doing.

When occupations have been surveyed for High and Low Mach people, lawyers are found to be the highest scorers in machiavellianism, closely followed by business executives, with doctors and teachers scoring lowest. So what are you, High Mach or Low Mach? Do the quiz on page 112 to find out the awful truth!

What is particularly different about High Machs is that while most of us can lie when required to do so, we cannot lie so easily in situations we feel strongly about. However, High Machs persuade with sincerity while holding the emphatically opposite conviction. So they have the greatest negotiating advantage over Low Machs when others cannot check the veracity of their assertions.[19]

High Machs cheat more than Low Machs because they are unconcerned by questions of morality and so can concentrate on winning the game by whatever means are most effective. They regard lying, deceit and manipulation as legitimate tactics.[20]

The key difference between manipulators and the rest of us is that while we tend to get distracted by relationships and are influenced by whether we like others or not, High Machs can flirt and appear good friends but never forget their own ambitions and always put these first, not second to loyalty or friendship.

Why should reality TV programmes that show us manipulation in action be such a modern obsession? Is it possible our interest in these formats is because manipulation has become the key issue of current times? When you are likely to encounter those around you for most of your life then deception is likely to be uncovered and does not make sense as a long-term strategy, as it could lead to being ostracized.

It is only in situations where you are unlikely to keep meeting your victims in the future that manipulation begins to make sense. So the reason why machiavellianism could be on the increase is that we live in more anonymous times, where, for example, we are much less likely to know our neighbours well.[21]

Increased geographic mobility means our backgrounds are more mysterious to each other, and even if our deceptions are uncovered, we won't be hanging around long enough for it to matter much. This might explain why manipulation could be burgeoning, because more people can now get away with it with less social cost.[22]

Because manipulation is essentially a cynical short-term strategy – the aim is to gain as much out of the other person before they realize they are being manipulated – psychologists speculate that manipulators develop from unstable families, or where there has been an early major disappointment or heartbreak in a romantic affiliation.

A childhood in which long-term relationships are rare means

manipulators never learn the benefits of long-term investment in relationships. Recent research by psychologist Nigel Barber of the Birmingham-Southern College in the USA confirms that machiavellian personality types are more frequently found in children from unstable families, for example where there are high rates of divorce.[23]

Psychologists Jon Sutton and Edmund Keogh of Glasgow Caledonian University and Goldsmiths College, London University, confirmed with their research that children as young as nine years old can display machiavellian personalities.[24] These manipulative youngsters were found to have already developed a lack of faith in human nature, not seeing others as fundamentally kind or honest. This could explain why they felt it was legitimate to be manipulative, as they believed everyone else was similarly scheming, and this could be due to a lack of supportive relationships in early childhood.

Research by psychologists Elinor O'Connor and Christopher Simms of University College Dublin has uncovered some intriguing differences between men and women in the way they manipulate.[25] Female manipulators were found to particularly favour the tactic of self-disclosure in relationships, partly because it is a subtle way of making people feel they should trust you, as you obviously believed in them by sharing a confidence.

Revealing things about yourself that are normally kept hidden is perceived positively by others, and inclines them to feel flattered that such an intimacy has been shared. It also prompts them to reciprocate by self-disclosing themselves, but they may reveal something actually truthful (unlike the first intimacy unveiled by the manipulator) but which should be kept secret, and therefore provide a possible weapon to be used against them in the future.[26]

Another intriguing finding is that more feminine men tend also to use self-disclosure as a manipulation tactic.

While the female manipulator uses self-disclosure to manipulate others into trusting her, the male manipulator seems too impatient to use a deepening relationship to their own ends, and instead relies on argumentative persuasion tactics. For example, manipulative men keen on persuading women to sleep with them early on in a relationship have been found by research to frequently use references to what everyone else is doing in bed.[27]

Another key gender difference in manipulation appears to be that while women emphasize to the victim the advantages of doing what they want, men focus on the problems that will accrue to you if you don't do as they wish. Machiavellian men tend to subtly intimidate, while women tend to lure.[28]

The first TV series of *Big Brother* surged in ratings and hit the headlines only after 'Nasty' Nick Bateman began to be seen by the audience for what he really was – a schemer and a liar. Yet he duped the rest of the household into becoming the most popular person in the house.

Note that the other household members were for the first few weeks totally in the dark about Nick's duplicitous character; at the beginning he was even the person least nominated for eviction. It was only being in intensive and continual contact with him that finally led them to rumble him.

Therefore a key point that manipulators are only too aware of is the need to manipulate secretly, as when people feel they are being manipulated there is a rapid build-up of resentment and resistance – as happened in the original *Big Brother* household when Nasty Nick's tactics were finally exposed.

The latest psychological research confirms that time seems to be the vital factor in uncovering manipulators for what they are, as they are likely to be most successful if others only come into contact with them for a short time.[29] This is because the longer you know and the closer you get to a manipulator, the more likely they are to slip up and for their true character to be revealed.

So time appears to be an indispensable weapon in the fight against manipulators, and asking for more time before making a decision when a manipulator is trying to get you to make a commitment will usually irritate them. This is therefore a good test – playing for more time – that will uncover the manipulators amongst us.

Also, because manipulators are carefully tailoring their behaviour to appear to be the right person at the right place at the right time, they often seem to be very different people in various social settings as they encounter contrasting demands. So manipulators will tend to 'compartmentalize' their lives, and will not like friends or associates from different parts of their lives, say from work or their social lives, meeting each other, thus allowing them to compare notes about the manipulator's ever-changing persona. A manipulator will therefore not readily allow you to mingle with others who know them from another part of their life.

For those of us who cannot consult so easily with others to check up on who is really plotting against us, as they did in the original *Big Brother* household, it is much more difficult to spot the manipulators amongst us.

It is interesting to note that in recent reality TV programmes the eventual winners have all been those who never appeared an overt threat to other contestants. Highly effective male competitors appear to have recently fallen down badly by being unable to suppress the instinctive male desire to draw attention to their strengths, and this merely alerted others to their threat, and eventually produced their downfall.[30]

It seems that in the game of manipulation, the real winners are careful to hide the threat they pose, so the competition can't respond until it is too late.

Then they carefully look flabbergasted and bewildered at being handed the prize at the end.

ARE YOU A MANIPULATOR?

MACHIAVELLIAN SCALE

Each statement is followed by two possible responses: agree or disagree. Read each statement carefully and decide which response best describes how you feel. Then tick the corresponding response. Please respond to every statement. If you are not completely sure which reply is more accurate, put the answer that you feel is most appropriate. Do not read the scoring explanation before filling out the questionnaire. Do not spend too long on each statement. It is important that you answer each question as honestly as possible.

		AGREE	DISAGREE
1	Everyone has a vicious streak, some just hide it better	A	B
2	Most people are basically good and kind	B	A

		AGREE	DISAGREE

| 3 | Completely trusting anyone is asking for trouble | **A** | **B** |

| 4 | Getting ahead is possible without cutting corners | **B** | **A** |

| 5 | The successful are more unlikely than the rest of us to be honest and good | **A** | **B** |

| 6 | The truth is important to mention when persuading | **B** | **A** |

| 7 | Important people need to be flattered | **A** | **B** |

| 8 | Most people cannot be easily fooled | **B** | **A** |

| 9 | Handling others often means saying what they want to hear | **A** | **B** |

| 10 | Most people do not need incentives to work really hard | **B** | **A** |

Score

Add up your score by totalling the number of As and Bs you have ticked.

8 or more As: You are definitely a High Mach because of your lack of concern with conventional morality. In your view lying and cheating and other forms of deceit are justified if they achieve your ends. The essence of your successful manipulation of others is your focus upon getting things done rather than long-range, more abstract goals. Hence you are more interested in tactics for achieving possible ends than in an inflexible striving for ultimate idealistic goals. This explains your success at work, but your relative failure in friendship and love.

Between 5 and 7 As: You are scoring above average in machiavellianism because of your relative lack of emotional involvement with most others. Your success in getting others to do what you want them to do is enhanced by viewing them as objects to be manipulated, rather than as individuals with whom one has empathy. One advantage you have in negotiation compared to Low Machs is your ability to control the outward appearance of your anxiety, so people have difficulty guessing what you really think in a given situation. You are missing out on enjoying the differences between people, as you tend to assume everyone else is more similar than they really are.

Between 3 and 4 As: You are average to below average in machiavellianism, because your greater emotional involvement with others means you tend to identify with their point of view, and once empathy occurs it becomes more difficult for you to use psychological leverage to influence others to do things they may not want to do. While High Machs can advocate a policy they disapprove of without then coming to approve of it, you tend to change your opinion, in effect converting your at first deceitful advocacy into an honest one. Your relative lack of distrust for others explains why you have been deceived in the past.

Between 0 and 2 As: You are Low Mach because your emotional needs seriously distort your perceptions of others; then you make errors in evaluating others, making it difficult for you to coolly manipulate them. You are more likely to get absorbed by the sociability of being with others than the goal of getting ahead, and hence you are more influenced by who you are with than able to influence them. Unlike High Machs you believe honesty itself is more important than the mere appearance of honesty. The problem is if you cannot learn to control your emotions you will always be an open book to High Machs who will manipulate you mercilessly.

One reason the manipulator works covertly is that it appears vital in today's cultural climate to keep your strong motivation to suceed secret. Many people even keep this secret from themselves. This leads to an important problem we discussed earlier in the book: 'goal conflict'. One conflict we are often trapped by is that our fear of failing in front of others prevents us taking the personal risks that could lead to eventual success.[31]

At the heart of motivation then is the delicate balance of striving in such a way as not to alienate others – indeed the best way of getting what we want is to get others on board to help us realize our ambitions. The alternative is that we find we can easily create a situation where others become obstacles to our ends.

For example, there is a psychological paradox at the heart of anyone's attempts to climb the ladder of success and in particular achieve promotion at work. On the one hand, you must demonstrate to your superiors that you can occupy a more dominant position in the future.[32] You have to therefore behave in a way that hints at 'dominance-potential' (as psychologists term it), yet on the other hand you cannot be so constantly striving for dominance that your bosses find you difficult to control or supervise.

This is the classic conundrum that most who are ambitious fail to grasp. Because their personalities exhibit a long-standing tendency to dominate interactions between people, they find it difficult to behave like subordinates, when in order to win promotion it is absolutely vital the boss feels comfortable supervising them.[33]

Dominance as a feature of personality has recently become of great interest to psychologists because it seems to predict who does indeed go on to achieve promotion at work. However, the key is to be able to control your 'striving for dominance'. Dominance can be measured using sophisticated scientifically devised personality tests, but you can also assess how dominant your workmates are more informally, by simply focusing on the way they talk to co-workers.[34] You can therefore usefully decide for yourself whether they are 'Hi-Dom' or 'Lo-Dom', which sounds a bit like some fetish service available from sleazy phone booths, but is an absolutely vital assessment to make when negotiating your way through the minefield of office politics.

Basically, psychologists have found a strong link between dominance, as measured in their formal testing, and certain conversational strategies. High-dominant people (Hi-Doms) tend to interrupt others – particularly subordinates – or at least those they regard as subordinates. They talk longer, take charge of the conversation by deciding when the topic is going to change, and state their preferences and opinions in a dogmatic and unyielding manner. They love to give instructions and advice, and tend to state strong personal preferences rather than waiting to hear what others have to say first.[35]

A common but difficult situation, which repeats all too frequently in offices, is that two co-workers aspire for a job promotion but only one can be successful – and so one eventually becomes the supervisor of the other. Because both candidates initially wanted to occupy what psychologists refer to as the 'high-dominance' position, the now-subordinate who aspired to be the supervisor will still psychologically manifest the initial wish to take charge.

In other words, psychologists predict they will become a very difficult subordinate and find it particularly arduous to adjust to this situation.

Psychologists have found that those who occupy 'low-dominance' positions at work but who aspire for a 'higher-dominance' position (i.e., promotion) tend to behave more dominantly than you would expect from their status in the office hierarchy. On the other hand, people who are in the same low-dominance position but who are happy with it – termed 'fulfilled low-dominance' by psychologists – supply the right amount of subordination to their superiors.[36]

Basically Hi-Doms in particular have a serious problem when it comes to playing the subordinate role, particularly if their aspirations for promotion have recently been thwarted. This is a recent finding by psychologists Marianne Schmid Mast and Judith Hall at Northeastern University in Boston, USA, in an extensive study of how dominance effects the way we interact with each other and how ultimately successful we become.[37]

This has important psychological implications for the way an office should be handled – it means that recently frustrated Hi-Doms should immediately be given some kind of activity or project that allows them to express their frustrated Hi-Dom personality in a more productive way. Otherwise all that will happen, if that frustrated Hi-Dom energy isn't creatively channelled, is they will become very difficult to control as subordinates.

How then to be the ideal subordinate – this is a skill that Hi-Doms in particular could learn with real benefit to their career aspirations. How to be the boss's pet?

Firstly ask the boss for advice, listen to it and follow it through. Bosses are more used to being asked for things and having to say no to subordinates, so it's a real pleasure to them to find themselves placed in a mentoring role. Bosses need the gossip and facts about what's really going on on the shop floor, which they are paranoid about not getting because they are in management, so become that vital source of information. Your acting as a confidante also makes them feel closer emotionally to you.

Your boss has enemies and rivals and is in a constant battle for dominance in the warfare of office politics, so help him or her win their battles and you will become an ally for life. Most employees are too focused on their own problems to think and explore the entanglements of their superiors. In fact, the ideal employee is the one who solves a boss's problems, not the other way round. Although most of us think our superiors should help us, the art of success is to ask yourself how can you help them.

Obviously there is a danger that you could just become your boss's lackey without any real benefit, so you need to link your success with the boss's. You have to make it in his or her interests that you get promoted and develop more power to help him or her in the future. You do this by explaining (subtly) how if you had more power, this would be more power to wield on their behalf.

You also need to test your boss periodically to see how willing they are to reward your efforts on their behalf in small ways as a signal that they are going to see you right in the long term. You do this by observing in particular their behaviour towards you when they are in the presence of their superiors – do they single you out for attention and speak positively of you to their bosses? This is a useful psychological test because it demonstrates if they can stop thinking about their own self-promotion for a while to consider yours.

If they don't, then move on. Find a boss who is willing to reward your efforts on their behalf.

Ultimately the key to promotability is visibility – make sure that you are the most discernible person in the workplace in terms of activity to your boss. Take on the projects that reflect their areas of interest.

If at this stage you are feeling nauseated that this is all too obsequious and sycophantic, then you are probably a Lo-Dom who is fulfilled by your subordinate role (nothing wrong with that, but could you park and wash my car please?). Alternatively you could be a Hi-Dom who can't bear adopting a Lo-Dom strategy when it's needed – you don't realize it yet but you are actually seen as a threat rather than an ally by your superiors.

Remember, if you can, that your tendency to behave relentlessly as a Hi-Dom is going to be particularly inappropriate when you are passed over for your next promotion.

What this psychological research suggests is that, particularly at work, 'emotional intelligence' – or the ability to handle your emotions and those of others – is still an essential skill it would be foolish to neglect.[38]

Office politics are commonly found to be the most troublesome aspect of trying to get on in the workplace. In particular, many who rely on talent and hard work – which *should* be the key criteria for advancement – often find that because they neglect or despise office politics they lose out in the long run.

They usually lose to the cunning manipulator who ends up getting promoted despite not working nearly as hard as the competition, and anyone who rises to the top of any social hierarchy has used Machiavelli whether he or she realizes it or not.

Even if you don't approve of Machiavelli one thing is for sure: he has been used against you and so it's best for your own protection that you are aware of his thought.

You might wonder why something written almost 500 years ago has any relevance to you, but remember that Napoleon Bonaparte said that *The Prince* is the only book worth reading. Mussolini declared that Machiavelli is 'the teacher of all teachers of politics', and *The Prince* is said to be on the bedside tables of all the major world leaders of the last 100 years.[39]

In this influential work, Machiavelli basically sets out the rules of power – rules for acquiring, wielding and maintaining power. Rules we can still learn from today if we want to negotiate the minefield of personal competition in general and office politics in particular.

The book was written in the form of advice to a hypothetical Prince who is trying to rule a kingdom he has just acquired. Since the publication of this seminal work it has unfairly acquired a reputation for advocating cold-hearted ruthlessness. Actually Machiavelli – who himself experienced torture from the rulers of his native Florence – was simply laying out the stark reality of human affairs, not celebrating the ruthless application of power.[40]

Mussolini also pointed out that for him the major problem with Machiavelli was 'he did not have enough contempt for humanity'.

Everyone needs to read *The Prince* because whether you agree with it or not the ideas in it will be used against you in your battles with competitors.

And if you still doubt the relevance of Machiavelli to today's office environment, here is something Machiavelli wrote almost 500 years before the Kelly inquiry:

> If sometimes you need to conceal a fact with words, do so in such a way that it does not become known. Or, if it does become known, make sure you have a ready and quick defence.

The key lesson is you may have your own agenda but have a defence on standby in case you suddenly have to defend your behaviour in public. So the first lesson of Machiavelli is to be aware there is a public agenda for your actions – the reasons people who observe you should conclude you do what you do – but behind this public face you will often have covert reasons that need to remain hidden. You could say Machiavelli was the father of spin.[41]

Machiavelli emphasized the importance of reputation in determining advancement and that this reputation could be entirely divorced from what a person is actually like. Given it's *reputation* that determines success in politics then you must work on yours to ensure it's what is needed to succeed. So it's important to start *backwards* from what an electorate or interview panel is looking for and supply that, rather than start forwards with what you are like and try to fit in. That means you need to focus on the elements of yourself that are closest to what is required reputation wise.[42]

You therefore need to focus on acts and alliances that are best for developing the necessary reputation. Machiavelli pointed out that all great leaders often perform acts that have no real practical benefit but that enhance mightily their reputation in a desired direction. Many leaders pick on a weaker nation and start a small war merely to enhance their reputation rather than to achieve any practical goal of assistance to their own country.[43]

Much of what is helpful in terms of personal advancement and so gaining others' attention might not even be fundamental to your company's business, but the key is to ensure you are seen to be the solver of problems and so attract others' respect and admiration. This obviously seems very machiavellian because you are pretending to be a team player when in fact you are acting for yourself.

This is another key point that many office workers forget and that Machiavelli emphasized: 'to pursue love is to lose power'.

What he means by this is manipulators never lose sight of their goal of personal advancement; to this end they will forge friendships and alliances, but they will never get distracted by the personal elements in these relationships.[44]

The machiavellian is therefore never completely open or honest in relationships, as this could be used against them if shifting sands means a friend develops an interest opposed to your own. You should be 'friendly' and have lots of 'friends' but if you want someone you can trust – a true friend – then get a dog – as Gordon Gecko the unscrupulous billionaire trader says in the classic machiavellian film *Wall Street*.[45]

Ultimately, all politics is about power and what determines who has the most power in a conflict or a negotiation, as in every office every day, is who is most dependent on the other. If your managers want you to do something at work that you simply don't want to do, but you are more dependent on them for a job than they are on you for what you bring to the office, then they have the power, not you.

So the art of gaining power over others is to make them dependent on you and yourself independent of them. It may take some time to create that dependence, but if you are behaving in a classic machiavellian way and therefore strategically, then you are willing to make a sacrifice today in order to win tomorrow.[46]

Machiavelli developed his ideas from the political machinations he saw around him. He saw at first hand a failed multiple assassination attempt where one celebrated Florentine family aspiring to rule tried to wipe out another while they both arrived hand in hand to an Easter Mass. When the attempt failed – within seconds – the ringleaders were immediately hanged.

Machiavelli concluded, 'Do unto others as they would do unto you only do it first and do it conclusively.'

The key uncomfortable question Machiavelli was asking was what are the necessary qualities of a person who rises up the ranks and ends up wielding power over others? In particular, is it better to be loved or feared? What kind of person should you be? Machiavelli concluded it's best to be *both* loved and feared. Most of us seem to err on the side of being one or the other, when we need both in our armoury.[47]

You may want your bosses to like you, and this is certainly desirable, but you don't want them to feel the relationship is so close they can take you for granted as there is no fear of you ever leaving.

At the heart of machiavellian thinking is the notion that we are constantly jostling for position in a social hierarchy and this idea seems alien to most people, who are content not to adopt such a competitive attitude to social and work situations. But it's vital to remember that there is a social component to any situation where motivation is involved. For example, a football match is also a social event. You won't win just by kicking the ball better than anyone else, but also by your interaction with other players on the pitch, and most vital of all, the winners are those who are able to ensure a social situation does not become an obstacle to their individual goals.

It is important to grasp that machiavellianism can be an extremely long-term project when it comes to using a relationship to mould someone into the kind of person it suits you for them to be.

Many couples I see in my marital therapy work at The Maudsley Hospital in South London are obviously primarily concerned about problems they discern in their partner's personality. But they are usually much less aware of perhaps an even more troubling issue: how their own persona is being slowly ground away, or distorted, by their relationship.

Lucy, a client of mine who was married for three decades to a successful businessman in the motor trade, only became fully aware of how her character had been moulded by him after he suddenly abandoned her for another woman. She came to see me because she was understandably upset at the unexpected desertion, after what she thought had been a successful family life with two happy children in their twenties.

However, as time went by she was surprised at all the ways she had adapted to his demands over the years, so that her personality had been completely transformed. On meeting a new younger male companion she discovered that she had almost lost touch with who she really was: her old political and cultural interests had to be rescued.

Lucy's personality changed in the hands of her husband – she lost her old friends, who found they had little in common with her any more. When she emerged blinking into the sunlight after the end of her marriage with her new-found freedom to give her old submerged personality an airing again, her friends came back, asking, 'Where has the old you been all these years?'

I have often found that some dominant partners hugely enjoy the moulding process – often a symptom of a determined personality – they prefer to work on someone who can be shaped into the form they want, rather than find material that is set in stone. So they seem to seek out a group who are pliant and willing to be carved up, in exchange for securities that come with relationships. Perhaps those not entirely confident about who they are in the first place are attracted to those who enjoy sculpting, because they are full of overweening certainty about what the world should look like.

So, perhaps, who you choose to settle down with becomes a key moment in the crossroads of life – a contrasting choice could result in you ending up an entirely different person.

This is because your personality, your attitudes, your preferences and your dispositions do not spring full-blown from a vacuum but are shaped by your experiences and, in particular, your significant relationships. We are used to the idea that our parents, and in particular their relationship with us, partly fashioned us into the kind of people we are today. However, what is only now beginning to be recognized by psychologists is the fact we are also significantly shaped by our partners.

Stephen Drigotas, a psychologist based in Texas, coined the term 'Michelangelo Syndrome' to capture the notion that we act like sculptors to our partners and shape them during our relationship.[48] Michelangelo Buonarroti described sculpting as a process whereby the artist releases a hidden figure from the block of stone in which it slumbers, a figure vibrant and divine, an 'ideal form'. Applied to close relationships, the Michelangelo metaphor describes a beneficent unfolding towards an ideal self.[49]

The idea is that the ideal partner is someone who facilitates us, through the deft use of the chisel of themselves, into becoming the kind of people we most wish to be. The dark side of the Michelangelo Syndrome is the idea that we can become shaped into the kind of person we would rather not be and indeed can end up horrified by the results.[50]

Even if you are not cohabiting with a determined sculptor, Drigotas argues that everybody's personality is probably a partial reflection of the shaping process produced by their partner. For example, one of the happiest married couples I know are James and Mary. When at a dinner party James will guide conversation towards topics that are good for his partner Mary – topics about which he knows Mary will be funny or knowledgeable.[51]

In a close relationship like this Mary flourishes, becoming a better and more interesting person. In contrast, some relationships stifle growth, blocking personal development or perverting the self. For example, Mary has a colleague Susan who is in a much less good relationship, where her partner Paul mocks Susan's beliefs and actually goes out of his way to create situations where she is likely to appear foolish. By varying their behaviour, a partner can bring out the best or worst in their associate's behaviour repertoire.[52]

But if Michelangelo Syndrome to a greater or lesser extent applies to all relationships, as Drigotas believes, then part of the secret of finding the right life-long partner is knowing who will help shape you into the kind of person you want to become. The implication is that you are in a better position to know who is right for you when you (a) have a sense of the kind of ideal self you aspire to and (b) know what kind of person will help you achieve that.[53]

Drigotas and psychologist colleagues have recently conducted ground-breaking research on sixty-three young people in strong relationships that confirms his theories. He found that being with someone who appeared to be able to help you become the kind of person you ultimately wanted to be was a strong predictor of personal well-being and satisfaction with the relationship.[54]

The intriguing implication is that if our partners promote movement towards or away from our ideal selves then it is vital to be mature and far-sighted enough to choose someone who will not always confirm our own view of the world. For example, I often see in my clinic the dependent and avoidant who feel the world is a dangerous place, and who therefore are afraid to take risks. These clients unconsciously seek out partners who confirm their view of reality. This kind of partner helps render my clients even more dependent and avoidant over time. So it is useful to have some awareness of the negative directions your personality is prone to travel in, and find someone who can arrest this process and even turn you around and move you on to a more positive bearing.[55]

The key ramification of this 'partner as sculptor' model of relationships is it suggests that quite a bit of hard work might need to be done by a mason encountering bits of difficult stone that need rounding off. Close partners will, for example, have to possess the ability and inclination to identify each other's weaknesses and draw attention to them rather than ignoring them.[56]

Drigotas also points out that, given how fraught all this chiselling could be, there is an important distinction between the related Pygmalion Syndrome and the Michelangelo Syndrome. In the Pygmalion Syndrome your partner is sculpting you according to their own view of what is the ideal you, which might not fit with your own perspective. In the Michelangelo Syndrome, you are being shaped into a form you personally desire.[57]

But all this talk of Pygmalion and Michelangelo Syndromes raises a troubling question: when your partner looks at you approvingly, are they admiring you or their own handiwork?[58]

5

DO YOU SUFFER FROM FALSE HOPE SYNDROME?

The greatest discovery of my generation is that a human being can alter his life by altering his attitudes

William James

To become rich know the difference between assets and liabilities – divest yourself of liabilities and garner assets

Robert Kiyosaki

The concept of hope has been interwoven with the Western psyche since classical antiquity in both its secular and sacred traditions. According to the pagan Greek myth, Hope was the last and only good spirit to escape from Pandora's box. St Paul exalted hope as one of the three most fundamental Christian virtues (I Corinthians 13:13); he also felt it necessary to exhort his followers to hope (Romans 8:34–5, 12:12, 15:12–13).

Dante identified the absence of hope with hell (*The Inferno*, canto iii, line 9); Pope wryly noted hope's perennial, and perennially frustrating, nature (*Essay on Man*, Epistle 1, 1733–4).

In the 1980s another psychological construct similar to hope was developed, that of optimism. Psychologists define optimism as a generalized expectancy that one will experience good outcomes in life. This definition makes no distinction regarding the agency through which outcomes occur, whether the individual's efforts, the efforts of others or outside forces. Optimism leads to persistence in goal-directed striving, and the most recent research has characterized optimism as the most powerful predictor of behaviour.[1]

But the key point here is that there is a difference between the kind of pointless hope or optimism that isn't based on any evaluation of how you might achieve your goals and the kind of hope rooted in an understanding of the mechanism by which difficulties can be overcome. The danger is to confuse one with the other. One helps you feel good but may not be so useful in achieving a goal.[2]

For example, around the same time each year with the arrival of Lent, it is traditional to consider how to improve one's fitness or health by giving something up like drink, smoking or over-indulgence. We like to imagine ourselves as fitter, healthier and sexier looking and then of course the next part of the daydream is how our lives will be different – who we could then pull or which Olympic event we would then dominate.

Psychologists at the Universities of New York and Hamburg have for the first time scientifically investigated whether this kind of daydream or wild fantasy is in fact a help or hindrance in achieving our goals. It's an important question because it turns out these daydreams about how our lives would be once we achieved our goals are not only common but a key part of many people's motivational strategy. The thought of turning Michelle Pfeiffer down for a date because Julia Roberts is on the line craving our new slim-line figure is just what we seem to need to get us out of bed on a cold spring morning for that dispiriting jog round the sodden park.

The psychologists investigated who actually achieved their goals of getting to date those they had a crush on, or landing a dream job, by following up students several years after they stated their aspirations. The surprising finding was that those who frequently fantasized about what would happen after they achieved their goals in the end were much *less* likely to be successful than those who simply had a clear idea of what they wanted and a positive expectation of achieving it.[3]

The last part is key – it turns out that optimism predicts a big effort and a strenuous striving produces better results, which feed back into more optimism. One theory as to why wild fanta-sizing about desired outcomes is so counter-productive when it comes to actually achieving goals is that if you mentally enjoy a desired future in the here and now, then this curbs current investment into a possible future. After all, if you are having a fantastic time fantasizing about that date with Julia Roberts, why bother going through the strain of actually getting fit?

Wild fantasies, it seems, start to replace striving, so the key lesson from this intriguing research is that achieving goals in life is all about positive expectations of future success. You should imagine the date with Julia Roberts is indeed possible, but you shouldn't get so absorbed in your fantasy that you forget to get out there and pound the streets to achieve your goal.

While overconfidence will help you keep your pecker up it won't necessarily help you achieve all your goals.

Many trying to improve their fitness and health have goals like losing a certain amount of weight or running a mile by a certain time – but the brutal truth according to the latest psychological research is that most of us will fail to achieve our health goals.

Yet despite persistently failing, we seem to try and try again to attain fitness targets.

On average we will make the same New Year resolutions ten times, about half of all alcoholics have returned to drinking following three months of intensive abstinence treatment, and according to Gamblers Anonymous only 7% achieve abstinence after two years.[4]

What keeps us going is the optimism that with a bit of tweaking in our health programmes we will eventually get there. Psychologists Janet Polivy and Peter Herman from the University of Toronto call this 'False Hope Syndrome' and this term represents a dramatic sea change in psychological thinking about how to actually achieve fitness targets.[5] Before, the theory was that we should keep ourselves motivated by imagining success was just around the corner. Now psychologists believe that it is unrealistic expectations of the ease with which fitness goals can be attained that explain why we don't prepare properly for personal change and ultimately fail.[6]

Instead of constantly investing in false hope as we start our next diet or fitness regime, better that we realistically understand that personal change is extremely difficult to attain and maintain, so that we set about trying to get where we want with a more sober and unsentimentally pragmatic approach.[7] This is not to say we should be gloomy, just that we should not keep expecting success to occur easily, and understand change requires planning and a comprehensive personal investment.

Oh, and one other thing the latest research has established: instead of aiming for weight *loss*, or measuring achievement by a negative, better to monitor our progress by positives, i.e., how many healthy meals we had last week, or how many times we make it to the gym.[8] This is a more realistic way to measure improvements, as losses like pounds shed are unlikely to be rewarding to monitor due to slow progress. Better to focus on the positive things you are doing to try and achieve your goals and keep patting yourself on the back for these.

HOW HOPEFUL ARE YOU?

Each statement is followed by two possible responses: agree or disagree. Read each statement carefully and decide which response best describes how you feel. Then tick the corresponding answer. Please respond to every statement. If you are not completely sure which reply is more accurate, put the one that you feel is most appropriate. Do not read the scoring explanation before filling out the questionnaire. Do not spend too long on each statement. It is important that you answer each question as honestly as possible.

		AGREE	DISAGREE
1	I can usually think of many ways to get out of a jam	A	B
2	My past experiences will probably not help me when it comes to the future	B	A
3	With any problem there are likely to be many solutions	A	B
4	Setbacks are a sign you should probably give up and try something different	B	A
5	I love learning new things	A	B

6   How hard I work at something is
     due to its pleasantness rather than
     its long-term implications | B | | A |

7   I enjoy work that will put me in
     new situations | A | | B |

8   I have strengths that are not useful
     in solving my main problems at
     the moment | B | | A |

9   I like meeting new people because
     they will usually end up liking me | A | | B |

10   There are a lot of problems in life
     where I have not had the right
     training to solve | B | | A |

Score

Add up your score by totalling the numbers of As and Bs in each
box you have ticked.

8 or more As: You are scoring very high indeed on being hopeful
about the future – this means that you usually expect things to
turn out well for you even when facing your darkest hour. There
are several possible reasons for this, including a generally
optimistic disposition whereby you tend to feel things will turn
out well in the world in any case. If your optimism is based on
your confidence about your own talents then this means you are
likely to approach your problems with much more energy than
most others – however, you need to appraise which problems you
can solve and which you can't as you have a slight tendency to
feel luckier than you might be.

Between 5 and 7 As: You are scoring above average on being
hopeful about the future and this is probably down to your
positive feelings about your problem-solving abilities combined
with your commitment to overcoming difficulty, which understandably leads you to be very optimistic about your future.
Because you don't feel quite as lucky as higher scorers it is probably the case that you avoid taking on certain projects because
you over-pessimistically assume you won't succeed. You may

need to be open-minded about what you are capable of.

Between 2 and 4 As: Although you are scoring around average to just below average for hope it may be you were more hopeful in the past. Perhaps a series of negative recent events has ground down your optimism so you are feel fairly bleak about your ability to cope with future difficulty. It may be that you feel let down by others as well and so now feel you can't trust others and this has led to a lack of confidence in the support you think you need to persist against difficulty. You need to avoid problems a little less and slowly rebuild your confidence in your ability to overcome obstacles, but pick smaller problems first. Learn to rely less on others and more on yourself as in fact most times it's what you bring to a situation that is the most valuable resource.

Between 0 and 1 A: You are scoring very low on hope for the future and this means you assume immediately in any situation that things will most probably not turn out well for you. This limits your assertiveness and indeed becomes a self-fulfilling prophecy – because you don't stick up for yourself you tend to get less out of life. Ask yourself why you are so convinced that you can't learn how to overcome your problems – they may seem overwhelming at the moment but acquiring the necessary skills is not beyond you, but can only happen if you feel more hopeful about yourself.

Wishful thinking and self-deception are instances of motivated believing. In the most straightforward sort of case, given by Professor Dion Scott-Kakures, a desire that his daughter be the most talented dancer in the company leads him to come to believe that his daughter is indeed the most talented dancer in the company.[9]

Wishful believing is a familiar, much-evidenced phenomenon. Studies have, for example, concluded that the actual link between a subject's self-appraisal of his or her intelligence and results from a standardized IQ test is very low; the correlation between an individual's judgement of his own physical attractiveness and others' judgements of that same individual's attractiveness is also extremely low;[10] the association between college athletes' judgements of their own ability and the judgements of their coaches is even lower still.[11] Psychologists note, moreover, that self-perceptions become more biased when the trait is highly desirable or undesirable, so they conclude that with virtually every conceivable positively valued trait, the majority of people think they are better than others.[12]

This raises immediate problems when it comes to tracking performance – you may recall I mentioned this in a previous chapter as a vital component of any successful motivational strategy.

A large part of assisting people to help themselves involves giving people feedback about themselves and their performance – if you want to improve yourself or your abilities you need feedback so as to ensure you are on the right track. Feedback at school and university for instance comes in the form of teachers' comments, coursework marks and exam results.

Actually a large part of success boils down very simply to reaction to feedback – particularly as the most useful feedback is that which is markedly discrepant to your own view of yourself.[13] So if you think you are a maths genius but get zero in the exam, this is useful feedback in preparing for applying for that Higher Maths degree. Much of education, therefore, turns on self-awareness and wrestling with this thorny issue. Indeed much of the stress of being a teacher is about cushioning the blow so that your pupils don't get too upset by the feedback on their performance but at the same time finding a way of keeping them motivated.

The latest psychological research by Dr Alain Morin of Mount Royal College, in Canada, has some useful insights into this area of self-awareness that are vital for those working with the less advantaged.[14]

If you stand in front of a mirror (thus becoming self-aware of that terrible haircut), chances are you compare what you see (real self) to some ideal of physical appearance that you aspire to. The inevitable discrepancy produces discomfort and then psychological mechanisms are naturally activated to strategically eliminate these unpleasant emotions. In a sense, teachers are always holding up mirrors to their pupils, trying to make them more self-aware.[15]

The initial reaction is simply to escape self-awareness by avoiding whatever is causing it – after going to the hairdresser's I avoid reflective surfaces like the plague. But obviously you cannot evade mirrors for ever (believe me I've tried) – so eventually you will have to face reality and try to reduce the discrepancy between the real self and the ideal self. How? Either by modifying the real self (a hat might just do it) or by changing the ideal self (you could lower your expectations about your looks).

Current psychological research shows that the bigger the discrepancy the stronger the tendency to avoid self-awareness.[16] For example, you might observe a discrepancy between your actual and ideal weight. If you are slightly overweight (small discrepancy), you will be likely to modify your diet and/or do exercises – i.e., to change the real self; however, if you are severely overweight (large discrepancy), you might feel discouraged before attempting anything and avoid the whole issue (escape self-awareness).

This is the danger of the kind of feedback that leaves a pupil disheartened.

When people observe a discrepancy and don't escape self-awareness, do they try to reduce the discrepancy by changing the real self, or, instead, the standard (the ideal self)? Do I wear a hat or try to lower my expectations about being able to pull Claudia Schiffer? Some pupils reject the negative feedback they get by saying education isn't for them or the standards expected of them are too high.[17]

If you are faced with feedback and you don't think you can respond by improving performance the key issue for you then becomes how to escape this uncomfortable self-focus. Drinking alcohol is one way to go about it. Another very popular activity in our society is watching TV. Lately Sophia Moskalenko and Steven Heine of the University of British Columbia in Canada conducted four studies aimed at showing that people who experience discrepancies watch more TV to escape self-awareness.[18]

In one study Moskalenko and Heine measured the amount of time participants watched television after receiving the result of a bogus IQ test. To create a discrepancy (and motivate participants to avoid self-awareness), Moskalenko and Heine informed some participants that they did very poorly on the IQ test. (Other participants received positive feedback or no feedback at all.) During a six-minute period in which television was available after the test scores were announced, participants who got good scores (no discrepancy) were observed watching TV for only two and a half minutes on average. Those who received no word on their score watched a little more TV – about three minutes. But people told that they had low IQ scores (discrepancy) turned to TV for an average of more than four minutes.

It would seem a lot of the unhelpful behaviour we observe in those suffering from various disadvantages is actually an attempt to escape self-focus. So an essential skill of the self-motivated is constantly trying to receive feedback, which assists in personal change rather than the attempt to run away from the self.[19]

This kind of motivated thinking lies at the heart of motivated behaviour, argues Dion Scott-Kakures, Professor of Philosophy at Scripps College, USA. Professor Scott-Kakures uses the ancient story of Troy to illustrate the point in his recent paper. Laocoon, as many will recall, was convinced that disaster would result when the gifted horse was brought within the walls of Troy. Indeed, he was certain the city would be destroyed. In at least some tellings of the story, he had scant evidence for his claims. After all, the Greeks had pulled up stakes and sailed off over that 'wine dark sea'.

But Laocoon feared the Greeks – even when bearing gifts; and, in consequence, he saw portents of catastrophe everywhere. He saw as Greek cunning what the other Trojans saw as evidence of Greek capitulation and fatigue before the impregnable walls. He saw an obvious and fearsome ruse where the others saw fitting homage to respected fellow warriors. Of course Laocoon was correct – but only adventitiously.

However unjustified may be the Trojans' belief about the significance of the horse, Professor Scott-Kakures argues we appear to have a grip on how the Trojans come to believe as they do: Cognition is driven and directed by desire.

In this regard Laocoon's motivated belief is more puzzling. He does not believe wishfully; he comes to believe just what he dreads. Yet his belief, as well, is motivated, driven by his fears – not his desires – that the Greeks have not departed and that the city will be destroyed. He comes to believe what is unwelcome.

In such cases, individuals come, on the basis of poor evidence, to believe just what they want not to be so.

Stock examples come readily to mind: the jealous husband, convinced that his wife is unfaithful; the successful student, convinced – once again – that she has failed her examinations; the frantic business executive, returning home – at great inconvenience – convinced she has left the gas stove burning; the anorexic, who believes she's overweight.

Scott-Kakures' goal here is to answer the question, 'What's in it?' for the unwelcome believer in a manner that casts light on the dynamics of motivated believing. Popular accounts of motivated believing have it that there 'must be some perceived gain' for the motivated believer.

In one recent study coffee drinkers and non coffee drinkers were exposed to purported research alleging the dangers of heavy coffee consumption to women. Women coffee drinkers judged the evidence as weaker than did the men or non-consuming women.[20]

One possibility is that because they found the connection at issue personally threatening these women, or some of them, were motivated to take a hypercritical stance. When confronted with evidence that has implications for optimistic beliefs, people evaluate it in a self-serving manner, applying more stringent criteria to evidence with less favourable implications to the self. Later studies indicate that such threatened subjects do, indeed, subject evidence to more painstaking scrutiny and appraisal.[21]

Significantly, when the consequences of heavy consumption are presented as far less dire, women coffee drinkers rate the evidence as no less compelling than other subjects. Thus the existence and, perhaps, even the extent of biased thinking co-varies with a subject's motivational constitution.

Of course, wishful believing is far more common than unwelcome believing; but this is very likely due to the fact that most people approach life with an optimistic stance. But while that may be true of most folks, it seems not to be true of all – certainly not Laocoon. Indeed psychologist E. Tory Higgins has argued that while most individuals are focused upon the presence of positive outcomes, others are focused upon the absence of negative outcomes.[22]

This characterological difference can be put to work to explain the sources of motivated wishful and unwelcome believing. A subject with a negative outcome focus will begin hypothesis testing with unpleasant possibilities. So, for Laocoon, the focus of hypothesis testing is the destruction of the city, while for the other Trojans it is the end of the siege. Even though Laocoon desperately wants the city not to be destroyed, his negative-outcome focus in concert with a confirmation of positivity bias will favour the confirmation of the feared possibility. Needless to say, there's an irony here, since, indirectly at least, the desire that a hypothesis not be the case results in its confirmation.

Professor Scott-Kakures asks us to imagine that it is the mid-1980s, just as news of AIDS and its symptoms (and in particular of Kaposi's sarcoma) is making its way into the informed public's awareness. Imagine further that Yuri, a well-informed fellow, sensitive to and fearful of AIDS (frankly, with little cause given his boring sexual history), emerges from the shower one morning, and notes the presence of a dime-shaped, purplish spot on his calf. 'I have AIDS,' he concludes. Devastated, his heart pounding, he emerges from the bathroom and, near tears, informs his wife of his just-discovered plight. After brief investigation, his wife discovers that the 'spot' is a bit of an aged and soiled wax ear plug of the sort that insomniac Yuri uses each night.

Laocoon and our other unwelcome believers are, as a clinician might call them, 'hyper-vigilant'. For reasons characterological or situational, they are all peculiarly focused on painful possibilities. In similar fashion, wishful believers may engage in intensive testing with the apparent aim of confirming some target proposition; they are, indeed, directionally driven. If the goal of such motivated believing is not anxiety reduction but is, in some sense to be clarified, the realization of the agent's goals and values, how are we to conceive of the role of motivation?

Scott-Kakures points out that in the Trojan myth, for Laocoon, the failure to believe that the horse is a danger will ensure the dreaded state of affairs. Thus, what may motivate the intensive testing of unwelcome believers like him is the desire to avoid a certain mistake or error, the costs of which are particularly vivid. It is, indeed, because he fears for the destruction of the city that Laocoon comes to believe that the horse is a danger.

What is central to pragmatic hypothesis testing accounts is another sort of cost to the settling of such questions: the cost of anticipated errors. Motivation for hypothesis testing is provided by a subject's regard for the costs of being mistaken.

The costliest error, the 'primary' error, is the error the subject is preponderantly motivated to avoid. This error is fixed by the aims, values and interests of the cognizer. Thus, in so far as a subject's hypothesis testing is sensitive to the avoidance of the costliest error, it serves to bring about what that subject values.

The most motivated and successful people harbour fears that their belief in their current strategy might be mistaken – hence their tendency to question their approach and be open-minded to other ideas. The less motivated and those who suffer from false hope syndrome tend to not fear enough being wrong and so overly believe their current approach is right.

As a result they are more prone to not achieving their goals.

6

GOALS, GOALS, GOALS!

The primary cause of success in life is the ability to set and achieve goals. That's why the people who do not have goals are doomed forever to work for those who do. You either work to achieve your own goals or you work to achieve someone else's goals

Brian Tracy

Though philosophers have traditionally been concerned with the pursuit of happiness, far greater wisdom would seem to lie in pursuing ways to be properly and productively unhappy. The stubborn recurrence of misery means that the development of a workable approach to it must surely outstrip the value of any Utopian quest for happiness

Proust

The Latin root of the word 'motivation' means 'to move'; hence, in this basic sense the study of motivation is the study of action. In life it seems you are always moving towards something or away from something else. Motivation can mean you are being pulled along by a future desire or pushed along by a drive, e.g., a desire for attention.

One of the key take-home messages about motivation is that many people are moving in a certain direction, but they are unaware of their eventual destination, though their arrival there is horribly inevitable. This explains much of the difficulty most people have with motivation. As I hope the perfect day exercise on page 66 illustrates, it is vital to know what you want, in particular to understand what you *really really* want as opposed to what you say you want.

There is also an issue over specificity of goals: many people want to be rich but they don't take the time to discover – through exercises like the perfect day – exactly how rich they want to be and what they would do with the money. If all they would use the money for is to 'spend more time with the kids' then it's possible they can do that now without depriving the kids of their time while they pursue wealth. Being crystal clear about your goals is one of the most powerful lessons from motivation theory.[1]

In my clinical experience it is never the case that anyone who comes to see me has a clear understanding of their true goals. Usually what they think they want is in marked contrast to what we discover together when we explore the issue of their true goals.

This naturally leads us to an attempt to understand goals, and that is what this chapter is about. Goals don't just happen on a football field; goals can have an extremely wide meaning, and the central point here is that one reason people don't achieve their goals is that they simply don't understand what those goals are.[2]

But motivation is also, at its core, about personal change. We appear driven to want to change the external environment – so we have more Ferraris on our front drive, for example – but actually to achieve more Ferraris we have to change as people – so we work harder or perform better. In order to lose weight we have to become the kind of person who is less fond of food and less loath to take the lift rather than the stairs.[3]

Maybe fundamentally we are not sure what kind of person we need to become in order to get what we want. Alternatively, it seems that many people are afraid of the kind of person they might become if they make the changes necessary to achieve their ambitions.[4]

At the heart of this problem of success depression, with which we started this book, is the surprising but increasingly accepted idea in psychology that we are not very good at predicting what will make us truly happy. For Harvard Professor of Psychology Daniel Gilbert has discovered that our ability to predict how good or bad we will feel after future events is surprisingly poor.[5]

One of his studies compared how Democrat and Republican voters in Texas predicted they would feel with how they actually felt after the right-wing George Bush Junior got elected Governor there. He found that Democrats felt surprisingly better about him than they thought they would, and Republicans were less enthused after the successful election than when Bush was just a possibility.

In another replication of this result, Gilbert asked more than 100 university professors before and after they found out about an important promotion, how they predicted they would feel before and how they actually felt after. Oddly, whatever happened in terms of success or failure, they were bad at predicting their future emotional state – those who achieved the sought-after promotion felt less happy than expected, and those who failed felt less bad than predicted.

Gilbert also found those in serious long-term romantic relationships predicted they would feel much worse if the relationship broke up than they actually felt when their affiliations did finish. Indeed, there was no significant difference in happiness between those who suffered a falling-out and those still in a relationship, despite the prediction that breaking up would cause much misery.[6]

Psychological research on how the general population reacts to a whole series of terrible events, like losing a child in a car accident, being diagnosed with cancer, becoming paralysed or being sent to a concentration camp, has oddly found these problems have less impact on long-term happiness than anticipated.[7]

In the most spectacular experimental demonstration of this effect, big-money national lottery winners were found not to be statistically significantly more happy than those paralysed following a major car accident, six months after each incident.[8]

This inability to anticipate correctly our future emotional states after important events could be one of the most profound discoveries of modern psychology, because every major decision we make in life is based on an implicit prediction of how happy or sad the outcome will make us. The judgement to marry or divorce, or to become a lawyer rather than a trumpet player, hinges on which choice we think will bring the greater emotional rewards.[9]

But if every decision we make is based on a consistently

flawed anticipation of our future emotional state then, Gilbert argues, it follows we go through life frequently failing to make the right choices.

Common examples of our poor emotional forecasting include our tendency to marry the wrong person (we think we will be happier with them than we turn out to be), shopping for groceries on an empty stomach (we think we will eat more than we eventually do) and whenever we say 'I'll just have one chip . . .'

While poor decision-making might be an unfortunate side effect of this phenomenon, one benefit is that this tendency seems to be a kind of 'psychological immune system', wired into our minds, which protects us from feeling too terrible when bad things happen to us. This system is in a constant battle with all the bad things that are always happening to us, perhaps to ensure we don't feel suicidal all the time.

This psychological immunity partly works by the rationalizations we wheel out to cope with crises, explains Gilbert. So when we are dumped by our girlfriends we eventually start thinking we never loved them that much anyway, and they were probably not right for us in the first place. These rationalizations can be surprisingly powerful; Gilbert quotes the example of the man who narrowly missed the opportunity to franchise the first McDonald's restaurant, and hence slimly missed the chance to become a billionaire, who noted many decades later, 'I believe it turned out for the best.'

We also constantly overestimate the impact of events on our emotional lives because we exaggerate to ourselves how we think we would feel after a possible future event as a way of motivating ourselves. So we say, 'If I fail the algebra test next week I will be doomed to a life of poverty and despair, so I'd better skip the party and stay at home and revise instead.' In fact, failing the test probably wouldn't have such a bad impact on us, but if we didn't think it would, we wouldn't be motivated to revise hard for it.[10]

We also tend to focus exclusively on the future event in question, so we fail to consider everything else that could be going on in our lives then, which will also impact on our mood. While we imagine the next big promotion in our career will make us happy for ever, which is why we then make excessive sacrifices for the boss, we forget that after the advancement, other aspects of life will continue as before. We will still get parking tickets and visits from the mother-in-law.[11]

If we became more aware of precisely how bad we are at predicting how we will feel in the future, this would have major implications for treatments of our psychological problems. For example, if a phobic realized he wouldn't feel quite as bad as he thinks he will when encountering a spider, he would stop being a spider phobic.[12]

The extreme insinuation of Gilbert's work is that we could all choose to live on a kind of 'Zen' planet where we declared, 'It doesn't matter what you do to me – I will be OK anyway.' Indeed, why should any of us bother to do anything, like vote, as whoever gets in, or whatever the results of our actions, it seems to make little difference to our happiness?

But Gilbert hastens to correct this misapprehension – he isn't saying events don't make a difference to our happiness, just that they make less of a difference than we consistently imagine they will.

However, our tendency to avoid taking risks in life is because we anticipate coping less well with disaster or failure than we would actually, and this should encourage us to gamble more. Even if things don't go as we hope, we will probably cope with adversity better than we predict. Gilbert is himself an example of this less risk-averse attitude: he is probably one of the only professors at Harvard not to have got a high school diploma, because he dropped out of school, preferring to go travelling rather than graduating.

Gilbert himself acknowledges that clearly there are many people who end up feeling worse after bad events than can be accounted for by his research – after all, suicide and depression do occur after relationship breakdown and job loss. But Gilbert's argument is that psychiatric disorder occurs when our psychological immune system malfunctions.

Yet what is fundamentally provocative about this work is it turns on its head our previous notion that it is the mentally ill who are deluded and irrational in their approach to the world. Instead it now seems it is the sane who constantly rationalize away the bad things that happen to them, because their psychological immune system is protecting them from reality.

The problem if we don't have a clear idea of our goals is that our lives can become rather aimless. Also, as all human behaviour is really an exercise of will and it follows that all human relations are essentially conflicts of will, we tend to end up following the life that others desire for us rather than the one we want for ourselves.[13]

One way of looking at this is that while the intellect decides ends, it is the will that provides the means and, therefore, the crucial movement towards these ends.

A passage from Tolstoy's *Anna Karenina* illustrates the vexed issue of how people behave in ways that seem at variance with what is required to get what they really want, leading to dramatic questions of whether what we really want lies more in the realm of the unconscious, according to economic psychologist Dr Harold Wolozin at the University of Massachusetts, USA.

The dilemma of Varenka and Koznyshev in *Anna Karenina* is that their actions ultimately defeat what they both desperately want, which is to get married. The scene was set when Varenka volunteered them to take her brother's children out to search for mushrooms:

> *They walked a few steps in silence. Varenka saw that he wanted to speak; she guessed what it was about and grew faint with joy and fear. They had gone so far that they could not be overheard by anyone, but still he did not speak. Varenka would have done better not to break the silence, for after a silence it would have been easier for them to say what they wanted to say than after talking about mushrooms; but almost against her will, almost by accident, Varenka said: 'So you haven't found anything? But then of course there are always fewer in the middle of the wood.'*
>
> *Koznyshev gave a sigh and made no answer. He was vexed that she should have spoken about the mushrooms. He wanted to bring her back to her first remark about her childhood; but as though against his own will, after a longish pause, he made a remark in reply to her last words.*
>
> *'I've only heard that white mushrooms grow mostly at the edge of the woods, though I can't tell which are the white ones.'*
>
> *A few more minutes passed; they had gone still further from the children and were quite alone. Varenka's heart was thumping so hard that she could hear it and she felt herself turning red, then pale, then red again.*
>
> *To be the spouse of a man like Koznyshev . . . seemed to her the height of happiness. Besides she was almost sure she was in*

love with him. And now in another moment it had to be decided.
She was terrified. Terrified of what he might and what he might
not say.

Now or never was the moment when he had to make their
position clear; Koznyshev, too, felt this. Everything about
Varenka – her look, her blush, her lowered eyes – showed that
she was in a state of painful suspense. Koznyshev saw it and was
sorry for her. He even felt that to say nothing now would be to
offend her. He quickly went over in his mind all the arguments in
favour of his decision. He repeated to himself the words in which
he had intended to propose to her. But instead of those words, by
some sort of unaccountable idea that came into his mind he
suddenly asked: 'What is the difference between a white and a
birch mushroom?'

Varenka's lips trembled with agitation when she replied:
'There is hardly any difference in the cap. It's the stalks that are
different.'

And the moment these words were uttered, both he and she
understood that it was all over, that what should have been said
would never be said, and their agitation, having reached its
climax, began to subside.

'The stalk of a birch mushroom,' said Koznyshev, who had
completely regained his composure, 'reminds me of the stubble
on the chin of a dark man who has not shaved for two days.'

'Yes that's true,' Varenka replied with a smile, and in-
voluntarily the direction of their walk changed. They began
walking toward the children. Varenka felt hurt and ashamed, but
at the same time she experienced a sense of relief.

When he got home and went over his reasons again,
Koznyshev came to the conclusion that his first decision had been
wrong. He could not be unfaithful to the memory of Marie.

In spite of their conscious will to consummate their longings into
a clear proposal of marriage, Varenka and Koznyshev both have
an unconscious will to do otherwise. Both are apprehensive and
self-conscious, both wholly absorbed with those few words that,
when spoken, will constitute a proposal: he has rehearsed his
overture, she her acceptance. Yet every time they are on the verge
of addressing each other, they find themselves skittering away.

Within the realm of concious will, they only know what they
have determined to do, and, in this bondage, they are no longer

capable of imagining the other or even of understanding how they have arrived at this particular moment, according to Dr Wolozin. So Koznyshev is reduced to repeating to himself the words he had intended to use, and Varenka to hearing her heart pounding, feeling herself turn red, then pale, then red again. And then 'unaccountably' and 'almost against their will', they discover themselves talking about mushrooms instead of marriage.[14]

Psychologists such as Dr Wolozin argue there are two main possibilities here. One is that while they both dearly want to get married they are so afraid of rejection that the goal of seeking marital union is confounded by the goal of avoiding the embarrassment of rebuff. As we have already suggested, in setting one goal we usually have to sacrifice another. If we want to diet to become thin then in order to attain the goal of slimness we have to give up the goal of satiety.[15]

It is the inability to give up goals that stymies us from achieving the other goals that are supposedly more important to us.

Of course the other possibility is that actually they don't really embrace the goal of marriage closest to their hearts and that unconsciously they don't really want to be united. In which case this is an issue of goal clarification.

Perhaps the most surprising thing about what I am going to suggest in this chapter is how much of life can be specified in terms of goals. We might be used to thinking of goals in the workplace or in sporting prowess, but would you realize that it's vital to use a 'goals approach' if you want to achieve whatever you desire in your personal life?[16]

Psychologists Frank D. Fincham from University College Cardiff and Stephen Beach from the University of Georgia in the USA point out that it is possible to analyse all human interaction and problems in terms of goals.[17]

Consider, for example, a relatively common conflict: a couple arguing over directions while travelling. Like many common-garden-variety situations in which conflicts occur, there is little obvious basis for conflict. Both partners want to get to the destination, and neither seems to benefit from arguing about directions. Yet, as it becomes clear that they are not on the correct road, here they go again. He becomes angry and asks why she cannot read a simple map. She retorts that there is nothing wrong with her map reading, that he must have missed a turn.

They progress through several increasingly hostile reproach-denial cycles until she suggests they stop and ask someone for directions. He drives on in stony silence, even angrier than he was prior to her suggestion. Everything happens quickly. Upon later inquiry, neither partner reports planning what they did, but both report a considerable number of very negative thoughts about the other in the silence that followed the brief eruption.

How does a goal analysis help us understand the conflict and discuss it with the couple?

Psychologists Fincham and Beach begin with three premises: (a) all behaviour is goal directed; (b) spouses don't always know what the goal is, even for their own behaviour (goals can be latent as well as consciously experienced); and (c) goals vary widely.

Upon accepting these premises, we can begin to talk with the couple about their argument in an intuitively clear way. We may explain that we can identify goals and changing goals on the basis of what is holding their attention and consuming their energy.

Fincham and Beach suggest we can ask the husband at what point he thinks he switched from focusing on finding his way to focusing on whose fault it was for being lost. This is an important moment, because it is the point at which his goals began to shift without his necessarily realizing it. Such a shift in attentional focus is a good indication that an emergent goal displaced his prospective goal of working jointly with his wife to find their way.

Attempting to find out more about his goal shift is likely to illuminate aspects of their interaction that characteristically precede a negative shift in his conflict behaviour. Likewise, we might ask the wife about the point at which she began to shift from her focus on helping her husband to defending herself or even counter-attacking.

What triggers the shift to the emergent goal for *this* husband and *this* wife? Are there similarities in the triggers that elicit this shift across conflict episodes?

Does a goal perspective help in any other ways? Yes, we can discuss with our clients the value of setting goals for themselves, examining the relation of the new goals to existing ones (e.g., are they consistent?), and being aware of when their prospective goals are displaced by emergent ones during an interaction. In particular, therapists can highlight the possibility that emergent goals are often self-identity goals (frequently activated automatically and outside awareness) and that responses often reflect attempts to avoid loss of face (usually manifest in over-learned conflict behaviour).[18]

In such circumstances, argue Fincham and Beach, conflict is most likely to escalate, become more global, and generate more rigid conflict behaviour as the original issues that provoked conflict are subsumed by issues of face-saving. It can be emphasized that captives of this process are usually quite unaware of it and often express puzzlement about why so much conflict can be generated by trivial issues (e.g., navigation/driving).

In addition, goal-setting can facilitate accomplishment in a variety of therapies, and concrete, small goals are especially useful in this regard. Setting concrete goals allows couples to think about opportunities to implement their goals, further facilitating accomplishment.

One resultant approach to helping a couple find more adaptive ways to manage conflict is to think through over-arching goals (e.g., I want to show I care and also get to the party), and then help the couple break the general goals into smaller, more concrete ones.

By becoming aware of these considerations, Fincham and Beach contend, spouses can more easily persevere in patterns designed to convey, for example, warmth and regard for the partner.

But if goal conflict is at the heart of much marital distress, is it possible it's also core to our dissatisfaction with ourselves?

Lack of self-control is obviously at the centre of a group of ill-nesses termed 'disorders of impulse-control'. These range from people who cannot control their tempers to people who cannot control their drinking, eating, smoking, drug-taking or spending. There is even some evidence that impulse-control disorders may have been on the increase over the last two to three decades in the West, which could account for the puzzling perceived increase in mental disorder, even in a time of greater prosperity.[19]

One possible explanation for the increase in the numbers of people unable to control their impulses may lie in our child-rearing practices. Because of our greater wealth we are in a better position than ever before to give our children the things they demand. However, this may work to their disadvantage, in that in the past when we told them they could not have the toy they wanted because we could not afford it, we were in-advertently teaching them self-control.[20]

But control does not just mean learning to stop doing something. It also means being able to start doing something you have put off, such as work, a new project, the redecorating, revising for an exam or regular exercise. Common to both scenarios is that a current behaviour needs to be stopped or decreased – because it causes suffering – and replaced by another action.[21] Usually, the reason change is difficult is that the present behaviour produces some positive consequences, albeit short-term ones (for example, a smoker gets pleasure from inhalation), while the behaviour the person would like to change to might be beneficial in the long term (stopping smoking will help prevent lung cancer). Often, the short-term reward proves more alluring and powerful than the long-term benefit.

When we change our behaviour in a way we would like we are exerting self-control. So if we can stop ourselves overspending, give up unhealthy foods or take up jogging – simply because we want to – we are demonstrating self-control.

The key to change is to start with what psychologists call an 'ABC analysis'. ABC stands for 'Antecedents, Behaviour and Consequences'.[22] This illustrates the fundamental principle that all behaviour occurs as a result of events that have already taken place – the antecedent (the shopaholic finding herself in a shopping mall) – and has consequences (the thrill of the purchase). To change behaviour you have to alter either the antecedents or the consequences, and often both.

It may not even be that the behaviour you are stuck with gives any apparent immediate benefits. The battered wife stays, not because she enjoys being beaten up, but more often because she fears the consequences of leaving immediately (not being able to cope alone and possibly never finding another partner) more than she fears the repercussions of staying with an abusive partner. She puts off leaving in the hope that things will change.

But why do we find it so easy to put off until tomorrow things we would be better doing today? Or why do we tend to have difficulty resisting the temptation to do something that gives us immediate pleasure but holds long-term negative consequences?

One theory is that these are universal human weaknesses. We evolved as animals in a rapidly changing and uncertain world. In such situations, where the future is difficult to foresee, immediate pleasures are at least certain, but the future less so, in which case a sacrifice for long-term benefit may be wasted effort.[23]

However, the world we now inhabit is very different from the haphazard one of the jungle we evolved in. The long-term benefit of giving up smoking or drinking is one we are much more likely to experience if only we could overcome our natural, perhaps even biological, tendency to grab the short-term benefit at the expense of the long-term gain.

In spite of this natural tendency, we can increase our self-control by using self-management techniques. The first step therapists take when teaching clients self-control is to check whether the patient believes the particular behaviour in question is actually under their command in the first place. Addiction models, which help clients to believe that, for example, they smoke because they are 'addicted', tend to erode the belief that they can learn to control themselves and so stop smoking. Clearly it is more difficult to feel that you can gain discipline if you believe you are out of control than if you believe the behaviour is under your power but that you just need some help to improve your self-management.[24]

To avoid arguments with those in favour of the addiction model, I prefer to suggest that the real issue is whether it is possible to gain control of yourself. There is much research to suggest you can, and the group of people who successfully learn to control themselves without seeking help have a stronger belief that it is feasible than those who are less successful in learning to control themselves.[25] So, for example, one of the most powerful predictors of who will drop out of a stop-smoking programme is how strongly each smoker believes he can gain control over his smoking. Those who do not have much faith in their ability to give up before they start a programme tend to be much less successful in the attempt.

Psychologists have termed this 'self-efficacy', a belief in your self's ability to succeed.[26] So, before you can start gaining self-control, you have to be convinced of your ability to do so. You can do this by focusing on previous similar successes in the past, as well as by checking with those who have achieved what you would like to, and seeing that they are not dramatically different from yourself.

The next step in self-management is to start monitoring the behaviour or aspect of self you would like to change.[27] This may sound like an obvious thing to do, but it is surprising exactly how much of our everyday behaviour is routine and goes on below the level of conscious awareness – for example, driving after you have been doing it for many years. Given that the behaviour you may want to change displeases you, one way of defending yourself against your upset is to pay less attention to yourself when you are doing it. So, if you suddenly decided that you wanted to change the way you drive, your first step would be to pay more attention to exactly how you drive now.[28]

Simply becoming more aware of the behaviour – 'self-monitoring', as psychologists term it – is a very powerful self-management technique, and often produces change by itself. One common self-monitoring strategy is to keep a diary of when and how you perform the behaviour you would like to change. For example, you might keep a diary of every cigarette you have during the day if you want to give up smoking, or every item of food if you want to reach a more healthy weight.[29] Keeping a record of a habit you wish to change has been found, in itself, to produce a modification. This may be because the diary raises your awareness of the aspect of yourself you are unhappy about, which raises your general unhappiness. You then seek to resolve this by making more effort to change.

So we have discussed goal conflict, tracking (keeping a diary) and the need for adequate resources as the key determinants of success or failure.

However, a vexed issue remains: why do we tend to adopt the goals we do? In particular, do we adopt goals in order to show off our attainments to others or for our own personal satisfactions?

Goals help guide behaviour, whether they are set in the class-room, at the office or on the playing field. Some situations promote the adoption of certain goals. For example, in college courses students might adopt the goal of outperforming other students. The context defines what is important. Within the context of these over-arching 'purpose goals', individuals may also pursue specific 'target goals' that help them work towards their purpose goals, contend Amanda Durik and Judith Harackiewicz, psychologists at the University of Wisconsin, USA.[30] For example, students might plan to attend every lecture, or try to study for more hours than their classmates. The motivational consequences of goal-setting depend on whether target goals match or are coherent with purpose goals.[31]

Another important factor is whether situational goals are concordant with individuals' internal strivings. Goal concordance refers to the degree to which goals serve the intrinsic needs of the individual. Concordance is especially important at the purpose-goal level because purpose goals provide the reasons for task engagement, and can affect the ease with which individuals internalize those reasons. If purpose goals are not concordant, individuals may not perceive the task as worthwhile. Individuals pursuing concordant goals display higher levels of self-determination, effort and intrinsic motivation, observe Durik and Harackiewicz.[32]

Achievement goals are focused on the attainment of competence, but vary in the type of competence pursued.[33] Mastery goals are focused on self-referenced skill development measured by improvement over time, whereas performance goals are focused on demonstrating high ability compared to others.[34] Individual differences in achievement strivings help clarify which achievement goals should be concordant for particular individuals. Need for achievement refers to the desire to master the environment, to do things well and to excel beyond others. Individuals who are high in achievement motivation (HAMs) enjoy challenges, seek competence feedback, and set both mastery and performance goals for themselves.[35] In contrast, individuals low in achievement motivation (LAMs) tend to avoid ability assessment, and are unlikely to set performance goals for themselves, note Durik and Harackiewicz.[36]

Two different motivational orientations, towards learning and performance goals, have become important in educational and instructional psychology, distinguishing between the aim to increase one's competence (learning goal) and the aim to demonstrate high competence or to avoid demonstrating low competence (performance goal).[37]

Research findings indicate that instead of trying to encourage unrealistically positive self-conceptions, it is possible to enhance learning and achievement by providing a setting that fosters the adoption of learning goals. Settings that highlight learning goals lay emphasis on individual learning progress and task enjoyment and avoid competitive, result-focusing elements.[38] Individuals with a low-ability concept benefit from such learning goal conditions, because they learn to evaluate achievement situations as an opportunity to enhance their abilities. And if they are encouraged to use these opportunities, they may finally have reason to believe in their abilities.[39]

Durik and Harackiewicz point out that this analysis is clearly applicable to competition, a pervasive phenomenon in our society. Whether competing for grades in classrooms, trophies in athletic contests or financial rewards in sales contests, individuals may view their behaviour as externally controlled and experience pressure to win. On the other hand, competition can lead some individuals to view activities as challenging and opportunities for feedback, making competition attractive.[40]

Moreover, individuals may actually receive positive feedback during the course of competition, which can promote perceived competence. Thus competition can be a double-edged sword, with the potential both to undermine intrinsic motivation by being perceived as controlling and to enhance intrinsic motivation by providing challenge and positive feedback, warn Durik and Harackiewicz.[41]

The very fact you are reading this probably sets you apart psychologically from most others – it probably means you are more concerned about achieving higher standards in performance than the average. In other words, you are bit of a perfectionist when it comes to your goals.[42] The problem is there is a strong link between perfectionism and feeling depressed, especially when you fail to achieve the high standards you frequently set yourself.

Setting tough goals is an integral part of elite sports performance, and a perfectionist attitude is probably beneficial to an athlete's performance – for the perfectionist nothing but the perfect performance is considered good enough.[43] But perfectionists also tend to focus overly on the few mistakes they make, rather than see all the positive aspects of their performance as well. They tend to have a difficult time forgetting errors, and as a result end up being plagued by self-doubt, which is counter-productive in attaining peak physical performance especially in competitive sports.[44]

Swedish psychologists at Stockholm University have recently been investigating this problem by studying the psychology of elite athletes. The subjects in the study were contenders for the Olympics – and their psychology has produced findings that could assist all of us in our attempts to get fitter, look better or excel on the sports field.[45] The researchers found that elite athletes who benefited from a perfectionistic attitude are also those whose sense of self-esteem *doesn't* come from their performance; they basically like themselves for who they are, regardless of whether they foul up on the track or not. Those prone to a fear of failure and therefore high anxiety when competing had too much of their fragile self-esteem tied up in doing well. The possibility of athletic failure had too severe consequences in terms of their sense of feeling good about themselves, so producing low self-confidence when competing. The conclusion is that if too much is at stake when you strive in sports or to get fitter, this will bring you down as you inevitably bump the occasional hurdle.

The secret of success is still to set high standards, but to do so not because your whole sense of self-esteem depends on it. You want to be the best, but you already know you are good enough anyway.[46]

7

HOW REWARDS REALLY REDUCE MOTIVATION

Leaders have no interest in proving themselves, but an abiding interest in expressing themselves

Warren Bennis

Tom said to himself that it was not such a hollow world, after all. He had discovered a great law of human action, without knowing it – namely, that in order to make a man or a boy covet a thing, it is only necessary to make the thing difficult to attain. If he had been a great and wise philosopher, like the writer of this book, he would now have comprehended that Work consists of whatever a body is obliged to do, and that Play consists of whatever a body is not obliged to do

Mark Twain

How could you motivate your six-year-old to read more? One strategy would be to offer her some reward for every hour she spent reading stories. The other would be to give her a colouring storybook that included pictures to be coloured, along with the stories to be read.[1]

The two approaches typify the motivational strategies used by managers, teachers and parents worldwide. They usually offer a reward, or try to link the task with something intrinsically more interesting. But the very latest psychological research is now questioning whether these tactics might, in fact, reduce motivation in the long run.[2]

It has been known for at least fifty years that rats trained to run to a goal for a large reward will run more slowly when subsequently offered a smaller reward. They run more slowly than rats trained with the same small reward, but no preceding large one.[3] It seems previous large rewards de-motivate you from pursuing smaller offers, even when that is all that is available.[4]

What's more, rats first given a smaller reward run even faster for a subsequently larger reward than if they had just been given the large reward, with no smaller reward preceding it. Smaller prior offerings enhance the motivational effect of a bigger future reward.

These findings suggest rewards have an inflationary tendency. To maintain high motivation you might have to offer ever-growing compensation. Parents, teachers and managers seem prone to being lured on to a 'reward treadmill' by their reluctant underlings.[5]

Confirmation that this effect may even be wired into our brains comes from research just published by neuroscientists Leon Tremblay and Wolfram Shultz at the University of Freibourg in Switzerland, who might just have found one of the holy grails of brain science, the reward centre.[6] They discovered that this is located in the orbito-frontal cortex, the part of the brain just above your eyeballs, and it is primarily activated when we are in the presence of an incentive.

Their research on monkeys found this centre does not increase its activity in relation to the absolute size of the reward. Instead, activity is more related to the comparative magnitude of the prize, so how excited your brain is by an incentive depends mostly on what else it has been offered recently.

As this is a fundamental property of our brains, and not simply due to a greedy personality, we might have to rethink the reward strategy so widely used on everyone from six-year-olds struggling with reading to city executives.

The controversy over rewards has a long intellectual history. The utilitarian view as advocated by Jeremy Bentham, the nineteenth-century British philosopher, was that all desired human behaviour could be encouraged by simply rewarding it.[7] Jean-Jacques Rousseau, the leading figure of Romanticism, argued that if you get an external reward for doing something, like money, after a while you come to see the activity merely as a means to an end, rather than as an opportunity for enjoyment, exploration or play. In other words, your intrinsic interest in an activity is reduced by receiving external rewards.[8]

According to this perspective, rewarding your six-year-old with a treat for reading will reduce her intrinsic interest in the direct pleasure of reading, as she focuses more on the benefit of the reward.[9] Children and staff in this situation seem keener on producing the evidence required to obtain the reward (sitting with a book or looking busy in the office) rather than actually accomplishing the desired task (reading or working).

Modern psychological research appears to be siding with the Romantics. Studies repeatedly find that those who are rewarded seem to work harder and produce more activity, but the product is of a lower quality, contains more errors and is less creative than the work of comparable non-rewarded subjects working on the same problems.[10]

Before the 1950s, the famous animal psychologist Harry Harlow showed that monkeys would repeatedly solve mechanical puzzles despite the absence of food or other extrinsic rewards.[11] This was an example of intrinsically motivated behaviour, which occurs when people engage in an activity primarily for its own sake, whereas extrinsically motivated behaviour is controlled by incentives that are not part of the activity.

In the 1970s experiments first appeared in which people were presented with an interesting task like playing games, creating art or solving puzzles for which they received various rewards, ranging from money, sweets and gold stars to praise.[12] A control group performed the activity without receiving any reward at all. Both groups were then observed during a non-reward period in which they were free to continue performing the task or to engage in some alternative activity.

It was repeatedly found that rewarding people stopped them continuing to do a task when no reward was available. It seemed the external reward changed their motivation from doing a task because they enjoyed it to doing it only for the reward.[13]

Several different theories seek to account for this effect. The 'Overjustification Hypothesis' is that if we are being paid handsomely this will become incorporated into our account of personal motivation.[14] But if the pay is poor, it would make no sense to offer up financial reward as the reason for our effort; since we like to see ourselves as rational beings, we are forced to conclude we must derive personal satisfaction from our badly paid work. Or perhaps we strive to make poorly paid work more interesting as a way of compensating for the lack of external rewards.[15]

If we already enjoy our work, but then start getting rewarded hugely for it, our understanding of our motivation may shift from intrinsic enjoyment to external incentives.[16]

Does this mean we should give up on rewards as a way of motivating people? Does the alternative strategy of trying to stimulate interest by pairing it with another pleasurable activity in fact work?

This approach was recently investigated for the first time by psychologist Tory Higgins and colleagues from Columbia University in New York, who tried to see whether allowing children to colour in picture books they could read as well would stimulate their interest in reading.[17] They found that reading and colouring as simultaneous activities produced a decline in interest in both activities!

The authors suggest that when engaging in two pleasurable activities each alternative can grab attention from the other, thus disrupting whichever activity is currently being engaged in, and the pleasure derived from it.

But an alternative explanation from the work on the reward centre in monkey brains could be that the presence of a reward reduces the pleasure normally obtained from another usually pleasurable task, if both take place close together. This is because the pleasure we get from anything seems to hinge on a comparison taking place in our reward centre, with whatever benefit we just received. If you have just been highly rewarded, another normally good reward pales in comparison to the just-received benefit.[18]

This would even suggest that combining something you don't normally like doing with something you do will make you dislike the unpleasant activity even more as you contrast it with the more pleasant task. So how then to motivate your truculent six-year-old, or your sullen staff?

The answer appears to come from an unexpected manoeuvre. If combining two tasks you normally like doing seems to reduce the pleasure you get from either, what happens if you associate two things you usually dislike? Higgins and colleagues at Columbia tested this scenario by asking school students to simultaneously undertake two assignments they had clearly indicated a dislike for. Both were highly boring – one was checking for spelling mistakes in a booklet and the other copying out sentences.[19]

In comparison with the group of school children who did either one or other of the tasks, the children who did both together seemed to find each more interesting by the end of the experiment. They chose to continue copying sentences and checking for spelling mistakes for over twice as much time afterwards, when in fact they were free to stop the tasks and do what they liked. Even more startling, 35% of the children asked to take the materials home after the experiment to continue the tasks in their own time!

Higgins and colleagues speculate that when people switch back and forth between disliked activities, this allows them to take a break from the negativity of each task if either is getting too awful. But perhaps an even more intriguing explanation is that the brain's reward centre is contrasting the impoverished reward with an even smaller incentive as alternative, and finding that the normally disliked activity seems preferable in contrast to the other option. In other words, practically anything can be made to appear pleasant if the alternative if awful enough.

The possibility that one could actually reduce the negativity of an activity by combining it with another unpleasant activity is one of the most intriguing results in modern incentive research. This suggests that the best way to engage your six-year-old's interest in reading is to offer her the alternative of doing some boring housework instead!

Let's imagine another two scenarios at a hypothetical place of work. Your boss comes to you and announces he or she is looking for volunteers for a new project – he or she declines to tell you anything about the proposition but successful completion will be accompanied by a big financial bonus. In another scenario he or she approaches you again but this time an alternative obscure proposal attracts no financial incentive. Instead the boss is so confident this is the kind of thing for which there will be so many volunteers given how attractive the job is in itself, that he or she may consider deducting a special privilege from those who were assigned the project.

Which job do you imagine from these facts is the more pleasant one to do?

The point of this thought experiment is to illustrate the little-considered fact that incentives, and in particular their size, in themselves convey a lot of information about the nature of the task being rewarded.[20] We guess that big incentives are required for jobs that would not naturally attract many suitable candidates, while you don't have to reward people for doing something they want to do anyway – quite the contrary. For example, you don't have to pay people to go to watch a key final in a popular sporting contest like Wimbledon or the Olympics – indeed you *charge* those people for the privilege of attending.[21]

Given this fact, is it possible that providing rewards can demotivate people – because they use the fact there is a reward to come to conclusions about how desirable the task is in itself?

Rewards become a controversial issue when psychological 'self-perception' and 'attribution' theories are taken into account. These are theories about what we make of ourselves, and what we deduce about why we do what we do. According to these fields, in fact, individuals constantly reassess the reasons for their and others' behaviour. As a result, these approaches emphasize the *informational* impact of rewards. A reward, and the size of it, vitally tells us something about how we would do the task without the reward in place.[22]

For example, should a child be rewarded for passing an exam, or paid to read a book? It is interesting how queasy we get about the idea of paying a child to learn to read. It seems like bribery – after all, shouldn't a child learn to read for other reasons rather than just because they are going to get paid? Shouldn't one learn to read because of the inherent benefit and pleasure that comes from reading?[23]

Yet contrast this negative view of incentives with how content we are to use incentives in most other arenas – like at work or to motivate other people or even ourselves. This debate goes to the heart of a conflict that runs deeply between two fields of study of human behaviour – economics and psychology – that come to opposite conclusions about the use of rewards.[24]

A central tenet of the field of economics is that individuals respond to incentives. Indeed, academic economists point out that in fields of study outside universities where there are huge financial rewards available, for example for economists and mathematicians in the financial services industries, it will be correspondingly difficult for scholarly institutions to retain bright people.[25]

Talented individuals tend to follow the incentives and leave universities to work in banks. The prediction therefore would be that for maths and economics you should find less bright people in these fields remaining in the universities, compared to areas where there is no external competition – perhaps theology or philosophy. The academics seem unwilling at the moment to demonstrate in this practical arena whether these predictions are true.

However, in the view of psychologists and sociologists, rewards and punishments are often seen as counter-productive, because they undermine what is termed 'intrinsic motivation'.

Over the past two decades, more than 800 research papers in sociology and psychology have explored what is now termed the 'intrinsic–extrinsic motivation dichotomy'.[26] Intrinsic motivation refers to performing an activity for itself, in order to experience pleasure and satisfaction inherent in the activity. On the other hand, extrinsic motivation pertains to where the goals of the individual extend beyond those inherent in the activity itself and where rewards are the key issue. Intrinsically motivated behaviour typically occurs in the absence of any apparent external rewards.

So, for example, you would be intrinsically motivated to study economics if you did so because you enjoyed the subject for itself and gained pleasure from the learning process. You would, in contrast, be extrinsically motivated if you were to study economics because you wanted to end up earning a lot of money working for an investment bank. In this latter case an external reward – a large salary – appears to be the motivating force, not the inherent pleasure of the study of the subject itself.

The intriguing idea that emerges from a lot of psychological research is that we actually find tasks themselves intrinsically less attractive when offered rewards to complete them. Somehow, being offered an extrinsic reward seems to 'crowd out' intrinsic motivations.[27]

Psychologists have come to this conclusion from a series of experiments that use what is termed a 'free-choice' measure. This consists of calculating the time spent on the activity when external rewards are no longer operative. In one experiment subjects are paid or given other external rewards for completing a task. Then the experimenter declares that the experiment is officially over and presents a pretext for leaving the participant alone for a period of time (typically eight minutes).[28]

During that period, the participant is surreptitiously observed through a one-way mirror. The participant has the opportunity to work on the experimental task, to read some magazines or to do something else. The rationale underlying the free-choice measure is that the more an individual persists at the experimental activity, after the experiment is officially over and therefore does so from 'free choice', the more he or she is intrinsically motivated.[29]

This measure is in line with the usual definition of intrinsic motivation, which states that intrinsically motivated behaviour typically occurs in the absence of any apparent external rewards. The finding from these experiments is that the more you pay people to do something, the *less* they tend to continue doing it when free to choose not to, and when rewards are no longer available.[30] In contrast, often the less external reward there is for doing a task, the less pay for example, the *more* people continue to do the task after the little reward there was in the first place is withdrawn.[31]

In a now classical experiment conducted by Deci and colleagues in 1975, college students were either paid or not paid to work for a certain time on an interesting puzzle.[32] Those in the no-reward condition played with the puzzle significantly more in a later unrewarded 'free-time' period than paid subjects, and also reported a greater interest in the task. This experiment has since been replicated many times, with numerous variations in design and in types of subjects.[33]

For instance, similar effects were found for high school students in tasks involving verbal skills, and for pre-school children in activities involving drawing with new materials.

This is an extremely odd and intriguing finding from psychology, running directly against a central theme of economics that incentives promote effort and performance, and yet there is indeed a lot of evidence from the field of economics that incentives do just that.[34]

In other words, in economics, contingent rewards serve as 'positive reinforcers' for the desired behaviour. In psychology, their effect is much more controversial. A long-standing paradigm clash has opposed proponents of the economic view to the 'dissonance theorists', who argue that rewards may actually impair performance, making them 'negative reinforcers', especially in the long run.[35]

The results from a variety of programmes aimed at getting people to lose weight, stop smoking or wear seat belts, either offering or not offering rewards, are consistent. Individuals in 'reward' treatments show better compliance at the beginning, but worse compliance in the long run, than those in the 'no-reward' or 'untreated controls' groups. Taken together, these many findings indicate a limited impact of rewards on 'engagement' (current activity) and a negative one on 're-engagement' (persistence).[36]

A related body of work transposes these ideas from the educational setting to the workplace.

Workers find control of their behaviour via incentives 'alienating', and as a result occupational psychologists criticize the use of performance-contingent rewards in the work setting. They conclude that there is no doubt that the benefits of piece-rate systems or pay-for-performance incentive devices can be considerably compromised when the systems undermine workers' intrinsic motivation.

Offering monetary incentives to subjects for answering questions taken from an IQ test strictly decreases their performance, unless the 'piece rate' is raised to a high enough level. Citizens in Swiss cantons where the government was considering locating a nuclear waste repository were recently surveyed and it was found that the fraction supporting siting of the facility in their community *fell* by half when public compensation was offered.[37]

This last study shows that incentives can actually be counter-productive, crowding out intrinsic motivation. This phenomenon can be documented experimentally, and it explains numerous observations about the economy. For example, in convincing a community to accept a toxic waste facility being sited near by, monetary incentives have often been counter-productive. Community members perceive themselves to be 'bribed'. By contrast, if the decision regarding the site is perceived as fair, opposition is often limited by a perceived civic duty. Once extrinsic incentives reach a certain level, they outweigh the crowding-out effect, but when the crowding-out effect is present, it is better to have no incentives at all than low incentives.[38]

The way to resolve the issue is to understand that rewards may be only *weak reinforcers* in the short term and that, as stressed by psychologists, they may have *hidden costs*, in that they become negative reinforcers once they are withdrawn.[39]

Why and how does this happen? Firstly rewards often distract attention from the process of task activity to the product of getting a reward. So current rewards may decrease the individual's willingness to persist, because they orient activity towards performance rather than progress. In other words, the individual is led by short-term rewards to sacrifice long-run pay-offs. Thus subjects who are paid to solve problems typically choose easier ones than those who do not expect any payment.[40]

The problem with any reward system is that workers or children soon work out how to 'play the system', obtaining maximum rewards for minimum effort, so distracting them from key engagement with the task at hand.[41] Obtaining the reward becomes the key motivation rather than doing the job well. In a sophisticated and rigorous reward system there is a very close link between doing the job well and gaining a reward but if the reward is powerful enough the players keep their eye on the reward and in so doing take their eye off the ball.

Reinforcement has two effects. First, predictably, it gains control of an activity, increasing its frequency. However, when reinforcement is later withdrawn, people engage in the activity even less than they did before reinforcement was introduced.

The tension between the short-term and long-term effects on motivation of offering a reward also suggests the following idea: once a reward is offered, it will be required – and 'expected' – every time the task has to be performed, perhaps even in increasing amounts. In other words, through their effect on self-confidence, rewards have a 'ratchet effect'.[42] This irreversibility may explain people's (e.g., parents') reluctance to offer them.

So an additional effect of rewards arises, namely that we now have a strategic incentive to appear demotivated in order to be given a higher bonus in the future.

The threat of punishment also has a positive (short-term) reinforcement effect in instances when we know that monitoring is effective, but only a negative one when we think that we can 'get away with it'. A familiar case is a teenager's heightened temptation to violate his (her) parents' strict prohibition on smoking in situations where they cannot catch him (her).[43]

You want someone (like your child) not to smoke because they have internalized your reasons for discouraging them – not simply because they fear the sanction you will impose if you catch them smoking. If your ability to catch them smoking is very imperfect your threats could have the consequence of increasing the incentive to smoke without being caught.[44]

A related argument, therefore, in support of the demotivating effect of rewards is the notion of 'forbidden fruits', as advanced by economists Roland B'enabou of Princeton University and Jean Tirole of MIT.[45] Let's go back to the example earlier in the chapter in which a higher reward is, in equilibrium, associated with a less attractive task. Therefore, bonuses (or higher wages when effort is observable) reduce intrinsic motivation because people assume that a lot of cajoling is required for an unpleasant job, while in contrast they assume things you are forbidden from doing, indeed for which there is a penalty, must by definition be desirable activities.

So, argues B'enabou and Tirole, forbidden fruits are the most appealing. Therefore, the optimal bonus could well be zero, perhaps even negative. A famous (literary) case B'enabou and Tirole use is that of Tom Sawyer demanding bribes from other boys to let them paint a fence in his place:

> There was no lack of material; boys happened along every little while; they came to jeer, but remained to whitewash ... And when the middle of the afternoon came, from being a poor poverty-stricken boy in the morning, Tom was literally rolling in wealth. He had a nice, good, idle time all the while – plenty of company – and the fence had three coats of whitewash on it! If he hadn't run out of whitewash he would have bankrupted every boy in the village.
>
> Mark Twain, *The Adventures of Tom Sawyer*

In daily life, parents are quite familiar with what we shall call the forbidden fruit effect: powerful or salient constraints employed by adults to enforce the prohibition of some activity often decrease the child's subsequent internalization of the adults' disapproval.[46]

The key point here according to B'enabou and Tirole is that every reward (including feedback) has two aspects, first a controlling aspect and second an informational aspect, which provides the recipient with information about his competence and self-determination. If you are going to be heavily punished for doing something then implicit in that condition is a message that the task must be something you probably naturally desire to do greatly.

By contrast, rewards that are discretionary (not contracted for) may well boost your self-esteem or intrinsic motivation, because of a different learning effect. The worker or child learns from the reward that the task was considered difficult (and therefore that he is talented), or that the supervisor or parent is appreciative of, proud of or cares about his performance – and therefore that it is worth repeating it.[47]

Giving a bicycle to a hard-working child, or a special pay rise or early promotion to a productive assistant professor, *unexpectedly* after the successful completion of a task will not lead him to infer that his behaviour was controlled. This is because the principal was under no obligation (no commitment) to reward any particular outcome. And receiving the reward is good news, because the agent initially did not know how to interpret his performance. The reward then provides the agent with an indirect measure of his performance.[48]

If a person's feelings of competence and self-determination are enhanced, his intrinsic motivation will increase. If his feelings of competence and self-determination are diminished, his intrinsic motivation will decrease. Some rewards or feedback will increase intrinsic motivation through this process and others will decrease it.[49]

Suppose that, at some later date, you again face the choice of whether to undertake the same or a similar task and that, come that time, you remember only that you chose to engage in it and the extrinsic incentives that were then offered, but not your intrinsic interest in the task.

For instance, an individual engaged in a long-term project similar to one he has undertaken before – writing a book, proving a theorem, running a marathon – may, at times, be seized by doubt as to whether the intellectual and ego-gratification benefits that successful completion is likely to bring will, ultimately, justify the required efforts – 'Why am I doing this?' He may then reflect that since he chose to embark on this project once again in spite of low financial and career incentives, the personal satisfaction enjoyed from previous completions (and which, at this later and perhaps somewhat stressful stage, he cannot quite recall) must have been significant. Hence it is worth persevering on the chosen path.[50]

So intrinsic motivation is a precious thing to be nurtured and often might get snuffed out by external rewards.

But the evidence is that the reason why we do many things is to obtain not so much financial reward but regard and respect from those around us. These could be called social rewards – like praise and admiration.[51]

While most of the psychology and management literature emphasizes the necessity of boosting and protecting the self-esteem of one's personal and professional partners, people often criticize or downplay the achievements of their spouse, child, colleague, coauthor, subordinate or teammate.

Such 'ego bashing' may reflect 'battles for dominance': by lowering the other's self-confidence, an individual may gain real authority within the relationship, enabling her to steer joint decisions or projects in a preferred direction. This generally comes at a cost, however, namely the risk of demotivating the partner from seeking good projects or from exerting effort at the implementation stage.

The two types of goals that can be considered as ranging from intrinsic orientation to extrinsic orientation may be thought of in alternative lights. Psychologists like Durik and Harackiewicz distinguish between learning goals and performance goals (you want to get good at the task or you want to be seen by others as good at it), other authors between task-oriented goals and self-oriented goals (you want to be good at it for its own sake or you want to be good at it because of what it then says about you), and still others between mastery goals and performance goals (similar to the categories before).[52]

To carry on with the initial distinction between learning goals and performance goals, it is noteworthy that students with learning goals are interested in acquiring new skills and improving their knowledge, even if they make some mistakes. On the other hand, students with performance goals are usually interested in obtaining positive evaluations of ability and avoiding negative evaluations.[53]

In many cases, these students prefer to obtain a positive evaluation of a fairly simple task rather than run the risk of receiving a negative evaluation of a more challenging and meaningful task. Therefore, whereas learning or task-oriented goals or mastery goals imply the search for development and skill improvement, performance or self-oriented goals reflect the student's desire to demonstrate competence to others, and obtain positive judgements of competence levels and avoid negative judgements. In short, Durik and Harackiewicz contend, students have learning goals to develop their ability, and performance goals to prove their ability.[54]

Csikszentmihalyi, a psychologist who is a world leader in the field of happiness and well-being, defined intrinsically motivated behaviour in terms of the immediate subjective experience that occurs when people are engaged in an activity.[55] Expert climbers, dancers, chess players, basketball players and composers describe their experiences when fully engaged in terms of an emotional state Csikszentmihalyi labelled 'flow', characterized by (a) a holistic feeling of being immersed in, and carried by, an activity; (b) a merging of action and awareness; (c) focus of attention on a limited stimulus field; (d) lack of self-consciousness; and (e) feeling in control of one's actions and the environment. Flow is only possible when a person feels that the opportunities for action in a given situation match his or her ability to master the challenges.[56]

The challenge of an activity may be concrete or physical, like the peak of a mountain to be scaled, or abstract and symbolic, like a story to be written or a puzzle to be solved. Recent research has shown that both the challenges and skills must be relatively high before a flow experience becomes possible.[57]

There has been a related recent upsurge in work on the concept of 'interest'. These researchers differentiate between individual and situational interest. Individual interest is a relatively stable evaluative orientation towards certain domains; situational interest is an emotional state aroused by specific features of an activity or a task.[58] Two aspects or components of individual interest are distinguishable: feeling-related and value-related interests.

Feeling-related interests refer to the feelings that are associated with an object or an activity – feelings such as involvement, stimulation or flow. Value-related interests refer to the attribution of personal significance or importance to an object or activity.[59]

For example, if students associate mathematics with high personal significance because mathematics can help them get prestigious jobs, then we would not speak of interest. Although feeling-related and value-related valences are highly correlated, it is useful to differentiate between them because some individual interests are likely to be based primarily on feelings, whereas other interests are more likely to be based on personal significance.[60]

Despite the large amount of research conducted by psychologists into how to motivate people, particularly those in the workplace, it still seems as if managers and organizations stubbornly persist in using deeply flawed and out-of-date understandings of how to get more from their workforce.[61]

There are two key theories of motivation still widely employed, despite the fact work psychologist Frederick Herzberg demonstrated eons ago that they basically don't work.

The first theory is known technically as the KITA – or 'Kick In The Ass' – approach, which basically means that you get punished, humiliated, sacked, have your wages docked and so on if you are not producing the goods at the rate your boss would like. This approach merely leads to most chronically demotivated employees investing huge effort in avoiding being caught not producing the goods, and so dreaming up complex schemes whereby the pretence of hard work is maintained.[62]

If only the boss could harness the deep motivation that is devoted to avoiding a KITA using guile and strategy to getting the actual job done.

The other theory is based on the sentiment of the popular phrase 'Show me the money', which originated from the film *Jerry Maguire* about the tactics of an unscrupulous and materialistic sports agent. This theory is based on a deeply dark view of human character that basically contends that we only do things because of the cheque afterwards. This ignores the obvious fact that some of the most motivated human behaviour occurs in areas where no financial reward is possible – e.g., the motivation of a mother to care for her child, or of a husband to please his wife, or of a golfer to improve his swing.

All that happens in motivational scenarios built on 'showing me the money' is that inevitably people demand more and more cash, in order to do less and less. Also employees redirect their work in order to focus on what directly gains financial compensation, which is not the same as that which is most helpful to each other or the organization as a whole. The other major problem with this approach is many employees naturally become jealous or resentful of their lack of financial reward compared to those they see reaping the benefits of 'show me the money'. They tend to take revenge by stealing covertly from the organization or fiddling the books, or some other vindictive strategy, so exacting their own rewards.

Actually the key to motivating a workforce comes from research that asked a very basic question. It is a question that goes to the heart of psychology of work, and yet few managers ever pose it themselves. The key question is: what do people find most rewarding about work?[63]

The answers are all psychological and often have little to do with money (beyond a general sense of being fairly paid) and certainly they have nothing at all to do with avoiding a KITA.[64]

Here are the most frequently cited and strongest rewards that people find motivating in the workplace: a sense of achievement, recognition from colleagues of your good work, enjoying aspects of the job in itself, a sense of responsibility (i.e., it matters if you don't do a good job), a sense of career advancement and, finally, a feeling of personal growth.[65]

What is fascinating about this catalogue is how little work environments are designed to produce any of the rewards on it. Meetings convened by senior managers, for example, which could be used to acknowledge good work from individuals, tend to turn into a chance for a good KITA instead.[66]

So what the latest thinking in the psychology of motivation finds is that the very opposite of what is usually being done at work needs to be implemented in order to improve drive. Instead of carrots and sticks, people actually need to be given more freedom to do the job the way they want to do it, rather than as dictated by 'policy', guidelines or managers. This gives them a sense of personal responsibility and ownership over their work. Workers also need some shared sense of what counts as doing a good job, which can also be feedback to them, so they can feel personal pride in better performance. Most times managers and workers don't actually agree on the key goals of the organization and as a result what an employee thinks is the aim of their work is not what the management agrees with.[67]

Workers also need to be given 'natural' units of work, which are more likely to be found personally rewarding as achievement is then more obviously discernible. For example, the way the NHS is increasingly managed means patients are divided between more teams who super-specialize in different aspects of care, so now no one doctor or nurse takes overall responsibility for the individual patient. No one doctor or nurse obtains a sense of responsibility for a patient or feels the benefit as that patient recovers.[68]

Managers and workers need to sit down together and think about how the work fits in with the long-term personal and career goals of the workers – this is the best way of retaining employee loyalty and stops them jumping ship as soon as a better job offer comes along. How the work helps you develop in terms of skills is vital in helping build a sense of improving capacity to deal with more difficult challenges.

This motivational strategy, with its multiple approaches to focusing on improving the psychological reward of going to work, is globally termed 'Job Enrichment'.[69] At its heart is the understanding that the most motivated people in the world tend to work extremely hard without much direct financial reward (they often are relentless even in the face of poor rewards – that's how we recognize them as being motivated). The deeply motivated are also those who work hard even if no one is checking up on them, again another sign of how we know they are motivated.

At the heart of job enrichment though are the notions of a worker understanding themselves better, or their manager developing a better sense of the individual worker, of what makes each of us different, and using these to help us form a deeper connection with our work.[70]

Job enrichment is the most effective way psychology knows to improve motivation, but it requires us to devote the necessary time to think more deeply about why we go to work and what we get out of it on a personal level. But time is often in apparently scarce supply, and we are often reluctant to devote this time to our working lives because we are trapped in a cycle of extreme busyness – but busy doing things which just demotivate us in the long run.[71]

Job enrichment initially feels really peculiar as a way of thinking about work, because it requires us to focus on the positive aspects of work and ourselves, to think about our positive qualities and to help our work play to those strengths, rather than to focus on problems and devote all our energies to fixing those. At the heart of job enrichment is the radical and disturbing idea that actually most people want to do a good job – they just find that turning up at work is usually a real turn-off.

8

DO YOU HATE YOUR JOB?

Much of the difference between failure and success lies in what you believe you are entitled to, so you may as well think big

David Schwartz

The world has never been a level playing field
David S. Landes

A CASE STUDY IN PRACTICAL INTELLIGENCE

Are dustbin men intelligent? Could you answer this real-life problem that the garbage collectors of Tallahassee, Florida, recently solved?

Many of the garbage collectors in Tallahassee are high school drop-outs, who because of their lack of educational success would traditionally perform poorly on academic or intelligence tests . . .

Tallahassee, priding itself on the service it provides to its citizens, requires garbage collectors to retrieve trash containers from the backyards of residents. The trash bins are issued by the city to each household, so they are not purchased with personal funds and therefore are identical.

Each resident fills a large trash container and leaves it in the backyard rather than placing it on the kerbside to be picked up. Trash collectors must locate and retrieve each

---

full container from the backyard, heave it into the truck, and then drag the empty container back to the yard. Each stop requires two trips to the backyard, one to retrieve the full can and another to return it when it is empty.

Can you work out how the garbage collectors developed a way of halving the time taken to do their rounds? Take a few minutes to think about the problem and it may help to draw a diagram from above of several houses, their trash cans in the back garden and the garbage collectors' truck. *Don't* read the answer before having a go at the solution.

Answer: Because trash bins are issued by the city and not purchased with personal funds, they are identical. The new routine consists of wheeling the previous house's empty container to the next house's backyard, leaving it to replace the full can, which is in turn wheeled to the truck to be emptied. Once emptied, this can is wheeled to the back yard of the next house to replace its full can, and so on. The new routine requires only one trip to each house, whereas the previous one required two trips. The solution had eluded the managers who trained the garbage collectors.

This year record numbers of school students obtained the highest grades, yet employers continue to complain that the young people they employ seem to lack the basic skills required to succeed at work. This has driven accusations that school exams must be getting easier.

But the real answer to this paradox could lie in a startling new study just published by the world's leading expert on intelligence, Professor Robert Sternberg, an eminent psychologist at Yale University. Sternberg's research reveals the existence of a totally new kind of intelligence that he refers to as 'practical intelligence'.[1]

Sternberg's astonishing finding is that practical intelligence, which predicts success in real life, has an inverse relationship with academic intelligence. In other words, the more practically intelligent you are, the less likely you are to succeed in the cloistered academic world of school or university. Similarly, the more paper qualifications you hold and the higher your educational grades, it appears, the less able you are to cope with actual problems of everyday life, and the lower your score on practical intelligence.

Many people clearly successful in their actual environments do badly in standard IQ tests and the business setting is no better example of this. Entrepreneurs and those who have built large businesses from scratch are frequently discovered to be high school or college drop-outs.

IQ as a concept is over a hundred years old and was supposed to explain why some people seemed to excel at a wide variety of intellectual tasks. But IQ ran into trouble when it became apparent that some high scorers failed to achieve in real life what would have been predicted by their tests.

So a decade ago came the concept of emotional intelligence or EQ, which was supposed to explain this deficit by suggesting that to succeed in real life you require emotional as well as intellectual skills, which pencil-and-paper academic tests did not measure.

Emotional intelligence includes the ability to motivate yourself and persist in the face of frustrations, to control impulses and delay gratification, to regulate moods and keep distress from swamping the ability to think, and the ability to understand and empathize with others.

While social or emotional intelligence was a useful concept in explaining many of the real-world deficiencies of the brainy, it in itself did not account for much more success in real life. Again, some of the most successful people in the business world appeared to be obviously lacking in social charms – people like Bill Gates; and the parallel 'rise of the nerds' exemplifies the recent discovery of a new group of overachievers who might benefit from some kind of finishing school.

Not all real-life difficulties that we face are solvable with just good social skills, and good social acumen in one situation might not generalize to another.

So the key problem with both academic and emotional intelligence was they both still only appeared to explain a small proportion of success in real life. For example, research has demonstrated that IQ tests predict between 4% and 25% of real-world success in life, like job performance.[2]

Sternberg's group at Yale started from the opposite position to the way intelligence research has historically been done. Instead of asking what is intelligence, and investigating whether it predicts real-world success, Sternberg asked what distinguishes people who are thriving in real life from the less successful.

Instead of measuring this form of intelligence with the traditional mathematical or verbal tests, practical intelligence is scored by your answers to real-life dilemmas such as 'If you were travelling by car and got stranded on a motorway during a blizzard, what would you do?' A key contrast between these different kinds of questions is that in academic tests there is usually only one correct response, whereas in practical intelligence tests, as in real life, there is often more than one right answer.[3]

The Yale group found that most of the really useful knowledge successful people have acquired is gained during the performance of everyday activities, but typically without conscious awareness of what is being learned. Although successful people's behaviour reflects the fact they have this knowledge, the flourishing are often unable to articulate what they know. This partly explains why this form of intelligence was so difficult to identify previously.

The notion that people acquire knowledge without awareness of what is being learned is reflected in the common language of the workplace, as people speak of 'learning by doing' in reference to knowledge that psychologists now refer to as 'tacit'. Professional 'intuition' and 'professional instinct' further imply that the knowledge associated with successful performance is 'tacit'.

The key point about tacit knowledge is that no one formally teaches it to you. Indeed, given how vital this knowledge is to success, it is usually surprisingly poorly conveyed, so you usually have to learn it yourself, with what Sternberg refers to as 'minimal environmental support'. In other words, no one communicates it to you and it doesn't appear in text books or training manuals.

Another key difference between this intelligence and others is that while academic knowledge is about knowing facts or knowing 'what', practical intelligence is instead about knowing 'how'. Often unsuccessful people are doing exactly the same procedure as successful people, they are just not doing it the same way.

For example, two people may ask for a pay rise at work, but

how they ask for the rise will determine who gets paid more.

Sternberg found that the best way of getting at this elusive practical intelligence was to ask successful people to relate examples of crucial incidents at work where they solved problems, demonstrating skills that they had learned during the performance of their jobs. It would appear that one of the best ways of improving your practical intelligence is to observe master practitioners at work, and in particular to focus on the skills they have acquired during the performance of their jobs.

Oddly enough this is the basis of much traditional training based on an apprenticeship model, which has been criticized by modern educationalists. Historically the junior doctor learned by observing the consultant surgeon at work and the junior lawyer by assisting the senior barrister in a case.

Another way in which practical intelligence appears to resolve a previously unexplained paradox is that it explains why performance on academic tests usually declines after formal education ends. Yet most older adults contend that their ability to solve practical problems increases over the years, despite the fact most psychological testing would measure a decline in intellectual ability.

The key implication for organizations and companies is to understand that practical intelligence might not be detectable by conventional auditing and performance-measuring procedures. Furthermore, inducting new or less capable employees into becoming more practically intelligent will involve more real-life contact and learning from the genuinely practically intelligent – something it would appear cannot be done via training manuals or courses.[4]

But perhaps the biggest challenge is in recruitment, as these new studies strongly suggest that conventional paper measures of ability, such as university results, are unlikely to be helpful in predicting who will be best at solving your company's real-life problems.

Indeed, this new research suggests we start looking at companies in a completely different way – and see them as places where a huge number of problems are being solved all the time, but where it may take new eyes actually to see the practical intelligence in action.

However, not only are most corporations not aware of practical intelligence; today they are evermore trying to squeeze the very best out of their employees. But increasingly it is realized that a major problem at work is not so much people not pulling their weight, but workers actively sabotaging a corporation's efforts. The following example comes from a recent survey of workplace sabotage published by Dr Maureen Ambrose and colleagues from the University of Central Florida:[5]

> I worked at the Janacka machine, which cuts the hides and skin of the pineapple. We usually worked a straight ten-hour shift, so a lot of people would just burn out. To combat that, people would try to get more breaks – we were only allowed two breaks per shift. To do this, they would send a pineapple the wrong direction, or send a glove down, and it would break the whole machine. If the Janacka machine shuts down, you can't cut the pineapple, the line can't go on. The whole production line shuts down. It takes at least three hours to fix, so you're getting paid for three hours at least for just sitting around.

This story came from a pineapple packer working in the US, who would obviously prefer to remain anonymous, but I am frequently told equally hair-raising examples of active sabotage from British workers as part of my consultancy projects.

As a consultant psychiatrist at The Maudsley Hospital in South London a lot of my work consists of seeing individuals who are troubled in some way, but whole organizations can get referred to psychiatrists and psychologists as well. Consultation with institutions is usually required when some problem is causing conflict between a group of workers, leading to a sharp decline in organizational effectiveness.

A psychiatrist or psychologist like myself will go in and interview each individual employee as well as managers, and then maybe convene a group meeting to air the often strongly held emotional issues that underlie the fraught relationships that can develop in today's pressurized companies.

But often a corporation will only realize that active sabotage has been occurring when a particular disgruntled employee leaves and suddenly effectiveness dramatically and mysteriously improves, or if saboteur collaborators fall out and rat on each other.

A car rental firm found the length of time their cars lasted before needing replacing jumped suddenly after one employee left. Later they found out this person had been dropping grit into the engines.

At one very large temp agency that consulted me, two disgruntled employees were anonymously sending out staff who could speak little or no English into jobs that required in-depth interview skills – they would ring up to listen in on the chaos that ensued. This sabotage was achieved by purposefully misplacing job skills in the filing system. The agency only found out what was going on when one collaborator fell out with the other over a boyfriend, and sent an anonymous explanatory note to the boss.[6]

Workplace sabotage is defined as behaviour intended to 'damage, disrupt or subvert the organization's operations for the personal purposes of the saboteur by creating unfavourable publicity, embarrassment, delays in production, damage to property, the destruction of working relationships, or the harming of employees or customers'.[7]

One increasingly common form of sabotage is sometimes glossed as 'whistle blowing' – which basically means passing on embarrassing or sensitive information to the press or competitors. Since sabotage is particularly likely when people have discovered they have got the sack, most companies have stringent procedures about getting those who have just heard the bad news out of the building as rapidly as possible, so limiting the possibility of a retaliatory strike.

Indeed the current vogue for sacking by mobile text message actually has a ruthless logic to it, which is the further away from the actual workplace someone is when they get the news of their redundancy, the less sabotage they can commit. Though it could be said that leaking this story to the press is itself a form of corporate sabotage.

But what a lot of companies don't realize is that resentment doesn't just lie in the sacked employee. There are many motives that lie seething beneath the surface in most workers, including feeling powerless, frustrated, or having suffered a recent injustice. What appears to be simple error and allowable inefficiency is actually active sabotage.

Other common motivations for workplace sabotage include making work easier, sheer boredom and a desire for mere fun. At one call centre some staff were putting callers on hold for extended periods as a way of livening up their day. They would pick their victims by using arbitrary criteria – like if they had pets or not – the game of finding out whether the caller had a pet (the workers hated pets) relieved the boredom of their jobs.

In my experience the basic underlying psychological motivation for sabotage is a sense of powerlessness – and this leads to such destructive behaviour as breaking machinery to gain unscheduled breaks, which can increase an individual's sense of control.

At one firm I consulted with, the phone-room employees were all women who felt discriminated against by what was perceived to be a male-dominated and anti-female management. So the women telephone operators deliberately took a certain number of the phone instructions down incorrectly and dispatched erroneous orders. Part of the revenge on the male managers was overhearing them having to placate irate customers.

But another goal of sabotage can be to make work easier, as Dr Maureen Ambrose, a world authority on workplace sabotage, points out. The classic example is the use of a 'tap' in aeroplane manufacturing. A tap is a steel screw that rethreads a nut so that a misaligned bolt will fit. In the short run, this makes work easier, but in the long run employees know that it weakens the strength of the connection. The use of a tap will be enormously detrimental to the organization as it leads to the production of unsafe products. Although many efforts to facilitate work are innocuous, sabotage such as this can have crippling cost to an organization or may even destroy it altogether.

Over and over again in my experience a central issue at the heart of sabotage is an employee's belief that he or she (or someone else) has been treated unfairly. An employee who feels unjustly treated may try to 'even the score' by committing sabotage. This would include anyone who has been shown disrespect, passed over for promotion, given additional responsibilities with no pay increase, denied adequate resources to do the job, or received what he or she considered inadequate credit for work performed.

The problem for employers is that individuals do not simply become dissatisfied with conditions they perceive to be unjust. They usually do something about them. Thus sabotage is a means to restore a state of equity in the eyes of its perpetrators.

Psychological research on workplace sabotage found that when individuals were treated in an unfair way, whereby they were not getting their fair share of the company's profits, they stole from the firm only if the theft could restore their perceived inequity (i.e., if the stolen item had value). But when individuals were treated in an interpersonally unfair way – they were slighted or ignored – they stole even if the item was of absolutely no value to them.[8]

Firms frequently don't realize that just because various items that are stealable – or easily damaged – would have no direct benefit to the saboteur, does not mean there is no motivation to sabotage. Even if the employee receives no obvious benefit at all, the fact he or she is damaging the company is enough motivation.

Some train crashes where rail line bolts have been interfered with or even accidents when parachutes have been tampered with could in fact be the result of workplace sabotage. Maureen Ambrose's research has established that when saboteurs target organizations, they hit their mark 98% of the time. However, when saboteurs target individuals, 81% of the time they do greater harm to the organization than to the individual. Saboteurs often damage other people besides their intended targets, which is why companies should have more vigorous anti-sabotage policies than they tend to.[9]

In my experience, the key to reducing sabotage is to ensure that any sense of injustice felt by employees in the work environment can be dealt with openly, effectively and, above all, immediately by management. The frequent attempt by managers to bury their heads in the sand in the hope that the plight of the more powerless workers will go away of its own accord merely results in a strong desire for revenge.[10]

Those who think they are winners in exploiting their subordinates don't usually realize how behind-the-scenes sabotage is quietly 'evening up the score'.

Recent research on the psychology of work stress from Japan has found that not all work is equally stressful. Patients who were admitted to hospital for serious depression were classified as doing modern industrialized work (e.g., office workers, managers, teachers and technicians), or as belonging to a traditional occupation group (e.g., farmers and skilled manual workers). The rate of depression was much higher for the industrialized occupation group. This finding seems to support the view that the incidence of depression could have increased recently due to modern work having got more stressful compared to what your grandfather did, toiling out in the fields or in the blacksmith's shop.[11]

One possibility is that traditional work was more autonomous – you had all summer to get the harvest in and you did it at your own pace. In contrast, modern office work is linked to deadlines set by other people, so you can't work at the speed you feel most comfortable with.[12] One solution to stress at work could be to try and regain some autonomy; for example, deadlines are a lot more negotiable than they appear at first glance.

When given a deadline by the boss, reply that the only way you can make it is if something else you are doing at the same time is put on the back burner. This kind of negotiation works best by getting a sense of the boss's priorities and putting to the back of the queue things he or she doesn't regard as vital to their own career progress. This comes back to a vital issue in handling work stress: prioritizing.[13]

The secret of work survival is not doing everything well when under pressure: it is doing the important things well – the less crucial things can be sacrificed to some extent. Often we are too busy to get a sense of priority and we kill ourselves over things that really aren't worth it. A good way to get a sense of what is important or not is ask yourself, will this appear important looking back on it in a year's time? If it seems everything you are doing will look vital in a year's time, ask the question again but this time from the perspective of ten years' time.

But even if you are not so frustrated in your work as to actively sabotage the corporation, sabotage is an issue in most workers' lives because they feel sabotaged themselves. We are disappointed with our progress and yet we find it difficult to put our finger on who did the sabotaging. Our sneaking suspicion is it must have been us ourselves but when we weren't noticing.

It's a well-known psychological phenomenon. You go to a school or university reunion to catch up with those friends you haven't seen for many years, but you are in for a shock.

The student who got all the prizes and the medals seems to have not achieved anything like their initial promise, and seems stuck in a dead-end job. At the reunion, they struggle to draw a veil over what must be years of painful effort in post-graduate training without much reward. A cloud seems to hang over them, a stark contrast to the confidence they used to exude before going into the examination halls all those years ago.

In contrast, the student who didn't turn up to lectures and was nearly booted out for poor grades now turns up to the reunion driving a Porsche and has made it to the management grade quicker than the rest of the year made it to office clerk.

These kinds of experiences raise the question of whether performance at university or school is any real guide to how we perform professionally afterwards. It's an important issue because usually there were peers or teachers in the cloistered environment of an undergraduate curriculum guiding you to gain the necessary skills to make it through the course. But once you leave, the expertise and talents it takes to succeed in the more chaotic and changing world of work seem more elusive.

To more precisely understand this phenomenon, psychologist Eamonn Ferguson and physician colleagues from the University of Nottingham have recently conducted a systematic review of previous research on predictors of success in the ultra-competitive world of specialist medicine.[14, 15]

They found that academic performance before you get to medical school, like your A-level grades, predicts only 23% of the performance at medical school itself. However, when it comes to whether your academic achievement at medical school explains your subsequent success as a senior doctor, it appears that only 6% of the post-university performance is explained by previous medical school undergraduate accomplishment.

One possible implication of this astonishing result is that the academic environment provided by preparation for A-levels and the testing scenario itself is not too different from what you then encounter when you arrive at medical school or university.

However, the predicament that greets you once you have qualified is very different from that which greeted you once you got into medical school or university. It may be that the skills required to perform well in busy jobs are very different from those needed in the more ordered and less chaotic world of university or school. Whatever the precise explanation, it would seem that medical school or university is actually not that good at preparing its graduates for future job success.

Perhaps one explanation for the massive variability in post-university performance not accounted for by pre-university academic training lies in the arena of personality.

In their review, Eamonn Ferguson and colleagues found eight personality factors that have emerged consistently as predictors of success in medical training: 'dominance', 'tolerance', 'sociability', 'self-acceptance', 'well-being', 'responsibility', 'achievement via conformance' and 'achievement via independence'.

It is particularly intriguing that independence of mind and also conformity seem to be key personality factors in predicting post-university and post-school success, as these would seem to be opposite ends of the personality spectrum.

But perhaps the findings can be reconciled. To compete successfully at post-university interviews your CV and career to date have to stand out from the crowd. You have to have done more interesting and original work in comparison to your competition. Some independence of mind is required to achieve this, otherwise your CV would look just like the rest of the herd's.

In contrast, conformity is needed during the everyday performance of your job to ensure you don't rock the boat or stand out in some way, which draws the attention of your boss or senior colleagues and makes them think you are difficult to get along with or a potential troublemaker.

So a careful balance between conformity and independence is needed, which depends on the context you find yourself in.

Another intriguing finding from Eamonn Ferguson's work is that where you stand in terms of a personality feature called 'locus of control' is important in success in medicine and other careers, but not in the way predicted by psychologists.

Psychologists argue that 'internals', who accept personal responsibility for what happens to them in life, are more likely to be successful in the long run, because they are willing to change strategy depending on how well they find themselves doing. 'Externals', in contrast, blame the world and not themselves for their predicament, and are therefore unlikely to brush up on their revision or interview technique in the face of failure. For them it was simply because the exam was too difficult or the interview unfair.

Ferguson is suggesting that 'defensive externalism' might be the key strategy. This is a tendency to accept personal responsibility for success but blame the world for your failures. When you pass the interview it's because you are brilliant, and when you fail it's because the panel were a bunch of myopic halfwits who couldn't see the best candidate when he or she was standing right there in front of them. So you never blame yourself for bad things that happen and instead assume they are down to an external environment that might change in the future.

Another interesting conflict in personality features that emerges as necessary for post-university success is 'responsibility' and 'dominance' versus 'tolerance'. Dominant people aren't often seen to be that tolerant so there seems to be a paradox here. But perhaps the apparent contradiction can be resolved by understanding that the leader of a firm wants junior staff who will fit in and adapt to the working environment at the start of a training programme. But at the same time the hope is that the junior staff will in time take more charge, anticipating issues the boss might have to deal with and solving them pre-emptively for him or her, and eventually even run the firm.

This is not to say the boss wants the firm taken over by the junior staff, but he or she wants them to show some initiative and remove some of the day-to-day hassle.

But how is it that most workers don't really know what their boss wants from them and find it so difficult to perform in ways that gain seniors' approval? One possible answer is that at university and at school the requirements of the course and the expectations of seniors are articulated fairly clearly in the syllabus and also there are peers and more senior students to help convey this valuable information.

Once you qualify, however, you enter a world where there appears to be a 'hidden curriculum'. This is a term used to describe those processes, pressures and constraints that fall outside the formal curriculum, and that are often unarticulated or unexplored.

The big question is how to uncover the hidden curriculum of post-university employment. Several different strategies are of use here. One is to grab the kind of applicant who has successfully applied for a job you aspire to and ask them the secret of their success. It is best to pump such people just after they have got the job they always wanted because then they are so flush with their success that they don't mind showing off a bit by bestowing advice on younger, more inexperienced protégés. If you try to approach them too long after they have got their job then the euphoria has abated, and they have begun to perceive you as possible future competition and won't be so munificent with their advice.

Identify the younger senior achievers who still feel companionship with junior staff and are still too young to feel entirely comfortable with the more senior staff in the firm, and approach them for advice on what is needed to succeed in this organization.

It is often worth asking your boss directly, especially before you take up a particular post, what are the kinds of qualities they are looking for and what in particular they have found most difficult with previous trainees. Talk to those who have done your job in the past about the big pitfalls to avoid and what most impressed. A useful but neglected question is to ask them to recall when the boss was most annoyed and with what.

One of the largest surveys ever conducted to investigate which jobs are the most stressful involved interviewing over 3,000 people and concluded that the job most associated with major mental health problems was being a lawyer.[16] Second came teaching and then secretarial work. Lawyers, according to this research, are almost four times more likely to be depressed than the average working person.

The study was conducted by doctors at America's top medical school, Johns Hopkins, where I worked for a while as a psychiatrist. The authors of the study, led by Dr William Eaton, were puzzled as to why these three professions should be associated with the most depression of all and suggested that perhaps it was down to the lack of control the individual working in these areas had over their workload.

Much research into occupational stress has found that it's not so much the workload you suffer that determines your stress levels as how much control you have over the way you do your job. The more individual autonomy you have from nine until five, the more protected you seem to be from developing emotional disturbance, or even the physical consequences of stress, like high blood pressure. Even if you have a lot of work to do, as long as you have some say in how it's done, this seems to buffer you from the effects of occupational stress.

TOP OF LEAGUE TABLE FOR STRESSFUL PROFESSIONS
    Lawyers
    Teachers
    Secretaries
    Waiters

However, psychologists have long been puzzled by why lawyers were the most depressed profession of all, given, for example, that lawyers in the USA long surpassed doctors as the highest paid professionals. Yet 52% of practising lawyers in a recent survey there described themselves as dissatisfied.[17]

The latest theory to explain this odd result comes from top American psychologist Professor Martin Seligman at the University of Pennsylvania. Seligman argues that the key thing about lawyers is they tend at heart to be pessimistic personality types.[18] When bad things happen in life, pessimists tend to assume these negative life events are permanent and global – they are going to last for ever and are going to undermine everything. The pessimist views bad events as pervasive, permanent and uncontrollable, while the optimist sees them as local, temporary and changeable. While pessimism is maladaptive in most endeavours, Professor Seligman found, surprisingly, that those entering law school get better grades the more pessimistic they are.

Pessimism is seen as a plus among lawyers because seeing troubles as pervasive and permanent is a component of what the law profession deems prudence. A prudent perspective enables a good lawyer to see every conceivable snare and catastrophe that might occur in any transaction. The ability to anticipate the whole range of possible problems and betrayals that non-lawyers are blind to is highly adaptive for the practising lawyer who can, by so doing, help his clients defend against these eventualities. The best lawyers are probably those most deeply pessimistic about human nature and who don't trust their own clients any further than the opposition. This scepticism helps them to be best prepared for any eventuality.

Unfortunately, a personality feature that makes you good at your profession does not always make you a happy person.

The key to solving lawyer unhappiness – and, given pessimism probably is at the heart of the success of many other professionals where prudence is a key factor, a key to helping many of us to be happier at work – is not to take home the pessimism that helps us do our jobs well.

It is vital to understand that gloomy views of others are helpful in getting your job done well but to take these views home and maintain them of your spouse, family or friends is likely to make you depressed about life in general.

Pessimistic lawyers are, according to Professor Seligman, also more likely to believe that their spouses are being unfaithful and this might explain why lawyers have the highest divorce rate compared to other professions.

Seligman argues that the way to banish the pessimistic view of the world from your home life is to imagine your life is like a courtroom and dispute, as in a court case, the kind of negative pessimistic thoughts that, left unchecked, will produce depression. So, for example, the catastrophic thoughts like 'My husband is probably unfaithful' that might plague you should be disputed by imagining they are uttered by an external person whose mission is to make your life miserable. You need to marshal the evidence against these thoughts and 'credibly dispute' them rather than allow yourself to wallow in a sea of pessimism.

So, for example, you should come up with a series of credible alternatives to the most pessimistic conclusion you might come to. If, for example, your spouse didn't smile at you today as you left for work, it could be that instead of plotting to poison you, they are actually worrying about something else, or even could be overly concerned about you. The key is to weigh the evidence rather than just the thought. Obviously if there is good evidence for your worst fear – you find your milkman's underwear amongst your spouse's – then you have every right to be pessimistic, but don't assume your pessimism is warranted without the right evidence.

Seligman isn't arguing you should dispense with the pessimism at work that produces such useful prudence; instead he advocates the use of what he calls 'flexible optimism' – which basically means being more optimistic when it comes to your private and personal life. This, he believes, will prevent depression no matter how pessimistic your job might otherwise make you.

Pessimism is a powerful approach in some professions as it helps to anticipate disaster at work and so prevent it happening – but if you take this pessimism home with you then you will always feel so depressed about life that there will be no point leaving the office.[19]

Having explored one key reason for unhappiness at work – your attitude to yourself and your job – let's turn our attention to another important cause: working for someone who makes your life a misery, an unreliable boss.[20]

London First, a business organization supported by over 300 of the capital's major businesses, has recently launched 'Teach First', an initiative targeting high-flying students who would normally go straight into business, which aims to encourage them to take up teaching instead as a career.[21]

Upon graduation from university, successful candidates will undergo eight weeks' intensive teacher training before starting in the classroom. Additional evening training and classroom support is provided throughout the first year, giving all Teach First recruits qualified teacher status. In their second year, Teach First graduates will receive training and mentoring from the organization's business sponsors.

The plan is to recruit 200 top graduates a year as teachers for challenging inner-city schools. Placements will last two years, at which point graduates will be free either to continue teaching or to go into business on fast-track recruitment schemes. Part of the key attraction of the scheme is the mentoring from businesses because mentoring is something workers are increasingly interested in.

Mentoring is the hot topic in occupational psychology at the moment because it has recently been found by psychologists to be a key component in career success.

For example, Rachel Day and Tammy Allen from the Department of Psychology at The University of South Florida have recently published one of the most extensive investigations into the practical benefits of mentoring.[22]

A mentor is an experienced employee who serves as a role model and provides support and direction to a protégé. Mentors provide feedback regarding career plans and interpersonal development and are committed to helping the protégé succeed in the working world.

Day and Allen found that being mentored was linked to an increased desire for upward mobility, risk taking and resilience to career barriers in employees, and this helped explain why mentoring gave rise to greater career achievement eventually. Mentorship was also found to be positively related to achieving a higher salary, as well as subjective reports of career success and performance.

Other research confirms that those who are mentored experience considerable benefits, such as higher salaries and promotions, they are more satisfied with their jobs, and they demonstrate greater career mobility and recognition than those who are not mentored.[23]

These startling results help explain the current enthusiasm for mentoring in progressive workplaces. For example, as a result of the Partnership in Policing initiative, another of London First's schemes, currently half the borough commanders and senior officers from City of London Police have a mentor from the business community.

Part of the key to mentors' success is not just the obvious career advice they provide but perhaps the more subtle psychological support. Obvious advantages to having a mentor include sponsorship, coaching, exposure/visibility, protection and the provision of challenging assignments. The less obvious but perhaps equally vital psychological functions relate more to the interpersonal aspect of the relationship, and include role modelling, counselling, friendship and acceptance.

Mentors have been found to be particularly helpful in two crucial aspects of careers: resilience and insight. Career resilience is the ability to adapt to changing circumstances, even when circumstances are discouraging or disruptive. It comprises characteristics such as belief in self, willingness to take risks and need for achievement. Career insight is the ability to be realistic about one's career and consists of establishing clear, feasible career goals and realizing one's strengths and weaknesses.

So why does mentoring produce such overwhelmingly positive effects on workers?

A key point about a mentor is that, given they are usually senior and successful, they rather obviously and concretely demonstrate the rewards that can be attained if a more junior individual sticks with a career. Many careers in their early stages are full of disappointments and a mentor may help you see that persistence will eventually be rewarded.[24]

Those scoring high in psychological tests for career motivation have been found by psychologists to differ from the rest of us because they simply work harder on those projects that most directly effect their career. On an average day there may be multiple tasks you are required to complete but actually only a very small number of them have promotion or career advancement implications. These are usually the activities that are most visible to seniors and the most relevant to their own advancement. The tendency to work at these key tasks and sacrifice the others explains why those scoring high on career motivation mysteriously seem to have greater career advancement opportunities than the rest of us.

Maybe the key point about mentors is that they help you know what in your job really is most relevant to your future, and what isn't.[25]

But exactly why mentoring works remains a puzzle. The recent research from the University of South Florida on mentoring found that just having a mentor, without the mentor having to be terribly active, seemed to powerfully enhance career motivation.[26]

Yet these findings are important because they may further encourage mentorships in organizations. Companies may be more willing to advance mentorships knowing that they relate so strongly to workplace motivation.

Perhaps the immense positive impact of mentors is telling us something about the more general failure of managers who should in an ideal world be providing a mentoring role but who are clearly not fulfilling that function.

Psychological research in the workplace has established that employees are more likely to be highly motivated when their managers are supportive, provide clear performance feedback, encourage subordinates to set career goals, initiate discussions related to development and career-related issues and make the job challenging.[27]

Basically, the more a manager behaves like a mentor, the more motivated their subordinates become.

You work hard, you are talented and you are keen to succeed and help the organization prosper along with yourself – so what's going wrong? Why is it you find your skills are underemployed and your best ideas to help yourself and others go to waste? In all probability, if all the previous statements are true, then the most likely possibility is that you are working for an idiot.

Everyone has worked for a boss who is, let's be blunt but accurate, a fool. The law of survival in the workplace usually means that the complete nincompoop whom you worked for and who made bad decisions relentlessly day after day has survived and prospered – like a cockroach after a nuclear strike – while those who suffered under them found their careers stifled, moved away or had to start medication to lower their blood pressure.[28]

The boss who is an idiot ensures no good deed goes unpunished, because somewhere deep inside the unstirring cerebrum is some realization that those who are creative and effective are a threat to the stupid and hopeless. This means if you want to survive working for an idiot you are going to have to change tactics or get a season ticket for my psychiatric clinic now.[29]

The first step in surviving the stupid, but in charge, is to stop appearing a threat by being overtly clever and effective. One deeply irritating habit of those who have a clearer sense of what they want to achieve in the office than the boss is the tendency to ask threatening questions – like what do you mean? Or what's the point of that? Or you do realize that if you do that then this disaster will happen?

These questions, particularly in a public forum, serve only to point out to the audience that your boss is an idiot and you aren't – but haven't we forgotten who is in charge? So who is going to suffer as a result?

The reason sensible employees tend to ask difficult questions of buffoon bosses is that rather understandably they haven't understood a word the boss has said. The key trick here is to find the one person in the office – usually the boss's best buddy – to translate. Get clarification from someone who can decipher the last incoherent communication from the management, rather than ask questions that make it clear what you really think of them. Find out more covertly what the boss is really trying to say, and then don't try to make too much sense of it. It almost certainly won't have a meaningful rationale.[30]

Instead, having got to the bottom of the boss's agenda, no matter how little sense it makes, endeavour to work within it. Battling the boss rarely wins any plaudits, particularly at promotion time. Identify the problem your boss is trying to solve (no matter how stupid or non-existent it is) and help them solve it. Once you have demonstrated you are effective in helping them, only then will they try to help you.

The second tip in working for a fool is to understand that they don't notice very much of what is going on around them – if they did then they wouldn't be so dumb. Given that the art of promotion is visibility, most of what you do should have been good enough to get you noticed by any reasonable boss, but as you are working for a fool, you are going to have to signpost your achievements a bit more clearly.

For example, if you offer to go out and get lunchtime sandwiches for everyone, when you come back with them walk up to the boss and ask which one they want before you offer them to the masses – you can't just wave the flag of what you do, you have to park a jumbo jet on their lawn for you to stop being invisible to them.

You will be reluctant to do this the first few times as it will seem very cheesy to parade your efforts so glaringly in front of the boss. Remember this wouldn't be necessary if you were dealing with any reasonable boss, but instead you have the misfortune to work for an idiot, and as a result you seem to be invisible. If you want to stop tripping over the invisibility cloak, it's time to do something about it rather than just moan on about the fool in charge.[31]

The third technique of dealing with moronic management is to find a covert way of getting out of the meaningless activity they insist on you doing, which is slowly driving you round the bend. Here you need to be more resourceful and instead of resentfully pointing out how useless the work they want you to do is, find a cover for appearing to do it while not bothering. A useful tip here, if challenged on what you are doing right now, is to claim to be producing a report. The great thing about reports is no one wants to read them or be involved in producing them, so they will quickly leave you alone.

The final and key point about working for an idiot is that it's the conviction that they are so wrong and you are so right that is slowly carving out an ulcer in your stomach. It could well be the case that your boss slipped through the evolutionary process unnoticed and is now in charge of much superior intellects to theirs. The key is to manage your upset so it doesn't drive you to an early grave, and this means allowing others the conviction they are right even when they palpably are not, without having to correct them or fix their misapprehension.[32]

Do what they think is right, at least for a while, even though you know it's wrong. Bide your time and wait, pick your battles carefully because sooner or later, sooner in the case of truly dumb bosses, they will need your help to bail themselves out of trouble, and that's when your value will be finally realized and you will reap rewards. But only if you haven't annoyed them by then, by letting them know what you truly think of them.

Four Types of Idiot Boss and How to Deal with Them

THE FOOLISH FRIEND

This boss wants to be your best friend – he or she wants to be one of the team and so loves the idea of socializing after work or discussing your personal life – David Brent of the hit TV series *The Office* is the Foolish Friend type of boss. Of course what the Foolish Friend doesn't quite grasp is that relationships at work aren't a substitute for the lack of friendships elsewhere in their life but they are trying to fill a hole (which is their personality), which explains why the only person who knows their name in their neighbourhood is the pizza delivery boy. You need to make the Foolish Friend boss believe that you are indeed their buddy, but without having to endure the request to baby-sit them at weekends. Ask their advice about key issues in your personal life – like what school to send the kids to and whether a vasectomy is the right way forward in your marriage. This makes the Foolish Friend boss feel they are part of your life in the way they want to, but means they also won't know that you are actively ignoring everything they say.

THE AGONY AUNT

This boss appears, at least on the surface, to be actively involved in trying to solve problems at work and therefore seems at first glance to pass as someone effective. Of course, when you probe a bit further you find the boss listens carefully, emotionally and sympathetically (they may even wipe a tear away as they hear your worst complaints), but then this boss blithely does nothing at all to really help. What is idiotic about this boss is their apparent expression of deep interest in their workforce because although they may be genuinely interested, actually they are so stupid they can do nothing to practically help. This kind of boss is very popular with those who like to be listened to and then

191

ignored, rather than just ignored up front. The key to dealing with this boss is to realize they are of no use whatsoever to you, and therefore you are wasting your time taking issues that need real leadership to them. Instead you need to find the real action-oriented people in the organization and start working with them. Meanwhile, you should get lots of people to ventilate all at once to the Agony Aunt in back-to-back meetings, so that this amateur psychotherapist gets overwhelmed by listening, and finally agrees to *do* something about the problem just to get everyone to shut up about it.

THE FANTASIST

This boss fervently believes many bizarre things about themselves and the organization, like they are doing a good job, people respect them and officialdom is relentlessly advancing the progress of humankind. This kind of boss loves to cross-dress – they periodically like to look like someone who looks organized and effective. The mistake most employees make when dealing with a Fantasist is to try and bring them back into contact with reality – this is a woeful waste of time and fantasy is a much nicer place for this boss to be. Instead you should use this boss's poor grip on logic and reality to generate many alternative worlds that are unlikely to be questioned by the Fantasist, but the consequence of which is to persuade the boss to do the things that need doing. This kind of boss neglects hard evidence and so puts great store on gossip, hearsay and rumour and it is precisely these kinds of stories that you have 'overheard' (made up) that you should use to great effect in meetings to get your boss galvanized to do the things you want. Remember you remain in control as long as your imagination is more fertile than theirs.

THE AGORAPHOBE

This boss hates leaving his own office and as a result has extremely little contact with the rest of the organization. They find that if you go out into the real world you get pestered with people pointing out things that need improving, so better to retreat into the safety of your own cave and read reports about how dreadful things are out there. The Agoraphobe starts off never leaving their department but as the condition gets worse they retreat further and further into a smaller and smaller space until they refuse to leave their favourite corner of their own room. The Agoraphobe needs to be gently coaxed outside, eyes blinking from the light, by incentives like unthreatening get-togethers with colleagues, where the Agoraphobe doesn't sense danger, like complaints or problems that need solving.

HOW IDIOT BOSSES GOT THAT WAY

Some achieve idiocy while others have idiocy thrust upon them. Remember most idiot bosses were hired by other idiots further up the food chain, so the fact you are working for one is probably an ominous indicator of the intelligence of those even more senior. This is important to bear in mind as the commonest temptation when dealing with an idiot boss is to go behind their back to those more senior. This is often a big mistake: who do you think hired your idiot supervisor in the first place?

Some idiots find dumbness the best way of operating in an organization as it protects them from the frustration of having meaningful goals or expectations and getting upset when these are difficult to achieve. You yourself might learn something valuable from this. Sometimes the best protection from an organization imposing itself upon you with unreasonable demands is to become an idiot. The danger of being competent and effective is that your reward is more and more demands upon you with little real benefit. So learn from the idiot boss and use idiocy and incompetence to your advantage but unlike the idiot boss, target your idiocy to improve its effectiveness. Suddenly become obviously really really stupid just when they are trying to allocate a big project that you hate. This is the smart thing to do.

It's been said that people rarely leave bad jobs, but instead flee bad bosses. Most of the severe work-related stress that I see in my clinics for sick doctors at The Maudsley Hospital can be put down, directly or indirectly, to the strain of serving under a disagreeable boss – be it a manager or a senior doctor. Actually, the key misunderstanding these clients seem to make is to label the boss 'bad' – characterizing them as hopeless simply encourages doctors to give up on *managing* the boss, which is actually the key to success in this fraught situation.

We tend to think of ourselves as being managed by our bosses, but when things are going awry it's in fact time to start managing them.

The first step to managing a 'bad' boss is to understand their motivation – by doing this you can work out why they are no good at their jobs, from your standpoint, and this reveals which tactics to then use to solve your problem. And yes it is *your* problem: the key is to start acting. Remember the difficulty almost certainly lies in the *relationship* between you and your boss, and this is the area that you need to rectify. In my experience most conflicts around working in the NHS and contending with difficult superiors boil down to a clash of personalities, but this can be corrected with the right kind of personal psychological expertise.[33]

Let's take a few examples of common problems with bosses and follow through what benefits a motivational analysis brings.

THE BOSS WHO IS A CHEAT

A very serious but unfortunately not uncommon predicament is when your boss is constantly taking credit for your work. Perhaps he or she let everyone in the last big department meeting think that your new idea was actually their accomplishment. This is the kind of situation that commonly produces fury in doctors, so in a rage they burst into the boss's office and let him or her have a piece of their mind in no uncertain manner. Although this will make you feel great for a short while – well, until you get back to your clinic – it is not usually conducive to a good long-term relationship with the boss. And remember they usually have more obvious power than you.

A motivational analysis of this situation would suggest there are, in fact, only a few reasons why a boss might steal your ideas. First the good news is at least it means they find you a valuable asset to the organization – if only because you come up with good ideas that they can then filch.

This kind of boss is usually insecure about their own ability and therefore extremely threatened by talented juniors, so it's absolutely imperative you don't do anything that makes them feel you pose a danger to them. This can lead to an extremely uncomfortable co-existence . . . or a posting to Outer Mongolia. This kind of boss usually responds to a lot of praise for their own work, as they are not used to getting these kinds of strokes, which you should then turn to your advantage. You must, however, protect your own work by presenting ideas you have as formally as possible, preferably at meetings where the proceedings are minuted or in memos that record for posterity who came up with what first.

The best defence against stealing is to have an audience who witness your ideas being presented. This doesn't mean you can't let your boss steal more minor ideas, as this merely encourages their dependence on you. Once they are utterly clingy, turn this to your advantage by requiring more compensation for your assistance in the future. There is no surer path to career advancement than when your boss feels their future is tied up with yours.

THE BOSS WHO IS WEAK

Another classic bad boss is the weak or reluctant manager – this is someone who won't resolve conflicts at work between different parties. This boss also won't stand up for their employees and refuses to take the kind of risks that lead to organizational development or expansion. Often, the core motivation here is that a boss like this simply wants to be liked by everyone, and therefore can't stand conflict. It's also possible they are too busy dealing with lesser priorities to see the bigger problems right under their nose. Frequently, such managers are reluctant to be managers at all, and would much rather be getting on with their own work as individuals. They have often been promoted into a management position against their wishes.

If you are dealing with a weak manager, identify the underlying motivation. For example, if your manager needs to be liked by everyone, avoid communications that suggest contentious or highly charged emotional issues. Where you can, it is vital you resolve conflicts yourself by coming up with the solution and offering to implement it for them. This kind of boss is pathetically grateful for help in facing the kind of confrontation that they would normally like to avoid. Also this sort of boss is hugely responsive to sympathetic noises from you about the stress of being a boss, and would welcome any offers you have to assist them in doing their job.

THE BOSS WHO IS JUST DOWNRIGHT NASTY

Perhaps the most difficult boss of all to deal with is what is commonly known as the nasty boss – the boss who appears to delight in humiliating and embarrassing their workers. It may look as though this boss only gets out of bed so as to cause as much misery as possible but if you analyse the motivation what you usually find is that this boss is merely extremely 'task focused'. In other words, they simply want to get the job done at whatever cost and don't care who they upset in their narrow focus on work performance.

The key to dealing with the nasty boss is to ensure they feel you are as task focused as they are, so you are going to help them hit the goal they have set themselves. Often bosses turn nasty because the goals they are pursuing are not understood or appreciated by their underlings – who they then perceive as obstacles to their own ambition. The key here is to start by identifying what their goals are and assuring them that these are indeed your goals as well. Get the boss to see you as an ally in a hostile world (the nasty boss tends to see the world in black-and-white terms – you are either the enemy or a friend). Then get into the kind of dialogue where feedback on how to better hit their targets is welcomed, so reducing the need for abuse.

One of the best boss-management strategies is to meet regularly, often in a non-work environment, like for a drink after work. You should suggest this first time round as an opportunity you would welcome to discuss some work issues. The fact you are willing to devote some time after work to discussing work usually goes down well with any committed boss.

If you can get the boss to see you as a human being rather than a mere employee, you are on the way to a better relationship. Just as it is helpful to you not to see them as merely a boss but as a person with their own feelings, sensitivities and needs.

Rarely it can be the case that your boss really is out to get you. In this case you need to focus not so much on developing a relationship with them – indeed you may need to backtrack from this if it has been tried and failed – but rather on developing your protection mechanisms, like forming allies, preferably senior ones.

WHAT TO DO WHEN IT'S WAR

In a situation where it really is war with your boss do remember that they will usually have more power over you and you should seriously consider changing jobs or bosses, before they do your career some serious damage. Doctors, because they tend to have strong views on the correct way of doing things, often stay much longer than they should in this dangerous situation, as they are incensed at the unfairness of their predicament. The fairness of the situation isn't as important, however, as personal survival. The key is to learn to live to fight another day – you can probably wage a retaliatory war against your boss much more effectively if you are not working under them. So get the hell out. The antidote to getting into a competitive retaliatory relationship with your boss is to understand that happiness is the best revenge.[34]

We often complain about our difficulties at work to others; indeed sometimes it seems we do little else when we socialize after another long, frustrating day. But if we find our dinner stories develop a pattern – incredulous accounts of the stupid scrapes that organizations like the NHS (where I work) find themselves in – then really, at the core, we are actually complaining about incompetent managers.

Everyone has worked for an incompetent manager at some time in their lives. Not only do such inadequate supervisors make life at work a misery, they are usually disastrous for the organizations in which they work. This is because they not only generate a huge amount of low morale, but they incompetently lead the company/hospital into catastrophe due to their inability to make good decisions.[35]

One classic sign that you are dealing with an incompetent manager is the way they deal with things going wrong. The incompetent immediately try to find someone to blame – a scapegoat – as a way of diverting attention from their own incompetence. Deep down, incompetent managers are insecure about their own competence, and are primarily motivated to ensure it never comes under scrutiny. By contrast, the truly competent constantly seek feedback in order to improve performance.

Incompetent managers also love 'blamestorming' – sitting

around in large groups trying to find someone outside the group to blame. Incompetent managers do this because they fail to see that it is organizations themselves that have responses that need to be addressed. Instead they prefer to castigate an employee, which allows the fundamental organizational problem to be brushed under the carpet.

Over and over again we see in major public inquiries into disasters that managerial incompetence is actually to blame, but in the private sector and some parts of the NHS it is these senior staff who have the best parachutes to bail out of the plunging organization when it suddenly loses cabin pressure.[36]

So how best to deal with an incompetent manager? This is a vital question for all doctors who labour under managerial ineptitude and usually they just learn to put up with it. The danger of this is that an incompetent manager is eventually going to mismanage things to the extent that disaster will happen and then blame will come your way.

The key to dealing with incompetent managers, argues Professor Adrian Furnham, a psychologist at University College London and expert on management psychology, is to understand which type you are dealing with and so tailor your responses to fit the diagnosis. The most effective classification system is to understand that all managers fit into one of three basic types: they are Sad, Bad or Mad.

The Sad manager is someone who had ambitions to be doing much better in life than they are now, but have found themselves doing a job they feel is well beneath them, because of bad luck or simply because others spotted their incompetence and rewarded it. This is the manager with unfulfilled promise or the one who has been passed over and still smarts under the pain of the humiliation. The Sad manager is so preoccupied with their grieving that they withdraw from active management, and so the lights are on but no one's home.

The key to dealing with the Sad manager is to get others around you to support and encourage them to take a more active role – or at least not get in the way of others who are keen to fill the vacuum. Beware that the Sad manager is particularly prone to jealousy if you are seen to be someone on the up, so get them to believe that a rise in your fortunes is good for them too, as you are keen to take them with you as you journey up the hierarchy. You need friends to help do the manager's job for them so you don't shoulder the responsibility yourself.[37]

The Bad manager is someone who is so preoccupied with their own advancement and empire that they are quick to see others as obstacles. Things you might do, which seem innocuous to you, appear to be a threat to their authority and easily anger them. The Bad or psychopathic manager divides the world simply into enemies or allies, and it's vital not to stray on to their radar inadvertently as an enemy, as they will then throw all their resources into pulverizing you. To the Bad manager there are no neutrals, you are either for them or against them, so store up some credit by being seen to be on their side, and in particular never be seen to publicly fraternize with the Bad manager's enemies. If you find yourself being goaded into a fight with a Bad manager make sure you have plenty of friends on your side as the size of the opposition is the only thing that will intimidate the Bad manager. They are like wolves who like to separate one of the scared animals from the herd before picking them off, so huddle together for protection.

The Mad manager has a grip on reality that seems tenuous at best. This is exhibited by the fact that your understanding of what was agreed at a meeting and what they think happened are usually completely divorced from each other. The Mad manager makes decisions and assumes everyone else knows about them without actually alerting anyone – so they assume others can read their mind. This is in fact a useful clue to the tactic you have to adopt with the Mad manager. You need to have several sources of information about what they are thinking, not just their memos. You need to use these sources to get a sense of what is really going on. You also need to make sure there are independent witnesses at any vital meetings so that you can corroborate later your version of reality. Here you need friends as witnesses.

The key each time, whether you are dealing with Sad, Bad or Mad managers, is to always have colleagues to help you with this demanding and stressful work.

Of course there is a fourth type of manager, but these are so rare that I left them out of the classification system, confident you are unlikely to meet one. These are not Sad, Bad or Mad, but Glad – they enjoy their job and bring such positivity to it they are a joy to work with.

If you encounter a Glad manager then embrace them, support

them, and never let them out of your sight in case some other organization poaches them, for competent managers are harder to find than weapons of mass destruction.

Having understood the different kinds of bosses and how to deal with them, the next step to a happy working life is learning how to say no to unnecessary or unrewarding work – no matter what kind of boss you are dealing with. The essential difficulty with troublesome bosses boils down to how to say no to them.

Saying yes when you really would prefer to say no is at the heart of much unhappiness at work. The yes/no issue is central to a fulfilling career because one of the main problems with working life in the twenty-first century is that job descriptions are generally incredibly vague, so your responsibilities could expand faster than the universe after the Big Bang.

Today, most workers begin by co-operating with requests to do extra things, in the naïve belief this will earn them credits that can be cashed in later. However, what inevitably happens is that despite your willingness to go the extra mile, when it comes to reciprocation from others, you arrive at your massive credit account to finally make a withdrawal, only to find the bank actually went bust years ago.

To survive in working life you need to acquire the art of saying no, and as a result draw a boundary around what you feel you are able to humanly do. Don't be over-burdened with what others can pile on your shoulders. If you never learn to say no then you will rapidly find working unbearable, as physicists have recently calculated that the amount of work it is possible to do if no boundary is drawn is indeed infinite.

Another benefit of knowing how to say no well is that this gives you more choice to shape your job into something you enjoy, and gain personal fulfilment from, rather than simply becoming a workhorse serving someone else's ambitions.

Saying no is not about being bloody-minded or avoiding work; it is instead about gaining some kind of control over what is usually an extremely chaotic occupational environment.

Many workers suffer from the tendency to be good-natured and obliging, and as a result they get exploited mercilessly by management. They find it takes too long to think of an objection when they are asked to do something, so usually end up giving in simply from lack of ability to think on their feet. So keep the following list of tips below handy and practise them in front of a mirror – you do want to keep that helpful eager expression on your face.

TEN TIPS FOR SAYING NO

1. Never say no to armed gunmen or managers

A few years ago I made a series for BBC Radio 4 on the art of hostage negotiation; I travelled the world with my producer, Sally Flatman, speaking to psychologists and psychiatrists who are behind the scenes when terrorists take hostages. A key lesson they taught is that whatever is demanded by the gunmen from, say, the hijacked plane – be it a million dollars or a helicopter to take them out of the country – the police negotiators never respond with a no, even when the answer actually is no. Instead they say things like 'We are working on it but it's difficult to get a helicopter with a big enough fuel tank for your purposes' – basically they play for time.

The reason you never explicitly say no is that to do so would inevitably evoke a retaliatory response. So the art of saying no is to not appear to say no while in fact avoiding giving a person what they ask for. Obviously this art, when played at the highest level, has to be done in an extremely sophisticated manner, as most gunmen are not entirely stupid (I am not so sure about NHS managers), and can often detect when they are being flannelled. The art of saying no is to appear as though you are giving a positive response while really saying no.

So the number-one tip in learning the Zen skill of saying no is to remove the word no or any negative response from your vocabulary, and to become extremely proficient at getting bogged down in difficulties in fulfilling the request.

2. Play for time, as in all contests eventually bad light always stops play

A major ally on your 'saying no' team is time. If you spend long enough not giving people what they want they usually turn to other, quicker, solutions, discover how to do without your help or learn that they never really wanted what they asked of you in the first place. So instead of saying no, learn to say yes, but take so long doing it that this becomes a no in reality. One way of harnessing time is simply to postpone saying yes by having other things to do before you can give an answer. Also there are all those things you need to find out about before you can give this decision your proper consideration. Then there are all those people you have to check with (you are extremely keen to do this, it's just that the secretaries or accounts dept will want to be consulted first as they will be affected).

3. Put the ball back in their court
Have they checked first with the chief executive? Have they taken this to the management committee? Have they considered what will happen if this or that occurs, as a result of this new thing they want you to do? You don't mind doing it but first, as you don't want to tread on anyone's toes and you want to do it properly, you need to make sure the person making the request has followed the correct protocol. Doesn't this conflict with other arrangements already in place? Wouldn't that compatibility need ensuring first?

4. Bury it in a committee
One of the public sector's favourite and most unproductive activities is meetings. Obviously most meetings are usually more obstructive than helpful in implementing change (how many statues in major capitals do you see erected to a committee as opposed to an individual?). So a good way of saying no is to take a request to a meeting for it to be discussed – sure enough someone somewhere at a meeting will find a good reason for not doing it, or at least get upset that they weren't consulted first.

5. Ask for clarification
A good way of returning fire is to bombard the person making the request with questions. What happens during the holidays? Who will do it during sick leave? When they say this needs doing within seven days, do they mean seven working days? What precisely does their memo mean? Pedantry is a most useful weapon in dealing with missives from above. The key here is that most memos, because they are brief, leave a universe of meaning open to conjecture – a veritable playground of possibilities. Enjoy!

6. Take the opportunity to bring up a thing you need from them
One of the most universal, but tacit, laws of human interaction is that of reciprocation – if you ask me for a favour it would

appear impolite, at the least, not to try to do me a favour in return. So whenever someone asks you to do something take the opportunity to immediately ask them for something – keep a handy list of things you need doing that can be whipped out at the slightest sign of favours coming your way. Remember that survival in the modern office is increasingly like the gunfight at the OK Corral: the fastest on the draw walks away.

7. Remember you work in a team and so there are always others you have to check with first
One danger of saying no is that you don't look like a team player, so turn this on its head by becoming the most bonded of team players. So teamy, in fact, that you want to check with *everybody* before you agree that this is a good thing to do, as you don't want to go out on a limb here. If your team is big enough you are bound to find someone sooner or later who objects and this is where the new idea gets scuppered – but not by you.

8. You think it's a great idea but do they realize it will mean you can't also do the great idea they had last week?
One way to scupper a manager's plans for more work for you is to demonstrate that this will mean their other pet project will get impeded by this new project. People don't like it when you say no, and will fight you when you do, but they are pulled up short when the sacrifice that will be made to get this new thing done is on *their* part. This has a tendency to clarify just how important the new project is if an old one of *theirs* is going to be forfeited on the altar of the new directive.

9. If a thing is worth doing, it's worth doing well, or not at all . . .
Judo is about using the force an opponent is coming at you with to their disadvantage and tripping them up. So the manager wants this new objective attained, but what's the point of doing it if it's not going to be done properly – let's certainly do it but let's do it *properly* and this will mean, of course, a lot of new resources as well . . .

10. If it's such a good idea how come not everyone is doing it?
A favourite management technique when you ask for something

is to point out that this thing isn't happening elsewhere, so using comparison as a way of saying no. You can use this to your own advantage as well. If a Trust wants to start a new policy, how come it's not happening in a nearby office? How is it others seem to survive without this marvellous new plan? Unfortunately, this technique can make you sound a bit like a five-year-old complaining to their parents about what the older siblings have that they don't.

But don't forget, *they* started it.

9

DON'T BLEED IN THE WATER
(HOW TO GET YOUR BOSS'S JOB)

The only way many companies can attract and keep the best people is by offering them more than merely money or prestige – they offer them the chance to make history

Warren Bennis

You are one of the Lords of the Earth, with unlimited potentialities. Within you is a power which, if properly grasped and directed, can lift you out of the rut of mediocrity and place you among the Elect of the Earth – the lawgivers, the writers, the engineers, the great industrialists – the Doers and the Thinkers. It rests with you only to learn to use this power which is yours – this Mind which can do all things

Robert Collier

It used to be said that sex and death were the last big taboos – the subjects you didn't bring up in polite company. Actually, the really gargantuan taboo in modern Britain is money – and in particular how much you earn. However, the fact you are so reluctant to discuss this is probably losing you significant sums.[1]

It is actually critical to know how much our colleagues earn, because unless we are properly aware of this, we are not in a strong position to negotiate a pay rise. It is probably the case that those who are earning the least for doing the same work are also the ones who least realize it – to know the true value of your labour you need to know what others are getting paid to do the same work.[2]

The best way to find this out is to contact agencies who supply temporary staff in your profession, as agency rates bear some relationship to full-time salaries – and it's legitimate for you to enquire about the pay as you might be considering doing agency work. Recruitment advertisements and agencies are also good sources of information on pay scales and perhaps most importantly the pay futures of different forms of work.[3]

You need to know what the highest-paid people doing your work are earning because no company is going to pay you significantly more than that ceiling.

However, there is always room for improvement of financial position and the start of negotiating for a rise is to work out how valuable you are to the company – this means calculating how much money they make out of you or how much revenue you generate for them. In the public sector it is possible to calculate how much money it might cost the organization if they were to lose someone as efficient as you.[4]

The best time to negotiate a pay rise is when circumstances have changed in the job and you are now generating significantly more earnings for the organization than when you first started at your current pay scale. If you can argue that your job is now different then this is a strong case for saying your pay should also be altered.[5]

It is also vital during the negotiation to be specific. Pointing out that the firm is now £250,000 a year better off because of your work, or that you saved them the equivalent because of your intervention, is a much more effective negotiating position than vaguely saying you are a good worker. But because we are usually nervous when asking the boss for more money we tend to fall back on being indistinct. Ambiguity ensures we feel we are not overtly pressurizing the boss, when in fact it is specifics and clarity that most impress the audience.[6] After all, if you don't take yourself seriously, then why should the boss?

The psychology of the precise timing of when to ask for more money is absolutely crucial and yet is usually handled incompetently. Most workers tend to pluck up the courage to ask for more at desperate times when they frantically need more money – this of course is usually during periods of general economic malaise and so also when the company is probably not doing particularly well.[7] Actually, the best time to ask for a pay rise, psychologically, is when the corporation is thriving. Not only is the boss feeling good and in an expansive frame of mind, but seniors are going to be more averse to rocking the boat and losing valuable staff just after a record quarter's performance.

Another good moment is when you have pulled off a particularly good performance at work and are getting praised by the boss. Most workers simply lap up the goodwill but aren't machiavellian enough to capitalize on this essential psychological moment. Now is absolutely the time to ask for more money. Above all else, the boss is going to feel a real charlatan if they can't follow up their glowing praise for you with tangible benefits at your request – it makes them seem phoney in praising you, which is a significant psychological pressure that needs to be exploited.

Again most people ask for a pay rise without any adequate knowledge of the financial health of the organization for which they work. A glance at the annual accounts could illuminate just how generous your boss could afford to be and also helps assess where the company is in terms of the business cycle – if it is on an upturn get in now before the downturn starts.[8]

The psychology of timing is even important in terms of picking your moment. Don't ask the boss for more money at a social gathering, passing them in the corridor or just after a huge amount has been spent on some extravagant project. Friday afternoon is a good time to ask for a pay rise because the boss can then spend the weekend worrying that you might leave. It also gives the boss time to work out how they are going to justify your increase to their own seniors. Whatever you do don't rush the boss into a decision. Use phrases like 'I would like you to think about' and 'at an appropriate time'. In order to surmount the stress and embarrassment of actually asking for more money it is vital to use formal phrases like 'salary arrangements', 'review' and 'market value'.[9]

In fact, the very best position from which to negotiate a pay rise is when you have covertly lined up another job to go to if you don't get your way. Actually, if you have been in a job for any length of time, chances are you could be lagging behind job-moving colleagues in terms of reward. People who change jobs frequently nab the market rate with each new position while those who stay with the same company for a number of years often receive increases only in line with inflation.[10]

But what if, despite all your psychological plotting, the boss still says no? If you don't get the desired result, don't threaten to leave: it simply isn't professional. A good phrase to use if you get turned down is, 'You can appreciate that I would not have mentioned this unless I had given it a lot of thought', which makes them think you are considering leaving, without actually saying so. Also, put your disappointment to one side, keep your wits about you and listen very carefully to *how* you are turned down, as this gives a good clue as to when to ask for more money in the future. If you get a flat rejection with no explanation or account of what you would have to do differently in order to secure more money, then you should seriously consider leaving if the salary is important to you.[11] If instead it is suggested you should ask again in a few months' time, then there is hope yet.

Most bosses are nervous at turning down a request for more money as they are worried that the employee could be upset or angry and retaliate. If you are gracious and polite at this moment, most bosses are so relieved that this is a great psychological point at which to ask for something *else*, like improved work conditions, more expenses or perhaps more training. There is a natural psychological tendency to feel a need to reciprocate if someone has done you the favour of not reacting badly to your intervention.[12]

Above all else don't forget that famous psychological principle: 'If you don't ask, you won't get.'

There is one sure-fire way to guarantee you are selected for promotion when the next opportunity for advancement within your organization comes round, and that is to have a close relative as the boss. The following advice is for those of you not fortunate enough to be in that position!

The first step to achieving promotion is to understand that if you are not inside your own family's business, or sleeping your way to the top, getting promoted isn't actually a right. A widespread misapprehension amongst those frequently passed over for promotion is that skills, hard work, loyalty and training make the key difference to moving up the job ladder. These *should* be important but are often surprisingly insignificant – a much more vital issue is one of *perception*. How you are perceived, particularly by your boss, is central rather than the reality of what you do.[13]

Often it is precisely those who are doing all the hard work in the organization who are too busy to give enough attention to the issue of how they are perceived by others.

Occupational psychologists argue that the key characteristic of those who get promoted is 'being self-aware'. This means having an understanding of what your employer really needs combined with knowledge of how you are perceived by your employer.[14]

So promotion is actually about managing the perceptions of key decision-makers.

To start you need to become more aware of the needs of your organization as a whole (the bigger picture). Often we are so bogged down with the day-to-day problems of our jobs we don't lift our heads above the parapet to see the company from the standpoint of the senior managers. To you the key problem might be getting the distribution of products right – to them it might be keeping customer complaints down.[15]

Find out the key concern that is keeping your boss up at night, and help become the solution to that problem. This is particularly effective as a promotion strategy if you then ensure that you are indispensable to the firm in continuing to solve that problem. Sometimes that means being brutally selfish in not sharing a particular skill or strategy you have with co-workers. Many is the time the person who solved a serious problem for the managers then got passed over for promotion because they made themselves dispensable by helping everyone else learn to solve the problem for themselves.[16]

So promotable people operate with a basic marketing principle – they 'focus on the needs of the buyer' – in this case the person who makes the decisions about career advancement. Again, the influential senior staff might not be obvious. It could be that it is not your immediate manager who makes the key decision about promotion but someone above him or her. So find out more about the decision-making process and close the sale of yourself with the right person, not someone who has relatively little influence on your career.[17]

To many people self-promotion seems to be the same as 'showing off', but in fact empty narcissistic self-promotion is like unfocused selling. It's not appropriate, and no one wants it.

Skilled marketeers are determined to communicate a match between what they have to offer and what the organization needs. There's no place for misplaced ego inflation; true marketing focuses on the need of the customer.

But influencing key people in the organization by communicating your achievements to them probably also means pushing the boundaries of your job or going the extra mile, and making them aware of this. It is about being in the right place at the right time. Find out when your manager is most anxious about his or her performance being evaluated and ensure that is precisely when you are seen by them to be making a big contribution to their success.[18]

Whilst hard work and skills *are* important they are nowhere near as important as visibility and awareness. Waiting for others to notice your attributes and talents is a poor way to climb the career ladder; you can be 'good' in a closet and no one will ever know it.

To this end, expectations are key as they have a powerful impact on our emotions, behaviour and, most importantly, our performance. When you expect no rise or promotion at work, most likely you will not get them because you don't have the confidence to be more visible to the management at vital moments.

But another key issue is to find out what the bosses' expectations are of you. One of the most common reasons for low employee morale and performance is poor communication of work expectations. This is because many expectations are not written anywhere. That, in and of itself, can cause some trouble. A head of a department might expect a new employee to do X, Y and Z. Yet the head probably won't provide a written list of expectations because they assume that the employee will already know these things. Yet some things that are obvious and normal for some might be considered silly and unnecessary by the newly hired. The answer is to not allow assumptions to overrun our lives.[19]

There are several practical things that can be done to help you gain that next big promotion at work; it's fatal simply to expect hard work and talent to be naturally rewarded.

1. *Be aware of the expectations at work*. Obviously, we have to be aware of our own expectations before we try to

communicate them to anyone else. Be honest with yourself. If you expect a promotion after you close a million-dollar deal then you need to name what you expect. In this first step, you should claim what you want, whatever it might be, and be honest with yourself and those around you. It is particularly vital that the expectations involved in taking on a new project are clearly articulated. Often you think you have agreed to do something extraordinary and beyond the call of duty for which there should be recompense, yet the boss thinks you are just doing your job.

2. *Find out what it takes to dazzle them*. Many times the expectations of a supervisor or manager can be quite different from those of the employees. Very few workers ever bother to find out what would actually impress their boss and what irritates them most. This is actually a very disarming question to ask of senior staff early on in your job.

3. *Seek feedback*. You need to find out how you are doing in the eyes of your boss long before that crucial promotion interview comes along. The more and the earlier the feedback you get the more you can adjust your performance to exceed the expectations of your boss or hit the buttons that will impress.

4. *Make sure what you are good at is valued by your organization*. It is advisable to check from time to time that your expectations of your job and others' expectations of you there are indeed aligned with the core of who you are. If you value freedom and entrepreneurship in your professional life, don't seek positions that will land you in an environment opposite to your true values. You can't get promotion by play-acting the part – sooner or later someone is going to see through the act and bring the curtain down.

How to Answer the Toughest Interview Questions

The interview for your next move up the career ladder is one of the most nerve-racking experiences of your life – or so you believe – but things needn't be this way. Actually there is only a limited number of questions you can get asked – and I supply the secret to answering them below. If you don't get asked precisely one of these questions, the chances are you will be asked a variant, and so you merely need to alter your answer a little to accommodate the small change in the bouncer being bowled at you.

THE QUESTION
So, tell us a little about yourself.

Variations
What makes you special? What adjectives describe you best? How would you describe your character?

Analysis
This is the granddaddy of all interview questions and yet it still seems to trip up most interviewees. Oddly, this is because most seem unprepared for it, plus it is so open they panic. Often candidates become terrified because they aren't sure what the interviewer is getting at. In fact, they are just trying to find an undemanding way to get the ball rolling. A more sophisticated questioner might be deliberately vague because they want to see how you fill an unspecified space and how you respond to an ambiguous stimulus – this often reveals more about you than a more structured question. Many candidates get into such a fright over this question they reveal personal details about themselves that are at best irrelevant to the job and at worst make any employer think again, because all they have heard is deeply personal material and nothing of relevance to the job.

The Answer
You should have anticipated this question and prepared the following kind of response. Start by saying a little about your background and history, e.g., a little about you before you went to medical school or before you chose to specialize. Link your past in some way to your current interest in this job. For example, if you are a doctor applying for a medical job, you

might talk about how your particularly intriguing experiences of gastroenterology at medical school shaped your current interest in this specialism and your latest research interests. Then move on to your past key accomplishments that are relevant to this position, starting with the oldest and moving forward in time. Comment on your personal strengths as revealed by these achievements. Then move on to how you see yourself developing in the future in a way that suits the position you are currently applying for. Your answer should have a kind of past-present-future structure to link yourself and your past to this interview and your future in the job.

The No-No

Never, in response to this question, ask a clarifying question such as, 'What exactly do you want to know?' The last thing the interviewer wants is to be put on the spot themselves – they will think this suggests you are going to be an argumentative colleague.

THE QUESTION

Where do you see yourself in five years' time?

Variations

What are your long-term goals? What kind of future do you envisage for your career?

Analysis

What they want to hear is whether the vision they have for their department is compatible with the direction you are travelling in. Are you, if applying for a medical job, intending to become an academic when they want someone primarily interested in providing a good service? Or are you hoping to turn part-time in the near future precisely when they want someone to set up an M.Sc., as well as supervise the new procedure lists?

The Answer

The key thing to communicate is you want to do more and more – you have an endless appetite for the kind of things they are thinking of throwing at you. But start humbly by saying that what happens in five years depends on your performance in this job and the feedback you get. Then you need to talk about the sort of career where you hope to build on what you are currently doing. In other words, make your long-term goal fit the job; don't make the classic error of forcing the job to fit your deeper ambitions. A good tactic is to find out beforehand what previous incumbents went on to do and whether they did it with the blessing of the interviewers or not.

The No-No

Don't give an answer that reveals hopelessly unrealistic expectations – don't aim to be somewhere further up the career ladder very much sooner than most others have made it. Don't say that in five years' time you want to be doing the interviewer's job (it happens). The key is that the interviewer wants confidence and ambition, not unbridled cravings for success, which suggest you will cut corners to get where you want to be. Nor do they want someone who will stagnate for the next five years. The key to success is endless forward movement and you need to indicate that is your understanding as well.

THE QUESTION
Tell us about your hobbies and interests.

Variations
What are your extra-curricula activities? How do you spend your evenings or weekends and how, for example, will that affect the on-call rota?

Analysis
They want to know that you have a healthy balance in your life but this is also a sneaky way of finding out more about you. For example, if you run the local amateur dramatic society, it reveals that you have the kind of organizational skills that mean you can probably handle their dream of reorganizing their department or clinics. If you do volunteer work for a local charity it suggests you have strong moral values in your life and won't fiddle the results for the accounts investigation.

The Answer
Show that you can successfully juggle a variety of tasks, work and other goals by indicating not just that you have hobbies and outside interests but that you exhibit real talent or achievement in them as well. Many a candidate has swung an interview his or her way by revealing they tried for the British Olympic team in their 'hobby' sport. People who have the kind of energy to play tennis on a floodlit court after work for a couple of hours are unlikely to get exhausted by a long day in the office.

The No-No
Don't mention your predilection for pub crawls, or your membership of the Legalize Cannabis Campaign, your chairmanship of the local Young Conservatives, Hunt Saboteurs, Anarchists for Gay Wales or the local Real Ale Society. Don't list a series of hobbies that show you have moved from one to another over a period of time, indicating you can't settle or focus on anything.

THE QUESTION
Tell us your worst quality.

Variations
If you could change one aspect of your personality what would it be? Tell me the worst decision you ever made.

Analysis
This question leads to bluff and counter-bluff in the poker game that is the psychology of the interview. Most candidates realize how dangerous it is to relate some weakness that is vital to the job – like having difficulty getting on with others when teamwork is essential. But the interviewer wants to see how honest you can still be about yourself, given you have to negotiate the minefield of not shooting yourself in the foot. The key thing this question is in fact getting at is how self-aware are you – how objective can you be about yourself? Can you see faults or are you blind to your weaknesses? How then are you going to take feedback when you start the job and they need you to realize that you have to change in some way?

The Answer
There are really only three kinds of weaknesses you can fairly safely identify: firstly, those that everybody has – as long as in mentioning them you don't suggest you have them worse than anyone else. Secondly, weaknesses that are entirely irrelevant to the job. And thirdly, weaknesses that you identified you had in the past, but which you have subsequently cured. A good answer might be that when you are very very tired you can forget the need to take a short break (who doesn't?). Another is that in the past at medical school, if you are applying for a medical job, you used to procrastinate a bit before getting down to revising but you have since learned your lesson. Although you hastily add that your previous procrastination habit wasn't so

bad that it meant you ever failed anything, and that as you hated having to work so hard just before an exam now you prepare well in advance.

The No-No

Remember that whatever weakness you identify the interviewer will realize there are probably three other worse ones you kept to yourself. So please don't pick your actual worst quality and describe it in detail – the interviewer will merely assume things are much worse than that, and that you chose to reveal the least dangerous aspect of your various vulnerabilities.

A new job may be the exact thing you need in your career right now, but the problem is most of us are psychologically very conservative when it comes to considering change of employment. We prefer the security of staying put, and the certainties it brings with it, compared to the unknown hazards of a new workplace or different employer. We rationalize to ourselves that things are bad here, but it's probably just as terrible everywhere else, so we might as well stay put. Or we hope things are going to get better shortly, which is why we linger in dead-end jobs.[20]

The danger is if we are no longer enjoying our work, or developing our careers through the current job, then it could be we are heading for burn-out. Or if we are not adding to our value to future employers in what we are doing now at best we are gradually slipping behind in the competitive race that career advancement is. It might be that your current job is not just boring or upsetting you – which could be impinging on your mental health and that of your family – but it could be damaging your career prospects in the long run. So how do you know when it's time to change jobs?[21]

In fact, often we have overstayed our welcome in a job and are secretly hating it, but haven't consciously realized this, because things have deteriorated so gradually we failed to notice we don't get the buzz from work we used to.

The clues that it's time to think about changing jobs start with how avoidant you are of work – for example, do you head home at the first sign of a little sniffle or sneeze? Do you take a lot of time off sick? Do you find any excuse not to make it in, like transportation disruptions or bad weather? An extremely good test is how often – if ever – you have decided to go home in the middle of the working day because of feeling ill or some other pretext. Most people, if they genuinely like their work, turn up relentlessly, and in particular never leave once they have arrived at work, unless of course we are talking about a genuine emergency.[22]

Often avoidance of work can present in subtle ways – for example, do you volunteer for assignments that will take you out of the office and help you avoid a lot of work? A lot of business travel is in fact an evasion – to avoid being at work because the office is hated so much. Perhaps you tend to assign yourself tasks that will ensure you spend a lot of time travelling between depots and so are in the car rather than having to sit at the desk.

Perhaps you welcome disruptions to work as when machinery breaks down, and at one extreme maybe you sabotage work so that you are given a break from time to time.

Even if you appear to be at work, are you really avoiding it? Do you not turn your phone off voice-mail or check your emails until quite late in the day? Do you try to lie low and ensure people don't realize you are at work and start giving you things to do? The key question here is how involved are you with your work? Do you find those enthusiastic people at meetings puzzling and perhaps irritating? Do you sit in meetings watching the clock and not making any contribution at all? Do you have no interest whatsoever in the organization's clients? In fact, any of these could be a sign that you have become too detached from work.[23]

One subtle but reliable test of how engrossed you really are with your work is how well you know your work colleagues. If their personal lives are a complete mystery to you, then it is likely you consciously or unconsciously spend little time with them because you are so keen to get away from work and this translates into not caring for them.

For those who are really engrossed and enjoying their jobs, the team they are working with becomes almost a second family to them – can you say that about your workmates? Sometimes your scorn for colleagues is actually an unconscious hatred for work. But maybe at this stage you think to yourself, so I hate my work, doesn't everybody? Does it matter?

It's vital to be honest with yourself about how much you enjoy your job so you can begin to think about change. If you are disgruntled, it is probably the case that your employers or colleagues have noticed. You may not realize that they actually know you hate your job.[24]

The problem then is that you become a target for 'downsizing' or redundancy if the firm hits a difficulty. The advantage of knowing before your employer does that you hate your job is it gives you the chance to start looking for new and better work while you still have a job, rather than having to pound the streets as one of the unemployed. Future employers are always much more impressed if you are moving jobs – because this looks as if it's your active decision to choose them – rather than asking for work when you don't have any.[25]

SHOULD YOU CHANGE YOUR JOB?

CAREER INVOLVEMENT SCALE

Each statement is followed by two possible responses: agree or disagree. Read each statement carefully and decide which response best describes how you feel. Then tick the corresponding answer. Please respond to every statement. If you are not completely sure which reply is more accurate, put the one which you feel is most appropriate. Do not read the scoring explanation before filling out the questionnaire. Do not spend too long on each statement. It is important that you answer each question as honestly as possible.

		AGREE	DISAGREE
1	I enjoy thinking about my career during my leisure time	A	B
2	There is no point doing any extra training for my job as it is usually irrelevant	B	A
3	I like solving problems thrown up by my job even when not at work	A	B
4	I stick to my point of view at work, regardless of what others then think of me	B	A

		AGREE	DISAGREE

5 I am more up to date on the latest advances linked to my work than most of my colleagues

      AGREE: **A**   DISAGREE: **B**

6 I throw away without reading most of the material sent to me by management

      AGREE: **B**   DISAGREE: **A**

7 What the managers think of me is important to me

      AGREE: **A**   DISAGREE: **B**

8 I have many strengths which are not relevant to my current career

      AGREE: **B**   DISAGREE: **A**

9 Others ask my advice when it comes to advancing themselves in my type of career

      AGREE: **A**   DISAGREE: **B**

10 There is no point in volunteering for extra work – it doesn't get you anywhere

      AGREE: **B**   DISAGREE: **A**

Score

Add up your score by totalling the number of As and Bs you have ticked.

More than 8 As: You are scoring very high indeed on being involved in a career that is almost perfect for your personality and interests. You are likely to have advanced further than most people in your line of work given the time you have been involved in this career and this is partly because you have a clear sense of the need to play politics as well as work hard in order to get on. You are so involved with your career, however, it is possible that your leisure and family life suffer as a result.

Between 5 and 7 As: You are scoring above average on being in the right career for your interests; however there are aspects of the job that you don't like and that lower your motivation from time to time. You need to think about whether you really are pre- pared to do all that is required to advance to the very top or whether you are satisfied with where you are now. You might need to learn to like to do the things, like boring administration, that others feel are essential to doing the job properly.

Between 2 and 4 As: Although you are scoring around average to just below average for personally identifying strongly with your career, it could be that there were times in the past when you had stronger drive and determination. This might be because things have happened to sap your drive recently. These may not all be linked to work itself. Whatever has happened you need to question now whether the apparent goal at the end of your career is alluring enough to provide the drive to help overcome obstacles along the way.

Between 0 and 1 A: You are scoring very low on personal involvement in your career and this means that you might be just doing this current job while strategically waiting for developments elsewhere that will lead to what you really want to do. Whatever the reason, it is likely that you don't enjoy the nine-to-five aspect of your life at the moment and need to ask whether the stress of work is pulling down your enthusiasm for the rest of life. It could be you will start to enjoy your life more when work is more attuned to your own interests. Perhaps you should seriously consider changing career.

10

MONEY, MONEY, MONEY

That's the thing about money – it makes you do things you don't want to do

From *Wall Street*, an Oliver Stone film

Money makes people listen. When you have it, then you have something others want and need. When you don't you become invisible

Earl G. Graves

When you go to a fairground clairvoyant they often offer to read your palm, but it now seems, thanks to recent scientific research into personality, that they should really offer to peek inside your wallet and read that instead. For it has now been established that the contents of your purse are as revealing about you as if you spilled all the beans on the analyst's couch.

You may not realize just how much we reveal about our personality through our attitudes to money, saving and spending, but current research has established that, for example, the number of credit cards you have is deeply predictive of many other aspects of your life.

Psychologist Celia Hayhoe and colleagues from the University of Kentucky in the USA lately found, in an in-depth study of over 400 people, that those of us with four or more credit cards are less likely to borrow from friends or relatives to meet financial emergencies.[1] We are more likely to prepare a list when shopping, to have had money used as a reward in our family of origin, and we are also more likely to be female.

Those of us with four or more credit cards are particularly likely to spend money because of the pleasure it brings, and this illustrates an issue that is rarely discussed in polite company: that we differ widely psychologically in our view of what money is *for*.[2]

For example, some believe that money should be retained, and these personality types feel guilty when spending and, as a result of this sentiment, frequently have great difficulty making a spending decision.

Others are convinced that money is a source of power, because it gives you autonomy and freedom, helping you to express your abilities and so allowing you to be who you really want to be. These people are likely to endorse the view that those with money are powerful because they attract many friends.[3]

Yet another personality type tends to see money as the main marker of achievement in life – they see assets as a symbol of success and believe that a person's salary reflects his or her intelligence.[4]

On this last point it seems that men and women tend to view money in particularly radically different ways and therefore have a different relationship with it. Men are more likely to perceive money as a source of power while women think of money in terms of the things it can be converted to.[5]

While gender seems to be a major influence on our attitudes to money, previous experience also seems a vital factor. Those who have experienced financial hardship in the past tend to more strongly link the possession of money with how they are judged by others. It seems that if you have undergone psychological distress associated with financial deprivation, this can leave you permanently emotionally scarred. If you feel you have been looked down upon in the past because of lack of money, you tend for ever afterwards to feel that others' assessment of yourself is determined by how much you have.[6]

On the more positive side, previous financial hardship seems to produce more generosity and sharing of financial resources in the future, perhaps because you can better identify with those going through tough times, and so are willing to provide assistance.[7] If it wasn't for this psychological research we might never have become so aware of how our personality is reflected in the way we spend and save, as money, that great taboo, is rarely openly discussed.[8]

But precisely because it isn't talked about, except in the privacy of the bank manager's office or the psychologist's consulting room, many unhelpful myths seem to grow up around money. Perhaps the most unhelpful one seems rather similar to the greatest myth from the other huge taboo of sex: size is everything.

An example of this comes from my own clinic. The identity and details of all the cases in this book have been changed to protect the anonymity of clients.

Bruce was sitting crying in front of me in my clinic at The Maudsley Hospital. He seemed to be in an unusual position. Getting upset when talking to a psychiatrist is not that strange, but Bruce had pulled up in the car park in the latest Porsche and wore a designer suit; yet, despite having all that money could buy, he was thinking of leaving his lucrative job.

To take the story back a step or two, Bruce had left school early without many qualifications and started working as a market stall trader. His father had developed cancer and Bruce had to take over his stall in order to keep his large family, consisting of five younger brothers and sisters, above water financially.

The hours were long but Bruce worked hard and gradually made enough money actually to start saving a bit. He then saw an opportunity to buy into a fleet of ice-cream vans and gradually began building a small business empire.

Then he made friends with some people in the City and eventually landed a job trading for a large merchant bank, despite his lack of qualifications. Soon he was getting the kind of annual bonus that was large enough to cover what most people he was at school with earned over twenty years. Somewhere along the line he found time to get married and have two kids. The long hours never seemed to sap his incredible drive. It was only when he came home one day to find an empty house and a note from his wife saying she had taken the children to her mother's for a trial separation that he woke up to the fact his workaholic lifestyle was destroying his marriage.

Bruce only came to see me because his wife threatened a divorce unless he sought psychological help. At first Bruce found it difficult to see what the problem was. He was furious that despite all he had bought his wife over the years – an enormous engagement ring, several fast cars and a huge house in Essex – she appeared so ungrateful.

Bruce also couldn't see what he could learn from coming to see me. He clearly earned much more than me and surely that meant he knew much more than I ever could about anything that was important?

Bruce was basically a hard-core materialist and this was evident from the fact he viewed the acquisition of wealth and possessions as central to his life, essential for his happiness and crucial in his definition of success. Materialism is now believed by psychologists to be a kind of personality type, a bit like extroverts, and the key feature of the materialist personality is they tend to value financial success significantly more than other life goals such as community, social affiliation or self-acceptance.

Bruce couldn't understand that his wife and children wanted to see more of him and didn't mind if that meant they had to make cut-backs in their otherwise extravagant lifestyle. The problem was that for Bruce financial success was central to his sense of identity.

We traced Bruce's materialism back to his childhood and in particular the grinding poverty of his parents and their tendency to see money as their salvation, given the precariousness of their circumstances. Bruce came to define himself by what he was worth partly because in his childhood he hadn't been given the chance to develop any other sense of identity or self.

Our work together in therapy was to help Bruce see that it was possible to view himself in multiple roles – certainly as a successful trader, but also as a father, a keen football player, a husband and a good friend to his mates down the pub. It was only when Bruce could see that there was more to life than simply devoting his best years and all his intelligence and energy to his employers at the bank rather than to his family that he began to take the risk of slacking off a bit.

Bruce's problem is actually incredibly common amongst high-flyers at work and this is because the chase for the next big pay rise begins to take over their lives. Starting to think about where their career is really going raises troubling fundamental questions.

For example, why exactly do you turn up at work each day? Psychologists argue there are only two basic answers to this question: the first is because you derive some intrinsic enjoyment from the work you do; the second is because you don't actually enjoy what you do that much but you turn up for the money. If your career is driven purely by the pursuit of money the latest research into the link between materialism and unhappiness might make sobering reading.

Materialism is defined by psychologists as comprising (a) a central focus on materialistic acquisitions; (b) belief that materialistic pursuits would enhance happiness; and (c) tendency to define success as based on material possessions.

But the latest research by psychologists LinChiat Chang and Robert M. Arkin of Ohio State University in the USA has found a strong link between materialism and basic unhappiness. No one knows exactly why this is but one theory is that materialists constantly compare how much they have with how much everyone else has and this chronic upward comparison with those doing slightly better than them means that no matter how much they have they never feel satisfied.

Another theory is that materialists haven't developed a strong confident sense of who they are and so try to compensate for this by owning expensive things, which they hope will impress everyone else. Materialists are trying to buy an identity rather than live one through their relationships.

Bruce came to see that his terrible shame of being a member of a poor family led to his current materialism; he hoped that driving a Porsche would impress others and prevent them ever feeling sorry for him.

Bruce eventually traded in the Porsche for something much less ostentatious with which he went to pick up his family and bring them home – he finally understood that the more he possessed, the poorer he was getting in terms of his relationships.

Psychologists Tim Kasser and Virginia Grow Kasser of Knox College in the USA propose that those who strongly value the pursuit of wealth and possessions basically had experiences early in their lives that made them feel rather insecure. As a result, they have difficulties both with their interpersonal relationships and with personal self-esteem.[9]

To investigate this theory they explored whether the dreams of people high and low in materialism differ in the presence of themes relevant to (a) insecurity; (b) poor relationships; and (c) fragile self-esteem.

People who focus on materialistic goals are commonly

thought by many psychologists to have a basic feeling of insecurity about their own worth. Such feelings of insecurity are likely to arise early in life when individuals have experiences that do not support their psychological need to feel close to others and to actualize their 'true selves'.

Kasser and Kasser point out that one of the first developmental tasks children face is learning to feel related and connected to others, while also recognizing that they have perspectives and emotions distinct from their parents. Unfortunately, not all parents support a child's developing autonomy and desire for relatedness.

Such controlling parental styles may lead children to feel relatively insecure about their own value as people. As a way to compensate for this feeling, such individuals may attempt to attain the money and goods that advanced free-market, capitalistic cultures suggest are a means towards security and a measure of success in life.

Kasser and Kasser also argue empirical evidence supports these hypothesized relationships between felt insecurity and materialism. For example, previous research showed that highly materialistic eighteen-year-olds were especially likely to have parents who were non-nurturant (i.e., cold, controlling, non-democratic), a parental style likely to lead to feelings of insecurity. Similarly, people high in materialism were found to be more likely to have divorced parents, an experience that made them feel less loved, and probably less secure.[10]

Feelings of insecurity can also be inculcated through cultural circumstances. That is, cultural experiences that do not support people's attempts to be close to others and to be in charge or their own lives are likely to conduce to high materialism. In this vein, highly materialistic individuals are likely to have been raised in disadvantaged socio-economic circumstances.[11]

In part because of these past experiences that made them feel rather insecure, people with a strong materialistic value orientation may have more difficulty satisfying their psychological need for intimacy and connection to others. That is, the non-nurturant environments that led to their insecurity may also lead such individuals to be rather pessimistic about the chances of positive future relationships, to ignore such desires and deny that they are important, or to use materialistic means as a compensatory strategy to attain at least some marginal satisfaction of their needs.[12]

This proposition is consistent with the popular notion that high materialists are so strongly concerned with the attainment of financial success that they ignore their other needs, to the detriment of their well-being.

Kasser and Kasser believe substantial evidence is supportive of the idea that materialists have more difficulty in their relationships with others. First, studies have found that, compared to those who care less about materialistic pursuits, people strongly oriented towards materialism do not view interpersonal relationships as very important.[13] Other research confirms that the relationships they do have are likely to be shorter and less satisfying. What's more, data reveals that people who espouse materialistic goals also tend to stereotype, objectify and manipulate other people, none of which is likely to improve their relationships.

The problematic relationships materialistic individuals experienced early in life, and continue to experience, may also impact their view of their 'worth' as a person. People with a strong materialistic value orientation will probably have two types of problems with their self-esteem. First, they are likely to have somewhat lower self-esteem or more frequent negative views of their own abilities and capacities. Second, they are likely to have a contingent sense of self-esteem, in which their sense of worth is dependent on external accomplishments and praise rather than a deep-rooted feeling of believing in themselves.[14] As a result, their sense of personal worth is unstable and fragile, being easily buffeted about by external circumstances.

In support of these claims, people with a strong materialistic value orientation also report low self-esteem. Additionally, materialistic individuals are strongly concerned with competition and rewards and are more ego-involved in their behaviour, both of which are signs of having a contingent self-esteem. Further, the idealized images materialistic individuals frequently view in commercials are likely to make them less sure of their own worth and less satisfied with their lives.[15]

As a means of complementing and validating previous research, psychologists Tim Kasser and Virginia Grow Kasser of Knox College in the USA set out to analyse and compare the dreams of people high and low in materialistic tendencies.[16] Freud's breakthrough work, *The Interpretation of Dreams* (1900), was among the first to suggest the importance of dreams in understanding personality and psychopathology, and the psychoanalytic approach remains the best-known way of interpreting and understanding dreams.[17]

Basic to a Freudian viewpoint are the ideas that all dreams represent a (typically sexual) wish fulfilment and that a distinction must be made between the surface, manifest content of the dream and its underlying, latent content (which can be understood only by free association).[18]

Although other thinkers have agreed that dreams provide an informative way to understand individuals' personalities, not everyone shares all of Freud's beliefs, and the distinction between manifest and latent content is often ignored or questioned.[19]

Kasser and Kasser's view is that dreams represent the attempt of the sleeping mind to integrate a variety of different experiences, memories, feelings and thoughts; as such, dreams are likely to express strong motivations, conflicts and emotions to which an individual may not always have conscious access.[20]

Although the distortion and symbolism in dreams can sometimes make their meaning seem rather opaque without reliance on esoteric knowledge of symbolic meanings, Kasser and Kasser believe the basic story of a dream may be unravelled in a way that sheds light on many important personality dynamics of the dreamer.[21]

Although subjects may distort their dream reports in order to avoid embarrassment or to look better to others, the dream itself is created at a time when higher level cognitive processes are essentially inactive; as a result, some material that the dreamer would consciously censor may still make its way into both the dream and the dream report, yielding a deeper look inside the person's psyche.[22]

Because dreams occur in a unique brain state, they speak a language especially likely to present issues important to the individual dreamer (regardless of whether the individual later pays attention to these issues).[23] Thus, by studying dreams, researchers have the opportunity to learn a great deal about people's personalities and issues which they may otherwise be unable or unwilling to share.[24]

Kasser and Kasser's study of materialists compared to non-materialists found that dreams with themes of insecurity were easily the most prevalent type reported in the two groups, with frequent mention of being attacked by people, monsters, animals and even vegetables.[25] Indeed, on the surface, there appeared to be no obvious difference between the frequency of such dreams for people high and low in materialism. However, a closer and more subtle examination of dreams in which danger was a prominent theme revealed three important distinctions.[26]

First, people high in materialism were more likely to report falling in their dream reports (5 vs. 1 for low materialists). Falling is one dream symbol interpreted by many theorists as representing a feeling of insecurity, as there is nothing to hold on to while one falls, one is out of control of one's own destiny, and one is heading downward. Further, falling may even represent some of the earliest worries of the young infant, especially as it begins to toddle about.[27] Falling was represented in a variety of different ways among those high in materialism.

A second way in which themes of insecurity were more prevalent in the dreams of those high in materialism was their frequent mention of death in either their dreams or their associations with the dreams. Seven people high in materialism either encountered death in their dreams or associated death with a dream, while this was true for only one person low in materialism.[28]

Death for many people is the ultimate insecurity. It represents such great loss, is so uncontrollable, and is so inherently inconceivable that some have viewed anxiety about death as the fundamental motivation governing personality.[29]

The final notable difference concerning insecurity was a tendency on the part of people low in materialism, not seen at all in their counterparts (0 vs. 6), to reframe what was originally seen as dangerous as actually not so.[30]

That is, while many subjects were frequently confronted with dangerous situations in their dreams and often felt scared by these situations, a substantial number of people low in materialism were able to see the scary situation as not so scary or dangerous.[31]

Kasser and Kasser's theory suggests that one of the several important reasons why highly materialistic individuals feel insecure about their worth is that in their development they were exposed to interpersonal situations that were non-nurturant.[32] People low in materialism, on the other hand, were more likely to have been raised in environments of love and autonomy support.[33]

Materialism is a classic two-edged sword when it comes to motivation. It clearly is highly motivating – but like a lot of pathological motivations, it takes the form of an itch that can never be fully scratched. The materialistically motivated will never achieve real fulfilment because the key goal – a psychological need which requires addressing – will never be met by material possessions.

11

SEE YOU AT THE TOP

*You can have everything in life if you will just help others
to get what they want*

Zig Ziglar

*If you are willing to have people not like you, you will go
far*

Chin-Ning Chu

If you stop and think for a minute, the chances are that you will
say that the people you know who are the most successful, and
enjoy life the most, are those who 'have a way' with other
people. Everyone hungers for appreciation and acceptance. If
you can genuinely provide these things you will have the key to
human influence.[1]

So if you want to motivate others, if you want them to do
something for you, a useful tactic is to ask them to help you
think about how to do it. This makes them feel appreciated for
their brain, not just their brawn, and they will be motivated to
demonstrate their intelligence. Let someone know you think
they can achieve something they had not thought of themselves,
and they will – because you have gone down a route of inspiration rather than persuasion.[2]

The evidence is that one of the intrinsic reasons why we do
things is to obtain not so much financial reward but social
rewards – like praise and admiration from those around us.[3]

While most of the psychology advice emphasizes the necessity
of boosting and protecting the self-esteem of one's personal and

231

professional partners, people often criticize or downplay the achievements of their spouse, child, colleague, co-author, subordinate or teammate.[4]

Such 'ego bashing' may reflect *battles for dominance*: by lowering another's self-confidence, an individual may gain real authority within the relationship, enabling her to steer joint decisions or projects in a preferred direction. This generally comes at a cost, however, namely the risk of demotivating the partner from exerting effort.[5]

There are two related forms of ego bashing: one is 'by omission', where your partner omits to report news favourable to yourself; the other is active 'disparaging', in which your partner explicitly belittles you. While both strategies lower your self-confidence, the first one is reversible (the news can always be revealed later on), whereas the second is not.[6]

We have suggested one powerful psychological tactic by which to try to get on with others and reduce conflict, which is to understand and supply their emotional or psychological needs.

However, what happens when their needs are in direct conflict with your own? A good analogy of this situation is what happens when we battle with our children. A child may want to stay up late while a parent may desire them to retire early. An appeal to meeting the child's emotional needs is unlikely to be met at this moment as this is in opposition to the parents'.[7]

Another strategy needs to be adopted and this can be most loosely referred to as 'consequences'. First we need to understand how this works with children before learning to apply it to adults.

One of the commonest problems parents come to me with, often in great distress, is the issue of 'difficult children'. 'Difficult children', generally speaking, refers to disobedience and a tendency to relentlessly behave in a way that parents have repeatedly explained is undesirable – so these children often don't appear to listen.[8]

Actually, the root cause of the problem of 'difficult children' is captured in the very phrase itself. Most child psychiatrists and psychologists when referred 'difficult children' tend to see the parents as well and work with the whole family in order to bring about changes.[9]

They do this because the location of the fundamental problem is very rarely only in the child – which is what most frustrated parents believe. The real location of the predicament is in the relationship that has evolved over time between the parents and the child. This is because all human behaviour (and yes that includes your children's) occurs very simply because of consequences. Consequences are what flows or follows on from a behaviour. Theoretically if something negative tends to happen after you do something you usually stop doing it and instead perform a behaviour that has more positive consequences.[10]

At this point most parents cry out in despair that they have indeed punished their child inexorably and yet the awful behaviour continues. But when you examine what the consequences are for a piece of naughty behaviour from a child you often discover that positive consequences flow. For example, parents often give a naughty child much more attention than they do one who is behaving well. Even if the attention is in the form of an irritated parent, to many children this is better than no attention at all.

Also the difficult child usually finds that their 'difficult' behaviour causes their parents so much stress that the parents tend to capitulate in order to achieve a quiet life. So parents may give chocolate treats or succumb to other demands because they are terrified of the consequence, i.e., the difficult behaviour.[11]

At the heart of much parental despair over the difficult child is the brutal fact that there is often a power struggle between 'us' and 'them', and 'they' (the children) have often won by the time the exhausted parents come to see me. This is because the consequences the parents feel they can mete out on a child as a result of naughty behaviour are not as aversive as the consequence the child can mete out on the parent. In that situation, when you cannot produce a consequence the child would rather avoid, you are going to suffer from endemic naughtiness.

So the key to dealing with a 'difficult child' revolves around producing immediate and consistent consequences to their bad behaviour that they would much rather avoid, but crucially, combining this with positive consequences when the child generates better behaviour. Part of the problem is exhausted parents are not as positive to their difficult children when the child is good – tending instead to be so relieved to have a quiet period that they stop interacting with the child at that moment.[12]

To start producing change in a difficult child we need to

introduce the idea of clear communication. It is very important that the behaviours that are targeted for reduction are very concretely defined: for example, hitting means striking someone else with the hand or an object, coming home late means arriving home any time after 5.00 p.m.

Also it should be explained clearly why these behaviours are undesirable. This is vital because positive discipline involves teaching how to generalize – you want your child to work out for themselves why approval and disapproval tend to flow from certain behaviours. This reduces the amount of parental effort involved in having to tell your child off for every new situation.[13]

If you have clearly communicated the issue and your child remains disobedient we come to the consequences you need to now introduce. The most favoured consequence parents use is a telling-off, but this is unlikely to work if you find yourself using it all the time without any benefit. You need to change tactic and use your imagination to come up with some other more effective consequences.

The most effective consequence advocated by child psychologists and psychiatrists is 'time-out', meaning that your child goes to a pre-determined spot in the home and remains there for a set period without any stimulation or attention from the outside world.[14]

The time-out area should be easily accessible, and in such a location that the child can be easily monitored while in time-out. For example, if most activity takes place on the first floor of the house, the time-out area should not be on an upper floor. A chair in the corner of the dining room is an excellent spot.

When a child is told to go into time-out, a parent should only say, 'Time-out for . . .' and state the particular offence. There should be no further discussion. Then use a kitchen timer with a bell. Set the timer for the length of the time-out and tell the child he or she must stay in time-out until the bell rings. Placing the kitchen timer on the table is a good way to keep the child informed of how much time he has left to serve. While in time-out, the child should not be permitted to talk, and the parent should not communicate with the child in any way. The child also should not make any noises, such as mumbling or grumbling. He or she should not be allowed to play with any toy, to listen to the radio or stereo, watch television or bang on the furniture. Any violation of time-out should result in automatic resetting of the clock for another time-out period.[15]

If time-out isn't working because of a failure to observe its rules then a parent needs to escalate to 'response cost'. This means finding something the child likes, and making it unavailable to them as a result of failure to do time-out. Select an activity or object you can take away. Tell the child that until they do the time-out, they will not be able to use the object or engage in the activity. For instance, you can remove the cord from the TV and tell them that they may not watch TV or play a video game until they do the time-out.

Remove privileges or objects that you can control. Make a list of objects or privileges (TV, ride bike, stay up late, go outside and play, etc.). Tell the child that each time the undesirable behaviour occurs, one item will be crossed off the list for that day. Each day the procedure starts again.[16]

The advantages of time-out are that it eliminates a lot of yelling and screaming on the part of the parents. It also increases the probability that parents are going to be consistent about what is going to be punished, when and how.

The child also learns to accept his own responsibility for undesirable behaviour. The parents are not punishing the child; rather the child is punishing himself. The child should be repeatedly told that the parents did not put them in time-out but that the child put themself in time-out.[17]

As a result the child more readily learns to discriminate which behaviours are acceptable and which are unacceptable and begins to learn more self-control.

By keeping a written record of time-outs, parents can see if the procedure is reducing the targeted behaviour. Also, rewards can be tied to receiving only a certain amount of time-outs in a day or a smaller time period.

The key reason parents find focusing on consequences difficult is that they fail to understand a fundamental law of human behaviour, which is that we can't change another person. What we can do is change ourselves and the way we react to others and we then usually find that others (our children) react differently to us and so change because we have changed. Getting our children to change usually has to start with us, according to the Child Development Institute in the USA, founded by Clinical Psychologist Dr Robert Myers.[18]

DISCIPLINE TIPS FOR PARENTS

- Never disagree about discipline in front of the children

- Never give an order, request or command without being able to enforce it at the time

- Be consistent: reward or punish the same behaviour in the same manner as much as possible

- Agree on what behaviour is desirable and not desirable

- Agree on how to respond to undesirable behaviour

- Make it as clear as possible what the child is to expect if he or she performs the undesirable behaviour

- Make it very clear what the undesirable behaviour is. It is not enough to say, 'Your room is messy.' *Messy* should be specified in terms of exactly what is meant: 'You've left dirty clothes on the floor, dirty plates on your desk, and your bed is not made.'

- Once you have stated your position and the child attacks that position, do not keep defending yourself. Just restate the position once more and then stop responding to the attacks

- Remember that your behaviour serves as a model for your children's behaviour

- If one of you is disciplining a child and the other enters the room, that other person should not step in on the argument in progress

- Reward desirable behaviour as much as possible by verbal praise, touch or something tangible such as a toy, food or money

- Both of you should have an equal share in the responsibility of discipline as much as possible

Now how do we extrapolate these tips to dealing with adults? Very simply, assume any adult with whom you want to improve your relationship is not a thinking mature person, but instead a child. You can use the same techniques. You are not going to be able to admonish an adult in the same way as children – but you can use 'contingency management' in precisely the same way. When it comes to adults, you can invoke negative consequences for undesirable behaviours and positive consequences for behaviours you prefer.[19]

This is using motivational theory to enhance your relationships.

However, there is a balance to be struck and it is also the case that when dealing with adults you should bide your time and understand that there are a group of people who are intolerant and impatient of others' differences. For these people, relationships become extremely stressful.

You have either met them or you are one yourself: control freaks – people who attempt to control those around them in order to relentlessly get their way. Even if you are not a control freak yourself the likelihood is your life is profoundly affected at work, or in intimate relationships, by a controlling person.[20]

Previously, those who appeared to need to be in control, who would prefer jobs, for example, where they were the ones who made key decisions, were thought to be much happier than those who have what psychologists call a 'low desire for control' over their lives. Control freaks are also more likely to be found at the senior level of most organizations because they appear to rise to the top (Tony Blair has been accused by critics of being the ultimate control freak).

Control freaks rise to the top because being in control of your life means you are more assertive when things do not go your way, so you are less likely to accept it when others try to control you to their own ends. A woman high in desire for control, for example, would be much less likely to accept her male partner neglecting her, deciding where they go on holiday or controlling the finances.[21]

Obviously being a bit of a control freak would make you more difficult to live with, as such control rapidly becomes oppressive, compared to someone who more passively gave up control. Relationship therapists argue that the issue of who is in control lies at the root of most relationship conflict.

Indeed the famous 'Bridget Jones Syndrome' of successful, attractive people in their thirties and forties being unable to settle down with someone could be due to an inability to relinquish control over one's life that a relationship inevitably entails, compared to the complete control of singledom. The problem is the longer one stays single the more difficult it is to stop being such a control freak.[22]

Now psychologists conclude that being a controlling person is great as long as things are going your way. But as soon as the unpredictable occurs or you suffer setbacks it would appear that you do much worse than others because you find it difficult to cope when things are beyond your control. Yale University psychiatrists recently found that being a control freak makes you three times more likely to suffer a serious depression in the face of an adverse life event, like a failure at work or a relationship breakdown. Other research has also found that control freaks when under stress are much more likely to develop heart disease.

The key difficulty controlling people have arises when they are faced with situations that psychologists describe as 'effort–reward' imbalance. In other words, where you put in a lot of effort but get much less reward than you were expecting, or none at all. Control freaks work hard because they assume they will be rewarded for their effort. The trouble is life is not that predictable, and often there is little relationship between the amount of effort you put in and what you get back, yet control freaks have never understood this, and can't stand it.[23]

Recent research by psychologists Ann Zak and colleagues working in New York confirms that control freaks blame their partners more when things go wrong in a relationship. The control freak reasons they themselves have been working hard to make things succeed, so it can't be their own fault when they don't. As a result, there tends to be much more conflict in relationships where a control freak is one of the partners. Compromise is difficult for a control freak because their need for control partly appears to arise out of a strong sense they are right and everyone else is wrong.

Control-freak research even holds out the promise of finally getting to the bottom of some puzzling behaviour, like the person who refuses to accept that a relationship is over, and persistently stalks or pesters their former partner. It would appear that control freaks cannot bear the loss of control apparent in the fact that others can leave them, and are trying to reassert their control by endeavouring to get the person back. If anyone is going to leave, it should be the control freak's decision not anyone else's. So beware if you are in a relationship with someone who is very controlling – it is likely that person won't accept it if you want to end the relationship in the future.[24]

Even more intriguing is the recent finding by psychologists that control freaks tend to increase their controlling behaviour when they are under stress. This is because when they find themselves losing control in one sphere of life – say due to increased stress at work – they tend to compensate by increasing their control of their partner. Or vice versa – it could be your boss's increased need to control his or her office reveals a recent loss of control in their personal relationships.

Research on control freaks has even suggested that women are more likely to be control freaks in intimate relationships while men are more likely to be control freaks at work. This controversial finding has been suggested to be theoretically because women need to compensate for their sense of less control in the domain outside the home, as they tend to be found in more subservient work than men. Or perhaps to compensate for their sense of loss of control over their lives when they start a family.[25]

Another intriguing finding is that control freaks seem to get lost in a vicious spiral of control and stress. This is because they try to deal with stressful relationships by exerting yet more control, which just produces more stress in the relationship leading to more attempts to control. This continues until the control freak loses their temper in a final attempt to regain control of the situation. So paradoxically those we know who are most prone to completely 'lose it' and appear out of control through rage are in fact most likely to be control freaks unable to cope with not always getting their way.

But where do all the problems of being a control freak come from? Are they made or is it genetic? The answer seems to be a bit of both – most controlling people have had controlling parents, but the surprising finding is that control freaks have often had over-protective parents who cushioned them from learning how chaotic and uncontrollable life can be.[26]

ARE YOU A CONTROL FREAK?

Each statement is followed by two possible responses: agree or disagree. Read each statement carefully and decide which answer best describes how you feel. Then tick the corresponding reply. Please respond to every statement. If you are not completely sure which response is more accurate, put the answer that you feel is most appropriate. Do not read the scoring explanation before filling out the questionnaire. Do not spend too long on each statement. It is important that you answer each question as honestly as possible.

		AGREE	DISAGREE
1	I like to keep tabs on what my partner is up to when I am not around	A	B
2	I find it easy to see other perspectives even when they are different from my own	B	A
3	I don't approve of the way my partner spends money and they know it	A	B
4	I don't mind if my partner is innocently socializing with members of the opposite sex	B	A
5	A lot of what others tell you simply isn't true	A	B
6	When I get what I want it is usually because I have been lucky	B	A
7	I can feel claustrophobic when sharing deep intimacy	A	B
8	It is never wise to plan too far ahead as the future is mostly unpredictable	B	A

		AGREE	DISAGREE

9   I often question others a lot before
accepting their version of events   A   B

10   Success in life depends on the luck
of being in the right place at the
right time   B   A

Score

Add up your score by totalling the numbers of As and Bs you have ticked.

8 or more Bs: You are definitely not a control freak; if anything it might be you who are being pushed around a bit by a control freak, either at home or at work. It could be that some previous significant but often unpleasant relationship was with a control freak and it has rendered you traumatized or intimidated by control freaks. You would do well to learn a bit more about their psychology in order to understand how to deal with them, rather than avoiding them as you perhaps tend to at the moment.

Between 6 and 7 Bs: You appear to be scoring average or below average for being a control freak, but there are some areas where you like to exert a lot of control – perhaps the finances or the domestic arena. It could be you don't trust others much in those areas, or you or your family have had some kind of problem in the past with one of these issues, which has left you very protective of your sway in this domain.

Between 4 and 5 Bs: There are times when you are such a control freak you make others wonder why they bother with you at all, but these occasions are usually linked to periods of strain in your life. As you can be very considerate at other times, others are willing to forgive your rigidities, but beware in the future: particularly if you are given enough rope by those around you, you could increasingly become over-controlling and could be gradually learning to control others via their insecurities, which will make you successful but disliked.

Between 0 and 3 Bs: You are scoring very high on being a control freak, and this could be an extremely ominous sign as the psychological research suggests people scoring this high might be prone to eventually using escalating aggression in order to keep getting their way. You are such a control freak others in relationships with you probably spend much of their time trying to ensure everything in your life is as you want it – so much so that they have stopped living their own lives as they would like.

WHAT YOU SHOULD DO IF YOU OR YOUR PARTNER IS A CONTROL FREAK

It is important to realize that despite their often aggressive and assertive exterior, at their core control freaks are rather insecure individuals. Part of the urge to control their partners stems from a fear of losing control, and therefore losing their partner altogether. In fact, control freaks are often the more dependent person in a relationship. Having spent so long and dispensed so much emotional energy getting others to behave in a way that is acceptable to them (e.g., by exerting control), they are terrified at the prospect of having to go through that all over again with a new partner. So although they might appear to leave others out of their plans for much of the time, in fact they would be very upset if they were abandoned.[27]

Often when people break up with a control freak, it is the control freak who comes crawling back, unable to cope outside the relationship. Remembering this is vital in dealing with a control freak, because otherwise you could have got so used to being controlled that you underestimate your own power in the relationship.

The very fact there are things in life that will drive your control-freak partner crazy if they are not 'just so' is your greatest weapon in wresting control from them. You should make it clear that you will stop co-operating with their need for control in areas of life most important to them, unless they concede some control to you in areas that are important to you.[28]

(1) Find out why it is so important to the control freak to get their way in the areas control appears most ridiculous. If you are the control freak ask yourself what you really fear will happen if you don't get your way. The answer will reveal an insecurity that needs confronting, as avoiding it is what is producing the controlling behaviour.

(2) Consider the real as opposed to imagined consequences of others or yourself not getting their or your way. Are these

consequences really worse than the corrosive effect of being a control freak?

(3) Point out to a control freak all the areas in life where you tolerate not getting your own way. If you are the control freak, recall times when things didn't go as you wished and think whether the imagined disaster really transpired.

(4) If you are a control freak allow others more control in one area in exchange for you getting more control where you need it most.

(5) Ultimately a control freak needs to tolerate imperfection. Get your control freak (or yourself if you are the one with the problem) to give up control and accept imperfection at least once every day.

Of all the things that can happen to your marriage or relationship, the most disrupting is extramarital sex. This is the most cited cause of divorce all around the world. Anguish, psychological pain, depression, anger and humiliation are among the many disturbing and very emotional experiences of the partner of someone who has been unfaithful.[29]

The latest psychological surveys suggest that there is a 40–76% probability that one member of a married couple will have an affair over the course of a marriage. What's more, what is now emerging from the most recent psychological research into couples' lives is that women in particular may have fundamentally misunderstood why a male partner goes off to have an affair.[30]

Women tend to believe that men stray because they are seeking exciting sex. Indeed, women are more likely than men to forgive an extramarital fling, because they rationalize to themselves that it was 'just something physical' and there was no 'emotional' involvement.

However, a new study by psychologists David Buss and Todd Shackelford from the University of Texas turns this female view of what men want on its head. They point to a survey by *Playboy* magazine that found that while women were more likely to have a fling because they were dissatisfied with the sex in a marriage, there was no link between the quality of marital sex and whether a man was unfaithful.

Intrigued by these findings, Buss and Shackelford conducted their own survey of over a hundred married couples, probing the reasons for infidelity. Astonishingly they found that more women than men said that in the future they were likely to flirt with others, engage in a passionate kiss, or have a one-night stand, a brief fling or even a serious affair.[31]

Consistently, the women overestimated the likelihood that the men would do these things. In other words, married women are convinced that the men in their lives are much more preoccupied about sex and likely to have a fling because of lust than the evidence suggests men actually are.

Women should perhaps pay particular attention to the fact men rated problems with love and affection in the marriage as much more likely to lead to a serious affair than dissatisfaction with marital sex. Oddly enough, it was the other way round for the women – dissatisfaction with marital sex was more predictive of a future serious affair than problems over love and affection in the marriage.[32]

So it seems that, while it is undoubtedly useful to ensure a man is happy in bed, it is even more important to pay attention to the emotional intimacy of the relationship, and to be sure that he feels loved and cherished.

Even more fundamentally, the study suggests that women, who usually pride themselves as the emotional experts in a relationship, may be seriously over-confident in their judgement of their ability to read the minds of their male partners.

A review of the latest scientific research has uncovered four key areas where a woman is most likely to misunderstand the male mind. It's in these domains she needs to improve her grasp of what is really going on in her relationship, in order to ensure the alliance has a strong future.[33]

(1) Why does he do that? – It's because he's stressed

If a woman gets together with her best female friends, and she is stressed, then it's likely to soon come out and be dealt with for two major reasons: the friends are likely to notice it or the woman herself will want to talk about it.

With men, however, owning up to being stressed and therefore vulnerable is not part of their competitive culture, so men are often stressed but deal with it in, to women, surprising ways. For example, one recent survey from Leeds University investigated that favourite male pastime: going to a bar for a drink after work. 9.5% said they go to drink alcohol, 5.5% said it was to go to meet women, but an overwhelming 85% said they went in order to relieve stress.[34]

So if you want to know why he does something puzzling like watch the television when there is nothing on worth watching, often the answer is because it's his way of dealing with stress. The key here is for women to see whether his approach to stress is working. If it does for him then best not to interfere with it – as long as it has no ominous future implications like alcoholism or obesity.

The fact that men often like to brood about their problems is often perceived by women as a distancing tactic that makes them feel pushed away from the man's life. Women need to learn to tolerate the male preference for knocking about the cave ruminating. A woman shouldn't interfere too much, but should also let the man know that she wants to be his sounding board, if and when he feels like talking.[35]

(2) For a man, winning isn't everything – it's the only thing

Men often won't read to the kids before bedtime or help with the dish-washing, and to women this is upsetting because it appears to them to be because he is lazy or just doesn't care. Instead what is often happening from the male perspective is that he doesn't feel he does these tasks well – and often women will indeed reinforce this impression by criticizing men as they see them lumbering around trying tentatively for the first time to help with the laundry.

Men like to be praised for doing things well – so for a man one reason he doesn't do something is not that he doesn't want to, but that he doesn't think he does it *well*, and so the activity makes him feel incompetent. Men particularly need to feel competent. They hanker to feel like winners. So to get him to do something, a woman needs to shower a man with praise no matter how disturbing his faltering efforts might appear. This advice counts for double in the bedroom.[36]

(3) He needs to feel he's important

The key social change over the last fifty years, indeed it's nothing less than a revolution, is that women now quite rightly feel they can do anything – be astronauts, run countries and fight in wars.

Women's lib has left men feeling a bit left behind, and in particular men now wonder what exactly they are needed for. Women often radiate a strong sense of independence but the problem with this is it can leave men feeling that they don't play an important role in their partners' achievements or progress through life.

It's vital that a woman makes her man feel that he has been an important part of the successes of her life. The key issue here is termed by marital therapists 'impact' – strong relationships are founded on both sides feeling they have an influence on the other. Women can now be so independent it can leave men feeling they have no real impact on their partners.[37]

(4) Don't attack him for your problems

One of the most intriguing findings from Buss and Shackelford's study involved a concept they termed 'Mate Value Discrepancy'. MVD is not something we like to talk about in polite company, but put simply it's the scientific attempt to quantify what is going on when someone very desirable marries someone much less so. All couples probably vary a little in MVD, and some much more than others (the 'what's *she* doing with *him?!*' couples).

Now when the man was thought much more desirable than the woman in a married relationship, as rated by researchers, although the woman *thought* he had a high chance of having an extramarital affair, he was much less likely to indulge, compared to her estimate. However, when the woman was much more desirable than the man, her chances of having an affair were much higher.[38]

To put it simply, a very attractive woman married to a less attractive man is to be trusted much less than when the attractiveness is distributed the other way round. To put it even more bluntly, desirable men are actually to be more trusted than women think they are.

This has an interesting but profound implication. Many women, because they don't think an attractive man is to be trusted in the long term, opt for a slightly less obviously desirable man, because it makes them feel more secure. However, they then come to resent the fact he is not what they really wanted.[39]

In my experience, at my busy marital therapy clinics at The

Maudsley Hospital, women are more acutely aware of MVD than men are, and tend to make choices they later regret because they go for security early on, but desire becomes more important to them later on.

Putting desire before security is something women often accuse men of, but they could actually learn a thing or too by not dismissing this tactic so out of hand.[40]

Extramarital affairs are common, and the opportunities for them are actually increasing all the time. More women in the workplace means couples spend less time together, plus men have more opportunity because they meet more women at work. And, of course, by being out of the house more women get to meet more men as well.

The latest psychological research suggests that women frequently make a fundamental mistake in their relationships, which it's vital to understand if affairs are to be effectively prevented. The women seem to believe that men are looking for better sex elsewhere, when in fact they are often looking for something more down to earth – a confidante and emotional support. Ironically these were the very things women said they were looking for when they considered an affair! It could even be that men use the sex of an affair as a bit of an excuse to rationalize their less-than-macho need for a listening ear and basic affection.

It would seem that men and women are not so much from different planets as some popular self-help books suggest; indeed this dangerous assumption left unchallenged could actually be the foundation of many an affair.

The key issue here is a misunderstanding of the goals of men by women. By analysing relationships from the standpoint of goals we can gain a deeper understanding of conflict.

TEN STEPS TO STOP WORK RUINING YOUR RELATIONSHIP

(1) *Don't keep competing for who has the more stressful life.* It is easy, when one partner is complaining that work or busy lives are getting in the way of the relationship to argue that you have 'more stress than they do', but your life is not a suffering contest and mutual support is ruined

by your relationship becoming a torment competition. Obviously your stress is major to you but no one else's stress should be more or less important in the overall scheme of things. You can express appreciation of your partner without devaluing yourself, and in fact the best way to elicit support from the other is to nurture them. The problem with couples leading busy lives today is they tend to turn to each other for help without understanding that you still need to give in order to get.

(2) *Don't assume that working hard at the office has no effect on your home life.* Just because you go home or spend time together doesn't mean your work isn't affecting your relationship – the issue is how draining your work is of your emotional and creative energy, and also if you have begun to reserve your dynamism for your career rather than your relationship. Remember you have a limited amount of energy available in a given space of time so regardless of when or where you spend it, drained is drained. Keep some of the best of you for others in your life, not just your boss.

(3) *Even small things you do together are important.* Quality time together does not mean always having a heavy and intense discussion at home – learn to appreciate each other's company whenever you are together by tuning out distractions. For example, when driving together switch off the radio and talk or, for the evening meal, switch off the TV and appreciate each other over the table.

(4) *Don't forget that many truly successful people have home lives too.* It is easy to assume that all achievement must be bought with sacrifices, that succeeding in your career must mean neglecting others in your life. Often it is the fear of not being productive that keeps people from slowing down occasionally or taking care to look after themselves or others close to them. Don't make sacrifices in your home life just for the sake of reassuring yourself if you are insecure about how hard you work. Tackle the insecurity rather than allowing it to unbalance your life.

(5) *Don't let the work 'you' become the home 'you'.* Often the way we have to behave at work in a competitive and aggressive occupational environment is not the most conducive way to conduct relationships at home. In an assertive world outside the home, revealing vulnerability is not the way to get on, yet this is essential in any intimate relationship, as it makes you more approachable. It also allows those close to you to show they love you and want to support you. Try to create a buffering space between home and work; so for example on the journey home from the office mentally prepare to leave the worries of work behind and take on the persona of someone devoted to their family. Learn to change out of work clothes as soon as you get home as one of the rituals whereby you leave work behind once past the front door.

(6) *Be sensitive to when your busyness has hurt others.* When people are close to you they may be loath to fully express to you when your busyness has led you to neglect them. So you may need to encourage them to be more up front about how they would like the relationship to change for the better if you were willing to slow down a bit.

(7) *What makes you a success at work is not what makes you popular at home.* The skills you use at work to get on are the aspects of your personality that are often most concretely rewarded with bonuses and praise, so encouraging you to believe that this is the way to be at home as well. In fact, home life usually requires a contrasting set of social skills, including the abandonment of perfectionism in favour of simply getting on with others. At work, achieving goals often matters more than relationships – but at home the goal becomes the relationship.

(8) *It is easy to feel snared by work, when it is you who has really built the trap.* There is always the temptation to blame work pressures for deficiencies in your home life, but remember these are just excuses and it is vital to take responsibility for your choices, particularly your priorities. Your lifestyle is very much under your control (don't blame your upbringing for this), so you can opt to live

more simply and ensure that pursuing wealth is not your only aim. No one on their deathbed ever wishes they had spent more time at the office.

(9) *Success at work can leave you feeling rusty at home skills.* If you have spent much of your time studying, working or achieving, and little time playing, touching, communicating or loving others, then after a while intimacy becomes an area of relative inexperience for you. Remember, in order to become comfortable with some aspect of human experience you often have to work at it and practise it, but the temptation after you notice you have got rusty is to stick at the things you get rewarded for, like working hard in the office. Be persistent in trying to re-learn those human skills you have neglected for your career success.

(10) *You matter more to your partner for who you are than what you produce.* After a while success in earning more or achieving other rewards from your career like prestige or perks can seduce you into believing that it is these benefits that are what your partner likes in you. In fact, this is hidden low self-esteem at work because soon you come to believe your value lies only in what you can produce rather than who you are. Then you come to believe your actual presence matters less to your partner than the luxuries you bring them from your work achievements. This reinforces workaholic tendencies because you come to believe your relationship will deteriorate if you don't keep bringing home the bacon. No matter how much praise your partner gives you for your achievements, they will always prefer more time with you than simply with your awards on the mantelpiece.

Ten Steps to More Love and Less Competition in your Relationship

(1) *If you know how to love, you know how to listen.* Really listening to someone, not just hearing their words but trying to understand what they are saying,

and so what they truly think and feel, without rushing to judge or lecture, is one of the greatest gifts you can bestow, and is a sign of true love. Included in really listening is the notion of empathy – the ability to not just feel sympathy for another's situation, but also to put yourself in their shoes and so feel what they must be feeling.

(2) *If you know how to love, you know how to remember.* Men in particular frequently don't understand why women get so upset when an important anniversary or birthday slips their mind, and so goes unmarked by a celebration meal, flowers or just a card. Men don't understand why a woman might deduce that such forgetfulness implies lack of love, yet ask these same men how often they have forgotten when United are playing, and they will respond, 'But that's different.' The difference is precisely one of how important these things are in your life. So loving is about remembering what is going on in the other person's life that is important to them, and indicating that you haven't forgotten.

(3) *If you know how to love, you know how to love yourself.* Our relationships with others often reveal our relationship with ourselves, so if we are tough with those who make mistakes we are similarly unforgiving of our own frailties. You can only properly love another when you love yourself, and treating others kindly involves knowing how to be compassionate with yourself. You can only feel you deserve love, proper mature love not dependency based on insecurity, when you have self-respect.

(4) *Love is never giving up on compliments or saying thank you.* It may seem a bit forced to keep complimenting or thanking the person you have clearly decided to spend the rest of your life with, but praise and thanks are a vital way of making others feel worthwhile and valued. Therefore it is crucial in any relationship that is to survive the long term for

compliments and saying thank you to be part of the everyday currency. Your appreciation for others should always be shown, even if you think it is blindingly obvious.

(5) *Love is the ability to say nice things without qualification.* When men are asked by marital therapists to give their wives five compliments there and then in the session, they often take a long time to come up with anything, indicating how much they have got out of the habit of seeing what is good in their partners. Wives, on the other hand, can more easily hand out compliments about their husbands but these often have a critical undertone, for example, 'I like your shirt now you have finally managed to buy something decent for yourself.' Her compliments are barbed – such statements are not truly loving.

(6) *Love can be tough too.* If you know how to love you don't sit by while the person you supposedly care for self-destructs via alcoholism, gambling or relentless weight gain. You do the uncomfortable, difficult thing that others haven't the courage to do, and confront the issue. This means you accept the risk of annoying the other person. The best love is also tough love – the love that has the long-term interests of the other person at heart, not just keeping quiet for short-term benefits. In such a relationship you always know where you really stand and what the other person really thinks because at its base is the security of true love.

(7) *Love is being able to put the other person first.* Many say they first realized what true love was when they finally understood they had met someone they were willing to give up their lives for – someone they were willing to put ahead of themselves in terms of needs. Obviously such a strong and selfless emotion should be reciprocated otherwise this love could be exploited by the psychopathic. So true love is not just being able to put another person first but being cautious with such powerful love to ensure such a gift is properly

recognized for what it is and so will not be abused. At its core, when we talk about putting the other person first, we are really talking about personal sacrifice, and the deepest love is when you are willing to sacrifice what you care for most. So the ambitious man who will make no career sacrifices for his intimate partner is really making a statement about what he truly loves most – his job rather than his woman. Obviously sacrifices should not be demanded of another needlessly, but a good test of whether another person really feels true love for you, when you are deciding who to spend your life with, is to think hard about what sacrifices they have actually made for you, rather than what sacrifices they say they will make for you.

(8) *Love is about forgiveness.* We live in a world where the strong need for revenge when we have been hurt is further encouraged by the suggestion that we all have a right to get even. But often the healthiest thing to do in order to preserve a relationship is to let go of hurt and anger and forgive – otherwise a spiral of hostility ensues. It is easier to do this if you understand that you yourself have had your mistakes forgiven, and mutual forgiveness breeds a deeper love. We all have a need for forgiveness, and the best way to encourage this is through forgiving those who have hurt us, and this is one of the deepest signs of love, precisely because it is so difficult to do. Perhaps one of the simplest and overlooked explanations for our spiralling divorce rates is we have forgotten the vital ability to forgive.

(9) *If you know how to love, you know how to shoulder responsibility.* Once you are involved in a loving relationship you stop living just for yourself and start living for another. This means you have responsibilities towards them – to ensure at the simplest level they are not worried about you if you are late home or, at the most profound, that they will have to grieve for you because you like speeding. When you enter another person's life, if you love them you don't want to be a burden to them, but instead take on the responsibility

of helping their life improve because you are now in it. Taking on this responsibility is why true love is difficult, often painful and certainly not always joyful. The best lovers are therefore not always the most flirtatious people, because they take responsibility sincerely.

(10) *Love is being able to say it.* If you can't say 'I love you' because you are embarrassed or have fallen out of the habit, your discomfort may say something important about your unfamiliarity with this deep, serious and important emotion. But it is important to be able to say 'I love you' or respond when it is said to you, by saying 'I love you too'. These three words are one of the most powerful ways of giving and receiving in a relationship, so don't neglect them.

TEN STEPS TO BEING MORE FORGIVING IN RELATIONSHIPS

(1) *Forgiving helps you to let go of the past and move on with your life.* We tend to think of forgiving as a passive and weak activity, which basically invites others to walk all over us and exploit us, but in fact psychologists now believe the ability to forgive is vital for our mental health. This is because forgiving allows us to move on with our lives and stop constantly seeking revenge whenever others do us wrong. If you constantly seek perfect fairness and justice then you get trapped, being upset at all the inequalities of the world, particularly in respect to yourself, and never get on with the rest of your life.

(2) *Forgiveness values people rather than what they can do for you.* Modern life tends to end up valuing others in terms of what they can do for you. The problem with this perspective is it ensures you never value people for their basic humanity. The ability to forgive means the capacity to see beyond the immediate costs and benefits of relationships, and see into the distant long term

where it may take years for your forgiveness to be returned in terms of good will. Treating people positively, even when they don't warrant it, reveals a profound valuing of them as human beings, which will be reciprocated eventually.

(3) *Forgiving makes you less hostile.* Psychological research has found that those who are less able to forgive score higher on personality measures of simmering resentment and a need to see harm come to transgressors. The problem is all this hostility makes it possible you will end up in trouble with the law, or even get caught picking a fight with someone able to do you more harm. Forgiving will save you getting yourself into a lot of trouble in the long run.

(4) *Forgiveness will save your marriage.* One of the great untold secrets of a long and successful marriage is the mutual ability to forgive – people will always hurt each other in relationships and if someone doesn't start the cycle of forgiving it is easy for retribution to escalate any dispute into a marriage-wrecking one. Remember to forgive your partner because you might need their forgiveness in the future!

(5) *Forgiveness stops you constantly judging others.* If you don't believe in forgiving then you will tend to sit in judgement on everyone else and this leads to a natural sense of superiority, which is much less socially attractive than the humility that accompanies a more forgiving attitude.

(6) *Forgiveness makes you more empathic.* Empathy is the ability to sense what others feel even though you are not in their situation – this vital social skill is really helpful in making others perceive they can open up and get close to you. Those who are empathic tend to be more forgiving, so if you are having difficulty forgiving others this usually means you are incapable of seeing the world from others' standpoints. In particular, you have difficulty making the emotional and intellectual

leap required to see things through others' eyes, and unless you start learning how to do this, then getting close to others will remain a problem for you.

(7) *Forgiving makes you more human.* Once you have been in the position yourself of needing to be forgiven by others, because you have transgressed, indeed once you have experienced the benefit of being forgiven rather than rightly punished, you tend to be more forgiving to others. This means not only that you earn others' gratitude for holding back from punishing them, but you appear more human and less holier-than-thou and self-righteous.

(8) *Forgiveness is good for your health.* There is now a wealth of research evidence that more forgiving people suffer less depression and anxiety, and have increased hope, better self-esteem, better relationships, higher life satisfaction and better physical health as well. No one knows whether the ability to forgive is directly responsible for all these remarkable benefits or if these occur merely because forgiveness implies the absence of hostility. Whatever the reason, if you cannot forgive, you might be more miserable than your enemies and even die before them – what kind of victory is that? No, the best revenge is to be happy.

(9) *Forgiveness doesn't mean having to be a doormat.* A common error is to assume forgiveness means you should let others walk all over you – far from it. Forgiveness does not mean you cannot retaliate when wrong is done to you or do your best to ensure others are warned you will not take being pushed around. However, forgiveness does mean you don't devote a huge amount of your energies to getting precisely even, or hitting back harder than you were hurt in the first place. Aiming to get even is not only very difficult but rarely achieves very much in the long run.

(10) *Forgive not because this helps your enemies but because it assists you.* You are not in the forgiving

business to make life easier for others, you are doing it as a gift to yourself, as this releases you from constantly reliving past hurts until they are compensated for. You will be less afraid of others and life when you learn the capacity to forgive, and the accompanying ability to let hurt go.

12

IS TIME RUNNING OUT?
TIME TO GET AHEAD

Often we are caught in a mental trap of seeing enormously successful people and thinking they are where they are because they have some special gift. Yet a closer look shows that the greatest gift that extraordinarily successful people have over the average person is their ability to get themselves to take action

Anthony Robbins

The unlikely fact that doing more gives you greater energy to achieve more is a timeless success secret

Frank Bettger

The latest psychological research has come up with a novel way of motivating people to support charitable causes – remind them that one day they are going to die.[1]

In the experiment, participants who were walking past a funeral home were randomly assigned to be interviewed by a researcher either directly in front of the funeral home or approximately 150 metres away from it. The funeral home was a brick building with a large sign clearly visible to the pedestrian that read 'Howe's Mortuary'. Another large sign also drew pedestrians' attention to the funeral home as they passed by. The interviewer positioned himself so that the participants were forced to face the front of the building, so that they could clearly see the funeral parlour as they were being interviewed for the study.[2]

The investigators found that those who were interviewed directly in front of the funeral home expressed a much more favourable attitude towards charitable causes than those interviewed three streets away from the mortuary. Reminded, it seems, of their mortality, people judged charitable organizations as more beneficial to society and more desirable to them personally and indicated that society needs charities more.[3]

But just because people become more pro-charity in their attitudes when reminded of their own ultimate demise, does this effect translate into actual giving?

Another related experiment found that if subjects are given money that they can choose to keep or donate, they are more likely to give money to charity after they are reminded of their own deaths. The subjects were asked to 'briefly describe the emotions that the thought of your own death arouses in you' and 'jot down as specifically as you can what you think will happen to you as you physically die and once you are physically dead'.[4]

The researchers who conducted this intriguing and macabre research, a team led by psychologists Dr Ewa Jones based in Munich and Dr Tom Pyszczynski in Colorado, conclude that these studies have practical implications for charities. They argue that the amount of money given to charity could be increased when the request is presented in the context of 'death reminders'.[5]

Before we scoff at this morbid and weird idea, it might be useful to remind ourselves that Charles Dickens, that master psychologist, anticipated this research finding in A Christmas Carol, according to Tom Pyszczynski.[6]

In the story the ghost of Christmas past and the ghost of Christmas present show Ebenezer Scrooge how his cruelty and selfishness have adversely affected his own life and the lives of others. However, it is not until the ghost of Christmas future shows Scrooge a glimpse of his own future, his name inscribed on the head of a tombstone, that his stinginess and greed give way to benevolence and compassion for others. Dickens is telling us that one should value kindness and concern for others over selfishness and material riches, or else die an insignificant and lonely death.

In other words, by doing the right things, Scrooge was able to manage his terror of absolute annihilation. The prospect of death seems to have a uniquely galvanizing way of getting people to re-evaluate their priorities.

This theory is known in modern psychological parlance as 'Terror Management Theory' and it proposes that self-esteem, the belief that one is a valuable person within the context of one's cultural conception of reality, provides protection from the fear of death. Fear of death as a primary motivation in daily life has traditionally not received that much attention, perhaps precisely because we spend most of our time trying to deny this reality.[7]

Existentialists argue that unlike any other organism, human beings possess intellectual capacities that make them painfully aware that one day they will die. This pairing of an instinctive desire for continued life with awareness of the inevitability of death creates the potential for paralysing terror. Psychologists posit that we defend against this terror by creating structures like religion, and the idea that by doing the right things, being moral and helpful to others, we ensure we are needed and valued. This reassures us that life has meaning plus value, and so consists of more than taking in food, expelling waste and temporarily clinging to survival on a clump of rock and dirt hurtling through space.[8]

This theory perhaps explains the puzzle of why in poorer societies, where people are perhaps daily reminded of their own mortality, there is so much more co-operation and charitable behaviour than in richer communities.

But do charities really encourage true and pure altruism if in reminding people of their own mortality they produce more generous behaviour?[9] And if, as Dickens' story and this research suggests, the heightened awareness of one's own inevitable demise encourages the 'Scrooges' of the world to become kinder to at least some of the 'Tiny Tims', should we quibble over the origins of such transformations?

Dickens' Scrooge is offered as a literary metaphor for the phenomenon of vivid, benevolent, yet enduring personal transformation occurring usually over a period of hours. The change involves relationships, spirituality and life priorities. There are usually two kinds of inner change. There is an 'insight' transformation – a consolidation of psychological processes that may have been building for years – and there is a 'mystical' transformation, which individuals are quite at a loss to explain.

These experiences have been collected together in a book called *Quantum Change*, with the book's first author, William Miller, a Distinguished Professor of Psychology and Psychiatry at the University of New Mexico. He received the Jellinek Memorial Award (sometimes called the 'Nobel Prize for research in alcoholism') for his meticulous research on cognitive behaviour methods for helping alcoholics return to controlled drinking. Yet his own eight-year follow-up of these alcoholics revealed that, despite their original behavioural orientation, over the long haul they often turned to abstinence and Alcoholics Anonymous.[10]

Each of the book's case histories, chosen from several dozen quantum change experiences, share many but not all of the following characteristics: ineffability, revelation, transience of the original experience (although the effects last for decades), passivity, unity with the cosmos, transcendence, awe, joy-love-peace and distinctiveness.

Epiphanies and spiritual insights, of course, are common after taking mind-altering drugs, evangelical religious conversion and temporal lobe seizures. They are also common in reports of mystical, 'white light', near-death or 'alien abduction' experiences.

For some of the subjects, changes were much broader than for others, but in all what was changed was 'me', the person's sense of self. Unlike many drug and some mystical and epileptiform experiences, the experiences reported always conveyed a sense of the sacred and a sense of responsibility towards others and the world about them. Even if the subjects didn't believe in God (and two-fifths of them did not), they became more spiritual, less materialistic and more compassionate towards others and themselves.[11] The book's most provocative finding is the uniform decrease in the value placed on 'wealth', 'attractiveness', 'popularity' and 'fitting in' and an increase in 'spirituality', 'personal peace', 'forgiveness' and 'loving'.

A limitation of the book is that not only is its evidence of character change retrospective but the authors also fail to provide corroboration of change by informants. However, since the book purports to be about only subjective experience, this failing is by no means a fatal flaw.[12]

The message of a quantum change came into consciousness with great force and certitude. As one physician reported, 'I can't even try in words to describe what it was like. When you take intravenous morphine you get this sudden euphoric thing . . . but drugs pale in comparison to what this felt like.' The change is also positive and benevolent. A Catholic woman wrote, 'I had a feeling of lightness and exhaustion – and tears . . . I just continued to be more involved in church activities. For example, we regularly go into the Bernalillo county jail for Bible study and to do services . . . I didn't realize that people living in a situation like prison have so much to give me . . . I often get more out of it than I think they do . . . I guess a lot of it had to do with my giving up my own defenses, my intellectualizing about it and letting my emotional side come through.'

But perhaps the unifying effect of these experiences, which often occur near death, and an implication of Terror Management Theory mentioned before, is the notion of taking a longer time perspective than we normally do in our busy lives. When you have been confronted with death and survived, priorities naturally change, and usually for the better. So is it possible we could boost our motivation to do good things by getting a sense of what we will feel like if our life was to end tomorrow and we hadn't devoted ourselves to those things that we actually feel are really important? This also raises the fundamental issue for motivational psychology of time perspective.[13]

How far ahead do you plan your life? Psychologists now believe that whether you tend to dwell on the past, present or future predicts more about your personality and the kind of life you will lead than any other aspect of your psychology. The latest research, led by Professor Philip Zimbardo, a psychologist at Stanford University, finds you can divide all people into just three groups, depending on what psychologists now call your 'time perspective'.[14]

Past Types

These are mostly directed towards the past, so they honour traditions and previous obligations, and never forget to repay a debt. They are very influenced by past mistakes and perhaps shy away too strongly from any chance of repeating them. They tend to be conservative in their tastes and fashions, and have a strong need to maintain the status quo, so they are reluctant to experience the unfamiliar, or deal with change.

Present Types

These live for the moment and think little about the past – they have few regrets – and they rarely consider the future consequences of their behaviour, so they tend not to plan ahead. Juvenile delinquents have been found to be 'here and now' types – unconcerned about reward and punishments in the near future. The present directed are best able to enjoy the moment, undistracted by past worries or future anxieties, but they are also unable to delay gratification or plan a path to realistic goals.

Future Types

These are good at setting and achieving goals, particularly distant and long-term ones. They are able to restrain themselves from succumbing to temptation, because of an enhanced ability to see negative future consequences more clearly. On the other hand, their ambitions lead them to neglect personal and social relationships.

So why does your type matter so much? Your time perspective has been found to predict how likely you are to succumb to various problems and how successful you will be in life.[15]

High achievers at school and university are found to be almost always future-looking types, because they grasp the long-term consequences of present behaviour better than low-achieving students do, and so are prepared to make the sacrifices that exam success requires.[16]

Complex or difficult tasks, like becoming the head of a large corporation, wooing a desirable but hard-to-get mate or winning an award, need careful future planning. Usually a sequence of steps needs to be strategically organized, and this requires you to be so future oriented that you are thinking several moves ahead all the time, particularly in comparison with your competition.[17]

This ability to break down a distant goal into smaller steps and see the sequence in which they need to be undertaken requires an aptitude to be involved with the future, with which past- and present-directed types just can't compete. But the problem with the future oriented is they are so busy planning ahead and worrying about the impending, they never take time to enjoy the success that all the careful scheming produces.[18]

Perhaps because they are preoccupied with prospective consequences, behave more responsibly and can't abandon themselves to risks or simply enjoying the moment, research confirms that future types tend to have fewer sexual partners. It is the present types who tend to have the highest number of sexual partners, and who also have sex more often, perhaps because they are more devoted to personal pleasure regardless of its consequences.

Drug addicts, alcoholics and the overweight, in fact anyone prone to dependency or excessive appetites, have now been found to be 'live for the moment' types. Because they are too fixed in the present and they don't consider the future enough, they never anticipate the impending consequences of their present actions. They go for the immediate pleasure of the drugs, drink or fattening food, and don't give adequate thought to the future problems created by excessive consumption.[19]

Another intriguing spin-off of being a 'here and now' type is a tendency to be poor at punctuality. This is because not planning ahead, and getting too absorbed in whatever you are doing right now, leads constantly to errors about how long it takes to get anywhere on time.[20]

Research confirms that addiction-prone personalities have little sense of a future beyond a year ahead, whereas most people have some thoughts about where they will be, or would like to be, some six to ten years into the future. However, few people tend to give much thought beyond that kind of time horizon, unless they are excessively future oriented.

Those who suffer from a very shortened future-time perspective might have developed it because they are not used to being able to influence the future anyway, as a result of frequent failures in the past. Many psychological problems are basically down to getting stuck in the past, for example car accident victims who are too scared to travel ever again because images and thoughts about the accident keep recurring.[21]

Often those who have faced a traumatic event so terrible their own view of their mortality is altered become more aware of death, and as a result tend not to be so confident of a long future. This foreshortening of their view of the future tends naturally to lead to a refocusing on the past, rendering it difficult for them to move forward.

Similarly, people filled with remorse are basically dwelling on the past; they allow a negative previous experience to completely determine their view of themselves. They do not permit themselves to see personal change as possible, therefore their past doesn't have to determine their future.[22]

Yet your time perspective may change as you get older. The aged may tend to become more past directed as they feel their future is getting shorter. Fears about their impending demise could lead to denial about the future, and so a preference for dwelling on the past.

A future-time perspective is analogous to a searchlight, which helps to illuminate the way ahead, highlighting objectives not yet in the present. The stronger your personal searchlight, the farther you will tend to see into the future and the brighter and clearer objectives will appear, and so the nearer and more real you will perceive them. As a consequence, future types are better able to plan future actions and to take precautions against future events.[23]

But it's not all good news for future types. Excessively future-oriented people cannot 'waste' time relating to family, friends or enjoying personal indulgences. Such a time pressure fuels high stress levels. Driven by the curse of having their ambitious goals realized by endless work, these people, successful in careers but unsuccessful in life, may need 'time therapy' to develop a broader perspective on time, allowing them to integrate work and play in their lives.[24]

Indeed the most future-oriented types behave morally and conscientiously today because they are concerned about their future even beyond death, a future life after death. Recent research confirms a link between future orientation and a religious and spiritual attitude to life – what psychologists call a 'transcendental future' type.[25]

As all the three different basic time orientations – past, present and future – contain their own advantages and disadvantages, the solution according to psychologists who specialize in the area is to develop a 'balanced' time perspective.

Balance means being able to switch flexibly between past, present and future views depending on your situation. Focusing on the future at the right time gives you wings to soar to new heights of achievement, while a past perspective establishes roots with tradition and grounds your sense of personal identity. A present focus nourishes daily life by allowing playfulness and enjoyment.[26]

It would appear that we need all three perspectives, operating harmoniously, to realize fully our human potential.

Tips on How to Develop a Healthier Attitude to Time

(1) Most people simply don't know what to do right now in order to achieve a distant goal in the future. The secret is to work backwards from a distant goal to nearer smaller goals you would have to achieve to make the distant objective possible. See remote aims as connected to where you are now by a sequence of smaller steps.

(2) As distant goals, like rising to the top of your company, or having children who grow into well-adjusted adults, can appear so remote, many past or present types find if difficult to sustain motivation over such a long period. Motivate yourself by seeking smaller successes at more modest targets, rather than getting disheartened because you can't achieve all you want immediately.

(3) Stop blaming yourself for past mistakes – if you knew then what you know now, it is unlikely you would have done what you did. As it is impossible to have perfect foresight mistakes are inevitable. Learn from your mistakes to build a better future rather than always dwelling in the past.

(4) When there is nothing more you can do to avert a future disaster, learn to stop worrying about it and retain the ability to enjoy the present, even when the future is uncertain, which it always is.

What Type Are You – Past, Present or Future?

PAST, PRESENT OR FUTURE SCALE

Each statement is followed by two possible responses: agree or disagree. Read each statement carefully and decide which response best describes how you feel. Then tick the corresponding answer. Please reply to every statement. If you are not completely sure which response is more accurate, put the one that you feel is most appropriate. Do not read the scoring explanation before filling out the questionnaire. Do not spend too long on each statement. It is important that you answer each question as honestly as possible.

		AGREE	DISAGREE
1	I don't like thinking about the future	A	B
2	I tend to lose my temper when provoked	B	A
3	Getting together with friends for a party is one of life's important pleasures	A	B
4	I make lists of things I need to do	B	A
5	Some things are worth doing just because they feel good	A	B
6	Extra money beyond what you strictly need should not be gambled with	B	A
7	I didn't finish many projects I have started doing because they got too boring	A	B
8	In life the destination is more important than the journey	B	A
9	It is important to take risks to put some excitement in your life	A	B

10   Every morning I try to plan my day
      ahead

AGREE: **B**   DISAGREE: **A**

Score

Add up your score by totalling the number of As and Bs you have ticked.

8 or more Bs: FUTURE TYPE

You are very oriented towards the future, which means you place a great value on doing future-inclined activities: for example you are willing to devote considerable financial and personal resources to long-term projects like education and professional training. These lead to immediately undesirable problems like these activities being an unsociable way to spend personal time, but ultimately a more desirable future state will be achieved. So it is likely you will attain higher status in life than most of your friends from school, but you will probably be less popular than they.

Between 4 and 7 Bs: PRESENT TYPE

You are very focused on the present compared to higher scorers and this means you tend to be impulsive, responding to how you feel from moment to moment, with your heart ruling your head. As a result, you are a bit of a sensation seeker, craving novelty and excitement.

Between 0 and 3 Bs: PAST TYPE

You tend to be much more past oriented than higher scorers. This means that significant events from times gone by tend to overly influence your view of the future, perhaps making you too cautious. Or it might be that something so positive happened to you before that you now devote yourself to trying to recapture what happened, not sufficiently realizing that the future is always different from the past.

Perhaps the most unhelpful attitude to the future is manifested by those who suffer from one of the deepest motivational problems: procrastination.

It is estimated that there are at least thirty popular self-help books that promise to help you overcome putting things off. Many of us put off tasks and decisions until tomorrow, despite the fact we know deep down that we can and should do them today.[27]

Psychologists estimate that 95% of college students engage in procrastination, and surveys have established that procrastination chronically affects up to 20% of the adult population.[28]

The tendency to put off till tomorrow things that you should do today strongly predicts less success in most spheres, from passing exams to keeping fit and general organization in life.

If you have a tendency to procrastinate then you will be constantly penalized for late payment of bills and filing application forms. You will tend to get to appointments late (because you put off starting your journey) and you will also tend to be sicker (because you put off going to the doctor at the earliest symptoms and wait instead until things get much worse).[29]

New research just published from the world's top expert on procrastination, Joseph Ferrari of DePaul University in Chicago, has also established that procrastinating needs treating vigorously because it destroys relationships.[30]

Ferrari found that partners in relationships with procrastinators become extremely frustrated with chronic dilatory behaviours, such as delaying housework or other tasks. Parents, best friends and other family members frequently also have strained relationships with procrastinators because everyone gets fed up with the unreliability of dawdlers to follow through what they say they will do.

But now the latest psychological research suggests procrastination is in fact a core part of your personality, which will need tackling vigorously if you are to achieve any of the meaningful goals you set yourself. But this research has come up with some surprising explanations for the tendency to procrastinate.[31]

Procrastination has proved one of the toughest psychological problems to treat, as students will readily testify – year after year they find themselves revising in a rush the night before an exam because they repetitively put off working until too late. This is despite their earnest vows to not repeat the same mistake next year.[32]

Yet research into procrastination is suggesting novel avenues of hope for procrastinators – for example, new research establishes that they tend to always believe they have more time available to complete a task than non-procrastinators, and it is actually this time distortion that explains their dawdling.[33]

Part of the reason they always mistakenly believe time is on their side is that they are bored by the tasks they have been set, and when you are bored time does indeed appear to pass more slowly. This suggests procrastinators should break down a long-term deadline into nearer mini-deadlines, to make the task more interesting by limiting the time available to complete it in. This way procrastinators experience that adrenaline rush that excites and panics them into finishing the usual night before their long-term deadlines.[34]

A study just published from the University of Groningen has found that procrastinators tend to accelerate more rapidly than better planners, for example, hastily starting revision for an exam. It could be that this ability to rev up dramatically from a standing start – to move from no work to a frenetic pace suddenly – in itself encourages dawdling in the first place.[35]

People who don't procrastinate perhaps hate the rapid acceleration required by procrastination if a deadline approaches. So they accelerate more slowly into working harder to complete a task in the allotted time. To do this they start working earlier, and so have a more relaxed time just before deadlines, unlike procrastinators who are inevitably burning the midnight oil before any end result.[36]

Oddly enough it appears the ability to successfully work very hard and rapidly ends up encouraging procrastination. So it is no longer strictly true to simply describe procrastinators as lazy; rather they appear to like working in binges followed by long intervals of inactivity.[37]

Another surprising finding from Dr Ferrari's research is the discovery that there is a sub-type of procrastination called decisional procrastinating. Decisional procrastinators tend to put off making a decision and as a result end up starting on tasks too late. But the tendency to put off making decisions was found by Ferrari to be strongly linked with a fear of making mistakes and excessive perfectionism. Having to take a decision involves accepting the risk of committing an error, so postponing decision-making is a way of avoiding this risk.[38]

But eventually the deadline gets so close that this forces your hand in making a decision, so you feel less to blame personally for having to make a judgement in a rush. You can always ascribe your final choice to your frantic situation with the urgent deadline looming – though of course unconsciously you engineered this situation all along.[39]

Ferrari also found that one common reason for

procrastination was simple uncertainty about how to perform a task, and given this hesitancy, putting the task off was simply a way of hoping a more obvious way to start would suggest itself given enough time.[40]

This naturally suggests that one effective cure for procrastination is to put off the task while you actively gather information about different ways of doing it. But even after you have reduced your uncertainty about how to start, Ferrari's research also suggests that procrastination is not just about finding the looming task unpleasant, but also about having more enjoyable alternative activities that are readily accessible.[41]

In other words, it is never simply the case that we put off doing things; rather we procrastinate because we are doing something more interesting instead. The solution to procrastination is therefore to render the alternative distractions we keep turning to less accessible than the main task we are supposed to be doing. Or we should ensure that distractions cannot be so easily completed without our being reminded of what we should have been doing instead.[42]

For example, if you are a student, you should move the TV far away from where you do your homework. As a working adult you should store your unpaid bills on the TV so they are always visible as you are watching your favourite soap, when you should be paying them instead.[43]

But psychologist Allan Blunt at Carleton University, Ottawa, has recently uncovered a new, previously unknown, motivation to procrastinate: it appears that simmering resentment explains dawdling. Putting off a task often occurs when we resent having to engage in it – this explains why the Government has to spend so much money on advertising campaigns encouraging us to hand in our income tax forms on time.[44]

So procrastination of this kind will take the form of an avoidant reaction to activities we feel have been imposed on us by others. In this case we do anything but the task we are meant to be doing as a way of relieving our resentment at being so imposed upon.[45]

The new discovery that resentment underpins much procrastination suggests the resentment should be tackled primarily by focusing on all the things you would like to do that are more personally meaningful, which you can't properly enjoy while the thing you are putting off is hanging over you.

Aim to reward yourself with a treat for task completion after you have finished, rather than soothing your resentment away before starting the activity with the distractions that just contribute to procrastination.[46]

ARE YOU A PROCRASTINATOR?
PUTTING-OFF SCALE

Each statement is followed by two possible responses: agree or disagree. Read each statement carefully and decide which answer best describes how you feel. Then tick the corresponding response. Please respond to every statement. If you are not completely sure which reply is more accurate, put the one that you feel is most appropriate. Do not read the scoring explanation before filling out the questionnaire. Do not spend too long on each statement. It is important that you answer each question as honestly as possible.

		AGREE	DISAGREE
1	I find it easy to be early for appointments	A	B
2	Shopping for presents is usually a last-minute rush	B	A
3	I plan what I am going to do on holiday before I get there	A	B
4	I rarely go to events where tickets sell out quickly	B	A
5	I usually pay bills before the reminder comes	A	B
6	My desk or room where I do paperwork is rarely tidy	B	A
7	I check my diary for up-coming events everyday	A	B

		AGREE	DISAGREE

8 When packing for holidays I usually
   forget at least one thing   **B**   **A**

9 I prefer to finish a project before moving
   on to something else   **A**   **B**

10 I usually spent the night before an exam
    revising until late   **B**   **A**

Score

Add up your score by totalling the number of As and Bs you have
ticked.

8 or more Bs: You are scoring very high indeed for procrastination, which means you tend to avoid doing things you don't
enjoy or find boring for as long as possible. What you may not
realize is that your frequent feelings of anxiety or depression may
be linked to your tendency to procrastinate. You may be getting
depressed thinking of the growing number of things that need
doing, and you are putting them off because thinking about
doing them makes you anxious. You should try the 'Swiss-cheese'
approach to all those activities you put off because you don't like
doing them – attack your mountain of undone activities by
burrowing into them at random in a small way whenever you have
a spare moment, thus making small holes in your workload.

Between 5 and 7 Bs: You are scoring above average for a
tendency to procrastinate, which probably means just before you
settle down to do the things you need to, your dawdling self finds
lots of excuses to put off work until later. You need to learn to
anticipate the excuses you tend to come up with and firmly dispel
them with rational argument. In particular, you must rehearse
this rebuttal of your usual excuses long before you get ready to
face the job that needs doing. At the moment you are relying too
much on others and ultimatums to provide the motivational
energy for you to get things done. Ask yourself how much you
really want the goals you have set yourself, or are they instead
goals others have set up for you?

Between 3 and 4 Bs: You are scoring around average to below
average for a tendency to dawdle and this means that although
you do get projects finished before deadlines, the last few weeks
are still more hectic than you had planned them to be. It may be

there are many things that end up distracting you from your goals, which means you rarely concentrate purely on one project for long enough to finish it before moving on to something else. Your ambition means you attempt too much at once, which is slowing you down in the long run. Work on only one project at a time and in a place that is devoid of distractions.

Between 0 and 2 Bs: Congratulations! You are scoring very low indeed for a tendency to dawdle and this means you instinctively already know that golden time-management rule: never have to be told about a deadline twice. Do tasks the minute you become aware they need doing without any delay at all – or in the office, never touch the same piece of paper twice and do paperwork the minute it lands on your desk. The problem for you is that others will have noticed that because of your efficiency you always have spare capacity to do more, and you may be exploited by others who dawdle. While being firm with dawdlers, you need to be more understanding of the emotional reasons that lead them never to do things until the last moment.

The technical definition of procrastination is: 'To voluntarily delay an intended course of action despite expecting to be worse off for the delay.'[47] Psychologists have become very interested in this widespread phenomenon in recent years because of its deep effects on our lives.

Because of procrastination you might put off work or career assignments until the last minute, and so will perform poorly in accounting for your time to your seniors. It could be you are putting off studying for some better qualifications that could enhance your job prospects, or postponing compiling your CV so you could apply for a position with better career opportunities.[48] Maybe you are delaying telling your partner some unwelcome news about an area of work that he or she won't want to hear about. But because you keep putting various things off, your life is becoming a misery, as these 'various things' hang ever present over you.[49]

Psychologists have found that procrastination is a deep problem that goes to the core of your personality. As a result of all the stress it produces, procrastination accounts for profound decrements to physical health amongst other problems. For example, procrastinators may have high levels of drinking, smoking and insomnia, and poorer physical health. Because procrastinators put off going to the doctor, they may even live shorter lives as a result, because diagnoses of serious complaints are made too late.[50]

Some procrastinators put work assignments off until the last minute because they have convinced themselves that they work better under pressure – a common myth. The panic and lack of time that suddenly result from procrastination turn a normally mundane or even boring task into a rollercoaster ride of emotion. Life may be more 'exciting' but the chore still gets done much more poorly than if the proper amount of time had been allocated.[51]

The key issue is that procrastination is linked to profoundly negative outcomes in our lives. It has been associated with depression, guilt, low exam grades, anxiety, neuroticism, irrational thinking, cheating and low self-esteem.[52] As a result, procrastination probably accounts for much of why many never realize their full potential and so it can be an extremely disabling psychological condition.

Why do we do it? There are two main theories as to why we procrastinate. The first is 'fear of failure' – we are worried we aren't going to do the task particularly well and so put if off and prefer to do things we are better at, like watching TV or playing football.[53] The other main reason is labelled 'task aversion' or, to put this in non-jargon speak – we hate doing a task because it's an awful bind compared to something more enjoyable like watching TV or playing football!

If you are a fear-of-failure procrastinator, you probably have a form of perfectionism, which means because you are afraid of not doing a task well, you don't do it at all. The answer here is to lower your standards and also get some early feedback about how you have started the task to guide you in your efforts. Focus more on getting started rather than doing well.[54]

Psychologist Barbara A. Fritzsche and colleagues from the University of Central Florida have recently published some research based on this principle, that suggests an ingenious but amazingly simple technique to help overcome the endemic problem of procrastination. Basically you should start the project in a very small way, and then get some immediate encouraging feedback on how you are doing.[55]

The encouraging feedback may help fear-of-failure

procrastinators by reducing unhelpful perfectionism – they feel they are not going to fail after all and so are more likely to persist. Benefits may also arise from the process of discussing the work, which is a subtle way of getting us to confront the reality of the task rather than simply avoid it. Also, having an earlier subsidiary deadline helps bring the future forward and appear nearer.[56]

The solution to the problem of task aversion is to concentrate on the way you make decisions about unpleasant chores, rather than the 'terrible' task itself. The reality is that you have to do it and that delaying is making your life a misery. This is because you are now worrying so much about the delay it detracts from the pleasurable things you would prefer to be doing instead.[57]

Swiss psychologists Cornelius J. König and Martin Kleinmann of the University of Zurich, who specialize in an area of psychology termed 'behavioural decision-making', have come up with an ingenious technique to help procrastinators, which is to get them to make decisions a bit more like non-procrastinators.[58]

Instead of asking 'What do you want to do right now?' (with the inevitable answer of going out instead of working), ask '*In what order* do you want to do your tasks?' Focusing on task order seems to dramatically aid planning and therefore perhaps helps ameliorate procrastination. If you choose to go out *after* working, you will probably be able to party more and without the worry of the consequences of not working. Putting business before pleasure usually *enhances* the pleasure.[59]

TEN TIPS TO POSTPONE PROCRASTINATION

(1) *Vague priorities increase procrastination.* The person who insists that everything is a high priority is more likely to end up not doing what is most helpful to them in the long run. Much better to set clear priorities and also get guidance about how to go about completion in a step-by-step manner – you need to know what's not important in order to better understand what really is.

(2) *Make sure you are in the right mood to make the right decision.* Because low mood is associated with

pessimism, if you are depressed you don't see the point of starting on big projects so keep putting them off. Do something morale-boosting instead, and then when you are feeling better sit down and draw up a list of tasks that need tackling and start on the most important.

(3) *Often we start a project but then get distracted* by a small interruption, which then leads to another distraction and before you know it you have abandoned what you were meant to be doing hours ago. The key here is to minimize distractions when you start something you have been putting off – this might mean taking the phone off the hook and switching off your email. Maybe unconsciously you are rather hoping the distractions will stop you from getting on with essential duties.

(4) *Sometimes we procrastinate because we are used to authoritarian parents* or other authority figures taking control of our lives. Procrastination can be a form of unconscious rebellion or expression of resentment over the lack of control in our lives. Actually, stopping postponing is the key way to take back control over the direction of our lives.

(5) *The enormity of the task can be overwhelming*, particularly if it has built up in size over time as we have postponed getting on to it. Break the mountain down into smaller hills, and so focus on achieving small gains in the first few days. The longest journey begins with but a single step. Focusing on taking that one step is easier than thinking about accomplishing the whole journey.

(6) *Reward yourself for doing the things you avoid* with the pleasurable activities that are normally your excuse for avoidance. If you go out partying instead of staying in and revising, turn this around by rewarding your studying with partying. It's the basic sequence that procrastinators get wrong.

(7) *Often procrastinators rationalize to themselves* why they are not doing what they should be doing by supplying ready-made excuses, like 'Everyone needs to socialize' and 'All work and no play makes Jack a dull boy.' The key here is to recognize that you have a choice about what you do and when you do it. You are not governed by myths. Understanding that you can select your own goals reduces the power of your subconscious mind to supply rationalizations about why you aren't doing what you should be.

(8) *Be specific and realistic about your goals.* If you want to be promoted, it's unlikely that the report hanging over you is going to achieve this in itself – but it could get you noticed, which is a step in the right direction. One reason we put work tasks off is that we feel they won't get us what we really want, which is actually probably down to us being too ambitious and impatient.

(9) *Prepare to get started.* Sometimes the key problem is getting started and one approach to this is to prepare to get started. Tidy your desk or organize the office in preparation for starting and sometimes this seems to help you move seamlessly into actually starting.

(10) *Often we feel a lot better for having started to do something we have been putting off.* Focus on the unpleasantness of having a task hanging over you and notice more how much you have to distract yourself from this by doing all those unnecessary things you do, instead of what you really should be doing.

The odd thing about time is that it's a valuable resource that we all theoretically have in equal amounts. Unless there is something fundamentally awry with physics and the local structure of the universe where you live, then the length of your day should be the same as mine. Yet some seem to be able to accomplish so much more in the average day, it's almost as if they were covertly given more time while the rest of us struggle along on half rations.[60]

Actually the secret to why you give a job that needs doing to a busy person is that the super-successful are simply more effective at time management. They have the same amount of time as the rest of us, they just use it more potently.

'Time management', the latest buzz term in work psychology, is about controlling your most valuable (and actually under-valued) resource. Consider what would happen if you spent your organization's money with as few safeguards as you spend time, and when was the last time *you* reviewed the way time is allocated at work?[61]

The signals that your time management might need improving include last-minute rushes to meet deadlines, meetings that achieve nothing, days that seem somehow to slip unproductively by, crises that loom unexpectedly from nowhere. This sort of environment leads to inordinate stress and poor performance.

The latest research on the link between mental health and time management from psychologist William Kelly of the George Fox University in Portland in the USA confirms that those who worry a lot tend to be guilty of poor time management. This strongly suggests that taking more control of time during the working day could be a key element in improving the quality of working life and mental health generally.[62]

Poor time management is often actually a symptom of over-confidence: techniques that are familiar and used to work in the past are simply re-employed with new tasks, despite the fact the work environment may have now changed radically. Most of us seem to think that keeping a well-ordered diary and planning our activity is what time management amounts to – but in fact it's a more profound way of looking at the working day.

The first step to managing your time more effectively is to get a better sense of how you actually apportion your time at the moment and to do this you need to compile an activity log or a personal time survey. The first time you use an activity log you may be stunned to see precisely how much time you squander! Memory is a very poor guide when it comes to this, as it can be too easy to forget time spent reading junk mail, talking to colleagues, dealing with interruptions, etc.[63]

Keeping an activity log means, without modifying your behaviour any further than you have to, noting down the things you do as you do them. In particular, every time you change activities, whether opening mail, making coffee, gossiping with colleagues or whatever, note down the time of the change. Changes in activity are key moments in a working day because frequently poor time management revolves around taking too long to shift activity. Also too often we alter our performance in response to cues like an interruption, rather than being fully in control of when things stop and start.

As time is usually wasted in changing between activities, it is useful to group similar tasks together, thus avoiding the start-up delay of each. The time log will show you where these savings can be made. You may want then to initiate a routine that deals with these on a fixed regular basis.

Another key issue to look for is how much of your time is spent doing jobs that others should be doing – a tendency not to delegate or apportion work or time to others is a sign of poor time management.[64]

The most important types of activity in the mantra of time management are those which will save you time: allocate time to save time, a stitch in time saves days. And most importantly of all, always allocate time to time management: at least five minutes each and every day.

The next key thing that should emerge from your time log is your alarm at seeing the length of time you spend doing essentially low-value tasks!

Examine each work activity and decide objectively how much time each was *worth* to you, and compare that with the time you actually spent on it. Specifically, if you have a task to do, decide beforehand how long it should take and work to that deadline – then move on to the next task.[65]

At the heart of time management is spending most of your time on what is important and little or no time on what isn't. Poor time management is usually the result of allocating more time to the less vital aspects of your job. One excellent way of ensuring that you concentrate on the right things is to agree them with your boss. A useful way of negotiating with your boss about how to improve the quality of your working life is not to try and avoid the tasks you hate, instead negotiate over time, and allocate more time to those things you really want to do. Bosses rarely agree to your refusal to take part in certain activities, but they tend to agree to reduced time allocated to these areas if this results in more time spent doing the things they agree are really important.[66]

You should therefore ask the following questions of your managers and yourself: What is the purpose of the job? What are the measures of success? Work out how your superiors decide whether you are good at your job or not. Find out what the key targets to be achieved are from their standpoint, and how achievement will be measured. Allocate as much time as possible to these areas and reduce the time spent on issues that don't interest senior staff.

The key question that surprisingly never gets asked is: What is exceptional performance? Find out what this is considered to be, and work out how to achieve it.

What are the priorities and deadlines? You need to know this so that when you are overloaded with work, you know what to focus on. What resources are available? This ensures that you are using all the tools at your command. What costs are acceptable? This lets you know the boundaries within which you can move. How does this relate to other people? What is the broader picture within which you have to work?[67]

If you have answers to these questions, you will know how to do your job in terms of time allocation in a much more rational way. It is only if you know what exceptional performance is that you can plan to achieve it using all the resources you have available.[68]

Finally, when you inspect your personal time survey, you should be asking yourself how much time is allocated to things you enjoy doing and which play to your strengths compared with those activities you detest and which you aren't very good at.[69] The key to a happier working life is restructuring your day so more time is devoted to the parts of work you enjoy and are good at, and other stuff is deprioritized. This usually requires your colleagues to think harder about their time management so it can mesh better with yours and you can allocate time between yourselves more effectively.[70]

Time is unlike any other resource – it's something you can never get back again so if you have spent it unwisely it's gone for ever. Better then to treat it with the respect it deserves. Remember the clock is ticking . . .

13

HOW THE TOUGH GET GOING WHEN THE GOING GETS TOUGH – SETBACKS AND HOW TO BOUNCE BACK

One doesn't discover new lands without consenting to lose sight of the shore for a very long time

André Gide

Instead of seeing change as the end of something – you could see it as a beginning

Spencer Johnson

OK, so the worst has happened and you find yourself being 'carpeted' in the boss's office. Something has gone dreadfully wrong at work and you have been fingered as the culprit.

This nightmare scenario is one we all hope fervently to avoid but no matter how perfect an employee you are, it is probably impossible to avoid finding yourself in the supervisor's bad books sooner or later. Although it's something we would rather not think about, it's probably how you handle this situation that bears a stronger link to eventual career success than how you deal with the boss when things go well.[1]

You certainly won't progress up the career ladder by smiling wanly back at the irate chair of the board and weakly saying, 'Well, nobody's perfect!' The other most common strategy in this fraught situation is to ardently deny culpability, but defensiveness in this situation will almost certainly create an unhelpful impression.

The worst-case scenario that inevitably follows from this

approach is to end up in a heated argument with the boss where you shoot down his or her position that you are at fault and he or she leaves with the impression that you are impossible to manage.

Actually, if you can handle your cock-ups well, because this is such a rare skill it is much more likely to help you succeed at work in the long run than your ability to handle the congratulations when you win awards.[2]

The first key tactic is never to find yourself in a position where when things go wrong you are the only one in the firing line. Always take people with you in the direction you are going and so get others to share ownership for your decisions so they are alongside you defending what happened. It's vital to ensure you are always with a group when in the firing line – meaning there is less likelihood of there being a bullet with just your name on it.[3]

This strategy is confused with blaming others – and this doesn't go down well. Instead this tactic is about never being identified as the sole culprit or person in charge when things go wrong. Learn from politicians when trying to acquire this knack – you will notice how in any inquiry into a cock-up at senior Government levels a posse of underlings are always trooping into the inquiry offices carrying the can for what their superiors did. This is because the senior personnel made sure any decisions appeared to be group ones.

It's also vital to consider what your boss is going to think about you after this nasty little conversation is over. What do you want him or her to remember about you when they dwell on the incident afterwards or have to explain it to their colleagues?

Too many try to win the argument that they were not at fault and miss the fact that their defensiveness leaves a bad impression. You might even win the quarrel on the basis of facts but you could miss the key issue, which is the impression you have created about yourself. The crucial question your boss is asking themselves is whether the incident or cock-up is going to happen again because you haven't learned your lesson.[4]

The worst-case scenario from the boss's standpoint is that not only haven't you learned anything about how to prevent this sort of incident happening in the future, particularly if you won't take responsibility by accepting some of the fault, but also you are some kind of loose cannon who is going to create more havoc in the future.[5]

So the steps to winning your boss round, even when you have cocked up, is to do the unusual thing when being criticized: search for agreement. Keep peppering your responses with agreements. This will catch your boss off guard – he or she wasn't expecting you to agree and not defend yourself. Accept that what went wrong is terrible and shouldn't happen again. Agree also that something needs to be done to prevent a repetition. None of these agreements mean you accept culpability, but they are the kind of positive response that makes your boss feel he or she is being listened to and is having an impact – which after all is their main aim.[6]

Another useful psychological strategy is to use words that bond you and your boss together – this subtly changes the ownership of the problem to both of you, and not just you alone. So use words like 'us' and 'we' a lot when discussing what went wrong. For example, 'Perhaps what we should do to prevent this happening again is . . .' or 'This is obviously not going to look good for us . . .'

Finally, remember that anyone is going to feel terrible after having been told off but in fact criticism is an inevitable part of a healthy work environment. Never receiving criticism at all would probably actually mean you are being denied an opportunity to improve. If you genuinely want to get better at what you do and ensure that others feel the same way about your progress, then it's vital to encourage feedback that allows you to address what needs to change.

Eventually you should develop such confidence in effectively dealing with criticism that you go out of your way to seek feedback on your performance. If you think you are perfect already, you almost certainly aren't.[7]

We now come to the thorny issue of failure and setbacks, of which there will be many on your way to attaining your perfect day.

The difference between successful people and the rest of us is not that the flourishing have never experienced failure – indeed the thriving have often endured many setbacks. The essential difference is their *response* to failure.[8]

Of all the possible responses to a disappointment, the worst one is to see this experience as for ever determining your future. So if for example you are rebuffed by someone you are attracted to, you interpret this as meaning you will never attract anyone you desire ever again. In fact because you believe things are now hopeless, you stop trying, and as a result it does indeed appear that the setback was as bad as you feared. It's not the misfortune that is ever the real problem but the new pessimism in your outlook.

But how come the tenacious never let themselves get so downcast? The key lies in their analysis of *why* the failure happened, and this is why it is essential to sit down and examine minutely and dispassionately what really went wrong, rather than jump off the deep end and conclude it's because failure is in your genes.[9]

The persistent conclude that setbacks are fundamentally caused by things that can change. It is this belief in change that separates them from the rest of us, who assume instead that adversity is permanent.

If they are the problem themselves, they believe they can bring about a personal transformation to correct whatever the personal deficit might be. So if they get rebuffed, they assume they need to improve their appearance or social skills, not that they are forever doomed to be outcasts.[10]

In fact the successful see failure as teaching them valuable lessons about what needs to alter within themselves in order that they may finally attain what they want. They are not as afraid of failure as the rest of us, and so are willing to be more daring and take more risks.

Obviously if you believe that any failure is a message of condemnation about your fundamental inadequacies, then you will indeed be afraid of flops, because their consequences become enormous. As a result, you will avoid testing yourself, and this leads to avoiding growth opportunities.[11]

The persistent are willing to consider even the deepest part of their personality as requiring change, in order that they may finally gain what they want. This explains why so many of the ultimately successful bounce back completely transformed. They see all success as being the inevitable consequence of just finding the right button of change to press. Indeed this is why the successful often have a history of repeatedly reinventing themselves until they get the right formula.

Failure is often better than therapy at pointing out what needs to change within ourselves in order that we can ultimately get what we want, because it tells us things about ourselves that sometimes our best friends won't, and which we wouldn't otherwise have learned in a thousand years.[12]

The key is to listen carefully to the failure so we can hear what it is trying to tell us.

TIPS FOR OVERCOMING FAILURE

(1) *Stop focusing on how terrible the problem is and instead concentrate on the solution.* The successful spend only 10% of their time thinking about their problems and 90% dwelling on solutions. The rest of us devote 90% of our time concentrating on the problem and only 10% attending to possible solutions.

(2) *Stop indulging in 'wishful thinking'* – fantasizing about how different your life would be if the failure hadn't occurred – and accept that the failure is now a challenge that you will have to deal with. In fact, you don't deserve your ultimate success if you cannot overcome challenges like this one.

(3) *Observe how others have dealt with similar failures* and seek out those who have successfully overcome them to see what you can learn from them. Don't ruminate and obsess about the failure with those who have succumbed to the same problem and are keen to share and reinforce your complaints – comforting though that may be.

(4) *See failure as being due to factors that can change.* These factors may lie within yourself, in the world at large or in other people, but remember that change is the one constant of the universe, so no failure can be due to a permanent factor.

Remember that if you have never experienced a failure then you probably were not trying to extend your boundaries enough, and were staying too far inside your comfort zone. All failure is the inevitable consequence of seeking to grow and pursue ambition. You should actually therefore pat yourself on the back for failing!

HOW TO COPE WITH STRESS

At the heart of the challenge of motivation is the fact that trying hard to attain a goal usually introduces more stress into your life. Those who eventually succeed are usually better at stress management. Resource depletion has been mentioned as one of the three key reasons why people don't attain their goals – and one key mental resource is your emotional stability and energy, which are depleted by poor stress management.

(1) *Take time out from stress* – if you are obsessing about a problem all the time you are unlikely to be creative and energetic when coming up with solutions, so distract yourself from time to time with pleasant enjoyable activities.

(2) *Get a good night's sleep* – most problems seem huge in the small hours but appear very different first thing in the morning, so don't skip sleep as a way of trying to manage your stress.

(3) *Ask for help or advice* – whatever problem you are facing, it is likely that others have faced it before and finding out what others have done in similar circumstances will almost certainly be helpful, so don't be too proud about researching others' solutions.

(4) *Confide in someone* – discussing stress with someone else who will listen non-judgementally is useful, as exploring it through conversation usually produces more solutions and a healthier perspective than keeping your problem just bottled up in your mind.

(5) *Make notes* – even if you have no one to confide in, writing down your problem and how you feel has been found to be helpful in gaining a better perspective on it.

(6) *Imagine someone else had this problem* – what would your advice be to them? Often a good way of gaining

perspective on a stressful situation is to think how you would advise someone else labouring in the same situation, as this objectivity helps take the emotional turmoil out of decision-making.

(7) *Focus on solutions not just problems* – going over the problem again and again in your mind just makes it larger and larger, so stop dwelling on what has gone wrong and focus instead on what the possible solutions might be.

(8) *Stop beating yourself up* – a large part of stress is the guilt or blame we heap upon ourselves for mistakes we have made that have landed us in trouble. Everyone makes mistakes; the issue now is how to help yourself, and the best way is to start being kind to yourself, so make friends with yourself rather than being your own worst enemy.

(9) *Be realistic* – a lot of stress is self-generated because you imagine something much worse that has not happened yet – so focus on what is actually likely to happen in the future, not your worst imaginings.

(10) *Do not be afraid of difficulty* – stress is an inevitable part of life. A large part of upset is a component we add ourselves because we are frustrated or upset that a bad thing has happened to us, and not someone else. Yet the only time you will not be facing stress is when you are not alive, so stop going on about how unfair your stress is and start dealing with it as an inevitable part of life.

Achievement appears to be the result of an emotional conflict between striving for success and avoiding failure. Hope for success and the anticipation of pride at winning or prevailing over others is said to encourage success-oriented individuals to strive for excellence. On the other hand, a capacity for experiencing shame was thought to drive failure-oriented persons to avoid situations where they believed themselves likely to fail. It was the balance – or more aptly the imbalance – between these two factors that was believed to determine the direction, intensity and quality of achievement behaviour.[13]

For example, failure-avoiding individuals were thought likely to avoid all but the simplest tasks, unless extrinsic incentives such as money or the threat of punishment were introduced to overcome their resistance. In effect, it was the difference in emotional reactions (pride vs. shame) that was thought to answer the question of why some individuals approach learning with enthusiasm and others only with reluctance, and why some choose easy tasks for which success is assured and others tackle problems for which the likelihood of success is exquisitely balanced against the chances of failure.

Winning in any tough competitive situation, be it work, play or sport, is in large part determined by mental attitude, and this boils down to motivation. For example, how motivated you are will predict how fit you become, because it explains your persistence in the face of obstacles when in training. But the mystery over motivation has always been why some are so much more tenacious when pursuing their goals than others. Now part of that enigma appears to have been resolved by some intriguing new research by psychologist Tory Higgins at Columbia University in New York.[14]

Higgins has established that all motivation is basically of two types, which he calls 'promotion' or 'prevention' pride, and depends on whether you have experienced success in the past or not. Challenging situations remind those with promotion pride of their past achievements and galvanize them to try and do even better than before.

But often a competitive situation merely reminds those dogged by memories of past failures to try and avoid a repetition of the humiliation of previous defeats – so these people work mostly to prevent failure rather than achieve success. Failure avoidance often leads you to be primarily cautious when confronted with a goal, so you tend to skirt risks and perhaps even evade challenging situations altogether. Promotion pride leads to a more adventurous and experimental approach, as you don't mind risking failure in your attempts to attain success.[15]

The key lesson from this new understanding that all motivation is one of two types is that if you suffer from prevention pride you should make a conscious effort to remind yourself of past successes. It may be that some of your caution over really going for it is your obsession with not landing flat on your face, and that you have failed to understand that no achievement can ever occur unless you expose yourself to the risk of failure.

So if you avoid practising or exercising as much as you could because you are afraid of looking bad in front of others, remember that all those who eventually succeed and look fantastic in the awards ceremony as they receive the gold medal are only there because they weren't afraid of failing.

How you lead your life has everything to do with what you expect. It is because you expect to get a rollicking from your boss if you don't turn up for work on time that you get out of bed in the morning. In psychology and psychiatry we now conclude that a person's expectations are perhaps one of the most revealing things about their personality, and will predict with unerring accuracy what their future holds.[16]

So, if there is an attractive member of the opposite sex at a party, those with positive expectations will tend to be more willing to take the risk of attempting to chat that person up, while those who tend to expect only a negative outcome from such an endeavour will prefer to hang around the bar and complain about how boring everyone is.[17]

Even if the person with positive expectations (we call these people in technical language 'optimists') has been summarily rejected after an attempt to chat someone up, they won't trip over their ego languishing around their ankles as they back away. Instead they will have another go with someone else because they don't believe a negative present outcome has much bearing on what will happen in the future.

Optimists famously assume a half-pint in a pint glass is half full while pessimists believe the same glass is half empty. People can be fairly reliably divided into half-full or half-empty types – or optimists and pessimists. Psychologists now believe this factor is one of the most important in personality. It predicts your future more than practically any other personality feature.[18]

The ability to keep trying in the face of setback is a key determinant of success in life. In fact, the vital difference between those who end up very successful and those who do not is not that both groups have not encountered failure. Successful people, if you quiz them during their more maudlin moments, will admit to having encountered a huge amount of flops. The essential difference is how they reacted to their past failures. They tried to learn whatever valuable lesson each defeat had to teach them about how they needed to change, and then got up and had another go.[19]

So then how do you remain optimistic in the face of dispiriting defeat?

The requisite factor psychological research has recently revealed is how you explain to yourself how your past successes and failures occurred. It is not so much then that your past determines your future – more the way you explain your past to yourself that will determine your expectations of the future, and it is these expectations that guide you through life.

The three key factors involved in any of your explanations for your past are called the three Ps: pervasiveness, permanence and personalizing.[20]

Pervasiveness refers to whether a success or failure in a part of your biography is assumed by you to have implications for the rest of your life. So let us say you got told off by your boss over a project they didn't like. A tendency towards pervasive explanations would imply that you then assume that not only were you useless in this project, but by and large you are pretty ineffectual at all projects and everything else in life.

You might then explain why you get rebuked by your boss as being because you are pretty hopeless at most enterprises anyway. If you explain past non-successes using a lot of pervasiveness, you will be prone to what psychologists call 'catastrophizing'. A setback is seen as a total disaster because in your eyes something going wrong in one part of your history has devastating implications for all aspects of your life.

Needless to say, catastrophizing is not good for you psychologically and in fact has been linked by recent research to a shorter life span. In particular, and psychologists don't know the reason for this mysterious research result yet, catastrophizers are more likely to suffer a sudden death from accidents or being physically attacked. It could be catastrophizers tend to put themselves in more dangerous situations because they feel unable to stop bad things happening to them anyway.[21]

Optimists do the opposite to catastrophizers and assume when a bad thing happens to them that this is an issue restricted purely to that small part of their lives, and has no implications at all for any other part of their existence. However, optimists do something interesting when it comes to their explanation for good events – they invoke pervasiveness, and assume any success in one part of their lives will spill over to the rest of their existence. They assume if they manage to chat up that super-model this also means they will get that rise they wanted from the boss.

The key technique here is to become pervasive whenever explaining the good things that have happened to you, and drop pervasiveness when accounting for the bad.[22]

The second P to pay attention to is permanence. If you indulge in this thinking habit you assume negative events will be a permanent feature of your landscape, so remonstrations from superiors means they will be upset with you for all time. If you subscribe to both permanence and pervasiveness then you will be prone to what psychologists term 'hopelessness' and there-fore also 'helplessness'.

This will mean that your negative past experiences will lead you to believe there is no point trying again whatever oppor-tunity comes your way. The interesting thing about the hopeless is that, even when presented with a chance to better themselves, they reject it because they assume setbacks in the past are permanent and pervasive.

Optimists, on the other hand, believe any problem they encounter is probably a temporary one, and conversely that good fortune is likely to last. They only invoke permanence when thinking about their past successes.[23]

The final P is personalizing and this is the tendency to internalize or blame ourselves for what happens to us – so if you do get that rise you personalize this success, assuming this was largely due to your hard work and negotiating prowess. You externalize this success if you deduce it was something the boss was going to do anyway. It appears to be important to internalize explanations when good things happen to you and externalize when bad events occur if you are to maintain your optimism.

Going back to the disgruntled boss – your rebuff would be explained by a pessimist as an internal one, due to the fact they found you personally unappealing. The optimist would assume it is simply because the boss was having an off day, or was not in the mood for your kinds of ideas, and the cold shoulder had nothing to do with you personally.[24]

Now you will have noticed that a fair amount of mental gymnastics is required here to keep using permanence, pervasiveness and personalizing only whenever thinking about the good things that have happened in your past and abandon them when dwelling on the bad.[25]

The fact of the matter is pessimists have indeed been found to be slightly more accurate than these rose-spectacled optimists when contemplating reality. But positive illusions about yourself, as required by optimism, are still good for you. They ensure you keep persisting in the face of adversity until your efforts prove successful, while the pessimists gave up a long time ago and as a result never get anywhere.

Recent research confirms that optimists live up to 19% longer than pessimists and this is for three main reasons. The immune system of optimists tends to be in better shape – they have more vigorous white blood cells which are active in fighting off germs. Optimists have more friends because they are more pleasant to be with than the Victor Meldrew pessimists, and we know more social support is linked to better health. Finally optimists persist much more than pessimists at healthy behaviours, like keeping fit.[26]

Optimists are more likely to be able to kick bad habits like smoking because they still assume they will eventually succeed despite the occasional relapse, while pessimists indulge in catastrophizing and decide that every relapse is the end of the world so what is the point of trying anyway. Optimists persist in going to the gym and taking regular exercise because even though they don't appear to be looking much better or losing any weight for the first few weeks, they assume they eventually will.

It is precisely because optimists keep trying that they eventually succeed while pessimists fail because their view of their past leads them to believe effort is a waste of time.

It is no accident that the family motto of possibly the greatest polar explorer of the twentieth century, Sir Ernest Shackleton, was '*Fortitudine vincimus*' – by endurance we conquer.[27]

There is, however, one key moment in life when it is wiser to revert to pessimism than be a relentless optimist: when the price of failure is huge. Getting rebuffed by the model will not have massive implications for your life, but optimistically assuming you are not over the limit before setting off after a drinks party to drive home could be disastrous if you kill someone. Be a pessimist when the consequences of optimism could be pretty terrible.

Hence the ideal when contemplating your past, evaluating your present and looking forward to your future, is to be a 'flexible optimist'.[28]

Having low self-confidence holds most people back, inhibiting them from pursuing their dreams and stopping them eventually leading the lives they would really like. This is because we all prefer to wait until we feel more confident before trying difficult things we have never attempted before. The danger of this strategy is if you put your life on hold expecting self-confidence to magically appear, you will end up waiting for ever.[29]

For example, many single lonely people do not go to parties or other social events because of the strain involved in risking rejection. Instead they resolve to wait until some mythical moment in the future when they will feel strong enough within themselves (in other words, until they have more self-confidence) before taking on the pressure of socializing. Of course, the longer they put off meeting others, the larger this hurdle grows in their minds, and the more their self-confidence ebbs away as their inexperience in mingling deepens.

The next common myth about self-confidence is that self-confidence comes from success. So the lonely believe the point of trying to meet others is to successfully start a new relationship, which will boost their self-confidence. The problem with this attitude is it means every relationship failure merely worsens their self-confidence, inhibiting them from trying to start other new affiliations.

A belief in success as the key to self-confidence only produces a fear of failure. Fear of failure spawns a reluctance to try new things. But all learning to attempt novel avenues in life necessarily involves making mistakes in the early stages. The really self-confident remain high in self-esteem despite their errors. Their failures and mistakes do not destroy their self-confidence, so they don't mind trying out new things, and risking a high probability of flopping. What is their secret?[30]

They have realized that success often doesn't elevate genuine self-confidence. Success in one sphere of life, like work for example, frequently boosts self-confidence in that area, but usually this means your self-confidence is only raised while you are performing the activity you are successful at. Once you start doing something else, which you are not so assured at, your self-confidence tends to disappear.

This explains why those whose self-confidence comes from being good at their jobs tend to end up becoming workaholics. They don't like experiencing the lower self-belief they encounter whenever they try some activity outside the office. So hugely successful businessmen can be painfully shy of women, or the most socially confident hostesses can be reduced to jelly at the prospect of an exam.[31]

Another reason success is a poor basis for self-confidence is that the universe rewards hard work and genuine talent in an extremely haphazard way. Often you will deserve achievement from your efforts, but yet will not receive it. Attainment in life is often down to others recognizing your worth and honouring it.

So if we found our self-confidence on success, we are really placing our sense of self-worth in the hands of others, particularly on whether they approve of us or not. If others' appreciation determines how much you believe in yourself, then your self-confidence will evaporate the moment you encounter those who disapprove of you, even if their reservations about you are more to do with their own problems than any you may have.

Instead, true self-confidence comes from one simple but very rare attitude. This is that you promise yourself, no matter how difficult the problem life throws at you, that you will try as hard as you can to help yourself. You acknowledge that sometimes your efforts to help yourself may not result in success, as often being properly rewarded is not under your control.[32]

All low self-confidence comes from a deep inner doubt that you are not doing everything you can to truly help yourself. That you cannot rely on yourself. Genuine self-assurance comes from the knowledge that whatever happens to you, good or bad, at least you tried to help yourself, even if you were not successful in the end. So the switch you need to make is to start praising yourself for trying, and stop waiting for success before you applaud yourself.[33]

The biggest boosts to your self-confidence come from endeavouring to help yourself, despite facing the most difficult circumstances. So the secret to self-confidence is to transform your usual approach, which was to wait until you felt better about yourself before having a go at what you have been procrastinating over. Instead, start feeling pleased with yourself because you made an attempt, despite the fact you were not brimming with self-confidence.

The truly self-confident are not always the most successful, but they are the most tenacious, as they are unrelenting in their attempts to help themselves, because they believe they are worth it.

Despite some people's apparent best efforts at achieving their goals, they still seem to perpetually fail. Perhaps the best way to understand success is to turn the question upside down; instead, we should focus on why we fail.

The startling conclusion of asking the question in this way is that we often fail *because we decide to*. This common behaviour is termed self-defeating, self-handicapping or self-sabotage in a new field of study, which is little known now but is likely to become the dominant self-help ideology.[34]

Sometimes failure has benefits, and we choose failure because it has some positive consequences, and success may have some negative repercussions.

This category of self-defeating behaviour is designated a 'trade-off'. Many trade-off situations involve an immediate and a distant goal, and we often make poor choices by focusing on the short-term consequences at the expense of the long-term.[35]

So, for example, the obese claim weight reduction is their dearest wish, a long-term goal, yet they may eat to cheer themselves up, mood management being a short-term goal. Self-sabotage is occurring here because their dearest wish is really to be cheerful, not thin, which is a lesser goal. It may be they would have to give up on cheerfulness for a while to achieve weight reduction. Certainly it might be impossible to keep both goals and expect to achieve them together.

Another trade-off we all make is the fact that failure produces sympathy from our friends and lovers, while success can often induce jealousy. We may often choose failure so as not to disrupt the status quo in our relationships, or simply to preserve sympathy.

A deeper problem with success is that once we start being

successful, it generates the expectation of future success among friends and even in ourselves. Poor performance means we escape such expectations, and therefore anxiety and pressure.

But perhaps the most startling reason for self-handicapping is that by doing it we manage to cloud the issue of whether success or failure tells us anything about ourselves. Given that discovering how attractive or intelligent we *really* are might be deeply painful, particularly if we don't feel we could do anything about it, the advantage of a self-defeating strategy is that it provides a ready excuse if we do fail. If you really did work very hard for your exam and still failed, the inevitable conclusion might be that you are not very smart.[36]

Success and failure have powerful implications for our view of ourselves and therefore our self-esteem, yet self-esteem is something we instinctively act to protect at all times. Sabotaging an upcoming performance provides an 'external' explanation for failure ('It was the drink, I didn't have enough time to revise'), other than our own ineptitude; an 'internal' explanation ('Maybe I'm not that clever') would be much more damaging to our view of ourselves.[37]

If success occurs despite the obstacles we place in its way, we can always claim even more ability for ourselves. We can say to ourselves, 'I succeeded despite all that I had to drink, therefore I must really be very good.'

The beauty of self-handicapping is that it has benefits regardless of whether we succeed or fail – we can preserve our sense of self-esteem whatever happens. However, the huge drawback is that self-handicapping inherently increases the probability of failure. Self-handicapping is thus the ultimate trade-off that sacrifices your chances for success in exchange for protection from the implications of failure.[38]

The exciting new message is if you want to succeed at whatever goal you set yourself, be it in your career or your relationships, the major obstacles you need to remove are not those erected by others, but the impediments you have placed in your own way!

Ten Steps to Greater Self-Esteem

(1) *Low self-esteem comes in many disguises: learn to recognize it for what it is.* The need to fit in and be popular is really low self-esteem in disguise, because always needing others' approval is a way of reassuring yourself when you don't have your own vote of confidence. If popularity is the most important thing to you, you will never allow your individuality to surface, and that is what is, in fact, most endearing about people. Being able to take the risk of being a bit different is the strongest evidence of high self-esteem.

(2) *Don't think praise is given so as not to hurt your feelings.* You have low self-esteem when you focus on what is wrong with you all the time; whenever anything positive happens, like when you're praised, it is always questioned or interpreted negatively. It is easy to obsess over criticism or failure and forget positive experiences. Remember, behind many acts you take for granted (like people stopping to talk to you, or enquiring how you are) is evidence that you are pleasant to be with and valued by others.

(3) *Don't let the past determine your future.* Often low self-esteem comes from childhood or teenage experiences when you were bullied or made fun of by your peers at school, or even your parents. These very hurtful memories can lie in your unconscious and determine how you feel about yourself years later. It is a mistake to base your view of yourself on the attitudes of those who were very young, immature or just plain disturbed, and who enjoyed making fun of others as a way of dealing with their own personal problems. Don't let your popularity or lack of it when younger be your measure of your self-worth now. You are elevating the judgement of your contemporaries at that young age to an importance it doesn't warrant.

(4) *Don't let others' opinions matter more than your own.* There will be those who have criticized you, found

fault or attempted to obstruct your career, and it is tempting to let others' rating of you influence the way you value yourself. But don't forget another's evaluation of you is only useful if it is not distorted by a personal agenda, emotional difficulties or feelings of competitiveness. Some of the greatest people in the world have had more enemies than friends. As long as you are willing to try and improve in response to suggestions that make sense to you, understand that often the right path in life is not the most popular with others.

(5) *Don't project your own hatred for yourself on to other people.* Low self-esteem means you think people constantly harbour terrible thoughts or evaluations about you behind a thin veneer of politeness. The more mundane truth is when you have low self-esteem no one can hate you as much as you do, and actually everyone else is so obsessed about what others are thinking about them that they simply haven't got the time or energy to invest in hating you that much!

(6) *High self-esteem means you can risk failing.* If you have low self-esteem you hate making mistakes or failing because you will use this as yet more evidence of how inadequate you really are. High self-esteem means you risk trying new things or learning from fresh encounters because you will not judge your entire worth as a human being from one or two things that go wrong. If you fear failure so much, then you will never take the risk of exploring further horizons, as these will always expose you to an elevated risk of new things going wrong. High self-esteem gives you the confidence to be more adventurous, so each day try something new, but forgive yourself beforehand for having the temerity to risk making a fool of yourself.

(7) *Stop comparing yourself to others as the only way of sensing your self-worth.* Competitiveness is often another mask for low self-esteem, because the constant need to compare yourself to others is really a

discomfort over being able to be content with yourself just as you are. If you always need someone to look down on before you feel good about yourself, your low self-esteem is showing just a tad. Remember that people who earn more than you, or are better looking, might have terrible personal problems you know nothing about. In fact, how do you compare people with each other unless you are able to reduce the whole complexity of life to simple measurable issues, like money or good looks? That is too trivial an approach – so do the more sensible thing and stop rating everyone and yourself competitively. Focus on trying to improve yourself without the distracting regard for how others are doing. .

(8) *Recognize your own achievements.* If you don't recognize your own achievements, it will be even more difficult for others to see them – it's difficult peering through another's low self-esteem to their good points. Some achievements we take for granted: for instance, if you broke a bad habit a while ago, the fact you haven't relapsed for many months should be a source of pride, but is easily taken for granted. You may have some weaknesses, but what about all those foibles that are so common, but that you aren't plagued with? Remember all the remarkable problems others have that you have managed to avoid.

(9) *Low self-esteem means you don't trust yourself.* If you keep fearing the disaster that lurks around the next corner, which your deep inadequacy is going to land you in, then your low self-esteem definitely needs putting back in its cage. All anyone can ever do is try to foresee future problems, act to prevent them as best you can, and then stop worrying about the next mess you think you will land yourself in. Remember that catastrophes have still befallen the best prepared, and the future is never going to be entirely within your control. If it was then people should be praying to you, not God.

(10) *Aim to make a small improvement each day in yourself.* When you wake in the morning resolve to tackle, in a small way, some part of your life that needs improvement. True self-confidence comes from the feeling you can do something about your problems, not that you are the best in the world. There is no greater achievement than to endeavour to constantly improve. If you think you are already the best, the danger is you might be lulled into feeling there is no room for improvement.

14

TAKE IT TO THE LIMIT

Usually when people are sad, they don't do anything. They just cry over their condition. But when they get angry, they bring about a change

Malcolm X

The top is not an overcrowded place – the top fairly begs for more to climb its heights

Edward Bok

Who do women prefer – a man who is a bit reckless or someone who is kind? The latest research will surprise you.[1]

From Hollywood films to car adverts, heroism is a celebrated male quality – but new research confirms women find heroism one of the most attractive features in a man, and this explains a host of previously puzzling aspects of sexual attraction: for example, why women so often fall for 'lovable rogues' and why men like to show off recklessly in front of women.[2]

How heroic or courageous someone is does not usually get revealed during relatively safe times – this only becomes apparent when we confront physical danger and a wide range of human responses gets displayed.[3] But a new study has found that heroism is a vital quality in determining attraction of women to men, and this psychological research could even explain why heroism has persisted in the gene pool.[4]

The persistence of heroism is a puzzle to evolutionary

psychologists, as often the heroic are the first to be killed in genuinely dangerous situations. For example, it was probably the bravest members of the New York emergency services who were first up the staircases of the Twin Towers on 11 September, and therefore it was the most courageous who lost their lives.[5]

The brave, who are likely to take repeated risks, could be expected to be rare, as, in terms of lifetime survival chances, the more risks taken, the greater the likelihood of eventual disaster. There is a debate as to the difference between bravery and foolhardiness, yet clearly we need some people willing to take risks. Many were probably saved by the risk-takers who didn't just run away on 11 September.[6]

Bravery and risk-taking are not completely unknown, even in a safe, comfortable, pampered society. They are especially found among young males, who show a striking gender bias in willingness to engage in behaviours that some might consider brave, but which are also extremely risky. For example, young men are more likely to risk unprotected sex, drive cars or motorbikes dangerously, gamble and take risky financial decisions, and take part in dangerous outdoor sports.[7,8]

But psychologists Susan Kelly and Robin Dunbar from Liverpool University have come up with an intriguing explanation from their just-published research: it could be young men are so risk prone because this is a reliable way of attracting women. After all, this is the period of their lives when both sexes' interest in each other is greatest.[9]

In a ground-breaking study entitled 'Who Dares Wins', Kelly and Dunbar conducted experiments on attraction and found that women prefer risk-prone brave males to risk-avoidant non-brave males, and also that men are aware of this preference. Bravery in a male was shown to be the strongest factor influencing female choice of short-term partners, long-term partners and male friends, with kindness as a characteristic playing a lesser part in their choice. When bravery was pitted against unselfishness, the surprising result was that women put much more weight on courage than kindness.[10]

Women deemed kindness important in friendships but, particularly for sexual relationships, a tendency to take risks in a man was preferred to unselfishness.

One explanation for this intriguing finding is that women in our ancestral and more dangerous past would have needed to choose male mates who were able to protect them from both animal and human predators, and so the women would have logically favoured skilled and courageous fighters.[11]

Women could be programmed still by their genes and brains to favour a brave mate rather than a more timid 'stay-at-home'. After all, we evolved in a dangerous environment where a man who would take risks was probably more likely to go out and find the best shelter and food and so a woman would prefer someone who would furnish these resources.

In the environments in which we evolved, the provision of meat by hunting is generally a male province, and hunting for game often involves some degree of personal risk, either from the prey itself or from a dangerous environment. So choosing a brave man as a mate would have ensured a woman and her children were likely to be fed, as well as protected from marauding other males.[12]

Kelly and Dunbar were also interested in comparing unselfish courage with selfish bravery. After all, one could argue that there is a difference between a risk-taker who goes in and rescues another person, so placing his own life in danger, and someone who just drives fast because he enjoys it.

In order to see what kind of person women were most attracted to, Kelly and Dunbar compared how eight contrasting male personality profiles fared in evoking female approval.[13]

Women were asked who they would favour. One possibility was Bill, who is a quiet but capable man, always ready to lend a hand, but unobtrusive about it. He works as a mechanic during the day, which allows him the flexibility he needs as a key member of the local lifeboat crew. Bill would be classed as brave but kind, in contrast to someone brave but more selfish like Frank, who likes to be outdoors whenever he can. He is attracted by danger, and spends many weekends and holidays rock-climbing. He has recently taken up free-fall parachuting. Similar to Frank was Edward, who is a bit of an action man. He is always on the go, and throws himself into his work. He used to be a steeplejack, but now works as a deep-sea diver. When not working he goes jet-skiing and plays tennis.[14]

In marked contrast to Edward and Frank there was also Charles, who is not brave but he is kind. Charles enjoys looking after people. He works as a nurse at present, but is considering training to be a counsellor as he thinks the prospects might be better. He is learning to play the clarinet, but doesn't practise as much as he should as he worries about disturbing the neighbours.[15]

The researchers found that of the eight possible choices, Edward and Frank, both brave but not kind, did much better than anyone else in their approval ratings by women for a short-term fling. Also, when bravery was pitted against unselfishness, bravery across all types of relationships, short- or long-term, carried much more weight in male attractiveness to women.

In Kelly and Dunbar's study, men were asked which of the male personality profiles they thought the women would be most attracted to, and the men were able to correctly predict the female preference for bravery over kindness. This means men know that women are attracted to risk-taking and suggests that exhibitions of bravery could be part of the male mating strategy. This, of course, also means a lot of brave behaviour could be much less unselfish than it first appears.[16]

But there are, of course, disadvantages to selecting a mate who habitually takes risks. Brave risk-taking men are likely to be prone to a higher mortality rate than risk-avoidant men, and so a woman choosing a risk-prone mate runs the risk of eventually being left alone with no support. This risk is reflected in Kelly and Dunbar's research, which found that for long-term relationships bravery had a little less impact than it did for short-term flings in terms of female attraction to brave men. Plus, unselfishness was more valued in long-term relationships than in short-term flings, but whatever the scenario – short-term or long-term relationships – brave men were still far more preferred to the non-brave, so it appears that to women the benefits outweigh the potential costs.[17]

This begins to explain the puzzling attraction so many woman feel towards the 'lovable rogue', as it now seems it is the scoundrel's risk-taking that proves so attractive.

Another intriguing finding from the research was that bravery was found most attractive when the man involved was 'professionally' brave (e.g., a fireman) as compared to someone who was brave only fitfully (as in a volunteer for a lifeboat charity). It would seem women prefer men who are consistently brave, and linked to this might be some element of dependability or professionalism – as opposed to fitful bravery, which could be reasoned to be more likely to end in disaster.[18]

The other fascinating implication of Kelly and Dunbar's research is that risk-taking attracts women only when it is on display in some way. Given that they discovered that men were aware that women found risk-taking attractive, it could be that much male risk-taking or bravado now becomes understandable in terms of 'showing off' rather like a male peacock displaying his colourful feathers to attract a mate.[19]

For example, studies of primitive tribes, where hunting is the main way of providing food, have found that often male hunters like to share their kills around the village, more than would make sense if they wanted their own families to be well fed. It seems the sharing around of the fruits of the hunt is a way of advertising their bravery to other possible female mates in the village.

When married women have affairs, they are more likely to have extramarital sex during their fertile periods and there is also research evidence that the kind of man a woman is most likely to have an extramarital affair with is a male with high testosterone levels. Testosterone is a hormone strongly linked with risk-taking behaviour. This all suggests that women are attempting to get the good genes of the risk-taker for their off-spring, so enhancing the reproductive potential of their children, but also getting the timid stay-at-home male type to take care of them.[20]

Kelly and Dunbar's research into the secret attraction many women harbour for the risk-taker also explains the puzzling phenomenon of women who stay with rogues who are obviously unfaithful. It could be that as the risk-taker is seen to be a good bet in terms of foraging successfully in a dangerous world, you might as well hang on to the risk-taker you know, rather than leave him for yet another risk-taker, where the long-term prognosis for fidelity is the same anyway.[21]

Freud famously asked in a fit of frustration, 'What do women want?' Increasingly the answer appears to be that women want it all – they want a man who is sensitive and kind in general but who is also macho in emergencies. This often presents a conflict for women as in the longer term they understand that kindness and sharing are extremely useful in a relationship, but they also realize that this kind of man is unlikely to rise to the top in a competitive world.[22]

The research evidence from all around the world is that

women place much greater store on status and wealth in what they find attractive in men than men do in women. So it seems that the ability to provide resources is a vital aspect of what women are looking for in a man. This also explains why ambition and industriousness are found by psychological research to be some of the most attractive male personality features to women.[23]

In the kind of dangerous world that we evolved to live in and that existed a hundred thousand years ago, bravery and risk-taking in a male mate would make it more likely that a female would be defended from danger and get to eat meat at mealtimes.

But the world we live in today has until quite recently seemed much safer, so physical bravery did not seem such an obviously useful feature and this might have been why women going for lovable rogues seemed so puzzling. In fact, the answer is women were obeying their stone-age genes, which were still driving them to pursue the physically strong risk-takers, as there hasn't been enough evolutionary time to allow these genes to adapt to the very new safer circumstances of modern life.[24]

But now the world is again a more dangerous place it would be intriguing to see if bravery becomes an even more obviously desired characteristic once again.

ADVICE FOR WOMEN FROM THE 'WHO DARES WINS' RESEARCH

(1) Although risk-taking men are more attractive because a man needs to take a few risks to succeed in life, ask yourself if his risk-taking is reckless, or he takes risks with some consideration for the consequences. If he is basically just reckless, can you deal with the fall-out when he takes one risk too far?

(2) If you find yourself getting bored in a relationship and are thinking of straying, maybe you should encourage your partner to take more risks – he may in fact be playing safe to protect you and hasn't realized he needs to take a few more risks to stop appearing boring.

(3) Remember that someone who gets used to successfully taking risks in their job might come to believe they can take

risks elsewhere in their life and get away with them, like perhaps taking risks with the relationship by chancing an affair. If your partner is used to taking risks in his career you should be more vigilant about his fidelity.

ADVICE FOR MEN FROM THE 'WHO DARES WINS' RESEARCH

(1) Kindness and unselfishness in men is valued by women but risk-taking and bravery is even more attractive, so while you shouldn't dispense with altruism, don't rely on it alone to attract her: bravery will be more impressive.

(2) Dates that involve some display of bravery, like a frightening rollercoaster ride or even a horror film, are more likely to impress – but only if you manage to stay calm yourself and don't turn to her for support when terrified. And yes you should go down to check what that noise was in the middle of the night; otherwise you will soon be alone in the house.

(3) It would now seem that the racy car is part of the armoury you need to attract women because it suggests a tendency to take risks. Think about what your lifestyle says about your bravery. Perhaps it's time to throw away the cardigans and give the SAS uniform a try instead . . .

The predominant view reflected in the media is that some degree of risk-taking is beneficial and even necessary for the health and survival of the species. Ironically, during the first half of the last century, physical risk-taking was viewed as evidence of pathology. Psychoanalytically oriented theorists regarded physical risk-taking as expressive of a death wish. Anna Freud reported that in treating high-risk sports participants, the activity typically served the function of allaying anxieties about 'masculine inadequacy', that is to say, 'castration fear'.[25]

More recently, the understanding is that a great number of human activities, including such physical pursuits as skydiving and driving cars at high speeds, are motivated by the need to raise an individual's level of stimulation and excitement.[26]

Are you an 'extremeophile'? That's the term scientists use for anyone or anything that thrives in an extreme environment – a locale that's extremely hot or cold, or is at a high altitude, is very windy, has high pressure (as in deep sea), no pressure (as in space) or is just plain inhospitable in other extreme ways.

You may have thought that the need to explore the outer reaches of the planet and put up with severe discomfort should have abated, given we seem to know everything there is to know about our world's surface (and satellites tell us even more than you can by actually being there). Surely we have now been everywhere there is to go.[27] But it appears that, mysteriously, now more than ever, extremeophiles thrive amongst us.

For example, the numbers climbing Mount Everest have exploded ever since Sir Edmund Hillary and Tenzing Norgay first achieved the summit in 1953. Now the fastest sherpa can apparently make the climb in just under eleven hours and other records have been tumbling spectacularly recently, including youngest (fifteen) and oldest (seventy) persons to make the climb, plus first black person to ascend to the summit. To celebrate the fiftieth anniversary of Hillary and Tenzing's achievement, there were so many climbers tackling Everest that they literally queued on its slopes to await their chance on the summit.[28]

Now, for £40,000, even the relatively inexperienced will be guided to the top, but why bother? Even before the present stampede, 1,200 had already reached the top, eighty-nine in one day in May 2001, so there hardly seems any point.[29]

But it seems the spirit of adventure is unquenchable in an extremeophile, no matter the danger, indeed perhaps because of it. Maybe it's because even Everest is getting old hat that there are a strange group amongst us who restlessly seek out ever more bizarre physically extreme challenges no matter the threat to ourselves or the inconvenience to others.

For example a lone seventy-eight-year-old American yachtsman nicknamed 'Ivan the Terrible', famous for sailing single-handed from the US to Britain, was recently criticized as a maritime risk by coastguards in Devon for setting sail yet again, after just being rescued five times in as many weeks.[30]

Also of note, the first Royal Navy team to organize an expedition to Everest recently spent more time rescuing other climbers who got into difficulties than anything else. On their way down from the summit they rescued an Australian suffering from snow blindness and frostbite and a Briton with a broken leg, while another marine, part of the Royal Navy team, had to abandon his ascent less than 300 metres short of the summit after suffering from frostbite.[31]

What drives these apparently foolhardy individuals who persist in risking life and limb for little real return in terms of scientific or geographical discovery? Indeed, the level of interest in exposing oneself to this kind of danger has, if anything, heightened. This raises the question of whether the aims of science and exploration were actually always just a thin veneer for adventurers and explorers, and there was always something more mysterious and altogether more psychological going on.[32]

The early mountaineers who really launched the hobby in Victorian times and made the expensive journey to the Alps almost as a rite of passage were British men from the wealthy classes who were expected to go on to run the Empire. Self-denial, hardship and comradeship under extreme conditions were part of the culture of the brutal public schools that moulded them. There was, therefore, a sense in which if you could conquer a mountain all by yourself then conquering a country seemed much less forbidding. Extreme conditions were character-building and helped you cope practically with other real problems.[33]

Indeed, some modern occupational psychotherapists still exploit this theory when they get corporate executives to pay vast sums for a day of running around in the wilds getting wet and uncomfortable. The belief is this will help the team close deals back in the comfort of their offices.

Mallory, one of the first British climbers to attempt Everest in the 1920s, remains the epitome of this kind of Victorian thinking – he used oxygen in some of his attempts but famously 'would have preferred not to'.[34]

There is a sense in which the modern pampering of technology and wealth protects us and softens us and we feel the need to get back to basics in order to toughen up, and also discover what we are actually capable of. Maybe when you have only yourself to rely on, or a few comrades on whom your life depends, you discover who you really are and bonds are formed between people that are much stronger than those that endure in other areas of modern superficial life.[35]

Dr Peter Suedfeld and Dr Daniel Steel, psychologists at the University of British Columbia, have recently reviewed the research literature on explorers and adventurers who try to survive in extreme environments and uncovered some extremely surprising and counterintuitive findings. While most popular accounts emphasize the deprivations, dangers and stresses, the actual psychological research evidence is overwhelming that for many if not most the sojourn is a cherished and important part of their life, perceived as an impetus to growing, strengthening and deepening, to be remembered with pride and enjoyment.[36]

Along with their accounts of hardship, cold, hunger and possible doom, early explorers, stuck in the ice in crumbling ships or ramshackle shelters, made diary entries exalting the grandeur of the polar environment, the transcendental feelings and the sense of appreciation for their colleagues. Current-day polar crews report many more positive than negative experiences. Both to space and to the polar regions, the return rate is high, and the disappointment of those who are frustrated in their desire to go back is profound. For example, in one recent study twenty-six of twenty-eight participants in a dangerous and uncomfortable undersea habitat study were willing to do it again.[37]

The long-term after-effects of such experiences are also strikingly positive. Both self-reports and scientific data show that people who have come through a demanding exploration mission are mentally and physically healthier, more successful and more insightful than they had been or than comparison-control subjects.

It appears that the whole enterprise calls to something deep inside many people. People who go in for these experiences usually like challenges, and most do quite well in meeting the ones they encounter. Members of crews often come back with a less superficial set of values, more tolerance and affection towards other people and higher self-confidence.[38]

But the key is to be psychologically the right kind of person before setting out on one of these expeditions, otherwise disaster could beckon. Now psychologists reckon the science of personnel selection for extreme adventures is so developed they can predict with an uncanny degree of accuracy who will survive and who will end up needing rescuing from the drifting ice.

Psychologists have repeatedly found three predominant personality types, accordingly dubbed the 'real right stuff', the 'wrong stuff' and the 'no stuff', among astronauts, underwater marine researchers and mountain climbers, which determine the success or failure of these kinds of mission. Intriguingly, more recent research has found these three different personality types exist amongst all of us, but it is extreme conditions that bring them out most clearly. So maybe there is a kernel of truth to the cod psychology idea that running around outdoors in the damp separates out more clearly who will survive in tough situations.[39]

The 'real right stuff' are good at communicating and are goal focused – they don't end up fighting with each other because they were ignored in a meeting, as long as the goal of the expedition is achieved. The 'wrong stuff' are those who are not team players, and they score high in comparison to those who have the right stuff on argumentativeness and competitiveness. Meanwhile those suffering from 'no stuff' types bascially haven't the necessary motivation to overcome the kind of obstacles that beset the average space or polar mission.[40]

The fact that successful explorers and adventurers are often team players may come as a surprise to those who emphasize the rugged individualism exemplified by the recurring image of a lone man pitted against nature. But the reality is that most successful missions to remote places or extreme conditions require a team of people behind the lone explorer to keep supply lines open or provide back-up. It is those missions that end in tragedy where an inability to collaborate effectively or take advice from others, even if it was just the rescue services, often is the real story behind the scenes.

But there clearly has to be a delicate balance here – just because explorers can work in a team doesn't mean they are the life and soul of the party – all the evidence indicates they tend to score lower on extroversion than the average person.

Extroversion is a measure of warmth, gregariousness and excitement-seeking. Since being in an isolated environment is usually characterized by prolonged periods of boredom and monotony, to cope with this you would need to be relatively introverted and less excitement-seeking, as most extroverts are. Also as the most frequently cited source of stress by explorers is missing family and friends, those best suited to coping with this are those who don't form strong attachments to others and therefore miss them less.[41]

So it seems there is a kernel of truth to the idea of the adventurer as the strong silent type who prefers his own company. In an increasingly social world where 'emotional intelligence' is now heavily valued and the ability to get on with others seems to mark you out for success or failure more even than technical ability, perhaps the less extrovert explorer finds a welcome refuge on a deserted ice floe.[42]

Modern psychology has moved on from the Victorian idea that somehow those able to endure hardship and deprivation and who were more self-reliant were therefore somehow superior to the rest of us and deserved to rule us – the idea that these are better values that we should all aspire to.[43]

Of course, almost any environment is extreme and unusual for some individuals and groups and familiar and survivable for others: a life-long Londoner suddenly alone in the frozen Arctic tundra would find the surroundings no less strange and dangerous, and probably would live no longer, than would the Inuk hunter plunked down in the middle of Piccadilly Circus.[44]

But is there any real point to modern adventuring? It has been noted that Mars bears an uncanny climatic resemblance to Greenland. Martian daytime temperature averages 15 degrees C and plummets down to -70 degrees C at night. Greenland offers a similar temperature flux due to geographic location and seasonal variation, therefore making it an ideal analogue to Mars – climatic, physiological and psychological. So unsupported polar expeditions offer us a wealth of research material into our psychology and biology at extremes that could prove useful when we attempt to explore Mars.[45]

It could be that modern explorers who appear at first glance mad today may be precisely who we need in a crisis in the future.

15

ARE YOU TRYING TOO HARD?

We strive to be Number One . . . But win or lose, it is the competition which gives us pleasure
Joe Paterno (coach of Pennsylvania State University's football team)

You can never really teach a person something, they have to learn it for themselves
John Whitmore

Jim Loehr, one of the authors of the motivational book *The Power of Full Engagement*, spent thousands of hours watching videos of professional tennis matches, trying to discover what the top players did that separated them from the rest. He found nothing. Then he started to notice what players did *between* points.

The top players generally had a much better way of relaxing after each point in order to prepare for the next one. In a match lasting two or three hours, these mini recovery rituals mattered. The player without them became fatigued, then lost concentration and points.

Why do so many people now feel tired all the time, given we have to physically exert ourselves much less than our grandparents did? They lived in an era without all the labour-saving devices we now have – so is modern tiredness a response more to stress and a hectic lifestyle than mere muscular effort?

Perhaps a clue lies in the fact that when people say they are tired what they really mean is they are 'tired of it', and the key to solving tiredness is to uncover what the 'it' is.[1]

Paradoxically, those who complain of being weary all the time are usually go-getters, perfectionists, who push themselves to work harder than most others – so whatever might be going on psychologically, they are not using their tiredness as an excuse for laziness.

Instead, perhaps because they always attempt to urge themselves to the limits of endurance, they leave no spare capacity to cope with added stress from the environment, on top of the pressure they put themselves under. This might produce added strain, which then leads to feelings of weariness. But being perfectionists, when they feel a bit below par, they avoid undertaking many tasks because of fears of performing just mediocrely, which is not acceptable to their high standards.

This terror of only middling accomplishment means that those who feel tired all the time perhaps avoid too much activity when trying to rest. Tired-all-the-time people seem to suffer from black-and-white thinking or extreme swings – they are either working frenetically or flat out on their backs from exhaustion. The solution would seem to centre on finding a middle path.[2]

Perhaps therefore feeling tired all the time is a clue to having over-pushed yourself for reasons to do with ambitions implanted by pushy parents or guilt over being seen as lazy. Maniacal rushing is down to deep insecurities that will never be appeased by sheer effort, no matter how much is achieved. If you never allow yourself to take a break, your body can only interrupt the constant striving by ceasing to function. Sometimes the sole permission we can give ourselves to rest, in a competitive world, is exhaustion.

Feeling tired all the time makes it more likely you will adopt passive ways of relaxing or taking a break from work, like watching the TV. Feeling drained, you will tend to assume that you are not up to physical exertion like exercise. Yet going for a brief walk, doing some stretching or some quick sit-ups, has been found to make people feel more energetic and stimulated afterwards.[3]

A small amount of exercise usually leaves people feeling energized. So paradoxically feeling tired all the time, if it results in a withdrawal from or avoidance of exercise, will lead to a vicious cycle whereby as more passive activities are indulged in, you feel weaker over time.

Often those who now feel tired all the time, because they were very active in the past, will tend to notice a more dramatic decline in fitness levels than those who were never particularly dynamic anyway. This more rapid change from being in shape ensures a stronger sense of physical weakening than that felt by those who probably have a lower baseline fitness anyway. This in turn produces deeper gloom about bodily deterioration when a comparison is made with a past time of much greater fitness.

Always resorting to passivity, due to lethargy, will also produce boredom, and often this is confused with tiredness, because tedium itself produces yawning and sleepiness. Again a vicious cycle of boredom produced by not doing much that is exciting leads to greater torpor, which in turn yields deeper doldrums.

Feeling tired all the time is a symptom that commonly precedes the onset of a serious depression, so persistent fatigue should be treated vigorously. Experts in fatigue find the most effective approach is gradually increasing activity of a social and physical nature. So start going out with friends and taking up gentle exercise like walking or cycling because sometimes too much rest makes tiredness worse.

TIPS ON HOW TO STOP FEELING TIRED ALL THE TIME

(1) *There is a difference between feeling calm tired and tense tired* – perhaps the issue is not so much exhaustion but stress. Aim to take the fundamental stress out of your life rather than temporarily resting but returning to high stress all the time.

(2) *Tiredness could mask boredom* – perhaps you need to rethink your goals if pursuing them is exhausting you. Goals that have real meaning for us energize rather than deplete us.

(3) *Learn proper relaxation* – often passive resting allows you to worry about problems while involving activities

provide a more complete distraction and therefore proper mental rest.

(4) *Perhaps you don't lack energy, you merely invest it in the wrong things* – if you work hard but have no energy left for your family or your love life then maybe you need to wind down more at work and wind up more at home.

(5) *In trying to solve the puzzle of what you are really tired of, don't be afraid to consider you could basically be tired of your life* – be prepared to think radically and imaginatively about changing your whole lifestyle if you want to stop tiredness.

Many who complain bitterly of stress at work are probably suffering from a surprisingly different complaint – although they don't at first realize this. Often they will blame work and various aspects of it, like how much there is, or the excessive and unreasonable demands from colleagues or managers. In fact, the true difficulty lies within the worker themselves and has been labelled recently 'work dependency', otherwise variously known in the past as 'work addiction' or 'workaholism'.

Work Dependency is the new term preferred by many occupational psychologists because it better captures the notion that someone prefers to be at work because work has become a crutch that is shoring up the other, less successful, parts of their emotional and personal lives.

Work dependents can be identified by their excessive involvement with work and neglect of other areas of their lives. Most work consistently long hours, including evenings and weekends, and when they can be convinced to take a holiday, he or she will usually bring work along or take calls from the office. Work dependents like to have control and, as a result, will rarely delegate to others, causing them to work even more hours. Despite the many hours they work, work dependents are not necessarily highly productive. In fact, many could be quite inefficient due to their excessive perfectionism.

For the work dependent, satisfaction derived from work is more important than any derived from family life and it is not uncommon for the work dependent to suffer from health problems such as stress-induced illnesses, chronic fatigue, increased levels of anxiety and substance abuse. These health consequences are alarming because current estimates are that one in four of the working population suffer from work dependency. Given the commitment required by traditional hard-working professions like medicine and the law, the prevalence is likely to be much higher in these professions.

A work dependent differs essentially from a work enthusiast, which is a person who is also highly involved in his or her work, but does not experience the same internal drive to work or the same dissatisfaction from work, because they are not driven to work for pathological reasons. These are usually a central insecurity and an avoidance of problems elsewhere in their lives.

Emotional dependency on your job is usually because you have a higher need to prove yourself at work and work-dependency behaviours usually therefore arise in response to feelings of low self-worth and insecurity.

The idea that work dependency stems from low self-esteem means the problem lends itself to a particular form of self-help psychotherapy referred to as 'Rational Emotive Behavioural Therapy' or REBT. A new research paper recently published by psychologists Rebecca Burwell and Charles Chen of the University of Toronto argues that REBT is the best approach for those suffering from work dependency.[4] REBT is so named because the central focus of the treatment approach is that by using your Rational brain you can defeat the irrational Emotional side that is producing the problems and this will eventually help you change your Behaviour, which is also a vital part of personal transformation.

Albert Ellis, the founder of REBT, believes that people hold several key irrational beliefs, from which their neurotic suffering stems. One of these beliefs is that we must 'impress, live up to the expectations of, and outdo the performances of other people'.[5] From this irrational belief people derive an intense drive towards perfectionism and approval from others, which is one of the defining characteristics of work dependency.

Perhaps the real problem with addressing work dependency is that it is not typically seen as a problem, often because the profession also embraces a puritan work ethic. There are few more devastating accusations you could make about a colleague than they are not fully committed or that they are even relaxed about their work. So unlike alcoholism or substance abuse, work dependency is quite an acceptable practice in hard-working professions.

A work dependent's devotion to his or her work often leads to promotions and higher levels of salary – rewards that simply serve to perpetuate the problem. To complicate matters further, in an organization like the NHS, which is underfunded and chaotically managed, employers may actually seek out the work dependent in order to get more hours for the same wage. This attitude only serves to spark the work dependent's feelings of insecurity and reconfirm to him or her that working long hours is the only way to ensure job marketability, reinforcing the work-dependent cycle of thinking, feeling and behaviour.

So due in part to the fact that work dependency is so accepted in many professions, and that its practice can be easily rational-ized, denial of the problem is another issue that therapists must contend with. Many who counsel work dependents argue 'denial of the problem may be the greatest hindrance to corrective action' and this state of denial may further intensify the work-dependency symptoms before it is dealt with. As a result of this endemic denial, it is often not the work dependent themselves who seek a referral for help but instead a spouse or family member.[6]

In order to benefit from therapies like REBT, this issue of denial needs to be tackled and can be assisted by recognizing the key signs of work dependency. These are: (a) an uncontrollable addiction; (b) an individual's desire to escape from personal issues faced outside work; (c) extreme need to control one's life; (d) a highly competitive nature; (e) parents that modelled workaholic behaviour; and (f) an impaired self-image and limited self-esteem.

Treatment using REBT involves examining core beliefs, dis-puting how strictly rational or reasonable they are and then replacing the more irrational beliefs with healthier more reason-able ideas.

For example:

Belief 1: I should be able to carry a full workload without becoming completely anxiety-ridden. I'm a total loser.
Healthier belief: It is no wonder that I suffer from anxiety. I rarely have time for myself. It would be nice if I could

take two courses at a time and work full time but this simply isn't realistic – not for me or for anyone. I will be able to accomplish more if I actually give more time to myself. I would only be a loser if I kept trying to keep up with the same old hectic pace.

Belief 2: I must get an A in all of my courses or I won't be able to pursue further education.
Healthier belief: I have received lots of As in my previous courses. To reduce the time I spend in my present study does not mean that I would never be able to get a good grade. If I use my time wisely and effectively, I will probably keep a good academic record. Even I do not receive an A for one course, it is not the end of the world. My other personal assets, such as my relevant work experience, can also have a positive impact on my application for the next job.

Belief 3: If my boss gives me a bad performance appraisal then I'll know for sure that I'm in the wrong field of work.
Healthier belief: I have received very good evaluation from my boss thus far. Chances are that I won't get a bad performance appraisal, but even if I did, I have to remember that this is only one person's judgement of my work. Lots of people have already told me that I have a lot of talent in my field.

Many irrational beliefs negatively affect the work dependent's self-perception. Such misperceptions often derive from and reflect the lack of self-confidence within the person, reinforcing a sense of low self-esteem. Thus a vicious cycle is established that REBT attempts to challenge with disputation. But a key part of REBT is also the behaviour element – in other words, besides disputing your irrational beliefs it is also important to act.

A key technique in REBT is 'substitution': to counteract the tendency of work dependents to take on more and more, they are instructed not to take on new tasks until they first get rid of another responsibility. For example, a work dependent should not take on any new work or related tasks until he or she has eliminated another task with a corresponding time value.

Following this rule will provide a more structured context for workers to maintain a balanced work life.

Another key approach of REBT responds to the fact that very often work dependents not only hold the irrational belief that leisure is a waste of one's valuable time, but they also have no knowledge of how to make leisure a part of their lives. After correcting such misperceived thinking and feelings, the therapy facilitates work dependents to gain more hands-on experience in learning how to 'play'.

Making a commitment to scheduling leisure time is important as it provides the client with a structure for action execution and reinforces behaviour change. In the case of most doctors referred to my clinic I argue they should attempt to 'play' at least twice per week, by doing activities that they enjoy, such as eating out with friends, watching movies or hiking.

Inability to delegate tasks to others is a key weakness of the work dependent. At work, the work dependent should ask administrative, secretarial or support staff to help rather than taking the time to do everything themselves. Because of the macho culture of medicine, asking colleagues for help is a particular difficulty for male doctors. They might practise not taking the lead role in all of their projects suggested by managers.

Work dependents have real difficulty setting boundaries.[7] Therefore using boundaries to control the work day appears to be another effective strategy. For example, try to leave work after an eight-hour day, even if all your tasks are not completed. Not only should you follow this eight-hour rule in a strict manner, but you should also remind yourself that any planning related to your work schedule must follow this eight-hour rule. In other words, only a reasonable and achievable workload is arranged in this work-time boundary, so that you will be able to finish your work within this length of time. This will hopefully give you a more balanced work life without falling behind in your work, reducing anxiety and distress.

Therapy with work dependents is essentially about helping the client to see that work is only a part of, and not the only component of, life.[8] Life is still worthy and meaningful even if a person devotes less time to his or her work. This can only follow after the client has begun to accept themselves non-judgementally a bit more. Clients need to accept the consequences of their endeavours, whatever the results. Whenever they are judged in any way, at work or at college, they need to peacefully accept it.

For example, instead of saying to themselves, 'I got a mediocre reference, I'll never get anywhere in life,' they could try saying, 'I got an average reference but I learned a lot from this job that will help me to work more effectively.' In other words, learn for yourself the REBT view that 'doing is more important than doing well'.

There are grave dangers that lurk in wait of those who don't address their work addiction.

The Prime Minister's recent cardiovascular difficulties came as a shock partly because he is so young and vigorous; it is difficult to imagine Tony Blair as being anything but at the peak of fitness. Speculation naturally turns to whether the stress of the job could be a factor and his difficulties coincided with the most difficult year of his career – a career that had until then moved ever relentlessly upwards.

We know that heart rhythm disturbances like those suffered by the Prime Minister are very closely linked to emotional turmoil. This is probably secondary to a surge of cardiac stimulant hormones like adrenaline, which force the heart to beat faster in preparation for the fight or flight in the face of an enemy that our evolutionary history has equipped us for.

It is no accident that sudden cardiac death has long been linked anecdotally with strong emotion and there are many documented cases of individuals experiencing cardiac arrest or sudden death in settings of acute grief, fear or anger. We know sudden death increases in populations experiencing emotionally devastating disasters such as earthquake or war.[9]

Medical research that closely monitors those vulnerable to heart rhythm disturbances finds that Monday is the most 'popular' day for an abnormal rhythm, probably because of the stress of returning to work after a relaxing weekend. It is interesting to note that the Prime Minister was admitted to hospital on a Sunday – perhaps a sign that the anticipated stress of the forthcoming week comes a bit earlier if you are running the country.[10]

The most precise investigation of the link between emotional state and heart rhythm disturbances was conducted by Rachel Lampert and colleagues at Yale University in New Haven in the

USA in 2002, where mood diaries were closely matched with electrocardiogram monitoring. Of all the emotions recorded, including anxiety, worry and sadness, it was the emotion of *anger* that was most frequently associated with the kind of heart rhythm disturbances experienced by the Prime Minister.[11]

This intriguing result fits in with the medical view dating as far back as the 1950s that one key risk factor for cardiovascular disease is being a 'Type A personality'. This personality type is characterized by competitiveness, excessive drive and an enhanced sense of time urgency. Basically the Type A pattern refers to any person involved in an aggressive and incessant struggle to achieve more and more in less and less time. A Type A can be spotted because their aggression, competitiveness and impatience lead to muscle tension as well as an alert and rapid speech style together with an accelerated pace of activities.[12]

Does this ring any bells?

As they are so 'goal directed' or, to use the less technical term, pushy, Type As naturally also suffer from irritation, hostility and an increased potential for anger. This is because they eventually find most others around them are not travelling as fast as they are, and so are getting in the way. As a result there is huge frustration at not getting their expected results – this leads to anger and adrenaline overload. Then you find yourself trying to rearrange your diary with your personal assistant as you are stretchered to the hospital with them jogging along beside you.[13]

It is intriguing to note that Tony Blair, in true Type A fashion, was holding meetings the very next day after leaving hospital, despite being told by his doctors to rest.

The problem with the Type A theory is that it has proved difficult to measure reliably and define precisely the Type A personality – everyone, after all, is a bit competitive from time to time. When does this fall over into the danger of being a Type A?

But new research by a Canadian psychologist promises to solve this problem from an unexpected direction, which has surprising and ominous pertinence to Tony Blair.[14]

Stewart McCann of University College of Cape Breton in Nova Scotia has recently found that the younger you are when you achieve greatness the shorter your eventual life span.[15]

First McCann looked at twenty-two different samples of high achievers like prime ministers, popes, Supreme Court justices,

Nobel Prize recipients, Oscar winners and signers of the US Declaration of Independence. In practically all of these groups, he found that the younger you are when you achieve greatness, the shorter your eventual life. This finding, he suggests, is explained by the fact that young high achievers almost certainly are the most pushy and score highest on the Type A personality test and this explains the link between fast success and a quick exit.[16]

Dr McCann has recently repeated his study – focusing most specifically on politicians, in particular almost 2,000 US governors. He also used special statistical techniques to eliminate the possibility that his first series of findings could be put down to some statistical artefact. Most ominously for the Prime Minister, who, at the age of forty-three, became the youngest Prime Minister since Lord Liverpool in 1812, McCann found again that governors elected to office at younger ages tended to have shorter lives.[17]

On average, former governors reached their posts at age forty-nine, but age at election ranged from twenty-three to eighty-one years. The average age of death was seventy, but ranged from thirty-two to one hundred and three. Comparing age of election to age of death, McCann discovered that men elected governor at a relatively young age also tended to die at an earlier age.

But it's not just the ongoing stress of simply serving as governor that is shortening their lives – the study took that into account with various measures of how much stress was experienced by each governor from their work.

Instead it seems the crucial variable is how quickly you get success, which must be linked surely to having a pushy personality. Probably the true story is about the ominous interaction between a high-stress job and a Type A personality.[18]

Women who often complain about the pushy men they have to contend with at work should also beware, as they are fast catching up with men in the heart disease stakes. The Type A personality, it seems, is not just a male preserve and McCann himself notes that a previous study of a small sample of women who had won an Academy Award for Best Supporting Actress suggested that early female achievers may also have a shorter lifespan.[19]

Given most of us are unlikely to be bothered with the problems of winning an Academy Award or waving to an election-night crowd, does this research have any relevance to us? Could the less than steroidal pushiness that we experience in our daily lives affect our hearts and life span? In fact, the most 'ordinary' group that McCann examined in his research were eminent psychologists, and the age at which they received their Ph.D. also correlated with their length of life.

If it does seem to be the case that even relatively ordinary pushiness can lead to heart disease, the key question becomes: can you get Type As to calm down and become more Zen-like and so get them to live longer?

This is something many enemy nations, like North Korea, who are worried about where the Prime Minister's boundless energy could take his attentions to next, are probably keen to know the answer to.[20]

There is much evidence that getting Type As to slow down and give up their goal-directed behaviour is very difficult. However, there is some evidence that getting them to take up moderate exercise does have a significant impact on reducing their cardiac vulnerability.

The problem is many Type As take up exercise with the gusto that they bring to the rest of their lives (have you seen the way Tony Blair plays tennis?) and sudden death has also been linked in epidemiological studies to vigorous exercise, partly because exercise is also a potent releaser of cardiac stimulant chemicals like adrenaline.[21]

The real difficulty though is that being a Type A is usually so highly rewarded in modern society that it proves very difficult for doctors worried about their patients' health to discourage the behaviour.

For example, during the last three years a lady with a Type A personality has become a modern icon and role model to young people, particularly adolescent boys, who are usually difficult to motivate. She is competitive, impatient, always alert and gets aggressive when frustrated. She tries to accomplish more and more in less and less time. Her name is Lara Croft.

It is intriguing that Lara Croft epitomizes the Type A personality because this was seen until recently as a very male preserve. Similarly men can somewhat obsessionally pursue a task, perhaps to distract themselves from other emotional issues in their lives.[22]

For example, Ray Mouney ran the equivalent of thirty-eight

marathons in six weeks, through Death Valley in California, a place where temperatures reach 40 degrees F and where hundreds of people have died. He did this ostensibly to raise £100,000 for charity – to help those with terminal muscle-wasting diseases, as suffered by his oldest son Luke.[23]

He gave up his job to throw himself into the full-time work of caring for his son, but it is notable that his wife Tish does not take part in the exhausting campaigning and fundraising role that Ray has also carved out for himself.

Does this reflect a deeply embedded difference between men and women in the way they cope with extreme stress? Could it be that men deal with strain, and in particular those situations where they are unable to control the world as they would like, by throwing themselves into obsessions – fundraising and incessant running in Ray Mouney's case.

Perhaps an obsession for a man is a way of regaining a sense of control when his world seems suddenly confused – as when his child is born with an incurable disorder. Also an obsession could serve as a useful distraction from an otherwise upsetting problem.[24]

If this is the case then a lot of previously puzzling male behaviour suddenly becomes understandable for the first time. For example, it could be that the obsession so many men have with work is simply a way of dealing with the emotional difficulties elsewhere in their lives. It's not the work so much they are attracted *to* – it's the emotional and relationship difficulties they are running away *from*. Men in particular might find their jobs more appealing than family commitments, because at work the rules are clearer, while complications and uncertainties lurk within intimate relationships.[25]

The way to diagnose whether this is the cause of your work addiction is if, as a man, your tension and nerves escalate towards the end of the working day, rather than at the beginning, as the prospect of reading a bedtime story to your child begins to loom.[26]

It is certainly already established in the field of psychology that men and women tend to get depressed or stressed for very different reasons.

Typically, women tend to become emotionally disturbed by a relationship difficulty or failure, like a marital breakdown. Yet men can often continue functioning at a surprisingly high level even though their marriage is in tatters. In contrast, men are more likely to become psychologically disturbed by a failure to realize an ambition – so life events like unemployment or a setback at work tend to hit them much harder than they would a woman.[27]

Perhaps becoming obsessive about a project – be it fundraising or achieving something at work – is in fact a masculine attempt to cope with stress, because it provides the antidote of a sense of achievement when something is going wrong elsewhere in life.[28]

If this theory is correct then it could be useful to know that if a man has become rather obsessive recently this is his way of dealing with upset. As men are less likely to openly talk about their precise difficulties than women are, it provides a clue that they are struggling to deal with something elsewhere in their lives, something they probably haven't acknowledged to others or even themselves.

Psychologists are now beginning to uncover just how profound are the differences between the way men and women cope with stress. These new findings hold out the promise of at last revealing why men and women differ so much in the kind of emotional problems they will get, though often facing the exact same difficulties.[29]

A recent study from Ben Gurion University in Israel of settlers facing the profound stress of relocation threat in the war-torn Golan Heights region found that while women derived a buffering effect on their stress from a supportive marriage, this had no buffering effect on men at all.[30]

What is particularly intriguing about this research is that the men and women were both facing exactly the same problem – the threat of having to move against their will.

The women in this study were also found to be much more likely than men to deal with stress by interacting in pairs or small groups. They turned to support from their friends and relatives when feeling distress.[31]

Men may not use relationships as a buffer when coping with stress because they find self-disclosure about personal difficulties a threat to their male pride. Their competitive instincts may rebel against the idea of acknowledging personal vulnerability.

This inability to self-disclose and use relationships as a support at times of stress could have profound implications – it might explain why men are so much more likely to kill themselves than women are – though women are supposed to be more prone to depression overall. Suicide prevention in men may require them to be encouraged to acknowledge how they are feeling to those close to them.[32]

Also men may not realize that not sharing their worries with their female partners and instead brooding on them alone as they seem to prefer to do in fact makes their wives and girlfriends feel alienated from their lives. This often starts the relationship deteriorating at times of stress when it could be a useful support.[33]

Men might resist sharing worries with a spouse partly because of their fear of being a burden on others, as an important part of masculine identity is independence from others. A recent University of Iowa study found that men who suffered a heart attack who confided in their spouses adjusted better over time, but their spouses indeed felt more distressed than the spouses who had not been confided in. So although using a close relationship as a stress buffer is helpful to the person suffering strain, it can raise the tension levels of the person being confided in.

An extreme example of where male tactics such as obsessiveness and refusal to talk about their stress can lead is the recent instances in the US of men who have suddenly snapped out of the blue, and taken guns to work to shoot colleagues. This has often occurred because the male obsession with work at a time of acute stress has led some small slight to be blown out of all proportion.[34]

In a study to investigate why postal workers in the US seemed particularly prone to this kind of violent way of dealing with stress (going berserk in the US is now even nicknamed going 'postal'), another intriguing gender difference emerged.

Psychologists at the University of South Carolina found female postal workers used 'pro-social' coping skills when faced with stress, like talking with colleagues, while men used what the researchers described as 'antisocial' coping, which meant silently brooding and drinking heavily.[35]

Researchers from Brock University in Canada recently found that the male equivalent of women's use of supportive relationships as a stress buffer was in fact work satisfaction. Men who were very satisfied with how their careers were progressing were extremely unlikely to develop emotional disorders, no matter how much stress they faced elsewhere in their lives.[36]

This could explain why men retreat into work as a way of coping – they instinctively know that if they can boost their careers this will give them the kind of self-confidence they need to get through stress.

Indeed it might even be that women could learn a bit from the male coping skill, and use an obsession with a healthy project as a distraction from an unsolvable problem, just as Ray Mouney did with all his fundraising for his son.[37]

In a unique experiment, psychologists from St Thomas's Hospital in London accompanied a three-month transatlantic sailing voyage crewed almost entirely by novices, to investigate how men and women would cope with the prolonged stress and isolation of such a remarkable venture.[38]

Surprisingly, self-esteem went up higher in the women compared with the men, from before to after the arduous journey, and this intriguing finding has been confirmed on more than one adventurous expedition.

This is the kind of trip – like running through Death Valley – that men are much more likely than women to undertake, often because they may feel less tied down by family commitments and are probably more prone to take risks.[39] Yet it seems the distraction from worries left at home, and the self-confidence surviving the exhausting expedition produced, might have been better for the women than the usual coping skills they would have employed if left back on the shore – of confiding and ruminating with supportive others.

Where men often go wrong is that the obsessions they retreat into are often too antisocial and too extreme to assist in personal growth.[40]

It would appear getting absorbed by an obsession, as long as it is a healthy one and not taken to an extreme, is an aspect of a type of male coping skill that women might benefit from. As ever, when it comes to dealing with stress, it would appear both men and women could benefit from each other's coping style.[41]

Another way of looking at this analysis is to contrast goals that arise from within – internally – and those that are suggested by our environment. For example, if everyone at work goes home at five o'clock this suggests a certain set of goals in relation to work-life balance. However, if one worker is going home much later than that this indicates perhaps a lack of congruence between an internal drive and his or her environment.

Women are usually better than men at matching their internal goals with their social environment. This may be because women have more social goals in the first place.[42]

A variety of goals in life can enhance interest and enjoyment, but what matters is the degree to which the goals supported by the environment are congruent with the chronic goals the individual brings to the situation. In other words, many people may appear to be pursuing a goal set for them by work or a relationship, yet actually the way they pursue that goal is influenced by an internal goal that is really driving them.[43]

So, for example, it might appear that someone who turns up early and leaves late at work is diligently attempting to accomplish the goals set by their bosses. The reality might be that they are driven by internal demons of ambition or a need for superiority over others, which appear at a superficial level to converge with work goals.

This goes back to the heart of the fundamental question of why we do what we do – is there an internal need that is being met by the pursuit of an apparently external goal? What if those internal needs will never be met by the external goals?[44]

A good example of where a psychological analysis of motivation can produce some surprising answers is when the issue of supposedly largely altruistic work is examined for motivation. Caring professionals, according to motivational analysis, can have a dark side.

For example, doctors like to place the blame for the stress they experience on the environment in which they work. It's the difficult patients, staff and clinical environment that are responsible for the frustrations and irritations that take the pleasure out of the practice of medicine. But the latest psychological thinking is that a good part of the real difficulty lies within doctors themselves, particularly in their personality.[45]

We already know that not everyone exposed to the same difficult clinical circumstances will experience the same stress. Certain personality traits and characteristics can increase the risk of burn-out, for example, or a strong need for approval. These personality features tend to lead clinicians to take on too much and not protect themselves enough by drawing a clear boundary around their personal lives.[46]

The motivation to become a doctor is seldom discussed in depth or investigated from a rigorous research standpoint. The little work that has been done suggests that people might pursue the caring professions, like medicine, partly because of some early childhood experience with illness in the family or another episode where suffering and empathy were a factor.[47]

The late Anthony Storr, a famous British psychiatrist, argued in his book *Dynamics of Creation* that those attracted to the therapeutic professions 'often have some personal knowledge of what it is like to feel insulted and injured . . . which actually extends the range of their compassion', and he also suggested that many of these individuals seem to have had depressed mothers.

A similar but certainly deeply controversial argument from psychoanalysts is that carers tend to have experienced some form of rejection from their parents, which could explain their interest in the emotionally vulnerable. Essentially then these individuals project their own needs on to others, rather than deal with their needs directly. The personal pain is repressed, and professional functioning provides a form of self-healing. You are really looking after other people as a way of looking after yourself. Caring for others is a way of dealing with unresolved personal conflicts.[48]

This Freudian perspective is obviously going to have its supporters as well as its critics, but ask anyone who isn't a doctor and never had any interest in becoming one what they think about medicine and it's obvious that to large numbers the urge to enter medicine seems mysterious. The fact you will have on a daily basis to confront misery and suffering seems an odd way to want to spend your life. Also there is the off-putting burden of shouldering the responsibility of taking care of people and doing something about their suffering.[49]

From this perspective it becomes clearer that there has to be a feature of personality in potential doctors that views these two fundamental challenges in such a way as not to render them insurmountable barriers to following this basically rather peculiar profession – peculiar if you start to think about it for too long.

The key feature of personality that could be implicated is linked to high self-esteem – in other words, you have to have a slightly grandiose belief in yourself and therefore in your ability to take on deep challenges and overcome them. One perspective in psychology calls this personality feature 'narcissism'. The idea that doctors might be fundamentally narcissistic could be helpful in understanding the many psychological problems clinical practice presents.[50]

The term 'narcissism' was inspired by Ovid's myth of Narcissus in *Metamorphoses* (AD8), in which a young Greek man falls in love with his reflection while gazing into a pool. Finding himself unable to unite with this loved object, Narcissus dies broken-hearted or, depending on the particular version of the story, drowns in his attempt to embrace his own reflection in the pool of water.

The myth is vital to keep in mind when considering the complexities of narcissism, a concept that has come back into vogue in psychotherapy. It is particularly concerned with the idea of a tragedy in terms of the way narcissists lead their lives, which arises from their self-love and self-obsession.[51]

Accordingly, psychiatrists refer to narcissistic traits in a personality as characterized by a grandiose façade that actually hides a deep sense of inadequacy. Indications of this disorder include a preoccupation with fantasies of unlimited success, power, brilliance, beauty or ideal love, a sense of 'specialness' or entitlement and envy.[52]

Narcissists are described by the *Diagnostic and Statistical Manual of Mental Disorders* as exhibiting pervasive patterns of grandiosity and self-importance, and as demonstrating their superiority. At the same time, these individuals seem to have an excessive need for attention and admiration and are particularly concerned with how well they are doing relative to others. This definition suggests that narcissists' dynamics are driven by a chronic need to obtain external validation for their overly positive self-views, because these rest on an essentially fragile and weak sense of self.[53]

Thus it appears that narcissists might be in a chronic state of ego-involvement, wherein self-esteem is contingent on performance outcomes. Indeed, recent studies on nonpathological narcissists (who are assumed to have qualitatively similar, merely less extreme, manifestations of the *DSM* phenomena) confirm that these individuals are preoccupied with ego concerns.[54]

Trait narcissists were found to view themselves and their accomplishments as superior to others and to find ways of discounting negative and augmenting positive feedback.

Furthermore, narcissists derogate others after negative feedback, thus creating an inferior other to whom they can feel superior. Narcissists' chronic desire to establish their superiority over others has interesting implications for how they are likely to define and experience enjoyable activities. Specifically, narcissists should be expected to approach and most enjoy activities that support their primary goal of satisfying these ego concerns.[55]

Thus, unlike many people who try to avoid highly evaluative situations (because they find them at least somewhat aversive), narcissists are likely to have more positive experiences in these situations.

Not only would narcissists be expected to prefer ego-involving situations, they might also respond less positively to mastery situations that lack the evaluative component. Narcissists latch on to tasks that afford chances for the pursuit of their chronic ego concerns and have positive experiences while engaged with those tasks.[56]

Presumably, this situation appeals to them because it provides the potential to display their ability and document their superiority. They are less interested when told to engage in a task merely for its own sake, without any evaluative component.

Does this begin to ring any bells yet if you are a doctor or know any doctors?

There have been no formal studies of the prevalence of narcissism amongst doctors but data on professions deemed to be similar suggest inductively that we should expect to find high levels of narcissitic difficulties in medicine.

For example, Andrea Halewood and Rachel Tribe from the Department of Psychology, University of East London, recently attempted to ascertain the levels of problems related to narcissism amongst trainee counselling psychologists using a narcissism scale.[57]

The results of the study, published in the journal *Psychology and Psychotherapy*, indicate that a high degree of narcissistic injury may be prevalent among trainee counselling psychologists. Consequently, the study suggested that therapeutic work could be affected in those trainees who fail to address their own narcissism.[58]

The important implication for the practice of clinical medicine is that, assuming those whose self-view is very positive have much more to lose when they receive negative feedback than people whose self-view is negative, they should experience a larger threat to their self-esteem after negative feedback. This leads naturally to a stronger motivation to re-establish their self-image by derogating or punishing the source of the threat to their ego or sense of superiority to others.

When psychologists collect data concerning daily experiences and emotional reactivity over several days they find greater mood variability and self-esteem instability for highly narcissistic individuals. One explanation for this comes from the finding that narcissistic participants in experiments constantly reveal more anger, anxiety and self-esteem fluctuations after failure than do less narcissistic individuals. Intriguingly high and low narcissists do not differ in their reactions to success.[59]

It would seem narcissistic anger is a response to perceived threats to the grandiose self-image of high narcissists.

So it is precisely because narcissists display self-aggrandizement and fantasies about unlimited ability and power that they react with rage, shame or humiliation when their self-esteem is threatened. Narcissism is a feeling of grandiosity used to bolster and enhance a rather fragile self-esteem.

The problem for doctors, for a large number of whom it might appear that narcissism could be an issue explaining their work stress, is that the practice of medicine inevitably exposes you to a large number of failure experiences. Particularly aggravating for the narcissist is that these experiences are not even directly linked to personal performance but appear to be endemic failures in the system in which doctors work. The hospital, the administration, other staff and also patients conspire to produce a strong sense of frustration and failure in clinicians.

A useful approach to these problems is to understand that at the root of narcissism is the idea of being wonderful and also, in particular, 'perfect'. This perfectionism becomes increasingly problematic for the clinician, owing to the demands of the work. Doctoring, particularly in the training phase, involves many feelings of doubt and uncertainty. The work is often frustrating for those who need a concrete sense of achievement. It is therefore no accident that in the hierarchy of medicine it is those specialities that offer the most obvious concrete signs of doing something for patients, e.g., the surgical branches, that are the most prestigious.

To survive as a doctor in increasingly difficult times it is important to balance the high self-esteem that supplies the confidence to tackle very difficult challenges on a daily basis with the regular puncturing this takes in the face of inevitable daily failure. It would seem desirable to derive a sense of self-esteem from factors that are not too closely tied to the variable daily experience of clinical practice. For example, a more general sense of improvement in clinical skills as the years go by. It would seem vital not to let your typical day grind you down and instead to keep a long-term perspective on what you are trying to achieve.

If doctors fail to work through their own grandiosity, exhibitionism, aggression and need for power, the potential for turning to their patients or their work to meet their emotional needs is enormous. An improved awareness of physicians' covert motivations for career choice should facilitate professional growth and maximize effective functioning.

Narcissism is not just an issue at work, it's also an important one in relationships.

One theory is that the simple reason we do anything is that we hope it will make us feel good about ourselves and help us to like ourselves.

'If you do not love yourself you will be unable to love others' is a popular sentiment that permeates self-help books and the current spate of popular prime-time TV dating programmes, such as *Would Like To Meet* and *Perfect Match*. But this view, that high self-esteem is good for you, has now been challenged by research published in the latest issue of the prestigious *Journal of Personality and Social Psychology*.[60]

There are several theories for why self-liking should promote relationships. Perhaps those who do not like themselves do not believe that others can love them, and thus avoid healthy relationships. Or perhaps if we do not love ourselves, we will naturally select bad relationships as part of an overall self-destructive strategy.

But properly testing this received wisdom of pop psychology for the first time, Dr Keith Campbell and colleagues from the University of Georgia took the relatively unusual step of interviewing those in relationships with people harbouring extremely high self-esteem. They found that those who strongly like themselves might indeed be confident, exciting and charming on a first date, but their likeability rapidly faded over time, as their grandiosity became apparent. People awed at the outset gradually lost patience with the one-upmanship, and the narcissist's constant demands for admiration.[61]

It seems that the dating programmes and self-help-book advice contain a small kernel of truth – people do view those with high self-esteem especially favourably on an initial encounter. But the impression becomes reversed over repeated interactions. At the first meeting, those who had high liking for themselves were indeed rated agreeable, competent, intelligent, confident and entertaining, but by the seventh interaction or date they were seen as arrogant, overestimating their abilities, tending to brag and hostile.

So it appears that although high self-esteem leads to attention and admiration in the short run – perhaps just long enough to do well on a TV programme – it also leads to rejection in the long run – after the cameras have stopped filming.[62]

Another recent study by Dr Campbell found that high self-esteem strongly predicted future infidelity, as those who like themselves a lot constantly wonder if they have found someone as good as they truly deserve, and so keep a constant roving eye out for better prospects. Indeed very high self-esteem is linked with a corresponding tendency to harbour disdain for everyone else. But precisely because they look down on all others, those with high self-esteem find it easier to flirt and be playful at the start of relationships, as they don't really care about being rebuffed by those beneath their standards anyway.[63]

James Masterson, a famous New York City psychiatrist, has been extensively quoted in the *New York Times* as an expert on excessively high self-esteem or narcissism. After his theories appeared in the press, twelve individuals approached him for treatment. He diagnosed each of them as suffering from narcissistic personality disorder but informed them that he was unable to see additional patients and suggested they see another member of his practice.[64]

Not one of the twelve narcissists returned for treatment – they each apparently wanted to be in therapy only if they worked with a famous psychiatrist and thus increased their own status and esteem in New York society. Therapy with just anyone was beneath them.

Are You a Work Addict?

WORK-ADDICTION SCALE

Each statement is followed by two possible responses: agree or disagree. Read each statement carefully and decide which response best describes how you feel. Then tick the corresponding response. Please respond to every statement. If you are not completely sure which response is more accurate, put the response that you feel is most appropriate. Do not read the scoring explanation before filling out the questionnaire. Do not spend too long on each statement. It is important that you answer each question as honestly as possible.

		AGREE	DISAGREE
1	At work I prefer doing a great variety of things, rather than specializing in one area	A	B
2	My perfect holiday is where there are few if any activities planned each day	B	A
3	Competition at work is good for you	A	B
4	I can forget about work easily in the first few days when I go away on holiday	B	A
5	Most people I meet don't take as much care and pride in their work as they should	A	B
6	It is pointless planning your career too far ahead as anything could happen	B	A
7	I find it easier to relax if I have just achieved a lot at work	A	B
8	I devote more energy and time to my relationships than work	B	A
9	People who win the lottery and give up work are heading for trouble	A	B

10   There is no point taking deadlines too
        seriously, they are just a rough guide | B | | A |

Score

Add up your score by totalling the numbers of As and Bs you have ticked.

8 or more As: You are scoring very high for work addiction. You are scoring high on the Protestant work ethic – you believe that hard work and time spent amassing wealth are the best antidotes to the sloth and permissiveness that dominate contemporary society. You need to try a few of the things your friends or partner have been exhorting for a long time now so that you can get work in perspective – like sleeping in late on the weekend.

Between 5 and 7 As: You are scoring average to just above average for work addiction. You are not quite as obsessive about work as higher scorers but you are scoring above average in having a positive attitude to working hard. Hence you are best suited to occupations demanding a concrete and pragmatic orientation towards work – like the financial services, the sciences or medical-related services. Some unhappiness in your life may be related to the lack of tangible reward for harder than average work in your current career. It may be that if you are a harder worker than many of your colleagues and this is not being recognized you should think of changing where you work or what you do. A lot of your effort may be due to work addiction rather than work of practical benefit to your career.

Between 3 and 5 As: You are scoring average to just below average for work addiction. You tend to be more creative and innovative than higher scorers who embrace the Protestant work ethic more closely than you. You are also more sensitive than those more obsessed with hard work, and your capacity for playful fantasy ensures you think there is a lot more to life than just hard work – you believe we work to live, not live to work. You are also less intolerant than higher scorers of those colleagues who do not work so hard and hence you are more pleasant to work with than work addicts. However, perhaps you are a little too tolerant of the merely lazy and make more excuses for them than you should – they may even exploit you a little.

Between 0 and 2 As: You are scoring very low on work addiction, so you are scoring very low in valuing hard work and this is partly because you have great difficulty conforming to what society tends to regard as appropriate behaviour. Hence the careers best suited to you are those that tend to attract the non-conformist like artists and musicians, where theoretical and abstract as well as humanistic values are embraced. You have plans of what you would like to do with your life, of which only a very few revolve around amassing wealth – you are much more interested in having fun. Your success in life is likely to come from inspiration rather than hard slog.

If there is one disorder your boss hopes you will catch it is probably work addiction. In the past we spoke of workaholic colleagues mostly with pity, but in these days of job insecurity, the first person to leave the office is now regarded as having committed work hara-kiri.[65]

It used to be called workaholism, when it wasn't taken seriously, and thought to afflict only a few. But today psychologists and psychiatrists have changed the name to work addiction, because they believe this better captures the compulsive quality of the problem, and that it can be just as dangerous as any other kind of addiction, like drink, food or drugs.

Work addicts are different to work enthusiasts who simply enjoy their work a lot but can maintain a proper balance in their lives. As with an alcohol addiction, where at the beginning you drink because it enhances your mood occasionally and eventually you drink in order not to feel bad, with work addiction you work because if you don't, you feel guilty and unworthy.[66]

Work addiction is probably the only disorder that can bring you fame, wealth, recognition and reward. This explains why it might be one of the least recognized and addressed psychological problems you could suffer from today. In an increasingly competitive business environment, it is work addicts who appear, at first glance, to be those most likely to gain bosses' admiration and rewards.

But because a work addict basically works just for the sake of working, often achieving very little in reality for their effort, the work addict is not the most efficient member of the team. What's more, work addiction brings costs, first felt outside the office – the work addict is particularly vulnerable to losing their relationships, be it friends, family or lovers. Perhaps the earliest sign of work addiction is where something upsetting at work will affect you at home much more than something painful in your personal life will affect you at work.[67]

Friends at work may be the last to disappear, but evaporate they surely will, bored to death by the work addict's inability to converse about anything other than ambition, money, success – well, basically work.

The roots of work addiction are believed to lie in childhood, when the work addict's family made him believe their love for him was conditional on his achievements. This leaves the work addict with feelings of inferiority (because he was never told he was good enough just as he is by his parents), so he embarks on a career of overdoing in an attempt to compensate for these feelings of poor self-worth.

The problem runs so deep that even when the work addict is at play or socializing, he is primarily motivated by his self-absorption with work. He will pick his friends, hobbies, lovers, even his wife, according to how they may help his career. So the work addict will take up golf, not because he likes the game but because he notes it's what the senior management play and he is looking for an entrée into their circle.

Because everything gets tailored to work, the work addict loses his individuality and becomes a non-person, just a work robot. He gets irritable with others who don't show the same commitment to work and his inability to delegate means others feel excluded from the work addict's team of one. Work addicts take on too much; to them, quiet periods mean they are not doing enough to advance their careers – but then they get into a panic over their sudden plethora of deadlines.[68]

Paradoxically, all this makes the work addict less than pleasant to work with, so his colleagues and seniors do their best to prevent him moving to their department, thus impeding the work addict's long-term promotion. Work addiction becomes a self-sabotaging strategy and also a self-perpetuating one; because the addict never feels his career is advancing fast enough, he work binges even more.[69]

Friends, family or lovers complain that the work addict, even when physically present, is emotionally unavailable to them. Either they are exhausted by work or have diverted too much of their emotional energy to that sphere of their lives. In fact, work addiction is now thought to be one of the major and previously unsuspected causes of marital disharmony. In one survey conducted by a business magazine, 80% of readers said their husbands worked too much. The children of work-addict fathers have been found to suffer just as much depression and anxiety as a result of parental neglect as the children of alcoholic fathers.

Work addiction is not simply bad for the health of those close to you, it's bad for you as well. Research has found work addicts, in particular those who are impatient or frankly hostile to others, are more prone to a variety of physical illnesses, including serious heart trouble. 'Karoshi', or death from overwork, has been blamed for 10% of all deaths of working men in Japan.[70]

There is a treatment for work addiction but you will, er, have to work at it. The five steps to recovery are:

(1) Firstly you need to stop rating yourself and other people's worth purely in terms of career success. There are many people who lead worthwhile and fulfilling lives but who never make it to the top of their profession. Just because you may not succeed in attaining all your ambitions at work, it does not mean your life, in its entirety, will have been a failure. In fact, you will have wasted your productive years if you continue to neglect social, family and romantic relationships for the sake of work. Become satisfied instead with a standard that is just good enough – releasing you to put more energy into the rest of your life.

(2) Do not believe that if you work hard enough you are saving yourself from more work in the future because you will have cleared your in-tray. Your in-tray will never be empty. Do not get obsessed with always having to complete everything straightaway. On your deathbed there will still be things in your in-tray that you will just have to leave there.

(3) Just because someone throws you a ball doesn't mean you have to catch it. Just because a fantastic opportunity has come up at work doesn't mean you have to always seize it. Every time you accept another

opportunity at work remember what you are automatically giving up in your home and family life, as well as general personal development.

(4) Learn to delegate. The work addict is overburdened because his perfectionism and need for control mean he would prefer the stress of doing a task himself than the strain of coping with another's imperfect strivings. But by being patient with others and taking the risk of delegating, the more others will learn from being entrusted with work and the better they will get. Plus their relationship with you will improve as they feel included and trusted by you.

(5) Finally you need to break your addiction for praise and approval from others for your work skills or talents, and replace it with more concern over what others think about your attitude to your friendships, personal and family life.

THE DANGER SIGNS OF WORK ADDICTION

(1) Always hurrying and staying busy

(2) Not delegating enough because you need to stay in control of everything

(3) Higher standards of perfectionism than most who are successful in your line of work

(4) Self-neglect because of work

(5) A frequent belief you are not good enough at your job

(6) When faced with a problem, you tend to prefer the solution that requires most work

THE SIX DIFFERENT TYPES OF WORK ADDICT

(1) *Pseudo work addict*: appears at first glance to be a work addict, but only because they want you to think

they are. They work hard when the boss is around but relax when left alone in the office. Their main aim is to gain power in the organization rather than to be productive, so every task taken on is with a view to its promotion implications.

(2) *Escapist work addict*: stays on the job or in the office simply because they would rather be anywhere but home – they are trying to escape from an unhappy domestic or family situation. They try to turn work relationships into a surrogate family and, though married, are therefore prone to having an affair at work.

(3) *Ex-work addict*: a bit like ex-alcoholics who decline the offer of a drink, the ex-work addict recovers by setting extremely rigid limits around their work time because they know they are in danger of relapsing into work addiction if they stay at work a minute longer than planned. They labour hard in the time they have set themselves for work, but are firm in not going over these self-imposed boundaries. They fear retaliation from a wife or lover who has threatened to leave if the work addiction returns.

(4) *Temporary work addict*: works hard because some recent development has made them feel insecure about their job prospects but when confidence in their job security returns will slack off again. They are capable of sustaining hard work only as long as there is a threatening consequence for slacking.

(5) *True work addict*: takes their work too seriously, believing it is more important than absolutely anything else in their lives, be it family, friends or children. They strive to accomplish only the highest standards and only derive any real satisfaction in life from achievement at work.

(6) *Binge worker*: doesn't work consistently and may take a long period of time off relaxing rather than working,

but then leaves too short a time to finish too many tasks, so ends up working in binges, which may leave them up into the small hours finishing projects. Gets a secret buzz from pressure and so may try to create it when none is around, partly because normal, more consistent work rates bore them.

16

DOES YOUR MOTIVATION COME FROM YOUR BODY OR YOUR BRAIN?

The successful start by doing something very simple that the unsuccessful tend not to – they show up

Frank Bettger

Refine and improve the quality of your thoughts and you will have little to fear from the world

Buddha

A key issue that raises its head whenever we start to think about motivation is whether much of our basic drive is determined by issues beyond our control – not just our background, but our gender, for example.

For example, perhaps one of the greatest causes of discontent in relationships between men and women is that sexual appetites seem to be different. Women's capacity for sex is in fact greater than men's, in the sense that women can have more sex and more orgasms than men can over a set period of time, yet the controversy continues to rage as to whether men and women have very different sex drives.

Psychologist Professor Baumeister from Case Western Reserve University in the USA appears to have finally resolved this age-old dispute. His recent review of the research indicates that the average young man gets sexually aroused several times a day while the average young woman only experiences this twice a week. Forty-five per cent of men but only 15% of women report masturbating at least once per week. Women are almost four times more likely than men to say they have never masturbated.[1]

If men and women have very different sex drives, then the number of times they end up having sex could be the result of a compromise within their relationship and does not reflect the number of times they really want sex. To get a true picture of how often each gender actually desires sex, a good place to look is at sex in gay male and lesbian relationships, as these are not constrained by what the opposite sex wants. Research into this issue has found that two years into a relationship, two-thirds of gay men are having sex at least three or more times per week, but the figure is only one-third of lesbians for this high rate of sex.

If men and women have very different sex drives then a key aspect of maintaining a healthy relationship as a couple could be how this difference is negotiated without recrimination. The ability to compromise is a vital element in any relationship's long-term survival. It would appear from the research that the only time a couple coincide in levels of sex drive is when a relationship is starting, passion is high and intimacy is rising. Understanding that, for the rest of your life, sex drive is unlikely to coincide is now a vital relationship survival skill.[2]

Why does the man who has everything – a wonderful career, trophy wife, adoring family – risk it all for a casual affair? The worlds of politics, sport and business are replete with examples of sex scandals wrecking the family lives or the careers of otherwise highly successful men. New research into the role of the male sex hormone testosterone promises to supply a biological answer for the first time.[3]

Testosterone has long been linked with the drive for dominance over others, even when more passive compliance might be in your best interests. For example, prison inmates who have high testosterone levels are more likely to have committed violent crimes, engaged in criminal activity at an early age, been more dominant in prison, violated prison rules more often and been judged more severely by parole boards than those with lower levels.[4]

Testosterone is related to a general sensation-seeking tendency. Sensation seeking can have positive or negative effects depending on one's social background and resources. Individuals low in socio-economic status often find the most exciting things to do are illegal, while those from higher classes can find activities that are both stimulating and socially acceptable, like driving fast cars instead of stealing them, arguing instead of fighting, playing competitive sports instead of brawling.

Although men usually have testosterone levels between twenty to forty times that of women, exactly how potent testosterone can be is demonstrated by studies that have found testosterone measures increase in women with the status of their professions and is higher in more aggressive women.[5]

In a 1995 study of female university students, testosterone was negatively associated with low frequency of smiling, the absence of which is sometimes regarded as an indicator of dominance. Another study in the same year found that women testing high on testosterone had more sexual partners and claimed to need less commitment from a man before engaging in sex. There is also a well-established link between the amount of previous sexual experience a man has and his testosterone levels; this measure even predicts the amount he thinks about sex.[6]

As testosterone is found in much higher concentrations in men, might its effect on male behaviour have been previously underestimated? Alan Booth and James Dabbs of Penn and Georgia State Universities published research in the early 1990s using 4,500 Army veterans, revealing that men producing more testosterone are less likely to marry and more likely to divorce.

What was particularly startling about their research was the finding that testosterone levels did not have to be abnormally high to have a negative effect on marriage. Men with mid-range levels of testosterone were more likely to report lower marital success than those with very low measures.[7]

Booth and Dabbs found that men in the top third of the population for testosterone concentrations are 50% less likely to ever get married. Of those who do marry, they are 43% more likely to get divorced, 31% more likely to separate temporarily because of marital strife, 38% more likely to have extramarital sex and 12% more likely to hit their wives.[8]

Now Allan Mazur and Joel Michalek from Syracuse University in the USA have developed this work further, having investigated 2,100 Air Force veterans who received four medical examinations over a ten-year period. The main finding was that testosterone fell and remained low when the men got married, but rose with divorce, the rise in levels *preceding* the divorce by two years, and remaining high until three years after the break-up.[9]

What is groundbreaking about their work is the finding that as testosterone appears to rise before the time of divorce, there is a strong suggestion that changes in the man's environment that cause these rises in testosterone may then make marital breakdown more likely.

This change might be the man's experience of dominance outside as well as inside the family home. Testosterone in non-human primates rises when males achieve or defend dominant positions, and falls when they are dominated.

This link between testosterone, dominance and competition could mean that men with high testosterone levels tend to carry contentious competitive behaviour to relations with the opposite sex. This would result in difficulty finding a spouse and therefore never marrying, or once married being unable to sustain the relationship and divorcing, or, if still married, having a poor-quality marriage.[10]

Aggression and dominant behaviour are well suited to gathering and amassing resources, and achieving and maintaining status, but unchecked they are not conducive to the co-operation and mutual support essential to intimate heterosexual relations. Sensation-seeking behaviour linked to testosterone may mean men with high testosterone become bored with marriage more quickly than others and so seek out other partners.

Much male interpersonal behaviour is overtly or subtly concerned with managing dominance and subordination, and testosterone is the hormone most strongly linked to men's position in a dominance hierarchy. Sports, quizzes, elections, criticism, competition for promotion and academic jousting all involve male attempts at achieving domination or reconciling themselves to subordination.[11]

Previously, research has found that athletes' testosterone levels rise shortly before their sports fixtures, as if in anticipation of the competition. This pre-competition boost of the hormone may make the individual more willing to take risks and may improve co-ordination, cognitive performance and concentration – all effects produced by testosterone. For one or two hours after athletic competition, testosterone levels of winners are higher than those of losers – and these results have been replicated in sports as different as tennis and wrestling.

Intriguingly, the male involved has to regard the win as important; otherwise the rise in testosterone is lessened or does not occur at all. For example, when researchers were surprised not to measure a rise in testosterone in winners and a drop in losers of amateur judo competitions, they were told afterwards by their subjects that they did not take the matches seriously, which could explain the lack of effect on testosterone.

While these results were obtained in physically taxing sports, would they be replicated in the less vigorous competition of everyday social interaction? Research has found that testosterone rises shortly before chess games, and in those who are challenged in the form of an insult, and testosterone levels of winners are high relative to those of losers following chess matches.[12]

Similar effects occur among sports fans who are not themselves participants. Following the 1994 World Cup soccer tournament in which Brazil beat Italy, testosterone increased significantly in Brazilian fans who had watched the match on television and decreased in Italian fans.

It seems therefore the act of competing for dominant status affects male testosterone in two ways: firstly, testosterone rises in the face of a challenge as if it were an anticipatory response to impending competition; secondly, after the competition, testosterone rises in winners and declines in losers.

A life-long pattern of success, competition or challenge could lead to continuously higher levels of testosterone, which might in turn influence a testosterone-driven need to dominate, compete or get restless in a marriage. Competitors with a previous history of success in their sport tend to have higher levels of testosterone after a competitive match than those with a previous history of losses, so the testosterone response to competition is to some extent determined by a history of previous success. This may go some way to explaining why winning and losing streaks occur.[13]

The function of the elevated testosterone following a win and the drop in testosterone following a loss is not known. One possibility is that winners are soon likely to face other challengers: the high testosterone prepares them for this. The drop in testosterone among losers may encourage withdrawal from other challenges, thus preventing injury.

High-testosterone aggressive behaviours are now seen by many social scientists as no longer functional in urban, industrialized cultures and, in fact, may be dysfunctional in terms of optimum psychological development. Teresa Julian and Patrick McKenry at Ohio State University found in a study of thirty-seven middle-aged men that lower testosterone levels were associated with better marital satisfaction and higher quality parent-adolescent relationships.

Perhaps a low-testosterone-driven sex-role convergence is a very adaptive coping mechanism at mid-life for men, when to move towards such traditionally defined female traits as passivity, sensuality, nurturance, affiliation and expressiveness may benefit a marriage and family life.

The implication of this new research is that to achieve a content family life, many married couples may have to re-consider seriously the role of a career that encourages competitiveness in the man and so raises his testosterone levels, in turn endangering the marriage.[14]

But Jeffrey Foss of the Department of Philosophy at Victoria University in British Columbia points out that chauvinists will rejoice at the finding that the will to compete is enhanced by testosterone. This produces a biological rationale for why men tend to dominate in society, because practically every man has higher testosterone levels than any woman.[15]

But maybe, Foss contends, competitive spirit is not always an advantage, particularly where persistent concentration and con-tinued co-operation are required. In his local school district, Foss notes that among 109 secondary school scholarships, seventy-one went to girls and only thirty-eight to boys. Yet boys led the girls in suspensions by a ratio of 78% to 22%. If the will to dominate, driven by testosterone, explains the greater tendency of men to misbehave and thus be suspended from school, it may also explain their poorer academic performance.[16]

Foss concludes that testosterone may be a mixed blessing, if a blessing at all.

A leading gynaecologist has recently claimed that female politicians are using testosterone implants to try to match their male counterparts in assertiveness and competitiveness. Harley Street doctor Malcolm Whitehead said he has prescribed the hormone for a number of women who wanted to 'beef up' their image in the macho world of politics. He commented: 'I have prescribed testosterone implants for female politicians in Westminster who want to compete better with their male colleagues in committee meetings and parliamentary debates. They claim the hormone boosts their assertiveness and makes them feel more powerful.'

His extraordinary claim – recently published in the *New Statesman* magazine – was greeted with disbelief in Westminster, but then which female MP was going to publicly admit to trying testosterone? Trade and Industry Secretary Patricia Hewitt said, 'MPs are far more likely to succeed if they use rational arguments rather than hormonal-fuelled rhetoric.'[17]

Margaret Beckett, Environment, Food and Rural Affairs Secretary, also denied using the implants, saying, 'Women don't have to be like men to be successful.' Conservative Julie Kirkbride added, 'I can't believe Margaret Thatcher would have resorted to this type of thing, and she got to the top in a man's world.'

But Mr Whitehead, who runs a trust offering advice to menopausal women, maintained he is increasingly being approached by women MPs wanting testosterone implants. The hormone is produced in small amounts by women – at levels up to ten times lower than those of men. However, as women age those levels can dip, just as female hormones do at the menopause. The lowering of testosterone levels at the menopause is associated with causing women to lose interest in sex, have lower energy levels and, in some cases, reductions in their confidence and mood.

Testosterone implants are meant to solve that problem. The treatment involves embedding a small pellet under the skin, which releases a fixed testosterone dose into the bloodstream over a six-month period.[18] Critics claim this has dangers, but Mr Whitehead dismissed that suggestion, saying: 'As long as they stay within the normal hormonal range, there is nothing to worry about. All the talk of deepening voices and beard growth is complete nonsense.'

Testosterone can't as yet be taken orally, but it can be taken as a transdermal skin patch, as a chemical that dissolves under the tongue, or as an injection.

The most sophisticated medical view now of hormone replacement therapy for women in the menopause is that it should probably include a touch of testosterone to assist mood and sex drive.

A key controversy though is that unlike the situation in men, we still lack enough data about how normal testosterone levels vary in women throughout their life span or even through the monthly menstrual cycle. So it's difficult to know from a blood test what would constitute abnormally low levels and what would therefore need topping up by treatment.

Given the definite advantages to women of taking testosterone in terms of mood and drive, some doctors suggest it should be tried without any hard evidence that the woman is suffering from an actual testosterone deficiency.[19]

Tory politician Ann Widdecombe haughtily denied that women MPs needed any artificial help to stand up to their male counterparts. She said: 'This appears to be a send-up. It is just silly.'

However, scientists investigating the role of testosterone in women don't share this scepticism. They believe that testosterone plays an important role in maintaining mental and physical functions of healthy women.

For example, a recent study from the University of Utrecht in the Netherlands found that taking testosterone dissolved under the tongue markedly improved normal women's sex drive and arousal. Just three to four hours after taking the testosterone the women reported a significant increase in 'genital responsiveness' and 'sexual lust'.

Another study by Dr Valerie Grant at the University of Auckland found that how dominant you were as a woman was strongly linked to how high your testosterone levels were.

A previous study had found higher testosterone levels in professional and managerial women compared to housewives and clerical workers. Related research confirms that women with higher testosterone levels perceive themselves as 'self-directed', 'action-oriented' and 'resourceful', whereas those with lower testosterone concentrations perceived themselves as 'conventional' and 'possessing a caring attitude'.[20]

Neuroendocrinologist Dr Helen Bateup and colleagues at the RockSeller University in New York recently examined how competing in rugby games affected the testosterone levels in women. In an intriguing and unique experiment, they performed blood tests on a nationally recognized college women's rugby team in order to investigate how women's hormones change in anticipation of and response to aggressive striving.[21]

Dr Bateup and her colleagues found testosterone levels in the female rugby players before their matches were strongly associated with subsequent team bonding, aggressiveness and being focused during the game.

Maybe the historical huge contrast in testosterone levels between men and women had an evolutionary basis that it might be dangerous to mess with.[22] Women's response to challenges may be more defensive in nature than men's – the female approach has been termed a 'tend-and-befriend' strategy to differentiate it from the 'fight-or-flight' response attributed to men, which their higher testosterone levels probably helps produce.[23]

For females in our evolutionary past fight may have put their offspring in danger, while flight may have been compromised by pregnancy or offspring care. Tending entails nurturing activities intended to protect and calm offspring and befriending involves creating and maintaining networks that provide resources and protection for self and offspring.

In this light it's important not to forget that the nickname given to testosterone by endocrinologists is the 'one-night-stand hormone' as it increases sex drive and risk-taking. So it's thought to underpin the much greater male propensity to seek unattached sex compared to women.

If female politicians really are taking testosterone or are having their levels boosted by being in the competitive atmosphere of Parliament, could these hormonal changes have wider political implications? Are we more likely in the future to see female MPs getting caught up in the kind of sex scandals that have so characterized male politicians?[24]

If this is the case it might mean that testosterone causes women politicians to lose one clear advantage female MPs historically had over the men: at least their families could trust them more.

But maybe the biological price women pay for traditionally less sexually adventuresome lives compared to men was a tendency to get more depressed.

According to the rather alarming statistics, approximately one in ten men and one in five women will suffer from clinical depression at some time in their lives. Yet despite its becoming one of the commonest problems that family doctors now encounter, the evidence is that clinical depression is not just often unrecognized by the lay public, but even GPs frequently miss it, rendering this one of the most undiagnosed conditions.

We have all experienced low mood, but when does that become clinical depression? The standard psychiatric view is that clinical depression occurs when your mood is so low for so long (at least two weeks) that you can no longer work effectively or conduct relationships properly – it interferes with what doctors refer to as 'activities of daily living'.[25]

When you are at such a low ebb for so long, your whole body and not just your mind becomes affected. As a result, you suffer loss of weight, loss of appetite and profound sleep disturbance – all signals that a more profound change is occurring throughout your brain and body, and depression isn't just simply 'all in the mind'.

New research from the University of the Wisconsin in the USA suggests that the line between clinical depression and ordinary everyday low mood might be more blurred than previously thought. The study found that unpleasant thoughts experienced for a short while could induce very similar brain activity changes to those found in the clinically depressed. Furthermore, these transient negative thoughts produced profound biological changes to the body's immune system that were measurable up to six months later.[26]

Professor Richard Davidson, with colleagues at Wisconsin and Princeton University, New Jersey, asked fifty-two men and women to recount both the best and worst events in their lives on paper. For their best experiences, the subjects were asked to write about an event where they experienced 'intense happiness or joy'. And for their worst experience they were asked to remember an event causing 'the most intense sadness, fear, or anger'. During this autobiographical task, the brain activity was measured, and intriguing changes were noted in the part of the brain that is associated with planning future activity.

Those experiencing lower mood when recalling their worst past experiences showed greater activity in the frontal right-hand side of the brain while those who had better mood throughout the tasks showed more activity in the frontal left-hand side the brain.[27]

The fact that this study found clinical depression and just thinking negative thoughts or having a generally pessimistic outlook on life are all associated with similar alterations in the part of the brain associated with planning is an intriguing take on depression. We already know that the depressed are not just those who have suffered negative life experiences; rather they tend to be more affected by these events because they assume that the bad things happening to them now have dramatically awful future consequences as well. For example, they believe a failure at an exam means they are failures in life generally ('globalizing') or that they will always fail future exams. For the first time this research shows a definite link between the most unhelpful ways of thinking and brain activity changes. The fact it's the part of the brain linked to planning tells us that it's the way you look at the future that has the most profound implications for your mood and mental health.

The Wisconsin study had other intriguing findings about the future, as the subjects involved were then given flu shots and their antibody levels were measured after two weeks, four weeks and six months. Antibodies are the vital chemicals the body produces when it's mounting resistance to infections from viruses and bacteria; they attack invading agents and neutralize them. The researchers found a clear link between strong activity in the frontal brain area and a large rise in antibodies, and vice versa.

The importance of this finding is that brain activity linking negative emotions to a lower immune response against disease has been revealed for the first time.

However, the study could not explain exactly how having a positive attitude boosts the immune system. The researchers say some evidence exists to suggest a link between the front of the brain and the immune system via a complex hormonal system governed by glands in the brain interacting with glands elsewhere in the body.[28]

Another study, this time by Italian and UK researchers, also found that depressed people have fewer lymphocytes and T-cells – white blood cells crucial for fighting disease.

But just because the body's immune system is being affected by negative emotions, does this mean the depressed are prone to more physical illnesses? In fact, another recent study confirms that happy people are three times less likely to get a cold, according to researchers who squirted cold virus up the noses of volunteers.

Psychologist Sheldon Cohen and his colleagues at Carnegie Mellon University, Pennsylvania, also found that the positive thinkers who do develop symptoms complain about them less.

The team studied over 300 initially healthy volunteers. First, each person was interviewed over two weeks to gauge his or her emotional state. Next the researchers squirted rhinovirus, the germ that causes colds, into each subject's nose.

Those scoring in the bottom third for positive emotions were found to be three times more likely to catch a cold than those scoring in the top third. One possible explanation for the protective effect of positive emotions is that happier volunteers were found to have lower blood levels of stress-related hormones such as cortisol, which influences high blood pressure.[29]

Cohen's team also assessed how those people who did catch a cold coped with the symptoms. This involved collecting the tissues used by volunteers to blow their noses and weighing them, to calculate the amount of mucus each person produced. The finding was that even when symptoms were physically the same, participants with a negative emotional style complained more.

Is there anything we can do to influence our prefrontal cortex, stay positive and so ward off depression and future physical illness?

In a small but highly provocative study, the same University of Wisconsin research team that produced the frontal brain findings found, for the first time, that a short programme in 'mindfulness meditation' produced lasting positive changes in both the brain and the function of the immune system.[30]

Again Richard Davidson, Professor of Psychology and Psychiatry, led the research into 'mindfulness meditation'. This is a technique often recommended as an antidote to the stress and pain of chronic disease, designed to focus one's attention intensely on the moment, noting thoughts and feelings as they occur but refraining from judging or acting on those thoughts and feelings.

In the University of Wisconsin study, participants were randomly assigned to one of two groups. The experimental group, with twenty-five subjects, received training in mindfulness meditation, and attended weekly classes and one seven-hour retreat during the study; they were also assigned home practice for an hour a day, six days a week. The sixteen members of the control group did not receive meditation training until after the study was completed.

The meditation group showed an increase of activation in the left-hand side of the frontal brain region. The research team also tested whether the meditation group had better immune function than the control group did. All the study participants got a flu vaccine at the end of the eight-week meditation course. Then, at four and eight weeks after vaccine administration, both groups had blood tests to measure the level of antibodies they had produced. While both groups (as expected) had developed increased antibodies, the meditation group had a significantly larger increase than the controls, at both four and eight weeks after receiving the vaccine.[31]

The key benefit of the meditation, now we can see that it produces activation in this vital planning part of the brain, could be to help prevent the tendency of the less happy to link present bad events with future negative ones. It could be that to guarantee a future freer of depression and physical illness, you need actually to *be* more positive about the future.

While some claim we are more depressed today than previous generations ever were, the largest scientific study investigating the issue, conducted by Harvard University psychiatrists, has found that depression rates have, in fact, stayed remarkably constant in most parts of the community over the last forty years.

However, there was one striking exception: women under the age of forty-five were found to be between two to three times as likely to get depressed today than women of the same age in the 1950s and the 1970s. Women born after the last war were found to be suffering rates of depression almost three times the rate of men and twice the rate of older women. The researchers suggest that the tendency of younger women to have such high rates of depression, in particular compared to men, appears to be a recent phenomenon and probably did not occur before the 1950s.[32]

Currently over one in five women will get a serious depressive illness at some time in their lives while this only applies to around one in ten men.

It would appear that something has happened since the 1950s that has had a massive impact on women born after the last war to make them today the group most prone to depression. Psychiatrists are still unsure what this factor is. One obvious possibility is the rise of unrealistically perfect images of women in the media, leading modern women to feel chronically dissatisfied with their appearance. This would suggest the rise is linked to the dramatic increase in eating disorders we have witnessed recently.

But another cause could be the major change in the number of women entering the workplace and abandoning the sole role of housewife and mother that has occurred since the 1950s.[33]

Research confirms that women who have jobs and children are much more prone to depression than women who work but don't have children. In particular, working women who have no assistance with childcare are most prone to depression.

The modern woman certainly works many more hours compared to men when all the roles that she performs are considered. Women often work full-time outside the home and then do nearly all the childcare and domestic work afterwards. They are also increasingly 'sandwiched' between caring for young children and caring for sick and older family members.

It could be that the new problem of having to juggle the various responsibilities of children, marriage and career has produced greater strain on modern younger women than their mothers had to contend with. However, psychological research into whether working outside the home increases a woman's chance of getting depression has found that generally employment protects women from depression.[34]

However, there have been some puzzling exceptions to this finding. For example, research has found that lower social class women benefit more from working outside the home than higher social class women, when it comes to depression.

It might be that poorer women compensate for the strain of working by a massive gain in financial comfort. But richer women don't really experience much material improvement in their circumstances, which means they simply experience the strain of work but no real benefit to them in terms of economic pampering.

Psychological research has found that employment is particularly beneficial for women in protecting them from depression if they are getting high job satisfaction, or are in unhappy marriages, or have husbands who assist with childcare and housework. It could be that some women who are in work they hate and are not getting the necessary support from their husbands with the family, or who are missing husbands and children they enjoy being with, would be better off mentally if they gave up work.[35]

But other research has found that many women are at greatest risk from getting depression when they have several young children at home. It might therefore be that the traditional female support from mothers, female relatives and friends, which women obtained before the 1950s, is now absent, because all these other women are off juggling their own competing modern demands.

Another theory is that depression is caused by the difficulty women experience getting positive feedback for their efforts. Because of family commitments they cannot be as successful in their careers as they should like to be, and so don't get the praise from colleagues that would cheer them up. Yet because of their jobs, they also feel permanently guilty about their family lives and are unable to obtain the praise and rewards from their families and husbands they might get if they stayed fully at home.[36]

The main difference between men and women's sense of well-being, therefore, could be in their ability to gain clear-cut rewards for their efforts. Men can experience a definite sense of achievement from career progression or a sense of a job well done. Women feel caught on a treadmill whereby immense effort in any sphere of life appears to leave them with no sense of achievement, merely guilt over what they have sacrificed elsewhere to attain their goals.

But another double whammy women suffer from is they tend to blame themselves for their lack of success at home or at work, rather than see that it is difficult circumstances that account for their unsatisfactory performance.

Another possible problem is termed by psychologists 'role conflict'. At home women need to be nurturing, empathic and sensitive, but in the workplace it is dominance, assertiveness and competitiveness that are valued, and it is having to continually oscillate between these opposite extremes that creates strain and eventually depression in women.[37]

Susan Nolen-Hoeksema, a psychologist at the University of Michigan who specializes in trying to explain why women get more depression than men, suggests it is the lack of control women feel in their busy lives that leads to a sense of chronic strain. It is this relentless pressure that produces depression in women.[38]

But the latest and surprising theory to explain the modern

tendency of women to get so depressed comes from psychologists who argue that men more than women 'suffer' from positive illusions about their own abilities. Men tend to see themselves as better than average at most things they try while women are more realistic about themselves.

As a result men have tended to be rather over-confident about themselves, which in fact is helpful in many work situations requiring decision-making, dominance and assertiveness. Women's greater realism about themselves is more attractive and, combined with a greater regard for others, this partly explains why they are better at getting on with others than men, whose arrogance and self-centredness is more likely to alienate.

Psychologists now suggest that in order to take on and try to solve the problems one faces in the world outside the home, the male tendency to be over-confident could in fact be helpful, as it makes you less likely to get depressed in the face of setbacks.[39]

Inside the home the traditional female role of getting on with others and nurturing them, praising them and boosting their self-esteem, has not left much room for women to feel they are better than the rest, as men tend to. But what women now need more than ever is a bit of male over-confidence to take on all the juggling they have to do.

Yet from research looking at how men and women on interview panels react to assured-looking women, it appears that women projecting confidence appeal to men but not to women. Amongst women the appearance of boldness in other females is disliked, and this might explain why women are so wary of appearing too self-assured.

If this research is right, then it could in fact be that women's main enemy in their fight to overcome their modern tendency to depression is other women.

However, it is intriguing to consider that the key gender difference between men and women – contrasts in testosterone levels – could also account for another key difference – the fact that men and women suffer very different rates of depression.

If there is a genetic and biological basis for depression, does that mean depression serves some kind of evolutionary function?

Depression is one of the key causes for low motivation – so understanding a possible purpose to depression is essential in resolving low motivational states.

One example of a provocative theory for depression based on evolutionary thinking is 'Seasonal Affective Disorder'. This is triggered by low light conditions found in winter, a traditional time of scarcity, and it is a condition that enforces withdrawal and perhaps reduced energy consumption at times when our ancestors would have suffered seasonal scarcity. The condition makes sense from an evolutionary standpoint, combined with the fact that in modern conditions it is no longer adaptive.[40]

Another puzzle about depression that might be amenable to evolutionary explanation is the fact that women suffer between two to three times the rate of depression as men. Women have traditionally been involved in child rearing whereas men have historically been the providers of food, material resources and protection. Depression, with its symptoms that produce withdrawal and a reduction in risk-taking, would have kept women sheltered from danger, in order to bear and care for children, whereas a depressed man would have been more impaired in the role of provider and protector.

Sex hormones may be important mediators of these evolutionarily selected behavioural differences. It is interesting to note the antidepressant, novelty-seeking and aggression-promoting effects of testosterone. It is also curious to observe in a woman's life cycle the increased incidence of depression in the first trimester of pregnancy and post partum. Both are critical periods for offspring and a lower level of activity by the mother – so keeping her out of danger – may have been reproductively advantageous in times past.

It is clear that even aversive states like pain have a positive evolutionary function and pain is a good analogy for considering the function of depression because there is a way in which we can think of depression as a kind of emotional pain. Physical pain is unpleasant but there is a good reason for this – in its insistent aversive state it draws our attention abruptly to a part of the body that might require urgent attention. Pain breaks through competing stimuli and gains our focus.

But pain doesn't just grab our attention: we work ceaselessly to try and fix the cause of the pain in order to remove the sensation. These are two key concepts in the evolutionary theory about the function of depression – it draws our attention to something that needs fixing and it motivates us to fix it.

If depression is an emotional pain, what is it drawing our attention to and what needs fixing?

One function of depression could be social – to draw attention to the depressed person in order to gain assistance. Perhaps the ability to feel empathy with the depressed and to imagine how horrible depression might be motivates the well to render assistance.

There is perhaps a link between the tears of the depressed adult patient and the tears of a baby – a baby's crying drives its parents to pay attention and do something to remedy the cause of the crying. Some regard the adult depressive episode as an attempt at an adaptation that has failed because while it's a strategy that works in a baby it doesn't function so well in adults and in fact the depressed are often shunned rather than comforted.[41]

Another theory is that depression is a kind of yielding signal in hierarchy conflicts, which is useful because if competitors never yielded even though they were losing they could go on to put themselves at greater risk in an aggressive conflict. This social yielding hypothesis proposes that depression is an adaptation for forcing the loser of a conflict to (a) cease competing with the winner, (b) accept the fact that he has lost and (c) signal submission and thereby stop oppressive behaviour by the winner.

The key feature about depression from this evolutionary standpoint is that the depressed clearly are no threat to anyone and are therefore left alone by the aggressive seeking to take out the competition. It is thus possible to conceive of conditions in our more aggressive, dangerous and competitive past when depression was adaptive. The withdrawal and submissive elements of depressive behaviour seem to fit this theory.

However, the very latest evolutionary theory about depression comes at it from a completely different angle. In a recent paper in the *Journal of Affective Disorders*, Paul Watson and Paul Andrews, biologists at the University of New Mexico, suggest what they term a 'social navigation' hypothesis as the underlying reason we have depression.[42]

The strength of their theory over previous evolutionary arguments is that they take much more account of our social lives – the fact that much of our behaviour is there because of its social impact – and also they place more weight than previous views on the cognitive elements of depression. This again is important as modern talking treatments increasingly emphasize the importance of the way depressives think.

The social navigation hypothesis first draws attention to the 'anhedonia', or loss of pleasure in previously enjoyable activities, of depression, something that had not previously received enough consideration by researchers. Perhaps the inability to feel pleasure helps the depressive to sustain cognitive effort on a problem by preventing cognitive distractions. Consistent anhedonia is a hallmark of depression and may reflect the importance of resisting hedonic distractions.

Depressives also tend to expend a huge amount of cognitive effort – what might be termed ruminating – and usually this reflects a preoccupation with their social situation and their relationships with others. Indeed, depressives outperform 'normals' on social tasks. Their person perception is better than that of 'normals'.

In one recent experiment the depressed were found to be better able to spot lying, manipulative and other deceptive behaviour compared to controls. It could be because of their ability to see through the phoneyness of everyday social life that they become depressed in the first place.

Depression leads to withdrawal – psychic and physical retardation – but inside the person there is actually a lot of mental activity. The social navigation hypothesis posits that at the heart of depression is a huge physical, emotional and mental diversion of effort from usual activities, like physical action and eating, to social cognition or rumination to try and solve some social problem.

We need to realign our thinking about treatment to include a social perspective as well as the need for medication. We know that married people not getting along with their spouses are an astonishing twenty-five times more likely to attract a diagnosis of major depression than people without marital unhappiness. Another study found that approximately 30% of new episodes of major depression are associated with marital dissatisfaction. We also know that recovery from depression is hastened by improvements in social relationships and strong social support.

There has only been one published randomized study comparing antidepressant medication with couple therapy. The couple therapy consisted of twelve to twenty sessions intended to 'help the patient and partner to gain new perspectives on the presenting problems, to attach different meanings to the depressive types of behaviour and to experiment with new ways of relating to each other'. In the study, conducted by Professor Julian Leff and colleagues at The Institute of Psychiatry in London, patients receiving medication only were three times more likely to drop out of the study. In comparison, the couple therapy group made significantly greater gains in mood improvement, which remained statistically significant at two-year follow-up.[43]

Our experience of pain leads to strong attempts to avoid it in the future and this is its key adaptive feature. Perhaps that's the point of depression – it is so aversive that having experienced it we try to avoid it in the future. This means we are cautious about our attachments and it is notable that women who are more prone to depression are also more cautious than men about entering relationships and selecting possible future partners. If we were less cautious about attachments because we had no fear about depression then attachment as a human phenomenon in its present form might not even exist at all.

But if now we can see that depression might have some evolutionarily positive purpose, what is the purpose of happiness?

The key evolutionary puzzle about happiness is you actually don't need to be happy to survive on a day-to-day basis. Maybe happiness has a fundamental social function in that when we are happy we are expansive and generous and in so doing we build up credit with partners, so they will tolerate us more when we eventually get depressed.

This is an important theory for motivational thinking. It suggests that one powerful reason to develop ourselves beyond conventional performance is that we will then be able to give back more to others, and this provides a strong glue to our social lives.

However, there is a clear tension between the 'selfish gene' or 'evolutionary psychology' approach to explaining our drives – stating that all our behaviour is driven by our selfish chromosomes' need to propagate themselves at the expense of others – and the fact that much of what we do is often indeed selfless. The strongly motivated can appear selfish or at least self-centred. Are they really? In a more competitive society where stronger motivations are encouraged, is it inevitable that selfishness becomes more prevalent?

New research about recent changes in our behaviour, from a surprising source, promises finally to resolve the continuing debate about whether our society is becoming more selfish.

The debate was ignited in 1995 by the publication of social philosopher Robert Putnam's hugely influential book, *Bowling Alone*. This employed the tendency of Americans to bowl by themselves, rather than to form leagues, as a metaphor for the relentless rise of a destructive individualism, argued to be pervasively threatening society.[44]

But definitive evidence for this trendy sentiment, currently dominating liberal thinking, that we are now less connected to each other and live in a more fragmented society, is difficult to find. Certainly in a *Guardian* website survey at the end of last year that posed the question 'Are British people becoming more selfish than they used to be?' 83% agreed and only 16% dissented.

However, the Institute of Fiscal Studies recently published a detailed study of giving to charity over the last two decades in Britain and found that the proportion of households giving to charity had declined by only a fifth of 1% per year since the mid seventies. But the average amount given to charity had also rapidly increased in real terms, so the growth in the average size of donations more than compensated for the small decline in participation.[45]

Also, a recent study published by the Institute of Volunteering found significant rises between 1981 and 1997 in the extent of volunteering – defined as unpaid work benefiting someone other than close relatives. As a result, by the late 1990s, between half to three-quarters of the British population were involved in formal or informal volunteer activities.

Therefore, while the perception of social critics like Putnam might be that we are getting more selfish, is this actually justified from concrete measures of our behaviour? The question is more difficult to answer than it would appear at first glance, because the conundrum besetting social scientists is defining what would count as a contrast to selfishness – the purely selfless act.

Even hard-nosed evolutionary biologists who subscribe to the 'selfish gene' theory agree that co-operation rather than selfishness is often a useful long-term strategy to ensure your genes will persist. Self-seeking individuals once identified as such by groups tend to be ostracized, as it makes no sense to provide assistance to them. You know they are going to shaft you once your back is turned, or that at best goodwill towards them will not be returned.

Co-operation and unselfish behaviour persist in a nature called 'red in tooth and claw'. For example, there is evidence that even vampire bats are altruistic. One researcher spent two years of his life staying up at night watching the activities of 610 vampire bats, and noted which other bats they regurgitated blood to. They donated blood to family members but they also donated on the basis of reciprocity.

As giving our time or resources to others often prompts reciprocation from them, a lot of apparently generous behaviour could be reinterpreted as a far-sighted strategy to gain co-operation. In other words, much so-called altruistic behaviour is really self-interested, just subtly so. Indeed once evolutionary psychologists had run their mathematical models of optimal survival behaviour through the computer, they found that human society should favour the evolution of a sneaky creature called the 'pseudo-altruist'.

This is someone who appears on the outside, and whenever under public scrutiny, to be as altruistic as the next charity worker, so gaining social approval and support from others. But when their behaviour is not observed, and so cannot gain opprobrium from the group, they act entirely selfishly. Pseudo-altruism does indeed seem to perfectly explain a lot of behaviour uncovered by psychology experiments probing exactly how altruistic we are.

For example, when subjects who did not know they were taking part in an experiment to examine altruism were asked to give a talk on the moral of the story of the Good Samaritan, they could do so competently. But to get to the place where they were to give the sermon it was engineered that they pass by a confederate of the experimenter lying at the side of the road clearly needing assistance. A surprisingly small number stopped to help.

One recent piece of research that threatens to flush out the pseudo-altruists amongst us comes from the National Blood Authority, who recently sponsored a seminar questioning the state of altruism in Britain today. The authority is directly interested in this question as Britain, in contrast to many other countries, relies on an entirely voluntary system for maintaining vital blood supplies to the Health Service. Here the population donates blood in the absence of any payment. This peculiarly British element to our culture was celebrated by Tony Hancock's famous reluctance to part with a whole 'armful' of blood in exchange for tea and biscuits.[46]

But what is particularly interesting about blood donation is that it remains one of the few areas where volunteering has proven definitely superior to a more commercial approach, as pertains in the USA where blood is paid for. When blood can be sold, you get precisely the wrong kind of people offering theirs – those who need money desperately tend to be drug addicts and the chronically ill, whose blood is frequently dangerous and of poor quality, replete with viruses. So when you pay 'top dollar' for blood, you then have to pay even more to screen it rigorously. But when you have a voluntary system, the kind of person who gives blood tends to be of particularly low risk for all sorts of undesirable features, even compared to the general population.

But not only is blood donation a supreme example of a system that works better if non-commercial considerations apply: it is also the perfect example of an anonymous gift. This is because it is not possible to specify to whom you should like the blood to go, and instead it disappears into the community. This means there is absolutely no chance of reciprocation and therefore no benefit to the donor in a voluntary system. So it could be argued this is the one act of perfect altruism remaining to us.

Richard Titmuss, an economist at the LSE in the 1970s, highlighted the wider philanthropic impact on society of blood donation in a famous book entitled *The Gift Relationship: from Human Blood to Social Policy*. He argued blood donation was of immeasurably deep significance, as it held out the possibility of strengthening the bond of the donor with the whole of society.

Given levels of blood donation reveal something fundamental about the individual's sense of obligation to society, recent data from the National Blood Authority should be a cause for concern. From below 1.5 million donors per year in the 1960s, donation rose steadily to just over 2 million donors by the early

1980s, but since then there has been a gradual decline in the proportion of the population giving blood. In particular, the number of blood donors classified as active has declined steadily since October 1999, since when the total reduction has been 5%. This is especially worrying because Government waiting-list initiatives and the constant innovation of new procedures means the medical need for blood is rising rapidly each year.

The authority's own in-depth interview research uncovered an intriguing reason why altruism might be declining as a value in our society. Many more people said they might like to give blood than actually do, and the gap seems to be largely accounted for by the issue of 'convenience'. People said they would be more willing to give blood if it could be made more convenient.

This is perhaps a big factor that critics like Putnam underestimate in explaining why our civilization appears more selfish. The increasing emphasis on convenience as a value in a society ever more dominated by conveniences like shopping channels and credit card donations means altruism will ultimately suffer, because those who need our help tend not to arrange their crises when it is most convenient for us to offer assistance.[47]

In the Good Samaritan experiment alluded to earlier, the more of a rush people were in the less likely they were to stop and help someone at the side of the road. So the busier we get and the more we value convenience, the less likely we are to exhibit altruism.

Incidentally, the other major finding from the Good Samaritan experiment was that physically attractive people lying at the side of the road get helped more often. So the major lesson appears to be that today, and increasingly in the future, if you find yourself in trouble, try to make yourself look as attractive as possible.

The old way of thinking about the psychology of giving, charity and volunteering was that these were sacrifices people made in terms of their time and money. As a result it was frequently a bit of a puzzle to psychologists why so many give of their time and money without much obvious benefit.

But a new review of the research into volunteering by sociologist John Wilson of Duke University in the USA reveals some surprising answers as to why people volunteer.

One of the most common reasons people give for not volunteering is they are too busy. But the answer can't be as easy as that. The research indicates that often it is those with most time on their hands who are least likely to volunteer and those with less time on their hands who do most charity work. For example, the unemployed are much less likely to do voluntary work than those with full-time jobs.

One theory that explains this odd result – the busier you are the more likely you are to give time to charitable causes – is the idea that people with time on their hands are in that state because they have difficulties, for whatever reason, in connecting with other people. The lack of charitable involvement is, in fact, a sign of social isolation.

In a sense, the busier you are the more you are likely to be involved in other people's lives. Perhaps it is being plugged into a network of relationships that indirectly leads to charitable involvement, because it means you are someone who is concerned with and entangled in the lives of others.

This might explain the intriguing gender differences that have recently been uncovered by research into men and women's different attitudes to volunteering.

For example, surveys have found that if one spouse volunteers for charity work it is most likely to be the wife and her attitude to charity seems to complement her husband's. If in a particular relationship he takes the initiative when it comes to charity the wife seems to dutifully follow his lead. The more he volunteers, the more she is likely to as well. But in contrast if it is the woman who takes the initiative in the relationship when it comes to charity, a husband's approach is one of substitution – the more she volunteers, the less he is likely to in response!

Research into the female personality in contrast to the male partly explains these results. Women are more altruistic, empathic, attach more value to helping others, feel more guilty when they have not been compassionate and believe they are expected to care for the personal and emotional needs of others. Basically it seems that women see volunteering as a natural extension of their roles as wives and mothers.[48]

In fact, the main reason women do not do even more for charity than men do is they really are constrained by time in a way men aren't, by care-giving responsibilities at home.

But the latest research findings suggest that men could be missing out because in fact volunteering appears to be good for you – mentally and physically.

For example, research into those who are involved with charitable work or giving has found they tend to enjoy better physical health, stay fitter into old age and indeed even live longer. Put down that crispbread and turn off the rowing machine – if you want to extend your life span, getting down to the local volunteer bureau might be better for you than going to the gym!

But charity is good for your mind as well. Research has found that charitable involvement raises self-esteem and self-confidence and increases overall life satisfaction. One theory about why these benefits accrue is that perhaps the altruistic features of charity involvement reduce the destructive levels of self-absorption that appear so prevalent in our modern society.

Another possible explanation is that volunteering tends to plug people into their community and extends their social networks, so giving them a sense of belonging and bringing meaning to their lives, which then improves their physical and mental health.

Perhaps charity engagement is actually a fundamentally important feature of your personality and upbringing and one of the most revealing things about you. One theory is it appears an extension of private behaviour into the public sphere. For example, driving an elderly neighbour for a medical check-up is what you would do for your own family, so doing it for others means you see a less clear boundary between your home and the outside world.

In other words, charity work is about seeing a connectedness between your self and the rest of the world, which means you have a fundamentally different relationship with others than those who steer clear of charities.

No one really knows why getting involved with charities is such a good thing for your physical and mental health. But the fact remains that the few hours a week or month that so many give to charity may in fact end up being the most important thing they do to live longer – although they see it as something they do in their 'spare' time.

There is also new research that finds that getting your children to do some volunteer work is hugely helpful in preventing them getting into trouble as adolescents with drugs, antisocial behaviour or dropping out of school. One theory is that volunteer work for charities tends to expose them to the 'right crowd' and ensures they establish friendships with those who are likely to be better role models, rather than those they might otherwise meet on the streets, hanging around with time on their hands.[49] And college students who do volunteer work for charities are likely to get better grades, compared with those who don't.

While the reasons for all these benefits from charity involvement are as yet unclear, the results indicate that giving time to charity is not a sacrifice, in fact it's good for you. Perhaps charity engagement is therapeutic because it helps us realize there are many less fortunate than ourselves and this makes us more grateful for the everyday advantages of our lives that we tend to take for granted.

Charity gives us a wider perspective on life and stops us getting so self-absorbed that our own troubles get magnified out of all proportion.

So it's an odd conclusion but it seems to be true that, rather than running away, moving towards people in trouble helps us with our own. If only those who do no charity work at all at the moment knew this – after all, the new research suggests they are the ones really in trouble!

The issue of how people explain their behaviour to themselves is vital in understanding and altering motivation. The latest psychological research has some intriguing and often counterintuitive things to say about how we explain why we behave altruistically, for example. Altruism is a key issue in the science of motivation because it seems most theories of motivation break down when it comes to trying to explain why people do things that aren't actually in their own interests.[50]

Although people engage in many acts of genuine compassion, their vocabulary for talking about their motives in these cases is extremely impoverished and emphasizes self-interest.

For example, their accounts for giving to charity generally emphasize pragmatic or instrumental reasons: 'It gave me something to do', 'I liked the other volunteers', 'It got me out of the house'. People seem loath to acknowledge that their behaviour may have been motivated by genuine compassion or kindness. Indeed, the people interviewed in one study into compassion seemed to go out of their way to stress that they were not 'a bleeding heart, a goody two-shoes, or a do-gooder'.

Why might people be inhibited from expressing the

compassion they feel for others? Perhaps when confronted by the innocent suffering of another, we face a conflict. This experience is disturbing because it threatens our belief that the world is just and hence prompts the impulse to help eliminate the injustice.

Were we to offer unconditional help we would confront difficult questions of the following kind: 'If this person or group is worthy of my assistance, are the myriad other similar victims whose suffering I am exposed to on a regular basis not also worthy of my help?' or 'If this type of person or group is worthy of help now are they not also worthy of help in the future?'

It is not easy to answer these questions negatively and deny any further commitments, yet to answer them affirmatively renders the would-be helper vulnerable to becoming a victim him- or herself. For this reason, psychologists argue, people may resist responding to appeals for unconditional help and instead rely on various psychological techniques (e.g., victim derogation) to convince themselves that help from them is unwarranted.

Linked to this is the idea that people may actually act upon their feelings of compassion but find ways of rationalizing the action by convincing themselves that their action comports with their self-interest. Self-interest then becomes an important way of finding psychological cover for helping.

Tax deductions in exchange for charitable donations may provide a case in point. When people receive a tax deduction in exchange for their assistance, they do not have to feel like a do-gooder. They can construe their action as something to feel good about, but not as something that implies a responsibility to help all victim groups or even this victim group in the future. It is the symbolic or psychological value of a tax deduction, and not merely its material value, that makes tax-deductible donations so attractive.

The wisdom of offering people psychological cover for their altruistic behaviour also may, knowingly or unknowingly, underlie the practice of offering potential charity donors some product (e.g., light bulbs, address stickers or magazine sub-scriptions) for their donations. The commonness of this practice suggests that the net profit elicited by product-for-donation exchanges might well exceed that elicited by strict charity appeals alone. If so, the explanation for the success of the strategy might reside in the fact that the offer of an exchange creates a *fiction* that permits people to act on their impulse to help without committing themselves to unwanted psychological burdens, such as an enduring, open-ended relationship with either the victim or similar victims. That is, the offer of an exchange permits people to feel good about doing 'their part' without committing themselves to a hard-to-live-up-to psychological contract.

In effect, the 'exchange fiction' provides the mask under which the altruist can express her compassion and concerns with justice without having to reveal, or even recognize, her motives – after all, she is merely engaging in an economic transaction.

Psychologist John Holmes and colleagues from the University of Waterloo, Ontario, recently tested this idea in an intriguing series of experiments.[51]

In one part of the study, participants were approached with a request to assist a charity by making a financial contribution either through a direct donation or by purchasing decorative candles. The theory was that when victim need was high, people should most wish to disguise their compassion, thereby rendering especially great the increment in financial yield produced by the offer of an exchange of a candle.

Consistent with the exchange fiction analysis, the offer of an exchange of a candle in the high-need condition produced significantly larger contributions than did the strict donation appeal.

The results of the series of experiments suggest that people often are inhibited from engaging in unambiguous acts of help. Specifically, the results demonstrate that people are more willing to act on their feelings of compassion when they are provided with a self-interested justification.

The major contribution of the present studies is the finding that helping behaviour is facilitated when the framing of the helping act permits people to see themselves as altruistic but not unconditionally so. Appeals to self-interest provide an excuse for helping. In effect, they provide people with the licence to act on their sympathies.

This takes us back to a famous psychological principle: when confronted with people behaving in undesirable ways (e.g., not volunteering), it is generally more effective to remove obstacles that inhibit them from taking the desired action than to provide them with additional reasons for taking the desired action.

This principle is vital in helping us to attain difficult goals because often we don't seem to be able to get our act together and are defeated by difficulties like obstacles and our own apathy or exhaustion.

Often instead of stoking up our sense of will-power and increasing our motivation we need to tackle the hurdles that defeat us.

17

IF YOU HAVE NO ENEMIES THEN YOU AREN'T STRIVING HARD ENOUGH

It's choice – not chance – that determines your destiny
Jean Nidetch

He who has a why to live can bear with almost any how
Frederick Nietzsche

Being motivated is all well and good; the problem is that appearing motivated has a nasty habit of putting others' backs up. Ambition is, particularly in Europe as compared to the USA, not something we own up to. Success it seems just happened to us inadvertently and we are as surprised as you were to win that Nobel Prize, and no, hard work behind the scenes had nothing to do with it.[1] So how should you handle your motivation publicly?[2]

Have you noticed how before any competitive situation – a football match, race, exam or interview – the competitors tend to explain carefully to all the other rivals why they are unlikely to do well? Recent injuries, difficulty finding time to revise or prepare, or problems with training are emphasized. Psychologists describe this strategy as an attempt to preserve self-esteem if failure subsequently occurs, by having a ready-made excuse to hand for why you didn't succeed. After all, consider the opposite pre-match strategy, which is to tell everyone how hard you have worked and prepared for the test – in which case if you do fail, you must be pretty hopeless given all the effort you put in.[3]

However recent research by psychologist Edward Hirt of Indiana University has revealed that men are more likely than women to go a step further and actually self-handicap themselves, to ensure they have an accessible excuse for subsequent poor performance.[4]

This explains the male tendency to stay up late drinking heavily the night before that crucial job interview, while women more sensibly get a good night's sleep. Indeed, this appears to play into the male need to appear to perform spectacularly well despite obvious handicaps; the batsman who goes out and scores a hundred for England after an all-night orgy gains much more admiration from men than women. The female view is to regard that kind of behaviour as foolish, taking unnecessary risks with possible failure.

But the problem with this male tendency to self-handicap is that this obsession with how you appear in the eyes of others should failure occur renders failure more likely.[5]

The Indiana University researchers suggest that another reason why men self-handicap much more than women is that women tend to believe success is down to effort, so any failure means you didn't try hard enough. However, men are more prone to see accomplishment as based on ability so, to men, floundering has more fundamental implications about their capacities. It would indeed appear that men fear failing in front of their mates more than women do, and so try harder to protect themselves from it by having a prepared or obvious excuse for failure.[6]

This could also explain why men do so badly in sticking to New Year's resolutions, because they try to keep them without wanting to make much public effort to succeed (just in case they fail). So one key tactic known to help us keep resolutions, which men will therefore tend not to use, is to tell as many people as possible about our new resolve. This helps because it means others are less likely to offer you those cigarettes you have given up, or that extra drink you are cutting down on; instead they turn up to partner you on your jog round the park.[7]

To overcome the tendency to self-handicap, become more aware of all those little things you do that in fact make defeat more likely. Also stop focusing and planning for failure, and concentrate instead on how to succeed. Don't dominate your life and conversation with excuses. Instead find those who have achieved, sweep their 'night before' orgy stories aside, and ask them a bit more about how they really prepared hard, to get some inside tips on how to succeed.

Finally take a leaf out of the female book. It appears women have much more respect for the person who tried really hard and still failed than the competitor who never made the effort in the first place, because they were obsessed with what others think. It would appear self-handicapping might impress those losers amongst your friends, but will just draw disdain from the real winners.[8]

Men have also long had a reputation for being the more arrogant and self-promoting sex, frequently boastful and over-confident about their abilities, while women have traditionally been seen as the more self-deprecating gender. Self-deprecation is a much more attractive approach to the way you present yourself; those who tell us openly how wonderful they are usually end up irritating us hugely. Self-publicists actually appear self-centred and pretentious, so having the opposite effect they desired, of impressing.[9]

But new research by psychologists Bryan Gibson and Daniel Sachau from the USA suggests that self-deprecation is part of a subtle armoury of strategies used to cleverly manipulate others. It now appears that self-deprecation is a far from honest approach to human relationships, and is in fact one of the most astutely manipulative strategies of all.[10]

Gibson and Sachau have for the first time analysed the various self-deprecating approaches and shown how they are used to manipulate others.

SANDBAGGING

Sandbaggers claim to be much worse at things than they know they really are – the basic tactic here is to lull the competition into a false sense of security. Your opponents relax too much as they assume they have the contest 'in the bag'.[11]

Also because you have adjusted everyone's expectations downwards about you, when you perform much better than they were anticipating, this puts you in an even better light than if they had been assuming you would be quite good all along. So this tactic also takes the pressure off you to live up to high expectations.[12]

'Sandbagging' as a term is thought to have originated from the practice of lighter horse race jockeys traditionally being handicapped by extra weight in the form of sandbags added to their saddles. A pool table or card shark 'sandbags' when he initially pretends to be not very good in order to encourage his adversaries to raise their stakes against him.

Advantages: If you are particularly fearful of 'choking' from nerves in a high-pressure situation then sandbagging, because it takes the pressure off you by ensuring that no one is expecting very much from you, helps to relax you and ensure a better performance.[13]

Disadvantage: Once you have used sandbagging a few times people around you will know that you tend to make out you are going to do much worse than you tend to and find your behaviour manipulative or boring.

MODESTY

The aim of modesty as a manipulation tactic is to be liked, particularly if your being good at something is likely to intimidate, alienate or render others jealous. Modesty is different to 'sandbagging', as modesty is about how you deal with your achievement after it's over, while sandbagging is all about how you set up others' expectations before your performance.[14]

There are several different ways of being modest – you could make out the task wasn't as difficult as it appeared to others, or that you got 'lucky' – but basically a recurrent theme is to blame any other agency than yourself for your ability to succeed.

Modesty is a highly effective method of ingratiating because it allows others around you to feel better about themselves in contrast to you, as you keep reassuring them about how mediocre you are in comparison despite your superior results.

Advantages: Modesty done deftly is an excellent strategy for deflecting hatred, which is inevitable if your success or ability is not shared by those around you.[15]

Disadvantages: If you are not careful modesty can appear 'false' and you end up looking even more smug than if you had more honestly accepted the reality of how you garnered your attainment. Alternatively, if you are particularly good at this strategy many people could even believe your modesty and not give you credit for your ability.

SUPPLICATION

This is a tactic whose aim is to get others to feel sorry for you and therefore to try and help you. In particular, the strategy is about gaining others' long-term assistance by advertising your supposed weaknesses. This is a way of gaining help from more powerful others, though the balance of power could be more equal than they realize.

By making others feel sorry for you, you make them feel masterful and also altruistic, and therefore good about themselves, only they don't know that you have been calculating this effect all along. Stressing your inability to fend for yourself and your dependency on others, you cleverly invoke the natural human tendency to feel obligated and responsible about helping those weaker than yourself.[16]

But you have to be careful who you try supplication on, as the self-made tend to have little sympathy for those who don't appear capable of helping themselves. Supplication works best on those who feel guilty about their own good fortune.

Supplication can only really work when your weakness appears to be something beyond your control, an accident or bad luck, so this has to be deftly done, as any detection by stronger parties that you are manufacturing your weakness could be terribly punished.

Advantages: A huge benefit of supplication is that it turns those who could be potentially powerful enemies, capable of destroying you, into those only too anxious to assist your cause.

Disadvantages: You may often have to appear weaker than you really are, and so wait patiently to be helped when you could always have more quickly got to a target under your own steam. This strategy requires such huge endurance that is most likely to eventually crack, leaving you losing your temper with people who will be very surprised because they had no idea how powerful you really were all along.[17]

SELF-HANDICAPPING

Self-handicapping is, as we've discussed earlier, about creating a situation where you have a ready excuse for failure should it happen, for example by not preparing properly for an interview or an exam by leaving it to the last minute. This ensures that should you fail, you can blame this on the fact you didn't have enough time to prepare, rather than accept that no amount of hard work by you would have produced the same poor result.

Self-handicapping is a way of protecting the ego from confronting the painful reality that you might have higher expectations of yourself than are really warranted. Self-handicapping allows you to persist with the dream or fantasy that you really could have performed or achieved as well as anyone else; it was just a bit of bad luck that stymied you. Self-handicapping is a particular favourite with those who can't bear to truly know whether they were good enough for the big time.[18]

Advantages: If you self-handicap but still succeed, you gain even more admiration from your audience because your devil-may-care approach is much more endearing, heroic and adventurous than those who meticulously prepare and leave nothing to chance.

Disadvantages: The problem with self-handicapping is it makes it less likely you will achieve what you are truly capable of if you gave yourself a clear run at your goal and didn't put self-inflicted obstacles in the way.

DEFENSIVE PESSIMISM

This tactic is all about convincing yourself that you are going to fail, or do much worse than is likely, in order to motivate yourself to work harder and prepare even better. Defensive pessimists are often secretly rather lazy and may not even enjoy what they are doing just for the sake of it, so they have to motivate themselves by using some other means, like the scary idea that total and abject failure is looming much more than it really is.[19]

People close to defensive pessimists usually end up finding these relationships exhausting, as they have to devote so much time to reassuring the defensive pessimist that it really will all be 'OK on the night'.

Advantages: Defensive pessimists tend to end up performing extremely successfully compared with most others and are widely acknowledged to be perfectionists.

Disadvantages: This strategy is exhausting as it leads you to constantly over-prepare and so eventually you don't even try to aim for certain possible goals, as the huge effort your excessive fear of failure would produce puts you off.[20]

ARE YOU A SELF-DEPRECATING MANIPULATOR?

Each statement is followed by two possible responses: agree or disagree. Read each statement carefully and decide which answer best describes how you feel. Then tick the corresponding response. Please reply to every statement. If you are not completely sure which response is more accurate, put the response that you feel is most appropriate. Do not read the scoring explanation before filling out the questionnaire. Do not spend too long on each statement. It is important that you answer each question as honestly as possible.

		AGREE	DISAGREE
1	The less others expect of me the better I like it	A	B
2	I like to show off a little about my abilities	B	A
3	I hardly ever dress as expensively as I can afford to	A	B
4	I don't get uncomfortable when others recognize how good I truly am	B	A
5	If others know how much I prepare behind the scenes, they would be surprised	A	B
6	I like name-dropping in conversations to strangers	B	A
7	I gain whatever advantage I can before a competition has even begun	A	B
8	I am not very good at hiding what I really think and feel	B	A
9	No success in life is possible without a fair amount of deceit	A	B
10	I don't tolerate fools easily	B	A

Score

Add up your score by totalling the numbers of As and Bs you have ticked.

8 or more As: You are scoring very high for using self-deprecating manipulation tactics and this is because you are keenly aware that what others think of you is a vital part of achieving success in life.

Between 5 and 7 As: You are scoring above average on using self-deprecating manipulation tactics, and this is because you can be quite a manipulative person, for example by insincerely flattering others. But personal pride in your own achievements means you do sometimes show off when you know deep down it could alienate others.

Between 3 and 4 As: You are scoring around average for self-deprecating manipulation tactics and this is because you believe that most people value honesty and that appearing overly modest is obviously crafty to most others. You don't care as much about arousing jealousy in others as higher scorers, so you may not be giving enough weight to the fact that if you are genuinely above average in some spheres of life most people prefer it if you downplay these personal advantages.

Between 0 and 2 As: You are scoring very low on using self-deprecating manipulation tactics, and this is partly because you don't care as much as higher scorers about what others think of you, and so you don't mind taking the risk of sometimes appearing over-confident or successful. You may be over-confident about your ability to succeed despite the enmity of the jealous.

So is being more competitive better for you? Early research revealed that competition can undermine intrinsic motivation. For example, psychologists found that participants who played an enjoyable activity under competitive conditions were less likely to return to the activity during a free-choice period than those who had played under non-competitive conditions.[21] When participants were told to focus all their attention on winning, competition reduced intrinsic motivation relative to a 'less controlling' competition (in which participants were told to try to solve puzzles faster than another participant) even though all participants in these conditions won.[22]

Achievement behaviour is motivated by different goals.

While some individuals are motivated to establish superiority over others, other individuals are motivated to improve their performance. Psychologists Robert Franken and Douglas Brown at the University of Calgary, Canada, have shown that it is possible to differentiate people who have an ego-orientation from those who have a task-orientation but that these two orientations are opposite to each other. They have also shown that children with a task-orientation are more motivated than those dominated by an ego-orientation.[23]

Questions like 'Will I look smart?' and 'Can I out-perform others?' reflect ego-involved goals. In contrast, with task-involved goals, individuals focus on mastering tasks and increasing their competence. Questions such as 'How can I do this task?' and 'What will I learn?' reflect task-involved goals.

While it has already been shown that some people tend to be more competitive than others, the reason or reasons for such differences are not immediately clear. There are at least three reasons why some people like competitive situations. One reason is that there are winners and losers in most competitive situations. If you like to win then you need to pit yourself against another person so that you can be the winner and they can be the loser.[24]

A second reason is that competitive situations provide you with people on whom you can model yourself, or simply a situation that fosters the mastery of a skill. In other words, the competitive situation would provide an ideal situation for improving one's performance. A third reason people may like competitive situations is that they can be a source of motivation. Competitive situations provide people with information about what is an acceptable or high level of performance. To the degree that people are motivated to be highly competent, they might be motivated to put forth greater effort in competitive situations.[25]

Not all people like competitive situations. So Franken and Brown argue it follows from the distinction between ego- and task-orientation that there are some people (task-oriented individuals) who are motivated almost solely by task-related variables. This would involve such things as the amount of challenge (difficulty) provided by the task or the ability to perform well at the task.

Their results suggest that being high in competitiveness motivation tends to undermine mastery and work motivation. Indeed, there is considerable evidence that co-operation is considerably more effective than interpersonal competition and individualistic effort in predicting success.

Many psychologists argue that competitiveness is generally negative when it comes to achievement, not only for the individual but for society. Others argue that competitiveness often has strong positive motivational qualities and can lead to creativity. In a study to assess whether competitiveness might be a good predictor of sport interest, the 'desire to win' and the 'motivation for high performance' (MHP) were found by Franken and Brown to be two distinct factors.[26]

This research provides evidence that people select competitive situations for different reasons. For some it is to improve their performance, having little or no regard for winning. For some winning is the most important thing. For still others, competition provides the motivation for putting forth effort, which presumably will lead to improved performance in the future.[27]

We live in a competitive world where people compete for jobs, money, the boss's attention, a lover's attention or just attention full stop. Even those who proclaim they are completely disinterested in competing for anything appear slightly miffed if you ignore them for those who compete more successfully for your time. However, some psychotherapists believe that the indiscriminate need many people appear to have to compete and win, or at any rate to avoid losing, is at the root of many psychological problems. Therapists argue that competition is in fact an attempt to enhance feelings of self-worth, and hence hides deeper feelings of insecurity and low self-esteem. In other words, the overly competitive individual actually feels a loser, or was made to feel a loser when young, and their competitiveness is a constant striving to compensate for feelings of being unloved, perhaps by competitive parents. The problem for the overly competitive is that practically all their activities seem designed to elicit admiration that they believe they deserve from others, yet such praise quickly goes stale. Hence the problem is to get the balance of competitiveness right. Too much and you find out exactly how lonely it can be at the top; too little and the bottom can also seem pretty forlorn. One of the solutions is to have a clear idea of what your goal in any competition actually is – otherwise you may find you have created a game for yourself that you cannot win.[28]

COMPETITION SCALE

Each statement is followed by two possible responses: agree or disagree. Read each statement carefully and decide which response best describes how you feel. Then tick the corresponding response. Please respond to every statement. If you are not completely sure which response is more accurate, put the response that you feel is most appropriate. Do not read the scoring explanation before filling out the questionnaire. Do not spend too long on each statement. It is important that you answer each question as honestly as possible.

		AGREE	DISAGREE
1	Losers usually have only themselves to blame	A	B
2	My talents are largely recognized by others	B	A
3	I praise more than criticize	A	B
4	I rarely feel powerless and insignificant	B	A
5	I like hearing bad things about others	A	B
6	I am frequently persuaded by another point of view	B	A
7	If others could gain by hurting me, they would do so	A	B
8	My parents were not as harsh disciplinarians as most	B	A
9	I am not as influential as I should be	A	B
10	I avoid risks as much as I can	B	A

Score
Add up your score by totalling the numbers of As and Bs you have ticked.

7 or more As: You are scoring high on the competitive scale, which means your love of competition is so deep you even like to turn situations that might usually be considered non-competitive into competitive ones: for example you constantly like to play little games with yourself and others where winning and losing becomes possible. It is only when you come to accept completely that you have a lot of ability that you can begin to give all the game-playing a rest.

Between 5 and 6 As: You are scoring higher on the need to compete than the average and this explains your enjoyment of the manipulation of others and perhaps even the pleasure you get from denigrating others. Your love of being admired and being the centre of attention means winning at anything and everything may eventually come to dominate your life. You need to learn that your excessive ambition is leading you to expect too much and hence you will inevitably fall short of your goals, producing perpetual disappointment and dissatisfaction with yourself.

Between 3 and 4 As: While you are interested in competing in some things and you do enjoy winning, you are scoring average or lower than average for competitiveness. You like too many other people too much to enjoy competing with them, and hence you tend not to turn to deceit to successfully manipulate others as easily as higher scorers. The problem is your sincerity might let you down when you need to be more controlling of others to get what you really want.

Between 0 and 2 As: You are scoring low in the competitiveness scale and hence you are well below average in the need to compete. This is because you do not have low self-esteem as regards what you think are the important things in life; hence you tend to be more contented than higher scorers. However, your lack of ambition may mean you lose out to higher scorers when you come up against them. They beat you, but you have more fun. However, you do have regrets about long-term choices you have made as a result of your avoidance of competition.

TEN STEPS TO BETTER FRIENDSHIPS

(1) A vital ingredient that is too often missing in relationships, and explains why so many people don't have the friendships they want, is time. People who give more

time to others have more friends, and the number of friends you have throughout your life is enormously dependent on how much time you have to spend on others. Research has found that the typical seventeen-year-old (who has generally a lot of time on their hands) has on average nineteen friends; this number drops to only twelve for the average twenty-eight-year-old, but rises again to sixteen friends for the average forty-five-year-old.

(2) When people are asked to focus only on the relationships that are most satisfying, intimate and close, however, the number of true friends drops dramatically from the higher numbers used to quantify acquaintances, and falls to around six on average. What separates a true close friend from an acquaintance seems to be loyalty and the ability to keep confidences. Practically this is most recognized as refraining from public criticism of a friend. So although we all enjoy a good gossip, true friends don't slander each other. Although you may find betraying another friend's confidences makes you temporarily the centre of attention, it will lose you respect and trust from those who were considering making you a good friend.

(3) The fact that friends choose to spend time with you is in itself a compliment and a boost to self-esteem. It is this effect of good friendship – enhancement of self-esteem – that is vital, so to be seen as a good friend you should learn how to make people feel good about themselves with praise and compliments. Perhaps the biggest compliment of all is to be interested and affected by other people's lives.

(4) But good friends are not just interested in us: they also support us in our viewpoints and our endeavours. They may not agree with everything we do, but our closest friends will tend to uphold our positions when we turn to them for support in the face of a hostile world. Because good friends will tend to share our core attitudes, places to find good friends include

organizations or activities that reflect our own approach to life.

(5) While reciprocation is the unstated rule of friendships, it is also true that if you never dare to ask a favour of a friend, then in a sense they are not really good friends. Helping friends without obvious expectation of an immediate return for our assistance is an essential ingredient to friendship. Those who don't ever ask for help don't build the kind of interdependence close friendship requires – so fiercely independent people don't tend to have too many friends.

(6) All friendships exist because of communication – if you don't communicate then your friendship will wither. In particular, good friendship involves not holding back from saying what you feel in the way you might with a more formal relationship. You should therefore care less about 'impression management' with a good friend.

(7) Usually friendships progress through deepening levels of self-disclosure. You notice the other person has revealed something personal about themselves, and you then feel able to reciprocate similarly. Self-disclosing involves trusting, and those who cannot properly self-disclose have difficulty building intimate friendships. If there is an imbalance in who is doing all the self-disclosing then a proper friendship cannot develop. Try to mirror the amount of self-disclosing the other person is achieving and take it slightly further in terms of what you reveal about yourself but without jumping too far ahead of them.

(8) Friends are lost most often when they move away and contact becomes more difficult because of geographical distance. A simple way to maintain friendships when this happens is to try and keep special days each year as those reserved for reunions with particular friends, so they get into the habit of keeping those days clear for you as well.

(9) Friendship also involves patience with those who are unable to reciprocate quite as you would like all the time. Know when a friend is truly incapable of returning the affection and attention you desire, and invest your valuable time elsewhere rather than getting resentful over a friendship that is not working. In particular, realize that we all change with time and friends can grow apart because of an alteration in life direction. Hanging on to friendships that are no longer appropriate reveals an anxiety over how to form new friendships (see step 4).

(10) Never give up on friends you have not heard from for a long time – nothing is lost by sending a card to reignite a friendship. If you see yourself as a good friend you will have the confidence to realize others won't want to lose the opportunity to rekindle a friendship with you. As friendship is one of the greatest gifts we can bestow, try to be generous with it.

18

WANT TO BE WORSHIPPED?

To give pleasure to a single heart by a single act is better than a thousand heads bowing in prayer

Mahatma Gandhi

Most people who succeed in the face of seemingly impossible conditions are people who simply don't know how to quit

Robert Schuller

One reason motivation is difficult to learn about is that most of those around us will not share explicity what really drives them or how they go about getting what they want, as this represents a severe danger to their social standing. It seems necessary for us to draw a veil over our desires and this means it is difficult for others to learn from our experiences.[1]

One example of this effect is what happens when you try to ask ordinary people why they take part in TV programmes. Practically no one of any sophistication admits that it's largely because they want to become famous. It is intriguing to observe the somersaults people turn in order to avoid confronting this reality.

It seems you can't switch on the television these days without being greeted by yet another reality TV series. For the first time, we are *all* having to confront the question: do I want to be famous?[2] Previously fame was for a select few, but now just by answering any of a plethora of advertisements in newspapers from TV companies asking for volunteers for the latest bizarre format, anyone can share their antics with the nation.

But is it really the case that the pure motivation for taking part is the desire for celebrity?

In fact, reality TV has a poor record in turning out 'celebs' who last the course and establish any kind of serious money or reputation. Most briefly flame into household status but then plummet back to obscurity abruptly – indeed so rapid is their disappearance from view that it seems hardly worth all the effort and loss of dignity.

To try and understand why so many are so willing to become camera fodder I spoke in detail to three women who all claim that fame had nothing to do with their motivation for taking part in some of the most high-profile reality TV projects. In all cases reality TV was responsible for some extremely stressful and degrading experiences and none said they would repeat the experience.[3]

In Judith's case, during a *Wife Swap* programme, she had to endure her own children attacking and ridiculing her partner and her. In a series called *Made For Each Other*, Della was compelled to reveal in front of millions how often she had sex while the quality of her sex life was picked over by experts and her husband. In a series called *How Clean Is Your House* the degrading state of Emma's home, in particular her toilet and kitchen, replete with mouse droppings, pet urine and mould, was held up for ridicule to the nation.

So why did they do it?

Judith is in her mid thirties, lives in Stevenage and has been married for twenty-two years. She has two young teenage daughters and a partner who is a trifle obsessive about household rules, order and cleanliness. Judith's episode of *Wife Swap* was filmed in August of last year and, amazingly to me, both Judith and her husband agreed to take part without ever having watched *Wife Swap* before, although a previous series had been broadcast before their filming. Apparently they were out of the country at the time and so missed it, but they made no attempt whatsoever to find out how the programme worked and how participants were presented to the viewing public. This is a startling admission given how carefully middle class and ordered her husband and she are about most other areas of their life.

Dr Persaud: So what were your overall feelings about this experience?

Judith: I suppose I didn't realize beforehand it would be so stressful. Of course I realized there would be conflict – I think I expected their children to perhaps go off in a strop for a while but eventually for the children to play along with the whole thing – but actually the children went berserk.

Dr Persaud: Why did you take part?

Judith: The production company kept describing this as a journey we would go on and that we would learn things about ourselves that would be useful. I suppose though that basically I was quite nosy about how other people live and I wanted to see for myself what other families get up to.

Dr Persaud: What surprised you most about the experience?

Judith: I suppose the extent to which the whole thing is manipulated by the production company. There was a scene, for example, where I appear to be asking the children of the other family to collect all their usual snack foods and put them in a box, which in fact I was asked to do by the production company. I would never have done that myself. There is a famous scene where I write down all the rules I expect the children to follow in the new family and they tear it up – but I never would have written down the rules – I was asked to by the production company. Also there is a scene at the end when we are reunited with our families at long last when Belinda lost her temper with me and was rude to me. Actually that was really engineered by the production team because first they kept us waiting for hours for that meeting. Then they plied us with drink, and then they made it pretty clear that none of us could go until they had what they wanted, which was film of conflict between us, so we just supplied it in order to get home at long last. Having been away from our families for ten days and not allowed to make contact, we were all desperate to get home and we would have done anything they asked at that moment. We had arranged childcare and they were so over schedule we had to keep ringing them up and ask them to stay a bit longer, which really wasn't fair to them at all.

Dr Persaud: Surely you realized that conflict is what the production company is interested in and so they are going to carefully engineer this? In the end doesn't that, plus the editing, mean the public is not given a fair representation of yourself? Does that not bother you?

Judith: I think we came over OK in the end but I suppose I was naïve about how they have everything so mapped out. They pretend to be going along not knowing what is going to happen next but in fact they know exactly what they want from you, and engineer the situation to produce this.

Dr Persaud: Your partner didn't allow you to go out much at all before the programme because he was jealous and he did come over a bit like a control freak with all the rules that had to be rigidly followed. I wonder if one of the reasons you took part was the hope that the programme would in some way get him to change?

Judith: I think the programme did make him realize that perhaps he does try and control the children too much. When we started out on this the programme-makers asked us what would I want to change about my husband, and I answered that I wanted him to relax and chill out a bit more and I think that has happened a little bit.

One can't help feeling that there is a sense about Judith of tremendous confidence in herself and her family as able to come over in a way that wouldn't create a bad impression. Hence her taking part in this notorious programme without even bothering to see it first. Yet this attitude perhaps borders on arrogance – she wanted to see how other families lived but she was pretty confident that her family would come over as in some way better than any other. She seems quite a competitive person – she kept comparing herself favourably to the other family involved in *Wife Swap*.

But she doesn't appear to have given much thought to how she or her family might come over to others – after all, we live in a culture where manifest competitiveness is frowned upon. On the programme she is filmed in her children's bedrooms checking they haven't been watching TV, by putting a hand on the TV to see whether it's warm or not, as apparently prescribed by her husband's extensive rules. These include regular children's room inspections and a system of fines for contraventions. Judith is proud of this way of running a family and believes no one would view any of this as at all peculiar.

This, of course, is pure gold to the TV company, who wanted to put together two families at extremes in attitudes to discipline and rules, so as to produce maximum conflict. But they also wanted families who would not appear conventional, as otherwise why would anyone watch? Judith, like most of those who appear on reality TV, had a confidence that she would come over in a positive way to most others, which was perhaps a bit misplaced, and which is precisely what reality TV is there to exploit. Judith also, perhaps unconsciously, wanted her relationship shaken up in some way and found that reality TV was a way of doing it – she now tells me that her husband does indeed allow her out more than before. Maybe in the end she manipulated the situation and got what she wanted from it, rather than the other way round.

Della Dabinis is forty, and has been married to Victor for sixteen years. They live in Kent and have two teenage children. Della had a serious twenty-three-hour-a-week cleaning obsession and it impacted significantly on their relationship. Her reality TV show was *Made For Each Other*.

Della: I suppose I was basically curious about what would happen and I also thought it would be a bit of fun – I thought we could explore our relationship a bit and that there would be good bits and negative sides as well but those would be shown. In the end, though, I think it was much too negative about our relationship and I wouldn't repeat the experience.
Dr Persaud: I'm interested you thought the programme was going to be about the good as well as the bad in your relationship. I appreciate that when you agreed to take part it was for the first series of *Made For Each Other* and so there was no earlier series to compare it with, so the fact the series focuses on relationships in fairly serious trouble might not have been immediately apparent. However, surely it would be obvious, when an important part of the concept of the series is that tapes of your marriage are analysed by a divorce lawyer and a psychotherapist and then you are given advice, that this is not going to be about relationships going at all well?
Della: But we weren't told who the experts were going to be – we were only told they were experts. It was only just as we were about to meet them that we were told who exactly they were, that it was a divorce lawyer and a therapist.
Dr Persaud: So that sounds as though you feel you were manipulated by the programme – are there other examples of that?

Della: Well, they kept pushing for us to have the cameras on in our bedroom and I am a fairly prudish and private person when it comes to sex, believe it or not, and so I wasn't keen on that at all. But they kept pushing and pushing and eventually we agreed to just a few minutes of us in the bedroom but it was just us hiding under the sheets. But I was really surprised when that was precisely the bit they used. Also they added in the commentary on the programme that we hadn't had sex in the entire two weeks of filming, which I feel was really unfair of them to say, because there was no way they could know if that was true or not.

Dr Persaud: But surely you knew that if they had footage of you in a bedroom there was the possibility of it being broadcast to millions of people and also there was a scene where you and your partner talk about how often you have sex – that must have been excruciating to have that broadcast to millions.

Della: I hated that bit but I suppose what happens is after a while you forget that it's all on TV and that it could be broadcast. But I did find the analysis of our relationship interesting and I was taking part to try and get another perspective on our relationship.

Dr Persaud: But you could have done that by seeing a marital therapist – you didn't need to have your private life exposed to millions of others.

Della: Well, I was disappointed with the outcome of the programme. I did feel that it dwelled on the negative side of things and that there are a lot of positives in our relationship and it didn't include any of those. However, it was an opportunity to be an outsider to look in and give me some valuable feedback about how I and we were doing. It did make me realize that I am a bit fussy.

I did speak to Victor, Della's partner, as well and he confided that he took part because he felt that Della was not going to listen to him about her obsessive cleaning and was more likely to pay attention to someone from the outside, like a TV company. It does appear that many are using reality TV in this way. There is a message or a change they want to get through to their partners or others in their lives, and they feel exasperated by not succeeding. They think the TV company might get through where they have failed. What is remarkable, though, is how grave the risks are that such contestants are willing to face in order to achieve this. One possibility is that they regard TV as familiar and so in a sense it feels to them that they are taking fewer risks than entering the more strange and frightening, though at least private, world of therapy.

Emma Jane, a trainee lawyer in her late twenties, lives in London in a shared house. Emma was in some senses the most intriguing of the three women interviewed as she was the only one who didn't watch her reality TV show when it was broadcast and in fact still hasn't seen the programme. Emma lives with two male flatmates who together conspired to inhabit one of the most filthy flats in Britain. *How Clean Is Your House* is a reality TV show that offers to inspect where you live, humiliate you, but then clean up the mess.

Dr Persaud: Why did you agree to take part in this programme? After all, it involved among other horrors the cameras poking about in your loo with a faeces-encrusted bowl and showed how you eat and cook in a kitchen infested with mice and their droppings.
Emma: I really didn't agree to do it because I wanted to be famous or anything like that; in fact it's an odd thing I know to say, for someone who has taken part in one of these programmes, but I don't actually like watching myself on TV. I don't even think I've properly seen myself on video. I don't like looking at pictures of myself. I haven't got a problem with the way I look; it's just that I am not into a career as a celebrity – I want to pursue my legal career.
Dr Persaud: But the law is a very conservative profession with a small 'c' – were you not worried that taking part in a dubious TV programme might damage your reputation and so impair any possible future career?
Emma: I banked on the fact that there are so many reality TV shows around now that it means no one is going to remember you. I definitely wouldn't have done it had I been further along with my career, as it would have definitely been a disaster for me then. I also figured that by the time I reached the higher reaches of law it really would all have been lost in the mists of time.
Dr Persaud: So if you were hoping, as it seems, not to be noticed or remembered – why did you do it in the first place?

Emma: The programme was offering some real practical help – they were going to send a team of expert cleaners into our disgusting flat, which hadn't been cleaned in ten years, and scrub it from top to bottom. To get professional cleaners in would have cost us several thousand pounds – money we just didn't have. I found living there a real strain and it was beginning to get me down. The fact that they solved my problem was a godsend. I knew there was a chance it could have turned out badly for me but it was a chance I was willing to take, given how awful and increasingly disheartening my living conditions were.

Dr Persaud: Why might it have turned out badly for you?

Emma: C'mon, this is car-crash television – it's all about showing people in their worst possible light and I was fully aware of that. But as I say I thought about it carefully and figured that most people who know me well are not going to be influenced by what they see about me on TV. Those I don't know well who I might meet in the future are likely to have forgotten all about it. I thought it was going to be a fairly obscure programme but in the end it turned out to have higher ratings than expected. Looking back on it, though, I was taking a particular risk as this was the first series and as it wasn't possible to see any of the shows before I didn't know whether they were out to stitch you up or not.

Emma is the only one of these women who gave a lot of thought to the possible downside and indeed it does seem as though she obsessed about this for a fair length of time before agreeing to take part. She had a practical problem that needed solving urgently – she was living in a tip and the strain of the horrible conditions was getting her down badly. It turns out that it was this stress that made her opt for taking the risk of taking part in a reality TV show. Whether the reward of getting the flat cleaned was really worth endangering her future career as a lawyer was surely questionable. After all, if the programme had turned out badly for her there would have been a real possibility her future in such a conservative world would have been at risk.

However, she then seemed to wonder if she hadn't taken too much of a risk in taking part as we discussed how it could have reflected badly on her judgement. She did concede that the real reason she did it – she did actually desperately need to get the flat cleaned – would not be apparent to most viewers. So she was vulnerable to being perceived as shallow and celebrity obsessed as most of the other reality TV participants of which she had such a low opinion.

While no one admits to wanting to be famous when interviewed on the subject, as this would be seriously uncool, this is probably a fairly common motivation that drives the reality TV format. Remember that for most of us reality TV is probably going to be the only opportunity we have to be famous. This presents a key decisive moment in our lives, and many opt to try out what could happen if they took part more out of curiosity than a burning desire to be famous – after all, none of these three women is interested in having another go.

However, there are other strong psychological forces at play here. One gets a sense that all the women interviewed, with the possible exception of Emma, quite enjoyed the massive attention they got from the TV company, and were seduced by this into revealing confidences about themselves and doing things they later regretted. It is perhaps no accident that none of them was completely content in her relationship, except for Emma who didn't appear to be in a relationship at the time of her filming. It's almost as if the TV crew and the programme are psychologically supplying something that is otherwise missing for participants, particularly if this is attention and respect.

The surprising finding that emerges from this investigation is that actually a strong motivation to take part in these risky shows, where your dignity and reputation could be destroyed, is the idea that TV can solve our relationship or emotional problems for us. Or, in Emma's case, her problems of the state of her physical environment.

All three of the women here could have sought therapy or obtained expert help for themselves through channels other than TV. Instead they decided to explore their relationships and their lives or environmental difficulties through the opportunity they perceived as provided by the TV formats – and this is certainly how it was sold to them by the production companies involved.

Although they all claim to have genuinely learned useful things about their relationships or themselves from taking part, the major problem is that all of these insights could surely have been obtained in a less exposing and risky manner, in the privacy of a consulting room. Given the alternatives, it seems a large price to pay to risk losing your dignity and reputation by having TV cameras invade your home and life. The reality of reality TV is that it is out to exploit and manipulate in the relentless quest for ratings. It's not so much a wolf in sheep's clothing as a basking shark in a feeding frenzy if it spots vulnerability.[4] This was something all these women discovered to their cost.

Also most of the supposed 'experts' that TV turns to are not what they seem – certainly in terms of my own fields of psychology and psychiatry I know of no reality TV show that actually uses properly qualified 'specialists'. Such shows use the veneer of psychological expertise when in fact the producer remains the person who calls the shots, literally.[5]

The real lesson is that if a TV company has become interested in your life, be afraid, be very afraid, because this doesn't mean that you are extraordinarily attractive or delightful, as most contestants are seduced into believing – no one wants to watch that, do they? Instead it means that TV has found something about you that will entertain and fascinate, but not in a necessarily positive way, millions of people at home, who will ask after watching you, why on earth did you agree to do that?

At the heart of much of the motivation – even if becoming nationally famous is not a primary goal – is the prospect of increased significance within your local community and increased attention from those close to you, for today the modern cult of celebrity has come to replace the hierarchies of yesteryear, and anyone seeking to rise to the top of a social group has to take this new shift in society into account.

For example, new psychological research suggests that modern worship of celebrities by the public means that celebrities have become the new 'gods', and celebrity devotion has begun to take the place of religion in many people's lives.

Several psychologists have begun to emphasize the similarity between the role of the modern celebrity and that of religious icons, and these latest results confirm that one way of explaining the modern obsession with fame is that celebrities play a similar role today to that played by religious figures in the past.[6]

The research – the product of a unique collaboration between British and US psychologists – was conducted on 307 British people generally representative of the population, and measured in detail different aspects of attitudes to religion and celebrity. The results were published in a paper entitled 'Thou shalt worship no other gods – unless they are celebrities: the relationship between celebrity worship and religious orientation' and published in the prestigious journal *Personality and Individual Differences*.

The major and surprising finding was that however religious interest was measured, the lower a person's religious conviction, the more likely they were to worship celebrities. This strongly suggests that following the famous has begun to replace religion in many people's lives – the major predictor of little interest in celebrities was having a prior and current strong religious conviction.[7]

The team of psychologists at Sheffield Hallam University and Southern Illinois University School of Medicine, led by John Maltby, used a questionnaire that measured the degree of celebrity worship in people's lives. This included asking people if they would try possibly unsafe drugs or activities if their favourite celebrity approved them, or if they believed that a favourite celebrity could be guilty of a crime.[8]

The concept of 'celebrity worship' as akin to religious worship was first advanced by Lynn McCutcheon, a Florida psychologist, who pointed out that much of the news today is dominated by celebrities, and the public are increasingly personally affected more by what happens to their favourite idol than by relationships with family or friends.[9] For example, recent research by the University of Oxford Centre for Suicide Research found a massive rise in suicides in England and Wales during the month following the death of Princess Diana.[10]

Apparently, as a direct result of Diana's death and funeral, suicides increased overall by 17% in the month afterwards. The impact was greatest on women, particularly women closest in age to Diana herself, who died at thirty-seven. The rate of suicide in women increased some 34% in the month following Diana's death, and in women aged twenty-five to forty-four the rate increased by over 45%.[11]

Another study found that national suicide rates went up nationwide in the USA whenever the *New York Times* reported celebrity suicides.[12] Also psychologists have lately reported that devoted but otherwise unrelated fans of recently deceased celebrities sometimes experience bereavement hallucinations – the usual reactions to loss in surviving loved ones.[13]

This suggests that for many their whole life's meaning and identity becomes centred on the world of celebrity, just as a sense of identity and meaning was previously more usually derived from religion. Sports stars like David Beckham have not only become role models for millions of young boys around the world, but they also influence their values and lifestyle in a way that religion may have provided guidance in the past.[14]

Some fan bases also often resemble religions: for example the strong similarities of *Star Trek* fans to a cult have been widely noted by sociologists, and include the way they organize, recruit and hold ceremonies – commonly known as 'conventions'.[15]

The obsessiveness of dedicated celebrity followers also resembles religious worship. For example, fans will frequently exclusively pursue an interest in one celebrity and denigrate competing stars, so resembling the exclusivity of worship demanded by many major religions. Fans will also often perform rituals that appear religious-like, for example ensuring they watch all of a celebrity's TV appearances and attempting to collect items that have been touched by a celebrity.[16]

Auctions of articles owned or touched by celebrities and the high values obtained attest to the special significance bestowed on these objects – this has a strong resemblance to the interest in objects supposedly touched or rendered significant by religious figures, like the Holy Grail or the Turin Shroud.[17]

Celebrity worshippers also frequently refuse to believe that their idols are capable of wrong-doing, so the illict behaviour of some stars is frequently forgiven and explained away, while similar behaviour by non-celebrities would perhaps not be. Recent psychological research on mock jury scenarios has confirmed that celebrities accused of rape are more likely to be acquitted by the public than non-celebrities.[18]

This adds credence to the notion that celebrities are revered in a devout way as if they were religious figures. They are similarly perceived by large numbers of the public to be operating under a different set of rules, which cannot be understood by ordinary mortals, and for which allowances must therefore be made.

David Giles, a media psychologist at the University of Coventry, recently argued in his book *Illusions of Immortality: A Psychology of Fame and Celebrity* that one explanation for the modern obsession with becoming famous is that it is a quest for immortality.[19] There is a sense that the genuinely famous live on through their reputations and images, so preserving a part of themselves for eternity, and as a result actually achieve the kind of afterlife promised by religion.

Also, just as many wanted to touch Jesus's raiment to benefit from his power and achieve miracle cures, so the throng today reaches out from behind their barriers to make some physical contact with the famous, and they indeed appear to be guided in crucial healthcare decisions by celebrities.[20]

Research recently published in the *Western Medical Journal* confirms that after Betty Ford spoke out about her radical mastectomy for breast cancer in 1974, detection rates for breast cancer rose dramatically in a phenomenon known to experts as 'the Betty Ford blip'. The public clearly try to emulate a celebrity's medical experience: for example, after Nancy Reagan, wife of the then-President Ronald Reagan, had a mastectomy, rates of the alternative procedure – lumpectomy – dropped dramatically, probably because women thought the President's wife got the best advice.[21]

The problem is that celebrities, according to doctors, do not, in fact, demonstrate god-like abilities when it comes to health choices, so the public could be dangerously misled by them.

For example, the *Western Medical Journal* points out that Katie Couric, a US TV personality from the *Today* show, recommended early screening for colon cancer, after her husband died of it at age forty-two. Couric urged younger people to have colonoscopies, and even underwent one herself on television, although cancer authorities do not advocate routine colonoscopy, especially for younger people.[22]

One final intriguing similarity between religion and celebrity worship has just been reported by psychologist Lynn McCutcheon in the *British Journal of Psychology*.[23] Just as religions tend to be dominated by men in their senior officials and past major figures, so it has been found that, perhaps surprisingly, men score higher than women on celebrity worship, and men have been found to gossip more than women about media celebrities.[24]

Perhaps men are more interested in the idea of being worshipped than women?

The idea of celebrity worship turning the famous into modern gods can also become a kind of self-fulfilling prophecy – recent research from the University of Nebraska Department of Finance confirms that celebrity endorsement of products can have a significant impact on a multinational company's total worth. For example, Tiger Woods' endorsement of Nike products was shown to influence the market value of the whole company depending on his performance in tournaments. This means that our worship of celebrities does indeed turn them into the most powerful people on the planet, gods in our midst.[25]

Another reason why fame has become such a dominant motivation today is not just that the opportunities for becoming famous have multiplied, but also that we appear as a population to be getting more extrovert. This means that becoming significant to others matters more – as this tends to be a pre-occupation of extroverts. This again means that politics and machiavellian conspiring are more attuned to more people's psychology than ever before.[26]

Have you ever wondered why young people today seem so different from when you were the same age? Does the younger generation seem more loud, confident, arrogant and exhibition-istic than when you were at that stage of life? You might have charitably put this down to the difficulty of remembering what you were like when younger – maybe you were just the same, it's just that the passing years have dimmed the memory.[27]

In fact, your first impression has been backed up by science – data from the largest analysis ever performed on how personality is changing over time, conducted on almost 17,000 subjects over the last forty years, has just been published. It firmly establishes that people's personalities have been dramatically changing. Basically each subsequent generation has been getting much more extrovert and assertive since the 1960s.[28]

Psychologists divide personality into two main types – extroverts and introverts. Extroverts are outgoing and sociable, while introverts prefer to be more alone, often find constant company overwhelming and don't like to be the centre of attention.

This new finding could provide a novel explanation for many puzzling phenomena, like the rise of reality TV programmes such as *Big Brother* and *Temptation Island*, where young people seem willing to do any bidding on camera. This is in stark contrast to their parents, who watch with shocked bemusement.[29]

According to this new research, reality TV could simply reflect an actuality at large in society – the younger generation is significantly more exhibitionistic than the age groups before.

Extroverts, while more sociable and the life and soul of the party, are also more impulsive and easily bored. This could also explain the dramatic modern rise in problems linked to impetuous tendencies, for example eating disorders such as bulimia, where young girls impulsively binge and then in a fit of regret throw up after meals.[30]

Bulimia, although widely regarded as extremely common in young girls today, was first identified by doctors as recently as 1979, suggesting this could be a genuinely new phenomenon. Now it would appear we have an explanation for its emergence – it arises out of a combination of the increasing impulsiveness, boredom and preoccupation with attracting others of the more extrovert personality produced by the modern age.[31]

While extroverts may appear on the surface to be having more fun than introverts, because they are more sociable and have more friends, their dependency on sensation-seeking and company makes them vulnerable to other problems like drug abuse, through peer pressure and the need for constant stimulation.[32]

Because of this problem of impulsiveness, all across the world the more extrovert a society is, the higher the murder, divorce, crime, accident and unemployment rates.

This latest psychological research not only explains the rise of these social ills, but it has revealed that the generation gap between parents and their children, in terms of their personality, appears to be growing.[33]

Each generation since the 1960s has been found to be dramatically more extrovert or outgoing and sociable than the previous one. In other words, the younger you are the more extrovert you will tend to be compared to your elders.

Jean Twenge, a psychologist at Case Western Reserve University in the USA, recently uncovered this remarkable result when she analysed every comparable study of personality since the 1960s and found that young people today are on average 50% more extrovert than people the same age in the 1960s.[34]

Also she predicts that if current trends continue, by the year 2010, college-age students will be almost twice as extrovert as students were in the 1960s. Another way of putting this is that the average student-age person in the year 2010 will be more extrovert than over 80% of the population of the same age in the 1960s.

This is a bit like finding yourself in a class at school today populated entirely by the most extrovert people from your classroom thirty years ago.

Explanations for this dramatic rise in extroversion include the fact that Western societies have undergone many changes since the 1960s and these could have had a dramatic impact on personality, ensuring that people gradually became more outgoing.

Family mobility increased, day care for young children became more common, parenting was less centred on establishing rules, and the economy increasingly moved towards service and away from industry.

Increased family mobility may have increased 'outgoingness' in children and adolescents, who for the first time had to learn how to interact with more and different people while they were growing up. Before, when families hardly moved, as a child you did not have to get to know such a wide range of new acquaintances as the modern child moving regularly with his or her parents has to.

The constant moves of families are encouraged not only by shifting work patterns, which remove young couples from their home towns and place them miles from where they were born, but also by rapidly rising property prices, which have invited young families to keep moving along the property ladder. Never before in history have so many young people had to learn to enter social networks in the workplace and in their neighbourhoods from scratch. This is a process that fosters sociability as an incessant lifestyle.

The widespread advent of day care for the young may be having the same effect. When day care was more unusual, young children were exposed to only their parents and the neighbours' children. Now they socialize with larger numbers of children, prompting them to be more outgoing, particularly if they are to make their mark or be noticed in the midst of such a large group.[35]

In addition, philosophies of child-rearing have changed; in general, child-raising has become progressively more permissive, allowing children to speak their minds, in contrast to the earlier doctrine of being 'seen and not heard'. This change has most likely encouraged assertiveness in children.

Those who are withdrawn or tend to keep to themselves are actively encouraged to change their behaviour, and increasingly school reports include comments on a student's progress towards development as a co-operative social person as well as academic advance.

For example, one psychologist noted that one parent was cautioned that her son was not developing socially because 'he would pick one or two friends to play with, and sometimes he was happy to remain by himself'.[36]

Also recently children have been allowed to express themselves more freely and teachers often do not so much plan what to teach students as ask them what they would like to learn about a topic. This encourages assertiveness towards authority figures, and a misplaced confidence, despite ignorance that would have ensured the older generation remained more subdued in the presence of their elders.

Perhaps this is an attempt to prepare children for the new environment they will meet on leaving school, as jobs in the new service-oriented economy involve dealing with people. The theory is that extroverts are better adapted to contemporary service-centred society.

Indeed, it is so obvious that companies are now looking for extroverts that psychologists who write career advice guides routinely include advice on how to cheat on the personality tests that are increasingly employed to weed out 'undesirable' personalities, like introverts. These psychologists strongly suggest that applicants should 'recognize that a display of too much introversion, a desire for reflection, or sensitivity is to be avoided'.

The current preoccupation with selecting extroverts in the workplace could be a mistake because it runs counter to one of the most well-established facts about introverts – they are what psychologists term more 'task-oriented' than extroverts.[37]

This basically means they get on with the job at hand rather than being constantly distracted by the need to 'connect' – i.e., chat – with fellow employees. The new vogue for open-plan offices also encourages extroversion because socializing is more possible, while introverts who just want to get on with work are discriminated against, because they find all the social interaction around them distracting. They could also be more easily identified and gossiped about as 'loners'.

Clearly the modern belief is that not only at work but in all

406

aspects of life, an active, extroverted, gregarious temperament tends to incline a person better towards the exciting pace of modern life.

For unlike past times, in the modern era there has been an increased emphasis on the pursuit of happiness and extroversion – socializing or getting on in relationships – has been seen as the key to happiness. This has produced a greater emphasis on social skills than there was in previous periods.

Today, modern thinking is if you are unhappy you should do something about it, and that something usually has to do with socializing: getting on better with others, joining a club or terminating your boring marriage and putting yourself back in the market again.

Extroverts are usually more optimistic than introverts and this over-optimism of the young in comparison to older generations explains their tendency to take more risks and, for example, not to save as much – because they never plan for or fear a 'rainy day'. They are also more likely to smoke and abuse drugs because they are over-optimistic about any possible damage to their bodies.[38]

Extroverts are much more experimental when it comes to sex and also more promiscuous; this could therefore also explain why we have such a problem with a high and climbing unwanted pregnancy rate in teenagers.

Perhaps because of extroverts' restlessness, extroversion also predicts greater marital instability, and therefore it could be rising extroversion in younger generations that explains the rocketing post-war divorce rate.

In addition, the role of women has changed tremendously over the time period in question; women are more likely to work than in previous decades. As a result, women have probably increased in dominance and assertiveness as their roles have changed over the last forty years. In particular, you need to be much more assertive if you are working outside the home, while assertiveness within the home could perhaps often be linked to greater martial instability.[39]

But most worryingly of all, we may now have entered a vicious upward spiral of extroversion because we live in a new media age where extrovert media like television dominate. Not many introverts are going to be given their own TV series to host – so extroversion as a value now dominates our society.

The modern pervasiveness of relentless affability could explain why many in the older generation, brought up in more introverted times, now are increasingly alienated by the new ruthlessly outgoing society we live in. They frequently find themselves forced to be more extrovert than they really feel comfortable with.

Yet key valuable characteristics of introverts that could be most valuable to modern society seem to have been abandoned in the rush to be gregarious. For example, the tendency introverts have, compared to extroverts, to think hard about themselves, rather than being so outwardly focused. This means that introverts are more aware when their behaviour drops below the standards they set themselves. Extroverts tend not to be so bothered when this happens because they don't introspect as much – they are too preoccupied with the impression they are creating in others. Extroverts are much more prone to immoral behaviour, breaking rules and the law. This could explain the decline in standards in public and private life we now see everywhere.[40]

It could well be that our politicians, public figures and a whole generation could in fact profoundly benefit from a dash more introspection, and a little less sociability.

In the 1992 presidential election, the rallying cry of Republicans was 'Bill Clinton doesn't have the character to be president!', indicating that in modern politics character matters. To test this idea Steven Rubenzer and colleagues at the Mental Health & Mental Retardation Authority of Harris County Houston, Texas, asked 115 experts who had written book-length biographies of a particular president or had other, protracted contact, whether professional or personal, with an American president to rate his personality using a standard personality test used by psychologists. The experts were instructed to base their ratings of their respective subject on the five-year period *before* they became president. This approach was adopted because a president is subjected to strong pressures by his role and the environment of the White House, which may reduce the amount of variability of behaviour among different people. Rating of presidential greatness was based on a nineteen-page questionnaire sent to 846 Ph.D.-holding historians who were members of the American Historical Association.

The data indicated that most modern presidents are clearly

extroverts, while early presidents often scored below average on this factor and this has been attributed to 'increased influence of the mass media in presidential selection.'.[41]

Presidents did differ dramatically among themselves in test scores, suggesting not only that it was possible to group presidents, but also suggesting that there is no one personality throughout history that defines a presidential 'type'. This also suggests that there may be multiple roads to the same goal of achieving the presidency.[42]

Of all dimensions of personality, 'openness to experience' produced the strongest association with the historians' ratings of greatness. As this is correlated with general cognitive ability, and research across a broad spectrum of jobs has confirmed that general mental ability is the best predictor of occupational attainments, the relationship between openness and ratings of presidential greatness could be partially explained by cognitive ability.[43] Conscientiousness was only moderately associated with historical greatness. Extroverted people tended to make somewhat better presidents but 'agreeableness' was of little value in predicting presidential greatness. In fact, 'disagreeable' presidents did somewhat better.[44]

'Tender-mindedness' (concern for the less fortunate) had only a moderate correlation with attaining historical greatness. Interestingly, historical greatness was predicted remarkably well by low scores on 'straightforwardness'.[45] Presidents who are not straightforward use a variety of tactics to persuade people and achieve their ends, they are not above tricking, cajoling, bullying or lying if necessary and appear to be true politicians, playing the right tune to each crowd.[46]

If becoming president can be seen as a measure of some kind of ultimate achievement, the power of this research is that it illuminates most starkly how to get to the top, given how self-deprecating and coy most people are when asked to explain the secret of their success.[47, 48, 49]

19

CONCLUSION: WHY IT'S NOT JUST THE SIZE OF YOUR CARROT THAT MATTERS

The number-one motivator of people is feedback on results

Anonymous

What will people say about you when you die?

Stephen R. Covey

When trying to understand controversial high achievers, like sports legend Mike Tyson, it is important to appreciate that any area of human achievement is full of enigmas.

For example, Lennox Lewis, the revered world champion, is not totally holy himself. After all it was Lennox who threw the first punch at Tyson during the infamous press conference, which led to the extraordinary mêlée that prompted Las Vegas boxing authorities to call off the forthcoming bout. It was only *after* Lennox's punch that Tyson sunk his teeth into Lewis's thigh.

Lennox Lewis said afterwards, 'I was shocked. You don't bite people unless your life is being threatened, you know, you can't breathe so you are biting the guy to get out. But this geezer actually wants to bite and eat people. He is definitely sick.'

Is Tyson merely 'sick', as the media often portrays him? Or is there a deeper psychological explanation for his bizarre behaviour – is the chess-playing Lennox being more perceptive than the press realizes when he suggests Tyson's tendency to bite his opponents lies in a more fundamental emotional issue, a response to a threat that Tyson continually sees all around him?

Mike Tyson was born on 30 June 1966 and was largely brought up by a single mother struggling to raise two other children in grinding poverty, while drifting through the roughest neighbourhoods in New York.

Tyson was reportedly a small softly spoken child, burdened, on top of all his other disadvantages, with a lisp. This oddity apparently rendered him an easy target for the neighbourhood bullies and as a result he was constantly ridiculed and pounded, even by the local girls.

Perhaps the crucial seeds of what was to happen years later were being planted then, for quite soon after this period Mike Tyson would regularly detonate into a frenzy if anyone used his neighbourhood nickname, 'Fairy Boy', given to him because of his high-pitched lisping voice.

It was also during this time – and here the enigma deepens – that Tyson became obsessed with pigeons. He built a coop, looked after large numbers of pigeons tenderly and, as time went by, became fascinated by watching his birds fly high above the sewers that trapped him.

Psychoanalysts might argue that part of his fascination with birds was their ability to fly away and escape from the places that clutched him. But it is perhaps most notable that he did not exhibit any cruelty at all to these vulnerable creatures. After all, harming animals as a child is a classic predictor of future severe antisocial personality disorder.

In fact, when a local thug, indeed probably a proper psychopath, broke the neck of one of his birds, this would appear to have been a key turning point in Tyson's life. Until then Mike had been considered a relatively retiring and un-assuming child, but at that moment something seems to have popped inside his head and he retaliated violently. In later press interviews Tyson is said to particularly treasure the memory of how he savagely beat up the person who killed one of his beloved birds.

Inevitably, given the neighbourhood and his family's circum-stances, he turned to crime, and by the age of twelve he had graduated from pickpocketing to mugging, eventually moving up to armed robbery.

After an arrest he was regarded by the authorities as such a dangerous villain that he was shipped to a reform school miles away from home. From there he was taken by admirers of his fighting prowess to a local boxing club run by an old trainer called Cus D'Amato, who rapidly became a close friend and took Tyson in to live with him. D'Amato became the father that Tyson never had, but he was criticized for not developing Tyson as a man as much as he did as a fighter. As the only father-figure Tyson ever had was a boxing trainer, this probably means he was taught to see life largely in terms of a fight.

Then just as it seemed things were going right in Tyson's life, Cus D'Amato died. Tyson had lost his mother to cancer a few years earlier, so within a short space of time and before he was yet twenty, the only people who had ever honestly approved of him, and on whom his fragile self-esteem was based, were gone.

The impact of these losses should not be underestimated – Tyson is said to have burst into tears when interviewed by a journalist about D'Amato years later, while at the funeral he confided to a friend he felt so alone he wanted to commit suicide.

Yet Tyson apparently rapidly recovered and then defeated Trevor Berbick in November 1986 when he was just over twenty years old to win the WBC title and become the youngest ever heavyweight champion of the world. He had won twenty-six of his first twenty-eight fights by knock-outs – fifteen of these in the first round. Tyson would later declare that winning the title was the most memorable night of his life because, 'I've never really had people accept me so fully before and haven't really been accepted that way since.'

But now without proper guidance and only Don King, the notorious fight promoter, to step into the vacuum, things began to go wrong. He hastily married the attractive actress Robin Givens, who was to humiliate him just a few years later by revealing on TV that he had been diagnosed as being manic-depressive and prescribed mood-stabilizing drugs like lithium and anti-depressants.

Then in Tokyo in February 1990, an unknown 42–1 outsider, James 'Buster' Douglas, beat him in the tenth round in what should have been an easy fight for a fit Tyson.

A divorce from Givens followed, and then in 1992 he was sentenced to six years for raping a Miss Black America contestant called Desiree Washington. But few know that in the trial the judge ruled inadmissible the fact that Miss Washington had in the past made rape allegations against both a high school classmate and her own father.

Tyson walked out of prison a year later than he would have if he had not stoutly maintained his innocence throughout, and he then returned to the ring with some victories, but he lost in November 1996 to Evander Holyfield.

Then in the third round of the June 1997 rematch he bit Holyfield's ear twice.

Fined $3m for his conduct by the Nevada State Athletic Commission, Tyson had his licence revoked for a year and rumours surfaced in the press that he was in deep financial trouble. The boxer was then involved in an altercation with two motorists after their car hit a vehicle driven by his second wife Monica. He later served one year of a suspended sentence for assaulting the motorists and he was released in 1999 weighing twenty stone.

While all this was going on he faced a psychiatric examination at the request of the Nevada State Athletic Commission before it would consider returning his licence following the ear-biting incident. The report received much publicity, for Tyson had revealed feeling depressed all his life, saying to the psychiatrists and neurologists from Massachusetts General Hospital, 'I have no self-esteem, but the biggest ego in the world.' The doctors concluded that returning to boxing would help alleviate some of the stresses that contributed to his depression.

It was clearly a high-risk strategy and the decision suggests the doctors feared that depriving Tyson of the one thing he was good at would leave no viable alternatives, in terms of a life purpose or goal, for the already extremely low fighter. They might have been worried about where Tyson's fearsome aggression would be directed next if he didn't get his licence back, and whether indeed it would be turned to himself, in the form of a suicidal impulse.

The team of experts concluded Tyson exhibited 'a constellation of neurobehavioural deficits', that he trusted no one, felt alone in the world and expected to be betrayed. They recommended he be allowed to fight only if he remained in therapy.

But the deeper problem was that Tyson clearly didn't take too well to being challenged in a therapeutic encounter: he later said of his meetings with the psychiatrists, 'They love to torture people's minds, they would have been great Nazis.' This is a very important statement because it shows that Tyson seemed to see persecution even in the very doctors who tried to help him and by arguing with the authorities that he should get his boxing licence back.

Tyson returned to the ring in 1999 to face relative no-hoper Francois Botha. Tyson's fifth-round victory was marred by claims that he was trying to break his opponent's arm by gripping it until it snapped. In the same year he hit another opponent after the bell sounded signalling the end of round one.

But Mike Tyson's comments actually suggest an underlying low self-esteem bubbling just beneath the surface of the intimidation and swagger. 'People like to watch animals fight,' he once said, 'that's why they like to watch me.' He also once confided to D'Amato that he regarded himself as too ugly to attract women, while in a TV interview he said, 'Where I come from I'm just the piece of gum on the bottom of your shoe.'

Tyson, as he himself admits, has based his whole life on intimidation; after all, that was the only way to survive as the short kid with the lisp in the ghetto. He also became tough to protect the bruises on the inside. Now, because his experience since childhood has been that everyone he meets takes advantage of him and abuses him, he sees imaginary slights everywhere. It was possibly this that triggered the brawl at the Lennox Lewis press conference, following an innocent gesture by Lewis's bodyguard to keep Tyson back.

He also suffers apparently from chronic problems with relationships – intimate or professional – as the string of sacked managers and trainers attests, as do the rape case and two divorces. It may be that the only relationship he truly understands is that between two fighters in the ring, so only when he boxes does he feel worthwhile. This explains why his encounters outside the ring so often get transformed by him to resemble those inside it.

While a possible future Lennox Lewis–Mike Tyson encounter would appear to be the most absorbing clash of the century for fight fans, for the psychiatrist the key battle Tyson now faces is the one for his mind.

The fear must be that there are now not enough people who genuinely care for Tyson to provide the support he needs. Yet such relationships are particularly vital right now, as he is apparently not allowed to take the antidepressants he is supposedly normally on, due to boxing regulations in the run-up to a fight.

The removal of his usual treatment could partly explain what happened in the 'Meltdown in Manhattan' press conference. But what the media and the public don't appreciate is that, given his terrible experiences, when he strikes out, it's not against any real opponent in the outside world, for whoever he is facing, he is probably really fighting internal demons.

From this case history and the series of examples and cases marshalled earlier in this book, I contend that there are many grave weaknesses with the traditional way behavioural science has thus far tried to understand motivation.

Psychologists generally have evaluated only one type of motivation at a time. Yet in everyday life people can pursue multiple types of reinforcements simultaneously, or they can switch from pursuing one type of reinforcement to another.[1]

For example, the person who reads a newspaper while eating is simultaneously pursuing intellectual satisfaction and food consumption. The person who puts down a newspaper to start a morning walk has switched from pursuing the satisfactions of intellectual activity to those of physical activity. Although such 'motivation switching' is a fundamental aspect of everyday behaviour, there are few psychological efforts to account for it.[2]

In virtually all psychological experiments on motivation reported to date animal and human participants are not permitted to switch motivation. By not studying in greater depth when people switch from seeking one reinforcer to another, psychologists may have underestimated the importance of individual differences in rates of satiation (individual differences in desired amounts of various reinforcers) argue Steven Reiss and Susan Havercamp, Psychologists at Ohio State University.[3]

Another reason, suggest Reiss and Havercamp, psychologists have underestimated individual differences in desired amounts of reinforcement concerns the tendency to study animals in deprivational states. Deprivation induces common motivation in animals who otherwise may have very different motivations.[4]

For example, the behavioural consequences of individual differences in appetite are temporarily obscured by deprivational procedures that make animals very hungry. The motivational principles that apply to starving animals may not generalize well to other animals who are not necessarily starving, and they may be even less applicable to the everyday lives of people. Whereas almost all starving people spend most of their time and energy searching for food, people who are not starving show considerable individual differences in the amount of time and energy devoted to the preparation and consumption of meals.[5]

Reiss and Havercamp ask us to consider the distinction between gluttony and hunger. A glutton is a person who habitually has a hearty appetite and overeats for pleasure – the dictionary indicates that gluttons are people who enjoy eating above other pleasures. Because gluttony is a personality (individual difference) concept, it applies to only some people. In contrast, hunger is a temporary situational state related mostly to how long it has been since one's last meal; the term 'hunger' is not a personality factor and potentially applies to anyone who has not eaten in a while.

Although all people are to some degree motivated to eat, the amount of time, effort and persistence devoted to the pursuit of food may vary significantly from one individual to the next. The amount of food required for satiation varies considerably from one person to the next, even when deprivational factors are held constant. This is recognized in everyday life by references to some people being 'good eaters' or having 'hearty appetites'. These phrases suggest recognition among lay people that there are stable individual differences in the motivational strength of rewards such as food.

The plain fact is that some people just like eating much more than most people. Similarly, the amount of time, effort and persistence people devote to the pursuit of happiness (positive mood) varies considerably from one individual to the next. The platitude 'everybody wants to be happy' trivializes potentially important individual differences in effort.[6]

Some people try to look at everything positively and make the most out of whatever happens. These people work at being happy and organize a large portion of their everyday lives to achieve it. Others make only token efforts to escape a life filled with burdens, boredom or misery. These observations are made not as a value judgement on people's lives but as a factual statement that individuals differ considerably in the effort they make to experience positive moods.

Individuals show important differences in the strength of their motivations. Some people are extremely interested in surviving, whereas alcoholics drink themselves to death. Some people panic in anxious situations, whereas others readily approach them. American football players withstand considerable physical pain that the more squeamish among us would avoid at all cost.

To the extent that psychological theories of motivation have all people equally motivated to do anything, such as seek pleasure or avoid anxiety, these theories are fundamentally flawed, contend Reiss and Havercamp.

The psychological study of motivation has also struggled to escape from stating the obvious. For example, the argument that everybody seeks pleasure can become tautological if work is defined as pleasure for workaholics. If both the hedonist and the workaholic are viewed as seeking pleasure, important differences in motivation are trivialized. The hedonist attends every gathering possible, whereas the workaholic can hardly relax and stop working long enough to enjoy a single party.[7]

When a person desires unusually large or small amounts of reinforcement, that person is said to be 'aberrantly motivated'. Aberrant motivation (very high reinforcement sensitivity or very low reinforcement sensitivity) is assumed to result from complex interactions among biological, developmental, conditioning, and cognitive factors.

Theoretically, aberrant motivation is a risk factor for aberrant behaviour. That is, the amount of reinforcement a person seeks (how much reinforcement is required to produce satiation) may be the key to understanding the development of aberrant behaviour in at least some, if not many, people.[8]

Reiss and Havercamp consider the example of a boy with a high sensitivity for attention. By definition, the boy should behave as if he is chronically 'starved' of attention, showing vigorous efforts to obtain as much attention as immediately as possible. For this child, engaging in inappropriate behaviour may be an effective strategy to obtain quickly a large amount of reinforcement.

Sometimes people develop aberrant behaviour because they want something too badly or too quickly. A person who has not eaten in a long time starts thinking about food constantly, so that obtaining food starts to dominate the person's behaviour. In a similar fashion, people who develop aberrant behaviour may want to be loved too much, may need companionship too often, may need to escape immediately from frustration, or may desire pleasure all the time. At times these motivations may be extremely strong and dominate the person's behaviour.[9]

Anxiety sensitivity is reduced when people believe that the experience of anxiety will not harm them.

Generally, several limitations may be noted to previous research on motivation. First, psychologists have widely assumed – but not critically examined – the hypothesis that everybody is equally motivated to seek pleasure/happiness and equally motivated to avoid anxiety. People actually show wide individual differences in the strength of these motives. Second, psychological theories of motivation have been unduly influenced by the study of animals in deprivational states.[10]

This approach has obscured the role of individual differences in what we find rewarding or motivating. Whereas starving animals spend almost all of their time and energy seeking large quantities of food, most people spend widely varying amounts of time and energy pursuing a much broader range of reinforcers. Third, psychologists have studied only one motivation at a time. This has obscured the importance of individual differences in rates of satiation. Whereas individual differences in satiation rates may seem unimportant when only one motivation is considered, they seem relevant to explaining motivation switching in which a person changes the type of reinforcement he or she is pursuing.

Aberrant motivation is indicated when a person wants too much of a particular type of reinforcement and/or is too intolerant of everyday levels of some aversive stimulus such as anxiety or frustration. Aberrant motivation may be a risk factor for psychopathology because people usually cannot obtain high amounts of reinforcement by behaving in socially appropriate ways. People sometimes resort to inappropriate behaviour as the best strategy to obtain a high amount of immediate reinforcement.[11]

However, aberrant behaviour rarely leads to enough reinforcement to satiate aberrant desires; people with aberrant motives rarely obtain what they want and are at risk of unhappiness.

Reiss and Havercamp's theory suggests that it is worth reconsidering when to use certain clinical strategies. For example, teaching people socially appropriate skills to obtain desired reinforcements has been a popular strategy. Although this strategy may be effective when the primary problem is a lack of skill, it may be ineffective when an important part of the person's problem is aberrant motivation. Teaching thieves employment skills may not work for those who crave immediate riches; in such cases, it may be necessary to reduce the greed for a durable and generalized treatment benefit.

Work on the question of motivation was greatly impeded in the field by the outlook of one of the most famous psychologists of the twentieth century: B. F. Skinner's behaviourism. Skinner argued that if psychology was to be a natural science in the same way as physics or chemistry, it should restrain itself to measuring things equally precisely, with numbers and instruments. Thus the appropriate study area for psychology was an examination of how the environment influenced behaviour. You could put a ruler up against the environment and therefore measure it and so gauge its impact on behaviour.[12]

Since you couldn't get a ruler inside the mind, and nothing there could be reliably measured, it was best to avoid speculating as to what was going on in there.

Skinner argued that in analysing behaviour it was intellectually bankrupt to invoke inner causes as explanatory constructs. Note that this is in marked contrast to the Freudian view, which is that we are at the mercy of a wide variety of dark and unconscious drives or motives.

Skinner argued, for example, that to say that a person eats because he or she is hungry is circular because we infer a state of hunger from the behaviour (eating) that we are trying to explain. 'If this state [hunger] is purely inferential if no dimensions are assigned to it which would make direct observation possible it cannot serve as an explanation,' Skinner said.[13] Hunger is simply a ghost that we've created and, in turn, projected on to the machine. This is what Skinner is referring to when he observes that the constructs invoked always seem to have the exact qualities necessary to explain the behaviour at hand.

Further, Skinner is right to say that even a complete understanding at the neural level of behaviour would not bring anything new to a functional analysis of behaviour. Even if we knew the exact neural mechanisms that produced hunger, this information is not directly observable to us in normal settings. Therefore, it would not preclude the need to know the antecedent conditions (e.g., number of hours of food deprivation) to predict the probability that a person will eat.

In fact, some of the most important findings in motivation theory come from positing the kind of internal states that Skinner so disappoved of because they couldn't be measured.[14]

For example, scientists using a blend of Skinner's ideas and evidence of internal states have discovered that how rewarding you find something depends on what frame of mind you are in. Scientists find that if they deprive laboratory rats of food and so create a motivated animal, and then feed it whilst in that deprived state, the same kind of food acts in the future as a greater source of reward even when the animal is not in a deprived state. The point here is that the *power* of a reward depends on the state of mind you are in. If someone corrects a chronic and extreme deprived state with a stimulus or reward, your brain has an extremely positive attitude to that reward long after the deprivation state has ceased.

At the opposite end of the spectrum in psychology was the idea that the only thing worth studying was our inner drives, though they were not directly observable – in which case the question became how to develop an instrument to gauge these.

Through the development of a novel observational method, Sigmund Freud made possible the collection of reliable data about man's inner life. The scientific hypotheses he formulated about these formed the initial version of psychoanalysis.[15]

Many of these first thoughts have had to be revised in the light of subsequent scientific findings about the operations of the central nervous system, but even these refuted propositions often had much value, as the famous American psychoanalyst John Gedo points out.

Most important, contends Gedo, was Freud's realization that human thought is usually unconscious. His understanding of the role of the automatic repetition of basic patterns of behaviour, of the fateful consequences of early childhood emotional vicissitudes in structuring enduring mental dispositions, and of the distinction between two distinct modes of thinking are the most significant among his many contributions.[16]

The new millennium marked the centenary of the birth of psychoanalysis. Its sole parent, Sigmund Freud, has been dead for over sixty years – indeed, he was born before the American Civil War, relatively early in the reign of Queen Victoria – yet his contribution to modern civilization has been so profound that his work stayed at the centre of attention (whether to be praised or denigrated) throughout the twentieth century.[17]

John Gedo summarizes Freud's life's work by stating that he invented a new scientific discipline that has steadily grown for over a hundred years and in every part of the developed world – an intellectual and organizational feat of some magnitude. Freud's scientific writings (in English translation) comprise twenty-four volumes and continue to be read, not only by professional psychoanalysts. In fact, so great has Freud's prestige been in educated circles that even today, two to four generations after its original publication, his oeuvre is commonly equated with the conceptual world of psychology.[18]

In the most general sense, the functions of the central nervous system were then conceptualized in power engineering terms (as if the brain were an electrical apparatus), a paradigm that turned out to be incorrect. Most of Freud's scientific errors followed from these invalid neurophysiological assumptions.

But, argues John Gedo, perhaps one of the most underrated of Freud's achievements was the insight that human behaviour is characterized by a variety of automatic repetitions. Freud observed that patients were never aware of any motive for these behaviours, nor could an observer discover any in every instance; hence Freud concluded that there has to be a fundamental biological basis, inherent in the organization of the central nervous system, for the tendency to repeat. The first type of repetition he discerned was that of patterns of behaviour and attitudes initially experienced in relation to the primary caretakers of childhood.

Freud observed that patients re-experienced these patterns vis-à-vis the analyst – a process he named 'transference'. In other words, you project your previous attitudes to significant others, you relive your prior patterns of relationships, by re-experiencing these with your therapist. If you had an authoritarian father you might project authoritarianism on to your therapist.[19]

Freud eventually observed the obligatory occurrence of repetitive behaviours that produce neither pleasure nor profit; as he put it, these compulsive repetitions are 'beyond the pleasure principle' that governs most unconsciously motivated activities. These were the instances for which Freud was never able to discover any motive, so that he was forced to provide a purely biological explanation for them. His commitment to an energetic model of mental functions led him to the mistaken conclusion that the compulsion to repeat is caused by the operation of entropy (that is, the loss of organization).[20]

Because this hypothesis turned out to be unacceptable to most psychoanalysts, the important observations it was meant to explain were for some time neglected. In recent years, theoretical biology has emphasized the need to perpetuate the organization of complex living systems; this overriding biological principle provides a rationale for the persistence of existing patterns, even if in current circumstances they violate the pleasure principle.

The mechanism of such persistence is now well understood in neurophysiological terms as the effects of repeated use on strengthening synapses. In other words, synaptic mechanisms such as long-term potentiation, which are thought to underlie learning and memory, favour repetitive behaviour because whatever one has done is easier to do again, contends US psychoanalytic writer Virginia Demos.[21]

The adult human brain contains about thirty billion neurons, which are densely overlapping, branching and interconnected, producing a hyperastronomical number of synapses: ten followed by at least a million zeros. And these synapses are themselves regulated by chemical and electrical processes that operate in variable and complex ways, further magnifying the complexity of connective possibilities and of dynamics. The brain is constantly active, responding to signals from internal and environmental sources that cause neurons to develop dendrites and branchings, thereby creating new connections and forming circuits or networks.[22]

Development in the brain is the result of lived experience, which leads to the proliferation of dendrites, axons and increasingly complex neural networks. Unused neurons die off.

The functional unit of mental activity is not what occurs in a single neuron, but is rather the activation of an integrated network of interconnecting neurons all at the same time, resulting in thought, memory, perception, feeling, etc. All information is represented in the brain by temporal configurations of interconnected neurons. The human brain is special both as an object and as a system – its connectivity, dynamics, mode of functioning, and relation to the body and the world are like nothing else science has yet encountered.[23]

So the latest research suggests that while our behaviour is

controlled by our brains, the experiences we have quite literally form our brains.

Doctors have known for a long time that stress can have crippling tangible effects on the body, directly contributing to numerous physical problems, like stomach ulcers, heart disease and asthma. But new medical research suggests we should be much more worried about stress, because there is good evidence it could also cause actual physical brain damage and directly shrink our grey matter.[24]

The finding partly came about through the study of one of the most stressful experiences of all – war. Back in the mid 1990s military combat veterans in the USA had their brains scanned with the very latest imaging machines. The surprising finding was that in those who had seen more action, who had been nearer and longer at the front line, the brain structure called the hippocampus tended to be significantly smaller.[25] It looked as if being at war actually caused parts of the brain to shrink and wither away.

The hippocampus – the word derives from the Greek for sea horse because this small paired structure near the centre of the brain resembles the shape of a sea horse – now appears to be the part of the brain most vulnerable to sustaining structural damage secondary to mental stress.

Stress causes an increase in a variety of hormones released into our bloodstream, but of most interest is a group called glucocorticoids, which raise the heart rate, boost the immune system and suppress energy-intensive systems such as reproduction. Such changes are clearly useful for an animal trying to escape from a predator, but a side-effect of decades of chronic stress is that over-exposure to these particular stress hormones seems to shrink your hippocampus.[26]

But do you have to go to war to damage your brain? Is less extreme stress still a danger? Sure enough, studies have now established that the longer you have experienced symptoms of mere depression, the smaller your hippocampus is.

For example, Yvette Sheline and her colleagues at Washington University School of Medicine in St Louis recently reported a brain imaging study that revealed that the hippocampi of depressed patients were on average 12% to 15% smaller than those of controls of the same age, height and level of education. Numerous other studies have found similar results. 'It is absolutely clear that really prolonged major depression is associated with loss of hippocampal volume,' concludes Robert Sapolsky of Stanford University – the first neuroscientist to discover from his work with primates how vulnerable the hippocampus was to stress.[27]

Exactly why the hippocampus shrinks is still open to debate, but we also know that the hippocampus is one of the few parts of the brain where new nerve cell growth occurs and this may be because it's a key part of the nervous system involved in memory. It now seems that when we lay down new memories it's because new nerve cells have grown in our hippocampus to code for these recollections.

The particular kind of memory coded for by the hippocampus is spatial memory – when you are looking for your misplaced keys it's your hippocampus that will be activated.[28]

Taxi drivers recently given brain scans by scientists at University College London had a larger hippocampus compared with other people – it appears that their extensive geographical knowledge leads to remarkable growth in this part of the brain. The hippocampus grew larger as taxi drivers spent more time in the job, so the chances of finding your destination are increased by hailing a cab driver with a larger hippocampus. The hippocampus is significantly bigger too in birds and animals for whom navigation is a vital part of their evolutionary strategy. For example, birds that use space around them to hide and locate food have larger hippocampal volumes than closely related species that do not.[29]

If the hippocampus codes for spatial memory and shrinks when stressed, it is intriguing to note that stress can have important effects on our memory. Traumatic stress often leads us to avoid a place where we experienced shock, or to become anxious as we get near that location again, particularly as a result of our vivid memories for the traumatic incident. For example, those involved in automobile accidents often become more upset as they get closer to the precise road where the event occurred, suggesting that the hippocampus which codes for spatial memory is playing a key role in how stress affects us.

Princeton University neuroscientist Elizabeth Gould has found that exposing monkeys to chronic stress blocks new nerve growth and perhaps it is cell destruction combined with a lack of new growth that produces the effects of stress on our hippocampus.[30]

Intriguingly, several treatments for depression might have the opposite effect. Some anti-depressants, for example, increase the amount of serotonin in the gaps between brain cells, and serotonin is a well-known promoter of cell growth. Ronald Duman of Yale University and his colleagues have found that rodents given anti-depressant drugs or electroshock therapy all have significantly more newly grown cells in the hippocampus. This suggests, Duman says, that increased nerve cell growth is a common effect of anti-depressant treatment and could even be the main mechanism by which anti-depressants work.[31]

Doctors had assumed that depression results from changes on a more molecular scale – an imbalance in chemical messengers that communicate among brain cells. But perhaps the real issue is the way the actual physical structure of the brain is altered in depression or stress.

A more natural anti-depressant – exercise – may also encourage brain cell growth. Exercise has been shown to increase the level of serotonin in the brain and can often help patients shake off mild depressive symptoms. Neuroscientist Fred Gage and colleagues at the Salk Institute for Biological Studies in California report that rats with access to a running wheel had more than twice as many newly growing brain cells as did mice with no running wheel. Since the rodents ran an average of nearly five kilometres per day for several months, it would seem that next time you pass an ardent jogger you should admire the size of their hippocampus.[32]

But one question continued to trouble scientists despite these exciting developments: how could they be sure that the smaller hippocampi that the depressed and stressed seemed to have was a consequence of stress? Perhaps it was still remotely possible that it was having a smaller hippocampus in the first place that predisposes some to mental problems? Which comes first – the small hippocampus or the large stress?[33]

Now a new study has just been published that appears to take a big step to resolving this vital question. Mark Gilbertson and colleagues at Harvard Medical School brain scanned seventy identical twins – one of each pair was a Vietnam combat veteran who had clearly been exposed to the huge stress of war, while the other had stayed at home and had no combat exposure. Sure enough the men who went to war, and who ended up suffering from Post Traumatic Stress Disorder (PTSD), also had smaller than average hippocampi.[34]

But more astonishing yet was the finding that their identical non-combat twin *also* had a smaller hippocampus, of roughly the same size as that of the twin who had served in war and then developed PTSD.

So one group went through combat trauma while their siblings were not in the war, yet both groups had small hippocampi. So instead of brain shrinkage happening as a consequence of the stress of trauma, a small hippocampus must have preceded the experience of war. The amazing finding suggests that having a smaller hippocampus predisposes you to develop traumatic stress, and may even predict that you will suffer from mental health problems if you are stressed.

It could well be, with more research to explore and confirm this finding, that a small hippocampus should be viewed as a risk factor for PTSD and thus, like a heart murmur, should be an exclusionary factor for some types of military service. It could even be that brain scanning our hippocampi might help predict who is going to develop depression or other mental illnesses in the future.

Just because identical twins were involved in the study does not mean that having a smaller hippocampus is a purely genetic effect. Identical twins can have much more similar foetal environments than do non-identical twins. A 'two hit' model is possible whereby early childhood stress caused the hippocampus to shrink a lot and it was this prior vulnerability combined with the second hit of stress from then fighting a war that later tipped those who finally got PTSD over the edge.[35]

Some support for this 'two hit' model comes from Mark Gilbertson's finding that those who developed PTSD had a shared higher chance of experiencing childhood abuse with their co-twin who had not gone to war.

Oddly enough the 'two hit' theory has dramatic implications for the population back home when an army is abroad fighting, which is that the first 'hit' could be happening as mothers who are pregnant experience the stress and uncertainty of war.[36]

Recent research by psychiatrist Jim Van Os and colleagues from Holland has found that the chances of a mother giving birth to a child who later grows up to develop schizophrenia went up by at least 28% if she was pregnant during the very stressful time of May 1940, when the Germans invaded the Netherlands. The maternal stress hormones or glucocorticoids that can damage the hippocampus in adult life might even be capable of damaging the hippocampus of an unborn child.[37]

It would seem that it is vital pregnant mothers try to stay as relaxed as possible during such troubled times and in particular ensure that their healthy diet remains undisturbed by perturbations of mood. Otherwise their stress, and in particular possible temporary loss of appetite, could affect the brain development of their unborn children, and become the first of the two hits needed to cause later problems like depression or traumatic stress.

In other words, to echo the words of one psychiatrist whom Robert Sapolsky likes to quote, and who oversaw a ward full of PTSD sufferers in an American Veterans' Administration hospital: 'You have to understand that these boys had a lot of mileage under the hood before they ever set foot in Vietnam.'[38]

But even given these constraints of biology, the latest neuroscience research still suggests that we are responsible for being the persons we are. This conundrum is admitted to by philosophers like Santayana who ask, if we are not responsible for ourselves and our outcomes, 'who then should be responsible?'[39]

We now know that the experiences we have shape our brains physically as well as mentally, but we also choose our experiences and these choices are shaped by our brains. It would seem that the latest neuroscience research is teaching us to be particularly careful about our freedom to choose what we do with our lives because, having chosen, our consequent experiences shape our brains, which might limit further choice. In other words, we should be vigilant about our current life choices because once chosen they could produce brain changes that then constrain future options.

Perhaps the most passionate modern advocate of personal responsibility for our lives was the philosopher Friedrich Nietzsche, and his polemical stance on freedom now appears to have become particularly relevant, thanks to the latest neuroscience findings about the brain.

Nietzsche was a German philosopher of the late nineteenth century who challenged the foundations of traditional morality and Christianity. He believed in life, creativity, health and the realities of the world we live in, rather than those situated in a world beyond. Central to Nietzsche's philosophy is the idea of 'life affirmation', which involves an honest questioning of all doctrines that drain life's energies, however socially prevalent those views might be. Robert Wicks, the famous New Zealand Philosopher, contends he is one of the first 'existentialist' philosophers; Nietzsche has inspired leading figures in all walks of cultural life, including dancers, poets, novelists, painters, psychologists, philosophers, sociologists and social revolutionaries.

In a well-known aphoristic work, *The Gay Science* (*Die fröhliche Wissenschaft*, 1882) – whose title was inspired by the troubadour songs of Provence (1100–1300) – Nietzsche set forth some of the existential ideas for which he became famous, namely, the proclamation that 'God is dead' and the doctrine of 'eternal recurrence' – the idea that one is, or might be, fated to relive for ever every moment of one's life, with no omission whatsoever of any pleasurable or painful detail.

Nietzsche's atheism – his account of 'God's murder' – was voiced in reaction to the concept of a single, ultimate, judgemental authority who is privy to everyone's hidden, and personally embarrassing, secrets; his atheism also aimed to redirect people's attention to their inherent freedom, in the presently existing world, and away from all escapist, pain-relieving, heavenly other worlds.

To a similar end, Nietzsche's doctrine of eternal recurrence was formulated to draw attention away from all worlds other than the one in which we presently live, since eternal recurrence precludes the possibility of any final escape from the present world. The doctrine also functions as a measure for judging someone's overall psychological strength and mental health, since Nietzsche believed that it was the hardest world view to accept and affirm. In 1887, *The Gay Science* was reissued with an important preface, an additional fifth book and an appendix of songs, reminiscent of the troubadours.

Nietzsche's own account of this peculiar idea of eternal recurrence is described in *The Gay Science* thus:

> How, if some day or night, a demon were to sneak after you into your loneliness and say to you: 'This life, as you now live it and have lived it, you will have to live once more and innumerable times more; and there will be nothing new in it, but every pain and every joy and every thought and every sigh . . . must return to you all in the same succession and sequence even this spider and this moonlight between the trees, and even this moment and I myself. The eternal hourglass of existence is turned over

and over and you with it, a mere grain of dust.' Would you not throw yourself down and gnash your teeth and curse the demon who spoke thus? Or have you once experienced a tremendous moment when you would have answered him: 'You are a god, and never did I hear anything more godlike!' If this thought were to gain possession of you, it would change you as you are, or perhaps crush you. The question in each and everything, 'Do you want this once more and innumerable times more?' would weigh upon your actions as the greatest stress. Or how well disposed would you have to become to yourself and to life to crave nothing more fervently than this ultimate eternal confirmation . . . ?

This idea has been captured beautifully by the Hollywood film *Groundhog Day*, which is probably the only commercial movie to be dedicated to explaining the Nietzschian philosophy of existentialism! Ken Sanes, a columnist and critic living in Boston, USA, has written several beautiful analyses of the film that explain its links with Nietzschian philosophy.

One of the key points about the film is that if we don't take control of our lives we are doomed to be the pawns of fate, and we only take responsibility for our lives when we fully grasp that there is no alternative to the current one. Sadly it seems that only if we were forced to live the same life we have led over and over again would we begin to take our decisions seriously. So maybe we should consider that possibility in order to get a better handle on our control over our destiny. The true test of whether you have led a life worth living is whether you would choose to repeat it ad infinitum, without any change whatsoever.

In the movie, actor Bill Murray plays Phil, an arrogant, Scroogelike weather forecaster who spends the night in a small remote town – Punxsutawney, Pennsylvania. He is there to make a broadcast the next day about the annual ritual of the 'coming out of the groundhog', which by local folklore is supposed to predict future weather, like the length of winter.

Bill Murray wakes up the next morning, does his story (which he finds tedious and beneath him) and is annoyed to discover that he is trapped in Punxsutawney (a town he hates) for a second night because of an unexpected snowstorm after the groundhog ceremony.

When he wakes up in his guest house room the next morning, something very peculiar appears to have happened to time: it is the morning of the day before all over again. Everything that happened to him the previous day – the man trying to start a conversation at the top of the stairs, the old high school acquaintance recognizing him on the street, the ritual of groundhog day – happens again, exactly as it did before. He alone appears to be aware that the same day has already happened.

And, once again, due to inclement weather, he is forced to spend the night. When he wakes up the next morning, it is the same day as yesterday and the day before, with the same oncoming snowstorm keeping him stuck in town and the same events repeating themselves like a broken record.

And so it goes, day after day, as this misanthrope of a human being, as described by Ken Sanes, finds himself trapped in Punxsutawney on groundhog day in what science fiction would refer to as a time loop. With each 'new' day, he alone remembers what happened in previous editions of the same day but no matter what he does, he seems trapped in time, fated to repeat the same day again and again.

At first Murray's character responds with bewilderment. Then he despairs and begins to treat life as a game – after all, he finds there are no consequences – he will wake up the next morning and repeat the day again, even if he breaks the law or smokes there is no jail or cancer to bother him. So he risks his life and gorges on food, expressing both his sense of hopelessness and his growing recognition that, no matter what he does, time will reset itself and he will wake up as if nothing had happened.

Then one day he discovers that someone actually likes him for who he is, and he finally figures out a constructive response to his situation – he begins to live his life in the day allotted to him, or, rather, he begins to live the life he never lived before.

For example, he begins to take piano lessons from a music teacher who is continuously surprised at how proficient he is, since she always believes it is his first lesson. Then, an encounter with death – an old vagrant dies – has a deep effect on him. At first, he can't accept the man's death and, in at least one subsequent edition of the day, he tries to be good to the old man, taking him out to eat (for a last meal) and trying, unsuccessfully, to keep him alive.

Ken Sanes, the US columnist and critic, argues in his essays on the film that it is only when Bill Murray's character stops trying to force death to relent that his final defences fall away and his compassion for the old man transfers to the living. He begins to use his knowledge of how the day will unfold to help people. Knowing that a child will always fall from a tree at a certain time, he makes it a point to be there and catch the child every time. Knowing that a man will choke on his meal, he is always at a nearby table in the restaurant to save him.

Slowly, he goes through a transformation. Having suffered himself, he is able to empathize with other people's suffering. Having been isolated from society, he becomes a local hero in Punxsutawney. Now, he sees the day as a form of freedom. As he expresses it in a corny TV speech about the weather that he gives for the camera, at the umpteenth ceremony he has covered of the 'coming out' of the groundhog: 'When Chekhov saw the long winter, he saw a winter bleak and dark and bereft of hope. Yet we know that winter is just another step in the cycle of life. But standing here among the people of Punxsutawney and basking in the warmth of their hearths and hearts, I couldn't imagine a better fate than a long and lustrous winter.'

In other words, having accepted the conditions of life and learned the pleasures afforded by human companionship, he is no longer like all those people who fear life's travails, and try to use the weather forecast, by human or groundhog, to control events. He accepts 'winter' as an opportunity.

Finally, the female TV producer of the weather programme falls in love with the good person he has become and she spends the night (although he falls asleep so there is no sex). They wake up in the morning. She is still there and it is finally the next day. Having tried to lead a worthwhile life for the first time and used his day properly, Bill Murray is at last liberated to move on and use his new-found tools of acceptance, positivity and generosity in the world.

What is so powerful about *Groundhog Day*, as analysed by Ken Sanes, is the way it lets us experience what it would be like to make a breakthrough like this in our own lives. The movie shows us a character who is like the worst in ourselves. He is arrogant and sarcastic, absorbed in his own discomforts, without hope and cut off from other people. Like us, he finds himself in an inexplicable situation, seemingly a plaything of fate.

But, unlike us, he gets the luxury of being stuck in the same day until he gets it right. Whereas most of us go semi-automatically through our (very similar) days, he is forced to stop and treat each day like a world unto itself, and decide how to use it.

In the end, he undergoes a breakthrough to a more authentic self in which intimacy, creativity and compassion come naturally – a self that was trapped inside him and that could only be freed by trapping him. Like many of the heroes of fiction, he can only escape his exile from himself by being exiled in a situation not of his choosing.

In telling this story, the movie hits on a message that is commonly found elsewhere and that appears to express an essential truth: when we get beyond denial and resentment over the conditions of life and death, and accept our situation, life ceases to be a problem and we can become authentic and compassionate. Murray's character makes two such breakthroughs: first he accepts being condemned to being stuck in the same day, and then he accepts the fact that everyone else is condemned to die.

Robert C. Solomon, writing in the *Journal of Nietzsche Studies*, points out that like such existentialists as Søren Kierkegaard and Jean-Paul Sartre, Nietzsche is a powerful defender of what one might call 'the existential self', the individual who 'makes himself' by exploring and disciplining his particular talents and distinguishes himself from 'the herd' and the conformist influences of other people.[40]

On the other hand, we cannot but recognize that we are all 'thrown into' our circumstances, born with (or without) certain talents and abilities to varying degrees and with or without dispositions to certain physical liabilities and limitations. We are all products ('victims' some would say) of our upbringing, our families, our culture. Even without bringing in such spooky words as 'fatalism', we recognize in ourselves and in others the heavy baggage of our backgrounds and the fact that our choices and our so-called autonomy are both quite limited.

Nietzsche's favourite 'pre-Socratic' philosopher, Heraclitus, presented a contrasting vision when he declared, 'Character is fate.'[41]

Nietzsche may be unclear about the extent to which character is agency and how character and specific actions are related, but he is very clear about the fact that we, whatever we are 'given' in our natures, are responsible for cultivating our character. Not that this is easy. Nietzsche describes giving style to one's character as 'a great art'. But whether rare or commonplace, whether limited to a few 'higher men' or something that we all do, cultivating one's character goes hand in hand with Nietzsche's conception of fatalism.

Nietzsche's watchword is 'Become who you are' (cf. the sub-title of *Ecce Homo*, '*Wie man wird, was man ist*'). This short phrase captures Nietzsche's position in a nonparadoxical way. One is in so far as one has predetermined and limited possibilities – one's talents, abilities, capacities, disabilities, limitations. A child at an early age (perhaps almost from birth) displays a real talent for music, for language, for spatial relations, for gym-nastics, for dancing, for leadership. But it is perfectly obvious that these promising possibilities are no more than that, that they require development, encouragement, training, practice and dedication.

As Sartre says in a much-quoted 1971 interview (in *New Left Review*), 'The idea I have never ceased to develop is in the end that a man can always make something out of what is made of him.' So, too, for Nietzsche. Nietzsche writes, 'What alone can our teaching be? – That no one gives a human being his qualities – neither God, nor society, nor his parents or ancestors, nor he himself.'

Nevertheless, we have those qualities, and we are responsible for the way in which we develop them.[42]

The basic problem is that humans are not good, sharing, generous creatures, according to the existentialist writer, C. S. Wyatt. Children are what we remain our entire lives . . . greedy, manipulative, brats. Some people disguise this fact better than others. Children are not nurtured to behave poorly. In fact, the challenge is to socialize a child. We struggle to be social creatures. Society is unnatural. Rules are difficult.

'Mine' is naturally a child's way of thinking. It is soon followed by 'I didn't do it!'

Existentialism as a philosophy and an approach to life as championed by Nietzsche requires the active acceptance of our nature. We spend our lives wanting more and more. Once we realize the futility of worldly desire, we try to accept what we have. We turn to philosophy or religion to accept less. We want to detach from our worldly needs – but we cannot do so. It is the human condition to desire. To want. To seek more, even when that 'more' is 'more of less'. It is a desire to prove some-thing to ourselves, as well as others.

The Philosopher Robert Olson contends that the existentialists, in contrast, mock the notion of a complete and fully satisfying life. The life of every man, whether he explicitly recognizes it or not, is marked by irreparable losses. Man cannot help aspiring towards the goods of this world; nor can he help aspiring towards the serene detachment from the things of this world that the traditional philosopher sought; but it is not within his power to achieve either of these ambitions, or having achieved them to find therein the satisfaction he had anticipated.

Existentialism, suggests Wyatt, assumes we are best when we struggle against our nature. Mankind is best challenging itself to improve, yet knowing perfection is not possible. Religions present rules, yet the believers know they cannot live by all those rules. The 'sin-free' life is beyond human nature. Is that any less reason to try to be good, generous, caring and compassionate?

In other words, first a man or woman exists, and then the individual spends a lifetime changing his or her essence. Without life there can be no meaning; in existentialism the search for meaning is the search for self. We define ourselves by living; suicide would indicate you have chosen to have no meaning.

Existentialism is about being a saint without God; being your own hero, without all the sanction and support of religion or society.

Anita Brookner, interview in *Writers at Work, Eighth Series*, ed.
George Plimpton (1988).

EPILOGUE

In his entrancing book, *The Enigma of Suicide*, George Howe Colt explores who considers this final act. He recounts how on one August day in 1937, H. B. Wobber, a forty-nine-year-old bargeman, took a bus to the Golden Gate Bridge, paid his way through the pedestrian turnstile, and began to walk across the mile-long span. He was accompanied by a tourist he had met on the bus, Professor Lewis Neylor of Trinity College in Connecticut.[1]

They had strolled across the bridge, which stretches in a single arch from San Francisco to the hills of Marin County, and were on their way back when Wobber tossed his coat and vest to Professor Neylor. 'This is where I get off,' he said quietly; 'I'm going to jump.' As Wobber climbed over the four-foot railing, the professor managed to grab his belt, but Wobber pulled free and leaped to his death.

Less than three months after the Golden Gate Bridge had opened to great fanfare, Wobber became its first-known suicide. Since then, according to former *Life* magazine staff writer George Howe Colt, more than 800 others have jumped, making it the number-one location for suicide in the entire Western world.

As with most suicide statistics the numbers are conservative. Only those who have been seen jumping or whose bodies are recovered are counted as bridge suicides. Colt suggests that more than 200 others may have leaped unseen in darkness, rain or fog, been swept out to sea and their bodies never found. A leap from the bridge is easy, quick and lethal; one merely steps over a chest-high railing. At 70–85 miles an hour the 240-foot fall lasts four seconds. If the force of the fall doesn't kill the jumper instantly, the fierce current will sweep him or her out to sea, to drown or be devoured by sharks. Of more than 800 people known to have fallen or jumped from the bridge since it opened, only nineteen have survived.[2]

By 1990 there had been 885 confirmed deaths including a depressed man who wrote in his suicide note, before stepping over the railing and leaping to his death, 'Why do you make it so easy?'

According to Colt, during the suicide prevention movement of the late sixties and early seventies, the debate over an anti-suicide fence came to a head. Bridge directors received hundreds of letters, about two-thirds opposing the barrier. Some argued it would spoil the view: why destroy the view for so many for the sake of so few?[3] Others felt it was a waste of money: why spend money on someone who wants to die? Many defended a person's right to suicide: 'If and when I decide to die I would prefer the bridge as an exit point and I don't want to be kept from it by a high, jail-like railing,' one woman wrote to the *San Francisco Chronicle*. 'There are worse things than death and one should be able to make that personal choice if necessary.'[4]

This is the core issue in the debate about suicide and raises the question: why do we need suicide prevention and emotional support services like the Samaritans? Also: why should we continue to live? What is the ultimate motivation that keeps us clinging on to existence? Most of our attempts to motivate ourselves to work and love seem trivial to the suicidal, for whom life has lost all meaning.[5]

In November 1953, Chad Varah, an Anglican clergyman in London, developed in the crypt of St Stephen Walbrook what was at first a telephone service staffed almost entirely by volunteers 'to befriend the suicidal and despairing'. Suffice it to say that in the past half century this enterprise has flourished and become an international movement. There are now over 203 Samaritan branches in the UK and Republic of Ireland alone, not to mention branches in almost eighty countries around the world.[6]

In 2002 the Samaritans received 4,660,000 contacts by phone, email, letter and face to face, in settings as diverse as prisons and local fairs.[7]

Varah himself is full of straightforward no-nonsense advice.

He writes: 'Between the fanatics who have the answers for everyone else, and the Samaritans who want to help people find their own answers, there is such a great gulf fixed that any attempt to co-operate would be a waste of time. Those who know that Jesus is the answer – whatever this may mean – before they heard the question – seem to Samaritans to be terribly insecure people using slogans to avoid facing the complexity of human existence; and doubtless they in turn see Samaritan tolerance as indifference to sin.'

Well, what gave Chad Varah the idea for the Samaritans? He writes that when he read in 1953 that there were three suicides a day in London his restless mind busied itself with the question, why?

In large part, formal therapy consists of helping the client reconceptualize the can'ts, the won'ts, the absolutes and the non-negotiables of the patient's present firmly held positions; to widen the stubbornly fixed blinders of present perceptions; and to think the unthinkable.[8]

There is a twentieth-century example of effective suicide prevention that precedes the Samaritans.

On 14 August 1945, in the Second World War, Japanese Emperor Hirohito – in the first ever address to his people – in his historic prescript of capitulation ordered his loyal subjects to surrender. This is a supremely important moment in suicidology given the Japanese nation's historically high suicide rate, and its strong belief in loss of face, honour, and suicide as an honourable way out of humiliation.[9]

Mass suicide across the nation was the most likely response to such a humiliating message of surrender from the Emperor. But in a few brief sentences, the Emperor touched on two main antidotes to suicide: a generational sense of the future and a personal redefining of what is intolerable.

His words are arguably the most effective suicide prevention speech ever made. Here in part is what he said (translated): 'It is according to the dictates of time and fate that we have resolved to pave the way for a grand peace for all the generations to come by enduring the unendurable and suffering what is unsufferable.'

Those few words saved thousands of lives.

Even if we can theorize about the function of depression and happiness, this doesn't mean we can use these theories to explain suicide fully. Many who contemplate suicide are not depressed and feel this is an expression of ultimate personal choice.[10]

Why choose to carry on living? This is the fundamental question at the heart of motivation. It is supremely relevant because often people feel suicidal because a goal they have set great store by has been placed beyond their reach and as a result for them life has lost all meaning. My final contention is that it is dangerous to elevate any goal to such a position in your life that to fail to achieve it would leave life empty and devoid of purpose.[11]

It is clear that the most motivated people in the world are those who pursue their goals with such a fervent dedication that somewhere there is a sense for them that failure would indeed be catastrophic in terms of personal meaning. This is why they are willing to make so many sacrifices in order to pursue what they desire.[12]

The ultimate conundrum about motivation is that you do need to chase your goals with that kind of passion if they are extremely difficult to achieve. But if in the end things don't pan out, then you need to be able to drop the goal and move on to something else.[13]

Why? Because ultimately we are each other's purpose in life and for a goal to have filled your life entirely means you have also pushed others – and yourself – away in the narrowing of consciousness required. In the pursuit of any goal, remember who you are doing it for. If it's just for yourself then achieving the goal means there is no one to share the moment with – and what's the point of that?[14]

Hamlet's question is at the heart of suicide – 'To be or not to be?' Yes or no? Light or total darkness? It's a question that has more relevance than ever before because actually it's easier to take your own life in contemporary industrialized society than ever before.

The Stoic philosopher Seneca, who lived at the time of Christ (4 BC–AD 69), pointed out, rather disdainfully, that the exits are everywhere; each precipice and river, each branch of each tree, every vein in your body will set you free. But actually once you have heavy industry and technology everywhere – like trains on tracks on which you can throw yourself – the exits multiply so that on your way home tonight there is much more opportunity to commit suicide effectively than there ever was for the caveman returning home of an evening. And yet we think we live in safer times.[15]

But it's not only the opportunity that has changed dramatically over time, but also our attitude to suicide.

During Classical Greek times, suicide was viewed in more than one way. It was tolerated and even lauded when done by patricians – generals and philosophers – but condemned if committed by plebeians or slaves, whose labours were necessary for the smooth functioning of a patrician–slave society.[16]

In classical Rome in the centuries before the Christian era, life was held rather cheaply, and suicide was viewed rather neutrally or even positively. Seneca said, 'Living is not good, but living well. The wise man therefore lives as well as he should not as long as he can . . . He will always think of life in terms of quality and not quantity . . . Dying early or late is of no relevance, dying well or ill is . . . life is not to be bought at any cost.'

A major change occurred in the fourth century with a categorical rejection of suicide by St Augustine (354–430). Suicide was then considered a crime because it precluded the possibility of repentance and violated the biblical Sixth Commandment relating to killing.[17]

Suicide was a greater sin than any other. This view was elaborated by St Thomas Aquinas (1225–74), who emphasized that suicide was a mortal sin in that it usurped God's power over man's life and death.

Neither the Old nor the New Testament directly forbids suicide, but by the year 700 the Catholic Church had proclaimed that a person who attempted suicide was to be excommunicated. The notion of suicide as sin took firm hold and for hundreds of years thereafter played an important part in the Western view of self-destruction.[18]

John Donne, Anglican Chaplain to the King, wrote in 1610 a book entitled Biathanatos – *a Declaration of that paradoxe or Thesis, that selfe-homicide is not so naturally a sin.*[19] The book was so explosive in its opposition to current theological thinking it had to wait until 1647, sixteen years after Donne's death, to be published. Amongst the many arguments he marshals is the provocative one that voluntary martyrdom is also suicide. Therefore it follows that the death of Christ himself was a suicide par excellence.[20]

David Hume (1711–76) was one of the first major Western philosophers to discuss suicide in the absence of the concept of sin. His famous essay 'On Suicide' was published in 1777, the year after his death, demonstrating the same prudence as John Donne in publishing his work posthumously, and the book was promptly suppressed.[21] The burden of the essay is to refute the view that suicide is a crime, arguing that suicide is not a transgression of our duties to God or to our fellow citizens or to ourselves. Hume states:

> Prudence and courage should engage us to rid ourselves at once of existence when it becomes a burden . . . If it be no crime in me to divert the Nile or Danube from its course, were I able to effect such purposes, where then is the crime in turning a few ounces of blood from their natural channel?

In the twentieth century the two giants of suicidal theorizing – Emile Durkheim (1858–1917) in France and Sigmund Freud (1856–1939) in Austria – played rather different roles.[22]

Durkheim, following Rousseau, sought to place the blame for suicide on society – or an individual's relationship with society. Freud, eschewing both the notions of sin and of crime, gave suicide back to man but put the locus of action in our unconscious mind.

In Durkheim's best-known work, *Le Suicide*, published in 1897 although, astonishingly, unavailable in English until 1951, he laid the foundations for a new discipline – sociology – using suicide as an example of how social pressures can direct individual behaviour.[23]

He demonstrated effectively that there are essentially three types of suicide. In one instance, the 'altruistic', the customs and rules of a group demand suicide under certain circumstances – like hara-kiri or suttee. In a sense suicide arises from an individual being too enmeshed in the expectations of those around him.[24]

Most suicides in the modern West, though, are what Durkheim termed 'egoistic'. Such a suicide occurs when an individual has too few ties to his society and so, being lonely and isolated, appeals to continue to live from neighbours or friends don't reach the individual or don't occur at all.

Finally Durkheim termed 'anomic' the suicide that occurs as the result of a breaking of a relationship between an individual and society – e.g., losing one's job or the death of a close friend or relative. Estrangement from one's usual ties encapsulates the anomic suicide.[25]

Freud never wrote directly on this topic but he and his followers advocated the view that suicide was really a kind of inwardly directed homicide.

In 1910 there was a meeting on the topic of suicide in Freud's apartment in Vienna. On that occasion Wilheim Stekel, a psychoanalyst, pronounced that no one kills himself except one who wishes the death of another. Rage at being let down or deserted by someone was turned inward on oneself because it could not be expressed outwardly. Psychodynamically, suicide was seen as murder in the 180th degree.[26]

Professor of Thanatology Emeritus at the University of California, Edwin Schneidman, argues that following the horrors of the Second World War, a major sea change occurred in Western thinking – the issue became not so much why do people kill themselves, but why do the rest of us bother to try and stay alive.

Existential thinking came to the fore with the idea of the principal task of man being to respond to life's apparent meaninglessness, despair and absurd quality. Albert Camus (1913–60) begins his essay 'The Myth of Sisyphus' (1942) by saying, 'There is but one serious philosophical problem and that is suicide.' Ludwig Wittgenstein (1889–1951) also stated that the main ethical issue for man is suicide.[27]

Karl Menninger, a famous American psychiatrist, published in 1938 a book that captures the prevailing pessimism of the time – *Man Against Himself*. The fundamental thesis is that we perform self-destructive acts all the time, not just when we are overtly suicidal. Deep down we are our own worst enemies because it is we who constantly initiate behaviours that are inimical to our own best interests, from saying the wrong thing to our boss all the way down to cutting our own throat.[28]

Currently the US Army uses a recruitment slogan: 'Be all that you can be.' The Army is talking about fulfilment, of using all one's capacities. The opposite of being all that you can be is living at much less than you could. This is the area of subsuicidal neurotic lives that is Menninger's focus. To attend to suicide only and miss the fact that most of us are probably living a subsuicidal neurotic existence is to fail to put suicide in context.[29]

Menninger argues that a lot of the bad things that happen to us and that we put down as accidents are actually unconscious attempts at suicide. He cites Freud's famous case of Herr K. K was a former lover of Freud's patient Dora and latterly the object of her accusations and hostilities, who came one day face to face with her on the street where there was much traffic.[30]

Confronted with the woman who had caused him so much pain, mortification and disappointment, as though in bewilderment and in his abstraction, he allowed himself to be knocked down by a car. Freud comments that this is an interesting contribution to the problem of indirect attempts at suicide.

But if suicide is difficult to study because the one person you want to ask about it is no longer around to explain, then attempted suicide projects its own problems. Those who attempt suicide and fail are often embarrassed at their cock-up and reluctant to discuss in detail the painful episode.

A notable modern exception is Al Alvarez, a poet, a poetry critic, an essayist, a journalist and in his own published words 'a failed suicide', who wrote a lyrical book about suicide, *The Savage God,* published in 1972. For Alvarez, suicide is chosen because essentially it represents an escape:

> [There is] a whole class of suicides . . . who take their lives not in order to die but to escape confusion, to clear their heads. They deliberately use suicide to create an unencumbered reality for themselves or to break through the patterns of obsession and necessity which they have unwittingly imposed on their lives.

Alvarez also writes about his own suicide attempt and his road to recovery from suicidal impulses:

> Then when death let me down, I gradually saw that I had been using the wrong language; I had translated the thing into Americanese. Too many movies, too many novels, too many trips to the States had switched my understanding into a hopeful alien tongue. I no longer thought of myself as unhappy; instead I had 'problems'. Which is an optimistic way of putting it, since problems imply solutions, whereas unhappiness is merely a condition of life that you must live with, like the weather. Once I had accepted that there weren't ever going to be any answers, even in death, I found to my surprise that I didn't much care whether I was happy or unhappy; 'problems and the problem of problems' no longer existed. And that in itself is already the beginning of happiness.

Alvarez argues that no man is promiscuous about suicide – each has a favourite method and once that doesn't work they are unlikely to try another. This is a key argument in suicide prevention.

The most popular argument against a barrier at the Golden Gate Bridge is that it simply wouldn't work; common sense says that suicidal people would simply go and kill themselves somewhere else.[31]

Berkeley psychologist Richard Seiden gathered the names of 515 people who had been restrained from jumping from the bridge dating back to its opening day. Checking their names against death certificates, he learned that only twenty-five had gone on to take their own lives. Although his research proved that people did not inexorably go on to commit suicide using another method, critics argued that people restrained from jumping were not truly bent on death. What about those who had jumped and lived?[32]

In 1975, psychiatrist David Rosen interviewed six people known to have survived leaps from the Golden Gate Bridge. None of the survivors had gone on to kill themselves; the six he interviewed all favoured the construction of an anti-suicide fence. They all said had there been a barrier, they would not have tried to kill themselves some other way.[33]

For many years the most popular method of suicide in Great Britain was asphyxiation – sticking one's head in the oven and turning on the gas. After the discovery of natural gas deposits in the North Sea in the fifties and sixties, most English homes converted from coke gas, whose high carbon monoxide content made it highly lethal, to less toxic natural gas. From 1963 to 1978 the number of English suicides by gas dropped from 2,368 to eleven and the country's overall suicide rate decreased by one-third. Despite England's varying unemployment rate and social stresses since then, it has remained at that lower level.[34]

Going back to the question of a barrier at the Golden Gate Bridge, a San Francisco friend once said to George Howe Colt, 'Ninety-nine per cent of us don't need it: is it fair to ruin the view for the sake of a few? If they want to die so much, why not let them?' This attitude is shared by many.[35]

How far is it from this condoning to the chorus one sometimes hears when a crowd has gathered at the base of a tall building to watch the weeping man on the ledge high above, shouting 'Jump, jump, jump'?

Fortunately, points out George Howe Colt in answer to the voices who cry 'Jump' there are many other voices that cry 'Live'. Not just the voices of family, friends, therapists and prevention centre volunteers but the voices of strangers.

When an eighteen-year-old girl stood on the edge of a seven-storey building in Mexico City, threatening to jump, Iganacio Canedo, an eighteen-year-old Red Cross male nurse, inched out towards her reports Colt. Canedo was tied to a long rope, held on the other end by a squad of firemen. 'Don't come any nearer,' shouted the girl. 'Don't or I'll jump.' Canedo grabbed for her and missed. The girl screamed and jumped. Canedo jumped after her, caught her in mid air and locked his arms around her waist.

They fell four floors before the rope snapped taut. Canedo's grip held and he and the girl were hauled back to the roof. 'I knew the rope would save me,' said Canedo. 'I prayed that it would be strong enough to support both of us.' There are dozens of similar stories of potential suicides saved by strangers who instinctively reached out.

As a term project for 'The Psychology of Death', a course taught by psychologist Ed Shneidman at Harvard, one student placed an ad in the personals section of a local underground newspaper: 'Male 21 student gives self 3 weeks before popping pills for suicide. If you know any good reasons why I shouldn't please write to Box d-673.'[36] According to Colt, within a month he had received 169 letters. While the majority were from the Boston area, others came from as far away as New York, Wisconsin, Kentucky, even Rio de Janeiro. They offered many reasons why he should stay alive. Some wrote of music, smiles, movies, sunny days, sandy beaches. Some quoted Rod McKuen, E. E. Cummings or Dylan Thomas.

They suggested he spend time with others less fortunate than himself; implored him to think of those he would leave behind; called him a coward and dared him to struggle and survive. Some referred him to a therapist. Others offered friendship, enclosing their telephone numbers or their addresses. A few enclosed gifts: two joints of marijuana, an advanced calculus equation, a Linus doll, magazine clippings on the subject of kindness, a photo of apple blossoms with the message 'We're celebrating Apple Blossom time'. Some simply broke down in the middle of their letters and pleaded 'Don't' or 'You just can't'.

The student was not actually contemplating suicide but the answers he received were real.

Whether they might have persuaded someone truly suicidal to stay alive or not is impossible to say. But if the forces that lead someone to suicide are numerous, those forces that combine to prevent someone from killing himself may be equally complex, whether they be anti-depressants, a prevention centre volunteer, a barrier on a bridge, a Linus doll or the voice of a stranger saying, 'I care.'

NOTES

Introduction

1. Turken, Hanna, 'Freud and Motivation', *American Journal of Psychoanalysis*, Vol. 60(2), Jun. 2001, 185-97 (Kluwer Academic, US).

2. Schoon, Ingrid; Parsons, Samantha; Sacker, Amanda, 'Socioeconomic Adversity, Educational Resilience, and Subsequent Levels of Adult Adaptation', *Journal of Adolescent Research*, Vol. 19(4), Jul. 2004, 383-404 (Sage Publications, US).

3. Schoon, Ingrid; Bynner, John, 'Risk and Resilience in the Life Course', *Journal of Youth Studies*, Vol. 6(1), Mar. 2003, 21-31 (Taylor & Francis, UK).

4. Berglas, Steven, *How Successful People Overcome Burnout*, 2001, (Random House, UK).

5. de Oliveira; José H. Barros, 'Forgiveness and Happiness: A Cross-cultural Approach', *Psicologia Educaca Cultura*, Vol. 7(2), Dec. 2003, 283-312 (Colegio Internato dos Carvalhos, Portugal).

6. Smith, Jonathan C.; Karmin, Aaron D., 'Idiosyncratic Reality Claims', *Perceptual & Motor Skills*, Vol. 95(3, Pt. 2), Dec. 2002, 1119-28 (Perceptual & Motor Skills, US).

7. Anonymous, 'Landscapes of Betrayal, Landscapes of Joy: Curtisville in the Lives of Its Teenagers', *Family Therapy*, Vol. 31(1), 2004, 46 (Libra Publishers, US). Kahneman, Daniel, 'Objective Happiness', in Kahneman, Daniel; Diener, Ed (Eds.), *et al*, *Well-being: The Foundations of Hedonic Psychology*, 1999, pp. 3-25 (Russell Sage Foundation, US).

8. Redelmeier, D.A.; Singh, S.M., 'Survival in Academy Award-winning Actors and Actresses', *Annals of Internal Medicine*, 134(10), 15 May 2001, 955-62 (UI: 11352696).

9. Schoon, Ingrid; Bynner, John, 'Risk and Resilience in the Life Course', *op. cit.*

10. Shah, James; Higgins, Tory; Friedman, Ronald S., 'Performance Incentives and Means: How Regulatory Focus Influences Goal Attainment, *Journal of Personality & Social Psychology*, Vol. 74(2), Feb. 1998, 285-93 (American Psychological Assoc., US).

11. Scott, Groves; David, L., 'Self-esteem Development', *Adolescence*, Vol. 24(96), Win. 1989, 861-9 (Editions Medecine et Hygiene, Switzerland).

12. Riordan, Catherine A.; Thomas, J.; Stephen, James; Marsha, K., 'Evidence for Self-serving Biases', *Journal of Sport Behavior*, Vol. 8(1), Mar. 1985, 42-53 (Univ. of South Alabama, US).

13. Polivy J.; Herman C.P., 'If At First You Don't Succeed: False Hopes of Self-change', *American Psychologist*, 57(9), Sep. 2002, 677-89 (American Psychological Assoc., US).

14. Lever, Joaquina Palomar, 'Poverty and Subjective Well-being', *Social Indicators Research*, Vol. 68(1), Aug. 2004, 1-33 (Kluwer Academic Publishers, Netherlands).

15. Goddard, H. Wallace, 'Handbook of Positive Psychology; Authentic Happiness', *Family Relations: Journal of Applied Family & Child Studies*, Vol. 53(1), Jan. 2004, 117-18 (Blackwell Publishing, UK).

16. Wisman, Jon D., 'The Scope and Promising Future of Social Economics', *Review of Social Economy*, Vol. 61(4), Dec. 2003, 425-45 (Taylor & Francis, UK).

17. Redelmeier, D.A.; Singh S.M., 'Longevity of Screenwriters Who Win an Academy Award: Longitudinal Study', *British Medical Journal*, Dec. 2001, 323(7327), 1491-6, 22-29.

18. Anonymous, 'Social Status and Life Expectancy in an Advantaged Population: A Study of Academy Award-winning Actors', *Annals of Internal Medicine*, 134(10), S-6, 15 May 2001.

19. Ward, Russell A.; Spitze, Glenna D., 'A Longitudinal View', *Journals of Gerontology Series B-Psychological Sciences & Social Sciences*, Vol. 59B(1), Jan. 2004, S2-S8 (Gerontological Society of America, US).

20. Barkow, Jerome H., 'Happiness in Evolutionary Perspective', in Segal, Nancy L.; Weisfeld, Glenn E. (Eds), *et al*, *Uniting Psychology and Biology: Integrative Perspectives on Human Development*, 1997, pp. 397-418 (American Psychological Assoc. US,) xxiii, 568pp.

21. Fawcett, Jan, 'The Pleasure Principle: Can the Study of Addictive Disorders and their Effects on the Brain Help our Understanding of Happiness?', *Psychiatric Annals*, Vol. 33(9), Sep. 2003, 541 (SLACK, US).

22. Miskie, B.; Near, S.; Hegele R., 'Survival in Academy Award-winning Actors and Actresses', *Annals of Internal Medicine*, 138(1), Jan. 2003, 77-8, Author reply, 77-8, 7.

23. Staud, R., 'Survival in Academy Award-winning Actors and Actresses', *Annals of Internal Medicine*, 138(1), Jan. 2003, 77-8, author reply 77-8, 7.

24. Goddard, H. Wallace, 'Handbook of Positive Psychology; Authentic Happiness', *Family Relations: Journal of Applied Family & Child Studies*, Vol. 53(1), Jan. 2004, 117-18 (Blackwell Publishing, UK). Higgins, E.T.; Friedman, R.S.; Harlow, R.E.; Idson, L.C.; Ayduk, O.N.; Taylor, A., 'Achievement orientations from subject histories of success: Promotion pride versus prevention pride', *European Journal of Social Psychology*, 31, 2001, 3-23.

25. Schoon, Ingrid; Bynner, John, 'Risk and Resilience in the Life Course', *op. cit.*

26. Fawcett, Jan, 'The Pleasure Principle: Can the Study of Addictive

Disorders and their Effects on the Brain Help our Understanding of Happiness?', *op. cit.*

27. Perneger, Thomas V.; Hudelson, Patricia M.; Bovier, Patrick A., 'Health and Happiness in Young Adults', *Quality of Life Research,* Vol. 13(1), Feb. 2004, 171-8 (Kluwer Academic Publishers, Netherlands).

28. Hill, Roderick, 'Happiness Since World War II', *Social Indicators Research*, Vol. 65(1), 2004, 109-23 (Kluwer Academic Publishers, Netherlands).

29. Pataki, Sherri P.; Clark, Margaret S., 'Self-presentations of Happiness: Sincere, Polite, or Cautious?', *Personality & Social Psychology Bulletin*, Vol. 30(7), Jul. 2004, 905-14 (Sage Publications, US). Poulton, R; Milne, B.J., 'Low fear in childhood is associated with sporting prowess in adolescence and young adulthood', *Behavior Research & Therapy*, Oct. 2002, Vol. 40(10), 1191-97.

30. Alarc, N. Reynaldo, 'Sources of Happiness: What Makes People Happy?', *Revista de Psicologia*, Vol. 20(2), 2002, 169-96 (Pontificia Univ. Catolica del Peru, Peru).

1 Why Do You Do That Thing You Do?

1. Argyle, M., 'Causes and Correlates of Happiness' in Kahneman, Daniel; Diener, Ed (Eds.), *et al, Well-being: The Foundations of Hedonic Psychology*, 1999, pp. 353-73 (Russell Sage Foundation, NY), xii, 593pp.

2. Weaver, Charles N., 'Happiness of Asian Americans', *Psychological Reports*, Vol. 93(3:2), Dec. 2003, 1032-4 (Psychological Reports, US).

3. Huberman, Bernardo A.; Loch, Christoph H., 'Status as a Valued Resource', *Social Psychology Quarterly*, Vol. 67(1), Mar. 2004, 103-14 (American Sociological Assoc., US).

4. Nowak, Martin A; Sasaki, Akira; Taylor, Christine; Fudenberg, Drew, 'Emergence of Cooperation', *Nature*, Vol. 428(6983), Apr. 2004, 646-50 (Nature Publishing Group, UK).

5. Hauert, Christoph; Doebell, Michael, 'The Evolution of Cooperation', *Nature*, Vol. 428(6983), Apr. 2004, 643-6.

6. Powers, Alice Schade; Day, Lainy B., 'Freud and the Unconscious: Brain, Behaviour and Evolution', Vol. 62(2), Aug. 2003, 69-71 (Karger, Switzerland).

7. Barrett, Louise, 'Animal Innovation', *Animal Behaviour,* Vol. 67(5), May 2004, 993-4 (Elsevier Science, Netherlands).

8. Vaden-Goad, Linda, 'Coming of Age', *Psychology of Women Quarterly*, Vol. 28(2), Jun. 2004, 184-6 (Blackwell Publishing, UK).

9. Kanazawa, Satoshi; Still, Mary C., 'Teaching May Be Hazardous to Your Marriage', *Evolution & Human Behavior*, Vol. 21(3), May 2000, 185-90.

10. Derry, Paula S., 'The Tending Instinct', *Sex Roles*, Vol. 50(11-12), Jun. 2004, 879-80 (Kluwer Academic Publishers, Netherlands).

11. Brownridge, Douglas A., 'Male-Female Attraction Comparison Effects', *Violence & Victims,* Vol. 19(1), Feb. 2004, 17-36 (Springer Publishing, US).

12. Slama, Mark, 'Sense and Nonsense: Evolutionary Perspectives on

Human Behavior', *Psychology & Marketing*, Vol. 21(6), Jun. 2004, 481-5 (John Wiley & Sons, US).

13. Brookfield, John F.Y., 'Human Evolution: A Legacy in our Genes?' *Current Biology*, Vol. 13(15), Aug. 2003, R592-R593 (Cell Press, US).

14. Miller, Geoffrey, *The Mating Mind: How Sexual Choice Shaped the Evolution of Human Nature*, 2000 (Doubleday, US).

15. Miller, Geoffrey, 'Evolution of Human Music through Sexual Selection' in Wallin, N.L.; Merker, B. (Eds.) *et al*, 2000, *The Origins of Music*, pp. 329-60 (MIT Press, US).

16. Kanazawa, Satoshi, 'Why Productivity Fades with Age: The Crime-Genius Connection', *Journal of Research in Personality*, Vol. 37(4), Aug. 2003, 257-72 (Elsevier Science, UK).

17. Kanazawa, Satoshi, 'The Relativity of Relative Satisfaction', *Evolution & Human Behavior*, Vol. 24(1), Jan. 2003, 71-3 (Elsevier Science Publishing, US).

18. Savage, Joanne; Kanazawa, Satoshi, 'Social Capital, Crime, and Human Nature', *Journal of Contemporary Criminal Justice*, Vol. 18(2), May 2002, 188-211 (Sage Publications, US).

19. Kanazawa, Satoshi, 'Bowling With Our Imaginary Friends', *Evolution & Human Behavior*, Vol. 23(3), May 2002, 167-71.

20. Kanazawa, Satoshi, 'Why Father Absence Might Precipitate Early Menarche: The Role of Polygymy', *Evolution & Human Behavior*, Vol. 22(5), Sep. 2001, 329-34.

21. Kanazawa, Satoshi, '*De Gustibus est Disputandum*', *Social Forces*, Vol. 79(3), Mar. 2001, 1131-63 (University of North Carolina Press, US).

22. Hennessy, Robin J.; Kinsella, Anthony; Waddington, John L., '3D Laser Surface Scanning and Geometric Morphometric Analysis of Cranofacial Shape as an Index of Cerebro-cranofacial Morphogenesis: Initial Application to Sexual Dimorphism', *Biological Psychiatry*, Vol. 51(6), March 2002, 507-14 (Elsevier Science, UK).

23. Zebrowitz, Leslie A.; Hall, Judith A.; Murphy, Nora A.; Rhodes, Gillian, 'Looking Smart and Looking Good: Facial Cues to Intelligence and Their Origins', *Personality & Social Psychology Bulletin*, Vol. 28(2), Feb. 2002, 238-49 (Sage Publications, US).

24. Mazur, Allan; Mueller, Ulrich, 'Facial Dominance', in Somit, A., Peterson, S. (Eds.), *Research in Biopolitics*, 1996, Vol. 4, pp. 99-111 (JAI Press, London).

25. Fabricius, Dirk, 'Guilt, Shame, Disobedience: Social Regulatory Mechanisms and the "Inner Normative System"', *Psychoanalytic Inquiry,* Vol. 24(2), 2004, 309-27 (Analytic Press, US).

26. Kanazawa, Satoshi; 'A New Solution to the Collective Action Problem: The Paradox of Voter Turnout', *American Sociological Review*, Vol. 65(3), Jun. 2000, 433-42 (American Sociological Assoc., US).

27. Kanazawa, Satoshi; Still, Mary C., 'The Emergence of Marriage Norms: An Evolutionary Psychological Perspective', [Chapter], Hechter, Michael (Ed.), Opp, Karl-Dieter (Ed.), *Social Norms*, 2001, pp. 274-304, xx, pp. 429 (Sage Publications, US).

28. Kanazawa, Satoshi, 'Outcome or Expectancy? Antecedent of Spontaneous Causal Attribution', *Personality & Social Psychology Bulletin*, Vol. 18(6), Dec. 1992, 659-68 (Sage Publications, US).

29. Tracer, David P., 'Selfishness and Fairness in Economic and Evolutionary Perspective: An Experimental Economic Study in Papua New Guinea', *Current Anthropology*, Vol. 44(3), Jun. 2003, 432-8 (University of Chicago Press, US).

30. Fonagy, Peter; Target, Mary, 'Evolution of the Interpersonal Interpretive Function: Clues for Effective Preventive Intervention in Early Childhood', in Coates, Susan W.; Rosenthal, Jane L. (Eds.), *et al, September 11: Trauma and Human Bonds, Relational Perspectives book series,* 2003, pp. 99-113 (Analytic Press, Hillsdale, NJ, US), xiv, p. 293.

31. Hyde, Janet Shibley; Oliver, Mary Beth, 'Gender Differences in Sexuality: Results from Meta-analysis' in Travis, Cheryl Brown; White, Jacquelyn W. (Eds.), *Sexuality, Society, and Feminism, Psychology of Women,* 2000, pp. 57-77 (American Psychological Assoc.) viii, p. 432.

32. Penton-Voak, I.S.; Jones, B.C.; Little, A.C.; Baker, S.; Tiddeman, B.; Burt, D.M.; Prett, D.I., 'Symmetry, Sexual Dimorphism in Facial Proportions, and Male Facial Attractiveness', Proceedings of the Royal Society of London, Series B, 268, 1617-23, 2001.

33. Buss, David M., 'Personality Evoked: The Evolutionary Psychology of Stability and Change', in Heatherton, Todd F.; Weinberger, Joel Lee (Eds.), *Can Personality Change?*, 1994, pp. 41-57 (American Psychological Assoc.) xiv, p. 368.

34. Miller, Alan S.; Kanazawa, Satoshi, *Order By Accident: The Origins and Consequences of Conformity in Contemporary Japan* [Authored Book], 2000, xi, pp. 156 (Westview Press, US).

35. Gibson, Eleanor J., 'What Psychology is About: Ruminations of an Opinionated Aged Psychologist', *Ecological Psychology*, Vol. 15(4), Oct. 2003, 289-95 (Lawrence Erlbaum, US).

36. Kanazawa, Satoshi, 'Comment: Why We Love Our Children', *American Journal of Sociology*, Vol. 106(6), May 2001, 1761-76 (University of Chicago Press, US).

37. Hinsz, Verlin B.; Matz, David C.; Patience, Rebecca A., 'Does Women's Hair Signal Reproductive Potential?', *Journal of Experimental Social Psychology*, Vol. 37(2), Mar. 2001, pp. 166-72 (American Psychological Assoc., US).

38. Berry, Diane S., 'Attractiveness, Attraction, and Sexual Selection: Evolutionary Perspectives on the Form and Function of Physical Attractiveness' in Zanna, Mark P. (Ed.), *Advances in Experimental Social Psychology*, 2000, Vol. 32, pp. 273-342 (Academic Press, US).

39. Kanazawa, Satoshi, 'General Intelligence as a Domain-Specific Adaptation', *Psychological Review*, Vol. 111(2), Apr. 2004, 512-23 (American Psychological Assoc., US).

40. Kanazawa, Satoshi, 'Can Evolutionary Psychology Explain Reproductive Behavior in the Contemporary United States?', *Sociological Quarterly*, Vol. 44(2), Spr. 2003, 291-302 (University of California Press, US).

41. Kanazawa, Satoshi, 'Reading Shadows on Plato's Cave Wall: Reply', *American Sociological Review*, Vol. 68(1), Feb. 2003, 159-60 (American Sociological Assoc., US).

42. Kanazawa, Satoshi, 'General Intelligence as a Domain-Specific Adaptation', *op. cit.*

43. Yamagishi, Toshio; Tanida, Shigehito; Mashima, Rie; Shimoma, Eri; Kanazawa, Satoshi, 'You Can Judge a Book by Its Cover: Evidence That Cheaters May Look Different from Cooperators', *Evolution & Human Behavior*, Vol. 24(4), Jul. 2003, 290-301.

44. Kanazawa, Satoshi; Frerichs, Rebecca L., 'Why Single Men Might Abhor Foreign Cultures', *Social Biology*, Vol. 48(3-4), Fall-Winter 2001, 321-8 (Society for the Study of Social Biology, US).

45. Fink, Bernhard; Penton-Voak, Ian, 'Evolutionary Psychology of Facial Attractiveness', *Current Directions in Psychological Science*, Vol. 11(5), Oct. 2002, pp. 154-8.

2 How to Have a Perfect Day

1. Prentice, W.C.H., 'Some Cognitive Aspects of Motivation' (1961), in Notterman, Joseph M. (Ed.), *The Evolution of Psychology: Fifty Years of the American Psychologist*, 1997, pp. 84-97 (American Psychological Assoc., US) xxv, p. 783.

2. Miller, William R.; Tonigan, J. Scott, 'Assessing Drinkers' Motivation for Change: The Stages of Change Readiness and Treatment Eagerness Scale (SOCRATES)', in Marlatt, G. Alan; VandenBos, Gary R. (Eds.), *Addictive Behaviors: Readings on Etiology, Prevention, and Treatment*, 1997, pp. 355-69 (American Psychological Assoc., US), xxv, p. 930.

3. Azar, Beth; Sleek, Scott, 'Motivation and Emotion', in Reich, Jill Nagy; Bulatao, Elizabeth Q. (Eds.), *et al, Close Up on Psychology: Supplemental Readings from the APA Monitor*, 1997, pp. 32-42 (American Psychological Assoc., US) ix, p.168.

4. Goldman, Bert A.; Mitchell, David F., 'Motivation', in Goldman, Bert A.; Mitchell, David F., *Directory of Unpublished Experimental Mental Measures*, 1995, Vol. 6, pp. 200-9 (American Psychological Assoc., US) viii, p. 387.

5. Smith, Joan Young, 'Vicarious Motivation', in Makosky, Vivian Parker; Whittemore, Linda Genevieve (Eds.), *et al, Activities Handbook for the Teaching of Psychology*, 1987, Vol. 2, pp. 239-40 (American Psychological Assoc., US) xiii, p. 345.

6. Boys, Christopher James, 'Mastery Orientation Through Task-focused Goals: Effects on Achievement and Motivation' [Dissertation Abstract], *Dissertation Abstracts International*, Vol. 64(7-A), 2004, 2379 (Univ. Microfilms International, US).

7. Berridge, Kent C., 'Motivation Concepts in Behavioral Neuroscience', *Physiology & Behavior*, Vol. 81(2), Apr. 2004, 179-209 (Elsevier Science, Netherlands).

8. Lam, Shui-fong; Yim, Pui-shan; Law, Josephine S.F.; Cheung, Rebecca W.Y., 'The Effects of Competition on Achievement Motivation in Chinese Classrooms', *British Journal of Educational Psychology*, Vol. 74(2), Jun. 2004, 281-96 (British Psychological Society, UK).

9. Gagne, F.; St. Pere, F., 'When IQ is Controlled, Does Motivation Still Predict Achievement?', *Intelligence*, 2002, Vol. 30(1), 71-100.

10. Bracken, Cheryl Campanella; Lombard, Matthew, 'Social Presence and Children: Praise, Intrinsic Motivation, and Learning With

Computers', *Journal of Communication*, Vol. 54(1), Mar. 2004, 22-37 (Oxford University Press, UK).

11. Ito, Kimio, 'Effects of Impression Motivation on Processing of In-group Persuasive Messages', *Japanese Journal of Experimental Social Psychology*, Vol 43(1), Dec. 2003, 52-62 (Japanese Group Dynamics Assoc., Japan).

12. Radovan, Marko, 'Factors Affecting the Motivation of Unemployed for Education', *Obzorja/Horizons of Psychology*, Vol. 12(4), 2003, 109-20 (Slovenian Psychological Assoc., Slovenia).

13. Tunstall, Pat, 'Definitions of the "Subject": The Relations Between the Discourses of Educational Assessment and the Psychology of Motivation and Their Constructions of Personal Reality', *British Educational Research Journal*, Vol. 29(4), Aug. 2003, 505-20 (Taylor & Francis, UK).

14. Hancock, Dawson R.; Flowers, Claudia P., 'An Investigation of the Motivation of Survey-Takers', *International Journal on E-Learning*, Vol. 2(3), Jul.–Sep. 2003, 5-12 (Association for the Advancement of Computing in Education, US).

15. Cho, Min-Haeng, 'The Strength of Motivation and Physical Activity Level During Leisure Time Among Youth in South Korea', *Youth & Society*, Vol. 35(4), Jun. 2004, 480-94 (Sage Publications, US).

16. Simons, Joke; Vansteenkiste, Maarten; Lens, Willy; Lacante, Marlies, 'Placing Motivation and Future Time Perspective Theory in a Temporal Perspective', *Educational Psychology Review*, Vol. 16(2), Apr. 2004, 121-39 (Kluwer Academic Publishers, Netherlands).

17. Terman, Lewis, M., 'The Discovery and Encouragement of Exceptional Talent', (chapter) in Notterman, J.M. (Ed), *The Evolution of Psychology: Fifty Years of the American Psychologist*, (American Psychological Assoc., US), pp. 306-20.

18. Razzino, Brian E.; Ribordy, Sheila C.; Grant, Kathryn; Ferrari, Joseph R.; Bowden, Blake S.; Zeisz, Jennifer, 'Gender-related Processes and Drug Use: Self-expression with Parents, Peer Group Selection, and Achievement Motivation', *Adolescence*, Vol. 39(153), Spr. 2004, 167-77 (Libra Publishers, US).

19. Zhang, Amy Y.; Harmon, Julie A.; Werkner, Janet; McCormick, Richard A., 'Impacts of Motivation for Change on the Severity of Alcohol Use by Patients with Severe and Persistent Mental Illness', *Journal of Studies on Alcohol*, Vol. 65(3), May 2004, 392-7 (Alcohol Research Documentation, US).

20. Roesch, Matthew R.; Olson, Carl R., 'Neuronal Activity Related to Reward Value and Motivation', *Science*, Vol. 304(5668), Apr. 2004, 307-10 (American Assoc. for the Advancement of Science, US).

21. Allart-van Dam, Esther; Hosman, Clemens M.H.; Keijsers, Ger P.J., 'A New Instrument to Assess Participant Motivation for Involvement in Preventive Interventions', *Journal of Clinical Psychology*, Vol. 60(6), Jun. 2004, 555-65 (John Wiley & Sons, US).

22. Pribyl, Charles B.; Sakamoto, Masahiro; Keaten, James A., 'The Relationship Between Nonverbal Immediacy, Student Motivation, and Perceived Cognitive Learning Among Japanese College Students',

Japanese Psychological Research, Vol. 46(2), May 2004, 73-85 (Blackwell Publishing, UK).

23. Schnoll, Robert A.; Rothman, Randi L.; Newman, Holly; Lerman, Caryn; Miller, Suzanne M.; Movsas, Benjamin; Sherman, Eric; Ridge, John A.; Unger, Michael; Langer, Corey; Goldberg, Melvyn; Scott, Walter; Cheng, Jonathan, 'Characteristics of Cancer Patients Entering a Smoking Cessation Program and Correlates of Quit Motivation: Implications for the Development of Tobacco Control Programs for Cancer Patients', *Psycho-Oncology*, Vol. 13(5), May 2004, 346-58 (John Wiley & Sons, US).

24. Jackson, Chris J.; Smillie, Luke D., 'Appetitive Motivation Predicts the Majority of Personality and an Ability Measure: A Comparison of BAS Measures and a Re-evaluation of the Importance of RST', *Personality & Individual Differences*, Vol. 36(7), May 2004, 1627-36 (Elsevier Science, Netherlands).

25. Gottfried, Adele Eskeles; Gottfried, Allen W., 'Toward the Development of a Conceptualization of Gifted Motivation', *Gifted Child Quarterly*, Vol. 48(2), Spr. 2004, 121-32 (National Assoc. for Gifted Children, US).

26. Olivier, M.A.J.; Steenkamp, D.S., 'Underlying Deficits in Achievement Motivation', *International Journal for the Advancement of Counselling*, Vol. 26(1), Mar. 2004, 47-63 (Kluwer Academic Publishers, Netherlands).

27. Cokley, Kevin O., 'What Do We Know About the Motivation of African American Students? Challenging the "Anti-Intellectual" Myth: Correction', *Harvard Educational Review*, Vol. 74(1), Spr. 2004, 113 (Harvard Education Publishing Group, US).

28. Tavani, Christopher M.; Losh, Susan C., 'Motivation, Self-confidence, and Expectations as Predictors of the Academic Performances Among Our High School Students', *Child Study Journal*, Vol. 33(3), 2003, 141-51 (SUNY Coll. at Buffalo, US).

29. Thatcher, Joanne; Reeves, Sue; Dorling, Debbie; Palmer, Anna, 'Motivation, Stress, and Cortisol Responses in Skydiving', *Perceptual & Motor Skills*, Vol. 97(3, Pt. 1), Dec. 2003, 995-1002.

30. Papacharisis, Vassilios; Goudas, Marios, 'Perceptions About Exercise and Intrinsic Motivation of Students Attending a Health-related Physical Education Program', *Perceptual & Motor Skills*, Vol. 97(3, Pt. 1), Dec. 2003, 689-96.

31. Smith, Alan D.; Rupp, William T., 'An Examination of Emerging Strategy and Sales Performance: Motivation, Chaotic Change and Organizational Structure', *Marketing Intelligence & Planning*, Vol. 21(3), 2003, 156-67 (Emerald, UK).

32. Sundstrum, L.; Fredrik, Devlin; Robert H.; Johnsson, Jurgen I.; Biagi, Carlo A., 'Vertical Position Reflects Increased Feeding Motivation in Growth Hormone Transgenic Coho Salmon (Oncorhynchus Kisutch)', *Ethology*, Vol. 109(8), Aug. 2003, 701-12 (Blackwell Publishing, UK).

33. Gard, Gunvor; Larsson, Agneta, 'Focus on Motivation in the Work Rehabilitation Planning Process: A Qualitative Study from the Employer's Perspective', *Journal of Occupational Rehabilitation*,

Vol. 13(3), Sep. 2003, 159-67 (Kluwer Academic Publishers, Netherlands).

34. Koka, Andre; Hein, Vello, 'The Impact of Sports Participation After School on Intrinsic Motivation and Perceived Learning Environment in Secondary School Physical Education', *Kineziologija*, Vol. 35(1), Jun. 2003, 5-13 (Fakultet za Fizicku Kulturu, Croatia).

35. Hull, Joseph T.; Wright, Kenneth P. Jr.; Czeisler, Charles A., 'The Influence of Subjective Alertness and Motivation on Human Performance Independent of Circadian and Homeostatic Regulation', *Journal of Biological Rhythms*, Vol. 18(4), Aug. 2003, 329-38 (Sage Publications, US).

36. Abel, Elizabeth; Tak, Sung Hee; Gortner, Eva-Maria, 'Reliability and Validity of Motivation for Sexual Health', *Western Journal of Nursing Research*, Vol. 25(5), Aug. 2003, 548-60 (Sage Publications, US).

37. Eisenberger, Robert; Shanock, Linda, 'Rewards, Intrinsic Motivation, and Creativity: A Case Study of Conceptual and Methodological Isolation', *Creativity Research Journal*, Vol. 15(2-3), Apr. 2003, 121-30 (Lawrence Erlbaum, US).

38. Navarro-Pertusa, Esperanza; Heredia, Esther Barber; Ferrer, Abilio Reig, 'Gender Differences in Sexual Motivation', *Psicothema*, Vol. 15(3), Aug. 2003, 395-400 (Colegio Oficial de Psicslogos del Principado de Asturias, Spain).

39. Murphy, Helen; Roopchand, Naomi, 'Intrinsic Motivation and Self-esteem in Traditional and Mature Students at a Post-1992 University in the North-east of England', *Educational Studies*, Vol. 29(2-3), Jun. 2003, 243-59 (Taylor & Francis, UK).

40. Schilling, Tammy A.; Hayashi, Carl T., 'Achievement Motivation Among High School Basketball and Cross-country Athletes: A Personal Investment Perspective', *Journal of Applied Sport Psychology*, Vol. 13(1), Mar. 2001, 103-28 (Taylor & Francis, UK).

41. Schneider, W.; Klauer, T.; Janssen, P. L.; Tetzlaff, M., 'Influence of Psychotherapy Motivation on the Course of Psychotherapy', *Nervenarzt*, Vol. 70(3), Mar. 1999, 240-9 (Springer Verlag, Germany).

42. Cooper, Joel, 'Unwanted Consequences and the Self: In Search of the Motivation for Dissonance Reduction', in Harmon-Jones, Eddie; Mills, Judson (Eds.), *Cognitive Dissonance: Progress on a Pivotal Theory in Social Psychology, Science Conference series*, 1999, pp. 149-73 (American Psychological Assoc., US), xviii, p. 411.

43. Harmon-Jones, Eddie, 'Toward an Understanding of the Motivation Underlying Dissonance Effects: Is the Production of Aversive Consequences Necessary?', in Harmon-Jones, Eddie; Mills, Judson (Eds.), *Cognitive Dissonance: Progress on a Pivotal Theory in Social Psychology, Science Conference series*, 1999, pp. 71-99.

44. Kanfer, Ruth; Heggestad, Eric D., 'Individual Differences in Motivation: Traits and Self-regulatory Skills' in Ackerman, Phillip L.; Kyllonen, Patrick C. (Eds.), *et al, Learning and Individual Differences: Process, Trait, and Content Determinants*, 1999, pp. 293-313 (American Psychological Assoc., US) xxii, p. 482.

3 Why Will-power Doesn't Exist

1. Aarts, Henk; Gollwitzer, Peter M.; Hassin, Ran R., 'Goal Contagion: Perceiving is for Pursuing', *Journal of Personality & Social Psychology*, Vol. 87(1), Jul. 2004, 23-37 (American Psychological Assoc., US).

2. Boxall, Peter; Macky, Keith; Rasmussen, Erling, 'The Causes and Consequences of Leaving and Staying with Employers', *Asia Pacific Journal of Human Resources*, Vol 41(2), Aug. 2003, 195-214 (Sage Publications, US).

3. Akella, Devi, 'The Story Factor: Secrets of Influence from the Art of Storytelling', *Management Learning*, Vol. 34(3), Sep. 2003, 404-5 (Sage Publications, US).

4. MacLeod, Robert B. (Ed.), *William James: Unfinished Business*, [Edited Book] (1969) (American Psychological Assoc., US), vi, 106pp.

5. Holm, Leila, 'Underachieving Young Men Preparing for Work', *British Journal of Guidance & Counselling*, Vol. 32(2), May 2004, 254-5 (Taylor & Francis, UK).

6. Duruz, Nicolas, 'To Be a Psychotherapist Tomorrow', *Psychotherapies*, Vol. 23(4), 2003, 233-40 (Medecine et Hygiene, Switzerland).

7. Thompson, David R., 'Fostering a Research Culture', *Nursing Inquiry*, Vol. 10(3), Sep. 2003, 143-4 (Blackwell Publishing, UK).

8. Berridge, Kent C.; Robinson, Terry E., 'Parsing Reward', *Trends in Neurosciences*, Vol. 26(9), Sep. 2003, 507-13 (Elsevier Science, Netherlands).

9. Benson, Suzanne G.; Dundis, Stephen P., 'Understanding and Motivating Employees: Integrating Maslow's Hierarchy of Needs, Training and Technology', *Journal of Nursing Management*, Vol. 11(5), Sep. 2003, 315-20 (Blackwell Publishing, UK).

10. Hancock, Dawson R.; Flowers, Claudia P., 'An Investigation of the Motivation of Survey-Takers', *op. cit.*

11. No authorship indicated, Editorial Note, *Journal of Consumer Psychology*, Vol. 14(3), 2004, 197 (Lawrence Erlbaum, US).

12. Ballon, Bruce; Kirst, Maritt; Smith, Patrick, 'Youth Help-seeking Expectancies', *Addiction Research & Theory*, Vol. 12(3), Jun. 2004, 241-60 (Taylor & Francis, UK).

13. Birgden, Astrid, 'Finding the Will and the Way', *Psychology, Crime & Law*, Vol. 10(3), Sep. 2004, 283-95 (Taylor & Francis, UK).

14. Derry, Paula S., 'The Tending Instinct', *Sex Roles*, Vol. 50(11-12), Jun. 2004, 879-80 (Kluwer Academic Publishers, Netherlands).

15. Lehtonen, Tuija; Tuomainen, Sirpa, 'A Tool to Motivate', *Recall*, Vol. 15(1), May 2003, 51-67 (Cambridge Univ. Press, US).

16. Forster, Jens; Friedmann, Ron, 'Context-dependent Creativity', *Zeitschrift für Psychologie*, Vol. 211(3), 2003, 149-60 (Hogrefe & Huber, Germany).

17. Bernstein, Irwin S., 'The Study of Things I Have Never Seen', *American Journal of Primatology*, Vol. 60(3), Jul. 2003, 77-84 (John Wiley & Sons, US).

18. Aghanwa, H. S.; Akinsola, A.; Akinola, D.O.; Makanjuola, R.O.A., 'Attitudes Toward Donation', *Journal of the National Medical*

Association, Vol. 95(8), Aug. 2003, 725-31 (National Medical Assoc., US).

19. Baker, Ellen K., 'Tending to Our Self' in Baker, Ellen K., *Caring for Ourselves: A Therapist's Guide to Personal and Professional Wellbeing,* 2003, pp. 37-58 (American Psychological Assoc., US), ix, p. 173.

20. Pyszczynski, Tom; Solomon, Sheldon; Greenberg, Jeff, 'Terror Management Research: Coping with Conscious and Unconscious Death-related Thoughts', in Pyszczynski, Tom; Solomon, Sheldon, *et al, In the Wake of 9/11: The Psychology of Terror,* 2003, pp. 37-70 (American Psychological Assoc., US), xiv, p. 227.

21. Lewin, Kurt; Gold, Martin, 'Intention, Will, and Need' in Lewin, Kurt; Gold, Martin (Eds.), *The Complete Social Scientist: A Kurt Lewin Reader,* 1999, pp. 83-115 (American Psychological Assoc., US) xi, p. 363.

22. Franzen, Michael D.; Iverson, Grant L., 'Detecting Negative Response Bias', in Snyder, Peter Jeffrey; Nussbaum, Paul David (Eds.), *Clinical Neuropsychology: A Pocket Handbook for Assessment,* 1998, pp. 88-101 (American Psychological Assoc., US), xxvii, 674pp.

23. Bjork, Daniel W., 'Burrhus Frederick Skinner: The Contingencies of a Life' in Kimble, Gregory A.; Wertheimer, Michael (Eds), *Portraits of Pioneers in Psychology,* Vol. 3. 1998, pp. 261-75 (American Psychological Assoc., US) xxii, p. 363.

24. Thayer, Paul W., 'A Rapidly Changing World: Some Implications for Training Systems' in Quinones, Miguel A.; Ehrenstein, Addie (Eds.), *Training for a Rapidly Changing Workplace: Applications of Psychological Research,* 1997, pp. 15-30 (American Psychological Assoc., US) xii, p. 345.

25. Tedeschi, James T.; Felston, Richard B., 'Social Identities and Coercive Actions' in Tedeschi, James T.; Felson, Richard B., *Violence, Aggression, and Coercive Actions,* 1994, pp. 249-328 (American Psychological Assoc., US) xii, p. 463.

26. 'Is a Graduate Degree in Psychology the Right Choice for You?' in *Getting In: A Step-by-Step Plan for Gaining Admission to Graduate School in Psychology,* 1993, pp. 11-26 (American Psychological Assoc., US) viii, p. 221.

27. Batten, Helen Levine, 'The Social Construction of Altruism' in Shanteau, James; Harris, Richard Jackson (Eds), *Organ Donation and Transplantation: Psychological and Behavioral Factors,* 1999, pp. 83-96 (American Psychological Assoc., US) x, p. 214.

28. Paludi, Michele A.; Epstein, Charles, 'The Influence of Role Models and Mentors on Career Development', in Makosky, Vivian Parker; Sileo, Chi Chi (Eds.), *et al, Activities Handbook for the Teaching of Psychology,* 1990, Vol 3, pp. 244-6 (American Psychological Assoc., US) xii, p. 372.

29. Klonsky, Bruce G., 'A Test Construction Package' in Makosky, Vivian Parker; Whittemore, Linda Genevieve (Eds), *et al, Activities Handbook for the Teaching of Psychology,* 1987, Vol. 2, pp. 23-29 (American Psychological Assoc., US) xiii, p. 345.

30. Fernald, Peter S.; Fernald, L. Dodge, 'Inferences and Observable Behavior' in Makosky, Vivian Parker; Whittemore, Linda Genevieve

(Eds.), *et al, Activities Handbook for the Teaching of Psychology*, 1987, Vol. 2, pp. 3-6.

31. Hill, James, 'Physical Activity and Obesity', *Lancet*, Jan. 2004, Vol. 363(9404), p. 182.

32. Rosen, James C., 'Improving Body Image in Obesity' in Thompson, J. Kevin (Ed.), *Body Image, Eating Disorders, and Obesity: An Integrative Guide for Assessment and Treatment*, 2001, pp. 425-40 (American Psychological Assoc., US) vii, p. 505.

33. Emmett, Paul J.; Veeder, William, 'Freud in Time: Psychoanalysis and Literary Criticism in the New Century', *Annual of Psychoanalysis*, Vol. 29, 2001, 201-35 (Analytic Press, US).

34. Nicholson, Nigel, 'An Evolutionary Perspective on Change and Stability in Personality, Culture and Organization' in Erez, Miriam; Kleinbeck, Uwe (Eds.), *et al, Work Motivation in the Context of a Globalizing Economy*, 2001, pp. 381-94 (Lawrence Erlbaum Assoc., Mahwah, NJ, US), x, pp. 439.

35. Leung, Kwok, 'Different Carrots for Different Rabbits: Effects of Individualism-Collectivism and Power Distance on Work Motivation', in Erez, Miriam; Kleinbeck, Uwe (Eds.), *et al, Work Motivation in the Context of a Globalizing Economy*, 2001, pp. 329-39.

36. Bohart, Arthur C.; Tallman, Karen, 'When the Active Client is Difficult' in Bohart, Arthur C.; Tallman, Karen, *How Clients Make Therapy Work: The Process of Active Self-healing*, 1999, pp. 167-200 (American Psychological Assoc., US), xvii, 347pp.

37. Wachtel, Paul L., 'Some Therapeutic Implications of the Interpersonal View', in Wachtel, Paul L., *Psychoanalysis, Behavior Therapy, and the Relational World: Psychotherapy Integration*, 1997, pp. 64-75 (American Psychological Assoc., US) xxiv, 484pp.

38. Lewin, Gertrud Weiss, 'Behavior and Development as a Function of the Total Situation' (1946), in Lewin, Kurt, *Resolving Social Conflicts and Field Theory in Social Science*, 1997, pp. 337-81 (American Psychological Assoc., US), v, 422pp.

39. Shade, Barbara J.; Kelly, Cynthia A.; Oberg, Mary, *Creating Culturally Responsive Classrooms* [Authored Book], 1997 (American Psychological Assoc., US), viii, 168pp.

40. Panksepp, Jaak; Nelson, Eric; Bekkedal, Marni, 'Brain Systems for the Mediation of Social Separation-distress and Social-reward: Evolutionary Antecedents and Neuropeptide Intermediaries' in Carter, Carol Sue; Lederhendler, I. Izja (Eds.), *et al, The Integrative Neurobiology of Affiliation: Annals of The New York Academy of Sciences*, 1997, Vol. 807, pp. 78-100 (New York Academy of Sciences, NY, US), xviii, 614pp.

41. Wingfield, John C.; Jacobs, Jerry; Hillgarth, Nigella, 'Ecological Constraints and the Evolution of Hormone-behavior Interrelationships' in Carter, Carol Sue; Lederhendler, I. Izja (Eds.), *et al, The Integrative Neurobiology of Affiliation: Annals of The New York Academy of Sciences*, 1997, Vol. 807, pp. 22-41 (New York Academy of Sciences, NY, US), xviii, 614pp.

42. Collier, George; Johnson, Deanne, 'Motivation as a Function of Animal Versus Experimenter Control' in Bouton, Mark E.; Fanselow,

Michael S. (Eds.), *Learning, Motivation, and Cognition: The Functional Behaviorism of Robert C. Bolles*, 1997, pp. 117-29 (American Psychological Assoc., US), xiii, 451pp.

43. Liese, Bruce S.; Vail, Belinda A.; Seaton, Kimberly A., 'Substance Use Problems in Primary Care Medical Settings: Is There a Psychologist in the House?' in Resnick, Robert J.; Rozensky, Ronald H. (Eds.), *Health Psychology Through the Life Span: Practice and Research Opportunities*, 1996, pp. 177-94 (American Psychological Assoc., US), xvii, 464pp.

44. McCombs, Barbara L.; Pope, James E., 'Goal Two: Understanding Motivation and How it Can be Enhanced' in McCombs, Barbara L.; Pope, James E., *Motivating Hard to Reach Students: Psychology in the Classroom: A Series on Applied Educational Psychology*, 1994, pp. 27-35 (American Psychological Assoc., US), vii, 123pp.

45. Toch, Hans, 'The Anatomy of Violence', in Toch, Hans, *Violent Men*, 1992, pp. 179-215 (American Psychological Assoc., US) xv, 286pp.

46. McKeachie, Wilbert J., 'Teaching Psychology: Research and Experience in Makosky, Vivian Parker (Ed.), *The G. Stanley Hall Lecture Series*, Vol. 6, 1986, pp. 169-91 (American Psychological Assoc., US), 191pp.

47. Clary, E. Gil; Snyder, Mark; Stukas, Arthur, 'Service-learning and Psychology: Lessons from the Psychology of Volunteers' Motivations' in Bringle, Robert G.; Duffy, Donna K. (Eds.), *With Service in Mind: Concepts and Models for Service-learning in Psychology, American Association for Higher Education*, 1998, pp. 35-50 (American Psychological Assoc., US), v, 217pp.

48. Murphy, Kristina, 'The Role of Trust in Nurturing Compliance', *Law & Human Behavior*, Vol. 28(2) Apr. 2004, 187-209 (Kluwer Academic Publishers, Netherlands).

49. Eyny, Yaniv S.; Horvitz, Jon C., 'Opposing Roles in Appetitive Conditioning', *Journal of Neuroscience*, Vol. 23(5), Mar. 2003, 1584-87 (Society for Neuroscience, US).

50. Ho, Adrian K.; Jernudd, Bjorn H., 'Conversational Repair', *Journal of Asian Pacific Communication*, Vol. 10(2), 2001, 205-25 (John Benjamins, Netherlands).

51. Ouweneel, Piet, 'Social Security and Wellbeing of the Unemployed in 42 Nations', *Journal of Happiness Studies*, 2002, Vol. 3(2), pp. 167-92.

52. Stinson, Bobby L. II; Friedberg, Robert D.; Page, Richard A.; Cusack, Michael J., 'Improving Athletic Performance and Motivating Athletes' in Vandecreek, Leon; Jackson, Thomas L. (Eds), *Innovations in Clinical Practice: A Source Book*, 2000, Vol. 18. pp. 349-67 (Professional Resource Press/Professional Resource Exchange, Inc., Sarasota, FL, US), x, 494pp.

53. Mann, Traci; Sherman, David; Updegraff, John, 'Dispositional Motivations and Message Framing: A Test of the Congruency Hypothesis in College Students', *Health Psychology*, Vol. 23(3), May 2004, 330-4 (American Psychological Assoc., US).

54. Ames, Daniel R.; Flynn, Francis J.; Weber, Elke U., 'It's the Thought That Counts: On Perceiving How Helpers Decide to Lend a Hand',

Personality & Social Psychology Bulletin, Vol. 30(4), Apr. 2004, 461-74 (Sage Publications, US).

55. Straub, Jurgen, 'Differentiating Psychological Action Theory, Decentring the Reflexive, Autonomous Subject', *Journal für Psychologie*, Vol. 10(4), Dec. 2002, 351-79 (Vandenhoeck & Ruprecht, Germany).

56. Cockerham, William C.; Snead, M. Christine; Dewaal, Derek, F., 'Health Lifestyles in Russia and the Socialist Heritage', *Journal of Health and Social Behavior*, Mar. 2002, Vol. 43(1), pp. 42-55. (American Sociological Assoc., US).

57. Oyserman, Daphna; Bybee, Deborah; Terry, Kathy; Hart-Johnson, Tamera, 'Possible Selves as Roadmaps', *Journal of Research in Personality*, Vol. 38(2), Apr. 2004, 130-49 (Elsevier Science, UK).

58. Cockerham, William C.; Snead, M. Christine; Dewaal, Derek, F.; 'Health Lifestyles in Russia and the Socialist Heritage', *Journal of Health and Social Behavior*, *op. cit.*

4 How to Bin Friends and Disregard People

1. Hochschild, A.R., 'Emotion Work, Feeling Roles, and Social Structure', *American Journal of Sociology*, 85(3), 1979, 551-75 (University of Chicago Press, US).

2. Pugliesi, K., 'The Consequences of Emotional Labor: Effects on Work Stress, Job Satisfaction, and Well-being', *Motivation and Emotion*, 1999, 23(2), 125-54 (University of California Press, US).

3. Brotheridge, C., Grandey, A., 'Emotional Labor and Burnout: Comparing Two Perspectives on "People Work"', *Journal of Vocational Behavior*, 60, 2002, 17-39 (Elsevier Science, US).

4. Gross, J.; Levenson, R., 'Hiding Feelings: The Acute Effects of Inhibiting Negative and Positive Emotions', *Journal of Abnormal Psychology*, 106(1), 1997, 95–103 (American Psychological Assoc., US).

5. Jackson, S.E.; Turner, J.A.; Brief, A.P., 'Correlates of Burnout Among Public Service Lawyers', *Journal of Occupational Behavior*, 8, 1987, 339-49.

6. Maslach, C., Schaufeli, W.B., 'Historical and Conceptual Development of Burnout', in Schaufeli, W.B.; Maslach, C.; Marek, T. (Eds.), *Professional Burnout: Recent Developments in Theory and Research,* 1993, pp. 1-16 (Taylor & Francis, Washington, DC, US).

7. Brotheridge, C.; Grandey, A., 'Emotional Labor and Burnout', *Journal of Vocational Behavior*, 60, 2002, *op. cit.*

8. *Ibid.*

9. Repacholi, Betty; Slaughter, Virginia; Pritchard, Michelle; Gibbs, Vicki, 'Theory of Mind, Machiavellianism, and Social Functioning in Childhood,' in Repacholi, Betty; Slaughter, Virginia (Eds.), *Individual Differences in Theory of Mind: Implications for Typical and Atypical Development, Macquarie Monographs in Cognitive Science*, 2003, pp. 67-97 (Psychology Press, NY, US).

10. McIlwain, Doris; 'Bypassing Empathy: A Machiavellian Theory of Mind and Sneaky Power' in Repacholi, Betty; Slaughter, Virginia (Eds.), *Individual Differences in Theory of Mind: Implications for Typical and Atypical Development, Macquarie Monographs in Cognitive Science*, 2003, pp. 39-66.

11. Hawley, Patricia H., 'Prosocial and Coercive Configurations of Resource Control in Early Adolescence: A Case for the Well-adapted Machiavellian', *Merrill-Palmer Quarterly*, Vol. 49(3) Jul. 2003, 279-309 (Wayne State Univ. Press, US).

12. Mazza, Monica; De Risio, Alessandro; Tozzini, Carola; Roncone, Rita; Casacchia, Massimo, 'Machiavellianism and Theory of Mind in People Affected by Schizophrenia', *Brain & Cognition*, Vol. 51(3), Apr. 2003, 262-9 (Elsevier Science, UK).

13. Day, Rachel L.; Coe, Rebecca L.; Kendal, Jeremy R.; Laland, Kevin N., 'Neophilia, Innovation and Social Learning: A Study of Intergeneric Differences in Callitrichid Monkeys', *Animal Behaviour*, Vol. 65(3), Mar. 2003, 559-71 (Elsevier Science, UK).

14. Scrimali, T.; Grimaldi, L.; Sala, L., 'Cognitive Psychotherapy: From Human Information Processing to the Logic of Distant Equilibrium Complex Systems', *Journal de Therapie Comportementale et Cognitive*, Vol. 12(3), 2002, 84-96 (Masson, France).

15. Aziz, Abdul; May, Kim; Crotts, John C., 'Relations of Machiavellian Behavior With Sales Performance of Stockbrokers', *Psychological Reports*, Vol. 90(2), Apr. 2002, 451-60 (Psychological Reports, US).

16. Haas, Heather, 'Extending the Search for Folk Personality Constructs: The Dimensionality of the Personality-relevant Proverb Domain', *Journal of Personality & Social Psychology*, Vol. 82(4), Apr. 2002, 594-609 (American Psychological Assoc., US).

17. Sabia, Daniel R., Jr., 'Machiavelli's Soderini and the Problem of Necessity', *Social Science Journal*, Vol. 38(1), 2001, 53-67 (Elsevier Science, US).

18. Hanley, James Evan, 'The Role of Non-cooperative Games in the Evolution of Cooperation' [Dissertation Abstract], *Dissertation Abstracts International*, Vol. 61(9-A), Apr. 2001, 3751.

19. Shen, Dong; Dickson, Marsha A., 'Consumers' Acceptance of Unethical Clothing Consumption Activities: Influence of Cultural Identification, Ethnicity, and Machiavellianism', *Clothing & Textiles Research Journal*, Vol. 19(2), 2001, 76-87 (International Textile & Apparel Assoc., US).

20. Bruene, Martin, 'Social Cognition and Psychopathology in an Evolutionary Perspective, *Psychopathology*, Vol. 34(2), Mar. 2001, 85-94 (S. Karger AG, Switzerland).

21. Arsenio, William F; Lemerise, Elizabeth A., 'Varieties of Childhood Bullying: Values, Emotion Processes, and Social Competence', *Social Development*, Vol. 10(1), 2001, 59-73 (Blackwell Publishers, UK).

22. Sutton, Jon; Keogh, Edmund, 'Components of Machiavellian Beliefs in Children: Relationships With Personality', *Personality & Individual Differences*, Vol. 30(1), Jan. 2001, 137-48 (Elsevier Science, UK).

23. Barber, Nigel, *Why Parents Matter*, 2000 (Bergin & Garvey, US).

24. Sutton, J.; Keogh, E., 'Components of Machiavellian Beliefs in Children', *Personality & Individual Differences*, Jun. 2001, Vol. 30(1), pp. 137-48 (Elsevier Science, UK).

25. O'Connor, E.M.; Simms, C.M., 'Self-revelation as Manipulation', *Social Behavior & Personality*, 1990, Vol. 18(1), 95-9 (Society for Personality Research, New Zealand).

26. Balestri, Massimo, 'Overt and Covert Narcissism and their Relationship to Object Relations, Depression, Machiavellianism, and the Five Factor Model of Personality' [Dissertation Abstract], *Dissertation Abstracts International: Section B: the Sciences & Engineering*, Vol. 59(7-B), Jan. 1999, 3680.

27. Smith, Robert J., 'Psychopathic Behavior and Issues of Treatment', *New Ideas in Psychology*, Vol. 17(2), Aug. 1999, 165-76 (Elsevier Science, UK).

28. Sullivan, Roger J.; Allen, J.S., 'Social Deficits Associated with Schizophrenia Defined in Terms of Interpersonal Machiavellianism', *Acta Psychiatrica Scandinavica*, Vol. 99(2), Feb. 1999, 148-54 (Munksgaard Scientific Journals, US).

29. Whiten, Andrew, 'The Shaping of Social Cognition in Evolution and Development: Commentary on Michael Tomasello's "Uniquely Primate, Uniquely Human"', *Developmental Science*, Vol. 1(1), Apr. 1998, 19-20 (Blackwell Publishers, UK).

30. Girodo, Michel, 'Undercover Probes of Police Corruption: Risk Factors in Proactive Internal Affairs Investigations', *Behavioral Sciences and the Law*, Vol. 16(4), Fall 1998, 479-96 (John Wiley & Sons, US).

31. Wilson, Geoffrey Thomas, 'Renaissance Machiavellism and the Subject of Psychoanalysis', *Dissertation Abstracts International*, Vol. 58(8-A), Feb. 1998, 3149.

32. Collins, Judith M.; Griffin, Ricky W., 'The Psychology of Counterproductive Job Performance', in Griffin, Ricky W.; O'Leary-Kelly, Anne (Eds.), *et al*, 'Dysfunctional Behavior in Organizations: Violent and Deviant Behavior; Monographs in Organizational Behavior and Industrial Relations', Vol. 23, 1998, Parts A and B, pp. 219-42, xxiii, 288pp (JAI Press, US).

33. Gomez, Juan Carlos; Nunez, Maria, 'The Social Mind and the Physical Mind: Development and Domains of Knowledge', *Infancia y Aprendizaje*, No. 84, 1998, 5-32 (Aprendizaje SL, Spain).

34. Barber, Nigel, 'Sex Differences in Disposition Towards Kin, Security of Adult Attachment, and Sociosexuality as a Function of Parental Divorce', *Evolution & Human Behavior*, Vol. 19(2), Mar. 1998, 125-32 (Elsevier Science Publishing, US).

35. Mast, Marianne Schmid; Hall, Judith A., 'Who is the Boss and Who is Not? Accuracy of Judging Status', *Journal of Nonverbal Behavior*, Vol. 28(3), Fall 2004, 145-65.

36. Girodo, Michel, 'Machiavellian, Bureaucratic, and Transformational Leadership Styles in Police Managers: Preliminary Findings of Interpersonal Ethics', *Perceptual & Motor Skills*, Vol. 86(2), Apr. 1998, 419-27 (Perceptual & Motor Skills, US).

37. Moore, Shirley; Ward, Michael; Katz, Barry, 'Machiavellianism and Tolerance of Ambiguity', *Psychological Reports*, Vol. 82(2), Apr. 1998, 415-18 (Psychological Reports, US).

38. Jagers, Robert J.; Smith, Paula; Mock, Lynne Owens; Dill, Ebony, 'An

Afrocultural Social Ethos: Component Orientations and Some Social Implications', *Journal of Black Psychology*, Vol. 23(4), Nov. 1997, 328-43 (Sage Publications, US).

39. Goody, Esther N., 'Social Intelligence and Language: Another Rubicon?' in Whiten, Andrew; Byrne, Richard W. (Eds.), *Machiavellian Intelligence II: Extensions and Evaluations*, 1997, 364-96, xii, 403pp (Cambridge Univ. Press, UK).

40. Miller, Geoffrey F., 'Protean Primates: The Evolution of Adaptive Unpredictability in Competition and Courtship' in Whiten, Andrew; Byrne, Richard W. (Eds.), *Machiavellian Intelligence II: Extensions and Evaluations*, 1997, 312-40, xii, 403pp.

41. Byrne, Richard W., 'The Technical Intelligence Hypothesis: An Additional Evolutionary Stimulus to Intelligence?' in Whiten, Andrew; Byrne, Richard W. (Eds.), *Machiavellian Intelligence II: Extensions and Evaluations*, 1997, 289-311, xii, 403pp.

42. Whiten, Andrew, 'The Machiavellian Mindreader' in Whiten, Andrew; Byrne, Richard W. (Eds.), *Machiavellian Intelligence II: Extensions and Evaluations*, 1997, pp. 144-73, xii, 403pp.

43. Strum, Shirley C.; Forster, Deborah; Hutchins, Edwin, 'Why Machiavellian Intelligence May Not Be Machiavellian', in Whiten, Andrew; Byrne, Richard W. (Eds.), *Machiavellian Intelligence II: Extensions and Evaluations*, 1997, pp. 50-85, xii, 403pp.

44. Whiten, Andrew; Byrne, Richard W. (Eds.), *Machiavellian Intelligence II: Extensions and Evaluations*, 1997, xii, 403pp.

45. Mason, E. Sharon; Mudrack, Peter E., 'Are Individuals Who Agree That Corporate Social Responsibility is a "Fundamentally Subversive Doctrine" Inherently Unethical?', *Applied Psychology*, Vol. 46(2), Apr. 1997, 135-52 (Taylor & Francis, US).

46. Aiello, Leslie C., 'Terrestriality and the Origin of Language' in Runciman, W.G.; Smith, John Maynard (Eds.), *et al*, *Evolution of Social Behaviour Patterns in Primates and Man* (Proceedings of The British Academy), Vol. 88, 1996, 269-89, vi, 297pp.

47. Joseph, Judith Jacqueline, 'The Role of Suspicion, Relational Development, and Length of Relationship in the Accuracy of Deception Detection by Married Couples', *Dissertation Abstracts International: Section B: the Sciences & Engineering*, Vol. 56(9-B), Mar. 1996, 5172 (Univ. Microfilms International, US).

48. Drigotas, Stephen, M., 'The Michelangelo Phenomenon and Personal Well-being', *Journal of Personality*, Feb. 2002, Vol. 70(1), 59-77 (Blackwell Publishing, UK).

49. Crow, T.J., 'Sexual Selection as the Mechanism of Evolution of Machiavellian Intelligence: A Darwinian Theory of the Origins of Psychosis', *Journal of Psychopharmacology*, Vol. 10(1), 1996, 77-87 (Sage Publications, UK).

50. Jha, Praveen Kumar, 'Personality Correlates of Machiavellians', *Indian Journal of Psychometry & Education*, Vol. 26(2), Jul. 1995, 65-70 (Indian Psychometric & Educational Research Association, India).

51. Byrne, Richard W., *The Thinking Ape: Evolutionary Origins of Intelligence*, 1995, ix, 266pp (Oxford Univ. Press, UK).

52. Lester, David, 'Personality Correlates of Correctly Identifying Genuine Suicide Notes', *Perceptual & Motor Skills*, Vol. 80(3, Pt. 1), Jun. 1995, 890 (Perceptual & Motor Skills, US).

53. Chasiotis, Athanasios, 'The Mystification of Homeostasis: Socioemotional Reciprocity as a Basic Psychological Dimension', *Gestalt Theory*, Vol. 17(2), Jun. 1995, 88-129 (Westdeutscher Verlag, Germany).

54. Merrill, Joseph M.; Laux, Lila F.; Lorimor, Ronald J.; Thornby, John I.; *et al*, 'Measuring Social Desirability Among Senior Medical Students', *Psychological Reports*, Vol. 77(3, Pt. 1), Dec. 1995, 859-64 (Psychological Reports, US).

55. Moore, Shirley; Katz, Barry, 'Machiavellian Scores of Nursing Faculty and Students', *Psychological Reports*, Vol. 77(2), Oct. 1995, 383-6 (Psychological Reports, US).

56. Wilson, Geoffrey, 'Renaissance Machiavellism and the Subject of Psychoanalysis', *Psychoanalysis & Contemporary Thought*, Vol. 18(4), 1995, 559-603 (International Universities Press Inc., US).

57. Drake, Daniel S., 'Assessing Machiavellianism and Morality-conscience Guilt', *Psychological Reports*, Vol. 77(3, Pt. 2), Dec. 1995, 1355-59 (Psychological Reports, US).

58. Sares, Timothy Andrew, 'Influence of Educational Attainment on Helpfulness, Civic Values, and Machiavellian Views', *Dissertation Abstracts International: Section B: The Sciences & Engineering*, Vol. 56(6-B), Dec. 1995, 3507.

5 Do You Suffer from False Hope Syndrome?

1. Herman, C. Peter; Polivy, Janet, 'Realistic and Unrealistic Self-Change Efforts', *American Psychologist*, Vol. 58(10), Oct. 2003, 823-4 (American Psychological Assoc., US).

2. Fletcher, Anne M., 'Renewed Hope for Self-Change' [Peer Reviewed Journal], *American Psychologist*, Vol. 58(10), Oct. 2003, 822-3.

3. Snyder, C. R.; Rand, Kevin L., 'The Case Against False Hope', *American Psychologist*, Vol. 58(10), Oct. 2003, 820-2.

4. Lowe, Michael R., 'Dieting: False Hope or Falsely Accused?', *American Psychologist*, Vol. 58(10), Oct. 2003, 819-20.

5. Clarke, David, 'Faith and Hope', *Australasian Psychiatry,* Vol. 11(2), Jun. 2003, 164-8 (Blackwell Publishing, UK).

6. Edey, Wendy; Jevne, Ronna F., 'Hope, Illness, and Counselling Practice: Making Hope Visible', *Canadian Journal of Counselling*, Vol. 37(1), Jan. 2003, 44-51 (Canadian Guidance & Counselling Assoc., Canada).

7. Snyder, C.R., 'Hope Theory: Rainbows in the Mind', *Psychological Inquiry*, Vol. 13(4), Oct. 2002, 249-75 (Lawrence Erlbaum, US).

8. Leventhal, John J., 'Good News or False Hope?', *Child Abuse & Neglect*, Vol. 25(9), Sep. 2001, 1137-8 (Elsevier Science, US).

9. Bohart, Arthur C., 'Focusing on the Positive, Focusing on the Negative: Implications for Psychotherapy', *Journal of Clinical Psychology*, Vol. 58(9), Sep. 2002, 1037-43 (John Wiley & Sons, US).

10. Snyder, C.R.; Rand, Kevin L.; King, Elisa A.; Feldman, David B.; Woodward, Julia T., '"False" Hope', *Journal of Clinical Psychology*, Vol. 58(9), Sep. 2002, 1003-22.

11. Held, Barbara S.; Bohart, Arthur C., 'Introduction: The (Overlooked) Virtues of "Univirtuous" Attitudes and Behavior: Reconsidering Negativity, Complaining, Pessimism, and "False" Hope', *Journal of Clinical Psychology*, Vol. 58(9), Sep. 2002, 961-4.

12. Polivy, Janet; Herman, C. Peter, 'If At First You Don't Succeed: False Hopes of Self-change', *American Psychologist*, Vol. 57(9), Sep. 2002, 677-89.

13. Kwon, Paul, 'Hope, Defense Mechanisms, and Adjustment: Implications for False Hope and Defensive Hopelessness', *Journal of Personality*, Vol. 70(2), Apr. 2002, 207-31 (Blackwell Publishers, US).

14. Morain, Alan, 'A Neurocognitive and Socioecological Model of Self-Awareness', *Genetic, Social and General Psychology* Monographs, Vol. 130(3), Aug. 2004, 197-222.

15. Gringras, Paul, 'The Potential and the Pitfalls', *Autism*, Vol. 4(3), Sep. 2000, 229-47 (Sage Publications, UK).

16. Polivy, Janet; Herman, C. Peter, 'The False-hope Syndrome: Unfulfilled Expectations of Self-change', *Current Directions in Psychological Science*, Vol. 9(4), Aug. 2000, 128-31 (Blackwell Publishers, US).

17. Polivy, Janet; Herman, C. Peter, 'The Effects of Resolving to Diet on Restrained and Unrestrained Eaters: The "False Hope Syndrome"', *International Journal of Eating Disorders*, Vol. 26(4), Dec. 1999, 434-47 (John Wiley & Sons, US).

18. Moskalenko, S.; Heine, S.J., 'Watching Your Troubles Away', *Personality and Social Psychology Bulletin*, Jan. 2003, Vol. 29(1), pp. 76-85 (Sage Publishing, US).

19. Bland, Jeffrey S.; Levin, Buck, 'Support for a Biopsychological Approach', *Advances*, Vol. 13(1), Win. 1997, 26-30 (John E. Fetzer Institute, US).

20. Scott-Kakures, Dion, 'High Anxiety: Barnes on What Moves the Unwelcome Believer', *Philosophical Psychology*, Vol. 14(3), Sep. 2001, 313-26.

21. Farber, L.H., *The Ways of the Will*, 1966, (Basic Books, NY, US).

22. Shah, James, Higgins, Tory, Friedman, Ronald S., 'Performance Incentives and Means: How Regulatory Focus Influences Goal Attainment', *Journal of Personality & Social Psychology*, Vol. 74(2), Feb. 1996, 285-93 (American Psychological Assoc., US).

6 Goals, Goals, Goals!

1. Dickson, Joanne M.; MacLeod, Andrew K., 'Approach and Avoidance Goals and Plans: Their Relationship to Anxiety and Depression', *Cognitive Therapy & Research*, Vol. 28(3), Jun. 2004, 415-32 (Kluwer Academic Publishers, Netherlands).

2. Harju, Beverly L.; Twiddy, Sarah E.; Cope, John G.; Eppler, Marion E.; McCammon, Michael, 'Relations of Women Exercisers' Mastery and Performance Goals to Traits, Fitness, and Preferred Styles of

Instructors', *Perceptual & Motor Skills*, Vol. 97(3, Pt. 1), Dec. 2003, 939-50.

3. Boys, Christopher James, 'Mastery Orientation Through Task-focused Goals: Effects on Achievement and Motivation' [Dissertation Abstract], *Dissertation Abstracts International*, Vol. 64(7-A), 2004, 2379.

4. Locke, Edwin A., 'Self-set Goals and Self-efficacy as Mediators of Incentives and Personality' in Erez, Miriam; Kleinbeck, Uwe (Eds.), *et al, Work Motivation in the Context of a Globalizing Economy*, 2001, pp. 13-26 (Lawrence Erlbaum Associates, Publishers, Mahwah, NJ, US), x, 439pp.

5. Gilbert, Daniel T.; Gill, Michael J.; Wilson, Timothy D., 'The Future Is Now: Temporal Correction in Affective Forecasting', *Organizational Behavior & Human Decision Processes*, Vol. 88(1), May 2002, 430-44 (Elsevier Science, UK).

6. Gilbert, Daniel T.; Ebert, Jane E.J., 'Decisions and Revisions: The Affective Forecasting of Changeable Outcomes', *Journal of Personality & Social Psychology*, Vol. 82(4), Apr. 2002, 503-14 (American Psychological Assoc., US).

7. Nissle, Sonja; Bschor, Tom, 'Winning the Jackpot and Depression: Money Cannot Buy Happiness', *International Journal of Psychiatry in Clinical Practice*, Vol. 6(3), Sep. 2002, 183-86, (Martin Dunitz, UK).

8. Dickson, Joanne M.; MacLeod, Andrew K., 'Brief Report: Anxiety, Depression and Approach and Avoidance Goals', *Cognition & Emotion*, Vol. 18(3), May 2004, 423-30 (Taylor & Francis, UK).

9. Fung, Helene H.; Carstensen, Laura L., 'Motivational Changes in Response to Blocked Goals and Foreshortened Time: Testing Alternatives to Socioemotional Selectivity Theory', *Psychology & Aging*, Vol. 19(1), Mar. 2004, 68-78 (American Psychological Assoc., US).

10. Kawada, Christie L.K.; Oettingen, Gabriele; Gollwitzer, Peter M.; Bargh, John A., 'The Projection of Implicit and Explicit Goals', *Journal of Personality & Social Psychology*, Vol. 86(4), Apr. 2004, 545-59 (American Psychological Assoc., US).

11. Braten, Ivar; Samuelstuen, Marit S.; Stromso, Helge I., 'Do Students' Self-Efficacy Beliefs Moderate the Effects of Performance Goals on Self-Regulatory Strategy Use?', *Educational Psychology*, Vol. 24(2), Apr. 2004, 231-47 (Taylor & Francis, UK).

12. Gollwitzer, Peter M., Fujita, Kentaro; Oettingen, Gabriele, 'Planning and the Implementation of Goals', in Baumeister, Roy F.; Vohs, Kathleen D. (Eds.), *Handbook of Self-regulation: Research, Theory, and Applications*, 2004, pp. 211-28 (Guilford Press, NY, US), xv, 574pp.

13. Nair, K.P. Sivaraman, 'Life Goals: The Concept and its Relevance to Rehabilitation', *Clinical Rehabilitation*, Vol. 17(2), Mar. 2003, 192-202 (Hodder Arnold, UK).

14. Wolozin, Harold, 'The Individual in Economic Analysis: Toward Psychology of Economic Behaviour', *Journal of Socio-Economics*, Vol. 31(1), 2002, 45-57.

15. Summers, Jessica Jane, 'Social Goals, Achievement Goals, and the Pathways of Peer Influence in 6th Grade' [Dissertation Abstract], *Dissertation Abstracts International*, Vol. 64(4-A), 2003, 1177.

16. Pulkkinen, Lea; Nurmi, Jari-Erik; Kokko, Katja, 'Individual Differences in Personal Goals in Mid-thirties' in Pulkkinen, Lea; Caspi, Avshalom (Eds), *Paths to Successful Development: Personality in the Life Course*, 2002, pp. 331-52 (Cambridge University Press, NY, US), x, 422pp.

17. Beach, Steven, R.H.; Fincham, Frank, D., 'Marital Therapy and Social Psychology: Will We Choose Explicit Partnership or Cryptommesia?, (Chapter in) Brewer, Marilynn, B.; Hewstone, Miles (Eds), *Applied Social Psychology: Perspectives on Social Psychology*, 2004, pp. 50-78 (Blackwell Publishers, Malden, MA, US).

18. Linnenbrink, Elizabeth A., 'The Dilemma of Performance Goals: Promoting Students' Motivation and Learning in Cooperative Groups' [Dissertation Abstract], *Dissertation Abstracts International*, Vol. 63(10-A), 2003, 3474.

19. Bauer, Jack J.; McAdams, Dan P., 'Growth Goals, Maturity, and Well-Being', *Developmental Psychology*, Vol. 40(1), Jan. 2004, 114-27 (American Psychological Assoc., US).

20. Krolak-Schwerdt, Sabine; Le Coutre, Christine, 'Impact of Different Processing Goals on Person Memory', *Psychologische Beitrage*, Vol. 44(3), 2002, 428-46 (Pabst Science Publishers, Germany).

21. Van Yperen, Nico W., 'Task Interest and Actual Performance: The Moderating Effects of Assigned and Adopted Purpose Goals', *Journal of Personality & Social Psychology*, Vol. 85(6), Dec. 2003, 1006-15 (American Psychological Assoc., US).

22. Berg, Michael B.; Janoff-Bulman, Ronnie; Cotter, Justin, 'Perceiving Value in Obligations and Goals: Wanting To Do What Should Be Done', *Personality & Social Psychology Bulletin*, Vol. 27(8), Aug. 2001, 982-95 (Sage Publications, US).

23. Karoly, Paul; Bouffard, Leandre; (Trans.), 'Mental Health and Psychopathology from the Standpoint of Personal Goals: Conceptual, Empirical, and Clinical Aspects', *Revue Quebecoise de Psychologie*, Vol. 21(2), 2000, 115-51 (Revue Quebecoise de Psychologie, Canada).

24. Rubin, Henry H., 'Longitudinal Investigation of Factors Influencing the Development of Educational Goals Among Low-income Black Students' [Dissertation Abstract], *Dissertation Abstracts International*, Vol. 41(9-A), Mar. 1981, 4177.

25. Hofer, Jan; Chasiotis, Athanasios, 'Congruence of Life Goals and Implicit Motives as Predictors of Life Satisfaction, *Motivation & Emotion*, Vol. 27(3), Sep. 2003, 251-72 (Kluwer Academic Publishers, Netherlands).

26. Bay, Darlene; Daniel, Harold, 'The Theory of Trying and Goal-directed Behavior: The Effect of Moving Up the Hierarchy of Goals', *Psychology & Marketing*, Vol. 20(8), Aug. 2003, 669-84 (John Wiley & Sons, US).

27. Grant, Heidi; Dweck, Carol S., 'Clarifying Achievement Goals and Their Impact', *Journal of Personality & Social Psychology*, Vol. 85(3), Sep. 2003, 541-53.

28. Durik, Amanda M; Harackiewicz, Judith M., 'Achievement Goals and Intrinsic Motivation: Coherence, Concordance, and Achievement Orientation', *Journal of Experimental Social Psychology*. Vol. 39(4), Jul. 2003, 378-85 (Elsevier Science, UK).

29. Ee, Jessie; Moore, Phillip J.; Atputhasamy, Lourdusamy, 'High-achieving Students: Their Motivational Goals, Self-regulation and Achievement and Relationships to their Teachers' Goals and Strategy-based Instruction', *High Ability Studies*, Vol. 14(1), Jun. 2003, 23-39 (Taylor & Francis, UK).

30. Watson, Melanie Lemaistre, 'Role of Social Academic Goals in Relationships Among Fifth-graders' Interest, Achievement Goals, and Academic Outcomes' [Dissertation Abstract], *Dissertation Abstracts International*, Vol. 63(6-A), Jan. 2002, 2138.

31. Durik, Amanda M.; Harackiewicz, Judith M., 'Achievement Goals and Intrinsic Motivation: Coherence, Concordance, and Achievement Orientation', *Journal of Experimental Social Psychology*, Vol. 39(4) July 2003, 378-85.

32. Fein, Steven; Hoshino Browne, Etsuko; Davies, Paul G.; Spencer, Steven J., 'Self-Image Maintenance Goals and Sociocultural Norms in Motivated Social Perception', in Spencer, Steven J.; Fein, Steven (Eds.), *et al, Motivated Social Perception: The Ontario Symposium*, 2003, Vol. 9. *Ontario Symposium on Personality and Social Psychology*, pp. 21-44.

33. Shah, James Y.; Kruglanski, Arie W., 'When Opportunity Knocks: Bottom-up Priming of Goals by Means and its Effects on Self-regulation', *Journal of Personality & Social Psychology*, Vol. 84(6), Jun. 2003, 1109-22.

34. Dupeyrat, Caroline; Marine, Claudette, 'Implicit Theories of Intelligence, Achievement Goals, and Learning Strategy Use', *Psychologische Beitrage*, Vol. 43(1), 2001, 34-52 (Pabst Science Publishers, Germany).

35. Valle, Antonio; Cabanach, Ramon G.; Nunez, Jose C.; Gonzalez-Pienda, Julio; Rodriguez, Susana; Pineiro, Isabel, 'Multiple Goals, Motivation and Academic Learning', *British Journal of Educational Psychology*, Vol. 73(1), Mar. 2003, 71-87 (British Psychological Society, UK).

36. Boekaerts, Monique; Niemivirta, Markku, 'Self-regulated Learning: Finding a Balance Between Learning Goals and Ego-protective Goals' in Boekaerts, Monique; Pintrich, Paul R. (Eds.), *et al, Handbook of Self-regulation*, 2000, pp. 417-450 (Academic Press, San Diego, US), xxix, 783pp.

37. Dowson, Martin; McInerney, Dennis M., 'What Do Students Say About Their Motivational Goals?: Towards a More Complex and Dynamic Perspective on Student Motivation', *Contemporary Educational Psychology*, Vol. 28(1), Jan. 2003, 91-113 (Academic Press, US).

38. Shechtman, Nicole, 'Talking to People Versus Talking to Computers: Interpersonal Goals as a Distinguishing Factor' [Dissertation Abstract], *Dissertation Abstracts International: Section B: the Sciences & Engineering*, Vol. 63(4-B), Oct. 2002, 2101.

39. Senko, Corwin; Harackiewicz, Judith M., 'Performance Goals: The

468

Moderating Roles of Context and Achievement Orientation', *Journal of Experimental Social Psychology*, Vol. 38(6), Nov. 2002, 603-10 (Academic Press, US).

40. Tanaka, Ayumi; Okuno, Takuhiro; Yamauchi, Hirotsugu, 'Achievement Motives, Cognitive and Social Competence, and Achievement Goals in the Classroom', *Perceptual & Motor Skills*, Vol. 95(2), Oct. 2002, 445-58.
41. Dignum, Frank; Kinny, David; Sonenberg, Liz, 'From Desires, Obligations and Norms to Goals', *Cognitive Science Quarterly*, Vol. 2(3-4), 2002, 405-27 (Heldref Publications).
42. Ryska, Todd A., 'The Effects of Athletic Identity and Motivation Goals on Global Competence Perceptions of Student-athletes', *Child Study Journal*, Vol. 32(2), 2002, 109-29 (Revue Francophone de la Deficience Intellectuelle).
43. Lecci, Len; MacLean, Michael G.; Croteau, Nicole, 'Personal Goals as Predictors of College Student Drinking Motives, Alcohol Use and Related Problems', *Journal of Studies on Alcohol*, Vol. 63(5), Sep. 2002, 620-30 (Alcohol Research Documentation, US).
44. Cury, François; Da Fonseca, D.; Rufo, M.; Sarrazin, P., 'Perceptions of Competence, Implicit Theory of Ability, Perception of Motivational Climate, and Achievement Goals: A Test of Trichotomous Conceptualization of Endorsement of Achievement Motivational', *Perceptual & Motor Skills*, Vol. 95(1), Aug. 2002, 233-44.
45. Balaguer, Isabel; Duda, Joan L.; Atienza, Francisco L.; Mayo, Cristina, 'Situational and Dispositional Goals as Predictors of Perceptions of Individual and Team Improvement', *Psychology of Sport & Exercise*, Vol. 3(4), Oct. 2002, 293-308 (Elsevier Science, UK).
46. Halama, Peter, 'From Establishing Beliefs Through Pursuing Goals to Experiencing Fulfilment: Examining the Three-component Model of Personal Meaning in Life', *Studia Psychologica*, Vol. 44(2), 2002, 143-54 (Slovak Academy of Sciences Inst. of Experimental Psychology, Slovak Republic).

7 How Rewards Really Reduce Motivation

1. Bracken, Cheryl Campanella; Lombard, Matthew, 'Praise, Intrinsic Motivation, and Learning With Computers', *Journal of Communication*, Vol. 54(1), Mar. 2004, 22-37 (Oxford University Press, UK).
2. Papacharisis, Vassilios; Goudas, Marios, 'Perceptions About Intrinsic Motivation', *Perceptual & Motor Skills*, Vol. 97(3, Pt. 1), Dec. 2003, 689-96.
3. Koka, Andre; Hein, Vello, 'Intrinsic Motivation and Perceived Learning Environment', *Kineziologija*, Vol. 35(1), Jun. 2003, 5-13 (Fakultet za Fizicku Kulturu, Croatia).
4. Eisenberger, Robert; Shanock, Linda, 'Rewards, Intrinsic Motivation, and Creativity: A Case Study of Conceptual and Methodological Isolation', *Creativity Research Journal*, Vol. 15(2-3), Apr. 2003, 121-30 (Lawrence Erlbaum, US).
5. Murphy, Helen; Roopchand, Naomi, 'Intrinsic Motivation and Self-

esteem', *Educational Studies*, Vol. 29(2-3), Jun. 2003, 243-59 (Taylor & Francis, UK).

6. Oldfather, Penny; West, Jane; White, Jennifer; Wilmarth, Jill, 'Goal 1: Understanding Social Constructivism as a Basis for Meaningful Learning and Intrinsic Motivation', in Oldfather, Penny; West, Jane, *et al, Learning Through Children's Eyes: Social Constructivism and the Desire to Learn Psychology in the Classroom,* 1999, pp. 7-23 (American Psychological Assoc., US), x, 125pp.

7. Tauer, John M.; Harackiewicz, Judith M., 'The Effects of Cooperation and Competition on Intrinsic Motivation and Performance', *Journal of Personality & Social Psychology*, Vol. 86(6), Jun. 2004, 849-61 (American Psychological Assoc., US).

8. Lust, John A., 'Rewards and Intrinsic Motivation: Resolving the Controversy', *Personnel Psychology*, Vol. 57(1), Spr. 2004, 259-61 (Personnel Psychology, US).

9. Berry, Tiffany Hinz, 'Exploring the Role of Intrinsic Motivation in a Sample of Latino Children Attending an After-school Enrichment Program' [Dissertation Abstract], *Dissertation Abstracts International: Section B: The Sciences & Engineering*, Vol. 64(5-B), 2003, 2416.

10. Husman, Jenefer; Derryberry, W. Pitt; Crowson, H. Michael; Lomax, Richard, 'Instrumentality, Task Value, and Intrinsic Motivation: Making Sense of Their Independent Interdependence', *Contemporary Educational Psychology*, Vol. 29(1), Jan. 2004, 63-76 (Elsevier Science, UK).

11. Koka, A.; Hein, V., 'Perceptions of Feedback and Learning Environment as Predictors of Intrinsic Motivation', *Psychology of Sport & Exercise*, Vol. 4(4), Oct. 2003, 333-46 (Elsevier Science, UK).

12. Tsigilis, Nikolaos; Theodosiou, Argiris, 'Temporal Stability of the Intrinsic Motivation Inventory', *Perceptual & Motor Skills*, Vol. 97(1), Aug. 2003, 271-80.

13. Pierce, W. David; Cameron, Judy; Banko, Katherine M.; So, Sylvia, 'Positive Effects of Rewards and Performance Standards on Intrinsic Motivation', *Psychological Record*, Vol. 53(4), Fall 2003, 561-79 (Kenyon Coll. Psychology Dept., US).

14. Vansteenkiste, Maarten; Deci, Edward L., 'Competitively Contingent Rewards and Intrinsic Motivation: Can Losers Remain Motivated?', *Motivation & Emotion,* Vol. 27(4), Dec. 2003, 273-99 (Kluwer Academic Publishers, Netherlands).

15. Waterman, Alan S.; Schwartz, Seth J.; Goldbacher, Edie; Green, Hope; Miller, Christine; Philip, Susheel, 'Predicting the Subjective Experience of Intrinsic Motivation: The Roles of Self-Determination, the Balance of Challenges and Skills, and Self-Realization Values', *Personality & Social Psychology Bulletin*, Vol. 29(11), Nov. 2003, 1447-58 (Sage Publications, US).

16. Bouffard, Thérèse; Marcoux, Marie-France; Vezeau, Carole; Bordeleau Luce, 'Changes in Self-perceptions of Competence and Intrinsic Motivation', *British Journal of Educational Psychology*, Vol. 73(2), Jun. 2003, 171-86 (British Psychological Society, UK).

17. Higgins, E.T., 'Social Cognition: Learning About What Matters in the Social World', *European journal of Social Psychology*, 30, 2000, 3-39.

18. Van Yperen, Nico W.; Hagedoorn, Mariet, 'Do High Job Demands Increase Intrinsic Motivation or Fatigue or Both? The Role of Job Control and Job Social Support', *Academy of Management Journal*, Vol. 46(3), Jun. 2003, 339-48 (Academy of Management, US).

19. Kim, Byoung Jr.; Williams, Lavon; Gill, Diane L., 'A Cross-cultural Study of Achievement Orientation and Intrinsic Motivation', *International Journal of Sport Psychology*, Vol. 34(2), Apr.–Jun. 2003, 168-84 (Edizioni Luigi Pozzi, Italy).

20. Reitman, David, 'A Modest Proposal for a New Diagnostic Classification: Intrinsic Motivation Deficit Disorder (IMDD)', *Behavior Therapist*, Vol. 26(5), Jun. 2003, 310-11 (Assoc. for Advancement of Behavior Therapy, US).

21. Frederick-Recascino, Christina M.; Schuster-Smith, Hana, 'Competition and Intrinsic Motivation: A Comparison of Two Groups', *Journal of Sport Behavior*, Vol. 26(3), Sep. 2003, 240-54 (Univ. of South Alabama, US).

22. Vitterso, Joar, 'Flow Versus Life Satisfaction: A Projective Use of Cartoons to Illustrate the Difference Between the Evaluation Approach and the Intrinsic Motivation Approach to Subjective Quality of Life', *Journal of Happiness Studies*, Vol. 4(2), 2003, 141-67 (Kluwer Academic Publishers, Netherlands).

23. Durik, Amanda M.; Harackiewicz, Judith M., 'Achievement Goals and Intrinsic Motivation: Coherence, Concordance, and Achievement Orientation', *Journal of Experimental Social Psychology*, Vol. 39(4), Jul. 2003, 378-85 (Elsevier Science, UK).

24. Urdan, Tim, 'Intrinsic Motivation, Extrinsic Rewards, and Divergent Views of Reality', *Educational Psychology Review*, Vol. 15(3), Sep. 2003, 311-25 (Kluwer Academic Publishers, Netherlands).

25. Sweeney, Bryan James, 'Variables Related to Intrinsic Motivation', *Dissertation Abstracts International: Section B: The Sciences & Engineering*, Vol. 63(6-B), Jan. 2002, 3027.

26. Hassandra, Maria; Goudas, Marios; Chroni, Stiliani, 'Examining Factors Associated with Intrinsic Motivation', *Psychology of Sport & Exercise*, Vol. 4(3), Jul. 2003, 211-23.

27. Reeve, Johnmarshall; Nix, Glen; Hamm, Diane, 'Testing Models of the Experience of Self-determination in Intrinsic Motivation and the Conundrum of Choice', *Journal of Educational Psychology*, Vol. 95(2), Jun. 2003, 375-92 (American Psychological Assoc., US).

28. Sandrock, Paul, 'Creating Intrinsic Motivation to Learn World Languages', *Modern Language Journal*, Vol. 86(4), Win. 2002, 610-12 (Blackwell Publishing, UK).

29. Charbonneau, Danielle; Barling, Julian; Kelloway, E. Kevin, 'Transformational Leadership and Sports Performance: The Mediating Role of Intrinsic Motivation', *Journal of Applied Social Psychology*, Vol. 31(7), Jul. 2001, 1521-34 (V.H. Winston & Son, US).

30. Holden, Angela Dorothy, 'A Study of the Relationship Between Participation in Employer-provided Professional Development Programs and Project Managers' Intrinsic Motivation, Job Satisfaction and Organizational Commitment' [Dissertation Abstract],

Dissertation Abstracts International, Vol. 63(2-A), Aug. 2002, 775 (Universidad de Guadalajara, Mexico).

31. Deci, Edward L.; Ryan, Richard M.; Koestner, Richard, 'The Pervasive Negative Effects of Rewards on Intrinsic Motivation: Response to Cameron', (2001) *Review of Educational Research*, Vol. 71(1) Spr. 2001, 43-51 (American Educational Research Assoc., US).

32. Cameron, Judy, 'Negative Effects of Reward on Intrinsic Motivation – A Limited Phenomenon: Comment on Deci, Koestner, and Ryan', (2001) *Review of Educational Research*, Vol. 71(1), Spr. 2001, 29-42 (American Educational Research Assoc., US).

33. Deci, Edward L.; Koestner, Richard; Ryan, Richard M., 'Extrinsic Rewards and Intrinsic Motivation in Education: Reconsidered Once Again', *Review of Educational Research*, Vol. 71(1), Spr. 2001, 1-27 (American Educational Research Assoc., US).

34. Makri-Botsari, E., 'Causal Links Between Intrinsic Motivation, Self-esteem, and Unconditional Acceptance', in Riding, Richard J.; Rayner, Stephen G. (Eds.), *Self Perception. International Perspectives on Individual Differences*, Vol. 2, 209-20 (Ablex Publishing, Westport, CT, US), vi, 292pp.

35. Cury, F.; Elliot, A.; Sarrazin, P., Da Fonseca, D.; Rufo, M., 'The Trichotomous Achievement Goal Model and Intrinsic Motivation: A Sequential Mediational Analysis', *Journal of Experimental Social Psychology*, Vol. 38(5), Sep. 2002, 473-81 (Academic Press, US).

36. Ferrer-Caja, Emilio; Weiss, Maureen R., 'Cross-validation of a Model of Intrinsic Motivation', *Journal of Experimental Education*, Vol. 71(1) Fall 2002, 41-65 (Heldref Publications, US).

37. Eisenberg, Jacob, 'The Effects of Reward Schemes, Individualism-collectivism, and Intrinsic Motivation on Teams' Creative Performance' [Dissertation Abstract], *Dissertation Abstracts International: Section B: The Sciences & Engineering*, Vol. 62(11-B), Jun. 2002, 5417.

38. Katz, Helene S., 'The Relationship of Intrinsic Motivation, Cognitive Style, and Tolerance of Ambiguity, and Creativity' [Dissertation Abstract], *Dissertation Abstracts International: Section B: The Sciences & Engineering*, Vol. 62(11-B), Jun. 2002, 5419.

39. Alexandris, Konstantinos; Tsorbatzoudis, Charalambos; Grouios, George, 'Intrinsic Motivation, Extrinsic Motivation and Amotivation', *Journal of Leisure Research*, Vol. 34(3), 2002, 233-52 (National Recreation & Park Assoc., US).

40. Henderlong, Jennifer; Lepper, Mark R., 'The Effects of Praise on Children's Intrinsic Motivation: A Review and Synthesis', *Psychological Bulletin*, Vol. 128(5), Sep. 2002, 774-95 (American Psychological Assoc., US).

41. Davis, Sid; Wiedenbeck, Susan, 'The Mediating Effects of Intrinsic Motivation, Ease of Use and Usefulness Perceptions on Performance in First-time and Subsequent Computer Users', *Interacting with Computers*, Vol. 13(5), May 2001, 549-80 (Elsevier Science, UK).

42. Tauer, John M., Harackiewicz, Judith M., 'Winning Isn't Everything: Competition, Achievement Orientation, and Intrinsic Motivation', *Journal of Experimental Social Psychology*, Vol. 35(3), May 1999, 209-38 (Academic Press, US).

43. Koestner, Richard; Losier, Gaetan F., 'Distinguishing Three Ways of Being Highly Motivated: A Closer Look at Introjection, Identification, and Intrinsic Motivation' in Deci, Edward L.; Ryan, Richard M. (Eds.), *Handbook of Self-determination Research*, 2002, 101-21 (University of Rochester Press, NY, US), x, 470pp.

44. Cameron, Judy; Pierce, W. David, *Rewards and Intrinsic Motivation: Resolving the Controversy* [Authored Book], 2002 (Bergin & Garvey, CT, US), vi, 255pp.

45. Boyd, Michael P.; Weinmann, Carol; Yin, Zenong, 'The Relationship of Physical Self-perceptions and Goal Orientations to Intrinsic Motivation for Exercise', *Journal of Sport Behavior*, Vol. 25(1), Mar. 2002, 1-18 (Univ. of South Alabama, US).

46. B'enabou, Roland and Tirole, Jean, 'Intrinsic and Extrinsic Motivation', *Review of Economic Studies*, 70, 2003, 489-520.

47. Spotnitz, Sharon Hertz, 'Intrinsic Motivation in Learning Disabilities' [Dissertation Abstract], *Dissertation Abstracts International: Section B: The Sciences & Engineering*, Vol. 62(2-B), Aug. 2001, 1120.

48. Sinclair, Christina Dawn, 'Dispositional Goal Orientations, Perceptions of the Motivational Climate and Intrinsic Motivation' [Dissertation Abstract], *Dissertation Abstracts International*, Vol. 62(2-A), Aug. 2001, 509.

49. Willems, Patricia Pulido, 'The Effects of Situated Cognition, Academic Efficacy, and Intrinsic Motivation on Education Students' Learning' [Dissertation Abstract], *Dissertation Abstracts International*, Vol. 61(12-A), 2001, 4676.

50. Campanella Bracken; Cheryl Marie, 'Praise, Intrinsic Motivation, and Learning' [Dissertation Abstract], *Dissertation Abstracts International*, Vol. 61(10-A), May 2001, 3812.

51. Coskun, Hamit, 'The Effects of Out-group Comparison, Social Context Intrinsic Motivation, and Collective Identity in Brainstorming Groups' [Dissertation Abstract], *Dissertation Abstracts International: Section B: The Sciences & Engineering*, Vol. 61(7-B), Feb. 2001, 3898.

52. Cameron, Judy; Banko, Katherine M.; Pierce, W. David, 'Pervasive Negative Effects of Rewards on Intrinsic Motivation: The Myth Continues', *Behavior Analyst*, Vol. 24(1), Spr. 2001, 1-44 (Society for the Advancement of Behavior Analysis, US).

53. Gottfried, Adele Eskeles; Fleming, James S.; Gottfried, Allen W., 'Continuity of Academic Intrinsic Motivation from Childhood Through Late Adolescence: A Longitudinal Study', *Journal of Educational Psychology*, Vol. 93(1), Mar. 2001, 3-13 (American Psychological Assoc., US).

54. Conti, Regina; Collins, Mary Ann; Picariello, Martha L., 'The Impact of Competition on Intrinsic Motivation and Creativity: Considering Gender, Gender Segregation and Gender Role Orientation',

Personality & Individual Differences, Vol. 31(8), Dec. 2001, 1273-89 (Elsevier Science, UK).

55. Nakamura, Jeanne; Csikzentmihalyi, Mihaly, 'The Construction of Meaning Through Vital Engagement', [References], (Chapter in) Keyes, Corey; L. M., Haidt, Jonathan (Eds), *Flourishing: Positive Psychology and the Life Well-lived,* 2003, pp. 83-104 (American Psychological Assoc., US).

56. Wiest, Dudley J.; Wong, Eugene H.; Cervantes, Joseph M.; Craik, LuAnn; Kreil, Dennis A., 'Intrinsic Motivation', *Adolescence,* Vol. 36(141), Spr. 2001, 111-26 (Editions Medecine et Hygiene, Switzerland).

57. Guay, Frederic; Boggiano, Ann K.; Vallerand, Robert J., 'Autonomy Support, Intrinsic Motivation, and Perceived Competence: Conceptual and Empirical Linkages', *Personality & Social Psychology Bulletin,* Vol. 27(6), Jun. 2001, 643-50 (Sage Publications, US).

58. Fonseca, Antonio Manuel; Brito, Antonio de Paula, 'Psychometric Properties of the Intrinsic Motivation Inventory', *Analise Psicologica,* Vol. 19(1), Jan.–Mar. 2001, 59-76 (Instituto Superior de Psicologia Aplicada, Portugal).

59. Wu, Chin-yu, 'Facilitating Intrinsic Motivation in Individuals with Psychiatric Illness: A Study on the Effectiveness of an Occupational Therapy Intervention', *Occupational Therapy Journal of Research,* Vol. 21(3), Sum. 2001, 142-67 (SLACK Inc., US).

60. Conti, Regina, 'Time Flies: Investigating the Connection Between Intrinsic Motivation and the Experience of Time', *Journal of Personality,* Vol. 69(1), Feb. 2001, 1-26 (Blackwell Publishers, US).

61. Woolger, Christi; Power, Thomas G., 'Parenting and Children's Intrinsic Motivation in Age Group Swimming', *Journal of Applied Developmental Psychology,* Vol. 21(6), Nov.–Dec. 2000, 595-607 (Elsevier/JAI Press Inc., US).

62. Herzberg, F., 'One More Time: How Do You Motivate Employees?', *Harvard Business Review,* January 2003, 87-96.

63. Venkatesh, Viswanath, 'Determinants of Perceived Ease of Use: Integrating Control, Intrinsic Motivation, and Emotion into the Technology Acceptance Model', *Information Systems Research,* Vol. 11(4), 2000, 342-65 (Inst. for Operations Research & the Management Sciences, US).

64. Marr, J., 'Flow, Intrinsic Motivation, and 2nd Generation Cognitive Science', *Athletic Insight: Online Journal of Sport Psychology,* Vol. 2(3), Oct. 2000 (N.P. Athletic Insight, US).

65. Kaplan, Avi; Middleton, Michael J.; Urdan Tim; Midgley, Carol, 'Achievement Goals and Goal Structures', in Midgley, Carol (Ed.), *Goals, Goal Structures, and Patterns of Adaptive Learning,* 2002, pp. 21-53 (Lawrence Erlbaum Associates, Publishers, Mahwah, NJ, US), xvii, 311pp.

66. Midgley, Carol (Ed.), *Goals, Goal Structures, and Patterns of Adaptive Learning, op. cit.*

67. Elliot, Andrew J.; Thrash, Todd M., 'Approach-avoidance Motivation in Personality: Approach and Avoidance Temperaments and Goals',

Journal of Personality & Social Psychology, Vol. 82(5), May 2002, 804-18 (American Psychological Assoc., US).

68. Schvaneveldt, Paul L.; Miller, Brent C.; Berry, Helen E.; Lee, Thomas R., 'Academic Goals, Achievement, and Age at First Sexual Intercourse: Longitudinal, Bidirectional Influences', *Adolescence*. Vol. 36(144), Win. 2001, 767-87 (Libra Publishers, US).

69. Roberts, Brent W.; Robins, Richard W., 'Broad Dispositions, Broad Aspirations: The Intersection of Personality Traits and Major Life Goals', *Personality & Social Psychology Bulletin*, Vol. 26(10), Oct. 2000, 1284-96.

70. Lang, Frieder R.; Carstensen, Laura L., 'Time Counts: Future Time Perspective, Goals, and Social Relationships', *Psychology & Aging*, Vol. 17(1), Mar. 2002, 125-39 (American Psychological Assoc., US).

71. Rodriguez Martinez, Susana; Cabanach, Ramon G.; Pineiro, Isabel; Valle, Antonio; Nunez, José Carlos; Gonzalez-Pienda, Julio A., 'Approach Goals, Avoidance Goals and Multiple Academic Goals', *Psicothema*, Vol. 13(4), Nov. 2001, 546-50 (Universidad de Oviedo, Spain).

8 Do You Hate Your Job?

1. Sternberg, Robert J., 'Our Research Program Validating the Triarchic Theory of Successful Intelligence: Reply to Gottfredson', *Intelligence*, Vol. 31(4), 2003, 399-413 (Elsevier Science, UK).

2. Gottfredson, Linda S., 'Dissecting Practical Intelligence Theory: Its Claims and Evidence', *Intelligence*, Vol. 31(4), 2003, 343-97.

3. Richardson, Ken, 'What IQ Tests Test', *Theory & Psychology*, Vol. 12(3), Jun. 2002, 283-314 (Sage Publications, UK).

4. Sternberg, Robert J., 'Successful Intelligence: A New Approach to Leadership' in Riggio, Ronald E.; Murphy, Susan E. (Eds.), *et al*, *Multiple Intelligences and Leadership*. *LEA's Organization and Management Series*, 2002, pp. 9-28 (Lawrence Erlbaum Associates, Publishers, Mahwah, NJ, US), xv, 264pp.

5. Ambrose, Maureen L.; Seabright, Mark A.; Schmike, Marshall; 'Sabotage in the Workplace: The Role of Organizational Injustice', *Organizational Behavior & Human Decision Processes*, Sep. 2002, Vol. 89(1), pp. 947-65 (Elsevier Science, UK).

6. Dutton, Chris, 'Mentoring: The Contextualisation of Learning – Mentor, Protégé and Organisational Gain in Higher Education', *Education & Training*, Vol. 45(1), 2003, 22-29 (Emerald, UK).

7. Cohen, Geoffrey L.; Steele, Claude M.; Ross, Lee D., 'The Mentor's Dilemma: Providing Critical Feedback Across the Racial Divide', *Personality & Social Psychology Bulletin*, Vol. 25(10), Oct. 1999, 1302-18.

8. Hylan, Ian; Postlethwaite, Keith, 'The Success of Teacher-pupil Mentoring in Raising Standards of Achievement', *Education & Training*, Vol. 40(2), 1998, 68-77 (Emerald, UK).

9. Allen, Tammy D., 'Mentoring Others: A Dispositional and Motivational Approach', *Journal of Vocational Behavior*, Vol. 62(1), Feb. 2003, 134-54 (Elsevier Science, US).

10. Reichert, Tiffany Michelle, 'A Mentor/Sponsorship Approach' [Dissertation Abstract], *Dissertation Abstracts International: Section B: The Sciences & Engineering,* Vol. 63(2-B), Aug. 2002, 1045 (Transaction Periodicals Consortium, Rutgers University, US).

11. Fagenson-Eland, Ellen A.; Baugh, S. Gayle, 'Personality Predictors of Protégé Mentoring History', *Journal of Applied Social Psychology,* Vol. 31(12), Dec. 2001, 2502-17 (V.H. Winston & Son, US).

12. Hoyle, John R., *Leadership and the Force of Love: Six Keys to Motivating with Love* [Authored Book], 2002, xiv, 120pp (Sage Publications, US).

13. Maki, Diane Mae, 'Work Motivators', *Dissertation Abstracts International,* Vol. 61(12-A), 2001, 4853.

14. Ferguson, Eamonn; James, David; O'Hehir, Fiona; Sanders, Andrea, 'Pilot Study of the Roles of Personality, References and Personal Statements in Relation to Performance Over the Five Years of a Medical Degree', *BMJ,* Feb. 2003, Vol. 326(7386), pp. 429-31 (*BMJ,* Publishing Group, UK).

15. Miles, Rhonda M., 'The Influence of Academic Motivation in At Risk High School Students' [Dissertation Abstract], *Dissertation Abstracts International,* Vol. 61(6-A), Jan. 2000, 2198.

16. Curtis, E. Carroll; Eaton, William W.; Gillepsie, Robin Mary; Manderscheid, Ronald W.; Wagener, Diane, 'Surveillance of Psychological Disorders in the Workplace: Panel Comments', (Chapter in), Keita, Gwendolyn Puryear; Sauter, Steven L. (Eds.), 1992, *Work and Well-being: An Agenda for the 1990s,* pp. 97-114 (American Psychological Assoc., US).

17. Kasl, Stanislav V.; Bernacki, Edward; Bromet, Evelyn; Curtis, E. Carroll; Eaton, William W.; Fine, Lawrence J.; Gillepsie, Robin Mary; Manderschied, Ronald W.; Murphy, Lawrence R.; *et al,* 'Surveillance of Psychological Disorders in the Workplace', (Chapter in), Keita, Gwendolyn Puryear; Sauter, Steven L. (Eds.), 1992, *Work and Well-being: An Agenda for the 1990s,* pp. 73-95 (American Psychological Assoc., US).

18. Brooks, Val, 'In the Lion's Den?', *Educational Studies,* Vol. 26(1), Mar. 2001, 101-14 (Lawrence Erlbaum, US).

19. Park, Nansook; Peterson, Christopher; Seligman, Martin E.P., 'Strengths of Character and Well-being', *Journal of Social and Clinical Psychology,* Oct. 2004, Vol. 23(5), pp. 603-19, (Guilford Publications, US).

20. *Ibid.*

21. Pawlak, Stacey A., 'The Academic Mentoring Process: A Survey of Important Aspects' [Dissertation Abstract], *Dissertation Abstracts International: Section B: The Sciences & Engineering,* Vol. 59(9-B), Mar. 1999, 5145.

22. Day, R.; Allen, T.D. (in Press), 'The Relationship Between Career Motivation and Self-Efficacy with Protégé Career Success', *Journal of Vocational Behavior.*

23. Wayne, Sandy J.; Liden, Robert C.; Kraimer, Maria L.; Graf, Isabel K.; 'The Role of Human Capital, Motivation and Supervisor

Sponsorship in Predicting Career Success', *Journal of Organizational Behavior*, Vol. 20(5), Sep. 1999, 577-95 (John Wiley & Sons, US).

24. Cohen, Geoffrey L.; Steele, Claude M.; Ross, Lee D., 'The Mentor's Dilemma: Providing Critical Feedback Across the Racial Divide', *Personality & Social Psychology Bulletin*, Vol. 25(10), Oct. 1999, 1302-18 (Sage Publications, US).

25. Hylan, Ian; Postlethwaite, Keith, 'The Success of Teacher-pupil Mentoring in Raising Standards of Achievement', *Education & Training*, Vol. 40(2), 1998, 68-77 (MCB Univ. Press, UK).

26. Fine, Leslie M.; Pullins, Ellen Bolman, 'Peer Mentoring in the Industrial Sales Force: An Exploratory Investigation of Men and Women in Developmental Relationships', *Journal of Personal Selling & Sales Management*, Vol. 18(4), Fall 1998, 89-103 (Pi Sigma Epsilon, US).

27. Gerstner, Charlotte Rees, 'Leadership Relationships and Work Group Effectiveness: A Multi-level Empirical Examination' [Dissertation Abstract], *Dissertation Abstracts International: Section B: The Sciences & Engineering*, Vol. 59(6-B), Dec. 1998, 3104.

28. Schmidt, Laura Christine, 'A Motivational Approach to the Prediction of Mentoring Relationship Satisfaction and Future Intention to Mentor' [Dissertation Abstract], *Dissertation Abstracts International: Section B: The Sciences & Engineering*, Vol. 58(11-B), May 1998, 6269.

29. McAdams, Dan P.; de St. Aubin, Ed (Eds.), *Generativity and Adult Development: How and Why We Care for the Next Generation*, 1998, xxiv, 511pp (American Psychological Assoc., US).

30. Cameron, R.J., 'Discipline in the United Kingdom', *School Psychology Review*, Vol. 27(1), 1998, 33-44 (National Assoc. of School Psychologists, US).

31. Cameron, R.J., 'Discipline in the United Kingdom', *op. cit.*

32. Gayle, Susan Catellier, 'Workplace Purpose and Meaning' [Dissertation Abstract], *Dissertation Abstracts International*, Vol. 58(5-A), Nov. 1997, 1809.

33. Levine, Jane Chamedes, 'Personal Creativity and Classroom Teaching' [Dissertation Abstract], *Dissertation Abstracts International*, Vol. 57(10-A), Apr. 1997, 4260 (Univ. Microfilms International, US).

34. Fitzsimmons, James Alan, 'Construction and Praxis' [Dissertation Abstract], *Dissertation Abstracts International*, Vol. 57(7-A), Jan. 1997, 2854.

35. Martin, Robert, Jr., 'A Case Study of a Mentoring Program' [Dissertation Abstract], *Dissertation Abstracts International*, Vol. 57(7-A), Jan. 1997, 2880.

36. Bell, Carl C., 'Promotion of Mental Health Through Coaching', *Journal of the National Medical Association*, Vol. 89(8), Aug. 1997, 517-20 (National Medical Assoc., US).

37. Giordano, Francesca G., 'The Whole Person at Work: An Integrative Vocational Intervention Model for Women's Workplace Issues', *Journal for Specialists in Group Work*, Vol. 20(1), Mar. 1995, 4-13 (Sage Publications, US).

9 Don't Bleed in the Water (How to Get Your Boss's Job)

1. Chaiken, Shelly L.; Gruenfeld, Deborah H.; Judd, Charles M., 'Persuasion in Negotiations and Conflict Situations', in Morton, D; Coleman, Peter T. (Eds.), *The Handbook of Conflict Resolution: Theory and Practice*, 2000, pp. 144-65, xiii, 649pp (Jossey, Bass, Wiley, US).

2. Boyer, Mark A., 'Coalitions, Motives, and Payoffs', *Social Science Computer Review*, Vol. 17(3), Fall 1999, 305-12 (Sage Publications, US).

3. Graber, Julia A.; Brooks-Gunn, Jeanne, ' "Sometimes I Think That You Don't Like Me"' in Cox, Martha J.; Brooks-Gunn, Jeanne (Eds.), *Conflict and Cohesion in Families: Causes and Consequences: The Advances in Family Research Series*, 1999, pp. 207-42, xiv, 362pp (Lawrence Earlbaum Assoc., US).

4. Large, Michael D., 'The Effectiveness of Gifts as Unilateral Initiatives in Bargaining', *Sociological Perspectives*, Vol. 42(3), Fall 1999, 525-42 (Univ. of California Press, US).

5. Mintu-Wimsatt, Alma; Lozada, Hector R., 'Personality and Negotiation Revisited', *Psychological Reports*, Vol. 84(3, Pt. 2), Jun. 1999, 1159-70 (Psychological Reports, US).

6. Rose, Suzanna; Danner, Mona J. E., 'Money Matters: The Art of Negotiation for Women Faculty' in Collins, Lynn H.; Chrisler, Joan C. (Eds.), *et al, Career Strategies for Women in Academe: Arming Athena*, 1998, pp. 157-86, xviii, 333pp (Sage Publications, US).

7. Schellenberg, James A., *Conflict Resolution: Theory, Research, and Practice* [Authored Book], 1996 (State University of New York Press, US), ix, 247pp.

8. Maier, Kurt M., 'An Investigation of the Interaction of Self-monitoring and Communicative Conditions in Negotiation Settings' [Dissertation Abstract], *Dissertation Abstracts International*, Vol. 53(3-A), Sep. 1992, 885.

9. Rahim, M. Afzalur (Ed.), *Theory and Research in Conflict Management* [Edited Book], 1990 (Greenwood Press, Westport, CT, US), x, 251pp.

10. Smith, H. W., *Introduction to Social Psychology* [Authored Book], 1987 (Prentice Hall, US), xi, 449pp.

11. Carnevale, Peter J., 'Mediation of International Disputes', *Applied Social Psychology Annual*, Vol. 6, 1985, 87-105 (Sage Publications, US).

12. Köszegi, Sabine; Kersten, Gregory, 'Joint Negotiation Teaching', *Group Decision & Negotiation*. Vol. 12(4), Jul. 2003, 337-45 (Kluwer Academic Publishers, Netherlands).

13. Neumann, Dirk; Benyoucef, Morad; Bassil, Sarita; Vachon, Julie, 'State of the Art E-Negotiation Systems', *Group Decision & Negotiation*, Vol. 12(4), Jul. 2003, 287-310.

14. Weiss, Joshua N., 'Sequencing in Negotiation and a Proper Acknowledgment', *Negotiation Journal,* Vol. 19(3), Jul. 2003, 267-8 (Blackwell Publishing, UK).

15. Lin, Xiaohua; Miller, Stephen J., 'Negotiation Approaches: Direct and Indirect Effect of National Culture', *International Marketing Review*, Vol. 20(3), 2003, 286-303 (Emerald, UK).

16. Swenson, Elizabeth V., 'Using Negotiation and Mediation to Resolve Disputes' in Benjamin, Ludy T.; Nodine, Barbara F. (Eds.), *et al,*

Activities Handbook for the Teaching of Psychology, Vol. 4, 1999, 350-4 (American Psychological Assoc., US), xiii, 408pp.

17. Volkema, Roger J., 'Demographic, Cultural, and Economic Predictors of Perceived Ethicality of Negotiation Behavior: A Nine-country Analysis', *Journal of Business Research*, Vol. 57(1), Jan. 2004, 69-78 (Elsevier Science, UK).

18. Arnfast, Juni Soderberg; Jorgensen, J. Normann; 'Code-Switching as a Communication, Learning, and Social Negotiation Strategy', *International Journal of Applied Linguistics*, Vol. 13(1), 2003, 23-53 (Blackwell Publishing, UK).

19. Humphrey, Stephen E.; Ellis, Aleksander P.J.; Conlon, Donald E.; Tinsley, Catherine H., 'Brokered Ultimatums: Applying Negotiation and Justice Theory', *Journal of Applied Psychology*, Vol. 89(3), Jun. 2004, 466-82 (American Psychological Assoc., US).

20. Rapaport, William J., 'What Did You Mean by That? Misunderstanding, Negotiation, and Syntactic Semantics', *Minds & Machines*, Vol. 13(3), Aug. 2003, 397-427 (Kluwer Academic Publishers, Netherlands).

21. Jaworski, Adam; Ylanne-McEwen, Virpi; Thurlow, Crispin; Lawson, Sarah; Jaworski, Adam, 'Social Roles and Negotiation of Status', *Journal of Sociolinguistics*, Vol. 7(2), May 2003, 135-63 (Blackwell Publishing, UK).

22. Seibert, Scott E.; Kraimer, Maria L.; Crant, J. Michael, 'What Do Proactive People Do? A Longitudinal Model Linking Proactive Personality and Career Success', *Personnel Psychology*, Vol. 54(4), Win. 2001, 845-74 (Personnel Psychology, US).

23. Linehan, Margaret; Scullion, Hugh, 'Challenges for Female International Managers: Evidence from Europe', *Journal of Managerial Psychology*, Vol. 16(3-4), 2001, 215-28 (MCB Univ. Press, UK).

24. Maman, Daniel, 'Who Accumulates Directorships of Big Business Firms', *Human Relations*, Vol. 53(5), May 2000, 603-29 (Sage Publications, UK).

25. Bedi, Anjali, 'The Effect of Demographic Diversity on the Quality of Exchange Relationship in a Leader-member Dyad' [Dissertation Abstract], *Dissertation Abstracts International: Section B: the Sciences & Engineering*, Vol. 60(12-B), 2000, 6402.

10 Money, Money, Money

1. Hayhoe, Celia Ray; Leach, Lauren J.; Turner, Pamela R.; Bruin, Marilyn J.; Lawrence, Frances C., 'Differences in Spending Habits and Credit Use of College Students', *Journal of Consumer Affairs*, Vol. 34(1), Sum. 2000, 113-33 (American Council on Consumer Interests, US).

2. Arndt, Jamie; Solomon, Sheldon; Kasser, Tim; Sheldon, Kennon M., 'The Urge to Splurge Revisited: Further Reflections on Applying Terror Management Theory to Materialism and Consumer Behavior', *Journal of Consumer Psychology*, Vol. 14(3), 2004, 225-9 (Lawrence Erlbaum, US).

3. Rindfleisch, Aric; Burroughs, James E., 'Terrifying Thoughts, Terrible Materialism? Contemplations on a Terror Management Account

of Materialism and Consumer Behavior', *Journal of Consumer Psychology*, Vol. 14(3), 2004, 219-24.

4. Arndt, Jamie; Solomon, Sheldon; Kasser, Tim; Sheldon, Kennon M., 'The Urge to Splurge: A Terror Management Account of Materialism and Consumer Behavior', *Journal of Consumer Psychology*, Vol. 14(3), 2004, 198-212.

5. Christopher, Andrew N.; Schlenker, Barry R., 'Materialism and Affect: The Role of Self-presentational Concerns', *Journal of Social & Clinical Psychology*, Vol. 23(2), Apr. 2004, 260-72 (Guilford Publications, US).

6. Webel, Charles; Stigliano, Tony, 'Are We "Beyond Good and Evil"? Radical Psychological Materialism and the "Cure" for Evil', *Theory & Psychology*, Vol. 14(1), Feb. 2004, 81-103 (Sage Publications, US).

7. Chang, LinChiat; Arkin, Robert M., 'Materialism as an Attempt to Cope With Uncertainty', *Psychology & Marketing*, Vol. 19(5), May 2002, 389-406 (John Wiley & Sons, US).

8. Kasser, Tim, *The High Price of Materialism* [Authored Book], 2002 (MIT Press, Cambridge, Mass., US), xvi, 149pp.

9. *Ibid.*

10. Martin, Nora M., 'Materialism, Ethics and Generation X' [Dissertation Abstract], *Dissertation Abstracts International*, Vol. 64(3-A), 2003, 993.

11. Roberts, James A.; Manolis, Chris; Tanner, John F. (Jeff) Jr., 'Family Structure, Materialism, and Compulsive Buying: A Reinquiry and Extension', *Journal of the Academy of Marketing Science*, Vol. 31(3), Sum. 2003, 300-11 (Sage Publications, US).

12. Watson, John J., 'The Relationship of Materialism to Spending Tendencies, Saving, and Debt', *Journal of Economic Psychology*, Vol. 24(6), Dec. 2003, 723-39 (Elsevier Science, UK).

13. Jantzen, Wolfgang, 'Psychological Materialism' in Robbins, Dorothy; Stetsenko, Anna (Eds.), *Voices within Vygotsky's Non-classical Psychology: Past, Present, Future*, 2002, pp. 101-12 (Hauppauge, Nova Science Publishers Inc., NY, US), xi, 187pp.

14. Harmon, Mark D., 'Affluenza: Television Use and Cultivation of Materialism', *Mass Communication & Society*, Vol. 4(4), 2001, 405-18 (Lawrence Erlbaum, US).

15. Kasser, Tim; Grow Kasser, Virginia, 'The Dreams of People High and Low in Materialism', *Journal of Economic Psychology*, Vol. 22(6) Dec. 2001, 693-719 (Elsevier Science, UK).

16. Buijzen, Moniek; Valkenburg, Patti M., 'The Effects of Television Advertising on Materialism, Parent-child Conflict, and Unhappiness: A Review of Research', *Journal of Applied Developmental Psychology*, Vol. 24(4), Sep. 2003, 437-56 (Elsevier Science, UK).

17. Noordhof, Paul, 'Not Old . . . But Not That New Either: Explicability, Emergence, and the Characterisation of Materialism' in Walter, Sven (Ed.), Inst. fur Philosophie; U. Saarlandes, *et al, Physicalism and Mental Causation: The Metaphysics of Mind and Action*, 2003, pp. 85-108 (Imprint Academic, Charlottesville, VA, US), vii, 362pp.

18. Goldberg, Marvin E.; Gorn, Gerald J.; Peracchio, Laura A.; Bamossy, Gary, 'Understanding Materialism Among Youth', *Journal of Consumer Psychology*, Vol. 13(3), 2003, 278-88.

19. Solomon, Sheldon; Greenberg, Jeffrey L.; Pyszczynski, Thomas A., 'Lethal Consumption: Death-denying Materialism' in Kasser, Tim; Kanner, Allen D. (Eds.), *Psychology and Consumer Culture: The Struggle for a Good Life in a Materialistic World*, 2004, pp. 127-46. (American Psychological Assoc., US), xi, 297pp.

20. Csikszentmihalyi, Mihaly, 'Materialism and the Evolution of Consciousness' in Kasser, Tim; Kanner, Allen D. (Eds.), *Psychology and Consumer Culture: The Struggle for a Good Life in a Materialistic World*, 2004, pp. 91-106.

21. Kosmicki, Frank X., 'Materialism, Attachment Style, and Relational Ethics: Interpersonal Correlates of Materialistic Orientation' [Dissertation Abstract], *Dissertation Abstracts International: Section B: The Sciences & Engineering*, Vol. 63(6-B), Jan. 2002, 3056.

22. Vercueil, Laurent, 'Materialism', *Epilepsy & Behavior*, Vol. 3(3, Pt. 1), Jun. 2002, 298 (Elsevier Science, UK).

23. Little, Eric G., 'Moderate Materialism: Toward a Unified Ontology of Consciousness' [Dissertation Abstract], *Dissertation Abstracts International*, Vol. 63(5-A), Dec. 2002, 1862.

24. Kihlstrom, John F., 'The Seductions of Materialism and the Pleasures of Dualism: Comment', *Journal of Consciousness Studies*, Vol. 9(11), Nov. 2002, 30-34 (Imprint Academic, US).

25. Kasser, Tim, 'The High Price of Materialism', *Psychological Record*, Vol. 53(1), Win. 2003, 153-4 (Kenyon Coll. Psychology Dept., US).

26. Burroughs, James E.; Rindfleisch, Aric, 'Materialism and Well-being: A Conflicting Values Perspective', *Journal of Consumer Research*, Vol. 29(3), Dec. 2002, 348-70 (Univ. of Chicago Press, US).

27. Ahuvia, Aaron C.; Wong, Nancy Y., 'Personality and Values Based Materialism: Their Relationship and Origins', *Journal of Consumer Psychology*, Vol. 12(4), 2002, 389-402.

28. Chang, LinChiat; Arkin, Robert M., 'Materialism as an Attempt to Cope with Uncertainty', *Psychology & Marketing*, Vol. 19(5), May 2002, 389-406 (John Wiley & Sons, US).

29. Sebastian, K.A.; Matthew, V. George, 'Relationship Between PSI Experience and Materialism – Spiritualism Orientation Among College Students of Kerala', *Journal of Indian Psychology*, Vol. 20(1), Jan. 2002, 38-42 (Inst. for Yoga & Consciouness, India).

30. Clarke, Irvine; Micken, Kathleen S., 'An Exploratory Cross-cultural Analysis of the Values of Materialism', *Journal of International Consumer Marketing*, Vol. 14(4), 2002, 65-89 (Haworth Press, US).

31. Saunders, Barbara, 'Materialism', in Saunders, Barbara; van Brakel, Jaap (Eds.), *Theories, Technologies, Instrumentalities of Color: Anthropological and Historiographic Perspectives*, 2002, pp. 189-99 (University Press of America, Inc., Lanham, MD, US), 407pp.

32. Swinyard, William R.; Kau, Ah-Keng; Phua, Hui-Yin, 'Happiness, Materialism, and Religious Experience in the US and Singapore', *Journal of Happiness Studies*, Vol. 2(1), 2001, 13-32 (Kluwer Academic, Netherlands).

33. Wan Jusoh; Wan Jamaliah, Heaney; Joo-Gim; Goldsmith, Ronald E., 'Self-ratings of Materialism and Status Consumption', *Psychological*

Reports, Vol. 88(3, Pt. 2), Jun. 2001, 1142-44 (Psychological Reports, US).

11 See You at the Top

1. Tucker, Corinna Jenkins; McHale, Susan M.; Crouter, Ann C., 'Conflict Resolution: Links with Adolescents' Family Relationships and Individual Well-being', *Journal of Family Issues*. Vol. 24(6), Sep. 2003, 715-36 (Sage Publications, US).

2. Jacobson, Steven Marvin, 'The Attachment, Caregiving, and Sexual Systems Relationship to Conflict Communication in Adult Pair-bond Relationships', *Dissertation Abstracts International: Section B: The Sciences & Engineering*, Vol. 64(5-B), 2003, 2440.

3. Lin, Su-Mei, 'Relationship Among Conflict Management Styles, Employees' Job Satisfaction and Team Effectiveness' [Dissertation Abstract], *Dissertation Abstracts International*, Vol. 64(5-A), 2003, 1750.

4. Alfonso, Laura Magdalena, 'Mentoring Relationships With Aggressive Children' [Dissertation Abstract], *Dissertation Abstracts International: Section B: The Sciences & Engineering*, Vol. 64(4-B), 2003, 1890.

5. Angus, Lynne; Korman, Yifaht, 'Conflict, Coherence and Change' in Fussell, Susan R. (Ed.), *The Verbal Communication of Emotions: Interdisciplinary Perspectives*, 2002, pp. 151-65 (Lawrence Erlbaum Associates, Publishers, US), viii, 294pp.

6. Peterson, Randall S.; Behfar, Kristin Jackson, 'The Dynamic Relationship Between Performance Feedback, Trust, and Conflict', *Organizational Behavior & Human Decision Processes*, Vol. 92(1-2), Sep.–Nov. 2003, 102-112 (Elsevier Science, UK).

7. Carstarphen, Berenike O.H.M., Jr., 'Shift Happens: Transformations During Small Group Interventions in Protracted Social Conflicts' [Dissertation Abstract], *Dissertation Abstracts International*, Vol. 64(2-A), 2003, 634.

8. Richards, Jane M.; Butler, Emily A.; Gross, James J., 'Emotion Regulation in Romantic Relationships: The Cognitive Consequences of Concealing Feelings', *Journal of Social & Personal Relationships*, Vol. 20(5), Oct. 2003, 599-620 (Sage Publications, US).

9. Bayazit, Mahmut; Mannix, Elizabeth A., 'Should I Stay Or Should I Go?', *Small Group Research*, Vol. 34(3), Jun. 2003, 290-321 (Sage Publications, US).

10. Hobman, Elizabeth V.; Bordia, Prashant; Irmer, Bernd; Chang, Artemis, 'The Expression Of Conflict', *Small Group Research*, Vol. 33(4), Aug. 2002, 439-65.

11. Bodin, Arthur M., 'Relationship Conflict – Verbal and Physical: Conceptualizing an Inventory for Assessing Process and Content' in Kaslow, Florence W. (Ed.), *Handbook of Relational Diagnosis and Dysfunctional Family Patterns: Wiley Series in Couples and Family Dynamics and Treatment*, 1996, pp. 371-93 (John Wiley & Sons. UK), xxvi, 566pp.

12. De Dreu, Carsten K.W.; Weingart, Laurie R., 'Task Versus Relationship Conflict, Team Performance, and Team Member Satisfaction: A Meta-analysis', *Journal of Applied Psychology*,

Vol. 88(4), Aug. 2003, 741-9 (American Psychological Assoc., US).

13. Chen, Dora W., 'Promoting the Development of Competent Conflict Resolution Skills', *Early Childhood Education Journal*, Vol. 30(4), Sum. 2003, 203-8 (Kluwer Academic Publishers, Netherlands).

14. Janz, Teresa Ann, 'Preventing "Wars" with Community Mediation' [Dissertation Abstract], *Dissertation Abstracts International: Section B: The Sciences & Engineering*, Vol. 63(7-B), Feb. 2003, 3516.

15. Burt, S. Alexandra; Krueger, Robert F.; McGue, Matt, Iacono, William, 'Parent-child Conflict and the Comorbidity Among Childhood Externalizing Disorders', *Archives of General Psychiatry*, Vol. 60(5), May 2003, 505-13 (American Medical Assoc., US).

16. Hobman, Elizabeth V.; Bordia, Prashant; Gallois, Cynthia, 'Consequences of Feeling Dissimilar from Others in a Work Team, *Journal of Business & Psychology*, Vol. 17(3), Spr. 2003, 301-25 (Kluwer Academic Publishers, Netherlands).

17. Waska, Robert, 'Craving, Longing, Denial and the Dangers of Change: Clinical Manifestations of Greed', *Psychoanalytic Review*, Vol. 89(4), Aug. 2002, 505-31 (Guilford Publications, US).

18. Colmenares, Fernando; Zaragoza, Felix; Hernandez-Lloreda, Maria Victoria, 'Grooming and Coercion', *Behaviour*, Vol. 139(11-12), Nov. 2002, 1525-53 (E.J. Brill Publishers, Netherlands).

19. Seguin-Levesque, Chantal; Laliberte, Marie Lyne N.; Pelletier, Luc G.; Blanchard, Celine; Vallerand, Robert J., 'Harmonious and Obsessive Passion', *Journal of Applied Social Psychology*, Vol. 33(1), Jan. 2003, 197-221 (V. H. Winston & Son, US).

20. Hall, Ruth L.; Greene, Beverly, 'Not Any One Thing: The Complex Legacy of Social Class', *Journal of Lesbian Studies*, Vol. 6(1), 2002, 65-74 (Haworth Press, US).

21. Kanoy, Korrel; Ulku-Steiner, Beril; Cox, Martha; Burchinal, Margaret, 'Marital Relationship and Individual Psychological Characteristics', *Journal of Family Psychology*, Vol. 17(1) Mar. 2003, 20-8 (American Psychological Assoc., US).

22. Kingsfogel, Kristen M., 'Testing the Integration of Social Learning and Attachment Theories' [Dissertation Abstract], *Dissertation Abstracts International: Section B: The Sciences & Engineering*, Vol. 63(4-B), Oct, 2002, 2062.

23. Zak, Ann; Coulter, Colleen; Giglio, Sabrina; Hall, Jennifer; Sanford, Stephanie; Pellowski, Nancy, 'Do His Friends and Family Like Me? Predictors of Infidelity in Intimate Relationships', *North American Journal of Psychology*, Vol. 4(2), 2002, 287-90 (North American Journal of Psychology, US).

24. Polzer, Jeffrey T.; Milton, Laurie P.; Swann, William B., 'Capitalizing on Diversity', *Administrative Science Quarterly*, Vol. 47(2), Jun. 2002, 296-324 (Council for Exceptional Children).

25. Ha, Soo Mi, 'Gender Differences in Organizational Conflict' [Dissertation Abstract], *Dissertation Abstracts International: Section B: The Sciences & Engineering,* Vol. 63(2-B), Aug. 2002, 1074.

26. Tyrell, Dennis E., 'Understanding Coping Strategies' [Dissertation Abstract], *Dissertation Abstracts International: Section B: The Sciences & Engineering*, Vol. 63(2-B), Aug. 2002, 1053.

27. Kennedy, Janet Krone; Bolger, Niall; Shrout, Patrick E., 'Conflict in Adult Intimate Relationships', *Journal of Personality*, Vol. 70(6), Dec. 2002, 1051-77 (Blackwell Publishers, US).

28. McCallum, Debra Moehle; Arnold, Susan E.; Bolland, John M., 'Women Talk About Stress', *Journal of Social Distress & the Homeless*, Vol. 11(3), Jul. 2002, 249-63 (Kluwer Academic/Plenum Publishers, US).

29. Randel, Amy E., 'Identity Salience', *Journal of Organizational Behavior*, Vol. 23(6), Sep. 2002, 749-66 (John Wiley & Sons, US).

30. Cramer, Duncan, 'Relationship Satisfaction and Conflict', *Journal of Psychology*, Vol. 136(1), Jan. 2002, 75-81 (Heldref Publications, US).

31. Holt, Melissa K.; Espelage, Dorothy L., 'Problem-solving Skills and Relationship Attributes', *Journal of Counseling & Development*, Vol. 80(3), Sum. 2002, 346-54 (American Counseling Assoc., US).

32. Kroeger, Christine; Hahlweg, Kurt; Braukhaus, Christoph; Fehm-Wolfsdorf, Gabriele; Groth, Thomas, 'Conflict Areas Within Intimate Relationships', *Verhaltenstherapie & Verhaltensmedizin*, Vol. 22(2), 2001, 123-36 (Pabst Science Publishers, Germany).

33. Tross, Susan, 'Reaching the Hard to Reach', *AIDS & Behavior*, Vol. 5(2), Jun. 2001, 131-9 (Kluwer Academic/Plenum Publishers, Netherlands).

34. Bono, Joyce E.; Boles, Terry L.; Judge, Timothy A.; Lauver, Kristy J., 'The Role of Personality in Task and Relationship Conflict', *Journal of Personality*, Vol. 70(3), Jun. 2002, 311-44 (Blackwell Publishers, US).

35. Beckerman, Nancy; Sarracco, Michele, 'Integrating Emotionally Focused Therapy and Attachment Theory', *Family Therapy*, Vol. 29(1) 2002, 23-32 (Libra Publishers, US).

36. Martins, Luis L.; Eddleston, Kimberly A.; Veiga, John F. 'Jack', 'Moderators of the Relationship Between Work-family Conflict and Career Satisfaction', *Academy of Management Journal*, Vol. 45(2), Apr. 2002, 399-409 (Academy of Management, US).

37. Spence, Susan H.; Najman, Jake M.; Bor, William; O'Callaghan, Michael; Williams, Gail M., 'Maternal Anxiety and Depression', *Journal of Child Psychology & Psychiatry & Allied Disciplines*, Vol. 43(4), May 2002, 457-70, (Blackwell Publishers, UK).

38. Shackelford, Todd K.; Buss, David M., 'Marital Satisfaction and Spousal Cost-infliction', *Personality & Individual Differences*, Vol. 28(5), May 2000, 917-28 (Elsevier Science, UK).

39. Metz, Michael E.; Epstein, Norman, 'The Role of Relationship Conflict', *Journal of Sex & Marital Therapy*, Vol. 28(2), Mar.–Apr. 2002, 139-64 (Taylor & Francis, UK).

40. Montoya-Weiss, Mitzi M.; Massey, Anne P.; Song, Michael, 'Getting it Together: Temporal Coordination and Conflict Management', *Academy of Management Journal*, Vol. 44(6), Dec. 2001, 1251-62 (Academy of Management, US).

12 Is Time Running Out? Time to Get Ahead

1. Onwuegbuzie, Anthony J., 'Academic Procrastination', *Assessment & Evaluation in Higher Education*, Vol. 29(1), Feb. 2004, 3-19 (Taylor & Francis, UK).

2. Jonas, Eva; Schimel, Jeff; Greenberg, Jeff; Pyszczynski, Tom, 'The

Scrooge Effect: Evidence That Mortality Salience Increases Prosocial Attitudes and Behaviour', *Personality & Social Psychology Bulletin*, Vol. 28(10), Oct. 2002, 1342-53 (Sage Publications, US).

3. Sayers, Colleen Rose, 'The Psychological Implications of Procrastination, Anxiety, Perfectionism, and Lowered Aspirations' [Dissertation Abstract], *Dissertation Abstracts International: Section B: The Sciences & Engineering*, Vol. 64(7-B), 2004, 3541.

4. Wolters, Christopher A., 'Advancing Achievement Goal Theory: Using Goal Structures and Goal Orientations', *Journal of Educational Psychology*, Vol. 96(2), Jun. 2004, 236-50 (American Psychological Assoc., US).

5. Jonas, Eva; Schimel, Jeff; Greenberg, Jeff; Pyszczynski, Tom, 'The Scrooge Effect: Evidence That Mortality Salience Increases Prosocial Attitudes and Behavior', *Personality and Social Psychology Bulletin*, Vol. 28(10), Oct. 2002, 1342-53.

6. Ferrari, Joseph R., 'Procrastination and Impulsiveness: Two Sides of a Coin?' in McCown, William G.; Johnson, Judith L. (Eds.), *et al, The Impulsive Client: Theory, Research, and Treatment*, 1993. pp. 265-76 (American Psychological Assoc., US), ix, 446pp.

7. Sagarin, Brad J.; Britt, M. Anne; Heider, Jeremy D.; Wood, Sarah E.; Lynch, Joel E., 'Bartering Our Attention', *International Journal of Cognitive Technology*, Vol. 8(2), Fall 2003, 4-17 (Practical Memory Inst., US).

8. Buehler, Roger; Griffin, Dale, 'Planning, Personality, and Prediction: The Role of Future Focus in Optimistic Time Predictions', *Organizational Behavior & Human Decision Processes*, Vol. 92(1-2), Sep.–Nov. 2003, 80-90 (Elsevier Science, UK).

9. Smith, Glenda, 'Perceptions of Stress in Urban Special Education Teachers Across Settings' [Dissertation Abstract], *Dissertation Abstracts International*, Vol. 63(12-A), 2003, 4275.

10. Miller, W.R.; C'de Baca, J., *Quantum Change: When Epiphanies and Sudden Insights Transform Ordinary Lives*, 2001 (Guilford Press, US).

11. Knaus, William, *The Procrastination Workbook: Your Personalized Program for Breaking Free from the Patterns that Hold You Back* [Authored Book], 2002 (New Harbinger Publications, Inc., Oakland, Calif., US), vi, 172pp.

12. Ferrari, Joseph R.; McCown, William, 'Procrastination Tendencies', *Journal of Clinical Psychology*, Vol. 50(2), Mar. 1994, 162-7 (John Wiley & Sons, US).

13. van Eerde, Wendelien, 'A Meta-analytically Derived Nomological Network of Procrastination', *Personality & Individual Differences*, Vol. 35(6), Oct. 2003, 1410-18 (Elsevier Science, UK).

14. O'Donoghue, Ted; Rabin, Matthew, 'Self-awareness and Self-control', in Loewenstein, George; Read, Daniel (Eds.), *et al, Time and Decision: Economic and Psychological Perspectives on Intertemporal Choice*, 2003, pp. 217-43 (Russell Sage Foundation, NY, US), xiii, 569pp.

15. Fritzsche, Barbara A.; Young, Beth Rapp; Hickson, Kara C., 'Individual Differences in Academic Procrastination Tendency and Writing Success', *Personality & Individual Differences*, Vol. 35(7), Nov. 2003, 1549-57 (Elsevier Science, UK).

16. Sirois, Fuschia M.; Melia-Gordon, Michelle L.; Pychyl, Timothy A., ' "I'll Look After My Health, Later": An Investigation of Procrastination and Health', *Personality & Individual Differences*, Vol. 35(5), Oct. 2003, 1167-84.

17. Michaelson, Peter, *The Phantom of the Psyche: Freeing Ourself from Inner Passivity* [Authored Book], 2002 (Prospect Books, Santa Fe, NM, US), v, 241pp.

18. McGrath, Joseph E.; Tschan, Franziska, 'Temporal Factors Affecting Social Psychological Phenomena' in McGrath, Joseph E.; Tschan, Franziska, *Temporal Matters in Social Psychology: Examining the Role of Time in the Lives of Groups and Individuals*, 2004, pp. 47-67 (American Psychological Assoc., US), viii, 227pp.

19. Assur, Agnia M., 'The Relationship of Academic Procrastination to Affective and Cognitive Components of Subjective Well-being' [Dissertation Abstract], *Dissertation Abstracts International: Section B: The Sciences & Engineering*, Vol. 63(8-B), Mar. 2003, 3968.

20. Mittendorf, Brian Gary, 'Information Revelation, Real Options, and Employee Incentives' [Dissertation Abstract], *Dissertation Abstracts International*, Vol. 63(7-A), Feb. 2003, 2608.

21. Montero, Judith, 'A Program Design for College Students' [Dissertation Abstract], *Dissertation Abstracts International: Section B: The Sciences & Engineering*, Vol. 63(6-B), Jan. 2002, 3017.

22. Wikman, Erik Charles, 'Experiences of Chronic Procrastination (with original composition)' [Dissertation Abstract], *Dissertation Abstracts International*, Vol. 63(6-A), Jan. 2002, 2151.

23. Steel, Piers David Gareth, 'The Measurement and Nature of Procrastination' [Dissertation Abstract], *Dissertation Abstracts International: Section B: The Sciences & Engineering*, Vol. 63(3-B), Sep. 2002, 1599.

24. Shiller, Virginia M.; Schneider, Meg F., ' "I Hardly Have Any!" Reducing Homework Blues' in Shiller, Virginia M.; Schneider, Meg F., *Rewards for Kids!: Ready-to-use Charts and Activities for Positive Parenting*, 2003, pp. 105-16 (American Psychological Assoc., US), xi, 131pp.

25. Shiller, Virginia M., Schneider, Meg F., *Rewards for Kids!: Ready-to-use Charts and Activities for Positive Parenting*, 2003, *op. cit.*

26. Elvers, Greg C.; Polzella, Donald J.; Graetz, Ken, 'Procrastination in Courses: Performance and Attitudinal Differences', *Teaching of Psychology*, Vol. 30(2), May 2003, 159-62 (Lawrence Erlbaum, US).

27. Gregersen, Tammy; Horwitz, Elaine K., 'Language Learning and Perfectionism: Anxious and Non-anxious Language Learners' Reactions to their Own Oral Performance', *Modern Language Journal*, Vol. 86(4), Win. 2002, 562-70 (Blackwell Publishing, UK).

28. Tykocinski, Orit E.; Ruffle, Bradley J., 'Reasonable Reasons for Waiting', *Journal of Behavioral Decision Making*, Vol. 16(2), Apr. 2003, 147-57 (John Wiley & Sons, US).

29. Hammer, Corey A.; Ferrari, Joseph R., 'Differential Incidence of Procrastination Between Blue- and White-collar Workers', *Current Psychology: Developmental, Learning, Personality, Social*, Vol. 21(4), Win. 2002, 333-8 (Transaction Publishers, US).

30. Ferrari, Joseph R.; Patel, Tina, 'Social Comparisons by Procrastinators: Rating Peers with Similar or Dissimilar Delay Tendencies', *Personality & Individual Differences*, Vol. 37(7), Nov. 2004, 1493-501 (Elsevier Science, Netherlands).

31. Pfister, Tammy Lodge, 'The Effects of Self-monitoring on Academic Procrastination, Self-efficacy and Achievement' [Dissertation Abstract], *Dissertation Abstracts International*, Vol. 63(5-A), Dec. 2002, 1713.

32. Senecal, Caroline; Julien, Etienne; Guay, Frederic, 'Role Conflict and Academic Procrastination: A Self-determination Perspective', *European Journal of Social Psychology*, Vol. 33(1), Jan.–Feb. 2003, 135-45 (John Wiley & Sons, US).

33. Wolters, Christopher A., 'Understanding Procrastination from a Self-regulated Learning Perspective', *Journal of Educational Psychology*, Vol. 95(1), Mar. 2003, 179-87 (American Psychological Assoc., US).

34. Rodger, Susan Christine, 'Teacher Clarity and Student Anxiety: An Aptitude-Treatment Interaction Experiment' [Dissertation Abstract], *Dissertation Abstracts International: Section B: The Sciences & Engineering*, Vol. 63(4-B), Oct. 2002, 2044.

35. Dewitte, Siegfried; Schouwenburg, Henri C., 'Procrastination, Temptations, and Incentives: The Struggle Between the Present and the Future in Procrastinators and the Punctual', *European Journal of Personality*, Vol. 16(6), Nov.–Dec. 2002, 469-89 (John Wiley & Sons, US).

36. Jackson, Todd; Weiss, Karen E.; Lundquist, Jessie J.; Soderlind, Adam, 'Perceptions of Goal-directed Activities of Optimists and Pessimists: A Personal Projects Analysis', *Journal of Psychology*, Vol. 136(5), Sep. 2002, 521-32 (Heldref Publications, US).

37. Cook, Jerry L.; Jones, Randall M., 'Congruency of Identity Style in Married Couples', *Journal of Family Issues*, Vol. 23(8), Nov. 2002, 912-26 (Sage Publications, US).

38. Gauthier, Lysanne; Senecal, Caroline; Guay, Frederic, 'Academic Procrastination in Graduate Students: The Role of the Student and of the Research Director', *European Review of Applied Psychology/ Revue Europeenne de Psychologie Appliquee*, Vol. 52(1), 2002, 25-40 (Editions du Centre de Psychologie Appliquee, France).

39. Perez-Aranibar; Cecilia Chau; Cordova, Hugo Morales; Espinoza, Micaela Wetzell, 'Coping Style and Performance Status in a Group of Oncological Inpatients', *Revista de Psicologia,* Vol. 20(1) 2002, 93-131 (Pontificia Universidad Catolica del Peru, Peru).

40. Al-Fa'uri, R.; Al-Omari, A., 'Analysis of Reasons of Wrong Decisions in Jordanian Commercial Banks', *Dirasat: Administrative Sciences*, Vol. 29(2), Jul. 2002, 445-71 (Univ. of Jordan, Jordan).

41. Skidmore, Ronald Leroy, ' "Why Can't I Seem to Get Anything Done?": Procrastination and Daily Hassles as Predictors of Student Performance and Engagement in a College Self-paced Introductory Psychology Course: The Relation to Motivational Orientation and Learning Strategies' [Dissertation Abstract], *Dissertation Abstracts International*, Vol. 63(1-A), Jul. 2002, 88.

42. Davis, Richard A.; Flett, Gordon L.; Besser, Avi, 'Validation of a New

Scale: Implications for Pre-employment Screening', *Cyberpsychology & Behavior*, Vol. 5(4), Aug. 2002, 331-45 (Mary Ann Liebert, US).

43. Buffone, Gary, *The Myth of Tomorrow: Seven Essential Keys for Living the Life You Want Today* [Authored Book], 2003 (McGraw-Hill, NY, US), x, 275pp.

44. O'Brien, William Kirkman, 'Applying the Transtheoretical Model to Academic Procrastination' [Dissertation Abstract], *Dissertation Abstracts International: Section B: The Sciences & Engineering*, Vol. 62(11-B), Jun. 2002, 5359.

45. Pychyl, Timothy A.; Coplan, Robert J.; Reid, Pamela A.M., 'Parenting and Procrastination', *Personality & Individual Differences*, Vol. 33(2), Jul. 2002, 271-85 (Elsevier Science, UK).

46. Walsh, James J.; Ugumba-Agwunobi, Godwin, 'Individual Differences in Statistics Anxiety: The Roles of Perfectionism, Procrastination and Trait Anxiety', *Personality & Individual Differences*, Vol. 33(2), Jul. 2002, 239-51.

47. Scher, Steven J.; Osterman, Nicole M., 'Procrastination, Conscientiousness, Anxiety and Goals: Exploring the Measurement and Correlates of Procrastination Among School-aged Children', *Psychology in the Schools*, Vol. 39(4), Jul. 2002, 385-98 (John Wiley & Sons, US).

48. Ross, Scott R.; Canada, Kelli E.; Rausch, Marcus K., 'Self-handicapping and the Five Factor Model of Personality: Mediation Between Neuroticism and Conscientiousness', *Personality & Individual Differences*, Vol. 32(7), May 2002, 1173-84 (Elsevier Science, UK).

49. Holmes, Richard Alan, 'The Effect of Task Structure and Task Order on Subjective Distress and Dilatory Behavior in Academic Procrastinators' [Dissertation Abstract], *Dissertation Abstracts International: Section B: The Sciences & Engineering*, Vol. 62(8-B), Mar. 2002, 3803.

50. Leahy, Robert L., 'Improving Compliance in the Treatment of Generalized Anxiety Disorder', *Journal of Clinical Psychology*, Vol. 58(5), May 2002, 499-511 (John Wiley & Sons, US).

51. Ariely, Dan; Wertenbroch, Klaus, 'Procrastination, Deadlines, and Performance: Self-control by Precommitment', *Psychological Science*, Vol. 13(3), May 2002, 219-24 (Blackwell Publishers, US).

52. Cassady, Jerrell C.; Johnson, Ronald E., 'Cognitive Test Anxiety and Academic Performance', *Contemporary Educational Psychology*, Vol. 27(2), Apr. 2002, 270-95 (Academic Press, US).

53. Hamel, Carole F.; Guse, Lorna W.; Hawranik, Pamela G.; Bond, John B., Jr., 'Advance Directives and Community-dwelling Older Adults', *Western Journal of Nursing Research*, Vol. 24(2), Mar. 2002, 143-58 (Sage Publications, US).

54. Perkins, David N., 'The Engine of Folly', in Sternberg, Robert J. (Ed.), *Why Smart People Can be So Stupid*, 2002, pp. 64-85 (Yale University Press, New Haven, CT, US), ix, 254pp.

55. Fritzsche, Barbara A.; Young, Beth Rapp; Hickson, Kara C., 'Individual Differences in Academic Procrastination Tendency and Writing Success', *Personality & Individual Differences*, Vol. 35(7), Nov. 2003, 1549-57 (Elsevier Science, UK).

56. Murdock, Kevin, 'Management of Procrastination in Distance Education

Courses Using Features of Keller's Personalized System of Instruction', *Dissertation Abstracts International*, Vol. 62(1-A), Jul. 2001, 98.

57. Davis, John K., 'The Effects of Culture on Academic Procrastination' [Dissertation Abstract], *Dissertation Abstracts International*, Vol 61(9-A), Apr. 2001, 3464.

58. Konig, Cornelius, J.; Kleinmann, Martin, 'Business Before Pleasure: No Strategy for Procrastinators?', *Personality & Individual Differences*, Vol. 37(5), Oct. 2004, pp. 1045-1057 (Elsevier Science, Netherlands).

59. Ferrari, Joseph R., 'Procrastination as Self-regulation Failure of Performance: Effects of Cognitive Load, Self-awareness, and Time Limits on "Working Best Under Pressure"', *European Journal of Personality*, Vol.15(5), Sep.–Oct. 2001, 391-406.

60. O'Regan, Fintan; Cooper, Paul, 'Ruby Tuesday', *Emotional & Behavioural Difficulties*, Vol. 6(4), Nov. 2001, 265-9 (Sage Publications, UK).

61. Lavoie, Jennifer A.; Pychyl, A.; Timothy, A., 'A Survey of Online Procrastination, Attitudes, and Emotion', *Social Science Computer Review*, Vol. 19(4), Win. 2001, 431-44 (Sage Publications, US).

62. Kelly, William E., 'No Time to Worry: The Relationship Between Worry, Time Structure, and Time Management', *Personality & Individual Differences*, Vol. 35(5), Oct. 2003, 1119-26 (Elsevier Science, UK).

63. Aguilar V. Javier; Martinez J. Mario; Valencia C. Alejandra; Romero S. Patricia; Vargas Q. Veronica, 'Interrelation of Factors Associated with Intrinsic Motivation', *Revista Mexicana de Psicologia*, Vol. 18(2), Jun. 2001, 265-72 (Revista Mexicana de Psicologia, Mexico).

64. Cheek, Cheryl; Jones, Randall M., 'Identity Style and Employment Histories', *Journal of Vocational Behavior*, Vol. 59(1), Aug. 2001, 76-88 (Elsevier Science, US).

65. Ferrari, Joseph R., 'Getting Things Done on Time: Conquering Procrastination' in Snyder, C. R. (Ed.), *Coping with Stress: Effective People and Processes*, 2001 (Oxford University Press, US), pp. 30-46, xvi, 318pp.

66. Olson, Douglas H.; Claiborn, Charles D., 'Interpretation and Arousal in the Counseling Process' in Hill, Clara E., (Ed.), *Helping Skills: The Empirical Foundation*, 2001 (APA Books, US), pp. 257-69, xviii, 463pp.

67. Onwuegbuzie, Anthony J.; Collins, Kathleen M.T., 'Writing Apprehension and Academic Procrastination Among Graduate Students', *Perceptual & Motor Skills*, Vol. 92(2), Apr. 2001, 560-62.

68. Roloff, Michael E.; Paulson, Gaylen D., 'Confronting Organizational Transgressions' in Darley, John M.; Messick, David M. (Eds.), *et al*, *Social Influences on Ethical Behavior in Organizations*, LEA's *Organization and Management Series*, 2001, pp. 53-68 (LEA, US), x, 246pp.

69. Kuo, Frances E., 'Impacts of Environment and Attention', *Environment & Behavior*, Vol. 33(1), Jan. 2001, 5-34 (Sage Publications, US).

70. Tice, Dianne M.; Bratslavsky, Ellen.; Baumeister, Roy F., 'Emotional Distress Regulation Takes Precedence Over Impulse Control: If You Feel Bad, Do It!', *Journal of Personality & Social Psychology*, Vol. 80(1), Jan. 2001, 53-67 (American Psychological Assoc., US).

13 How the Tough Get Going When the Going Gets Tough – Setbacks and How to Bounce Back

1. Hannigan, Ben; Edwards, Deborah; Burnard, Philip, 'Stress and Stress Management', *Journal of Mental Health*, Vol. 13(3), Jun. 2004, 235-45 (Taylor & Francis, UK).

2. Lee, Joseph K. L., 'Job Stress, Coping and Health Perceptions', *International Journal of Nursing Practice*, Vol. 9(2), Apr. 2003, 86-91 (Blackwell Publishing, UK).

3. Friedman, Merle; Higson-Smith, Craig, 'Building Psychological Resilience' in Paton, Douglas; Violanti, John M. (Eds.), *et al*, *Promoting Capabilities to Manage Posttraumatic Stress: Perspectives on Resilience*, 2003, pp. 103-18 (Charles C. Thomas Publisher, Ltd., Springfield, IL, US), xxii, 222pp.

4. Burke, Ronald J., 'Work Stress and Coping', in Frydenberg, Erica (Ed.), *Beyond Coping: Meeting Goals, Visions, and Challenges*, 2002, pp. 83-106 (Oxford University Press, UK), xiii, 253pp.

5. Snipes, Dawn-Elise, 'Gender Differences in the Perception of Stressors' [Dissertation Abstract], *Dissertation Abstracts International: Section B: The Sciences & Engineering*, Vol. 64(3-B), 2003, 1536.

6. Griva, Konstadina; Joekes, Katherine, 'UK Teachers Under Stress: Can We Predict Wellness on the Basis of Characteristics of the Teaching Job?', *Psychology & Health*, Vol. 18(4), Aug. 2003, 457-71 (Taylor & Francis, UK).

7. Dobreva-Martinova, Tzvetanka, 'Occupational Role Stress: Its Association with Individual and Organizational Well-being' [Dissertation Abstract], *Dissertation Abstracts International: Section B: The Sciences & Engineering*, Vol. 63(4-B), Oct. 2002, 2096.

8. Lu, Luo; Tseng, Hui-Ju; Cooper, Cary L., 'Managerial Stress, Job Satisfaction and Health', *Stress Medicine*, Vol. 15(1), Jan. 1999, 53-64 (John Wiley & Sons, US).

9. Dobreva-Martinova, Tzvetanka; Villeneuve, Martin; Strickland, Lloyd; Matheson, Kimberly, 'Occupational Role Stress: Its Association with Individual and Organizational Well-being, *Canadian Journal of Behavioural Science*, Vol. 34(2), Apr. 2002, 111-21 (Canadian Psychological Assoc., Canada).

10. Bekker, M.H.J.; Hens, G.; Nijssen, A., 'Work Stress and Gender', *Gedrag & Gezondheid: Tijdschrift voor Psychologie & Gezondheid*, Vol. 29(4), Oct. 2001, 241-58 (Uitgeverij De Tijdstroom BV, Netherlands).

11. Bekker, Marrie H.J.; Nijssen, Angelique; Hens, Gonnie, 'Stress Prevention Training: Sex Differences in Types of Stressors, Coping, and Training Effects', *Stress & Health*, Vol. 17(4), Jul. 2001, 207-18 (John Wiley & Sons, US).

12. Fiedler, Edna R.; Della Rocco, Pam; Schroeder, David J.; Nguyen, Kiet T., 'The Relationship Between Aviators' Home-based Stress to Work Stress and Self-perceived Performance' [Report], F.A.A. Office of Aviation Medicine Reports, DOT-FAA-AM-00-32, Oct. 2000, 7pp (Aviation Medicine, US).

13. Konradt, Udo; Schmook, Renate; Wilm, Andreas; Hertel, Guido, 'Selective Results on Stress, Strain', *Health Education Research*, Vol. 15(3), Jun. 2000, 327-38 (Oxford University Press, UK).

14. de Vries, Thomas A.; Hoogstraten, Johan, 'The Relationship Between Work Stress and Concomitant Symptoms of Burn-out', *Gedrag & Gezondheid, Tijdschrift voor Psychologie & Gezondheid*, Vol. 28(2), Apr. 2000, 63-8 (Uitgeverij De Tijdstroom BV, Netherlands).

15. Jurkat, Harald B.; Reimer, Christian, Schroeder, Kerstin, 'Expectations and Attitudes of Medical Students Concerning Work Stress and Consequences of their Future Medical Profession', *Psychotherapie, Psychosomatik, Medizinische Psychologie,* Vol. 50(5), May 2000, 215-21 (Georg Thieme Verlag, Germany).

16. Lu, Luo; Tseng, Hui-Ju; Cooper, Cary L., 'Managerial Stress, Job Satisfaction and Health', *Stress Medicine,* Vol. 15(1), Jan. 1999, 53-64 (John Wiley & Sons, US).

17. Lindquist, Thalina L.; Cooper, Cary L., 'Using Lifestyle and Coping to Reduce Job Stress and Improve Health in "At Risk" Office Workers', *Stress Medicine,* Vol. 5(3), Jul. 1999, 143-52.

18. Mesch, Debra J.; McGrew, John H.; Pescosolido, Bernice A.; Haugh, Diana F., 'The Effects of Hospital Closure on Mental Health Workers: An Overview of Employment, Mental and Physical Health and Attitudinal Outcomes', *Journal of Behavioral Health Services & Research*, Vol. 26(3), Aug. 1999, 305-17 (Aspen Publishers, US).

19. Boey, Kam Weng, 'Coping and Family Relationships in Stress Resistance', *International Journal of Nursing Studies*, Vol. 35(6), Dec. 1998, 353-61 (Elsevier Science, UK).

20. Terry, Deborah J.; Callan, Victor J., 'Employee Adjustment to Large-scale Organisational Change', *Australian Psychologist*, Vol. 32(3), Nov. 1997, 203-10 (Australian Psychological Society, Australia).

21. Portello, Jacqueline Yvonne, 'Dimensions of Managerial and Professional Women's Stress: Interpersonal Conflict and Distress' [Dissertation Abstract], *Dissertation Abstracts International: Section B: The Sciences & Engineering,* Vol. 57(6-B), Dec. 1996, 4072.

22. Carnevale, Franco Angelo, 'Striving to Care: A Qualitative Study of Stress' [Dissertation Abstract], *Dissertation Abstracts International: Section B: The Sciences & Engineering*, Vol. 56(10-B), Apr. 1996, 5413.

23. Terry, Deborah J.; Callan, Victor J.; Sartori, Geoffrey, 'Employee Adjustment to an Organizational Merger: Stress, Coping and Intergroup Differences', *Stress Medicine*, Vol. 12(2), Apr. 1996, 105-22.

24. Greenglass, Esther R., 'Gender, Work Stress, and Coping: Theoretical Implications', *Journal of Social Behavior & Personality*, Vol. 10(6), 1995, 121-34 (Select Press, US).

25. Terry, Deborah J.; Tonge, Linda; Callan, Victor J., 'Employee Adjustment to Stress: The Role of Coping Resources, Situational Factors, and Coping Responses', *Anxiety, Stress, & Coping*, Vol. 8(1), 1995, 1-24 (Taylor & Francis, UK).

26. Duquette, Andre; Kerouac, Suzanne; Sandhu, Balbir K.; Ducharme, Francine, *et al*, 'Psychosocial Determinants of Burnout', *International Journal of Nursing Studies*, Vol. 32(5), Oct. 1995, 443-56 (Elsevier Science, UK).

27. Hatton, Chris; Brown, Rachel; Caine, Amanda; Emerson, Eric, 'Stressors, Coping Strategies and Stress-related Outcomes', *Mental Handicap Research*, Vol. 8(4), 1995, 252-71 (BILD Publications, UK).

28. Murphy, Lawrence R.; Hurrell, Joseph J. Jr.; Sauter, Steven L.; Keita, Gwendolyn Puryear (Eds.), *Job Stress Interventions* [Edited Book], 1995 (American Psychological Assoc., US), xiii, 439pp.

29. Spielberger, Charles Donald; Sarason, Irwin G; Brebner, John M.T.; Greenglass, Esther; Laungani, Pittu; O'Roark, Ann M. (Eds.), *Stress and Emotion: Anxiety, Anger, and Curiosity* [Edited Book], (1995) (Taylor & Francis Inc., US), xvi, 300pp.

30. Havlovic, Stephen J.; Keenan, John P., 'Coping with Work Stress: The Influence of Individual Differences' in Crandall, Rick; Perrewe, Pamela L. (Eds.), (1995), *Occupational Stress: A Handbook. Series in Health Psychology and Behavioral Medicine*, pp. 179-92 (Taylor & Francis Inc., US), xv, 307pp.

31. Crandall, Rick; Perrewe, Pamela L., (Eds.), *Occupational Stress: A Handbook* [Edited Book], 1995 (Taylor & Francis Inc., US), xv, 307pp.

32. Hedin, Anna Elisabeth, 'Perceived Total Workload Stress, Stress Symptoms, and Coping Styles of Working Women' [Dissertation Abstract], *Dissertation Abstracts International*, Vol. 56(4-A), Oct. 1995, 1253.

33. Keita, Gwendolyn Puryear; Hurrell, Joseph J., Jr. (Eds.), *Job Stress in a Changing Workforce: Investigating Gender, Diversity, and Family Issues* [Edited Book], 1994 (American Psychological Assoc., US), xix, 345pp.

34. Koeske, Gary F.; Kirk, Stuart A.; Koeske, Randi D., 'Coping With Job Stress: Which Strategies Work Best?', *Journal of Occupational & Organizational Psychology*, Vol. 66(4), Dec. 1993, 319-35 (British Psychological Society, UK).

35. Kaye, John; Moyer, Diane; Zecca, Denise; Soucar, Emil, 'A Feminist Reaction', *Journal of Mental Health Counseling*, Vol. 15(4), Oct. 1993, 461-64 (American Mental Health Counselors Assoc., US).

36. Dewe, Philip, 'The Appraisal Process: Exploring the Role of Meaning, Importance, Control and Coping in Work Stress', *Anxiety, Stress, & Coping*, Vol. 5(1), May 1992, 95-109 (Taylor & Francis, UK).

37. Rice, Phillip L., *Stress and Health*, (2nd Ed.) [Authored Book], 1992 (Brooks Cole, US), xx, 436pp.

38. Rees, David W.; Smith, Simon D., 'Work Stress Assessed by the Occupational Stress Indicator', *British Journal of Occupational Therapy*, Vol. 54(8), Aug. 1991, 289-94 (Coll. of Occupational Therapists, UK).

14 Take It to the Limit

1. Zaromatidis, Katherine; Carlo, Regina; Racanello, Dennis, 'Sex, Perceptions of Attractiveness, and Sensation Seeking', *Psychological Reports*, Vol. 94(2), Apr. 2004, 633-36 (Psychological Reports, US).

2. Rudin-Brown, Christina M.; Parker, Heather A., 'Behavioural Adaptation: Implications for Preventive Strategies', *Transportation Research Part F: Traffic Psychology & Behaviour*, Vol. 7(2), Mar. 2004, 59-76 (Elsevier Science, Netherlands).

3. Morgan, Susan E.; Palmgreen, Philip; Stephenson, Michael T.; Hoyle, Rick H.; Lorch, Elizabeth P., 'Associations Between Message Features and Subjective Evaluations of the Sensation Value', *Journal of*

Communication, Vol. 53(3), Sep. 2003, 512-26 (Oxford University Press, UK).

4. Stephenson, Michael T., 'Examining Adolescents', *Human Communication Research*, Vol. 29(3), Jul. 2003, 343-69 (Oxford University Press, UK).

5. Ostaszewski, Pawel, 'Temperament and the Rate of Discounting of Subjective Value of Delayed Rewards and Punishment', *Studia Psychologiczne*, Vol. 35(2), 1997, 111-39 (Wydawnictwo Instytutu Psychologii-Polska Akademia Nauk, Poland).

6. Stephenson, Michael T., 'High Sensation Seekers: What Works and Why', *American Journal of Health Behavior*, Vol. 27 (Suppl. 3), 2003, S233-S238 (PNG Publications, US).

7. Yonts, Nikki Eileen J.R., 'Beliefs About Firearms and Exposure to Violent Media' [Dissertation Abstract], *Dissertation Abstracts International: Section B: The Sciences & Engineering*, Vol. 63 (10-B), 2003, 4946.

8. Rosenbloom, Tova, 'Sensation Seeking and Risk Taking in Mortality Salience', *Personality & Individual Differences*, Vol. 35(8), Dec. 2003, 1809-19 (Elsevier Science, UK).

9. Kelly, Susan; Dunbar, R.I.M., 'Who Dares, Wins: Heroism Versus Altruism in Women's Mate Choice', *Human Nature*, Vol. 12(2), 2001, 89-105 (Aldine de Gruyter, US).

10. Lourey, Emma; McLachlan, Angus, 'Elements of Sensation Seeking', *Personality & Individual Differences*, Vol. 35(2), Jul. 2003, 277-87 (Elsevier Science, UK).

11. Rosenbloom, Tova, 'Risk Evaluation and Risky Behavior of High and Low Sensation Seekers', *Social Behavior & Personality*, Vol. 31(4), 2003, 375-86 (Society for Personality Research, New Zealand).

12. Lovelace, Laneel, 'Dysfunctional Anxiety and Disinhibition as Mutually Exclusive Constructs' [Dissertation Abstract], *Dissertation Abstracts International: Section B: The Sciences & Engineering*, Vol. 63(7-B), Feb. 2003, 3478.

13. Hans, Jason Walter, 'A Rural Adolescent Sample' [Dissertation Abstract], *Dissertation Abstracts International: Section B: The Sciences & Engineering*. Vol. 63(6-B), Jan. 2002, 2995.

14. Slater, Michael D., 'Sensation-seeking as a Moderator of the Effects of Peer Influences, Consistency with Personal Aspirations and Perceived Harm on Marijuana and Cigarette Use Among Younger Adolescents', *Substance Use & Misuse*, Vol. 38(7), 2003, 865-80 (Marcell Dekker, US).

15. Lissek, S.; Powers, Alice Schade, 'Sensation Seeking and Startle Modulation by Physically Threatening Images', *Biological Psychology*, Vol. 63(2), May 2003, 179-97 (Elsevier Science, UK).

16. Neely, Gregory; Lundstroem, Ronnie; Bjoerkvist, Bertil, 'Sensation Seeking and Subjective Unpleasantness Ratings of Stimulus Intensity', *Perceptual & Motor Skills*, Vol. 95(3), Dec. 2002, 706-12.

17. Oishi, Shigehiro; Schimmack, Ulrich; Colcombe, Stanley J., 'The Contextual and Systematic Nature of Life Satisfaction Judgements', *Journal of Experimental Social Psychology*, Vol. 39(3), May 2003, 232-47 (Elsevier Science, UK).

18. Thiffault, Pierre; Bergeron, Jacques, 'Fatigue and Individual Differences in Monotonous Simulated Driving', *Personality & Individual Differences*, Vol. 34(1), Jan. 2003, 159-76 (Elsevier Science, UK).

19. Krcmar, Marina; Greene, Kathryn, 'Predicting Exposure To and Uses of Television Violence', *Journal of Communication*, Vol. 49(3), Sum. 1999, 24-45 (Oxford University Press, UK).

20. Palmgreen, Philip; Donohew, Lewis; Lorch, Elizabeth Pugzles; Hoyle, Rick H.; Stephenson, Michael T., 'Tests of Sensation Seeking Targeting', *American Journal of Public Health,* Vol. 91(2), Feb. 2001, 292-6 (American Public Health Assoc.).

21. Palmgreen, Philip; Donohew, Lewis; Lorch, Elizabeth Pugzles; Hoyle, Rick H.; Stephenson, Michael T., 'A Controlled Time Series Approach', in Hornik, Robert C. (Ed.), *Public Health Communication: Evidence for Behavior Change*, 2002, pp. 35-56 (Laurence Erlbaum Assoc., US), xv, 435pp.

22. Holmes, Samantha Dionne, 'Sensation Seeking and Negative Emotional Recovery' [Dissertation Abstract], *Dissertation Abstracts International: Section B: The Sciences & Engineering,* Vol. 61(10-B), May 2001, 5620.

23. Stephenson, Michael T.; Palmgreen, Philip, 'Sensation Seeking and Perceived Message Sensation Value', *Communication Monographs,* Vol. 68(1), Mar. 2001, 49-71 (National Communication, US).

24. Daderman, Anna Maria; Wirsen Meurling, Ann; Hallman, Jarmila, 'Different Personality Patterns in Sensation Seekers', *European Journal of Personality*, Vol. 15(3), May–Jun. 2001, 239-52 (John Wiley & Sons, US).

25. Oishi, Shigehiro; Schimmack, Ulrich; Diener, Ed, 'Pleasures and Subjective Well-being', *European Journal of Personality*, Vol. 15(2), Mar.–Apr. 2001, 153-67.

26. D'Silva, Margaret; Usha, Grant; Harrington, Nancy; Palmgreen, Philip; Donohew, Lewis; Lorch, Elizabeth Pugzles, 'Drug Use Prevention for the High Sensation Seeker: The Role of Alternative Activities', *Substance Use & Misuse*, Vol. 36(3), 2001, 373-85 (Marcel Dekker, US).

27. Carton, S.; Le Houezec, J.; Lagrue, G.; Jouvent, R., 'Relationships Between Sensation Seeking and Emotional Symptomatology', *Addictive Behaviors*, Vol. 25(5), Sep.–Oct. 2000, 653-62 (Elsevier Science Inc., US).

28. Gunnarsdottir, E. Dianna; Pingitore, Regina A.; Spring, Bonnie J.; Konopka, Lukasz M.; Crayton, John W.; Milo, Tom; Shirazi, Parvez, 'Individual Differences', *Addictive Behaviors*, Vol. 25(5), Sep.–Oct. 2000, 641-52.

29. Davis, Rachel Sue, 'Audience Segmentation for Communication Interventions' [Dissertation Abstract], *Dissertation Abstracts International*, Vol. 60(12-A), 2000, 4232.

30. Brocke, Burkhard; Beauducel, André; John, Regina; Debener, Stefan; Heilemann, Hubert, 'Sensation Seeking and Affective Disorders', *Neuropsychobiology*, Vol. 41(1), Jan. 2000, 24-30 (S. Karger AG, Switzerland).

31. Omar, Alicia G.; Delgado, Hugo Uribe; Paris, Laura E., 'Personality

and Sensation Seeking in Adolescents', *Revista Mexicana de Psicologia*, Vol. 16(1), Jun. 1999, 167-73 (Revista Mexicana de Psicologia, Mexico).

32. Parent, Elena C.; Newman, Denise L., 'The Role of Sensation-seeking in Alcohol Use and Risk-taking Behavior', *Journal of Alcohol & Drug Education*, Vol. 44(2), Win. 1999, 12-28 (American Alcohol & Drug Information, US).

33. Garland, Thomas A., 'The Relationship Between the Diagnosis of Adults, Gender and Sensation Seeking' [Dissertation Abstract], *Dissertation Abstracts International: Section B: The Sciences & Engineering*, Vol. 60(5-B), Dec. 1999, 2338.

34. Puopolo, Mindy R., 'The Development of a Sensation Seeking Scale for the MMPI-2' [Dissertation Abstract], *Dissertation Abstracts International: Section B: The Sciences & Engineering*, Vol. 60(3-B), Sep. 1999, 1313.

35. Stephenson, Michael Taylor, 'Message Sensation Value and Sensation Seeking as Determinants of Message Processing' [Dissertation Abstract], *Dissertation Abstracts International*, Vol. 60(3-A), Sep. 1999, 0581.

36. Suedfeld, Peter; Steel, G. Daniel, 'The Environmental Psychology of Capsule Habitats', *Annual Review of Psychology*, 2000, Vol. 51 pp. 227-53 (Annual Reviews, US).

37. Steele, G.D.; Suedfeld, P., 'Temporal Patterns of Affect in an Isolated Group', *Environment and Behavior*, 1992, 23, pp. 749-65.

38. Pierson, Annick; le Houezec, Jacques; Fossaert, Arnaud; Dubal, Stephanie; Jouvent, Roland, 'Frontal Reactivity and Sensation Seeking an ERP Study in Skydivers', *Progress in Neuro-Psychopharmacology & Biological Psychiatry*, Vol. 23(3), Apr. 1999, 447-63 (Elsevier Science, US).

39. Breslin, F. Curtis; Sobell, Mark B.; Cappell, Howard; Vakili, Shervin; Poulos, Constantine X., 'The Effects of Alcohol, Gender, and Sensation Seeking on the Gambling Choices', *Psychology of Addictive Behaviors*, Vol. 13(3), Sep. 1999, 243-52 (American Psychological Assoc./ Educational Publishing Foundation, US).

40. Dsilva, Margaret Usha, 'Individual Differences and Choice of Information Source: Sensation Seeking in Drug Abuse Prevention', *Communication Reports*, Vol. 12(1), Win. 1999, 51-7 (Western States Communication Assoc., US).

41. Cheong, Jeewon; Nagoshi, Craig T., 'Effects of Sensation Seeking, Instruction Set, and Alcohol/Placebo Administration on Aggressive Behavior', *Alcohol*, Vol. 17(1), Jan. 1999, 81-6 (Elsevier Science, US).

42. Ostaszewski, Pawel, 'Temperament and the Rate of Discounting of Subjective Value of Delayed Rewards and Punishment', *Studia Psychologiczne*, Vol. 35(2), 1997, 111-39 (Wydawnictwo Instytutu Psychologii-Polska Akademia Nauk, Poland).

43. Harrington, Nancy Grant; Donohew, Lewis, 'Jump Start: A Targeted Substance Abuse Prevention Program', *Health Education & Behavior*, Vol. 24(5), Oct. 1997, 568-86 (Sage Publications, US).

44. Esterly, Richard W.; Neely, William T., *Chemical Dependency and Compulsive Behaviors* [Authored Book], 1997 (Lawrence Earlbaum, US), viii, 108pp.

45. Pliner, Patricia; Melo, Nancy, 'Effects of Manipulated Arousal and Individual Differences in Sensation Seeking', *Physiology & Behavior*, Vol. 61(2), Feb. 1997, 331-5 (Elsevier Science, US).

15 Are You Trying Too Hard?

1. Robinson, B.E., 'Workaholism: Bridging the Gap Between Workplace, Sociocultural, and Family Research', *Journal of Employment Counseling*, 37, 2000, 31-47 (National Employment Counseling Assoc., US).
2. Porter, G., 'Organizational Impact of Workaholism: Suggestions for Researching the Negative Outcomes of Excessive Work', *Journal of Occupational Health Psychology*, 70, 1996, 70-83 (APA Journals, US).
3. Caproni, P.J., 'Work/Life Balance: You Can't Get There from Here', *The Journal of Applied Behavioral Science*, 33, 1997, 46-56 (Sage Publications, US).
4. Burwell, R.; Chen, Charles, S.P., 'Applying REBT to Workaholic Clients', *Counselling Psychology Quarterly*, 2002, Vol. 15, No. 3, pp. 219-28 (BrunnerRoutledge Publishing, US).
5. Ellis, A., 'Changing Rational-Emotive Therapy (RET) to Rational Emotive Behavior Therapy (REBT)', *Journal of Rational-Emotive and Cognitive-Behavior Therapy*, 13, 1995, 85-90 (Sage Publications, US).
6. Robinson, B., *Chained to the Desk: A Guidebook for Workaholics, Their Partners and Children, and the Clinicians Who Treat Them*, 1995 (University Press, NY, US).
7. Seybold. K.C.; Salomone, P.R., 'Understanding Workaholism: A Review of Causes and Counseling Approaches', *Journal of Counseling and Development*, 73, 1994, 4-9 (Sage Publications, US).
8. Spence, J.T.; Robbins, A.S., 'Workaholism: Definition, Measurement and Preliminary Results', *Journal of Personality Assessment*, 58, 1992, 160-78 (Lawrence Erlbaum Assoc., US).
9. Burke, Ronald J., 'Workaholism Components, Job Satisfaction, and Career Progress', *Journal of Applied Social Psychology*, Vol. 31(11) Nov. 2001, 2339-56 (V.H. Winston & Son, US).
10. Chamberlin, Christine May, 'Workaholism, Health, and Self-acceptance' [Dissertation Abstract], *Dissertation Abstracts International*, Vol. 62(4-A), Oct. 2001, 1332.
11. Lampert, Rachel; Baron, Suzanne J.; McPherson, Craig A.; Lee, Forrester A.; 'Heart Rate Variability During the Week of September 11, 2001', *JAMA*, Aug. 2002, Vol. 288(5), pp. 575 (American Medical Assoc., US).
12. Burke, Ronald J., 'Workaholism in Organizations: The Role of Organizational Values', *Personnel Review*, Vol. 30(6), 2001, 637-45 (MCB Univ. Press, US).
13. Porter, Gayle, 'Workaholic Tendencies and the High Potential for Stress Among Co-workers', *International Journal of Stress Management*, Vol. 8(2), Apr. 2001, 147-64 (Kluwer Academic/ Plenum Publishers, US).
14. Kanai, Atsuko; Wakabayashi, Mitsuru, 'Workaholism Among

Japanese Blue-collar Employees', *International Journal of Stress Management*, Vol. 8(2), Apr. 2001, 129-45.

15. McCann, Stewart J.H., 'Achievement Age-death Correlations Alone Cannot Provide Unequivocal Support for the Precocity-longevity Hypothesis', *Journal of Psychology*, July 2004, Vol. 138(4), pp. 293-302 (Heldref Publications, US).

16. McCann, Stewart J. H., 'Younger Achievement Age Predicts Shorter Life for Governors', *Personality & Social Psychology Bulletin*, Feb. 2003, Vol. 29(2), pp. 164-9 (Sage Publications, US).

17. McCann, Stewart J.H., 'The Precocity-longevity Hypothesis: Earlier Peaks in Career Achievement Predict Shorter Lives', *Personality & Social Psychology Bulletin*, Nov. 2001, Vol. 27(11), pp. 1429-39 (Sage Publications, US).

18. Robinson, Bryan E., 'Workaholism and Family Functioning: A Psychological Profile of Family Members' in Robinson, Bryan E.; Chase, Nancy D. (Eds.), *High-performing Families: Causes, Consequences, and Clinical Solutions, The Family Psychology and Counseling Series*, 2001, pp. 3-22 (American Counseling Assoc., US), xviii, 189pp.

19. Shumate, Jean Irene, 'Stress, Burnout, and Coping Strategies Among Washington State High School Principals' [Dissertation Abstract], *Dissertation Abstracts International*, Vol. 60(8-A), Mar. 2000, 2760.

20. Burke, Ronald J., 'Workaholism and Divorce', *Psychological Reports*, Vol. 86(1), Feb. 2000, 219-20 (Psychological Reports, US).

21. Carroll, Jane J.; Robinson, Bryan E., 'Depression and Parentification Among Adults as Related to Parental Workaholism and Alcoholism', *Family Journal: Counseling & Therapy for Couples & Families*, Vol. 8(4), Oct. 2000, 360-7 (Sage Publications, US).

22. Bonebright, Cynthia A.; Clay, Daniel L.; Ankenmann, Robert D., 'The Relationship of Workaholism with Work-life Conflict, Life Satisfaction, and Purpose in Life', *Journal of Counseling Psychology*, Vol. 47(4), Oct. 2000, 469-77 (American Psychological Assoc., US).

23. Robinson, Bryan E., 'A Typology of Workaholics with Implications for Counselors', *Journal of Addictions & Offender Counseling*, Vol. 21(1), Oct. 2000, 34-48 (American Counseling Assoc. / International Assoc. of Addictions & Offender Counselors, US).

24. Flowers, Claudia; Robinson, Bryan E.; Carroll, Jane J., 'Criterion-related Validity of the Marital Disaffection Scale as a Measure of Marital Estrangement', *Psychological Reports*, Vol. 86(3, Pt. 2), Jun. 2000, 1101-3 (Psychological Reports, US).

25. Burke, Ronald J., 'It's Not How Hard You Work But How You Work Hard: Evaluating Workaholism Components', *International Journal of Stress Management*, Vol. 6(4), Oct. 1999, 225-39.

26. Burke, Ronald J., 'Workaholism and Extra-work Satisfactions', *The International Journal of Organizational Analysis*, Vol. 7(4), 1999, 352-64 (Center for Advance Studies in Management, US).

27. Burke, Ronald J., 'Workaholism in Organizations: Gender Differences', *Sex Roles*, Vol. 41(5-6), Sep. 1999, 333-45 (Kluwer Academic/Plenum Publishers, US).

28. Robinson, Bryan E., 'Workaholic Children: One Method of Fulfilling

the Parentification Role' in Chase, Nancy D. (Ed.), *Burdened Children: Theory, Research, and Treatment of Parentification*, 1999, pp. 56-74 (Sage Publications, US), xiii, 199pp.

29. Chase, Nancy D. (Ed.), *Burdened Children: Theory, Research, and Treatment of Parentification* [Edited Book], 1999, xiii, 199pp.

30. Harris, Keith Wynn, 'The Psychophysiology of Marital Interaction: Differential Effects of Support and Conflict', *Dissertation Abstracts International: Section B: The Sciences and Engineering*, Vol 62(2B). Aug. 2001, 1080 (Univ. Microfilms International, US).

31. Robinson, Bryan E.; Kelley, Lisa, 'Adult Children of Workaholics: Self-concept, Anxiety, Depression, and Locus of Control', *American Journal of Family Therapy*, Vol. 26(3), Fall 1998, 223-38 (Brunner/Mazel, US).

32. Robinson, Bryan E., 'The Workaholic Family: A Clinical Perspective', *American Journal of Family Therapy*, Vol. 26(1), Jan.–Mar. 1998, 65-75 (Brunner/Mazel, US).

33. Perez-Prada, Engracia, 'Personality at Work' [Dissertation Abstract], *Dissertation Abstracts International: Section B: The Sciences & Engineering*. Vol. 57(7-B), Jan. 1997, 4763.

34. Scott, Kimberly S.; Moore, Keirsten S.; Miceli, Marcia P., 'An Exploration of the Meaning and Consequences of Workaholism', *Human Relations*, Vol. 50(3), Mar. 1997, 287-314 (Sage Publications, UK).

35. Kanai, Atsuko; Wakabayashi, Mitsuru; Fling, Sheila, 'Workaholism Among Employees', *Japanese Psychological Research,* Vol. 38(4), 1996, 192-203 (Japanese Psychological Assoc., Japan).

36. Cournut, Jean, 'Metapsychology of Character and Permanence of Ego Splittings', *Revue Française de Psychanalyse*, Vol. 60 (Spec. Issue), 1996, 1597-1618 (Presses Universitaires de France, France).

37. Spanias, Photini Andreou, 'A Study of the Effects of Teacher Personality Types on Student Math Anxiety' [Dissertation Abstract], *Dissertation Abstracts International*, Vol. 57(3-A), Sep. 1996, 1027.

38. Kuhn, Rosemary Elizabeth, 'Sailing as a Transformational Experience', *Dissertation Abstracts International*, Oct. 2001, Vol. 62(4-B), 2113.

39. Landis-Kleine, Cathy; Foley, Linda A.; Nall, Loretta; Padgett, Patricia, *et al*, 'Attitudes Toward Marriage and Divorce Held by Young Adults', *Journal of Divorce & Remarriage*, Vol. 23(3-4), 1995, 63-73 (Haworth Press, US).

40. Schibsted, James Andrew, 'A Recovery Strategy for Workaholic Pastors' [Dissertation Abstract], *Dissertation Abstracts International*, Vol. 55(8-A), Feb. 1995, 2435.

41. Ishiyama, F. Ishu; Kitayama, Akio, 'Overwork and Career-centered Self-validation Among the Japanese: Psychosocial Issues and Counseling Implications', *International Journal for the Advancement of Counselling*, Vol. 17(3), Sep. 1994, 167-82 (Kluwer Academic, Netherlands).

42. Spence, Janet T.; Robbins, Ann S., 'Workaholism: Definition, Measurement, and Preliminary Results', *Journal of Personality Assessment*, Vol. 58(1), Feb. 1992, 160-78 (Lawrence Erlbaum, US).

43. Fassel, Diane; Schaef, Anne Wilson, 'A Feminist Perspective on Work Addiction' in Van Den Bergh, Nan (Ed.), *Feminist Perspectives on Addictions*, 1991, pp. 199-211 (Churchill Livingstone, US), xv, 222pp.

44. Adderholdt-Elliott, Miriam, 'Perfectionism and the Gifted Adolescent' in Bireley, Marlene; Genshaft, Judy (Eds.), *Understanding the Gifted Adolescent: Educational, Developmental, and Multicultural Issues, Education and Psychology of the Gifted Series*, 1991, pp. 65-75 (Teachers College, US), xiv, 288pp.

45. Haas, Ruth C., 'Workaholism: A Conceptual View and Development of a Measurement Instrument' [Dissertation Abstract], *Dissertation Abstracts International*, Vol. 50(5-B), Nov. 1989, 2190.

46. Lenk, Wolfgang, 'Self-administered Psychotherapeutic Treatment for a Lipoma', *Hypnose und Kognition*, Vol. 5(1), Apr. 1988, 45-52 (MEG Stiftung, Germany).

47. Bieber, Irving, 'Work Dysfunction', in Howells, John G. (Ed.), *Modern Perspectives in Psychosocial Pathology, Modern Perspectives in Psychiatry*, 1988, pp. 268-80 (Brunner/Mazel, UK), viii, 358pp.

48. Phillips, Elizabeth A., 'Codependency: A Real Problem' in Dickman, Fred; Challenger, B. Robert (Eds.), *et al, Employee Assistance Programs: A Basic Text*, 1988, pp. 194-203 (C.C. Thomas, US), xxiv, 493pp.

49. Booth-Kewley, Stephanie; Friedman, Howard S., 'Psychological Predictors of Heart Disease: A Quantitative Review', *Psychological Bulletin*, Vol. 101(3), May 1987, 343-62 (American Psychological Assoc, US).

50. Naughton, Thomas J., 'A Conceptual View of Workaholism and Implications for Career Counseling and Research', *Career Development Quarterly*, Vol. 35(3), Mar. 1987, 180-7 (American Counseling Assoc., US).

51. Spruell, Geraldine, 'Work Fever', *Training & Development Journal*, Vol. 41(1), Jan. 1987, 41-5 (American Society for Training & Development, US).

52. Pietropinto, Anthony, 'The Workaholic Spouse', *Medical Aspects of Human Sexuality*, Vol. 20(5), May 1986, 89-96 (Hospital Publications, Inc., US).

53. Maslach, Christina, 'Stress, Burnout, and Workaholism' in Kilburg, Richard R.; Nathan, Peter E. (Eds.), *et al, Professionals in Distress: Issues, Syndromes, and Solutions in Psychology*, 1986, pp. 53-75 (APA Books, US), 299pp.

54. Homer, Jack B., 'Worker Burnout: A Dynamic Model with Implications for Prevention and Control', *System Dynamics Review*, Vol. 1(1), Sum. 1985, 42-62 (John Wiley & Sons, US).

55. Joseph, Bill, 'Process Communication Management: "The Micro Chip of the O.D. World" ', *Organization Development Journal*, Vol. 3(3), Fall 1985, 65-7 (Organization Development Institute, US).

56. McMillan, Lynley H.W.; O'Driscoll, Michael P.; Brady, Elizabeth C., 'The Impact of Workaholism on Personal Relationships' [Peer Reviewed Journal], *British Journal of Guidance & Counselling*, Vol. 32(2), May 2004, 171-86 (Taylor & Francis, UK).

57. Robinson, Bryan E., 'Chained to the Desk: A Guidebook for Workaholics, Their Partners and Children, and the Clinicians Who Treat Them' [Authored Book], 2001 (New York University Press, NY, US), xvi, 255pp.

58. Halewood, Andrea; Tribe, Rachel, 'What is the Prevalence of Narcissism Amongst Counsellors?', *Psychology and Psychotherapy: Theory, Research & Practice*, 2003, Vol. 76, pp. 87-102.

59. Vonk, Roos; Ashmore, Richard D., 'Thinking About Gender Types: Cognitive Organization of Female and Male Types', *British Journal of Social Psychology*, Vol. 42(2), Jun. 2003, 257-80 (British Psychological Society, UK).

60. Campbell, W.K.; Foster, C.A.; Finkel, E.J.; 'Does Self-love Lead to Love for Others?', *Journal of Personality & Social Psychology*, 2002, Vol. 83, pp. 340-54.

61. Campbell, W.K.; Foster, C.A.; 'Narcissism and Commitment in Romantic Relationships', *Personality & Social Psychology Bulletin*, 2002, 28, 484-95.

62. Hicks, Randall Blair, 'Shame and the Adult Male Survivor' [Dissertation Abstract], *Dissertation Abstracts International: Section B: The Sciences & Engineering*, Vol. 62(11-B), Jun. 2002, 5376.

63. Flowers, Claudia P.; Robinson, Bryan, 'A Structural and Discriminant Analysis of the Work Addiction Risk Test', *Educational & Psychological Measurement*, Vol. 62(3), Jun. 2002, 517-26 (Sage Publications, US).

64. Masterson, James F.; 'The Personality Disorders: A New Look at the Developmental Self and Object Relations Approach', *Phoenix*, 2000, vi, pp. 276 (Zeig, Tucker & Co, US).

65. Solomon, Zahava; Ginzburg, Karni; Neria, Yuval; Ohry, Abraham, 'Coping with War Captivity: The Role of Sensation Seeking', *European Journal of Personality*, Vol. 9(1), Mar. 1995, 57-70 (John Wiley & Sons, US).

66. Donohew, Lewis; Palmgreen, Philip; Lorch, Elizabeth Pugzles, 'Attention, Need for Sensation, and Health Communication Campaigns', *American Behavioral Scientist*, Vol. 38(2), Nov. 1994, 310-22 (Sage Publications, US).

67. Ball, Samuel A.; Carroll, Kathleen M.; Rounsaville, Bruce J., 'Sensation Seeking, Substance Abuse, and Psychopathology in Treatment-seeking and Community Cocaine Abusers', *Journal of Consulting & Clinical Psychology*, Vol. 62(5), Oct. 1994, 1053-7 (American Psychological Assoc., US).

68. Lorch, Elizabeth Pugzles; Palmgreen, Philip; Donohew, Lewis; Helm, David, *et al*, 'Sensation Seeking', *Human Communication Research*, Vol. 20(3), Mar. 1994, 390-412 (Oxford Univ. Press, US).

69. Zuckerman, Marvin; Ulrich, Roger S.; McLaughlin, John, 'Sensation Seeking and Reactions to Nature Paintings', *Personality & Individual Differences*, Vol. 15(5), Nov. 1993, 563-76 (Elsevier Science, UK).

70. Stanforth, Nancy, 'Fashion Innovators, Sensation Seekers, and Clothing Individualists', *Perceptual & Motor Skills*, Vol. 81(3, Pt. 2), Dec. 1995, 1203-10.

16 Does Your Motivation Come from Your Body or Your Brain?

1. Vohs, Kathleen, D.; Baumeister, Roy, F., 'Sexual Passion, Intimacy and Gender', (Chapter in) Mashek, D.J., Aron, A.P. (Eds), *Handbook of Closeness and Intimacy*, 2004, pp. 189-199 (Lawrence Erlbaum Associates, US).

2. Pilz, Kevin Michael, 'Maternal Allocation and Offspring Effects' [Dissertation Abstract], *Dissertation Abstracts International: Section B: The Sciences & Engineering*, Vol. 63(12-B), 2003, 5613.

3. Kanazawa, Satoshi, 'Why Productivity Fades with Age: The Crime-genius Connection', *Journal of Research in Personality*, Vol. 37(4), Aug. 2003, 257-72 (Elsevier Science, UK).

4. Cashdan, Elizabeth, 'Hormones and Competitive Aggression in Women', *Aggressive Behavior*, Vol. 29(2), 2003, 107-15 (Wiley-Liss, US).

5. Neave, Nick; Wolfson, Sandy, 'Testosterone, Territoriality, and the "Home Advantage"', *Physiology & Behavior*, Vol. 78(2), Feb. 2003, 269-75 (Elsevier Science, US).

6. Aikey, Jeremy L.; Nyby, John G.; Anmuth, David M.; James, Peter J., 'Testosterone Rapidly Reduces Anxiety (*Mus Musculus*)', *Hormones & Behavior*, Vol. 42(4), Dec. 2002, 448-60 (Academic Press, US).

7. Mazur, Allan; Booth, Alan, 'Testosterone and Dominance in Men', *Behavioral & Brain Sciences*, Jun. 1998, Vol. 21(3), pp. 353-97 (Cambridge Univ. Press, US).

8. Wagner, John D.; Flinn, Mark V.; England, Barry G., 'Hormonal Response to Competition Among Male Coalitions', *Evolution & Human Behavior*, Vol. 23(6), Nov. 2002, 437-42 (Elsevier Science Publishing, US).

9. Mazur, Allan, Michalek, Joel, 'Marriage, Divorce and Male Testosterone', *Social Forces*, Sep. 1998, Vol. 77(1), pp. 315-30 (Univ. of North Carolina Press, US).

10. Gonzalez-Bono, E.; Salvador, A.; Serrano, M.A.; Ricarte, J., 'Testosterone, Cortisol, and Mood in a Sports Team Competition', *Hormones & Behavior*, Vol. 35(1), Feb. 1999, 55-62.

11. Campbell, Anne; Muncer, Steven; Odber, Josie, 'Aggression and Testosterone: Testing a Bio-social Model', *Aggressive Behavior*, Vol. 23(4), 1997, 229-38.

12. Gray, Peter B.; Kahlenberg, Sonya M.; Barrett, Emily S.; Lipson, Susan F.; Ellison, Peter T., 'Marriage and Fatherhood are Associated with Lower Testosterone in Males', *Evolution & Human Behavior*, Vol. 23(3), May 2002, 193-201.

13. Van Duyse, Els; Pinxten, Rianne; Eens, Marcel, 'Effects of Testosterone', *Hormones & Behavior*, Vol. 41(2), Mar. 2002, 178-86 (Academic Press, US).

14. Gaffney, Ben T.; Huegel, Helmut M.; Rich, Peter A., 'The Effects of *Eleutherococcus Senticosus* and *Panax Ginseng* on Steroidal Hormone Indices of Stress and Lymphocyte Subset Numbers in Endurance Athletes', *Life Sciences*, Vol. 70(4), Dec. 2001, 431-42 (Elsevier Science, US).

15. Foss, Jeffrey, *Science and the Riddle of Consciousness: A Solution*, 2000, Kluwer Academic/Plenum Publishers, US), xiii, pp. 225.

16. Duyse, Els Van; Pinxten, Rianne; Eens, Marcel, 'Does Testosterone Affect the Trade-off Between Investment in Sexual/Territorial Behaviour', *Behaviour*, Vol. 137(11), Nov. 2000, 1503-15 (E.J. Brill Publishers, Netherlands).

17. 'Who's on the Testosterone? Women Trying to Survive in the Macho World of Politics Are Resorting to Hormonal Help', (Features), *New Statesman*, July 7, 2003, by Bernard Mallee.

18. Gonzalez-Bono, E.; Salvador, A.; Serrano, M.A.; Ricarte, J., 'Testosterone, Cortisol, and Mood in a Sports Team Competition', *Hormones & Behavior*, Vol. 35(1), Feb. 1999, 55-62 (Academic Press, US).

19. Suay, F.; Salvador, Alicia; Gonzalez-Bono, E.; Sanchis, C.; Martinez, M.; Martinez-Sanchis, S.; Simon, V.M.; Montoro, J.B., 'Effects of Competition and its Outcome on Serum Testosterone, Cortisol and Prolactin', *Psychoneuroendocrinology*, Vol. 24(5), Jul. 1999, 551-66 (Elsevier Science Ltd/Pergamon, US).

20. Hurst, J.L.; Barnard, C.J.; Tolladay, U.; Nevison, C.M.; West, C.D., 'Behavioural Predictors of Welfare', *Animal Behaviour*, Vol. 58(3), Sep. 1999, 563-86 (Academic Press, US).

21. Bateup, Helen S.; Booth, Alan; Shirtcliff, Elizabeth A.; Granger, Douglas A., 'Testosterone, Cortisol and Women's Competition', *Evolution & Human Behavior*, May 2002, Vol. 23(3), pp. 181-92 (Elsevier Science, UK).

22. Galeotti, Paolo; Saino, Nicola; Sacchi, Roberto; Moller, Anders Pape, 'Song Correlates with Social Context, Testosterone and Body Condition', *Animal Behaviour*, Vol. 53(4), Apr. 1997, 687-700.

23. Gravance, Curtis G.; Casey, Patrick J., Erpino, Michael J., 'Progesterone Does Not Inhibit Aggression Induced by Testosterone Metabolites', *Hormones & Behavior*, Vol. 30(1), Mar. 1996, 22-25.

24. Cashdan, Elizabeth, 'Hormones, Sex, and Status in Women', *Hormones & Behavior*, Vol. 29(3), Sep. 1995, 354-66.

25. Mazur, Allan, 'A Neurohormonal Model of Social Stratification Among Humans: A Microsocial Perspective', in Ellis, Lee (Ed.), *Social Stratification and Socioeconomic Inequality, Vol. 2: Reproductive and Interpersonal Aspects of Dominance and Status*, 1994, pp. 38-45 (Greenwood Publishers, US), xi, 262pp.

26. Zielinski, William J.; Vandenbergh, John G., 'Testosterone and Competitive Ability: Laboratory and Field Studies', *Animal Behaviour*, Vol. 45(5), May 1993, 873-91.

27. Davidson, Richard J.; Kabat-Zinn, Jon; Schumacher, Jessica; Rosenkranz, Melissa; Muller, Daniel; Santorelli, Saki F.; Urbanowski, Ferris; Harrington, Anne; Bonus, Katherine; Sheridan, John F., 'Alterations in Brain and Immune Function Produced by Mindfulness Meditation', *Psychosomatic Medicine*, Vol. 65(4), Jul.-Aug. 2003, 564-70 (Lippincott Williams & Wilkins, US).

28. Albert, D.J.; Jonik, R.H.; Walsh, M.L., 'Hormone-dependent Aggression', *Neuroscience & Biobehavioral Reviews*, Vol. 16(2), Sum. 1992, 177-92 (Elsevier Science, UK).

29. Cohen, Sheldon, 'Social Relationships and Health', *American Psychologist*, Vol. 59(8), Nov. 2004, 676-84 (American Psychological Assoc., US).

30. Archer, John, 'The Influence of Testosterone on Human Aggression', *British Journal of Psychology*, Vol. 82(1), Feb. 1991, 1-28 (British Psychological Society, UK).

31. Albert, D.J.; Jonik, R.H.; Walsh, M.L., 'Aggression by Testosterone Implants', *Physiology & Behavior*, Vol. 47(4), Apr. 1990, 699-703 (Elsevier Science, US).

32. Albert, D.J.; Petrovic, D.M.; Walsh, M.L., 'Competitive Experience Activates Testosterone-dependent Social Aggression Toward Unfamiliar Males', *Physiology & Behavior*, Vol. 45(4), Apr. 1989, 723-7 (Elsevier Science, US).

33. Albert, D.J.; Dyson, E.M.; Walsh, M.L., 'Competitive Behavior in Male Rats: Aggression and Success Enhanced by Medial Hypothalamic Lesions As Well As by Testosterone Implants', *Physiology & Behavior*, Vol. 40(6), 1987, 695-701 (Elsevier Science, US).

34. Salvador, Alicia; Simon, Vicente; Suay, Fernando; Llorens, Luis, 'Testosterone and Cortisol Responses to Competitive Fighting in Human Males: A Pilot Study', *Aggressive Behavior*, Vol. 13(1), 1987, 9-13.

35. Bradford, John M.; Pawlak, Anne, 'A Single Case Study', *Canadian Journal of Psychiatry – Revue Canadienne de Psychiatrie*, Vol. 32(1), Feb. 1987, 22-30 (Canadian Psychiatric Assoc., Canada).

36. Mazur, Allan, 'A Biosocial Model of Status in Face-to-face Primate Groups', *Social Forces*, Vol. 64(2), Dec. 1985, 377-402 (Univ. of North Carolina Press, US).

37. Perse, Elizabeth M., 'Sensation Seeking', *Communication Reports*, Vol. 9(1), Win. 1996, 37-48 (Western States Communication Assoc., US).

38. Nolen-Hoeksema, Susan; Keita, Gwendolyn Puryear, 'Women and Depression', *Psychology of Women Quarterly*, Vol. 27(2), Jun. 2003, 89-90 (Blackwell Publishing, UK).

39. Neria, Yuval; Solomon, Zahava; Ginzburg, Karni; Ohry, Abraham, 'The Experience of Captivity: The Role of Sensation-seeking', *Psychologia: Israel Journal of Psychology*, Vol. 5(2), 1996, 188-98 (Israel Psychological Assoc., Israel).

40. Bonnelle, Kathleen P., 'A Profile of Sensation Seekers: Risk Taking and Risk Reduction Behaviors' [Dissertation Abstract], *Dissertation Abstracts International: Section B: The Sciences & Engineering*, Vol. 56(8-B), Feb. 1996, 4625.

41. Heino, Adriaan; van der Molen, Hugo; Wilde, Gerald J.S., 'Differences in Risk Experience Between Sensation Avoiders and Sensation Seekers', *Personality & Individual Differences*, Vol. 20(1), Jan. 1996, 71-9 (Elsevier Science, UK).

42. Watson, Paul J.; Andrews, Paul W., 'Toward a Revised Evolutionary Adaptationist Analysis of Depression: The Social Navigation Hypothesis', *Journal of Affective Disorders*, Vol. 72(1), Oct. 2002, 1-14 (Elsevier Science, UK).

43. Leff, J; Everitt, B., 'Is Couple Therapy Better Than Antidepressant Drugs?': Commentary reply, *British Journal of Psychiatry*, Vol. 178, Feb. 2001, 181-82 (Royal College of Psychiatrists, UK).

44. Putnam, Robert D., *Bowling Alone: The Collapse and Revival of American Community*, 2000, (Simon & Schuster, US).

45. Banks, James, 'Patterns in Household Giving: Evidence from Household Data Voluntas', Vol. 10(2), 55-66, January 1999.
46. Razafimanalina, R.; Mormede, P.; Velley, L. 'Preference-aversion', *Behavioural Pharmacology*, Vol. 7(1), Jan. 1996, 78-84 (Lippincott Williams & Wilkins, US).
47. Mustillo, Sarah; Wilson, John; Lynch, Scott M., 'Legacy Volunteering: A Test of Two Theories of Intergenerational Transmission', *Journal of Marriage & Family*, Vol. 66(2), May 2004, 530-41 (Blackwell Publishing, UK).
48. Musick, Marc A.; Wilson, John, 'Volunteering and Depression: The Role of Psychological and Social Resources in Different Age Groups', *Social Science & Medicine*, Vol. 56(2), Jan. 2003, 259-69 (Elsevier Science, UK).
49. Cronin, Christopher, 'Using the Sensation Seeking Scale', *Measurement & Evaluation in Counseling & Development*, Vol. 28(1), Apr. 1995, 3-8 (American Counseling Assoc., US).
50. Sheer, Vivian C., 'Sensation Seeking Predispositions and Susceptibility', *Journal of Applied Communication Research*, Vol. 23(3), Aug. 1995, 212-29 (National Communication Assoc., US).
51. Holmes, John G.; Miller, Dale T.; Lerner, Melvin J., 'Committing Altruism Under the Cloak of Self-interest: The Exchange Fiction', *Journal of Experimental Social Psychology*, Vol. 38(2), Mar. 2002, 144-51 (Elsevier Science, UK).

17 If You Have No Enemies Then You Aren't Striving Hard Enough

1. Thompson, Ted, 'Re-examining the Effects of Noncontingent Success on Self-handicapping Behaviour', *British Journal of Educational Psychology*, Vol. 74(2), Jun. 2004, 239-60 (British Psychological Society, UK).
2. Schimel, Jeff; Arndt, Jamie; Banko, Katherine M.; Cook, Alison, 'Not All Self-affirmations Were Created Equal: The Cognitive and Social Benefit of Affirming the Intrinsic (vs Extrinsic) Self', *Social Cognition*, Vol. 22(1), Feb. 2004, 75-99 (Guilford Publications, US).
3. Shepperd, James A.; Kwavnick, Kimberley D., 'Maladaptive Image Maintenance' in Kowalski, Robin M.; Leary, Mark R. (Eds.), *The Social Psychology of Emotional and Behavioral Problems: Interfaces of Social and Clinical Psychology*, 1999, pp. 249-77 (American Psychological Assoc., US), x, 403pp.
4. Hirt, Edward R.; McCrea, Sean M.; Boris, Hillary I., '"I know you self-handicapped last exam": Gender Differences in Reactions to Self-handicapping', *Journal of Personality & Social Psychology*, Jan. 2003, Vol. 84(1), pp. 177-93 (American Psychological Assoc., US).
5. Urdan, Tim, 'Predictors of Academic Self-Handicapping and Achievement: Examining Achievement Goals, Classroom Goal Structures, and Culture', *Journal of Educational Psychology*, Vol. 96(2), Jun. 2004, 251-64 (American Psychological Assoc., US).
6. Laux, Lothar, 'A Self-presentational View of Coping with Stress' in Appley, Mortimer H.; Trumbull, Richard (Eds.), *Dynamics of Stress: Physiological, Psychological, and Social Perspectives, The Plenum*

Series on Stress and Coping, 1986, pp. 233-53 (Plenum Press, NY, US), xvii, 342pp.

7. Haugen, Richard; Ommundsen, Yngvar; Lund, Thorlief, 'The Concept of Expectancy: A Central Factor in Various Personality Dispositions', *Educational Psychology*, Vol. 24(1), Feb. 2004, 43-55 (Taylor & Francis, UK).

8. Carron, Albert V.; Burke, Shauna M.; Prapavessis, Harry, 'Self-Presentation and Group Influence', *Journal of Applied Sport Psychology*, Vol. 16(1), Mar. 2004, 41-58 (Assoc. for the Advancement of Applied Sport Psychology, Canada).

9. Prapavessis, Harry; Grove, J. Robert; Eklund, Robert C., 'Self-Presentational Issues in Competition and Sport', *Journal of Applied Sport Psychology*, Vol. 16(1), Mar. 2004, 19-40.

10. Gibson, Bryan; Sachau, Daniel; Doll, Bruce; Shumate, Roberta, 'Sandbagging in Competition: Responding to the Pressure of Being the Favourite', *Personality and Social Psychology Bulletin*, Vol. 28(8), Aug. 2002, 1119-30.

11. Rhodewalt, Frederick; Tragakis, Michael W., 'Self-handicapping and School: Academic Self-concept and Self-protective Behavior', in Aronson, Joshua (Ed.), *Improving Academic Achievement: Impact of Psychological Factors on Education*, 2002, pp. 109-34 (Academic Press, San Diego, California, US), xxvii, 395pp.

12. Leahy, Robert L., *Overcoming Resistance in Cognitive Therapy*, [Authored Book], 2001 (Guilford Press, New York, US), x, 309pp.

13. Walker, Joan Marie Turner, 'Student Self-regulated Learning' [Dissertation Abstract], *Dissertation Abstracts International: Section B: The Sciences & Engineering*, Vol. 64(3-B), 2003, 1529.

14. Jalloul, Mona El-Sibai, The Relationship of Motivation, Goal Theory, and Perceptions of School Culture of Seventh Grade Arab-American Students' [Dissertation Abstract], *Dissertation Abstracts International*, Vol. 64(3-A), 2003, 778.

15. McCrea, Sean Michael, 'Prefactual and Counterfactual Thinking in Self-handicapping: Hiding Behind Alternative Worlds' [Dissertation Abstract], *Dissertation Abstracts International: Section B: The Sciences & Engineering*, Vol. 63(12-B), 2003, 6144.

16. Edmonds, Heidi Kay, 'Grade Retention and Children's Academic Self-efficacy and Use of Self-protective Strategies' [Dissertation Abstract], *Dissertation Abstracts International*, Vol. 63(11-A), 2003, 3852.

17. Eddings, Stacy Kay, 'Gender Differences in Self-handicapping: The Role of Self-construals' [Dissertation Abstract], *Dissertation Abstracts International: Section B: The Sciences & Engineering*, Vol. 64(1-B), 2003, 463.

18. Prapavessis, Harry; Grove, J. Robert; Maddison, Ralph; Zillmann, Nadine, 'Self-handicapping Tendencies, Coping, and Anxiety Responses Among Athletes', *Psychology of Sport & Exercise*, Vol. 4(4), Oct. 2003, 357-75 (Elsevier Science, UK).

19. van Eerde, Wendelien, 'A Meta-analytically Derived Nomological Network of Procrastination', *Personality & Individual Differences*, Vol 35(6), Oct. 2003, 1410-18 (Elsevier Science, UK).

20. Thompson, Ted; Hepburn, Jonathan, 'Causal Uncertainty, Claimed

and Behavioural Self-handicapping', *British Journal of Educational Psychology*, Vol. 73(2), Jun. 2003, 247-66 (British Psychological Society, UK).

21. Shields, Christopher A.; Paskevich, David M.; Brawley, Lawrence R., 'Self-Handicapping in Structured and Unstructured Exercise: Toward a Measurable Construct', *Journal of Sport & Exercise Psychology*, Vol. 25(3), Sep. 2003, 267-83 (Human Kinetics, US).

22. Rhodewalt, Frederick; Tagakis, Michael W., 'Self-Esteem and Self Regulation: Toward Optimal Studies of Self-Esteem: Comment', *Psychological Inquiry*, Vol. 14(1), Jan. 2003, 66-70 (Lawrence Erlbaum, US).

23. Martin, Andrew J.; Marsh, Herbert W.; Williamson, Alan; Debus, Raymond L., 'Self-handicapping, Defensive Pessimism, and Goal Orientation: A Qualitative Study of University Students', *Journal of Educational Psychology*, Vol. 95(3), Sep. 2003, 617-28 (American Psychological Assoc., US).

24. Dorman, Jeffrey P.; Adams, Joan E.; Ferguson, Janet M., 'Psychosocial Environment and Student Self-handicapping in Secondary School Mathematics Classes: A Cross-national Study', *Educational Psychology*, Vol. 22(5), Dec. 2002, 499-511 (Taylor & Francis, UK).

25. Schoneman, Sean William, 'The Role of the Cognitive Coping Strategy of Defensive Pessimism Within the Social-evaluative Continuum' [Dissertation Abstract], *Dissertation Abstracts International: Section B: The Sciences & Engineering*, Vol. 63(6-B), Jan. 2002, 3024.

26. Kass, Joanne, 'The Relationship of Self-handicapping and Self-esteem, to the Symptom Reporting Behavior of Primary Care Patients' [Dissertation Abstract], *Dissertation Abstracts International: Section B: The Sciences & Engineering*, Vol. 63(6-B), Jan. 2002, 2995.

27. Franken, Robert, E.; Brown, Douglas J., 'Why Do People Like Competition? The Motivation for Winning, Putting Forth Effort, Improving One's Performance, Performing Well, Being Instrumental, and Expressing Forceful/Aggressive Behavior', *Personality and Individual Differences*, Vol. 19, Issue 2, Aug. 1995, 175-84.

28. Yamauchi, Hirotsugu; Miki, Kaori, 'Longitudinal Analysis of the Relations Between Perceived Learning Environment, Achievement Goal Orientations, and Learning Strategies: Intrinsic-extrinsic Regulation as a Mediator', *Psychologia*, Vol. 46(1), Mar. 2003, 1-18 (Psychologia Society, Japan).

18 Want to Be Worshipped?

1. Whitson, David, 'Masculinities and Moralities', *Journal of Gender Studies*, Vol. 13(2), Jul. 2004, 173-5 (Taylor & Francis, UK).

2. Ferris, Kerry O., 'Seeing and Being Seen: The Moral Order of Celebrity Sightings', *Journal of Contemporary Ethnography*, Vol. 33(3) Jun. 2004, 236-64 (Sage Publications, US).

3. Page, Ruth E., 'Contradictory Patterns of Representation', *Discourse & Society*, Vol. 14(5), Sep. 2003, 559-79 (Sage Publications, US).

4. Batra, Rajeev; Homer, Pamela Miles, 'Brand Image Beliefs', *Journal of Consumer Psychology*, Vol. 14(3), 2004, 318-30 (Lawrence Erlbaum, US).

5. Maltby, John; Day, Liz; McCutcheon, Lynn E.; Martin, Matthew M.; Cayanus, Jacob L., 'Celebrity Worship', *Personality & Individual Differences*, Nov. 2004, Vol. 37(7), pp. 1475-82 (Elsevier Science, Netherlands).

6. Maltby, John; Houran, James; Lange, Rense; Ashe, Diane; McCutcheon, Lynn E., 'Thou Shalt Worship No Other Gods – Unless They Are Celebrities: The Relationship Between Celebrity Worship and Religious Orientation', *Personality & Individual Differences*, Vol. 32(7), May 2002, 1157-72 (Elsevier Science, UK).

7. Maltby, John; Houran, James; McCutcheon, Lynn E., 'A Clinical Interpretation of Attitudes and Behaviors Associated with Celebrity Worship', *Journal of Nervous & Mental Disease*, Vol 191(1), Jan. 2003, 25-29 (Lippincott Williams & Wilkins, US).

8. Martin, Matthew M.; Cayanus, Jacob L.; McCutcheon, Lynn E.; Maltby, John, 'Celebrity Worship and Cognitive Flexibility', *North American Journal of Psychology*, Vol. 5(1), 2003, 75-80 (*North American Journal of Psychology*, US).

9. McCutcheon, Lynn E.; Maltby, John, 'Personality Attributions About Individuals High and Low in the Tendency to Worship Celebrities', *Current Research in Social Psychology*, Vol. 7(19), 2002, 325-39 (Univ. of Iowa, US).

10. Raj Persaud, 'Suicides Rise After Diana's Death', *BMJ*, Nov. 2000, Vol. 321: 1243.

11. Giles, David C.; Maltby, John, 'The Role of Media Figures in Adolescent Development: Relations Between Autonomy, Attachment, and Interest in Celebrities', *Personality & Individual Differences*, Vol. 36(4), Mar. 2004, 813-22 (Elsevier Science, UK).

12. Pluchon, C.; Simonnet, E.; Toullat, G.; Gil, R., 'Face Naming and Recognition of Famous People', *Revue Neurologique*, Vol. 158(6-7), Jul. 2002, 703-8 (Masson, France).

13. Roehm, Michelle L.; Roehm, Harper A.; Boone, Derrick S., 'A Comparison of Alternatives for Within-Program Brand Exposure', *Psychology & Marketing*, Vol. 21(1), Jan. 2004, 17-28 (John Wiley & Sons, US).

14. Acchione-Noel, Sylvia Catherine, 'Dual Processes in Face Recognition' [Dissertation Abstract], *Dissertation Abstracts International: Section B: The Sciences & Engineering*, Vol. 64(2-B), 2003, 978.

15. Kane, Thomas Henry, 'Last Acts: Automortography and the Cultural Performance of Death in the United States, 1968–2001' [Dissertation Abstract], *Dissertation Abstracts International,* Vol. 63(12-A), 2003, 4314.

16. Belfi, Brian Joseph, 'Stalker Habilitation Program: A Dialectical Behavior Approach' [Dissertation Abstract], *Dissertation Abstracts International: Section B: The Sciences & Engineering*, Vol. 63(11-B), 2003, 5504.

17. Martin, Brett A.S.; Bhimy, Andrew C.; Agee, Tom, 'Infomercials and Advertising Effectiveness: An Empirical Study', *Journal of Consumer Marketing*, Vol. 19(6) 2002, 468-80 (Emerald, UK).

18. Parnaby, Patrick F.; Sacco, Vincent F., 'Fame and Strain: The Contributions of Mertonian Deviance Theory to an Understanding of the Relationship Between Celebrity and Deviant Behaviour', *Deviant*

Behaviour, Vol. 25(1), Jan.–Feb. 2004, 1-26 (Taylor & Francis, UK).

19. Giles, David, *Illusions of Immortality: A Psychology of Fame and Celebrity*, [Authored book], (St Martin's Press, US).

20. McCutcheon, Lynn E.; Ashe, Diane D.; Houran, James; Maltby, John, 'A Cognitive Profile of Individuals Who Tend to Worship Celebrities', *Journal of Psychology*, Vol. 137(4), Jul. 2003, 309-22 (Heldref Publications, US).

21. Stack, S., 'Media Coverage as a Risk Factor in Suicide', *Journal of Epidemiology & Community Health*, Vol. 57(4), Apr. 2003, 238-40 (BMJ Publishing Group, UK).

22. Casey, Mary K.; Allen, Mike; Emmers-Sommer, Tara; Sahlstein, Erin; Degooyer, Dan; Winters, Alaina M.; Wagner, Amy Elisabeth; Dun, Tim, 'When a Celebrity Contracts a Disease: The Example of Earvin "Magic" Johnson's Announcement That He Was HIV Positive', *Journal of Health Communication,* Vol. 8(3), May-Jun. 2003, 249-65 (Taylor & Francis, UK).

23. Chen, Ning, 'A Study of the Mechanism of Psychological Processing of Celebrity Advertisement Spokesmen of Different Ages', *Psychological Science*, Vol. 26(1), Jan. 2003, 37-40 (Editorial Board of Psychological Science, China).

24. Fraser, Benson P.; Brown, William J., 'Media, Celebrities, and Social Influence: Identification with Elvis Presley', *Mass Communication & Society*, Vol. 5(2), 2002, 183-206 (Lawrence Erlbaum, US).

25. McCarley, Nancy G.; Escoto, Carlos A, 'Celebrity Worship and Psychological Type', *North American Journal of Psychology*, Vol. 5(1), 2003, 117-20 (North American Journal of Psychology, US).

26. Martin, Matthew M.; Cayanus, Jacob L.; McCutcheon, Lynn E.; Maltby, John, 'Celebrity Worship and Cognitive Flexibility', *North American Journal of Psychology,* Vol. 5(1), 2003, 75-80.

27. Louie, Thérèse A.; Obermiller, Carl, 'Consumer Response to a Firm's Endsorser (Dis)association Decisions', *Journal of Advertising*, Vol. 31(4), Win. 2002, 41-52 (CtC Press/JOA, US).

28. McCutcheon, Lynn E., 'Machiavellianism, Belief in a Just World, and the Tendency to Worship Celebrities', *Current Research in Social Psychology, Http://Www.Uiowa.Edu/,* Vol. 8(9), 2003, 131-9 (Univ. of Iowa, US).

29. McCutcheon, Lynn E.; Maltby, John, 'Personality Attributions About Individuals High and Low in the Tendency to Worship Celebrities', *Current Research in Social Psychology, Http://Www.Uiowa.Edu/,* Vol. 7(19), 2002, 325-39.

30. Maltby, John; Houran, James; McCutcheon, Lynn E., 'A Clinical Interpretation of Attitudes and Behaviors Associated with Celebrity Worship', *Journal of Nervous & Mental Disease*, Vol. 191(1), Jan. 2003, 25-9 (Lippincott Williams & Wilkins, US).

31. Jenkins, Rob; Burton, A. Mike; Ellis, Andrew W., 'Covert Face Recognition', *Cognition*, Vol. 86(2), Dec. 2002, B43-B52 (Elsevier Science, Netherlands).

32. Greene, Ernest; Fraser, Scott C., 'Observation Distance and Recognition of Photographs of Celebrities' Faces', *Perceptual & Motor Skills*, Vol. 95(2), Oct. 2002, 637-51.

33. Schweinberger, Stefan R.; Pickering, Esther C.; Jentzsch, Ines; Burton, A. Mike; Kaufmann, Juergen M., 'Event-related Potential Evidence for a Response of Inferior Temporal Cortex to Familiar Face Repetitions', *Cognitive Brain Research*, Vol. 14(3), Nov. 2002, 398-409 (Elsevier Science Publishers BV, US).

34. Twenge, Jean M., 'Birth Cohort Changes in Extraversion: A Cross-temporal Meta-analysis, 1966-1993', *Personality & Individual Differences*, Vol. 30(5), Apr. 2001, 735-48 (Elsevier Science, UK).

35. Sukhdial, Ajay; Aiken, Damon; Kahle, Lynn, 'A Scale for Measuring Sports Fans' Old-school Orientation', *Journal of Advertising Research*, Vol. 42(4), Jul.–Aug. 2002, 71-81 (Advertising Research Foundation, US).

36. Person, Ethel S., *Feeling Strong: The Achievement of Authentic Power* [Authored Book], 2002 (William Morrow & Co., Inc., NY, US), xx, 412pp.

37. Stafford, Marla Royne; Stafford, Thomas F.; Day, Ellen, 'A Contingency Approach: The Effects of Spokeperson Type and Service Type on Service Advertising Perceptions', *Journal of Advertising*, Vol. 31(2), Sum. 2002, 17-35 (CtC Press/JOA, US).

38. Gardner, Sue; Herbert, Camilla, 'The Modern Media – Avoiding Pitfalls, Advancing Psychology', *Psychologist*, Vol. 15(7), Jul. 2002, 342-5 (British Psychological Society, UK).

39. Pirkis, Jane; Francis, Catherine; Blood, Richard Warwick; Burgess, Philip; Morley, Belinda; Stewart, Andrew; Putnis, Peter, 'Reporting of Suicide in the Australian Media', *Australian & New Zealand Journal of Psychiatry*, Vol. 36(2), Apr. 2002, 190-7 (Blackwell Science Asia, Australia).

40. McCutcheon, Lynn E., 'Are Parasocial Relationship Styles Reflected in Love Styles?', *Current Research in Social Psychology, Http://Www.Uiowa.Edu/*, Vol. 7(6), 2002, 82-93.

41. McCutcheon, Lynn E.; Lange, Rense; Houran, James, 'Conceptualization and Measurement of Celebrity Worship', *British Journal of Psychology*, Vol. 93(1), Feb. 2002, 67-87 (British Psychological Society, UK).

42. Dean, Dwane Hal; Biswas, Abhijit, 'Third-party Organization Endorsement of Products: An Advertising Cue Affecting Consumer Prepurchase Evaluation of Goods and Services', *Journal of Advertising*, Vol. 30(4), Win. 2001, 41-57 (CtC Press/JOA, US).

43. Rubenzer, Steven J,; Faschingbauer, Thomas R.; Ones, Deniz S., 'Assessing the US Presidents Using the Revised NEO Personality Inventory', *Assessment*, Vol. 7(4), Dec. 2000, 403-20 (Sage Publications, US).

44. Hale, Libbe, 'The Archetype of the Stranger in Contemporary American Culture' [Dissertation Abstract], *Dissertation Abstracts International: Section B: The Sciences & Engineering*, Vol. 62(1-B), Jul. 2001, 599.

45. Knight, Jennifer L.; Guiliano, Traci A.; Sanchez-Ross, Monica G., 'Famous or Infamous? The Influence of Celebrity Status and Race on Perceptions of Responsibility for Rape', *Basic & Applied Social Psychology*, Vol. 23(3), Sep. 2001, 183-90 (Lawrence Erlbaum, US).

46. Ferris, Kerry O., 'Through a Glass, Darkly: The Dynamics of Fan-celebrity Encounters', *Symbolic Interaction*, Vol. 24(1), 2001, 25-47 (Univ. of California Press, US).

47. Erdogan, B. Zafer; Baker, Michael J.; Tagg, Stephen, 'Selecting Celebrity Endorsers: The Practitioner's Perspective', *Journal of Advertising Research*, Vol. 41(3), May–Jun. 2001, 39-48 (Advertising Research Foundation, US).

48. Baum, Matthew A., 'Going Private: Public Opinion, Presidential Rhetoric and the Domestic Politics of Audience Costs in US Foreign Policy Crises', *Journal of Conflict Resolution*, Vol. 48(5), Oct. 2004, 603-31 (Sage Publications, US).

49. Deluga, Ronald, J., 'Relationship Among American Presidential Charismatic Leadership, Narcissism and Rated Performance', *Leadership Quarterly*, Vol. 8(1), Spr. 1997, 49-65 (Elsevier Science, Netherlands).

19 Conclusion: Why It's Not Just the Size of Your Carrot that Matters

1. Uchtmann, Roger G., 'Visions of the Emerald Beyond: 5th Lucerne Conference on Consciousness, Physics and Arts, "Space, Time and Beyond", January 18-19, 2003', *Journal of Consciousness Studies*, Vol. 10(8), Aug. 2003, 71-8 (Imprint Academic, US).

2. Esman, Aaron H., 'From Philosophy to Psychotherapy: A Phenomenological Model for Psychology, Psychiatry, and Psychoanalysis', *American Journal of Psychiatry*, Vol. 161(7), Jul. 2004, 1314-15 (American Psychiatric Assoc., US).

3. Reiss, Steven; Havercamp, Susan, 'The Sensitivity Theory of Motivation: Implications for Psychopathology', *Behavior Research and Therapy*, Vol. 34, Issue 8, Aug. 1996, 621-32.

4. Daniels, Victor, 'The World in Your Head: A Gestalt View of the Mechanism of Conscious Experience' [Peer Reviewed Journal], *Philosophical Psychology*, Vol. 17(2), Jun. 2004, 311-14 (Taylor & Francis, UK).

5. Zhu, Jing, 'Understanding Volition', *Philosophical Psychology*, Vol. 17(2), Jun. 2004, 247-73 (Taylor & Francis, UK).

6. Bechtel, William; Van Leeuwen, Cees (Eds.), Editorial [Peer Reviewed Journal], *Philosophical Psychology*, Vol. 17(2), Jun. 2004, 147 (Taylor & Francis, UK).

7. Smith, David L., 'Implicit Philosophies and Therapeutic Theories: How Theoretical Constructs Conceal Phenomena', *Humanistic Psychologist*, Vol. 32(2), Spr. 2004, 198-218 (Sage Publications, US).

8. Mulvibill, Beverly A.; Cotton, Janice N.; Gyaben, Susan L., 'Best Practices for Inclusive Child and Adolescent Out-of-School Care: A Review of the Literature', *Family & Community Health*, Vol. 27(1), Jan.–Mar. 2004, 52-64 (Lippincott Williams & Wilkins, US).

9. Bender-Junker, Birgit, 'Emotions in Practice: Feelings and Their Social Domains', *Gestalt Theory*, Vol. 25(4), Dec. 2003, 246-55 (Westdeutscher Verlag, Germany).

10. Dreher, Barbara (Ed.), 'Machiavellian Philosophy', *American Journal of Alzheimer's Disease & Other Dementias*, Vol. 18(4), Jul.–Aug. 2003, 197-8 (Prime National Publishing, US).

11. Höll, Kathleen, 'Philosophical Anarchism', *International Gestalt Journal*, Vol. 26(2), Fall 2003, 47-70 (Center for Gestalt Development, US).

12. Ashcroft, Richard E., 'Constructing Empirical Bioethics', *Health Care Analysis*, Vol. 11(1), Mar. 2003, 3-13 (Kluwer Academic Publishers, Netherlands).

13. Bormuth, M., 'Karl Jaspers as Pathographer', *Fundamenta Psychiatrica: Psychiatrie und Psychotherapie in Theorie und Praxis*, Vol. 16(4), Dec. 2002, pp. 154-9 (Schattauer, Germany).

14. Brett, George Sidney, 'The Progress of Psychology: General Survey' in Muirhead, J. H., (Ed.), Brett, George Sidney, *A History of Psychology: Vol. III. Modern Psychology*, 1921, pp. 242-72. (George Allen & Unwin Ltd., London, UK), 346pp.

15. Gedo, John, E., 'The Enduring Scientific Contributions of Sigmund Freud', *Perspectives in Biology and Medicine*, Vol. 45(2), Spring 2002, 200-211.

16. Brett, George Sidney, 'Representative Types of Theory', in Muirhead, J.H. (Ed.), Brett, George Sidney, *A History of Psychology: Vol. III. Modern Psychology*, 1921, pp. 168-201.

17. Brett, George Sidney, 'From Fechner to Wundt', in Muirhead, J.H., (Ed.), Brett, George Sidney, *A History of Psychology: Vol. III. Modern Psychology*, pp. 127-67.

18. Brett, George Sidney, 'The Transition in Germany' in Muirhead, J.H. (Ed.), Brett, George Sidney, *A History of Psychology: Vol. III. Modern Psychology*, pp. 63-86.

19. Brett, George Sidney. 'The Transition in Germany' in Muirhead, J.H., (Ed.), Brett, George Sidney, *A History of Psychology: Vol. III. Modern Psychology*, pp. 36-62.

20. Brett, George Sidney, 'The Transition in Britain and France' in Muirhead, J.H. (Ed.), Brett, George Sidney, *A History of Psychology: Vol. III. Modern Psychology*, pp. 11-35.

21. Demos, E. Virginia, 'Psychoanalysis and the Human Sciences: The Limitations of Cut-and-Paste Theorizing', *American Imago*, Vol. 58(3), Fall 2001, 649-84.

22. James, William, 'The Perception of Time', in James, William, *The Principles of Psychology*, 1 & 2, 1890, 605-42 (Henry Holt and Co., Inc., NY, US), xii, 697pp.

23. Lilly, Frank A., Bramwell-Aejskind, Gillian, 'The Dynamics of Creative Teaching', *Journal of Creative Behavior*, Vol. 38(2), 2004, 102-24 (Creative Education Foundation, US).

24. Jack, Anthony I.; Prinz, Jesse J., 'Searching for a Scientific Experience: Comment', *Journal of Consciousness Studies*, Vol. 11(1) Jan. 2004, 51-6 (Imprint Academic, US).

25. Strong, Michael; Baron, Wendy, 'An Analysis of Mentoring Conversations with Beginning Teachers: Suggestions and Responses', *Teaching & Teacher Education*, Vol. 20(1), Jan. 2004, 47-57 (Elsevier Science, Netherlands).

26. Todt, Oliver, 'Regulating Under Uncertainty', *Safety Science*, Vol. 42(2), Feb. 2004, 143-158 (Elsevier Science, Netherlands).

27. Sheline, Yvette I.; Gado, Mokhtar H.; Kraemer, Helena C., 'Untreated Depression and Hippocampal Volume Loss', *American Journal of*

Psychiatry, Aug. 2003, Vol. 160(8), 1516-18 (American Psychiatric Assoc., US).

28. Becker, Janet E., 'Attitudes Toward Referral Behavior', *Health & Social Work*, Vol. 29(1), Feb. 2004, 36-45 (NASW Press, US).

29. McCaughtry, Nate, 'The Emotional Dimensions of Pedagogical Content', *Journal of Teaching in Physical Education*, Vol. 23(1), Jan. 2004, 30-47 (Human Kinetics, US).

30. Kozorovitskiy, Yevgenia; Gould, Elizabeth, 'Adult Neurogenesis: A Mechanism for Brain Repair?', *Journal of Clinical & Experimental Neuropsychology*, Vol. 25(5), Aug. 2003, 721-32 (Swets & Zeitlinger, Netherlands).

31. Dias, Brian G; Banerjee, Sunayana B.; Duman, Ronald S.; Vaidya, Vidita A., 'Differential Regulation of Brain Derived Neurotrophic Factor Transcripts by Antidepressant Treatments in the Adult Rat Brain', *Neuropharmacology*, Vol. 45(4), Sep. 2003, 553-63 (Elsevier Science, UK).

32. Rhodes, Justin S.; van Praag, Henriette; Jeffrey, Susan; Girard, Isabelle; Mitchell, Gordon S.; Garland, Theodore Jr.; Gage, Fred H., 'Exercise Increases Hippocampal Neurogenesis to High Levels But Does Not Improve Spatial Learning in Mice Bred for Increased Voluntary Wheel Running', *Behavioral Neuroscience*, Vol. 117(5), Oct. 2003, 1006-16 (American Psychological Assoc., US).

33. Quintanilla L.; Sarriá E., 'Realism, Animism and Theory of Mind: Cultural and Universal Characteristics of Mental Knowledge', *Estudios de Psicologia*, Vol. 24(3), 2003, 313-35 (Fundacion Infancia y Aprendizaje, Spain).

34. Gilbertson, Mark W.; Shenton, Martha E.; Ciszewski, Aleksandra; Kasai, Kiyoto; Lasko, Natasha B.; Orr, Scott P.; Pitman, Roger K., 'Smaller Hippocampal Volume Predicts Pathologic Vulnerability to Psychological Trauma', *Nature Neuroscience*, Vol. 5(11), Nov. 2002, 1242-47, (Nature Publishing, UK).

35. Giessner, Ulrike, 'The Power Principle in Nietzsche, Adler, and Freud', *Zeitschrift fur Individualpsychologie*, Vol. 26(1), 2001, 64-9 (Ernst Reinhardt Verlag, Germany).

36. Nerlich, Brigitte; Clarke, David, D., 'Mind, Meaning and Metaphor: The Philosophy and Psychology of Metaphor in 19th-century Germany', *History of the Human Sciences*, Vol.14(2), May 2001, 39-61 (Sage Publications, UK).

37. Spauwen, J; Krabbendam, L; Lieb, R.; Wittchen, H.U.; van Os, Jim, 'Early Maternal Stress and Health Behaviours and Offspring Expression of Psychosis in Adolescence', *Acta Psychiatrica Scandinavica*, Vol. 110(5), Nov. 2004, 356-64. (Blackwell Publishing, UK).

38. Domino, Brian; Conway, Daniel W., 'Optimism and Pessimism from a Historical Perspective', in Chang, Edward C. (Ed.), *Optimism & Pessimism: Implications for Theory, Research, and Practice*, 2001, pp.13-30 (American Psychological Assoc., US), xxi, 395pp.

39. Wicks, Robert, 'Friedrich Nietzsche', *The Stanford Encyclopedia of Philosophy*, Fall 2004, Edward N. Zalta (Ed.).

40. Soloman, Robert C., 'Nietzsche on Fatalism and "Free Will"', *Journal of Nietzsche Studies*, Spr. 2002, 23, pp. 63-87.
41. Wyatt, C.S., *Introduction to Existentialism*, 2005, (Tameri, CA, US).
42. Olson, R.G., *An Introduction to Existentialism*, 1962, (Dover Publications, US).

Epilogue
1. Shneidman, E., *Comprehending Suicide: Landmarks in 20th Century Suicidology*, 2001 (American Psychological Assoc. US).
2. Colt, George, *The Enigma of Suicide*, 1991, (Summit Books, US).
3. Hall, Barry; Gabor, Peter, 'Peer Suicide Prevention in a Prison', *Crisis: Journal of Crisis Intervention & Suicide*, Vol. 25(1), 2004, 19-26.
4. van Engeland, Herman, 'Parasuicidal Behavior in Adolescence: Possibilities and Limits of Prevention', *Kindheit und Entwicklung*, Vol. 13(1) 2004, 38-46 (Hogrefe & Huber, Germany).
5. Becker, Katja, EI-Faddagh, Mahha, Schmidt, Martin H., 'Cybersuicide or Werther-Effect Online: Suicide Chatrooms or Forums in the World Wide Web', *Kindheit und Entwicklung*, Vol. 13(1), 2004, 14-25 (Hogrefe & Huber, Germany).
6. Becker, Katja, 'Suicidality in Childhood and Adolescence – Introduction to the Special Issue', *Kindheit und Entwicklung*, Vol. 13(1), 2004, 1-4.
7. Moller, H.J., 'Suicide, Suicidality and Suicide Prevention in Affective Disorders', *Acta Neurologica Scandinavica*, Vol. 108 (Supp. l418), Oct. 2003, 73-80 (Blackwell Publishing, UK).
8. Zaloshnja, Eduard; Miller, Ted R.; Galbraith, Maury S.; Lawrence, Bruce A.; DeBruyn, Lemyra M.; Bill, Nancy; Hicks, Kenny R.; Keiffer, Michael; Perkins, Ronald, 'Reducing Injuries Among Native Americans: Five Cost-outcome Analyses', *Accident Analysis & Prevention*, Vol. 35(5), Sep. 2003, 631-9 (Elsevier Science, Netherlands).
9. Pritchard, Colin; King, Elizabeth, 'A Comparison of Child-sex-abuse-related and Mental-disorder-related Suicide in a Six-year Cohort of Regional Suicides: The Importance of the Child Protection-psychiatric Interface', *British Journal of Social Work*, Vol. 34(2), Mar. 2004, 181-98 (Oxford University Press, UK).
10. Abe, Ryo; Shioiri, Toshiki; Nishimura, Akiyoshi; Nushida, Hideyuki; Ueno, Yasuhiro; Kojima, Maki; Kitamura, Hideaki; Akazawa, Kohei; Someya, Toshiyuki, 'Economic Slump and Suicide Method: Preliminary Study in Kobe', *Psychiatry & Clinical Neurosciences*, Vol. 58(2), Apr. 2004, 213-6 (Blackwell Publishing, UK).
11. Towl, Graham J., 'Suicide in Prisons', *British Journal of Forensic Practice*, Vol. 5(3), Aug. 2003, 28-32 (Pavilion Publishing, UK).
12. Conner, Kenneth R., 'A Call for Research on Planned vs. Unplanned Suicidal Behavior', *Suicide & Life-Threatening Behavior*, Vol. 34(2), Sum. 2004, 89-98 (Guilford Publications, US).
13. Lunsky, Y., 'Suicidality in a Clinical and Community Sample of Adults with Mental Retardation', *Research in Developmental Disabilities*, Vol. 25(3), May–Jun. 2004, 231-43 (Elsevier Science, Netherlands).
14. Ham, Peter, 'Suicide Risk Not Increased with SSRI Antidepressants', *Journal of Family Practice*, Vol. 52(8), Aug. 2003, 587-8 (Dowden Health Media, US).

15. Waern, Margda; Rubenowitz, Eva; Wilhelmson, Katarina, 'Predictors of Suicide in the Old Elderly', *Gerontology*, Vol. 49(5), Sep.–Oct. 2003, 328-34 (Karger, Switzerland).

16. Bongar, Bruce, *The Suicidal Patient: Clinical and Legal Standards of Care* (2nd Ed.) [Authored Book], (American Psychological Assoc., US), 2002. xxvi, 376pp.

17. Bongar, Bruce Michael, 'Risk Management: Prevention and Postvention' in Bongar, Bruce Michael, *The Suicidal Patient: Clinical and Legal Standards of Care,* pp. 163-204 (American Psychological Assoc., US), 1991, xix, 311pp.

18. Bongar, Bruce Michael, 'Inpatient Management and Treatment of the Suicidal Patient' in Bongar, Bruce Michael, *The Suicidal Patient: Clinical and Legal Standards of Care,* pp. 133-61.

19. Bongar, Bruce Michael, 'Suicide: Legal Perspectives', in Bongar, Bruce Michael, *The Suicidal Patient: Clinical and Legal Standards of Care,* pp. 33-59.

20. Bongar, Bruce Michael, 'The Knowledge Base', in Bongar, Bruce Michael, *The Suicidal Patient: Clinical and Legal Standards of Care,* pp. 1-32.

21. Bongar, Bruce Michael, 'Management and Treatment of the Suicidal Patient', in Bongar, Bruce Michael, *The Suicidal Patient: Clinical and Legal Standards of Care,* pp. 103-31.

22. Bongar, Bruce Michael, *The Suicidal Patient: Clinical and Legal Standards of Care.*

23. Berman, Alan L.; Jobes, David A., 'Prevention and Postvention' in Berman, Alan L.; Jobes, David A., *Adolescent Suicide: Assessment and Intervention,* pp. 227-65 (American Psychological Assoc., US), 1991, vi, 277pp.

24. Berman, Alan L.; Jobes, David A., *Adolescent Suicide: Assessment and Intervention.*

25. Ivanoff, André; Hayes, Lindsay M., 'Preventing, Managing, and Treating Suicidal Actions in High-risk Offenders' in Ashford, Jose B.; Sales, Bruce Dennis (Eds.), *et al, Treating Adult and Juvenile Offenders with Special Needs,* pp. 313-31 (American Psychological Assoc., US), x, 518pp.

26. Violanti, John M., 'Violence Turned Inward' in VandenBos, Gary R.; Bulatao, Elizabeth Q. (Eds.), *Violence on the Job: Identifying Risks and Developing Solutions,* 1996, pp. 229-49 (American Psychological Assoc., US), viii, 439pp.

27. McIntosh, John L.; Santos, John F.; Hubbard, Richard W.; Overholser, James C., 'Prevention, Ethics, and Unresolved Issues' in McIntosh, John L.; Santos, John F., *et al, Elder Suicide: Research, Theory and Treatment,* 1994, pp. 199-232 (American Psychological Assoc., US), xiii, 260pp.

28. Peck, Michael, 'Youth Suicide' in Wass, Hannelore; Corr, Charles A. (Eds.), *Childhood and Death. Series in Death Education, Aging, and Health Care,* 1984, pp. 279-90 (Hemisphere Publishing Corp., Washington, DC, US), xvi, 392pp.

29. Pfeffer, Cynthia R., 'Death Preoccupations and Suicidal Behavior in Children' in Wass, Hannelore; Corr, Charles A., (Eds.), *Childhood and Death, Series in Death Education, Aging, and Health Care,* pp. 261-78 (Hemisphere Publishing Corp., Washington, DC, US), xvi, 392pp.

30. Douglas, Julie; Cooper, Jayne; Amos, Tim; Webb, Roger; Guthrie, Elspeth; Appleby, Louis, ' "Near-fatal" Deliberate Self-harm: Characteristics, Prevention and Implications for the Prevention of Suicide', *Journal of Affective Disorders*, Vol. 79(1-3), Apr. 2004, 263-8 (Elsevier Science, UK).

31. Novick, Lloyd F.; Cibula, Donald A.; Sutphen, Sally M.; Novick, Lloyd F., 'Adolescent Suicide Prevention', *American Journal of Preventive Medicine*, Vol. 24 (Supp. 14), May 2003, 150-6 (Elsevier Science, UK).

32. Read, Benjamin; Seiden, Richard; Moyer, James, 'Suicide Prevention in Public Places', [Chapter], Berman, Alan L. (Ed.), *Suicide Prevention*, pp. 3-24 (Springer Publishing Co., US).

33. Rosen, David H., 'The Serious Suicide Attempt: Five-year Follow-up Study of 886 Patients', *JAMA: Journal of the American Medical Association*, Vol. 235(19), May 1976, 2105-09 (American Medical Assoc., US).

34. Schwartz, Robert C.; Rogers, James R., 'Suicide Assessment and Evaluation Strategies: A Primer for Counselling Psychologists', *Counselling Psychology Quarterly*, Vol. 17(1), Mar. 2004, 89-97 (Taylor & Francis, UK).

35. Azrael, Deborah; Hemenway, David; Miller, Matthew; Barber, Catherine W.; Schackner, Robert, 'Youth Suicide', *Suicide & Life-Threatening Behavior*, Vol. 34(1), Spr. 2004, 36-43 (Guilford Publications, US).

36. Schneidman, Edwin S., 'Suicide', *Suicide & Life-Threatening Behavior*, Vol. 11(4), Win. 1981, 198-220 (Guilford Publications, US).

INDEX

SIMPLY IRRESISTIBLE
How to catch and keep your perfect partner
By Dr Raj Persaud

As psychology advances its understanding of the mind and brain, perhaps the last remaining bastion of mystery about why we do what we do relates to love and attraction. However, recent research suggests that even the mysteries of attraction are being revealed – which is great news for those amongst us who would rather not leave seduction to chance.

In this illuminating follow-up to his acclaimed bestseller, *The Motivated Mind*, Dr Raj Persaud draws on the very latest research to show not only how to increase your attractiveness generally, but how to become absolutely irresistible to anyone. For example, do you know . . .

- that experiments on dating can predict with over 80% accuracy who will be attracted to who by whether just a few simple conversational strategies are used on a date?

- why abnormally low lighting is strongly associated with romance, why women wear blusher on their cheeks, or lipstick to enhance their pouting lips? Or

- that seeking to be agreeable on a date is not actually the most attractive or successful strategy to use.

- And for anyone out there who is looking for that rare combination of brains and beauty, there is reassuring news: current research reveals that it is indeed perfectly possible to guess a person's IQ from the way they look.

Frank, witty and packed with useful questionnaires and invaluable advice, *Simply Irresistible* is the essential guide on how to catch – and keep – your perfect partner.

0 593 05588 8

COMING SOON FROM BANTAM PRESS

BANTAM PRESS